MAINE
Pages 274-299

MAINE

BOSTON
Pages 50-127

CONNECTICUT
Pages 194-225

RHODE ISLAND
Pages 168-193

MASSACHUSETTS
Pages 132-167

0 kilometres   10

0 miles   10

EYEWITNESS *TRAVEL GUIDES*

NEW ENGLAND

DK EYEWITNESS *TRAVEL GUIDES*

NEW ENGLAND

DORLING KINDERSLEY
LONDON • NEW YORK • SYDNEY • DELHI
PARIS • MUNICH • JOHANNESBURG
www.dk.com

A DORLING KINDERSLEY BOOK

www.dk.com

PRESIDENT Pierre Léveillé
VICE PRESIDENT, FINANCE Natalie Watanabe
MANAGING EDITOR Carolyn Jackson
MANAGING ART DIRECTOR Diane Denoncourt
PRODUCTION MANAGER Michelle Turbide
DIRECTOR, BUSINESS DEVELOPMENT Christopher Jackson

EDITOR Neale McDevitt
ART DIRECTORS Michel Giguère, Anne-Marie Lemay
SENIOR RESEARCH EDITOR Heather Mills
RESEARCHERS Tal Ashkenazi, Jessica Braun, Genevieve Ring
PICTURE RESEARCHER Linda Castle
MAP COORDINATOR Peter Alec Fedun
SENIOR EDITOR, PRODUCTION Brian Parsons
INDEXER Linda Cardella Cournoyer
PREPRESS PRODUCTION Martin Francoeur, Jean Sirois

MAIN CONTRIBUTORS
Eleanor Berman, Patricia Brooks, Tom Bross, Patricia Harris, Pierre
Home-Douglas, Helga Loverseed, David Lyon

PHOTOGRAPHERS
Alan Briere, Ed Homonylo, David Lyons

ILLUSTRATORS
Gilles Beauchemin, Martin Gagnon, Vincent Gagnon, Stéphane
Jorisch, Patrick Jougla, Luc Normandin, Jean-François Vachon

MAPS
Dimension DPR

Filmwork by Colourscan, Singapore
Printed and bound by Graphicom

First published in Great Britain in 2001
by Dorling Kindersley Limited
80 Strand, London WC2R 0RL

**The information in every
DK Eyewitness Travel Guide is checked regularly.**
Every effort has been made to ensure that this book is as up-to-date as
possible at the time of going to press. Some details, however, such as
telephone numbers, opening hours, prices, gallery hanging arrangements,
and travel information are liable to change. The publishers cannot accept
responsibility for any consequences arising from the use of this book.
We value the views of our readers very highly. Please write to: Senior
Publishing Manager, DK Eyewitness Travel Guides, Dorling Kindersley,
80 Strand, London WC2R 0RL. Or contact us via: travelguides@dk.com

CONTENTS

HOW TO USE
THIS GUIDE *6*

Sailboat off the Cape Cod coast

INTRODUCING
NEW ENGLAND

Vermont's dazzling fall foliage

West Quoddy Head Light, Maine

BOSTON

NEW ENGLAND REGION BY REGION

TRAVELERS' NEEDS

Mansion in Waterbury, Vermont

SURVIVAL GUIDE

Costumed interpreter at
Plimoth Plantation,
Plymouth, Massachusetts

Mark Twain House
in Hartford,
Connecticut

How to Use this Guide

This guide helps you to get the most from your visit to New England. *Introducing New England* maps the region and sets it in its historical and cultural context. Each of the six states, along with the city of Boston, has its own chapter describing the important sights using maps, pictures, and detailed illustrations. Suggestions on restaurants, accommodations, shopping, entertainment and outdoor activities are covered in *Travelers' Needs*. The *Survival Guide* has tips on everything from changing currency in New England to getting around in Boston.

BOSTON

Boston has been divided into five sightseeing areas, each one opening with a list of the sights described. All the sights are numbered and plotted on an *Area Map*. The detailed information for each sight is presented in numerical order, making it easy to locate within the chapter.

Sights at a Glance lists the chapter's sights by category: Historic Streets and Squares; Historic Buildings, Churches, Museums, and Theaters; Waterfront Sights; Gardens and Zoos; and Parks and Cemeteries.

1 Area Map

For easy reference, the sights are numbered and located on a map. The sights are also shown on the Boston Street Finder *on pages 122–7.*

A locator map shows where you are in relation to other areas of the city center.

2 Street-by-Street Map

This gives a bird's-eye view of the heart of each sightseeing area.

A suggested route for a walk covers the more interesting streets in the area.

All pages relating to Boston have yellow thumb tabs.

Stars indicate the sights that no visitor should miss.

3 Detailed Information on Each Sight

All the sights in Boston are described individually. Addresses, telephone numbers, opening hours, and information on admission charges and wheelchair access are also provided. The key to all the symbols used in the information block is shown on the back flap.

1 Introduction
The landscape, history, and character of each state is described here, showing how the area has developed over the centuries and what it has to offer the visitor today.

NEW ENGLAND REGION BY REGION
In this book, New England has been divided into the six states, each of which has a separate chapter. The most interesting sights to visit have been numbered on the *Pictorial Map*.

Each state of New England can be quickly identified by its color coding, which is shown on the inside front cover.

2 Pictorial Map
This shows the road network and gives an illustrated overview of the whole state. All the sights are numbered, and there are also useful tips on getting around the state.

Story boxes explore specific subjects further.

3 Detailed Information
All the important towns and other places to visit are described individually. They are listed in order, following the numbering on the Pictorial Map. Within each town or city, there is detailed information on important buildings and other sights.

For all the top sights, a Visitors' Checklist provides the practical information you will need to plan your visit.

4 The Top Sights
These are given two or more pages. Historic buildings are dissected to reveal their interiors; museums and galleries have color-coded floor plans; national parks have maps showing facilities and trails.

Stars indicate the best features and works of art.

INTRODUCING
NEW ENGLAND

Putting Northern New England on the Map

COMPRISED OF VERMONT, NEW HAMPSHIRE, and Maine, this northern section is New England at its most rural and, often, wildest. Although Vermont also has its high ground in the form of the Green Mountains, it is famous for its rolling farmland. New Hampshire is known for its White Mountain range and the series of spectacular passes, or notches, that nature has carved between the peaks. Massive, but sparsely populated, Maine is covered in dense forest and an intricate network of lakes, streams, and rivers. It also boasts a coastline as rugged as any found on the Eastern Seaboard.

MA

CT

RI

KEY TO COLOR CODING

Northern New England

■ Vermont

■ New Hampshire

□ Maine

CANADA

UNITED STATES OF AMERICA

New England

PACIFIC OCEAN

Gulf of Mexico

ATLANTIC OCEAN

MEXICO

CANADA

KEY

▬ Interstate

▬ Major road

▬ Minor road

— Railroad

✈ International airport

🚉 Train station

Lake Memphremagog

Derby Line

VERMONT

Lake Champlain

St. Albans

Plattsburgh

Berlin Beth

Burlington

Essex Junction Danville

St. Johnsbury

Shelburne

Waterbury

Littleton Pinkha Notch

Montpelier

Barnet

Jacks

Franconia Bretton Woods

NEW YORK

Lincoln *WHITE* North Conw

Middlebury

GREEN MTN NATIONAL FOREST Randolph

MOUNTAIN NATIONAL FOREST

KEY

Fair Haven Rutland

White River Junction

Laconia

Woodstock

Windsor

Fort Edwards Manchester

GREEN MTN NATIONAL FOREST

Claremont

Concord

Bellows Falls

Roches

Manchester

NEW HAMPSHIRE

Bennington

Keene

Saratoga Springs

Wilmington Brattleboro

Schenectady

Greenfield

Albany

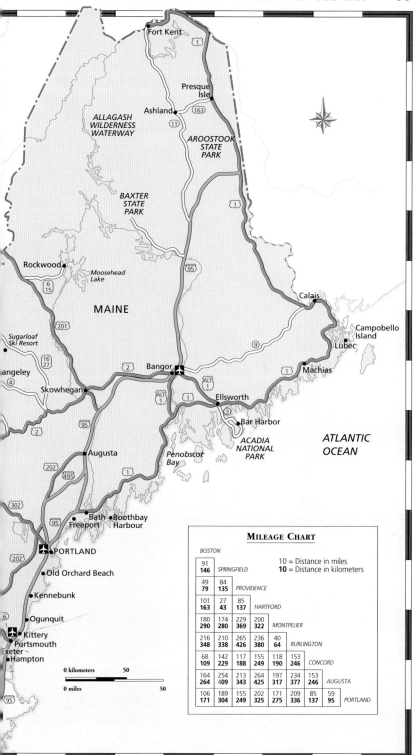

MILEAGE CHART

BOSTON									
91 / **146**	SPRINGFIELD								
49 / **79**	84 / **135**	PROVIDENCE							
101 / **163**	27 / **43**	85 / **137**	HARTFORD						
180 / **290**	174 / **280**	229 / **369**	200 / **322**	MONTPELIER					
216 / **348**	210 / **338**	265 / **426**	236 / **380**	40 / **64**	BURLINGTON				
68 / **109**	142 / **229**	117 / **188**	155 / **249**	118 / **190**	153 / **246**	CONCORD			
164 / **264**	254 / **409**	213 / **343**	264 / **425**	197 / **317**	234 / **377**	153 / **246**	AUGUSTA		
106 / **171**	189 / **304**	155 / **249**	202 / **325**	171 / **275**	209 / **336**	85 / **137**	59 / **95**	PORTLAND	

10 = Distance in miles
10 = Distance in kilometers

Putting Southern New England on the Map

MUCH SMALLER IN SIZE THAN the northern section, southern New England – Massachusetts, Rhode Island, and Connecticut – traditionally has been the industrial and cultural hub of the region. Massachusetts is the historical center of the New England colonies, with the first settlers disembarking at Plymouth in 1620. Ever-popular Cape Cod is a wonderful mix of beaches and understated charm. The smallest state in the country, tiny Rhode Island contains some of New England's most extravagant mansions, some found along the spectacular Cliff Walk in Newport. Connecticut's proximity to New York City to the south has graced many of its towns and cities with a cosmopolitan flavor.

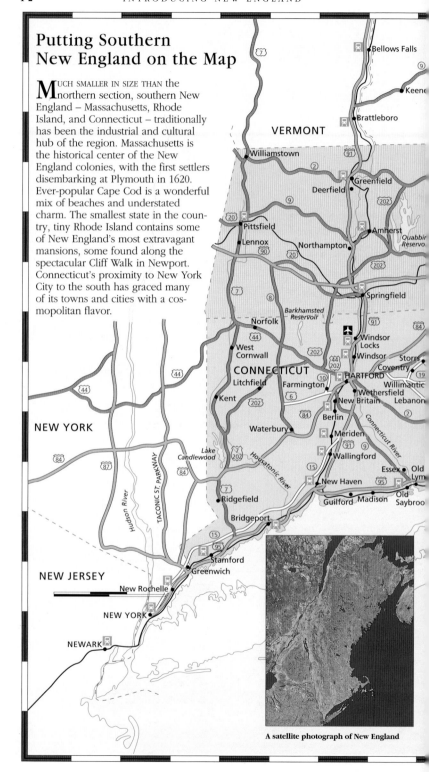

Bellows Falls

Keene

Brattleboro

VERMONT

Williamstown

Greenfield

Deerfield

Amherst

Quabbin Reservo

Pittsfield

Lennox

Northampton

Springfield

Norfolk

Barkhamsted Reservoir

Windsor Locks

Windsor

Storrs

Coventry

West Cornwall

CONNECTICUT

Litchfield

Farmington

HARTFORD

Willimantic

Kent

Wethersfield

Lebanon

New Britain

Berlin

Connecticut River

Waterbury

Meriden

NEW YORK

Lake Candlewood

Housatonic River

Wallingford

Essex

Old Lym

New Haven

Old Saybroo

Ridgefield

Guilford

Madison

Bridgeport

Hudson River

TACONIC ST. PARKWAY

Stamford

NEW JERSEY

Greenwich

New Rochelle

NEW YORK

NEWARK

A satellite photograph of New England

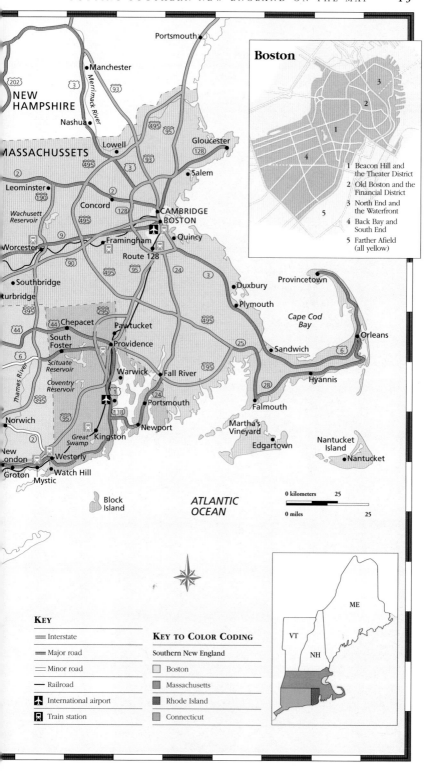

Boston

1 Beacon Hill and
  the Theater District
2 Old Boston and the
  Financial District
3 North End and
  the Waterfront
4 Back Bay and
  South End
5 Farther Afield
  (all yellow)

Portsmouth

NEW
HAMPSHIRE

Manchester

Merrimack River

Nashua

MASSACHUSSETS

Lowell

Gloucester

Leominster

Salem

Wachusett
Reservoir

Concord

CAMBRIDGE
BOSTON

Worcester

Framingham

Quincy

Route 128

Southbridge

Duxbury

Sturbridge

Plymouth

Provincetown

Chepacet

Pawtucket

Cape Cod
Bay

South
Foster

Providence

Orleans

Scituate
Reservoir

Warwick

Fall River

Sandwich

Thames River

Coventry
Reservoir

Hyannis

Portsmouth

Norwich

Falmouth

Great
Swamp

Kingston

Newport

Martha's
Vineyard

New
London

Westerly

Edgartown

Nantucket
Island

Groton

Watch Hill

Nantucket

Mystic

Block
Island

ATLANTIC
OCEAN

0 kilometers   25

0 miles   25

KEY

Interstate

Major road

Minor road

Railroad

International airport

Train station

KEY TO COLOR CODING

Southern New England

Boston

Massachusetts

Rhode Island

Connecticut

ME

VT

NH

A Portrait of New England

For many people, New England is white-steepled churches, craggy coastlines, and immaculate village greens. However, the region is also home to the opulence of Newport, Rhode Island, the beautiful suburban communities of Connecticut, and the self-assured sophistication of Boston – as well as the picture-postcard villages, covered bridges, timeless landscapes, and back-road gems.

From its beginning, the region has been shaped by both geography and climate. Early explorers charted its coastline, and communities soon sprang up by the sea, where goods and people could be ferried more easily from the Old World to the New. Much of the area's early commerce depended heavily on the ocean, from shipping and whaling to fishing and boat-building. Inland the virgin forests and hilly terrain of areas such as New Hampshire, Vermont, and Maine created communities that survived and thrived on independence. The slogan "Live free or die" on today's New Hampshire license plates is a reminder that the same spirit still lives on. New England

Uncle Sam puppet

winters are long and harsh, and spring can bring unpredictable weather. As the 19th-century author Harriet Martineau (1802–76) declared, "I believe no one attempts to praise the climate of New England." Combined with the relatively poor growing conditions of the region – glaciers during the last Ice Age scoured away much of New England's precious soil – this has meant that farming has always been a struggle against the capricious forces of nature. To survive in these northeastern states required toughness, ingenuity, and resourcefulness, all traits that became ingrained in the New England psyche. Indeed, the area today is as much a state of mind as it is a physical space.

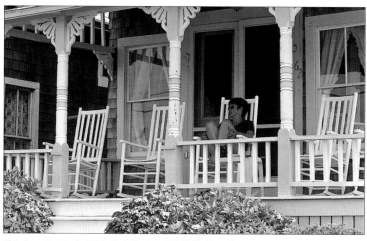

Victorian cottage in the Trinity Park district in Oak Bluffs, Massachusetts

◁ **White steeple of the Town Hall in Fitzwilliam, New Hampshire**

Former frontier outpost, Old Fort Western in Augusta, Maine – a view into New England's past

Few places in America – if any – are richer in historical connections. This is where European civilization first gained a toehold in America. And even long after the American Revolution (1776–83), New England continued to play an important role in the life of the developing nation, supplying many of its political and intellectual leaders. That spirit endures. An intellectual confidence, some may call it smugness, persists; some people would say it is with good reason since it was New England that produced the first flowering of American culture. Writers such as Henry David Thoreau (1817–62), Ralph Waldo Emerson (1803–82), Louisa May Alcott (1832–88), and Herman Melville (1819–91) became the first American writers of an international caliber. Even in the 20th century, New England still figured largely in the arts and letters, while to this day the famous preparatory schools and the Ivy League universities and other institutions

Statue of Samuel de Champlain

New England-born Louisa May Alcott

of higher learning continue to draw some of America's best and brightest to the region.

MOUNTAINS AND SEASHORE

From the heights of the White Mountains – the highest terrain in the northeastern US – to the windswept seashore of Cape Cod, New England offers a stunning range of landscapes. And while industrialization and urbanization have left their stamp, there is plenty of the wild past still in the present. The woods of Maine, for example, look much as they did when American writer and naturalist Henry David Thoreau visited them more than 150 years ago. Vermont's Green Mountains would be instantly recognizable by the explorer Samuel de Champlain (1567–1635) who first saw them almost 400 years ago. But it is not only the countryside that has endured; there are homes scattered throughout New England that preserve an array of early American architectural styles, from Colonial to Greek Revival. Just as the terrain is varied, so, too, is New England's population. The earliest settlers to the region were mostly of English and Scottish stock. Even by the early 19th century New England was still a relatively homogenous society, but this changed dramatically during the mid-1800s as waves of Irish immigrants arrived, driven from their homeland by the potato famines.

This altered the political balance of the area. Whereas the earliest leaders tended to be of British ancestry – men such as President John Adams (1735–1826) and John Hancock (1737–93), signatories of the

Machine Shed inside the Boott Cotton Mill Museum in Lowell, Massachusetts

their descendants directly from the Pilgrims who first came here aboard the *Mayflower*.

OUTDOOR ACTIVITIES

Despite the area's proximity to some of America's most populated areas – a mere 40-mile (64-km) commute separates Stamford, Connecticut, and New York City – it offers a wealth of outdoor activities. There is something here to keep just about any sports enthusiast satisfied. For canoeists and white-water rafters, there are the beautiful Allagash and Connecticut rivers and a captivating collection of lakes.

Rafting on the Kennebec River

Declaration of Independence – now Irish-born politicians came to the fore. In 1884 one such man, Hugh O'Brien (1827–95), won the mayoral race in Boston. Meanwhile immigrants from Italy, Portugal, and eastern Europe also arrived, as well as an influx of French-Canadians, who flocked to the mill towns looking for employment. Still, the Irish represented a sizable part of the New England community and their impact on New England society and politics continued to grow, culminating in the election of John F. Kennedy (1917–63) in 1960 as America's first Roman Catholic president. Today some of the fourth-, fifth-, and sixth-generation Irish Americans have ascended to the top of New England's social hierarchy, although there remains a special cachet for people who can trace

For skiers, resorts such as Killington, Stowe, and Sugarloaf offer some of the best skiing in the eastern US. The region's heavy snowfalls provide a wonderful base for cross-country skiers and snowshoers as well. There's biking on the back roads of New Hampshire and excellent hiking on the Appalachian Trail and Vermont's Long Trail, considered by many as one of the best hiking trails in the world.

Of course, many popular outdoor activities center around the ocean. There's kayaking among the islands and inlets of the Maine shoreline, wind surfing off Cape Cod, and ample opportunities for sailing, fishing, swimming, and scuba diving up and down the entire New England coast.

Fisherman with a large striped bass

The Landscape and Wildlife of New England

CONSIDERING ITS PROXIMITY to major cities, rural
New England boasts a surprisingly diverse collection of wildlife, including many species of birds,
moose, bears, beavers, and, rarely, bobcats. The
topography of the region includes rolling hills,
dense woodlands, rugged mountains, and a coastline
that is jagged and rocky in some areas and sandy
and serene in others. Northern Maine has the closest
thing to wilderness found in the eastern United
States, with hundreds of square miles of trackless
land and a vast network of clear streams, rivers, and
lakes. New England is also home to the White,
Green, and Appalachian mountain ranges.

*Bald eagles are found around
water, making Maine their
favorite New England state.*

COASTLINE

From the crenelated coastline of Maine,
which measures almost 3,500 miles
(5,630 km) in length, to the sandy beaches
of Connecticut, the New England shoreline is richly varied. Here visitors find various sea and shore birds, many attracted
by the food provided by the expansive
salt marshes that have been created by
barrier beaches. A few miles offshore,
there is excellent whale-watching.

MOUNTAIN LANDSCAPE

The western and northern parts of New
England are dominated by the Appalachian
Mountains, a range that extends from
Georgia to Canada. The highest point is
6,288-ft (1,917-m) Mount Washington,
also known for drastic weather changes
at its summit. Birch and beech trees are
plentiful at elevations up to 2,000 ft
(610 m). At the highest elevations, pine,
spruce, and fir trees are most common.

*The great blue
heron is the
largest of the
North American
herons. This
elegant bird is
easily spotted in
wetlands and on
lakeshores.*

*White-tailed deer can
be found in a range
of habitats, from forest edges to open
woodland. They are
frequently spotted
on mountainsides up
to 2,000 ft (610 m).*

*Whales are plentiful off the coast,
particularly in the Gulf of Maine
from early spring to mid-
October. Finbacks, minke,
and right whales are most
common, but humpbacks
generally put on the
best show, often leaping
out of the water.*

*Coyotes were once
all but extinct in the
region, but in recent
years their numbers
have exploded. They
tend to live in forested
and mountainous
areas, but might be
seen in urban areas.*

NATIONAL WILDLIFE REFUGE

With 93 million acres (38 million ha) under its control, the National Wildlife Refuge (NWR) offers protection for some of the country's most ecologically rich areas. The NWR system began in 1903 when President Theodore Roosevelt (1858–1919) established Pelican Island in Florida as a refuge for birds. Thirty-one refuges are located in New England, including ten in Massachusetts, five in Rhode Island, four in New Hampshire, nine in Maine, two in Connecticut, and one in Vermont. The New England refuges offer some of the best bird-watching in the region.

Rachel Carson National Wildlife Refuge, a vast wetland stop for migratory birds

LAKES AND RIVERS

The rivers and lakes of New England provide fishermen, canoeists, and vacationers in general with a world of outdoor pleasures. The network of waterways is particularly extensive in Maine, which has more lakes than any state in the northeastern United States. Among the rivers, the Connecticut is New England's longest, at more than 400 miles (644 km) in length. It runs from the Canadian border along the Vermont-New Hampshire border through Massachusetts and Connecticut.

FORESTS

The logging industry and the switch to agricultural and grazing land – especially for sheep – decimated many of the forests of New England in the 19th and early 20th centuries, but the tide has turned. Vermont, for example, has far more forests today than it did 100 years ago. In the lower elevations, the trees are mostly deciduous, such as ash, maple, and birch, but higher up in the mountains coniferous trees such as balsam fir predominate.

Mallard ducks are a frequent sight throughout New England wetlands. The birds can be seen from April to October, when they migrate to warmer climes.

The pigeon hawk, also known as the merlin, can be found throughout New England, even in urban areas.

Chipmunks are seen virtually throughout rural New England, especially in the forests.

Moose *are common in Maine, northern Vermont, and New Hampshire. Although they can be spotted in the woods, they are most often seen along the shores of lakes. Drivers should be wary of moose, especially at dawn and dusk.*

Raccoons are commonly seen in wooded areas. They often pay visits to campsites, brazenly foraging for food with dexterous paws.

Fall Foliage

T HE COOL WEATHER IN THE FALL signals more than back-to-school time in New England. It also sounds a clarion call to hundreds of thousands of visitors to head outdoors to gaze in wonder at one of Nature's most splendid offerings: the annual changing of leaf colors. Planning foliage tours is an inexact science, however. Generally, leaves start to change earliest in more northern areas and higher up mountainsides. On some mountains in northern New England, for example, the leaves will begin changing color as early as August. In general, the peak period varies from early October in the northern part of the region to late October in the southern section. But this can differ, depending on the weather. Cooler temperatures than normal tend to speed up the leaf-changing timetable and vice versa.

Young boy during fall's pumpkin harvest

Blue sky
The rich palette created by the foliage is made even more dramatic by a backdrop of a deep blue fall sky.

VERMONT'S FALL COLORS
While each of the New England states offers something for "leaf peepers," none can top Vermont. With its rich mix of deciduous trees, the Green Mountain State is anything but just green in late September and October. Inns and hotels tend to be booked up months in advance on the key weekends as the Vermont countryside swells with one of its biggest influx of out-of-state visitors.

Forest floor
Fallen leaves are more than just beautiful to the eye. They will eventually decay and replenish the humus layer.

Nature's paint box
One of the most remarkable features of the fall foliage season is how it transforms the scenery. Here Quechee Gorge, Vermont's Grand Canyon, has changed its verdant green cloak for one of many colors.

Maple leaf
The maple tree is one of the most common trees in New England. Its leaves change to yellow, red, or orange.

WHY LEAVES TURN

The changing of leaf colors is not just a capricious act of Nature. It is a direct response to the changing realities of the seasons. As daylight hours diminish, the leaves of deciduous trees stop producing the green pigment chlorophyll. With the disappearance of chlorophyll, other pigments that had been hidden behind the chlorophyll's color now burst into view. More pigments are produced by sugars that remain trapped in the leaves. The result is a riotous display that makes this the high point of the year for many visitors. Two of the most spectacular areas for color are Litchfield Hills, Connecticut *(see pp208–209),* and Camden, Maine *(see pp286–7).* Foliage hotlines give updates and are listed on page 379.

A single crimson leaf aglow on the forest floor

Fall hiking
Hikers should wear bright clothing and stick to well-marked trails and paths in the fall as this is also hunting season in the area.

The Appalachian Trail

A common squirrel

THE APPALACHIAN TRAIL is one of the longest footpaths in the world at 2,168 miles (3,490 km). From its southern terminus at Springer Mountain in the state of Georgia to its northernmost point on the summit of Mount Katahdin, Maine, the trail crosses 14 states and two national parks as it wends its way through forests, meadows, and mountains. The trail travels through five of the six New England states, missing only Rhode Island, and reaches its highest point in the northeast on windswept Mount Washington *(see p267)* in New Hampshire. Each year about 400 intrepid souls, called "thru hikers," complete the journey in a single trip. The vast majority of people, however, choose to walk the trail in smaller, more manageable sections. The trail is usually marked by rectangular white blazes painted on trees and rocks, and overnight hikers can take advantage of primitive shelters that are situated roughly every 10 miles (16 km).

APPALACHIAN TRAIL

☐ *New England*

··· *Appalachian Trail*

Hanover, New Hampshire
Home of Dartmouth College, Hanover is located on the Appalachian Trail. This stretch of the trail, called the Dartmouth Outing Club section, runs through a series of scenic valleys and mountain passes.

Vermont's lush *green cloak becomes a brilliant patchwork in the fall, a popular time to hike this section of the trail.*

Mount Greylock is one of the highlights of the Massachusetts section.

The Connecticut section runs through the Housatonic Highlands and the valley along the Taconic Range.

Burlington

St. Johnsbu

Montpelier

Hanover

Rutland   Lebanon

Conco

Brattleboro

Bennington

Worceste

Pittsfield

Springfield

Hartford

Waterbury

New Haven

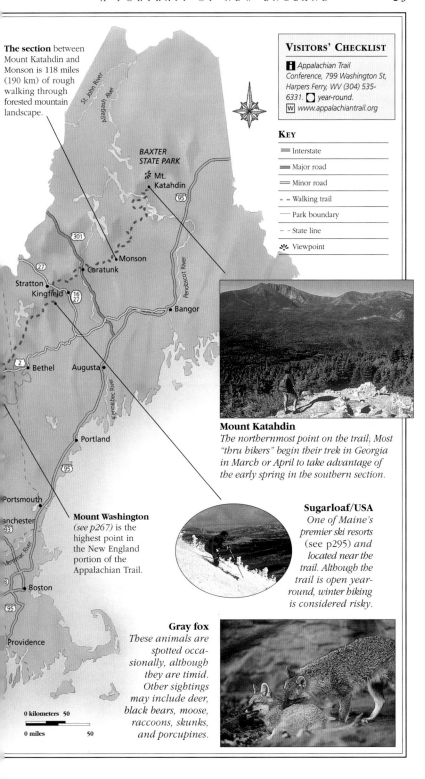

The section between Mount Katahdin and Monson is 118 miles (190 km) of rough walking through forested mountain landscape.

St. John River

Allagash River

BAXTER STATE PARK

Mt. Katahdin

95

301

Monson

27

Caratunk

Stratton

Kingfield

16
27

Bethel

Augusta

Penobscot River

Kennebec River

Bangor

Portland

95

Portsmouth

anchester

93

Merrimac River

3

Boston

95

Providence

2

0 kilometers 50

0 miles   50

VISITORS' CHECKLIST

ℹ️ *Appalachian Trail Conference, 799 Washington St, Harpers Ferry, WV (304) 535-6331.* ◐ *year-round.* Ⓦ *www.appalachiantrail.org*

KEY

━━ Interstate

━━ Major road

━━ Minor road

- - Walking trail

— Park boundary

- - State line

☆ Viewpoint

Mount Katahdin
The northernmost point on the trail. Most "thru hikers" begin their trek in Georgia in March or April to take advantage of the early spring in the southern section.

Mount Washington *(see p267)* is the highest point in the New England portion of the Appalachian Trail.

Sugarloaf/USA
One of Maine's premier ski resorts (see p295) and located near the trail. Although the trail is open year-round, winter hiking is considered risky.

Gray fox
These animals are spotted occasionally, although they are timid. Other sightings may include deer, black bears, moose, raccoons, skunks, and porcupines.

Maritime New England

Whaleboat figurehead

IT WAS THE SEA that helped open up the region to settlement in the 17th century. The sea also provided New Englanders with a way of life. In the early years, ships worked the fertile waters off Cape Cod for whales, fish, and lobster. Whaling reached its zenith in the 19th century, when hundreds of whaleboats fanned out to the uttermost ends of the Earth in search of new grounds for whales. Today the best places to explore the area's rich maritime and whaling history and traditions are the New Bedford Whaling National Historical Park and the New Bedford Whaling Museum in New Bedford, Massachusetts *(see p121)*, and Mystic Seaport *(see pp214–15)* in Connecticut.

Ropes and pulleys *were important for hoisting sails and lowering the whaleboats.*

Antique whaling harpoons
Harpoons and lances were hand-forged in New Bedford. Harpoons were thrown to attach a line to the whale. When the leviathan tired of pulling boat and men, the lance was used for the kill.

NEW ENGLAND'S WHALERS

Competition in 19th-century whaling was fierce. In 1857 some 330 whalers sailed out of New Bedford, Massachusetts, alone. The *Catalpa*, portrayed by C.S. Raleigh in his late-1800s painting, is an example of a well-outfitted whaler.

Whaleboats were lowered into the water to hunt and harpoon whales. Whale oil was used for illumination and was a valuable commodity.

Maritime art
Maritime influences still appear throughout New England. This contemporary chest by Harriet Scudder depicts an early whaling scene.

THE ICE TRADE

The cold winters of northern New England provided the source of a valuable export in the 19th century. In the days before mechanical refrigeration, ice from the region's frozen rivers, lakes, and ponds was cut up into large blocks, packed in sawdust, and shipped as far away as India. To keep the ice from melting, engineers designed ships with special airtight hulls. The ice trade finally collapsed in the late 1800s when mechanical methods for keeping perishables cool began to make ice obsolete for refrigeration in an increasing number of places in the world.

Harvesting ice

Barks were popular whaling vessels in the 19th century because they were maneuverable and could undertake long voyages.

Scrimshaw
New England sailors killed long periods of inactivity on the sea making etchings on whale teeth or jawbones. Ink and tobacco juice added color.

Whale carcasses were secured to the sides of the ship so that the blubber could be stripped and boiled onboard for its oil.

Lighthouses
Nearly 200 lighthouses dot New England's coast, testimony to the area's maritime ties.

Lobster industry
In colonial times, lobster was so common it was used as fertilizer. Today it is considered a delicacy.

New England Architecture

Scrolled door pediment

NEW ENGLAND ARCHITECTURE encompasses a variety of styles. In the early years of colonization, the influences of England predominated. But after the Revolutionary War (1775–83), the new republic wanted to distance itself from its colonial past. Drawing on French Neo-classicism, the newest European style of the late 18th century, American architects brought into being a distinctive American version known as Federal. In its efforts to define itself, New England did not reject foreign ideas, however, as evidenced by the Greek Revival style of the early 19th century and the adaptation of English and French Revival styles for the next 100 years.

First Church of Christ in West Hartford, Connecticut

COLONIAL STYLE

Colonial style, the style of the period when America was still a British colony, has two aspects: the homes of ordinary people and the more elaborate architecture of public buildings, mansions, and churches. The large wooden houses built in towns and rural areas in New England between 1607 and 1780 constitute one of the area's architectural treasures. Numerous examples survive, and the style has many regional variations. The famous Connecticut "saltbox" houses are an example. They featured distinctive close-cropped eaves and a long back roof that projected over a kitchen lean-to.

Eleazer Arnold House chimney, Providence, Rhode Island

Roof
Shingles became the main roofing material and were frequently used for walls as well.

Chimney
The large chimney provided a vital outlet for smoke.

Jethro Coffin House was built in 1686 and is the oldest surviving structure in Nantucket, Massachusetts. A slot beside the front door allowed inhabitants to see who was standing outside.

Windows
Small casement windows were fitted with diamond-shaped panes of glass imported from England.

Door
In keeping with the practical Colonial aesthetics, doors featured a simple, vertical-board design.

Casement window

GEORGIAN STYLE

The term Georgian, or Palladian, refers to the mainstream classical architecture of 18th-century England, which drew on designs of 16th-century Italian architect Andrea Palladio (1508–80). In the colonies and England, these elegant buildings marked the presence of the British ruling class.

Pedimented dormers, Ladd Gilman House, in Exeter, New Hampshire

Roof
Roofs were less steeply pitched than earlier Colonial-era designs. A delicate balustrade crowns the roof.

Windows
Georgian windows were usually double-hung sash with 6 panes.

Doors
Doors featured a raised-panel design with six or more panels and classical moldings.

Vassall/Craigie/ Longfellow House, built in 1759, displays typical style features. Its facade has classical columns and a triangular pediment.

FEDERAL STYLE

American architects viewed the Federal style as a distinctive national statement. Some Federal buildings drew on both Greek and Roman architecture, representing the tenets of democracy and republicanism. Federal style is more restrained than Georgian, with less intricate woodwork.

The Colony House in Newport (see pp182–7), Rhode Island

Fanlights
Fanlights, frequent in Georgian archi-tecture, were also found in Neo-classical design.

Roof
Neoclassical roofs were often flat.

Facade
Neoclassical facades were less decorated than Georgian. Often stories were separated by bands of stone called string courses.

Gardner-Pingree House is known for its graceful propor-tions and beautiful doorway.

GREEK REVIVAL STYLE

Popular between 1820 and 1845, this style is a more literal version of classical architecture than the Federal style. Greek Revival buildings typically borrowed the facades of ancient Greek temples, often sensitively re-creating them in wood.

Samuel Russell House in Middletown, Connecticut, features a white exterior common in Greek Revival structures.

Providence, Rhode Island, church door

Facade
The "temple fronts" of Greek Revival buildings were inspired by the archeological discoveries in Greece and Turkey in the 18th century.

Columns
These Corinthian columns faithfully follow conventions of ancient Greek architecture.

New England Universities

NEW ENGLAND IS NOT ONLY THE CRADLE of American civilization, it is also the birthplace of higher education in the New World. Harvard University *(see pp110–17)* was founded in 1636, only 16 years after the Pilgrims arrived at Plymouth Rock *(see pp148–9)*. Four of the country's eight renowned Ivy League colleges are located in New England: Harvard, Brown *(see p175)*, Dartmouth *(see p263)*, and Yale *(see pp222–5)*. Here higher learning goes hand in hand with tradition and culture. Many of America's most famous art collections and natural history museums are found on campus grounds. As well, many of the top-ranked liberal arts colleges are found here, including Bowdoin, Wellesley, and all-women Smith College.

1764 Rhode Island College, later Brown University, is founded in Providence, Rhode Island

1853 Franklin Pierce, graduate of Bowdoin College in Brunswick, Maine, is elected 14th president of the United States

1636 Harvard University is founded in Cambridge, Massachusetts; 12 students enroll in the inaugural year

1701 Puritan clergymen found Collegiate School in Saybrook, Connecticut

1778 Phillips Academy is founded by educator Samuel Phillips in Andover, Massachusetts

1781 John Phillips, uncle of Samuel, founds Phillips Exeter Academy in Exeter, New Hampshire

1801 Daniel Webster graduates from Dartmouth and goes on to an illustrious career as US statesman and orator

1640	1680	1720	1760	1800	1840

1640	1680	1720	1760	1800	1840

1642 Physics becomes a mandatory subject at Harvard, using text by Aristotle

1777 Brown's University Hall building is used as barracks for Colonial troops during War of Independence

1817 Harvard Law School is established

1832 Yale Art Gallery is founded after US artist John Trumbull donates some 100 pieces of art from his personal collection

1717 Collegiate School is moved to New Haven, Connecticut, and is renamed Yale in 1718 in honor of benefactor Elihu Yale

1844 Yale graduate Samuel Morse sends world's first telegraphic message in Morse code

1852 The Harvard crew wins inaugural Harvard-Yale Regatta – beginning one of the longest rivalries in US college sports

1861 Massachusetts Institute of Technology (MIT) is founded

1868 William Dubois is born. Dubois would go on to become the first black to earn a Ph.D. from Harvard

1919 Philanthropist and Brown University graduate John D. Rockefeller, Jr. donates 5,000 acres (2,025 ha) of Maine's Mount Desert Island for use as a preserve. His further gifts would form almost one-third of Acadia National Park *(see pp288–9)*

1925 S.J. Perelman graduates from Brown; goes on to win Academy Award for screenplay of *Around the World in 80 Days* (1956)

1957 Theodore Geisel (Dr. Seuss), Dartmouth alumnus, publishes *The Cat in the Hat*

1992 Yale graduate Bill Clinton is elected 42nd president of the United States

2000 Academy Award-winner Elizabeth Shue *(Leaving Las Vegas)* graduates from Harvard with a degree in political science

| 1880 | 1920 | 1960 | 2000 |
| 1880 | | 1960 | 2000 |

1877 Former slave Inman Page becomes first African-American to graduate from Brown

1861 Yale awards country's first Ph.D. degrees

1920

1946 Percy Bridgman becomes first Harvard physicist to receive Nobel Prize in Physics

1969 Women are admitted to Yale's undergraduate program

NEW ENGLAND BOARDING SCHOOLS

New England boasts the most prestigious collection of college preparatory, or "prep," schools in the US. The two preeminent institutions are Phillips Academy in Andover, Massachusetts, and Phillips Exeter Academy *(see p256)* in Exeter, New Hampshire. Both are private, coeducational schools and attract the sons and daughters of some of the country's wealthiest and most influential families. Other prominent prep schools include Choate Rosemary Hall in Wallingford, Connecticut, and Groton in Groton, Massachusetts.

Campus of Phillips Exeter Academy

Literary New England

WRITING IN HIS SEMINAL WORK *Democracy in America* (1835), French historian Alexis de Tocqueville (1805–1859) declared, "The inhabitants of the United States have, then, at present, no literature." Less than two decades later that scenario had changed radically. By then, writers such as Ralph Waldo Emerson (1803–82), Henry David Thoreau (1817–62), and Nathaniel Hawthorne (1804–64) were creating works that would take their place among the classics of 19th-century literature – and that was just in one town, Concord *(see pp144–5)*, Massachusetts. Since that first flowering, New England writers have been taking their place among the best in the world.

Author Nathaniel Hawthorne (1804–64)

In 1854 he published *Walden; or, Life in the Woods,* in which he outlined how people could escape a life of "quiet desperation" by paring away the extraneous, anxiety-inducing trappings of the industrial age and living in harmony with the natural world.

Ralph Waldo Emerson, speaking to Transcendentalists in Concord

FATHER OF TRANSCENDENTALISM

Born in Boston, Ralph Waldo Emerson graduated from Harvard University in 1821 and became the pastor of the Second Church (Unitarian) in Boston in 1829. In many ways Emerson turned his back on his formal religious education in the 1830s when he founded the Transcendentalism movement. Among other things, Emerson's writings espoused a system of spiritual independence in which each individual was responsible for his or her own moral judgments. Moving to Concord in 1834, the popular essayist and lecturer soon became known as the "Sage of Concord" for his insightful teachings.

Concord was also the birthplace of Emerson's most famous disciple, Henry David Thoreau. A one-time school teacher, Thoreau worked as a pencil maker before quitting to undertake his lifelong study of nature. Deeply influenced by the Transcendentalist belief that total unity with nature was achievable, Thoreau built a small cabin at Walden Pond *(see p145)* in 1845, living as a recluse for the next two years.

Henry David Thoreau's simple grave in Concord, Massachusetts

19TH-CENTURY LITERARY FLOWERING

It was also in Concord that Nathaniel Hawthorne penned *Mosses from an Old Manse* in 1846. Hawthorne later returned to his hometown, Salem *(see pp136–7)*, Massachusetts, where he wrote his best-known work, *The Scarlet Letter* (1850). Moving to Lenox in western Massachusetts, Hawthorne became friends with Herman Melville (1819–91), who wrote his allegorical masterpiece *Moby-Dick* (1851) in

Illustration from Herman Melville's *Moby-Dick*

Visitor on the porch of the Robert Frost house in New Hampshire

neighboring Pittsfield. The book drew its inspiration from the voyage that Melville made from New Bedford, Massachusetts, to the South Seas aboard the New England whaler *Acushnet*.

Like Melville, Mark Twain (1835–1910) was not a New Englander by birth. However, it was during his long stay in Hartford *(see pp198–9)*, Connecticut, that he penned the novels that would vault him into worldwide prominence, including *The Adventures of Tom Sawyer* (1876), *The Adventures of Huckleberry Finn* (1885), and *A Connecticut Yankee in King Arthur's Court* (1889).

19TH-CENTURY WOMEN AUTHORS

Although opportunities for women were limited in 19th-century America, several New England female writers still managed to leave their mark on literature. One of the region's most famous – and mysterious – literary figures was Emily Dickinson (1830–86). Born in Amherst *(see p162–3)*, Massachusetts, she was educated at the Mount Holyoke Female Seminary *(see p162)* before withdrawing from society in her early 20s. Living the rest of her life in her family's home, Dickinson wrote more than 1,000 poems – the vast majority of which remained unpublished until after her death. Today her finely crafted poems are

Cover of sheet music for Harriet Beecher Stowe's *Uncle Tom's Cabin*

admired for their complex rhythms and intensely personal lyrics.

The greatest single indictment of the slavery that would catapult America into civil war came from the pen of Harriet Beecher Stowe (1811–96), who would later become Mark Twain's next door neighbor in Hartford. *Uncle Tom's Cabin; or, Life Among the Lowly* (1852) told the story of a slave family's desperate flight for freedom to a rapt, largely sympathetic audience worldwide. Louisa May Alcott (1832–88) – yet another Concord resident – left a lasting and loving portrait of domestic life in the United States during the Civil War in *Little Women* (1868), a perennial favorite of children.

20TH CENTURY

In the 20th century, New England continued to play a defining role in American literature, spawning native writers as diverse as "Beat" chronicler Jack Kerouac *(see p142)* and the "Chekhov of the suburbs," John Cheever (1912–82). The region has also provided a fertile base for transplanted New Englanders. The poet Robert Frost (1874–1963), a native of San Francisco, lived most of his life in Vermont and New Hampshire, and the mountains, meadows, and people of the region figure prominently in his poetry, which won the Pulitzer Prize an unprecedented four times. Poet and novelist John Updike (b.1932) has lived much of his life in Ipswich, Massachusetts, and set both *Couples* (1968) and *The Witches of Eastwick* (1984) in the northeast. Novelist John Irving was born in Exeter, New Hampshire, in 1942. Much of his later fiction is set in New England, including *The World According to Garp* (1978) and *Cider House Rules* (1985). Perhaps the area's best-known living writer is Stephen King (b.1947). The prolific master of the macabre and author of such horror stories as *The Shining* (1977) is a longtime resident of Bangor, Maine, where his Gothic-style home is one of the town's biggest tourist attractions.

Fright master and longtime Bangor resident Stephen King

NEW ENGLAND
THROUGH THE YEAR

NEW ENGLAND is really a year-round tourist destination – depending on what it is people are looking to do. Generally, spring is the shortest season. Occurring sometime between April and June, spring can be short-lived but glorious, with wildflowers bursting forth in colorful bloom. Summer is the busiest tourist period. With the good weather stretching from mid-June into early September, this part of the year is characterized by warm temperatures that have people flocking to lakes and the ocean. Fall is when New England is at its most beautiful, with its lush forests changing from green to a riot of gold, red, and orange. The peak fall-foliage period generally occurs from mid-September to late October. Winter, which usually lasts from December to mid-April, is often marked by heavy snowfalls – a boon for winter sport enthusiasts.

Colorful hot-air balloon

Cars decorated with flowers in Nantucket's Daffodil Festival

SPRING

NEW ENGLAND'S shortest season is sometimes little more than a three-week interval between winter and summer. As well as being the prime time for maple syrup tapping, spring brings with it a host of festivals.

APRIL

Boston Marathon *(third Monday, April)*, Boston, MA. The world's oldest and most prestigious marathon.
Patriot's Day *(third Monday, April)*, Lexington and Concord, MA. Costumed reenactments of the pivotal battles that were waged at the outset of the Revolutionary War.
Daffodil Festival *(late April)*, Nantucket, MA. The town is decked out in millions of yellow daffodils.

MAY

Annual Civil War Living History and Battles Encampment *(early May)*, Hammonasset Beach State Park, CT. Civil War reenactment complete with battles.
Main Street in May *(May)*, Plymouth, NH. Antique cars, sidewalk musicians, and children's activities are highlights of this annual event.
Gaspee Days *(mid-May–mid-June)*, Cranston and Warwick, RI. Reenactment of the burning of a British schooner.
Brimfield Antique Show *(May, July, and September)*, Brimfield, MA. Dealers from across the US sell their wares.
Lobsterfest *(late May)*, Mystic, CT. A lobsterbake popular with both locals and visitors.

Patriot Days celebration in Lexington, Massachusetts

Delicious lobsters served up during Mystic's Lobsterfest

JUNE

Harvard-Yale Regatta *(early June)*, New London, CT. This is a classic college showdown.
Taste of Hartford *(early June)*, Hartford, CT. One of New England's largest outdoor food festivals.
Discover Jazz Festival *(early June)*, Burlington, VT. Jazz, blues, and gospel are the highlights of this popular festival.
International Festival of Art and Ideas *(mid-June–July)*, New Haven, Hartford, Stamford, and New London, CT. A showcase of some of the world's best performance and visual arts.

SUMMER

NEW ENGLAND summers can be hot and humid. This is vacation time for students and families, making the region a very busy place, especially the coastline and beaches.

AVERAGE DAILY HOURS OF SUNSHINE

Hours

Jan Feb Mar Apr May Jun Jul Aug Sep Oct Nov Dec

Sunshine Chart
New England's weather can vary greatly from year to year. Generally, the short spring is cloudy and wet, giving way to better weather in June. July and August are usually the sunniest months. Bright fall days out among the colorful foliage are spectacular.

JUNE

Circus Smirkus *(early June–mid-August)*. This international youth circus stages shows around New England.

Windjammer Days *(late June)*, Boothbay Harbor, ME. Shoreside events complement parade of graceful sailboats.

Stowe Flower Festival *(late June)*, Stowe, VT. Seminars and tours of formal gardens.

Northwest Connecticut Balloon Festival *(late June)*, Goshen, CT. Mass-ascensions, hot-air balloon rides, car and motorcycle show, and fireworks highlight this festival.

Storm Trysail Club Block Island Race Week *(late June)*, Block Island, RI. This week-long event is the largest sailing event on the coast.

Williamstown Theater Festival *(late June–August)*, Williamstown, MA. Acclaimed festival of classical and new theater productions.

Jacob's Pillow Dance Festival *(late June–late August)*, Becket, MA. Ballet, jazz, and modern dance are featured in the country's oldest dance festival.

JULY

Independence Day Celebrations *(July 4th)*, throughout New England. Parades, fireworks, and concerts mark the anniversary of US independence.

Tanglewood Music Festival *(early July–late August)*, Lenox, MA. Boston Symphony and Boston Pops orchestras give concerts on beautiful estate *(see p167)*.

Riverfest *(July)*, Hartford, CT. Fireworks and free concerts along the Connecticut River.

Vermont Quilt Festival *(July)*, Northfield, VT. A premier quilting celebration.

Mozart Festival *(July and August)*, Burlington, VT. A celebration of the music of Wolfgang Amadeus Mozart.

Schooner Days *(mid-July)*, Rockland, ME. Highlights of this maritime festival include boat races and a parade of classic windjammers.

Newport Music Festival *(mid-July)*, Newport, RI. Classical music concerts are held inside the city's mansions.

Newport Regatta *(mid-July)*, Newport, RI. This huge regatta attracts some 300 boats.

Guilford Handcrafts Exposition *(mid-July)*, Guilford, CT. This event features pottery, glass, pewter, jewelry, folk art, and quilts.

Lowell Folk Festival *(late July)*, Lowell, MA. Dance troupes, musicians, and ethnic food are served up here.

AUGUST

Maine Lobster Festival *(early August)*, Rockland, ME. Lobster and live entertainment are on the menu at this event.

Ben & Jerry's Newport Folk Festival *(early August)*, Newport, RI. One of the country's top folk festivals, held at Fort Adams State Park.

League of New Hampshire Craftsmen Annual Fair *(early August)*, Newbury, NH. The oldest crafts fair in the US features craft

Popular Schooner Days in Rockland, Maine

demonstrations, workshops, performing arts, and 200 booths selling crafts of extremely high quality.

Addison County Fair *(early August)*, New Haven, VT. This is one of the state's largest agricultural fairs.

Mystic Outdoor Arts Festival *(mid-August)*, Mystic, CT. This art show attracts 300 artists.

Newport JVC Jazz Festival *(mid-August)*, Newport, RI. International jazz stars gather to perform in this celebration of music.

Downtime Concord Fiddling Championship *(late August)*, Concord, NH. An annual fiddling tournament that attracts both the young and the old.

Brooklyn Fair *(late August)*, Brooklyn, CT. The country's oldest continuously running agricultural fair has ox pulls and livestock shows.

Champlain Valley Exhibition *(late August–early September)*, Essex Junction, VT. Horse shows and midway rides are part of this huge fair.

July 4th road markings

AVERAGE MONTHLY PRECIPITATION

MM												Inches
300												12
240												9
180												6
120												3
60												
0	Jan	Feb	Mar	Apr	May	Jun	Jul	Aug	Sep	Oct	Nov	Dec	0

Precipitation Chart
Spring is called "mud season" by locals, thanks to rainy skies and melting snow. Summer can be unpredictable, but is generally dry. Snow usually starts in December.

AUTUMN

MANY PEOPLE consider the fall to be New England's most beautiful season. Bright, crisp autumn days are made more glorious by the brilliant fall foliage *(see p20–21)*.

SEPTEMBER

Rhode Island Heritage Festival *(September 4th)*, Providence, RI. Thirty ethnic communities celebrate their heritage and culture with music, song, dance, arts, and food demonstrations.
Windjammer Weekend *(early September)*, Camden, ME. A celebration of Maine's fleet of classic sailing ships.
Vermont State Fair *(early September)*, Rutland, VT. One of the most popular agricultural fairs in the state.
Classic Yacht Regatta *(early September)*, Newport, RI. More than 100 vintage wooden yachts are on parade in this regatta.
Woodstock Fair *(early September)*, South Woodstock, CT. The state's second-oldest agricultural fair includes crafts, go-cart races, livestock shows, and petting zoos for children.
Mount Washington Old Car Show *(early September)*, North Conway, NH. Some 300 antique cars, trucks, and motorcycles are on display.
Norwalk Oyster Festival *(early September)*, East Norwalk, CT. This nationally acclaimed celebration includes fireworks, antique boats, and lots of oyster sampling.
The Big "E" *(last two weeks of September)*, Eastern States Exhibition Ground, West

A Harvest Festival, this one in Keene, New Hampshire

Springfield, MA. One of New England's biggest fairs, complete with rodeos, rides, and a circus.
Harvest Festivals *(late September)*, throughout New England. Parades, apple picking, and hay rides are just some of the festivities held around the region to celebrate the fall harvest.
Sugar Hill Antique Show *(late September)*, Sugar Hill, NH. A popular, long-running antique show attracts numerous dealers and their wares.
Northeast Kingdom Fall Foliage Festival *(late September–early October)*, throughout northern Vermont.

Different towns hold foliage-related bus tours, hiking parties, and family events.

OCTOBER

Sled Dog Derby *(October–April)*, Hanover, NH. Top dog teams and mushers compete.
Mozart Festival *(October–April)*, Burlington, VT. A celebration of the works of Wolfgang Amadeus Mozart.
Woonsocket Autumnfest *(early October)*, Woonsocket, RI. Live music, craft displays, a midway, and a Columbus Day parade top events.
New England Bach Festival *(October)*, Brattleboro, VT. A month-long musical celebration of Johann Sebastian Bach.
Haunted Happenings *(October)*, Salem, MA. A 10-day festival celebrating the city's witch-related past *(see pp136–9)* and Halloween.
PumpkinFire *(late October)*, Providence, RI. Elaborate pumpkins are created in this carving competition.

NOVEMBER

Holiday Craft Exhibition and Sale *(mid-November–December 31st)*, Brookfield,

Brilliant colors, heralding Northeast Kingdom Fall Foliage Festival

AVERAGE MONTHLY TEMPERATURE

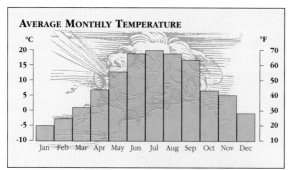

Temperature Chart
New England temperatures vary greatly through the year. In the summer, temperatures of 90° F (32° C) are not quite frequent, while the thermometer can dip to 0° F (-18° C) or lower in winter. In general, it is warmer along the coast and in the southern section of New England.

CT. Hundreds of craft artists put unique wares up for sale.

Thanksgiving Celebration *(mid–late November)*, Plymouth, MA. Thanksgiving traditions of the past are celebrated in historic homes. Visitors can also take part in a Victorian Thanksgiving at Plimoth Plantation *(see pp150–51)*.

Festival of Light *(late November–early January)*, Hartford, CT. Constitution Plaza is transformed into a spectacular world of more than 200,000 white lights.

WINTER

NEW ENGLAND WINTERS are often marked by heavy snowfalls, particularly in the mountainous areas farther inland. Temperatures can also plunge drastically overnight and from one day to the next. This, of course, is a boon for people who enjoy winter sports, as New England has some of the most popular ski centers in the eastern US.

DECEMBER

Christmas at Blithewold *(throughout December)*, Bristol, RI. Traditional Christmas celebrations are celebrated in this beautiful mansion.

Festival of Trees and Traditions *(early December)*, Hartford, CT. Hundreds of beautiful trees and wreaths are on display.

Festival of Lights *(early December)*, Wickford Village, RI. This family-oriented festival includes tree- and window-decorating competitions, hayrides, and live music.

Wolfgang Amadeus Mozart, feted in Burlington, Vermont

Christmas Tree Lighting *(early December)*, Boston, MA. The enormous tree in front of the Prudential Center is lit up with thousands of bright lights.

Candlelight Stroll *(mid-December)*, Portsmouth, NH. The town's historic Strawbery Banke district *(see pp254–5)* is resplendent with antique Christmas decorations and thousands of candles.

Boston Tea Party Reenactment *(mid-December)*, Boston, MA. Costumed interpreters bring to life the famous protest that precipitated the Revolutionary War.

First Night Celebrations *(December 31st)*, throughout New England (except Maine). A series of family-oriented celebrations, started in Boston in 1976 and now celebrated around the world. Music, art, and a host of festivities.

Vermont Farm Show *(late January)*, Barre, VT. Vermont's premier winter show includes a variety of

agricultural displays and livestock exhibits.

Brookfield Ice Harvest *(late January)*, Brookfield, VT. Ice sculptures and ice-cutting demonstrations are featured here.

Chinese New Year *(late January–early February)*, Boston, MA. The location for this colorful festival is Boston's Chinatown.

National Toboggan Championships *(February)*, Camden, ME. Daredevils of all sizes and ages come to compete in this high-speed, often hilarious, event.

Stowe Derby *(late February)*, Stowe, VT. This is one of the oldest downhill and cross-country skiing races in the country.

New England Spring Flower Show *(March)*, Boston, MA. Meticulous landscaped gardens and thousands of new blooms announce the colorful end of winter.

St. Patrick's Day Parade *(March 17th)*, Boston, MA. One of the country's longest-running and most famous parades. Post-parade festivities are held throughout the city, including a reception at historic Faneuil Hall.

Musicians in Boston's St. Patrick's Day Parade

The History of New England

THE EARLY HISTORY *of New England is the history of the United States itself, for it is here that civilization first gained a toehold in America and where much of the drama of forming a new country was played out. But even after the rest of the country had been populated, New England continued to exert influence on the political, economic, and intellectual life of the country.*

No one can say for sure which Europeans first made landfall in New England. Some historians claim that the Vikings, after first reaching Newfoundland around AD 1000, eventually ventured as far south as Massachusetts. Others suggest that Spanish, Portuguese, or Irish explorers were the first Old World visitors. But one thing is sure: none of these peoples actually discovered the area. Native Americans already had called the region home for several thousand years. They were descendants of nomads from central Asia who had journeyed to what is now Alaska via the then-dry Bering Strait between 20,000 and 12,000 years ago. Slowly they migrated east.

Paul Revere

The earliest fossil evidence of human activity in the area dates back to 9000 BC. By the time the first European came ashore, the region was populated by about 20,000 Native Americans. Most of them were members of the Algonquin "nation," a loose conglomeration of a dozen or so tribes that occasionally engaged in violent internecine struggles. Their inability to unite would later prove a fatal flaw when confronted by a common foe – white settlers. Unlike their Asian ancestors, the Algonquins, also known as Abenakis ("people of the dawn"), had given up nomadic life. They ate moose, deer, birds, and fish, but grew crops, too – maize, called Indian corn, beans, and pumpkins.

Map of the Northeast, printed in England a month after the Declaration of Independence was signed

◁ *Native American Indians Cooking and Preparing Food c.1850 by J. Fumagalli*

Embarkation and Departure of Columbus from the Port of Palos, undated painting by Ricardo Balaca

THE AGE OF DISCOVERY

The voyage of Christopher Columbus (1451–1506) to the New World in 1492 fired the imagination of maritime nations in Europe. Soon seafarers from England, France, and Spain were setting forth to explore the New World on behalf of their respective kings and queens. In 1497 the Italian explorer John Cabot (c.1425–1499) reached New England from Bristol, England, and claimed the land, along with all the territory north of Florida and east of the Rocky Mountains, for his English patron, Henry VII (1457–1509). By the end of the 16th century, helped largely by the 1588 defeat of the Spanish Armada, England was beginning to achieve mastery of the seas.

King James I (1566–1625)

In 1606 England's King James I (1566–1625) granted a charter to two ventures to establish settlements in America. The Virginia Company was assigned an area near present-day Virginia; the Plymouth Company was granted rights to a more northern colony. This second group ran into trouble early on. One of its ships strayed off course and was captured by the Spanish near Florida. Another ship made it to New England, but had to turn back to England before winter arrived. In May 1607 two ships left Plymouth, England, with approximately 100 colonists. Three months later they made landfall at the mouth of the Kennebec River, where the settlers constructed Fort St. George. Their first winter proved to be an especially cold and snowy one, and the furs and mineral wealth fell far short of what the colonists expected. After just a year, the so-called Popham Colony was abandoned.

Despite this inauspicious beginning, the Plymouth Company hired surveyor John Smith (1580–1631) to conduct a more extensive evaluation of the territory. In 1614 Smith sailed along the Massachusetts coast, observing the region. His findings, published in *A Description of New England*, not only coined the name of the region, but also painted a glowing picture of this new land and its "greatnessse" of fish

TIMELINE

25,000-12,000 BC Central Asian nomads cross Bering Strait to become first North Americans	**7,000-1,000 BC** Warming temperatures lead to development of New England's forests

25,000 BC		10,000 BC		AD 1000	1500

10,000 BC Humans move into New England area after deglaciation

Leif Eriksson in Viking boat

AD 1000 Vikings sail to Newfoundland, Canada, and move south along the coast and timber. Of all the places in the world, concluded Smith, this would be the best to support a new colony.

COLONIAL NEW ENGLAND

While the explorers of the early 17th century probed the shoreline of New England, events were taking place in Europe that would have a far-reaching impact on the settlement of the New World. The Reformation of the 16th century and the birth of the Protestant faith had created an upheaval in religious beliefs – particularly in England, where Henry VIII (1491–1547) had severed ties with Rome and had made sure that parliament declared him head the Church of England.

Protestant Puritans believed that the Church of England, despite its claim to represent a reformed Christianity, was still rife with Catholic practices and that their faith was being debased in England, especially after James I, who was suspected of having Catholic sympathies, succeeded Elizabeth I in 1603. Puritans were persecuted for their beliefs and found themselves facing a stark choice: stay at home to fight against overwhelming odds or start anew somewhere else.

A small, radical faction of Puritans, known as Separatists, emigrated to Holland. The lifestyle of the Dutch did not live up to the demanding standards

Puritan governor addresses Colonists in 1621

of the Separatists' stern orthodoxy. As a result, they negotiated a deal with the Plymouth Company to finance a "pilgrimage" to America. In September 1620 they set sail. After a grueling 66-day voyage, their ship, the *Mayflower*, landed at what is now Provincetown *(see p156)*, Massachusetts.

It was a short-lived stay. The barren, sandy coast seemed a forbidding place, so the ship sailed on to Plymouth Rock *(see pp148–9)*, where the fatigued Pilgrims disembarked on December 26, 1620. During the winter of 1620–21, half of the Pilgrims succumbed to scurvy and the rigors of a harsh New England winter. But with the arrival of spring, the worst seemed to be behind them. The settlers found an ally among the indigenous people in Squanto (d.1622), a member of the Pawtuxet tribe who had been taken to England in 1605. Squanto had returned to the New World in 1615, and when word reached him that the English had arrived, he soon helped them negotiate a 50-year peace treaty between the Pilgrims and the chief of the local Wampanoag tribe. Squanto also taught the newcomers how to live in their adopted home. He showed them how to shoot and trap, and told them which crops to grow. The first harvest was celebrated in the fall of 1621 with a three-day feast of thanksgiving.

Pilgrims board the *Mayflower* in 1620

1497 John Cabot explores North American coast	1607 First North American colony founded at Jamestown	1614 John Smith names territory New England	1620 Pilgrims land at Plymouth, Massachusetts, aboard the *Mayflower*	
1500	**1600**		**1615**	**1620**
1492 Christopher Columbus discovers the New World	1602 Captain Bartholomew Gosnold lands on Massachusetts coast *John Smith*		1616 Smallpox epidemic kills large number of New England Indians	*First feast of thanksgiving* 1621 Pilgrims celebrate feast of thanksgiving

The Battle of Bunker Hill

George III of England

THE FIRST MAJOR BATTLE of the Revolutionary War took place in Boston on June 17, 1775, and actually was fought on Breed's Hill. The Americans had captured heavy British cannon on Breed's and Bunker hills overlooking Boston Harbor, which gave them a commanding position. Britain's first two attacks on Breed's Hill were repelled by the outnumbered defenders. The Colonial soldiers were running low on ammunition, however, which gave rise to commander Colonel William Prescott's orders, "Don't fire until you can see the whites of their eyes!" Reinforced with 400 fresh troops, British forces made a bayonet charge and seized the hill, forcing the Americans to retreat to nearby Bunker Hill. The British suffered more than 1,000 casualties to approximately 150 for the Americans. The battle reinforced the confidence of the American troops that had first been kindled by their successes at Lexington and Concord.

Bunker Hill Monument, *a granite obelisk, honors Colonial casualties.*

IN THE HEAT OF THE BATTLE

John Trumbull's 1786 painting Battle of Bunker Hill *depicts the hand-to-hand combat of the skirmish, fought mainly with bayonets and muskets. Victory came at a price. As one British soldier commented, "It was such a dear victory, another such would have ruined us."*

Colonial General Joseph Warren dies in final moments of battle after being shot in the head.

Declaration of Independence
Less than a year after the battle, the Second Continental Congress adopted the Declaration of Independence, which outlined the framework for democracy in the United States.

Attack on Breed's Hill
Prior to the infantry assault on the Colonial position, British men-of-war bombarded Breed's Hill with cannonade. Portions of nearby Charleston caught fire and burned during the bombing.

A British officer prevents grenadier's *coup de grâce.*

British Firelocks
Loading a musket involved shaking gunpowder into a pan just above the trigger as well as into the barrel itself. The powder in the barrel was then tamped down with a small rod. This time-consuming process meant that soldiers stood unprotected on the battlefield as they reloaded.

British troops storm Colonial positions with renewed vigor after having suffered massive casualties on first two attempts.

British Major John Pitcairn collapses into his son's arms after being shot in chest, only to die while receiving medical treatment for his wounds.

COLONEL WILLIAM PRESCOTT

Born in Groton, Massachusetts, William Prescott (1726–95) led the Colonial forces during the battle of Bunker Hill. In the initial stages of the fight, British warships bombarded the Americans' fortified position with heavy cannon. The untested Colonial troops were taken aback, especially when a private was decapitated by a cannonball. Sensing his men were disheartened, Prescott, covered in the slain soldier's blood, leapt atop the redoubt wall and paced back and forth in defiance of the bombs bursting around him. His brave gesture galvanized the troops, who went on to make one of the most courageous stands of the Revolutionary War.

Death of Metacomet (King Philip) in 1676

COLONIAL NEW ENGLAND

From this modest beginning, the settlement began slowly to prosper and expand. Within five years the group was self-sufficient. Nine years later the Massachusetts Bay Company was founded, which sent 350 people to Salem *(see pp136–9)*.

A second, much larger group joined the newly appointed governor, John Winthrop (c.1587–1649), and established a settlement at the mouth of the Charles River. They first called their new home Trimountain, but renamed it Boston in honor of the town some of the settlers had left in England.

During the 1630s immigrants started spreading farther afield, creating settlements along the coast of Massachusetts and New Hampshire, and even venturing inland. However, the colonists' gain proved to be

the Natives' loss. Initial cooperation between both groups gave way to competition and outright hostility as land-hungry settlers moved into Indian territory. War first erupted with the Pequot tribe in 1637, which resulted in their near annihilation as a people. The hostility reached its peak at the outset of the King Philip's War (1775–6), when several hundred members of the Narragansett tribe were killed by white settlers near South Kingston, Rhode Island.

WEAKENING TIES

The sheer distance dividing England and New England and the fact that communication could move no faster than wind-borne ships meant that there was very little contact between Old World and New. The colonists were largely self-governing, and there was no representation from them in the British parliament. Efforts by London to tighten control over the colonies were sporadic and in most cases successfully resisted until the Seven Years War between Britain and France (1756–1763) assured British domination of North America.

Ironically, British success created the conditions that lessened the colonists' dependence on the mother country and also led to their growing estrangement. The colonies, especially New England, would come to feel that they no longer had to rely on British protection against the French in Canada and their Indian allies. Moreover, Britain's efforts after 1763 to derive a revenue from the colonies to help cover the debt incurred by the war and to contribute to imperial defense

England's George III (1738–1820)

TIMELINE

Harvard booster

1636 Harvard is founded, becoming America's first college

1656 Puritans of Massachusetts Bay Colony begin systematic persecution of newly arrived Quakers with imprisonment, banishment, and hanging

1676 King Philip's War ends when Wampanoag chief Metacomet is betrayed and killed

| 1630 | 1660 | 1675 | 1690 |

1630 Puritans led by John Winthrop found Boston

1636 Murder of two colonists, supposedly by Pequot Indians, sparks the beginning of Pequot War

Salem gravestone

1692 Salem witch trials begin, leading to the execution of 20 people met growing resistance. The cry of "No taxation without representation" would become a rallying call to arms for the independence movement, with the most vocal protests coming from New England.

The taxation issue came to a head under the reign of King George III (1738–1820), who ascended the throne of Great Britain in 1760. The Hanoverian king believed that the American colonists should remain under the control of Britain, and enacted a series of heavy taxes on various commodities, such as silk and sugar. In 1765 British parliament passed the Stamp Act, which placed a tax on commercial and legal documents, newspapers, agendas, and even playing cards and dice. The act had a galvanizing effect throughout New England as its incensed inhabitants banded together and refused to use the stamps. They even went so far as to hold stamp-burning ceremonies.

Parliament eventually repealed the act in 1766, but this did not end the issue. In fact, at the same time that the Stamp Act was rescinded, it was replaced by the Declaratory Act, which stated that every part of the British Empire would continue to be taxed however the parliament saw fit. To make sure that the colonists would not flout the law, the British sent two regiments to Boston to

Paul Revere's 1770 engraving of the Boston Massacre

British stamp for American colony goods

enforce its control. The troops, called Redcoats for their distinctive uniforms, proved decidedly unpopular. A series of small skirmishes between them and local sailors and workers culminated in the Boston Massacre (March 5, 1770), in which the British soldiers opened fire on an unruly crowd, killing five, including a free black man, Crispus Attucks.

REVOLUTIONARY SPIRIT

After the massacre an uneasy truce ensued. A simmering distrust remained between the two sides, and it only needed a suitable provocation to boil over again. That provocation came in the form of yet another proclamation – this one giving the East India Company the right to market tea directly in America, thus bypassing American merchants. When three ships arrived in Boston Harbor in 1773 with a shipment to unload, a group of about 60 men, including local politicians Samuel Adams (1722–1803) and John Hancock (1737–93), disguised themselves with Indian headdresses and then boarded the ships. They dumped 342 tea chests, valued at £18,000, into the harbor. The Boston Tea Party (see p89) was celebrated by the colonists as a

Protesters during the 1773 Boston Tea Party

1704 The *Boston News Letter*, America's first newspaper, is published	**1737** John Hancock, an original signatory of the Declaration of Independence, is born	*John Hancock's signature*		**1773** New taxes spur Boston Tea Party
1710	**1725**	**1740**	**1750**	**1770**
	1713 Boatyard in Gloucester, Massachusetts, produces America's first schooner		**1770** British soldiers kill five in Boston Massacre	

Crowd in Philadelphia celebrating the signing of the Declaration of Independence on July 4, 1776

justifiable act of defiance against an oppressive regime. Parliament responded by passing the Intolerable Acts of 1774. These included the closing of the port of Boston by naval blockade until payment was made for the tea that had been destroyed.

On September 5, 1774, 56 representatives from the various American colonies, including New England, met in Philadelphia to establish the First Continental Congress to consider how to deal with grievances against Britain. The first concrete step toward nationhood had been taken.

Minutemen repelling the British, who were tryint to march through to Concord

Although the British troops garrisoned in Boston in the mid-1770s represented a formidable force, a large part of New England lay beyond their control. In the countryside, locals stockpiled arms. In 1775 the royal governor of Massachusetts, General Thomas Gage (1721–87), learned about such a cache at Concord (see pp144–5), 20 miles (32 km) west of Boston. He ordered 700 British soldiers to travel there under cover of darkness and destroy the arms.

The Americans were tipped off by dramatic horseback rides from Boston by Paul Revere and William Dawes. By the time the troops arrived at Lexington a few miles to the east of Concord, 77 colonial soldiers had set up a defensive formation, slowing the British advance. The Redcoats pressed onward to Concord, where close to 400 American patriots, called Minutemen for their ability to muster at a moment's notice, repelled the British attack. By the end of that day, April 19, 1775, 70 British had been killed and the casualty toll was 273. American losses were 95.

TIMELINE

1774 British navy imposes blockade of Boston Harbor	**1775** Battles at Concord and Lexington mark beginning of Revolutionary War	**1783** Treaty of Paris signals end to Revolutionary War	**1789** George Washington becomes first president of the United States	*George Washington*

1775	1780	1785	1790	1795

1774 First Continental Congress held in Philadelphia	**1776** Second Continental Congress ratifies the Declaration of Independence	**1781** Colonial forces win decisive battle over British at Yorktown, Virginia	**1791** First mechanical cotton mill of Samuel Slater at Pawtucket, Rhode Island. *Slater Mill*	

Boston shipbuilding c.1850

The days of discussion were now clearly over. Colonial leaders signed the Declaration of Independence on July 4, 1776, and the American Revolution had begun. For the next six years the war would be waged first on New England soil, but then mostly beyond its borders in key battles at places such as Valley Forge, Pennsylvania, and Yorktown, Virginia. Although the fighting ceased in 1781, the war officially came to an end with the signing of the 1783 Treaty of Paris.

A NEW INDUSTRIAL POWER

The fledgling United States of America was rich in natural resources, especially in New England. The region had excellent harbors that gave it access to the West Indies, Europe, and farther afield, where a developing maritime trade *(see pp24–5)* with the spices, teas, and other riches of the Far East proved increasingly lucrative. Indeed, New England ships became a familiar sight at docks from Nantucket *(see p153)* to New Guinea and from Portsmouth *(see pp252–3)* to Port-au-Prince, Haiti. New England also became a world center for the whaling

Antique harpoon

industry, as local ships plied the Seven Seas in search of the leviathans of the deep, which were killed for their oil, baleen, and blubber. The burgeoning shipbuilding industry that had sprung up along the coast also supplied a fleet of fishing boats that trolled the Grand Banks and the waters off Cape Cod, returning with their holds full of cod and halibut.

Ultimately it was an invention of the Industrial Revolution that transformed New England into an economic powerhouse. In the late 18th century, the first of Richard Arkwright's (1732–92) cotton spinning machines was imported to North America from England and installed on the Blackstone River at Pawtucket *(see pp172–3)*, Rhode Island. Previously cotton had been processed on individual looms in homes. Arkwright's device permitted cotton spinning to be carried out on factory-sized machines, which increased productivity a thousandfold. Soon mills sprang up, mainly in Massachusetts, in towns such as Lowell *(see pp142–3)*, Waltham, and Lawrence.

Richard Arkwright's sketch for his revolutionary cotton spinning machine

1800 National census results: 5.3 million people

Noah Webster

| 1805 | 1810 | 1815 | 1820 | 1825 |

1806 New Haven's Noah Webster publishes *Compendious Dictionary of the English Language*

1820 Maine gains independence from Massachusetts and becomes 20th state in the Union

By the mid-19th century, New England held two-thirds of America's cotton mills. The region offered two main advantages: a ready supply of rivers to power the mills' machinery and an increasing flow of cheap labor. Escaping the Potato Famine in the 1840s, numerous Irish immigrants fled to Massachusetts, where the mill towns beckoned with dormitory housing for their employees. Despite their numbers, however, this group faced discrimination.

Irish peasant contemplating failed crop

In Boston many such newcomers settled in squalid tenements along the city's waterfront. Eventually the Irish would come to dominate Boston politics and social order, but for much of the 19th century they faced a daily struggle just to survive.

The extent of industrialization was felt in a relatively small area of New England, mostly Massachusetts, Rhode Island, and Connecticut. In the hinterland of Vermont, New Hampshire, and Maine, farming and logging remained the key industries well into the 20th century. These far-flung regions provided some of the manpower for the heartland's factories, as people left the hardscrabble life of subsistence farming for new lives farther south. Northern New England also helped supply the factories with some of their raw materials. The forests of Vermont, for example, were hacked down to make grazing land for sheep, which supplied wool for the textile mills.

ABOLITIONIST NEW ENGLAND

New England's role in 19th-century America was not merely one of economic powerhouse. The region also dominated the fields of education, science, politics, and architecture, as well as serving as the cultural heart of the nation, with Boston and its environs producing some of the nation's most influential writers and thinkers. The Massachusetts capital was also the center of a prominent protest against slavery, which was firmly entrenched in the southern states and reviled in much of the North.

William Lloyd Garrison (1805–79) began publishing a newspaper called *The Liberator* in 1831. In Garrison's view, "There is only one theme which should be dwelt upon till our whole country is free from the curse – SLAVERY." His polemics in *The Liberator* drew the wrath of pro-slavery forces. The House of Representatives of the southern state of Georgia offered $5,000 for his arrest. But Garrison continued publishing his newspaper, never missing an issue until it ceased publication at the end of the Civil War (1861–65), when slavery had been expunged from American society.

Some residents of New England towns went beyond merely reading and writing about the injustices of slavery. Stirred by Garrison and the so-called abolitionist movement, some antislavery exponents offered safe houses for what came to be known as the Underground Railroad. This loosely

Abolitionist William Lloyd Garrison

TIMELINE

Colt six-shooters

1835 Connecticut's Samuel Colt invents the six-shooter handgun

1851–2 *Uncle Tom's Cabin* appears in serial form in *The National Era* newspaper

1861 Civil War begins

1830	1845	1860

1831 Abolitionist William Lloyd Garrison publishes first edition of anti-slavery newspaper *The Liberator*

1840 Ireland's first Potato Famine devastates country

1851 Herman Melville publishes *Moby-Dick*, written in the southern Berkshires

1865 Civil War ends, leaving some 620,000 Americans dead connected network of escape routes helped slaves fleeing the South make their way to freedom in the North and in Canada, beyond the reach of slave hunters. Towns such as Plymouth *(see pp148–9)*, Massachusetts, Portland *(see pp280–83)*, Maine, and Burlington *(see pp232–5)*, Vermont, served as key "stations" on the slaves' road to freedom. The Underground Railroad was immortalized in Harriet Beecher Stowe's novel *Uncle Tom's Cabin; or, Life Among the Lowly* (1852).

DECLINING POWER

In the latter part of the 19th century there were signs that the days of New England's industrial preeminence were over. The transcontinental railroad had opened up the West to an army of new immigrants, which flooded in after the Civil War. The New World was a far, far bigger place than it had been when the Pilgrims landed, and the opportunities were boundless. The Great Plains encompassed thousands of square miles of arable land that New England farmers could only dream about. And for those looking for a more temperate climate, many other areas of the US now beckoned.

Meanwhile, the exploitation of natural resources and the development of new technologies were changing the face of industry. The discovery of petroleum meant that whale oil lost its economic importance, while steam engines offered a way of powering mills that no longer required river water-power – one of the natural advantages upon which the region had relied.

Cover of sheet music based on Harriet Beecher Stowe's *Uncle Tom's Cabin* by artist Louisa Corbauy

These problems were compounded by the fact that local labor was organizing to fight for better pay and working conditions, driving some factories to move to the South where labor costs were cheaper. Between 1880 and 1923, the South's share of the cotton-weaving industry rose from 6 percent to almost 50 percent.

The call for unionization even reached into the ranks of the police force, sparking one of America's most bitter labor confrontations. In 1919 Boston's men in blue sought to affiliate themselves with the American Federation of Labor. The city's police commissioner refused the request, and the entire force went on strike. Boston was beset by a

Child laborer in cotton spinning plant

Ralph Waldo Emerson

1875

1882 Massachusetts-born poet/philosopher Ralph Waldo Emerson dies

1884 Mark Twain publishes *The Adventures of Huckleberry Finn*, a novel he wrote at his home in Hartford, Connecticut

Modern Red Sox fan

1890

1897 Country's first subway is opened in Boston

1910

1903 Boston Red Sox win first World Series baseball championship wave of crime and riots, prompting the governor to send in the militia. By the time order was restored, at least five people had been killed and dozens had been wounded.

The loss of New England's economic importance was accompanied by a wave of change in the social makeup of the region. What had long been a homogeneous society – largely Protestant and of English or Scottish descent – was transformed by a rapid influx of immigrants. By the turn of the 20th century more than two-thirds of the residents of Massachusetts had at least one parent born outside the country.

The Depression of the 1930s hit the inhabitants of New England particularly hard. Unemployment in some towns topped 40 percent and wages plunged dramatically. World War II provided a temporary boost to the economy as shipyards and munition factories worked overtime to provide the military with the tools of their trade. However, with the return of peace, New England struggled to find its way in the new postwar era, and its economy continued to have its difficulties. The glory

Women making shell casings in a munitions plant during World War II

days, at least economically speaking, seemed to be irretrievable.

NEW ENGLAND REBIRTH

Even in its worse decline, as factories crumbled and residents headed for greener pastures, New England still possessed advantages that set the stage for recovery. One important factor was its concentration of higher educational institutions *(see pp28–9)*. As the Manufacturing Age gave way to the Information Age beginning in the 1960s, knowledge and adaptability became increasingly valuable commodities. With their well-endowed

Unknown artist's depiction of Harvard University campus c.1857

TIMELINE

Calvin Coolidge

1914–1918 World War I

1923 Vermont's Calvin Coolidge is sworn in as country's 30th president by his father

1929 Stock market crash marks beginning of Great Depression

Depression soup kitchen

1915	1925	1935	1945	1955

1939–45 World War II: US enters conflict in 1941

1954 World's first nuclear submarine is built in Groton, Connecticut

Falmouth Heights Beach in Cape Cod

England's stunning physical beauty: the craggy coastline of Maine, the beaches of Cape Cod *(see pp156–9)*, the picturesque Vermont villages, and the coiled-up mountains of New Hampshire. As America became more prosperous and its workers had more free time in which to spend their mounting disposable income, tourism became an even bigger business than manufacturing had once been. The skiers, fishermen, beachcombers, antique hunters, campers, and others who flocked to the Northeast year-round pumped billions of dollars into the states' economies. By the 1990s tourism ranked alongside manufacturing as one of New England's most profitable industries.

research facilities, venerable institutions such as Harvard University *(see pp112–17)* and the Massachusetts Institute of Technology *(see p111)* attracted a new generation of young entrepreneurs looking to cash in on this newest opportunity. Meanwhile a son of one of Boston's most prominent families was proving that New England's impact on the national political scene was not over yet. John F. Kennedy *(see p152)*, the great-grandson of an Irish potato-famine immigrant, became American's first Catholic president in 1960.

John Fitzgerald Kennedy

Somehow, it seems fitting. After all, it was the beauty of the area that had helped convince people such as John Smith, close to four centuries ago, that New England had a viable future. And now, that same natural beauty is proving to be both timeless and lucrative, helping to bring about a renaissance in the prosperity of the place where American society had begun so tenuously so many years before.

Starting in the mid-1980s, companies producing computer software and biomedical technology set up shop in the Boston suburbs and southern New Hampshire. The meteoric growth of high-tech industries represented a second revolution of sorts – proving far more valuable than the Industrial Revolution of the previous century. Meanwhile certain businesses, such as the insurance trade, weathered the shifts in the economy better than traditional manufacturing ventures, with Hartford *(see pp198–201)*, Connecticut, continuing to serve as the insurance capital of the nation.

One thing that all the economic upheavals did not change was New

Vermont's trademark rural landscape

1961 Massachusetts-born John F. Kennedy becomes first Catholic president	1990 Thieves make off with artwork valued at $100 million from Boston's Isabella Stewart Gardner Museum		2000 Vermont becomes first state to legally recognize same-sex marriages
1960	**1970**	**1980**	**1990**	**2000**

1968 Senator Robert Kennedy is assassinated in Los Angeles

1963 President Kennedy is assassinated in Dallas

Robert F. Kennedy

1999 John F. Kennedy, Jr. dies in plane crash off Martha's Vineyard

BOSTON

Boston's Best

THE CITY OF BOSTON's Athenian self-image is manifested in dozens of museums, galleries, and archives, paramount of which is the Museum of Fine Arts. The city's importance in America's history has left it with an unique legacy of old buildings, with much fine religious and civic architecture, including Trinity Church and Massachusetts State House. This strong architectural heritage continues to the present day, and includes modern structures such as the John Hancock Tower. Boston's wealth of sights, along with its many parks and gardens, make it a fascinating city to explore.

Boston Common and Public Garden
At the heart of the city, the spacious common, and smaller, more formal Public Garden, provide open space for both sport and relaxation.

Trinity Church
Perhaps Boston's finest building, this Romanesque Revival masterpiece by Henry Hobson Richardson was completed in 1877.

John Hancock Tower
Dominating the Back Bay skyline, with its mirrored façade reflecting the surroundings, the John Hancock Tower is New England's tallest building.

Museum of Fine Arts
One of the largest museums in North America, the M.F.A. is famous for its Egyptian, Greek, and Roman art, and French Impressionist paintings.

Old State House
The seat of British colonial government until independence, the building later undertook many different uses. It now houses a museum on the revolution.

Old North Church
Dating from 1723, this is Boston's oldest surviving church. Due to its role in the Revolution, it is also one of the city's most important historical sites.

0 kilometers 0.5

0 miles 0.5

New England Aquarium
This aquarium displays a huge array of creatures from the world's oceans. Researchers here are also involved in key international fish and whale conservation programs.

Massachusetts State House
Built in the 1790s as the new center of state government, the Charles Bulfinch-designed State House sits imposingly at the top of Beacon Hill.

John F. Kennedy Library and Museum
The nation's best-loved president is celebrated here in words and images – video clips of the first president to fully use the media make this a compelling museum.

The Freedom Trail

From Boston Common to Paul Revere House

Boston has more sites directly related to the American Revolution than any other city. The most important of these sites, as well as some relating to other freedoms gained by Bostonians, have been linked together as "The Freedom Trail." This 2.5-mile (4-km) walking route, marked in red on the sidewalks, starts at Boston Common and eventually ends at Bunker Hill in Charlestown. This first section weaves its way through the central city and Old Boston.

Elegant Georgian steeple of Park Street Church

Nurses Hall in Massachusetts State House

Central City

The Freedom Trail starts at the Visitor Information Center on Boston Common ① (see pp64–5). This is where angry colonials rallied against their British masters and where the British forces were encamped during the 1775–76 military occupation. Political speakers still expound from their soapboxes here, and the Common remains a center of much activity.

Walking toward the northwest corner of the Common gives a great view of the Massachusetts State House ② (see p68–9) on Beacon Street, designed by Charles Bulfinch as the new center of state governance shortly after the Revolution. Along Park Street, at the end of the Common, you will come to Park Street Church ③ (see p66), built in 1810 and a bulwark of the antislavery movement. The church took the place of an old grain storage facility, which in turn gave its name to the adjacent Granary Burying Ground ④, one of Boston's earliest cemeteries and the final resting place of patriots John Hancock and Paul Revere (see p120). Continuing along Tremont Street you will come to King's Chapel and Burying Ground ⑤ (see p76). The tiny cemetery is Boston's oldest, containing, among others, the grave of city founder John Winthrop. As the name suggests, King's Chapel was the principal Anglican church in Puritan Boston, and more than half of its congregation fled to Nova Scotia at the outbreak of the Revolution. The box pew on the right just inside the front entrance was reserved for condemned prisoners to hear their last sermons before going to the gallows on Boston Common.

Heart of Old Boston

Head back along Tremont Street and turn down School Street, where a hopscotch-like mosaic embedded in the sidewalk commemorates the site of the First Public School ⑥, established in 1635. At the bottom of the street is the Boston Globe Store ⑦ *(see p77)*, a landmark more associated with Boston's literary emergence of 1845–65 than with the Revolution.

The Old South Meeting House ⑧, a short way to the south on Washington Street, is a graceful, white-spired brick church, modeled on Sir Christopher Wren's English country churches. As one of the largest meeting halls in Revolutionary Boston, "Old South's" rafters rang with many a fiery speech urging revolt against the British. A few blocks along, the Old State House ⑨ presides over the head of State Street. The colonial government building, it also served as the first state legislature, and the merchants' exchange in the basement was where Boston's colonial shipping fortunes were made. The square in front of the Old State House is the Boston Massacre Site ⑩, where British soldiers opened fire on a taunting mob in 1770, killing five and providing ideal propaganda for revolutionary agitators.

Follow State Street down to Congress Street and turn left to reach Faneuil Hall ⑪, called the "Cradle of Liberty" for the history of patriotic speeches made in its public meeting hall. Donated to the city by Huguenot merchant Peter Faneuil, the building was built primarily as Boston's first central marketplace.

The red stripe of the Freedom Trail comes in handy when negotiating the way to the North End and the Paul Revere House ⑫ on North Square. Boston's oldest house, it was home to the man known for his famous "midnight ride" *(see p120)*.

(see p77)

TIPS FOR WALKERS

Starting point: Boston Common. Maps available at Boston Common Visitor Center.
Length: 2.5 miles (4 km).
Getting there: Park Street Station (T Green and Red lines) to start. State (Orange and Blue lines) and Haymarket (Orange and Green lines). T stations also on route. Follow red stripe on sidewalk for the full route.

Faneuil Hall, popularly known as "the Cradle of Liberty"

WALK

Boston Common ①
Boston Globe Store ⑦
Boston Massacre Site ⑩
Faneuil Hall ⑪
First Public School Site ⑥
Granary Burying Ground ④
King's Chapel and Burying Ground ⑤
Massachusetts State House ②
Old South Meeting House ⑧
Old State House ⑨
Park Street Church ③
Paul Revere House ⑫

0 meters 250
0 yards 250

KEY

••• Walk route

Ⓣ Subway

ℹ Tourist information

Old State House, the seat of colonial government

The Freedom Trail

From Old North Church to Bunker Hill Monument

DISTANCES BEGIN to stretch out on the second half of the Freedom Trail as it meanders through the narrow streets of the North End, then continues over the Charles River to Charlestown, where Boston's settlers first landed. The sites here embrace two wars – the War of Independence and the War of 1812.

View from Copp's Hill terrace, at the edge of Copp's Hill Burying Ground

The North End

Following the Freedom Trail through the North End, allow time to try some of the Italian cafés and bakeries along the neighborhood's main thoroughfare, Hanover Street. Cross through the Paul Revere Mall to reach Old North Church ⑬ (see p87), whose spire

Gravestone at Copp's Hill Burying Ground

is instantly visible over the shoulder of the statue of Paul Revere on horseback. Sexton Robert Newman hung two lanterns in the belfry here, signaling the advance of British troops on Lexington and Concord in 1775. The church retains its 18th-century interior, including the traditional box pews.

The crest of Copp's Hill lies close by on Hull Street. Some of Boston's earliest gallows stood here, and Bostonians would gather in boats below to watch the hangings of heretics and pirates. Much of the hilltop is covered by Copp's Hill

Burying Ground ⑭. This was established in 1660, and the cemetery holds the remains of several generations of the Mather family – Boston's influential 17th- and 18th-century theocrats – as well as the graves of many soldiers of the Revolution. Boston's first free African American community, "New Guinea," covered the west side of Copp's Hill. A broken column marks the grave of Prince Hall, head of the Black Masons, distinguished veteran of the Revolution, and prominent political leader in the early years of the Republic. The musketball-chipped tombstone of patriot Daniel Malcolm records that he asked to be buried "in a stone grave 10 feet deep" to rest beyond the reach of British gunfire.

Traditional box pews inside Old North Church

WALK

View of Bunker Hill Monument
from Charlestown harborfront

KEY

● ● ● Walk route

0 meters   250

0 yards   250

Charlestown

**Lion carving,
USS *Constitution***

The iron bridge over the Charles River that links the North End in Boston with City Square in Charlestown dates from 1899. Across the bridge, turn right along Constitution Road, following signs to Bunker Hill Pavilion ⑮, a privately sponsored multimedia show about the first pitched battle of the Revolution, fought here in 1775. The visitors' center for the nearby Charlestown Navy Yard ⑯ shares the building, and it is worth visiting to get an overview of the site. The colonial navy had been no match for the might of Britain's naval forces during the Revolution, and building a more formidable naval force became a priority. This was one of several shipyards that were set up around 1800. Decommissioned in 1974, the yard is now maintained by the National Park Service.

Lying at her berth alongside Pier 1, the USS *Constitution* is probably the most famous ship in US history and still remains the flagship of the US Navy. Built at Hartt's shipyard in the North End, she was completed in 1797. In the War of 1812, she earned the nickname "Old Ironsides" for the resilience of her live oak hull against cannon fire. Fully restored for her bicentennial, the *Constitution* occasionally sails under her own power.

The granite obelisk that towers above the Charlestown waterfront is Bunker Hill Monument ⑰, commemorating the battle of June 17, 1775 that ended with a costly victory for British forces against an irregular colonial army, which finally ran out of ammunition. British losses were so heavy, however, that the battle would presage future success for the colonial forces. As a monument to the first large-scale battle of the Revolution, the obelisk, based on those of ancient Egypt, was a prototype for others across the US.

Defensive guns at Charlestown Navy Yard with view of the North End

BEACON HILL AND THE THEATER DISTRICT

B Y THE 1790s, the south slope of Beacon Hill, facing Boston Common, had become the main seat of Boston's wealth and power. The north slope and the land up to the Charles River, known as the West End, was much poorer. Urban renewal has now cleared the slums of the West End, and the gentrification of Beacon Hill has made this one of Boston's most desirable neighborhoods. The area south of Boston Common is more down-to-earth, and home to the city's Theater District.

SIGHTS AT A GLANCE

Historic Streets and Squares

Bay Village ⑰
Beacon Street ⑥
Charles Street ①
Chinatown ⑯
Downtown Crossing ⑭
Louisburg Square ②
Mount Vernon Street ③

Historic Buildings, Museums, and Theaters

African Meeting House ⑫
Boston Athenaeum ⑩
Colonial Theater ⑮
Hepzibah Swan Houses ⑤
Massachusetts State House pp68–9 ⑪
Museum of Science and Science Park ⑬
Nichols House Museum ④
Park Street Church ⑧
Shubert Theater ⑱
Wang Center for the Performing Arts ⑲

Parks and Cemeteries

Boston Common and Public Garden ⑦
Granary Burying Ground ⑨

KEY

☐ Street-by-Street map *see pp60–61*

Ⓣ "T" station

ℹ Tourist information

P Parking

GETTING THERE

This area is well served by public transportation. Park Street, Chinatown, Boylston, Charles/M.G.H., and Science Park "T" stations are closest to the main sights. Buses 43 and 55 go to Boston Common.

| 0 meters | 250 |
| 0 yards | 250 |

◁ **Front view of the Massachusetts State House, seen from Boston Common**

Street-by-Street: Beacon Hill

Lion door knocker, Beacon St.

From the 1790s to the 1870s, the south slope of Beacon Hill was Boston's most sought-after neighborhood – its wealthy elite decamped only when the more exclusive Back Bay (*see pp92–101*) was built. Many of the district's houses were designed by Charles Bulfinch and his disciples, and the south slope evolved as a textbook example of Federal architecture. Elevation and view were all, and the finest homes are either on Boston Common or perched near the top of the hill. Early developers abided by a gentleman's agreement to set houses back from the street, but the economic depression of 1807–12 resulted in row houses being built right out to the street.

Cobblestone street, once typical of Beacon Hill

Louisburg Square
The crowning glory of the Beacon Hill district, this square was developed in the 1830s. Today, it is still Boston's most desirable address **2**

Charles Street Meeting House was built in the early 18th century to house a congregation of Baptists.

Key

– – – Suggested route

PINCKNEY STREET

LOUISBURG SQUARE

MOUNT VERNON STREET

CEDAR STREET

CHARLES STREET

CHESTNUT STREET

Back Bay and South End

DE LUCA'S MARKET

"FRESHEST BY FAR SINCE 1905"

★ **Charles Street**
This elegant street is the main shopping area for Beacon Hill. Lined with upscale grocers and antique stores, it also has some fine restaurants **1**

Star Sights

★ Charles Street

★ Nichols House Museum

★ **Nichols House Museum**
This modest museum offers an insight into the life of Beacon Hill resident Rose Nichols, who lived here from 1885 to 1960 ❹

LOCATOR MAP
See Street Finder map 1

0 meters	50
0 yards	50

Mount Vernon Street
Described in the 19th century as the "most civilized street in America," this is where the developers of Beacon Hill (the Mount Vernon Proprietors) chose to build their own homes ❸

→ **Massachusetts State House**

WALNUT STREET

SPRUCE STREET

BEACON STREET

Boston Common

Hepzibah Swan Houses
Elegant in their simplicity, these three Bulfinch-designed houses were wedding gifts for the daughters of a wealthy Beacon Hill proprietress ❺

Beacon Street
The finest houses on Beacon Hill were invariably built on Beacon Street. Elegant, Federal-style mansions, some with ornate reliefs, overlook the city's most beautiful green space, Boston Common ❻

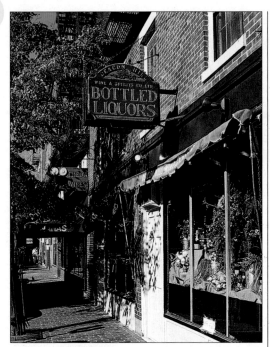

Charles Street, lined with shops catering to the residents of Beacon Hill

Charles Street ❶

Map 1 B4. ⓣ *Charles/ MGH.*

THIS STREET originally ran along the bank of the Charles River, although subsequent landfill has removed it from the riverbank by several hundred feet. The main shopping and dining area of the Beacon Hill neighborhood, the curving line of Charles Street hugs the base of Beacon Hill, giving it a quaint, village-like air. Many of the houses remain residential on the upper stories, while street level and cellar levels were converted to commercial uses long ago. Though most of Charles Street dates from the 19th century, widening in the 1920s meant that some of the houses on the west side acquired new façades. The Charles Street Meeting House, designed by Asher Benjamin in 1804, was built for a Baptist congregation that practiced immersion in the then adjacent river. It is now a commercial building. Two groups of striking Greek Revival row houses are situated at the top of Charles

Street, between Revere and Cambridge Streets. Charles Street was one of the birthplaces of the antique trade in the US and now has some two dozen antique dealers.

Louisburg Square ❷

Map 1 B4. ⓣ *Charles/ MGH, Park Street.*

HOME TO millionaire politicians, best-selling authors, and corporate moguls, Louisburg Square is perhaps Boston's most prestigious address. Developed in the 1830s as a shared private preserve on Beacon Hill, the square's tiny patch of greenery surrounded by a high iron fence sends a clear signal of the square's continued exclusivity. On the last private square in the city, the narrow, Greek

Revival bow-fronted town houses sell for a premium over comparable homes elsewhere on Beacon Hill. Even the on-street parking spaces are deeded. The traditions of Christmas Eve carol singing and candlelit windows are said to have begun on Louisburg Square. A statue of Christopher Columbus, presented by a wealthy Greek merchant in 1850, stands at its center.

Mount Vernon Street ❸

Map 1 B4. ⓣ *Charles/ MGH, Park Street.*

IN THE 1890s the novelist Henry James called Mount Vernon Street "the most civilized street in America," and it still retains that air of urbane culture. Most of the developers of Beacon Hill, who called themselves the Mount Vernon Proprietors, chose to build their private homes along this street. Architect Charles Bulfinch envisioned Beacon Hill as a district of large freestanding mansions on spacious landscaped grounds, but building costs ultimately dictated much denser development. The sole remaining example of Bulfinch's vision is the Second Harrison Gray Otis House, built in 1800 at No. 85 Mount Vernon Street. The current Greek Revival row houses next door (Nos. 59–83), graciously set back from the street by 30 ft (9 m), were built to replace the single mansion belonging to

Columbus Statue, Louisburg Square

Otis's chief development partner, Jonathan Mason. The original mansion was torn down after Mason's death in 1836. The three Bulfinch-designed houses at Nos. 55, 57, and 59 Mount Vernon Street were built by Mason for his daughters. No. 55 was ultimately passed on to the Nichols family *(see p63)* in 1883.

OLIVER WENDELL HOLMES AND THE BOSTON BRAHMINS

In 1860, Oliver Wendell Holmes wrote that Boston's wealthy merchant class of the time constituted a Brahmin caste, a "harmless, inoffensive, untitled aristocracy" with "their houses by Bulfinch, their monopoly on Beacon Street, their ancestral portraits and Chinese porcelains, humanitarianism, Unitarian faith in the march of the mind, Yankee shrewdness, and New England exclusiveness." So keenly did he skewer the social class that the term has persisted. In casual usage today, a Brahmin is someone with an old family name, whose finances derive largely from trust funds, and whose politics blend conservatism with *noblesse oblige* toward those less fortunate. Boston's Brahmins founded most of the hospitals, performing arts bodies, and museums of the greater metropolitan area.

Oliver Wendell Holmes (1809–94)

Drawing room of the Bulfinch-designed Nichols House Museum

Nichols House Museum **4**

55 Mount Vernon St. **Map** 1 B4.
℡ (617) 227-6993. **Ⓣ** Park Street.
◐ May–Oct: noon–5pm Tue–Sat;
Nov–Apr: noon–5pm Mon, Wed,
Sat. **●** Jan. **🖾 🚫 🍴**

THE NICHOLS HOUSE MUSEUM was designed by Charles Bulfinch in 1805 and offers a rare glimpse into the tradition-bound lifestyle of Beacon Hill. Modernized in 1830 by the addition of a Greek Revival portico, the house is nevertheless a superb example of Bulfinch's domestic architecture. It also offers an insight into the life of a true Beacon Hill character. Rose Standish Nichols moved into the house at 13 when her father purchased it in 1883. She left it as a museum in her 1960 will. A woman ahead of her time,

strong-willed and famously hospitable, Nichols was, among other things, a self-styled landscape designer who traveled extensively around the world to write about gardens.

Hepzibah Swan Houses **5**

13, 15 & 17 Chestnut St. **Map** 1 B4.
Ⓣ Park Street. **●** to the public.

THE ONLY WOMAN who was ever a member of the Mount Vernon Proprietors *(see p62)*, Mrs. Swan had these houses built by Bulfinch as wedding presents for her daughters in 1806, 1807, and 1814. Some of the most elegant and distinguished houses on Chestnut Street, they are backed by Bulfinch-designed stables that face onto Mount Vernon Street. The deeds restrict the height of the stables to 13 ft (4 m) so that her daughters would still have a view over Mount Vernon Street. In 1863–65, No. 13 was home to Dr. Samuel Gridley Howe, abolitionist and educational pioneer who, in 1833, founded the first school for the blind in the US.

Beacon Street **6**

Map 1 B4. **Ⓣ** Park Street.

BEACON STREET IS LINED with urban mansions facing Boston Common. The American Meteorological Society occupies No. 45, which was built as Harrison Gray Otis's last and finest house, with 11 bedrooms and an elliptical room behind the front parlor where the walls and even the doors are curved. The elite Somerset Club stands at Nos. 42–43 Beacon Street. In the 1920s to 1940s, Irish Catholic mayor James Michael Curley would lead election night victory marches to the State House, pausing at the Somerset to taunt the Boston Brahmins within. The Parkman House at No. 33 Beacon Street is now a city-owned meeting center. It was the home of Dr. George Parkman, who was murdered by Harvard professor and fellow socialite Dr. John Webster in 1849. Boston society was torn apart when the presiding judge, a relative of Parkman, sent Webster to be hanged. The family lived as recluses here from 1859 to 1908 before giving the house to the city. The headquarters of the Unitarian Universalist Association, an international church, and its publishing arm, Beacon Press, occupy premises at No. 25.

Elegant Federal-style houses on Beacon Street, overlooking Boston Common

Boston Common and Public Garden ❼

Acquired by Boston in 1634 from first settler William Blackstone, the 48-acre (19-ha) Boston Common served for two centuries as common pasture, military drill ground, and gallows site. British troops camped here during the 1775–76 military occupation. As Boston grew in the 19th century, the Boston Common became a center for open-air civic activity and remains so to this day. By contrast, the 24-acre (10-ha) Public Garden is more formal. When the Charles River mudflats were first filled in the 1830s, a succession of landscape plans were plotted for the Public Garden before the city chose the English-style garden scheme of George F. Meacham in 1869. The lagoon was added to the garden two years later.

The Public Garden, a popular green space in the heart of the city

Make Way for Ducklings
Based on the classic children's story by Robert McCloskey, this sculpture is of a duck and her brood of ducklings.

The Ether Monument memorializes the first use of anesthesia in 1846.

★ George Washington Statue
Cast by Thomas Ball from bronze, with a solid granite base, this is one the finest memorial statues in Boston. It was dedicated in 1869.

CHARLES STREET

Statue of Edward Everett Hale

Lagoon Bridge
This miniature, ornamental bridge over the Public Garden lagoon was designed by William G. Preston in 1869 in a moment of whimsy. The lagoon it "spans" was constructed in 1861.

Statue of Reverend William Ellery Channing

The Swan Boats, originally inspired by Wagner's *Löhengrin,* have been a feature of the Public Garden lake since 1877.

★ Shaw Memorial
This relief immortalizes the Civil War's 54th regiment of Massachusetts Infantry, the first free black regiment in the Union Army, and their white colonel Robert Shaw.

VISITORS' CHECKLIST

Map 1 B4. Ⓣ *Park Street, Boylston Street, Arlington.* Ⓒ *24 hrs.* **Visitors' Center** 146 *Tremont St.; (617) 426-3115.* Ⓒ *8:30am–5pm Mon–Fri, 9am–5pm Sat–Sun.* **Swan Boats** *Boston Public Garden.* Ⓒ *(617) 522-1966.* Ⓒ *Jun–Aug:10am–5pm daily; mid-May and Sep: 10am–4pm daily.* 🅦 *www.bostonusa.com*

The Soldiers and Sailors Monument, erected in 1877, features prominent Bostonians from the time of the Civil War.

Blackstone Memorial Tablet recalls the purchase of the common in 1634 and is cited as proof that it belongs to the people.

Park Street subway

Brewer Fountain was purchased at the Paris expo of 1867.

Visitors' Center

Parkman Bandstand
This bandstand was built in 1912 to memorialize George F. Parkman, who bequeathed $5 million for the care of Boston Common and other parks in the city.

The Flagstaff

0 meters 100
0 yards 100

STAR FEATURES

★ Shaw Memorial

★ George Washington Statue

Central Burying Ground
This graveyard, which dates from 1756, holds the remains of many British and American casualties from the Battle of Bunker Hill (1775). The portraitist Gilbert Stuart is also buried here.

Park Street Church at the corner of Tremont and Park Streets

Park Street Church ❽

1 Park St. **Map** 1 C4.
☎ *(617) 523-3383.* Ⓣ *Park Street.*
🕐 *Jul–Aug: 9am–3:30pm Tue–Sat;*
Sep–Jun: by appointment. ✝
Jul–Aug: 10:45am, 5:30pm Sun;
Sep–Jun: 9am, 10:45am, 5:30pm Sun.
🚫 ♿ Ⓦ *www.parkstreet.org*

PARK STREET CHURCH'S 217-ft
(65-m) steeple has punc-
tuated the intersection of Park
and Tremont Streets since its
dedication in 1810. Designed
by English architect Peter
Banner, who adapted a design
by the earlier English architect
Christopher Wren, the church
was commissioned by parish-
ioners wanting to establish a
Congregational church in the
heart of Boston. The church
was, and still is, one of the
city's most influential pulpits.

Contrary to popular belief,
the sermons of Park Street
ministers did not earn the
intersection the nickname of
"Brimstone Corner." Rather,
the name came about because

the US militia, based in
Boston, stored its gunpowder
in the church basement as
safekeeping against bombard-
ment from the British navy.

In 1829, William Lloyd
Garrison (1805–79), fervently
outspoken firebrand of the
movement to abolish slavery,
gave his first abolition speech
from the Park Street pulpit.

In 1849 a speech entitled
The War System of Nations
was addressed to the
American Peace Society by
Senator Charles Sumner.
Much later, in 1893, the
anthem *America the Beautiful*
by Katharine Lee Bates
debuted at a Sunday service.
Today the church continues,
as always, to be involved in
religious, political, cultural,
and humanitarian activities.

Granary Burying Ground ❾

Tremont Street. **Map** 1 C4. Ⓣ *Park
Street.* 🕐 *8am–4:30pm daily.*

NAMED AFTER the early grain
storage facility that once
stood on the adjacent site of
Park Street Church, the Granary Burying Ground dates
from 1660. Buried here were
three important signatories to
the Declaration of Independence – Samuel Adams, John
Hancock, and Robert Treat
Paine, along with Benjamin
Franklin's parents, merchant-
philanthropist Peter Faneuil,
and some victims of the
Boston Massacre.

The orderly array of gravestones, often featured in films
and television shows set in
Boston, is the result of modern groundskeeping. Few
stones, if any, mark the actual
burial site of the person memo-
rialized. In fact, John Hancock
may not be here at all. On the
night he was buried in 1793,
grave robbers cut off the hand
with which he had signed
his name to the Declaration
of Independence, and some
believe that the rest of his body
was removed during 19th-
century construction work.

Boston Athenaeum ❿

10 Beacon St. **Map** 1 C4.
☎ *(617) 227-0270.* Ⓣ *Park Street.*
🕐 *Jun–Aug: 9am–8pm Mon, 9am–
5:30pm Tue–Fri; Sep–May: 9am–4pm
Sat.* Ⓦ *www.bostonathenaeum.org*

ORGANIZED IN 1807, the
collection of the Boston
Athenaeum quickly became
one of the country's leading
private libraries. Sheep farmer
Edward Clarke Cabot won the
1846 design competition to
house the library, with plans
for a gray sandstone building
based on Palladio's Palazzo
da Porta Festa in Vicenza,
a building Cabot knew from
a book in the Athenaeum's
collection. From this initial
commission, Cabot went on
to become the first president
of the Boston Society of
Architects. Among the Athenaeum's major holdings are the

Granary Burying Ground, final resting place for Revolutionary heroes

Stone frieze decoration on the Renaissance Revival-style Athenaeum

personal library that once belonged to George Washington and the theological library supplied by King William III of England to the King's Chapel (*see p76*). In its early years the Athenaeum was Boston's chief art museum, but when the Museum of Fine Arts was proposed, it graciously donated much of its art, including unfinished portraits purchased in 1831 from the widow of the painter Gilbert Stuart.

Massachusetts State House ⓫

See pp68–9.

African Meeting House ⓬

8 Smith Court. **Map** 1 C3.
🎫 *(617) 725-0022.* ⓣ *Park Street.* ◯ *Memorial Day–Labor Day:10am–4pm daily; Labor Day–Memorial Day 10am–4pm Mon–Fri.* ⬤ *public hols.* 📷 ✏️
🔲 *www.nps.gov/boaf*

BUILT FROM TOWN HOUSE plans by Asher Benjamin, the African Meeting House was dedicated in 1806. The oldest black church building in the US, it was the political and religious center of Boston's African American society. The interior is plain and simple but rang with the oratory of some of the 19th century's most fiery abolitionists: from Sojourner Truth and Frederick Douglass to William Lloyd Garrison, who founded the New England Anti-Slavery Society in 1832. The meeting house basement was Boston's first school for African American children until the adjacent Abiel Smith School was built in 1831. When segregated education was barred in 1855, however, the Smith School closed. The meeting house became a Hasidic synagogue in the 1890s, as most of Boston's African American community moved to Roxbury and Dorchester. The synagogue closed in the 1960s, and in 1987 the African Meeting House reopened as the linchpin site on the Black Heritage Trail.

Museum of Science and Science Park ⓭

Science Park. **Map** 1 B2.
🎫 *(617) 723-2500.* ⓣ *Science Park.* ◯ *Labor Day–July 3: 9am–5pm Sat–Thu, 9am–9pm Fri; July 4–Labor Day 9am–7pm Sat–Thu, 9am–9pm Fri.* ⬤ *Thanksgiving, Dec 25.* 📷
♿ 🐾 🔲 *www.mos.org*

THE MUSEUM OF SCIENCE straddles the Charles River atop the flood control dam that sits at the mouth of the Charles River. The Science Park that has developed around it includes a large-format cinema and planetarium.

With more than 1,000 interactive exhibits covering natural history, medicine, astronomy, the physical sciences, and computing, the Science Museum is largely oriented to families. The Mugar Omni Theater contains a five-story domed screen with a multidimensional wrap-around sound system, and shows mostly educational films, usually with a natural science theme. The Charles Hayden Planetarium offers daily shows about stars, planets, and other celestial phenomena.

Holmes Alley, once an escape route for slaves on the run

BLACK HERITAGE TRAIL

In the first US census in 1790, Massachusetts was the only state to record no slaves. During the 19th century, Boston's substantial free African American community lived principally on the north slope of Beacon Hill and in the adjacent West End. The Black Heritage Trail links several key sites, ranging from the African Meeting House to several private homes, which are not open to visitors. Among them are the 1797 George Middleton House (Nos. 5–7 Pinckney Street), the oldest standing house built by African Americans on Beacon Hill, and the Lewis and Harriet Hayden House (No. 66 Phillips Street). Escaped slaves, the Haydens made their home a haven for runaways in the "Underground Railroad" of safe houses between the South and Canada. The walking tour also leads through mews and alleys, like Holmes Alley at the end of Smith Court, once used by fugitives to flee professional slave catchers.

Free tours of the Black Heritage Trail are led by National Park Service rangers – (617) 742-5415 – and are offered from Memorial Day weekend to Labor Day, 10am, noon, and 2pm daily, departing from the Robert Gould Shaw Memorial.

Massachusetts State House ⓫

THE CORNERSTONE OF the Massachusetts State
House was laid on July 4, 1795, by Samuel
Adams and Paul Revere. Completed on January
11, 1798, the Charles Bulfinch-designed center
of state government served as a model for the
US Capitol Building in Washington and as
an inspiration for many of the state capitols
around the country. Later additions were made,
but the original building remains the archetype
of American government buildings. Its dome,
sheathed in copper and gold, serves as the
zero mile marker for Massachusetts, making
it, as Oliver Wendell Holmes *(see p63)*
remarked, "the hub of the universe."

The State House, from Boston Common

The Great Hall
is the latest addition to the State
House. Built in 1990, it is lined with
marble and topped by a glass dome,
and is used for state functions.

★ **House of Representatives**
*This elegant oval chamber was built for
the House of Representatives in 1895. The
Sacred Cod, which now hangs over the
gallery, came to the State House when it first
opened in 1798, and it has since hung over
any place where the representatives have met.*

Main Staircase
*Beautiful stained-glass
windows decorate the
main staircase. They
illustrate the varied state
seals of Massachussets
from its inception as a
colony through to
modern statehood.*

STAR SIGHTS

★ **Nurses Hall**

★ **House of
Representatives**

The Wings of the State
House, thought by many
to sit incongruously with
the rest of the structure,
were added in 1917.

Hall of Flags
Flags carried into battle by regiments from the state of Massachusetts are housed here. They are displayed beneath a stained-glass skylight depicting seals of the original 13 colonies.

★ Nurses Hall
This marble hall is lined with murals depicting critical events leading up to the American Revolution. The name derives from the statue of an army nurse here, erected to honor all the nurses who took part in the Civil War.

Administrative offices
can be found on the upper floors of the building.

The dome was sheathed in copper in 1802 to prevent water leakage, and, in 1872, gilded in 23-carat gold.

Entrance

Doric Hall
George Washington is among the historical figures represented here. The center doors of the hall are opened only for a state governor at the end of his term or for a visiting head of state.

Senate Chamber
Prior to 1895, this was the meeting chamber of the House of Representatives. Situated directly beneath the State House's magnificent dome, the chamber features a beautiful sunburst ceiling, also designed by Charles Bulfinch.

Brattle Book Shop, a Boston literary landmark

Downtown Crossing ⓮

Washington, Winter & Summer Sts.
Map 4 F1. Ⓣ *Downtown Crossing.*

As an antidote to heavy traffic congestion, this shopping-district crossroads, at the intersection of Washington, Winter, and Summer Streets, was laid out as a pedestrian zone between 1975 and 1978. Downtown's department stores are the main focal points of the area, notably Macy's and Filene's, although the area also offers a range of other outlets, including bookstores, camera stores, and jewelers. The Lafayette Center has a selection of more popular stores.

The busy Macy's department store is one of a chain found throughout the US, with the most well-known store in New York. The Filene's empire has its heart in Boston, however, as it was founded here by William Filene in 1881. It is now the biggest and best-known department store in New England. The flagship store on Washington Street was completed in 1912 and is best known for its Bargain Basement, introduced in 1908. This became the store's trade-mark, and it is still operating, although it is no longer run by Filene's. There are remarkable bargains to be found, and you will see all kinds of Bostonians here, lured by the low prices.

Another well-known store in the area is Brattle Book Shop, just off Washington Street on West Street. Founded in 1825, this bibliophiles' treasure-house is packed with more than 250,000 used, rare, and out-of-print books, as well as back issues of magazines, maps, prints, postcards, and manuscripts. Outside the store are bins of bargain books priced between $1 and $5.

Colonial Theatre ⓯

106 Boylston St. **Map** 4 E2.
◖ *(617) 426-9366.* Ⓣ *Boylston.*
◒ *phone to check.* ♿

Clarence h. blackall designed 14 Boston theaters during his architectural career, among them the Colonial, which is the city's oldest theater to have been in continuous operation under the same name. Although plain outside, the interior is impressively opulent. Designed by H.B. Pennell, the Rococo lobby has chandeliers, gilded trim, and lofty arched ceilings. The auditorium is decorated with figures, frescoes, and friezes.

The theater opened on December 20, 1900 with an extravagant performance of the melodrama Ben Hur. Today the theater is best remembered for premiering lavish musical productions, such as *Ziegfeld Follies.*

Gilt cherub, the Colonial Theatre

Chinatown ⓰

Bounded by Kingston, Kneeland, Washington & Essex Sts. **Map** 4 E2. Ⓣ *Chinatown.*

This area is the third largest Chinatown in the US after those in San Francisco and New York. Pagoda-topped telephone booths, as well as a three-story gateway guarded by four marble lions, set the neighborhood's Oriental tone.

The first 200 Chinese to settle in New England came by ship from San Francisco in 1870, recruited to break a labor strike at a shoe factory. Another wave of immigration from California in the 1880s was prompted by an economic boom that led to job openings in construction. Boston's Chinese colony was fully established by the turn of the 19th century. Political turmoil in China immediately following World War II, and more recent arrivals from Vietnam, Laos, Korea, Thailand, and Cambodia, have swelled Chinatown's population. Along with the area's garment and textile industries, restaurants, bakeries, food markets, and dispensers of Chinese medicine are especially numerous along the main thoroughfare of Beach Street, as well as on Tyler, Oxford, and Harrison Streets.

Colorful August Moon Festival, held in Boston's Chinatown

Bay Village ⑰

Bounded by Tremont, Arlington & South Charles Sts. **Map** 4 D2. Ⓣ *New England Medical Center, Boylston.*

ORIGINALLY AN expanse of mud flats, the Bay Village area was drained in the early 1800s and initially became habitable with the construction of a dam in 1825. Many carpenters, cabinetmakers, artisans, and house painters involved in the construction of Beacon Hill's pricier town houses built their own modest but well-crafted residences here. As a result there are many similarities between the two neighborhoods.

Fayette Street was laid out in 1824 to coincide with the visit of the Marquis de Lafayette, the French general who allied himself with George Washington. Bay Street, located just off Fayette Street, features a single dwelling and is generally regarded as the city's shortest street. In 1809, poet and short-story writer Edgar Allen Poe was born in a boarding house on Carver Street, where his thespian parents were staying while in Boston on tour with a traveling theatrical company.

In the 1920s, at the height of the Prohibition era, clandestine speakeasies gave Bay Village its still-prevalent bohemian ambience. More recently, the neighborhood has become a center for Boston's gay community.

Bay Village's Piedmont Street is well known for the W. S. Haynes Company at No. 12, which has been hand-crafting flutes and piccolos since 1888, and has acquired among musicians a world-wide reputation for its instruments.

Shubert Theatre ⑱

265 Tremont St. **Map** 4 E2.
Ⓕ *(617) 482-9393.* Ⓣ *Boylston, New England Medical Center.*
◯ *phone to check.* ♿
Ⓦ *www.boston.com/wangcenter*

THE 1,650-SEAT Shubert Theatre rivals the Colonial Theatre *(see p 70)* for its long history of staging major pre-Broadway musical productions.

The vast Grand Lobby of the Wang Center for the Performing Arts

Designed by the architects Charles Bond and Thomas James, the theater features a white Neoclassical façade with a pair of Ionic columns flanking a monumental, Palladian-style window over the entrance. The theater first opened its doors in 1910, and during its heyday many stars walked the boards, including Sarah Bernhardt, W.C. Fields, Cary Grant, Mae West, Humphrey Bogart, Ingrid Bergman, Henry Ford, and Rex Harrison. Today, dance, theater, musicals, and opera are showcased here.

Wang Center for the Performing Arts ⑲

270 Tremont St. **Map** 4 E2.
Ⓕ *(617) 482-9393.* Ⓣ *Boylston, New England Medical Center.*
◯ *phone to check.* ♿
Ⓦ *www.boston.com/wangcenter*

OPENED IN 1925 as the Metropolitan Theatre and later named the Music Hall, New England's most ornate variety theater was inspired by the Paris Opera House, and was originally intended to be a movie theater. Designed by Clarence Blackall, the theater's auditorium was once one of the largest in the world. The theater was restored, transformed, and renamed as the Wang Center for the Performing Arts in 1983. The five-story Grand Lobby and seven-story auditorium are designed in Renaissance Revival style, with gold chandeliers, stained glass, ceiling murals, and jasper pillars.

Today the theater is used primarily as a venue for Broadway road shows, visiting Opera productions, concerts, and motion-picture revivals. It is also the main performance venue for the prestigious Boston Ballet troupe.

THE HISTORY OF BOSTON'S THEATER DISTRICT

Boston's first theater opened in 1793 on Federal Street. Fifty years later, with patronage from the city's social elite, Boston had become a major tryout town and boasted a number of lavish theaters. The US premiere of Handel's *Messiah* opened in 1839, the US premiere of Gilbert and Sullivan's *H.M.S. Pinafore* in 1877, and the premiere of Tchaikovsky's *First Piano Concerto* in 1875. In the late 19th century theaters came under fire from the censorious Watch and Ward Society. Later, in the 20th century, dramas such as Tennessee Williams' *A Streetcar Named Desire* and Eugene O'Neill's *Long Day's Journey into Night* debuted here. Musicals included *Ziegfeld Follies*, Gershwin's *Porgy and Bess*, and works by Rodgers and Hammerstein.

A Streetcar Named Desire, starring a young Marlon Brando and Jessica Tandy

Old Boston and the Financial District

British Lion, Old State House

T HIS IS AN AREA OF BOSTON where old and new sit one on top of the other. Some of its sights, situated in the older part of the district closest to Boston Common, predate the American Revolution. Much of what can be seen today, though, was built much more recently. The north of the district is home to Boston's late 20th-century, modernist-style City Hall and Government Center, while to the east is the city's bustling Financial District. This once formed part of Boston's harbor waterfront, a district built on mercantile wealth. Today, the wharves and warehouses have been replaced by skyscrapers belonging to banks, insurance companies, and high-tech industries.

SIGHTS AT A GLANCE

Historic Buildings and Churches

Bell Atlantic Building **11**
Boston Globe
  Store **4**
Custom House **10**
Faneuil Hall **8**
Government
  Center **7**
King's Chapel and
  Burying Ground **2**
Old City Hall **3**
Old South Meeting
  House **5**
Old State House
  pp78–9 **6**
Omni Parker House **1**
Quincy Market **9**

KEY

▨	Street-by-Street map *see pp74–5*
Ⓣ	"T" station
🚉	Train station
ℹ	Tourist information
🅿	Parking

`0 meters 300`
`0 yards 300`

GETTING THERE

This area is well served by public transportation. Bowdoin, Government Center, State, and Haymarket "T" stations are located at the heart of the district. The area is also served by buses 6, 7, 92, 93, 352, 353, 354, and 355.

◁ **Custom House, Boston's original skyscraper and one of the most distinctive buildings on the city skyline**

Street-by-Street: Colonial Boston

AN IMPORTANT PART of Boston's Freedom Trail *(see pp54–7)* runs through this historic core of the city, the site of which predates American Independence. Naturally, the area is now dominated by more recent 19th- and 20th-century development, but glimpses of a colonial past are prevalent here and there in the Old State House, King's Chapel and its adjacent burying ground, and the Old South Meeting House. Newer buildings of interest include the Omni Parker House, as well as the towering skyscrapers of Boston's financial district, located on the northwest edges of this area.

Irish Famine memorial, Washington Street

Government Center

★ King's Chapel and Burying Ground

A church has stood here since 1688, although the current building dates from 1749. The adjacent cemetery is the resting place of some of the most important figures in US history ❷

SCHOOL STREET

PROVINCE STREET

Omni Parker House

This hotel (see p307) first opened its doors in 1855, then underwent many renovations. Famed for its opulence, the hotel also gained a reputation in the 19th century as a meeting place for Boston intellectuals. The current building was erected in 1927 ❶

0 meters 50

0 yards 50

Old City Hall

This building served as Boston's City Hall from 1865 to 1969. Today it houses a number of offices and a trendy French restaurant ❸

STAR SIGHTS
─────────────
★ Old South Meeting House
─────────────
★ Old State House
─────────────
★ King's Chapel and Burying Ground

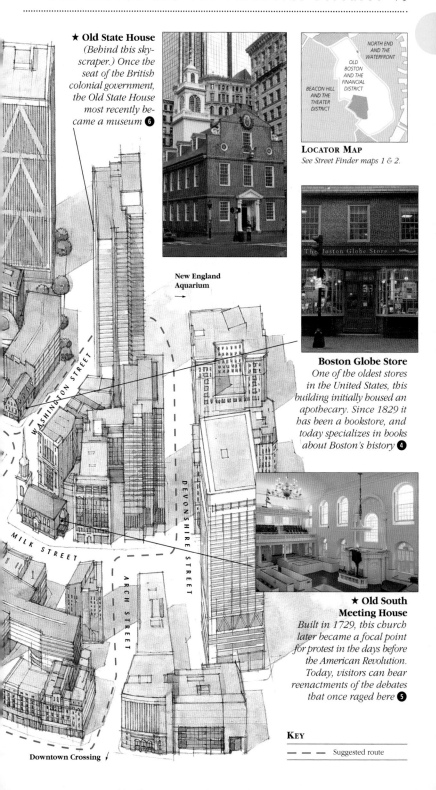

★ **Old State House**
(Behind this sky-scraper.) Once the seat of the British colonial government, the Old State House most recently became a museum ❻

LOCATOR MAP
See Street Finder maps 1 & 2.

NORTH END AND THE WATERFRONT

OLD BOSTON AND THE FINANCIAL DISTRICT

BEACON HILL AND THE THEATER DISTRICT

New England Aquarium →

Boston Globe Store
One of the oldest stores in the United States, this building initially housed an apothecary. Since 1829 it has been a bookstore, and today specializes in books about Boston's history ❹

WASHINGTON STREET

DEVONSHIRE STREET

MILK STREET

ARCH STREET

★ **Old South Meeting House**
Built in 1729, this church later became a focal point for protest in the days before the American Revolution. Today, visitors can hear reenactments of the debates that once raged here ❺

KEY

---- Suggested route

Downtown Crossing ↙

Omni Parker House ❶

60 School St. **Map** 1 C4.
🅒 *(617) 227-8600.* Ⓣ *Park Street, State, Government Center.*
🅦 *www.omnihotels.com*

Harvey D. Parker, raised on a farm in Maine, became so successful as the proprietor of his Boston restaurant that he achieved his ambition of expanding the property into a first-class, grand hotel. His Parker House opened in 1855, with a façade clad in white marble, standing five stories high, and featuring the first passenger elevator ever seen in Boston. It underwent several, rapid transformations during its early years, with additions made to the main structure in the 1860s and a 10-story, French chateau-style annex completed later that century. The building saw many successive transformations, and its latest 14-story incarnation has stood across from King's Chapel on School Street since 1927.

This hotel attained an instant reputation for luxurious accommodations and fine, even lavish, dining, typified by 11-course menus prepared by a French chef.

Among Parker House's many claims to fame are its Boston Cream Pie, which was first created here, and the word "scrod," a uniquely Bostonian term for the day's freshest seafood, still in common usage. Two former Parker House employees later became recognized for quite different careers. Vietnamese revolutionary leader Ho Chi Minh worked in the hotel's kitchens around 1915, while black activist Malcolm X was a busboy in Parker's Restaurant in the 1940s.

Simply decorated, pure white interior of King's Chapel on Tremont Street

PARKER HOUSE GUESTS

Boston's reputation as the "Athens of America" was widely acknowledged when members of a distinguished social club began meeting for lengthy dinners and lively intellectual exchanges in 1857. Their get-togethers took place on the last Saturday of every month at Harvey Parker's fancy new hotel. Regular participants included New England's literary elite *(see pp30–31)*: Henry Wadsworth Longfellow, Ralph Waldo Emerson, Nathaniel Hawthorne, and Henry David Thoreau, to name a few. Charles

John Wilkes Booth, infamous Parker House guest

Dickens participated while staying at the Parker House during his American speaking tours, and used his sitting-room mirror to rehearse the public readings he gave at Tremont Temple next door. The mirror now hangs on a mezzanine wall. In 1865, actor John Wilkes Booth, in town to see his brother, a fellow thespian, stayed at the hotel and took target practice at a nearby shooting gallery. Ten days later, at Ford's Theatre in Washington, he pulled a pistol and shot Abraham Lincoln.

King's Chapel and Burying Ground ❷

58 Tremont St. **Map** 1 C4.
🅒 *(617) 523-1749.* Ⓣ *Park Street, State, Government Center.* ⬜ *Jul–Aug: 9am–4pm Mon & Thu–Sat, 1–3pm Sun; Apr–Jun & Sep–Oct: 10am–3pm Mon, Fri & Sat; Nov–Mar: 10am–3pm Sat.* ✝ *11am Sun, 12:15pm Wed.* 🅦 *www.kings-chapel.org*

British crown officials were among those who attended Anglican services at the first chapel on this site, which was built in 1688. When New England's governor decided a larger church was needed, the present granite edifice – begun in 1749 – was constructed around the original wooden chapel, which was dismantled and heaved out the windows of its replacement. After the Revolution, the congregation's religious allegiance switched from Anglican to Unitarian. The sanctuary's raised pulpit – dating from 1717 and shaped like a wine glass – is one of the oldest in the US. High ceilings, open arches, and clear glass windows enhance the sense of spaciousness and light. The bell inside the King's Chapel is the largest ever cast by Paul Revere *(see p120)*.

Among those interred in the adjacent cemetery, Boston's oldest, are John Winthrop and Elizabeth Pain, the inspiration for adultress Hester Prynne in Nathaniel Hawthorne's moralistic novel *The Scarlet Letter.*

Old City Hall ❸

45 School St. **Map** 2 D4.
📞 (617) 227-3370. Ⓣ *Park Street, State, Government Center.*
◻ *Only restaurant and café open to public.*

A FINE EXAMPLE of French Second Empire architectural gaudiness, this was Boston's City Hall from 1865 to 1969 – it was superseded by the rakishly modern New City Hall structure at nearby Government Center *(see p80)*. The renovated 19th-century building now accommodates offices and an elegant French restaurant, Maison Robert *(see p329)*.

Previous occupants have included such flamboyant mayors as John "HoneyFitz" Fitzgerald and James Michael Curley. Statues here memorialize Josiah Quincy, Boston's second mayor, and Benjamin Franklin, who was born around the corner on nearby Milk Street.

19th-century French-style façade of Boston's Old City Hall

Boston Globe Store ❹

258 Washington St. **Map** 2 D4.
📞 (617) 523-9552. Ⓣ *Park Street, State, Government Center.*
◻ *9am–6pm Mon–Fri, 9:30am– 5pm Sat, 11am–4pm Sun.*
Ⓦ *www.globestore.boston.com*

A DORMERED GAMBREL roof crowns this brick landmark, which opened as Thomas Crease's apothecary shop in 1718 and was reestablished as the Old Corner Bookstore in 1829.

Moving in 16 years later, the Ticknor & Fields publishing company became a gathering place for a notable roster of authors: Emerson, Hawthorne, Longfellow, Thoreau, early feminist writer Margaret Fuller, and *Uncle Tom's Cabin* novelist, Harriet Beecher Stowe. The earliest editions of William Dean Howells' erudite *Atlantic Monthly* periodical were printed here – with Julia Ward Howe's rousing tribute to American Civil War bravado, *The Battle Hymn of the Republic*, first appearing in the February 1862 issue. Now owned and managed by the city's leading newspaper, the *Boston Globe*, the corner store specializes in books about Boston past and present.

The Boston Globe Store, specializing in books about the history of Boston

Old South Meeting House ❺

310 Washington St. **Map** 2 D4.
📞 (617) 482-6439. Ⓣ *Park Street, State, Government Center.* ◻ *Apr– Oct: 9:30am–5pm daily; Nov–Mar: 10am–4pm daily.*
Ⓦ *www.oldsouthmeetinghouse.org*

B UILT IN 1729 for Puritan religious services, this edifice, with a tall octagonal steeple, had colonial Boston's biggest capacity for town meetings. In 1765 a group of merchants and businessmen took the name "the Sons of Liberty" to protest the hated Stamp Act. Their outbursts against British taxation and the Stamp Act in particular drew increasingly large and vociferous crowds to the pews and upstairs galleries.

During a candlelit protest rally on December 16, 1773, fiery speechmaker Samuel Adams flashed the signal that led to the Boston Tea Party down at Griffin's Wharf several hours later. The British retaliated by turning Old South into an officers' tavern and stable for General John Burgoyne's 17th Light-horse Regiment of Dragoons. Displays, exhibits, and a multimedia presentation

entitled *Voices of Protest* relive those raucous days as well as more recent occurrences well into the 20th century. The Meeting House offers a series of lectures covering a wide range of New England topics and also holds occasional chamber music concerts and organ recitals. The downstairs shop has a selection of merchandise, including books, craft and scrimshaw reproductions, board games with historical themes, pottery, glassware, cards, jewelry, and the ubiquitous tins of "Boston Tea Party" tea.

Directly across Washington Street, sculptor Robert Shure's memorial to the 1845–50 Irish Potato Famine was added to the small plaza here in 1998.

Old South Meeting House, in stark contrast to the modern city

Old State House 6

DWARFED BY THE TOWERS of the Financial District, this was the seat of British colonial government between 1713 and 1776. The royal lion and unicorn still decorate each corner of the eastern façade. After independence, the Massachusetts legislature took possession of the building, and it has had many uses since, including produce market, merchants' exchange, Masonic lodge, and Boston City Hall. Its wine cellars now function as a downtown subway station. The Old State House houses two floors of Bostonian Society memorabilia and a video presentation documenting the change from colony to republic.

Old State House amid the sky-scrapers of the Financial District

A gold sculpture of an eagle, symbol of America, can be seen on the west façade.

West Façade
A Latin inscription, relating to the first Massachusetts Bay colony, runs around the outside of this crest. The relief in the center depicts a local Native American.

Entrance

Keayne Hall
This is named after Robert Keayne who, in 1658, gave £300 to the city so that the Town House, predating the Old State House, could be built. Exhibits in the room depict events from the Revolution.

★ Central Staircase
A fine example of 18th-century workmanship, the central spiral staircase has two beautifully crafted wooden handrails. It is one of the few such staircases still in existence in the US.

SITE OF THE BOSTON MASSACRE

A circle of cobblestones below the balcony on the eastern façade of the Old State House marks the site of the Boston Massacre. After the Boston Tea Party, this was one of the most inflammatory events leading up to the American Revolution. On March 5, 1770, an angry mob of colonists taunted British guardsmen with insults, rocks, and snowballs. The soldiers opened fire, killing five colonists. A number of articles relating to the Boston Massacre are exhibited inside the Old State House, including a musket found near the site and a coroner's report detailing the incident.

Cobbled circle: site of the Boston Massacre

The tower is a classic example of Colonial style. In 18th-century paintings and engravings it can be seen clearly above the Boston skyline.

British Unicorn and Lion
A royal symbol of Britain, the original lion and unicorn were torn down when news of the Declaration of Independence reached Boston in 1776.

★ **East Façade**
This façade has seen many changes. An earlier clock from the 1820s was removed in 1957 and replaced with an 18th-century replica of the sundial that once hung here. The clock has now been reinstated.

Council Chamber
Once the chambers for the royal governors, and from 1780 chambers for the first governor of Massachusetts (John Hancock), this room has seen many key events. Among them were numerous impassioned speeches made by Boston patriots.

The Declaration of Independence was read from this balcony in 1776. In the 1830s, when the building was City Hall, the balcony was enlarged to two tiers.

STAR SIGHTS

★ **East Façade**

★ **Central Staircase**

New City Hall and Government Center, a main city focal point

Government Center ❼

Cambridge, Court, New Sudbury & Congress Sts. **Map** 2 D3.
Ⓣ Government Center.

THIS CITY CENTER development was built on the sight of what was once Scollay Square, demolished as part of the trend for local urban-renewal that began in the early 1960s. This trend had already seen the building of the strikingly Modernist concrete and brick New City Hall, which stands on the eastern side of the square and houses government offices and a concert hall.

Some viewed the development as controversial; others did not lament what was essentially a disreputable cluster of saloons, burlesque theaters, tattoo parlors, and scruffy hotels. The overall master plan for Government Center was inspired by the outdoors vitality and spacious-ness of Italian piazzas. Architects I.M. Pei & Partners re-created some of this feeling by surrounding Boston's new City Hall with a vast terraced plaza covering 56 acres (23 ha), paved with 1,800,000 bricks. Its spaciousness makes it an ideal place for events such as skateboard contests, political and sports rallies, food fairs, patriotic military marches, and concerts.

Faneuil Hall ❽

Dock Sq. **Map** 2 D3.
Ⓒ (617) 635-3105. Ⓣ Government Center, Haymarket, State. **Great Hall**
Ⓞ 9am–5pm daily. ♿ 🖉 🎧

A GIFT TO Boston from the wealthy merchant Peter Faneuil in 1742, this Georgian, brick landmark has always functioned simul-taneously as a public market and town meeting place. Master tinsmith Shem Drowne modeled the building's grass-hopper weathervane after the one on top of the Royal Exchange in the City of London, England. Revo-lutionary gatherings packed the hall, and as early as 1763 Samuel Adams used the hall as a platform to suggest that the American colonies should unite against British oppression and fight to establish their independence; hence the building's nickname "Cradle of Liberty" and the bold posture of the statue of Sam Adams at the front of the building. Toward the end of the 18th century it became apparent that the existing Faneuil Hall could no longer house the capacity crowds that it regularly attracted. The commission to expand the building was undertaken by Charles Bulfinch, who completed the work from 1805 to 1806. The building then remained unchanged until 1898, when

Sam Adams statue, in front of Faneuil Hall

it was expanded even more according to long-standing Bulfinch stipulations. Faneuil Hall was restored in the 1970s as part of the wider redevelopment of Quincy Market.

Quincy Market ❾

Between Chatham & Clinton Sts.
Map 2 D3. Ⓒ (617) 338-2323. Ⓣ Government Center, State. Ⓞ 10am–9pm Mon–Sat, noon–6pm Sun. ♿ Ⓦ www.faneuilhallmarketplace.com

THIS IMMENSELY popular shopping and dining complex attracts nearly 14 million people every year. It was developed from the buildings of the old Quincy Market, which was the city's meat, fish, and produce market. These build-ings had fallen into disrepair before they underwent a widely acclaimed restoration in the 1970s. The 535-ft (163-m) long Greek Revival-style colon-naded market hall is now filled with a selection of fast food stands and a comedy nightclub, located in the spectacular central Rotunda. Completing the ensemble are twin North and South Market buildings – these individual warehouses have also been refurbished to accommodate numerous boutiques, stores, restaurants, and pubs, as well as upstairs business offices.

Gallery of the Greek Revival main dome in Quincy Market's central hall

Custom House ❿

3 McKinley Square. **Map** 2 E3.
📞 *(617) 310-6300.* Ⓣ *Aquarium.*
Museum ☐ *8am–11pm daily.* ☒
www.marriott.com/vacationclub/BOSCH

BEFORE LANDFILL altered
downtown topography,
early Boston's Custom House
perched at the water's edge.
A temple-like Greek Revival
structure with fluted Doric
columns, the granite building
had a skylit dome upon com-
pletion in 1847. Since 1915,
however, it has supported a
495 ft (150 m) tower with a
four-sided clock. For the best
part of the 20th century, the
Custom House was Boston's
only bona fide skyscraper.

The public has free access
to a small museum of maritime
history in the 19th-century
rotunda, with many objects
on loan from the Peabody
Museum in Salem.

**Greek Revival Custom House tower,
one of Boston's most striking sights**

Telephone Men and Women at Work, **Bell Atlantic Building**

Bell Atlantic Building ⓫

185 Franklin St. **Map** 2 D4.
📞 *(617) 743-4747.* Ⓣ *State,
Aquarium.* **Museum** ☐ *24 hours
daily.* ♿

DATING FROM 1947 and
overlooking the south
side of Post Office Square,
this Art Deco building is still
in use today. Dean Cornwell's
monumental 160-ft (49-m)
long *Telephone Men and
Women at Work* mural –
populated by 197 life-size
figures – has circled the lobby
since 1951 and is a truly remarkable work of art. The
small museum at street level
features an accurate restoration of Alexander Graham
Bell's Court Street laboratory,
complete with his tools,
books, workbench, and one

of his garret window-frames
overlooking a diorama of
Scollay Square. The exhibit
was constructed from parts
of Bell's original workshop,
put to one side and lovingly
preserved when the house
where he lived was demol-
ished in the 1920s. It was
opened on June 3, 1959,
coincidentally the 84th
anniversary of the invention
of the telephone. The world's
first commercial telephone
and first telephone switch-
board, both dating from May
1877, are also displayed in
the museum.

The beautifully landscaped
Post Office Square, on the
northern side of the Bell
Atlantic Building, is a small
island of green situated amid
the soaring skyscrapers of the
financial district. Vines climb
a 143-ft (44-m) long trellis
along one side of the park,
and a fountain made of green
glass cascades on the square's
Pearl Street side. A focal point
for the whole district, the
grassy square comes into its
own during the warmer
months of the year, when
office workers can be
seen sprawling across
its well-kept lawns.

The square is also
overlooked by down-
town's main post office,
housed in the John W.
McCormack courthouse
building, and Le Meridien
Hotel *(see p307),* a classic
Renaissance Revival show-
piece completed in 1922.

ALEXANDER GRAHAM BELL (1847–1922)

A native of Edinburgh, Scotland, and son of a deaf
mother, Bell moved to Boston in 1871 to start a
career teaching speech to the deaf. Two years
later he was appointed as professor of vocal
physiology at Boston University. Bell worked
in his spare time on an apparatus for trans-
mitting sound by electrical current. History
was made on March 17, 1876, when Bell
called to his assistant in another room: "Mr.
Watson, come here. I want you." The first
demonstration of the "telephone" took place
in Boston on May 10, 1876, at the Academy
of Arts and Sciences. By 1878, he had set up
the first public telephone exchange in New
Haven, Connecticut.

NORTH END AND THE WATERFRONT

HIS WAS BOSTON's first neighborhood, and one that has been key to the city's fortunes. Fringed by numerous wharves, the area prospered initially through shipping and shipbuilding, with much of America's early trade passing through its warehouses. The more recent importance of finance and high-tech industries, however, has seen the waterfront evolve, its

Statue in Old North Church garden

old warehouses transformed into luxury apartment blocks and offices. Away from the waterfront, the narrow streets of the North End have historically been home to European immigrants, drawn by the availability of work. The area today is populated largely by those of Italian descent, whose many cafés, delis, and restaurants make it one of the city's most distinct communities.

SIGHTS AT A GLANCE

Historic Sites and Churches
Clough House ②
Copp's Hill Burying
  Ground ①
Old North Church
  p87 ③
Paul Revere House ⑤
Paul Revere Mall ④

Waterfront Sights
Boston Tea Party Ship ⑧
Children's Museum ⑨
New England Aquarium
  pp90–91 ⑦
Waterfront Wharves ⑥

```
0 meters          450
0 yards           450
```

KEY

▦	Street-by-Street map *see pp84–5*
Ⓣ	"T" station
🚌	Bus station
P	Parking

GETTING THERE
This area is well served by public transportation. Aquarium "T" station is located toward the south of the area, near Long Wharf. The area is also served by buses 6, 92, 93, and 111.

◁ **Boston Tea Party Ship, with the Financial District in the background**

Street-by-Street: North End

Old North Church clock

THE MAIN ARTERIES of this area are Hanover and Salem Streets. Topped by the Old North Church, Salem Street is indicative of this area's historical connections – indeed the Old North Church is one of Boston's premier Revolutionary sights. In general the area consists of narrow streets and alleys, with four- and five-story tenements, many of which are now expensive condominiums. Hanover Street, like much of the area, has a distinctly Italian feel, while just south of here is North Square, site of the famous Paul Revere House (*see p88*).

Clough House
Period furnishings can be seen in this house by Ebenezer Clough, who also helped build the Old North Church ❷

Charlestown

Copp's Hill Burying Ground
During the American Revolution, the British used this low hilltop to fire cannon at American positions across Boston Harbor. Created in 1659 it is the city's second oldest graveyard ❶

★ **Old North Church**
Built in 1723 and famous for the part it played in Paul Revere's midnight ride (see p120), this is Boston's oldest religious building. On festive occasions, the North End still rings with the sound of its bells ❸

KEY

— — — Suggested route

STAR SIGHTS

★ **Old North Church**

★ **Paul Revere House**

★ **Paul Revere Mall**

Government Center

0 meters   50

0 yards   50

★ Paul Revere Mall
Linking the Old North Church to Hanover Street, this tree-lined mall dates only from 1933. Its antique feel is enhanced by a statue of Paul Revere, which was sculpted in 1885 ❹

LOCATOR MAP
See Street Finder map 2

St. Stephen's Church echoes the North End's Italian theme, though only by chance. Long before the first Italians arrived, Charles Bulfinch incorporated Italian Renaissance features and a bell tower into his renovation of an earlier church building.

Hanover Street is the most Italian of all Boston's streets, brought to life by restaurants and cafés, as well as the day-to-day activities of its ethnic community.

↘ **The waterfront**

★ Paul Revere House
This is the house where Paul Revere began his midnight ride (see p120). Revere's home from 1770 to 1800, it is now a museum ❺

Slate tombstones of Boston's early settlers, Copp's Hill Burying Ground

Copp's Hill Burying Ground ❶

Entrances at Charter & Hull Sts.
Map 2 D2. ⓣ *Government Center, North Station.* ◻ *8am–5pm daily.*

EXISTING SINCE 1659, this is Boston's second-oldest cemetery after the one by King's Chapel *(see p76)*. Nicknamed "Corpse Hill," the real name of the hill occupied by the cemetery derives from a local man by the name of William Copp. He owned a farm on its southeastern slope from 1643, and much of the cemetery's land was purchased from him. His children are buried here. Other more famous people interred here include Robert Newman, the sexton who hung Paul Revere's signal lanterns in the belfry of Old North Church *(see p87)*, and Edmund Hartt, builder of the USS *Constitution (see p119)*. Increase, Cotton, and Samuel Mather, three generations of a family of highly influential colonial period Puritan ministers, are also buried here. Hundreds of Boston's Colonial-era black slaves and freedmen are also buried here, including Prince Hall, a free black man who founded the African Freemasonry Order in Massachusetts.

During the British occupation of Boston, the site was used by British commanders who had an artillery position here. They would later exploit the prominent hilltop location during the Revolution, when they directed cannon fire from here across Boston harbor toward American positions in Charlestown. King George III's troops were said to have used the slate headstones for target practice, and pockmarks from their musket balls are still visible on some of them.

Copp's Hill Terrace, directly across Charter Street, is a prime observation point for

Decorative column, Copp's Hill

Quiet, leafy street, typical of the area around Copp's Hill

views over to Charlestown and Bunker Hill. It is also the site where, in 1919, a 2.3-million-gallon molasses tank exploded, creating a huge, syrupy tidal wave that killed 21 people.

Clough House ❷

21 Unity St. **Map** 2 E2.
ⓣ *Haymarket, Aquarium.* ◻ *Jun–Sep: 10am–2pm Wed.*

EBENEZER CLOUGH was a master mason and one of the Sons of Liberty who participated in the Boston Tea Party. One of two masons who helped to build the neighboring Old North Church *(see p87)*, he was also the head of a syndicate that laid out Unity Street in 1710 and built a series of six town houses here. The only building to survive is the one at No. 21 Unity Street, which was built in 1712 and was the house in which Ebenezer Clough himself lived. In a bad state of decay for many years and in danger of demolition, the house was saved when the Reverend P. Kellet, vicar of Christ Church, launched a fund-raising campaign in 1962. A rather austere three-story building, it is typical of much of Boston's colonial architecture. Now fully restored to its former condition, the house has finely executed window and door lintels, decorated with raised brick panels over the first-floor windows and simple, carved-brick detailing over the door. The Heritage Room on the second floor features typical period furnishings and household accessories.

Clough House once stood alongside an identical brick residence, which was acquired by Benjamin Franklin in 1748. He bought the house for his two widowed sisters but never lived here himself. It was demolished in the 1930s to make way for the Paul Revere Mall *(see p88)*.

Old North Church™ ❸

CHRIST EPISCOPAL CHURCH is the official name of Boston's oldest surviving religious edifice, which dates from 1723. It was built of brick in the Georgian style similar to that of St. Andrew's-by-the-Wardrobe in Blackfriars, London, designed by Sir Christopher Wren. The church was made famous on April 18, 1775, when sexton Robert Newman, aiding Paul Revere *(see p120)*, hung a pair of signal lanterns in the belfry. These were to warn the patriots in Charlestown of the westward departure of British troops, on their way to engage the revolutionaries.

VISITORS' CHECKLIST

193 Salem St. **Map** 2 E2.
📞 (617) 523-6676.
Ⓣ *Haymarket, Aquarium, North Station.* 🅾 *Jul–Aug: 9am–5pm daily.* ✝ *9am, 11am & 4pm Sun (also 5pm Jul–Aug).* 📷 ♿ 🎧
Ⓦ www.oldnorth.com

★ **Box Pews**
The traditional, high-sided box pews in the church were designed to enclose footwarmers, which were filled with hot coals or bricks during wintry weather.

★ **Bell Tower and Steeple**
Views from the top of the bell tower, such as this one toward the Financial District, are well worth the climb. Famous as the place where Robert Newman hung his lanterns, the tower contains the first set of church bells in North America, cast in 1745.

Entrance

STAR SIGHTS

★ **Bell Tower and Steeple**

★ **Box Pews**

Bust of George Washington
This marble bust of the first US president, modeled on an earlier one by Christian Gullager, was presented to the church in 1815.

Paul Revere Mall ④

Tileston St. **Map** 2 E2.
Ⓣ *Haymarket, Aquarium.* ♿

THIS BRICK-PAVED plaza gives the crowded neighborhood of the North End a precious stretch of open space between Hanover and Unity Streets. A well-utilized municipal resource, the Mall is always full of local people: children, teenagers, young mothers, and older residents chatting in Italian and playing cards or checkers. Laid out in 1933, and originally called the Prado, its focal point is Cyrus Dallin's equestrian statue of local hero Paul Revere, which was originally modeled in 1885. However, it was not sculpted and placed here until 1940. Bronze bas-relief plaques on the mall's side walls commemorate a number of North End residents who have played an important role in the history of Boston. Benches, a fountain, and twin rows of linden trees complete the space, which has a distinctly European feel.

At the north end of the Mall, across Unity Street, is Old North Church *(see p86)*, one of the city's most important historical sites. To the south is busy Hanover Street, which is lined with numerous Italian cafés and restaurants.

Paul Revere House kitchen, as it was in the 18th century

Paul Revere House ⑤

19 North Sq. **Map** 2 E2.
📞 *(617) 523-2338.* Ⓣ *Haymarket, Aquarium.* ◯ *mid-Apr–Oct: 9:30am–5:15pm daily; Nov–mid-Apr: 9:30am–4:15pm daily.* ● *Jan–Mar: Mon.* 🎫 ♿ 🚫 📷
Ⓦ *www.paulreverehouse.org*

THE CITY'S oldest surviving clapboard frame house is historically significant, for it was here in 1775 that Paul Revere began his legendary horseback ride to warn his compatriots in Lexington of the impending arrival of British troops. This historic event was later immortalized in a boldly patriotic, epic

poem by Henry Wadsworth Longfellow *(see p110)*. It begins "Listen, my children, and you shall hear of the midnight ride of Paul Revere."

Revere, a Huguenot descendent, was by trade a versatile gold- and silversmith, copper engraver, and maker of church bells and cannons. He and his second wife, Rachel, mother of eight of his 16 children, owned the house from 1770 to 1800. Small leaded casement windows, an overhanging upper story, and nail-studded front door all contribute to make it a fine example of 18th-century Early American architecture. In the courtyard along one side of the house is a large bronze bell, cast by Paul Revere for a church in 1804 – Revere made nearly 200 church bells. Three rooms in the house contain period artifacts, including original pieces of family furniture, items made in Revere's workshop, and colonial banknotes. The house, which by the mid-19th century had become a decrepit tenement fronted by stores, was saved from demolition by preservationists' efforts led by one of Revere's great-grandsons.

Next door, the early 18th-century Pierce-Hichborn House is the earliest brick town house remaining in New England.

View toward the Custom House and the Financial District, across Christopher Columbus Park

Rowes Wharf development, typical of Boston's waterfront regeneration

Waterfront Wharves ❻

Atlantic Avenue. **Map** 2 E4.
Ⓣ *Aquarium.*

BOSTON'S WATERFRONT is fringed by many wharves, reminders of the city's past as a key trading port. One of the largest of these is Long Wharf, established in 1710 to accommodate the boom in early maritime commerce. Once extending 2000 ft (610 m) into Boston Harbor and lined with shops and warehouses, Long wharf provided mooring for the largest ships of the time.

Running along the waterfront and past Christopher Columbus Park, Harbor Walk connects Long Wharf with other adjacent wharves, such as Union, Lewis, and Commercial wharves. Dating from the early 1800s, most are now converted to fashionable harborside apartments. Rowes Wharf, to the south of the waterfront, is a particularly fine example of such revitalization.

Built of Bostonian red brick, this modern development features a large archway that links the city to the harbor. It comprises the luxury Boston Harbor Hotel, opulent condominiums, offices, and a marina.

New England Aquarium ❼

See pp90–91.

Boston Tea Party Ship ❽

Congress St. Bridge. **Map** 2 E5.
☎ (617) 338-1773. Ⓣ *South Station.* ⬚ *Jun–Sep: 9am–6pm daily; Oct–May: 9am–5pm daily.* 🅿
🅆 www.historictours.com/boston

GRIFFIN'S WHARF, where the Boston Tea Party took place on December 16, 1773, was buried beneath landfill many years ago. Since 1973, the Danish-built sailing brig *Beaver II* has been anchored on Fort Point Channel a short distance south of the old Griffin's Wharf site. The vessel resembles one of the three original British East India Company ships involved in the Tea Party protest. Today, modern-day patriots toss imitation bales of tea overboard, re-creating one of the acts of defiance that prompted Britain to put the Massachusetts Bay Colony under martial law.

On an adjacent pier, ship models, Tea Party memorabilia, and other educational exhibits are displayed in a museum.

Children's Museum ❾

300 Congress St. **Map** 2 E5.
☎ (617) 426-8855. Ⓣ *South Station.* ⬚ *mid-Jun–Aug: 10am–5pm Sat–Thu, 10am–9pm Fri; Sep–mid-Jun: 10am–5pm Tue–Sun.* 🅿 ♿ 🅆 www.bostonkids.org

OVERLOOKING Fort Point Channel, a rejuvenated 19th-century wool warehouse contains one of the country's best children's museums. There are many interesting exhibits, and youngsters can participate in games and learning activities, and even climb through a two-story maze.

The Factory exhibit lets children work on a real assembly line and make their own spinning tops. The City Slice exhibit is a cross-section of a working city street, showing a dissected house, street, and car. Careers can be sampled as children work on a mini-construction site, or act in a simulated TV studio. An international flavor is added by a visit to the silk merchant's house transplanted from Kyoto, and to Teen Tokyo.

Playing on the mini-construction site at Boston's Children's Museum

New England Aquarium ➐

THE WATERFRONT'S prime attraction dominates
Central Wharf. Designed by a consortium of
architects in 1969, the aquarium's core encloses
a vast four-story ocean tank, which contains an
innumerable array of marine animals. A curving
walkway runs around the outside of the tank from
top to bottom and provides viewpoints of the
interior of the tank from different levels. Also
resident at the aquarium are colonies of penguins,
while the recently added west wing contains an
outdoor tank with harbor seals. The *Discovery*
exhibit, a tank floating separately from the aquarium, features shows performed by sea lions.

Edge of the Sea Tidepool
*A fiberglass shore recreates a
world where the land meets the
sea. It is home to animals such as
horseshoe crabs and sea urchins.*

Penguin Pool
*One of the main attractions
of the aquarium, the
penguin pool runs
around the base of the
giant tank. It contains
African, rockhopper,
and blue penguins.*

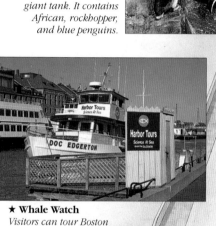

★ **Whale Watch**
*Visitors can tour Boston
Harbor, where whales can
often be seen. Tours
also explore aspects
of oceanography,
such as studying
the harbor's
ecosystem.*

**Main
entrance**

Harbor Seals
*The west wing, an outdoor tank
covered by a steel canopy, is home
to a lively colony of harbor seals.*

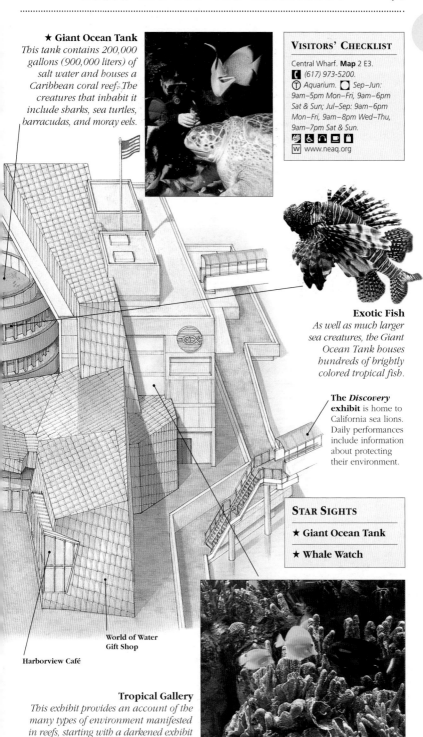

★ Giant Ocean Tank
This tank contains 200,000 gallons (900,000 liters) of salt water and houses a Caribbean coral reef. The creatures that inhabit it include sharks, sea turtles, barracudas, and moray eels.

VISITORS' CHECKLIST

Central Wharf. **Map** 2 E3.
🄵 *(617) 973-5200.*
🅣 *Aquarium.* 🄾 *Sep–Jun: 9am–5pm Mon–Fri, 9am–6pm Sat & Sun; Jul–Sep: 9am–6pm Mon–Fri, 9am–8pm Wed–Thu, 9am–7pm Sat & Sun.*
🄿 🄳 🄾 🄿 🄵
🅦 www.neaq.org

Exotic Fish
As well as much larger sea creatures, the Giant Ocean Tank houses hundreds of brightly colored tropical fish.

The *Discovery* exhibit is home to California sea lions. Daily performances include information about protecting their environment.

STAR SIGHTS

★ Giant Ocean Tank

★ Whale Watch

World of Water Gift Shop

Harborview Café

Tropical Gallery
This exhibit provides an account of the many types of environment manifested in reefs, starting with a darkened exhibit of deep-water reef fishes and ending with a brightly lit, Pacific coral reef.

BACK BAY AND SOUTH END

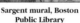

Until the 19th century Boston was situated on a narrow peninsula surrounded by tidal marshes. Projects to fill Back Bay began in the 1850s and were made possible by new inventions such as the steam shovel. The Back Bay was filled by 1880, and developers soon moved in. Planned along French lines, with elegant boulevards, Back Bay is now one of Boston's most exclusive neighborhoods. The more bohemian South End, laid out on an English model of town houses clustered around squares, is home to many artists and Boston's gay community.

Sargent mural, Boston Public Library

SIGHTS AT A GLANCE

Historic Streets and Squares
Boylston Street ❽
Commonwealth Avenue ❹
Copley Square ❼
The Esplanade ❶
Newbury Street ❺

Historic Buildings, Churches, and Museums
Boston Center for the Arts ⓬
Boston Public Library ❾

First Baptist Church ❸
Gibson House Museum ❷
Institute of Contemporary Art ⓫
John Hancock Tower ❿
Trinity Church pp98–9 ❻

KEY

▦	Street-by-Street map *see pp94–5*
Ⓣ	"T" station
🚆	Train station
🚌	Bus station
ℹ	Tourist information
🅿	Parking

GETTING THERE

The area has good public transportation. Arlington, Copley, and Hynes/ I.C.A. "T" stations serve the Back Bay. Back Bay/ South End and Prudential "T stations serve the South End. The area is served by buses 1, 8, 9, 10, 39, 43, 49, 55, and 302.

0 meters	450
0 yards	450

◁ **View of Back Bay's characteristic row houses, from the top of the John Hancock Tower**

Street-by-Street: Back Bay

T HIS FASHIONABLE DISTRICT unfolds westward
from the Public Garden *(see pp64–5)* in a grid
that departs radically from the twisting streets
found elsewhere in Boston. Commonwealth
Avenue, with its grand 19th-century mansions
and parkland, and Newbury and Boylston Streets
are its main arteries. Newbury Street is a magnet
for all of Boston wanting to indulge in some
upscale shopping, whereas the more somber
Boylston Street bustles with office workers.
Copley Square anchors the entire area and is the
site of Henry Hobson Richardson's magnificent
Trinity Church *(see pp98–9)* and the 60-story
John Hancock Tower *(see p101)*, from which
there are some magnificent views of Boston.

**Weekly summer and fall farmers'
market, Copley Square**

Copley Square
*This square was a marsh
until 1870. It took on its
present form only in the late
20th century as buildings
around its edges were completed. A farmers' market,
concerts, and folk-dancing
feature regularly* ❼

Fenway Park ←

COMMONWEALTH AVENU

NEWBU

DARTMOUTH STREET

BOYLSTON STREET

Boylston Street
*The site of the Prudential
Center and the Institute
of Contemporary Art (see
p101), Boylston Street is
also the location of the
fabulous New Old South
Church (see p100)* ❽

**★ Boston
Public Library**
*One of the first free
public libraries in the
world, this building
was designed by
Charles McKim. Inside
are murals by John
Singer Sargent* ❾

**South
End**

First Baptist Church
By Henry Hobson Richardson (see p96), this church is a fine example of his Romanesque Revival style ❸

Beacon Hill

COMMONWEALTH AVENUE

CLARENDON STREET

STREET

Public Garden

LOCATOR MAP
See Street Finder map 3

BEACON HILL AND THE THEATER DISTRICT

BACK BAY AND SOUTH END

Commonwealth Avenue
Envisioned as Boston's Champs-Elysées, this avenue boasts beautiful town houses and a tree-lined central mall ❹

★ Newbury Street
High fashion outlets, galleries, and restaurants characterize this street – Boston's most fashionable, and a great place for people-watching ❺

★ Trinity Church
Acknowledged as Henry Hobson Richardson's Romanesque Revival masterpiece, this is one of the most important churches in the US. ❻

KEY

− − − − Suggested route

STAR SIGHTS

★ Newbury Street

★ Trinity Church

★ Boston Public Library

0 meters   50
0 yards   50

The Esplanade ❶

Map 1 A4. ⓣ *Charles/ MGH.*
⬚ *24 hrs daily.* ♿ �ⓦ *www.ci.boston.
ma.us/parks/openspaces*

R UNNING ALONG the Boston
side of the Charles River,
between Longfellow Bridge
and Dartmouth Street, are the
parkland, lagoons, and islands
known collectively as the
Esplanade. While the park is
used most extensively for inline skating, cycling, and strol-
ling, it is also the main access
point for boating on the river
and the site of the city's
leading outdoor concert space.

In 1929, Arthur Fiedler, then
the young conductor of the
Boston Pops Orchestra, chose
the Esplanade for a summer
concert series that became a
tradition. The Hatch Memorial
Shell was constructed in 1939,
and its stage is widely used
by musical ensembles and
other groups throughout the
summer. Fourth of July concerts by the Boston Pops,
which are followed by fireworks, can attract upward
of 500,000 spectators.

**Fountains at the Esplanade,
next to the Charles River**

Gibson House Museum ❷

137 Beacon St. **Map** 1 A4.
📞 *(617) 267-6338.* ⓣ *Arlington.* ⬚
*May–Oct: 1pm–3pm Wed–Sun; Nov–
Apr: 1pm–3pm Sat–Sun.* 🖼 🚫 ⬚
ⓦ *www.fisher.edu/backbay/gibson*

A MONG THE FIRST houses
built in the Back Bay, the
Gibson House preserves its
original Victorian decor and
furnishings throughout all six
stories. The 1860 brownstone
and red-brick structure was

designed in the popular
Italian Renaissance Revival
style for the widow Catherine
Hammond Gibson, who was
one of the few women to own
property in this part of the
city. Her grandson Charles
Hammond Gibson, Jr., a noted
eccentric, poet, travel writer,
horticulturalist, and bon vivant,
arranged for the house to become a museum after his death
in 1954. As a prelude to this,
Gibson began to rope off the
furniture in the 1930s, thus
inviting his guests to sit on the
stairs to drink martinis made
with his own bathtub gin.

One of the most modern
houses of its day, the Gibson
House boasted such technical
advancements as gas lighting,
indoor plumbing in the basement, and coal-fired central
heating. Visitors can see a full
dinner setting in the dining
room or admire the whimsical
Turkish pet pavilion. It is
Gibson's preservation of the
1860s decor (with some modi-
fications in 1888) that makes
the museum a true time cap-
sule of Victorian life in Boston.

The original Victorian-style library of the Gibson House Museum

First Baptist Church ❸

110 Commonwealth Ave. **Map** 3 C2.
📞 *(617) 267-3148.* ⓣ *Arlington.*
⬚ *for Sunday worship.* ✝ *11am
Sun.* 🚫 ♿

T HE ROMANESQUE-STYLE First
Baptist Church on the corner of Commonwealth Avenue
and Clarendon Street was
Henry Hobson Richardson's
first major architectural
commission and became an
instant landmark when it was
finished in 1872. Viewed from
Commonwealth Avenue, it is
one of the most distinctive
buildings of the city skyline.

Richardson considered the
nearly freestanding bell tower,
which he modeled roughly
on Italian campaniles, to be
the church's most innovative
structure. The square tower
is topped with a decorative
frieze and arches protected
by an overhanging roof. The
frieze was modeled in Paris
by Bartholdi, the sculptor who
created the Statue of Liberty,
and was carved in
place by Italian arti-
sans after the stones
were set. The faces
in the frieze, which
depict the sacraments,
are likenesses of prom-
inent Bostonians of
that time, among them
Henry Wadsworth
Longfellow and Ralph
Waldo Emerson. The
trumpeting angels at

**Detail of Bartholdi's frieze atop the distinctive
square tower of the First Baptist Church**

the corners of the tower gave the building its nickname, "Church of the Holy Bean Blowers."

Four years after the church was completed, the Unitarian congregation dissolved because it was unable to bear the expense of the building. The church stood vacant until 1881, when the First Baptist congregation from the South End took it over.

Commonwealth Avenue ❹

Map 3 B2. Ⓣ *Arlington, Copley, Hynes Convention Center/ ICA.*

BACK BAY was Boston's first fully planned neighborhood, and architect Arthur Gilman made Commonwealth Avenue, modeled on the elegant boulevards of Paris, the centerpiece of the design. At 200 ft (61 m) wide, with a 10ft (3 m) setback from the sidewalks to encourage small gardens in front of the buildings, Commonwealth became an arena for America's leading domestic architects in the second half of the 19th century. A walk from the Public Garden to Massachusetts Avenue is like flicking through a catalog of architectural styles. Few of the grand buildings on either side of the avenue are open to the public, although the Boston Center for Adult

Education at No. 5 can be toured by appointment. The mansion, built in 1912 in Italianate style, was a late addition to Back Bay. Textile industrialist owner Walter C. Baylies later added a ballroom modeled on the Petit Trianon in Versailles.

A statue of the fervent abolitionist William Garrison (1805–79) stands on Commonwealth Avenue's central mall.

William Garrison statue on Commonwealth Avenue

🏛 Center for Adult Education

5 Commonwealth Ave. ☎ *(617) 267-4430.* ◯ *Apr–Sep: 10am–6pm Mon–Sat, noon–6pm Sun; Oct– Mar: 10:30am–5:30pm (last admission: 30 mins before closing).* ● *May 11.* 🎨 ∅ ♿ 📷 🎧 ⬤ ⓦ www.bcae.org

Newbury Street ❺

Map 3 C2. Ⓣ *Arlington, Copley, Hynes Convention Center/ ICA.*

NEWBURY STREET is a Boston synonym for "stylish." The elegant Ritz-Carlton Hotel on the corner with Arlington Street sets an elegant tone for the street that continues with a mix of prestigious and often

well-hidden art galleries, stylish boutiques, and some of the city's most *au courant* restaurants.

Churches provide vestiges of a more decorous era. The Church of the Covenant at No. 67 Newbury is open for viewing for a few hours a week, and contains the world's largest collection of Louis Comfort Tiffany stained-glass windows. A chorus and orchestra perform a Bach cantata each Sunday at Emmanuel Church on the corner of Newbury and Berkeley Streets.

The Newbury Street Mural at the corner of Newbury and Dartmouth highlights the street's role as a place to be seen. It depicts 72 of the famous and not so famous, from Sam Adams to Tom Yawkey, who owned the Boston Red Sox for 44 years. Modern-day aspiring celebrities may be spotted at the sidewalk tables of Newbury's "hottest" restaurants, such as Sonsie *(see p331).*

⛪ Church of the Covenant

67 Newbury St. ☎ *(617) 266-7480.* ◯ *noon–1pm Tue, Thu.* 🎨 ∅ ♿ 📷 🎧 ⓦ www.churchofthecovenant.org

Stylish Newbury Street, with its elegant shops, galleries, and restaurants, the epitome of Boston style

Trinity Church ❻

ROUTINELY VOTED one of America's 10 finest buildings, this masterpiece by Henry Hobson Richardson dates from 1877. Trinity Church was founded in 1733 near Downtown Crossing, but the congregation moved the church to this site in 1871. The church is a granite and sandstone Romanesque structure standing on wooden piles driven through mud into bedrock, surmounted with granite pyramids. John LaFarge designed the interior, while some of the windows are designed by Edward Burne-Jones and executed by William Morris.

The Bell Tower was inspired by the Renaissance cathedral at Salamanca, central Spain.

Bas-relief in Chancel
On the wall of the chancel, behind the altar, are a series of gold bas-reliefs. This one shows St. Paul before King Agrippa.

★ **North Transept Windows**
Designed by Edward Burne-Jones and executed by William Morris, the three stained-glass windows above the choir relate the story of Christmas.

Parish House

The Pulpit is covered with carved scenes from the life of Christ, as well as portraits of great preachers through the ages.

Chancel
Designed by Charles Maginnis, the present-day chancel was not dedicated until 1938. The seven windows by Clayton & Bell of London show the life of Christ.

David's Charge to Solomon
Located in the baptistry, to the right of the chancel, this beautiful window is also the result of a partnership between Edward Burne-Jones and William Morris. The story shown is one of the few in the church from the Old Testament.

VISITORS' CHECKLIST

Copley Sq. **Map** 3 C2.
(617) 536-0944.
Copley. 8am–6pm daily. 8am, 9am, 11am & 6pm Sun. **concerts.**
www.trinitychurchboston.org

John LaFarge's lancet windows show Christ in the act of blessing. They were designed at the request of Phillips Brooks – he wanted LaFarge to create an inspirational design for the west nave, which he could look at while preaching.

★ West Portico
Richardson disliked the original flat façade of Trinity Church, and so modeled the deeply sculpted west portico after St. Trophime in Arles, France. It was added after his death.

Carving of Phillips Brooks and Christ

PHILLIPS BROOKS

Born in Boston in 1835 and educated at Harvard, Brooks was a towering charismatic figure. Rector of Trinity Church from 1869, he gained a reputation for powerful sermons. From 1872 Brooks worked closely with Henry Hobson Richardson on the design of the new Trinity Church – at least five sculpted likenesses of him can be seen in and around the building.

Main Entrance

STAR SIGHTS

★ **West Portico**

★ **North Transept Windows**

The New Old South Church on the corner of Copley Square

Copley Square ❼

Map 3 C2. Ⓣ *Copley.*

NAMED AFTER John Singleton Copley, the great Boston painter born nearby in 1737, Copley Square is a hive of civic activity surrounded by some of Boston's most striking architecture. Summer activities include weekly farmers' markets, concerts, and even folk-dancing.

The inviting green plaza took years to develop; when Copley was born it was just a marshy riverbank, which remained unfilled until 1870. Construction of the John Hancock Tower in 1975 anchored the southeastern side of Copley Square, and the Copley Place development completed the square on the southwestern corner in 1984. Today's Copley Square, a wide open space of trees, grass, and fountains, took shape in the heart of the city in the 1990s, after various plans to utilize this hitherto wasted space were tendered.

A large plaque honoring the Boston Marathon, which ends at the Boston Public Library, was set in the sidewalk in 1996 to coincide with the 100th race. As well as pushcart vendors, the plaza has a booth for discounted theater, music, and dance tickets.

Boylston Street ❽

Map 3 C2. Ⓣ *Boylston, Arlington, Copley, Hynes Convention Center/ ICA.*

A BRASS TEDDY BEAR sculpture, outside F.A.O. Schwarz, is one of Boylston Street's principal landmarks. It is a reproduction of the toy company's famous New York's Fifth Avenue symbol. The French Academic-style building at the corner of Boylston and Berkeley Streets was originally built for the Museum of Natural History, forerunner of the Museum of Science (*see p67*). Its present occupant is the upscale clothier Louis. The Art Deco building at the corner of Arlington and Boylston houses Shreve, Crump & Low, Inc., Boston's finest jewelers.

Some notable office buildings stand on Boylston Street. The lobby of the New England building at No. 501 features large historical murals and dioramas depicting the process of filling Back Bay. The central tower of the Prudential Center dominates the skyline on upper Boylston Street. Adjoining the Prudential is the Hynes Convention Center. It was

enlarged in 1988 to accommodate the city's burgeoning convention business.

The Italian Gothic-style **New Old South Church**, at the corner of Dartmouth, was built in 1874–5 by the congregation that had met previously at the Old South Meeting House (*see p77*).

🛉 **New Old South Church**
Tremont St. 🄲 *(617) 523-3383.*
◯ *Apr–Sep: 10am–6pm Mon–Sat, noon–6pm Sun; Oct–Mar: 10:30am–5:30pm (last admission: 30 mins before closing).* ● *May 11.* 🖼 🛉
Jul–Aug: 10:45am, 5:30pm Sun; Sep–Jun: 9am, 10:45am, 5:30pm Sun.
🚫 ♿ 🖻 🄽 🆆 *www.oldsouth.org*

Boston Public Library ❾

Copley Square. **Map** 3 C2.
🄲 *(617) 536-5400.* Ⓣ *Copley.*
◯ *Apr–Sep: 9am–9pm Mon–Thu, 9am–5pm Fri–Sat; Oct–May: 9am–9pm Mon–Thu, 9am–5pm Fri–Sat, 1pm–5pm Sun.* ● *public hols.* ♿
🖻 🄽 🆆 *www.bpl.org*

FOUNDED IN 1848, the Boston Public Library was America's first metropolitan library for the public. It quickly outgrew its original building, hence the construction of the Italian *palazzo*-style Copley Square building in 1887–95. Designed by Charles McKim, the building is a marvel of fine wood and marble detail. Bates Hall, on the second floor, is particularly noted for its soaring barrel-vaulted ceiling. Sculptor Daniel Chester French fashioned the library's huge bronze doors, Edward Abbey's murals of the Quest for the Holy Grail line the book request room, and John Singer Sargent's murals of Judaism and Christianity cover a third-floor gallery.

The library's circulating collection is housed in the 1971 Boylston Street addition, a modernist structure by architect Philip Johnson.

The vast Bates Hall in the Boston Public Library, noted for its high barrel-vaulted ceiling

John Hancock Tower ⑩

200 Clarendon St. **Map** 3 C2.
📞 (617) 572-6429. Ⓣ Copley.
🕐 9am–11pm Mon–Sat;
May–Oct: 10am–11pm Sun; Nov–Apr:
noon–11pm Sun. 🔴 Thanksgiving,
Dec 25. 📷 ♿ 🎧
Ⓦ www.cityviewboston.com

THE TALLEST BUILDING in New England, the 740-ft (226-m) rhomboid that is the John Hancock Tower cuts into Copley Square, with its mirrored façade reflecting the surroundings. The innovative design has created a 60-story office building that shares the square with its neighbors, the Romanesque Trinity Church and the Italian Renaissance Revival Copley Plaza Hotel, without dwarfing them.

The observatory on the 60th floor offers breathtaking views of Boston and New England in three directions. All around the observatory visitors can hear a recorded narrative, and telescopes are available for close-up views.

Institute of Contemporary Art ⑪

955 Boylston St. **Map** 3 A3.
📞 (617) 266-5152. Ⓣ Hynes
Convention Center/ ICA. 🕐 12pm–
5pm Wed–Sun, 12pm–9pm Thu.
🔴 public hols. 📷 ♿ 🎫
Ⓦ www.icaboston.org

THIS RICHARDSONIAN Romanesque brick-and-stone building was renovated in 1975 under the direction of leading Boston architect Graham Gund, and is renowned for its open design. Its new function was to house the Institute of Contemporary Art, which is one of the oldest non-collecting art organizations in the US. As there is no formal collection, the I.C.A. is able to mount cutting-edge art exhibitions that reflect the latest innovations from the contemporary art world. One of the I.C.A.'s curatorial strengths has been its broadly international vision as it has forged an identity apart from the New York art scene.

View over Back Bay and the Charles River from the John Hancock Tower

Boston Center for the Arts ⑫

539 Tremont St. **Map** 4 D3.
📞 (617) 426-5000. Ⓣ Back Bay/
South End. **Cyclorama** 🕐 9am–
5pm Mon–Fri. **Mills Gallery**
🕐 1–4pm Sun–Wed, 7–10pm
Thu–Sat. 🔴 public hols. 📷 for
performances. 🚫 ♿ 🎫
Ⓦ www.bcaonline.org

THE CENTERPIECE of a resurgent South End, the B.C.A. complex includes three theaters, an art gallery, and artists' studios as well as the Boston Ballet Building, home to the company's educational programs, rehearsal space, and administrative offices.

Richardsonian Romanesque-style façade of the Institute of Contemporary Art

The Tremont Estates Building at the corner of Tremont Street, an organ factory in the years after the Civil War, now houses artists' studios, rehearsal space, and an art gallery. The largest of the B.C.A. buildings is the circular, domed Cyclorama, which opened in 1884 to exhibit the 50-ft (15-m) by 400-ft (121-m) painting *The Battle of Gettysburg* by the French artist Paul Philippoteaux. The painting was removed in 1889 and is now displayed at Gettysburg National Historic Park. For many years, the Cyclorama was Boston's leading venue for indoor events such as boxing, and was also the city's wholesale flower market. Today it is a challenging performance and exhibition space.

The Mills Gallery houses exhibitions focusing on emerging contemporary artists, with a strong emphasis on multimedia installations and shows with confrontational, and often provocative, themes.

FARTHER AFIELD

MOST OF BOSTON's historic sights are concentrated in the central colonial and Victorian city. However, the late 19th and 20th centuries saw Boston expand into the surrounding area. What were the marshlands of the Fenway now house two of Boston's most important art museums, the Museum of Fine Arts and the Isabella Stewart Gardner Museum (see p105). Southeast of the city center, Columbia Point was developed in the mid-20th century and is home to the John F. Kennedy Library and Museum (see p104). West of central Boston, across the Charles River, lies Cambridge, a city in its own right and sometimes referred to as the "Socialist Democratic Republic of Cambridge," a reference to the politics of its two major colleges, Harvard and the Massachusetts Institute of Technology. Harvard Square (see pp110–11) is a lively area of bookstores, cafés, and street entertainers. Charlestown, east of Cambridge, is the site of the Bunker Hill Monument (see p118) and the Charlestown Navy Yard, where the US's most famous warship, the USS Constitution, is moored.

Statue of William Prescott, Bunker Hill Monument

SIGHTS AT A GLANCE

Towns
Cambridge ❼
Charlestown ❽

Museums and Historic Sites
Isabella Stewart Gardner
  Museum ❺
John F. Kennedy Library
  and Museum ❶
John F. Kennedy National
  Historic Site ❹

Lexington ⓫
Lincoln ⓬
Museum of Fine Arts
  pp106–9 ❻
Quincy ⓭
Wellesley College ❾

Gardens and Zoos
Arnold Arboretum ❸
Franklin Park Zoo ❷
Broadmoor Sanctuary ❿

KEY

▨	Main sightseeing area
☐	Urban area
✈	Airport
🚉	Train station
══	Highway
══	Major road
══	Minor road
──	Railroad

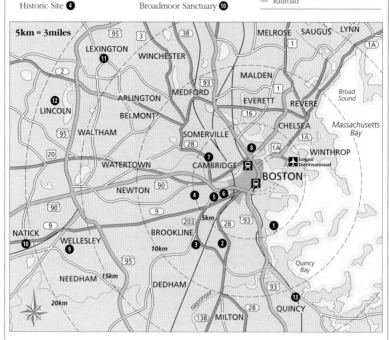

◁ Central courtyard of the *palazzo*-style Isabella Stewart Gardner Museum

John F. Kennedy Library and Museum ❶

Columbia Point, Dorchester.
📞 (617) 929-4523. Ⓣ JFK/ U Mass.
🕐 9–5 daily. ● Jan 1, Thanksgiving,
Dec 25. 🖼 ♿ 🎥 📷 ⌨
www.cs.umb.edu/jfklibrary/museum.htm

THE SOARING WHITE concrete
and glass building housing
the John F. Kennedy Library
stands sentinel on Columbia
Point near the mouth of the
Boston Harbor. This striking
white and black modern building by the architect I. M. Pei
is equally dramatic from the
interior, with a 50-ft (15-m)
wall of glass looking out over
the water. Exhibitions extensively chronicle the 1,000
days of the Kennedy presidency with an immediacy
uncommon in many other
historical museums. Kennedy
was among the first poli-
ticians to grasp the power of
media. The museum takes full
advantage of film and video
footage to use the president's
own words and image to tell
his story: his campaign for the
Democratic Party
nomination, landmark
television debates
with Republican
opponent Richard
M. Nixon (who later
became infamous
for the Watergate
Scandal), and his
many addresses to
the nation.
     Several rooms re-
create key chambers
of the White House
during the Kennedy
administration,
including the Oval Office;
gripping film clips capture the
anxiety of nuclear brinks-
manship during the Cuban
missile crisis as well as
the inspirational spirit of the
space program and the
founding of the Peace Corps.
Recently expanded exhibits
on Robert F. Kennedy's role
as Attorney General touch on
both his deft handling of race
relations and his key advisory
role to his brother. The combination of artifacts, displays,
and television footage
evoke both the euphoria
of "Camelot" and the numb
horror of the assassination.

**Lowland gorilla with her baby in the simulated
natural environment of Franklin Park Zoo**

Franklin Park Zoo ❷

1 Franklin Park Rd. 📞 (617) 541-
5466. Ⓣ Forest Hills. 🚌 16 from
Forest Hills subway. 🕐 Apr–Sep:
10am–5pm Mon–Fri, 10am–6pm
Sat–Sun; Oct–Mar: 10am–4pm daily.
● Jan 1, Thanksgiving, Dec 25. 🖼
♿ ⌨ www.zoonewengland.com

THE ZOO, originally planned
as a small menagerie, has
expanded dramatically over
the past century and long ago
discarded caged enclosures
in favor of simulated natural
environments. Lowland gor-
illas roam a forest edge with
caves for privacy, lions lounge
around a rocky kingdom,
while zebras, ostriches, and
giraffes are free to graze on
open grassland. The Butterfly
Landing is a dense garden
within a large hooped en-
closure where as many as
1,000 butterflies flit from
flower to flower, especially on
a warm afternoon. New Age
and light classical music aug-
ment the sense of fantasy. In
the small petting zoo youngsters can meet farm animals.

Arnold Arboretum ❸

125 Arborway, Jamaica Plain.
📞 (617) 524-1717. Ⓣ Forest Hills.
🚌 39. 🕐 sunrise–sunset daily.
Visitors Center 🕐 10am–4pm
Mon–Fri, noon–4pm Sat–Sun. ●
public hols. ♿ ⌨ www.arboretum.
harvard.edu

FOUNDED BY Harvard
University in 1872 as
a living catalog of all the
indigenous and exotic trees
and shrubs adaptable to
New England's climate, the

Dramatic, modern structure of the John F. Kennedy Library and Museum

Arboretum is planted with more than 15,000 labeled specimens. It is the oldest arboretum in the US and a key resource for botanical and horticultural research. The Arboretum also serves as a park where people jog, stroll, picnic, and paint.

The park's busiest time is on the third Sunday in May – Lilac Sunday – when tens of thousands come to revel in the sight and fragrance of the lilac collection, one of the largest in the world. The range of the Arboretum's collections guarantees flowers from late March into November, beginning with cornelian cherry and forsythia. Blooms shift in late May to azalea, magnolia, and wisteria, then to mountain laurel and roses in June. Sweet autumn clematis bursts forth in September, and native witch hazel blooms in October and November. The Arboretum also has fine fall foliage in September and October.

A large scale model of the Arboretum can be seen in the Visitors' Information Center just inside the main gate.

John F. Kennedy National Historic Site ❹

83 Beal St, Brookline. **[** (617) 566-7937. ⓣ *Coolidge Corner.* ◯ *mid-March–Nov: 10am–4:30pm Wed–Sun.* ● *Thanksgiving.* 🎟 🚫
ⓦ *www.nps.gov/jofi*

THE FIRST HOME of the late president's parents, this Brookline house saw the birth of four of nine Kennedy children, including J.F.K. on May 29, 1917. Although the Kennedys moved to a larger house in 1921, the Beal Street residence held special memories for the family, who repurchased the house in 1966 and furnished it with their belongings circa 1917 as a memorial to John F. Kennedy. The guided tour includes a taped interview with J.F.K.'s mother Rose. A walking tour takes in other neighborhood sites relevant to the family's early years.

Central courtyard of the *palazzo*-style Isabella Stewart Gardner Museum

Isabella Stewart Gardner Museum ❺

280 The Fenway. **[** (617) 566-1401. ⓣ *MFA.* ◯ *11am–5pm Tue–Sun.* ● *Jan 1, Thanksgiving, Dec 25.* 🎟 🚫 🚻
ⓦ *www.boston.com/gardner*

THE ONLY THING more surprising than a Venetian *palazzo* on The Fenway is the collection of more than 2,500 works of art inside. Advised by scholar Bernard Berenson,

the strong-willed Isabella Stewart Gardner turned her wealth to collecting art in the late 19th century, acquiring a notable collection of Old Masters and Italian Renaissance pieces. Titian's *Rape of Europa*, for example, is considered his best painting in a US museum. The eccentric "Mrs. Jack" had an eye for her contemporaries as well. She purchased the first Matisse to enter an American collection and was an ardent patron of James McNeill Whistler and John Singer Sargent. The paintings, sculptures, and tapestries are displayed on three levels around a stunning skylit courtyard. Mrs. Gardner's will, which was instrumental in the setting up of the museum, stipulates the collection should remain assembled in the manner that she originally intended. Unfortunately, her intentions could not be upheld; in 1990 thieves made off with 13 of these priceless works, including a rare Rembrandt seascape, *Storm on the Sea of Galilee*, then conservatively valued in the region of $200 million.

THE EMERALD NECKLACE

Best known as designer of New York's Central Park, Frederick Law Olmsted based himself in Boston, where he created parks to solve environmental problems and provide a green refuge for inhabitants of the 19th-century industrial city. The Emerald Necklace includes the green spaces of Boston Common and the Public Garden (*see pp64–5*) and Commonwealth Avenue (*see p97*). To create a ring of parks, Olmsted added the Back Bay Fens (site of beautiful rose gardens and gateway to the Museum of Fine Arts and the Isabella Stewart Gardner Museum), the rustic Riverway, Jamaica Pond (sailing and picnicking), Arnold Arboretum, and Franklin Park (a golf course, zoo, and cross-country ski trails). The 5-mile (8-km) swath of parkland makes an excellent bicycle tour or ambitious walk.

Jamaica Pond, part of Boston's fine parklands

The Museum of Fine Arts ❻

Tᴴɪꜱ ᴍᴜꜱᴇᴜᴍ ᴏᴘᴇɴᴇᴅ ɪɴ 1876 on Copley Square and moved to its present location in the Fenway in 1909. It is the largest art museum in New England and one of the five largest in the United States, with a permanent collection of approximately 500,000 objects, ranging from Egyptian artifacts to paintings by John Singer Sargent. The original Classical-style building was augmented in 1981 by the addition of the West Wing, designed by I. M. Pei.

★ Japanese Temple Room
This room was created in 1909 to provide a space in which to contemplate Buddhist art. The M.F.A. has one of the finest Japanese collections outside Japan.

American Silver
The revolutionary Paul Revere (see p120) was also a noted silversmith and produced many beautiful objects, such as this ornate teapot.

First floor

Entrance

★Egyptian Mummies
Among the museum's Egyptian and Nubian art are these coffins of Nes-mut-aat-neru (700–675 BC) of Thebes.

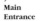

Main Entrance

★ Copley Portraits
John Singleton Copley (1738–1815) painted the celebrities of his day, hence this portrait of a dandyish John Hancock.

A two-headed amphora from Athens (530–520 BC) is among the Classical Greek artifacts.

★ **Impressionist Paintings**
Boston collectors were among the first to appreciate French Impressionism. La Japonaise (1876) by Monet is typical of the M.F.A. collection.

Second floor

KEY

 Art of Africa, Oceania, and the Ancient Americas

☐ American paintings, decorative arts, and sculpture

☐ Ancient Egyptian, Nubian, and Near Eastern art

☐ Asian art

☐ Classical art

☐ Contemporary art

☐ European paintings, decorative arts, and sculpture

☐ Musical instruments

☐ Works on paper

☐ Special/temporary exhibitions

☐ Nonexhibition space

Medieval frescoes
and French silverware feature among the exhibits of European decorative art.

Sargent Murals
John Singer Sargent spent the last years of his life creating these murals for the M.F.A.'s domed rotunda.

Court level

GALLERY GUIDE

Classical, Far Eastern, and Egyptian artifacts can be seen on both floors of the museum. American decorative arts and painting are on the first floor, while European decorative arts and paintings are on the second.

Ram's Head
Once part of a much larger statue, this marble Greek ram's head dates from the 4th century BC.

STAR EXHIBITS

★ **Copley Portraits**

★ **Impressionist Paintings**

★ **Egyptian Mummies**

★ **Japanese Temple Room**

Exploring the Museum of Fine Arts

IN ADDITION TO THE major collections noted below, the Museum of Fine Arts has important holdings in the arts of Africa, Oceania, and the ancient Americas. The museum also houses collections of works on paper, contemporary art, and musical instruments. Several galleries, large and small, are devoted to temporary thematic exhibitions. The modern West Wing of the museum houses a seminar room, lecture hall, and well-stocked bookstore. An important research center, the museum has played a major role in the excavation of artifacts around the world.

11th-century, silver Korean ewer

Boston Harbor by the Luminist painter Fitz Hugh Lane (1804–65)

AMERICAN PAINTINGS, DECORATIVE ARTS, AND SCULPTURE

THE AMERICAN PAINTING galleries on the first floor begin with the Colonial portrait gallery. The M.F.A. owns more than 60 portraits by John Singleton Copley, perhaps America's most talented 18th-century painter, as well as works by Gilbert Stuart and Charles Willson Peale. The next gallery houses 19th-century landscapes, including harbor scenes by Fitz Hugh Lane, an early Luminist painter. Farther on are the lush society portraits of John Singer Sargent and those of other late 19th-century artists who constituted the "Boston School." There are also notable seascapes by Winslow Homer, who often painted on the Massachusetts coast, as well as the muscular figure portraiture of Thomas Eakins. The large and airy Lane Gallery of Modern Painting and Sculpture presents a sampling of works by 20th-century masters including Stuart Davis, Jackson Pollock, Georgia O'Keeffe, and Arthur Dove.

A corridor gallery of American silver leads from the first-floor rotunda eastward to the American decorative arts galleries. Two cases contain tea services and other pieces by Paul Revere *(see p88)*. The next gallery traces the development of the Boston style of 18th-century furniture through a definitive collection of desks, high chests, and tall clocks. The reconstructed Oak Hill dining room, parlor, and bedroom from an early 19th-century mansion evoke the well-to-do lifestyle of the Federal era. Earlier period rooms are found on the Court Level, along with a gallery of ship models and an outstanding collection of contemporary crafts.

EUROPEAN PAINTINGS, DECORATIVE ARTS, AND SCULPTURE

EUROPEAN PAINTINGS and sculpture from the 16th to the 20th centuries are on the second floor of the museum. They begin with 17th-century Dutch paintings, including a number of portraits by Rembrandt. The Koch Gallery of European Paintings from 1550 to 1700 is impressive both for the drama of the space – a great hall with travertine marble walls and high, wooden coffered ceiling – and for the range of art works, which ranges from Francisco de Zurbarán and El Greco to Paolo Veronese, Titian, and Peter Paul Rubens.

Boston's 19th-century collectors enriched the M.F.A. with wonderful French painting: the museum features several paintings by Pierre François Millet (the M.F.A. has, in fact, the largest collection of his work in the world) as well as by other well-known 19th-century French artists, such as Édouard Manet, Pierre-Auguste Renoir, and Edgar Degas. One of the museum's most popular galleries displays *La Japonaise* (1876) by Claude Monet and *Dance at Bougival* (1883) by Renoir. The M.F.A.'s Monet holdings are unsurpassed outside of Paris, and there is also a good collection of paintings by the

La Berceuse by the Dutch painter Vincent van Gogh (1853–90)

Part of the Processional Way of Ancient Babylonia (6th century BC)

Dutch artist Vincent van Gogh. Early 20th-century European art is also exhibited.

The M.F.A. is also well known for its extensive collection of European decorative arts. A series of galleries displays tableware, ceramics, and glass clustered by period from the early 17th to early 20th centuries. An impressive array of 18th-century French silver is displayed in a gallery where the walls are painted with Neoclassical Louis XVI-style motifs – these were originally installed in the town house of a New York banker. There is also a striking display of 18th-century Chinese export porcelain, which is set against the imported backdrop of a Parisian hotel's Louis XV-style interior.

ANCIENT EGYPTIAN, NUBIAN, AND NEAR EASTERN ART

THE M.F.A.'S COLLECTION of Egyptian and Nubian materials is unparalleled outside of Africa and derives primarily from M.F.A.-Harvard University excavations along the Nile, which began in 1905. The first floor houses a 1998 installation showing Egyptian Funerary Arts, which uses the M.F.A.'s superb collection of mummies from nearly three millennia to illustrate the technical and art historical aspects of Egyptian burial practices. The adjacent gallery of Ancient Near East artifacts displays Babylonian, Assyrian, and Sumerian reliefs. Another gallery is devoted to ancient Nubia, the cultural region around the Nile stretching roughly between the modern African cities of Aswan and Khartoum.

The Egyptian and Nubian collections continue on the second floor. Highlights include two monumental sculptures of Nubian kings from the Great Temple of Amen at Napata (620–586 BC and 600–580 BC). A few of the galleries are set up to re-create Nubian burial chambers, which allows cuneiform wall carvings to be displayed in something akin to an original setting; a superb example is the offering chapel of Sekhem-ankh-Ptah from Sakkara (2450–2350 BC).

CLASSICAL ART

THE M.F.A. BOASTS one of America's top collections of Greek ceramics, particularly red- and black-figure vases, which are displayed in a large gallery on the first floor, as well as in smaller

Roman fresco, excavated from a Pompeian villa (1st century AD)

galleries on the second floor. In general, the Classical galleries of the museum are arranged thematically to highlight the influence of Greek arts on both Etruscan and Roman art. The Etruscan gallery on the first floor has several carved sarcophagi, while the Roman collection on the second floor features grave markers, portrait busts, and a series of wall panel paintings unearthed in Pompeii in an M.F.A. expedition of 1900–01.

ASIAN ART

THE ASIAN COLLECTIONS, occupying some of the most elegant galleries in the M.F.A., are said to be the most extensive under one roof in the world. The first-floor galleries are primarily devoted to Indian, Near Eastern, and Central Asian art. Among the highlights are Indian sculpture and changing exhibitions of Islamic miniature paintings and Indian narrative paintings.

Tang Dynasty Chinese Horse (8th century)

A beautiful stairway adorned with carved lions and a portal of a dragon in the clouds announces the entrance to the main Chinese and Japanese galleries on the second floor. Extensive holdings and limited display space mean that specific exhibitions change often, but the M.F.A.'s exhibitions of Japanese and Chinese scroll and screen paintings is, nevertheless, unmatched in the West. The strength of the M.F.A.'s Japanese art collection is largely due to the efforts of collectors such as Ernest Fenollosa and William Bigelow Sturgis. In the 19th century they encouraged the Japanese to maintain their traditions, and salvaged Buddhist temple art when the Japanese imperial government had withdrawn subsidies from these institutions. The Buddhist Temple Room is considered to contain some of the finest examples of Asian temple art in the world.

Cambridge ❼

PART OF THE GREATER BOSTON metropolitan area, Cambridge is, nonetheless, a town in its own right and has the mood and feel of such. Principally a college town, it is dominated by Harvard University and other college campuses. It also boasts a number of important historic sights, such as Christ Church and Cambridge Common, which have associations to the American Revolution. Harvard Square is the area's main entertainment and shopping district.

Site of the Washington Elm, on Cambridge Common

🏛 Longfellow National Historic Site

105 Brattle St. ☎ (617) 876-4491. ◯ May–Oct: 10am–4:30pm Wed–Sun. ⬛ Ø ⬛ ✓ ⓦ www.nps.gov/long

This house on Brattle Street, like many around it, was built by Colonial-era merchants loyal to the British Crown during the Revolution. It was seized by American revolutionaries and served as George Washington's head-quarters during the Siege of Boston.

The poet Henry Wadsworth Longfellow boarded here in 1837, was given the house as a wedding present in 1843, and lived here until his death in 1888. He wrote his most famous poems here, including *Tales of a Wayside Inn* and *The Song of Hiawatha*. Longfellow's status as literary dean of Boston meant that Nathaniel Hawthorne and Charles Sumner, among others, were regular visitors.

🏛 Harvard Square

☎ (617) 497-1630. ⬛ ⓦ www.harvardsquare.com

Even Bostonians think of Harvard Square as a stand-in for Cambridge – the square was the original site of Cambridge from around 1630. Dominating the square is the Harvard Cooperative Society ("the Coop"), a Harvard institution, that sells inexpensive clothes, posters, and books. Harvard's large student population is very much in evidence here, adding color to the character of the square. Many trendy boutiques, inexpensive restaurants, and numerous cafés cater to their needs. Street performers abound, especially on the weekends, and the square has long been a place where pop trends begin. Club Passim, for example, has incubated many successful singer-songwriters since Joan Baez first debuted here in 1959.

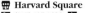

Street musician, Harvard Square

🏛 Cambridge Common

Set aside as common pasture and military drill ground in 1631, Cambridge Common has served as a center for religious, social, and political activity ever since. George Washington took command of the Continental Army here on July 3, 1775, beneath the Washington Elm, now marked by a stone. The common served as the army's encampment from 1775 to 1776. Today the ball fields and playgrounds are popular with families. In 1997 the first monument in the US to the victims of the Irish Famine was unveiled on the common.

🏠 Christ Church

Garden St. ☎ (617) 876-0200. ◯ 8am–5pm daily. ✝ 8am, 12:30pm & 5pm Sun. Ø ⬛ ⓦ www.christchurch.com

With its square bell tower and plain, gray shingled edifice, Christ Church is a restrained example of an Anglican church. Designed in 1761 by Peter Harrison, the architect of Boston's King's Chapel (*see p76*), Christ Church came in for rough treatment as a barracks for Continental Army troops in 1775 – British loyalists had almost all fled Cambridge by this time. The army even melted down the organ pipes to cast musket balls. The church was restored for services on New Year's Eve, 1775, when George Washington and his wife, Martha, were among the worshipers. Anti-Anglican sentiment remained strong in Cambridge, and Christ Church did not have its own rector again until the 19th century.

Simple interior of Christ Church, designed prior to the Revolution in 1761

⛩ Radcliffe Institute for Advanced Studies

Brattle St. 📞 *(617) 495-1573.* ♿
🌐 www.radcliffe.edu

Radcliffe College was founded in 1879 as the Collegiate Institution for Women, when 27 women began to study by private arrangement with Harvard professors. By 1943, members of Harvard's faculty no longer taught separate undergraduate courses to the women of Radcliffe, and in 1999 Radcliffe ceased its official existence as an independent college. It is now an institute for advanced study promoting scholarship of women's culture. The first Radcliffe building was the 1806 Federal-style mansion, Fay House, on the northern corner of what became Radcliffe Yard. Schlesinger Library, on the west side of the yard, is considered a significant example of

**Stained glass,
Radcliffe Institute**

Colonial Revival architecture. The library's most famous holdings are an extensive collection of cookbooks and reference works on gastronomy.

⛩ M.I.T.

77 Massachusetts Ave. 📞 *(617) 253-4795.* **MIT Museum** ⏰ *10am–5pm Tue–Fri, noon–5pm Sat–Sun.* **Hart Nautical Gallery** ⏰ *9am–5pm daily.* **List Visual Arts Center** ⏰ *noon–6pm Tue–Sun, 6–8pm Fri.* 📷 🚫 ♿ 🛍 🌐 www.mit.edu

Chartered in 1861 to teach students "exactly and thoroughly the fundamental principles of positive science with application to the industrial arts," the Massachusetts Institute of Technology has evolved into one of the world's leading universities in engineering and the sciences. Several architectural masterpieces dot M.I.T.'s 135-acre (55-ha) campus along the Charles River, including Eero

Saarinen's Kresge Auditorium and Kresge Chapel, built in 1955. The Wiesner Building is a major collaboration between architect I. M. Pei and several artists, including Kenneth Noland, whose relief mural dominates the atrium. The building houses the **List Visual Arts Center**, noted for its avant-garde art.

The **Hart Nautical Gallery** in the Rogers Building focuses on marine engineering, with exhibits ranging from models of ships to exhibits of the latest advances in underwater research. The **M.I.T. Museum** blends art and science with exhibits such as Harold Edgerton's groundbreaking stroboscopic flash photographs, and the latest holographic art.

CAMBRIDGE TOWN CENTER

Cambridge Common ①
Christ Church ②
Harvard Square ③
Harvard University Museums *(see pp114–17)* ④
Harvard Yard *(see pp112–13)* ⑤
Longfellow National Historic Site ⑥
Radcliffe Institute for Advanced Studies ⑦

KEY

🅿 Parking

ℹ Tourist information

✝ Church

🚇 Subway

BROOKLINE ↙

M.I.T.
BOSTON →

0 meters   400
0 yards   400

Harvard Yard

IN 1636 Boston's well-educated Puritan leaders founded a college in Newtowne. Two years later cleric John Harvard died and bequeathed half his estate and all his books to the fledgling college. The colony's leaders bestowed his name on the school and rechristened the surrounding community Cambridge after the English city where they had been educated. The oldest university in the US, Harvard is now one of the world's most prestigious centers of learning. The university has expanded to encompass more than 400 buildings, but Harvard Yard is still at its heart.

Holden Chapel
Built in 1742, the chapel was the scene of revolutionary speeches and was later used as a demonstration hall for human dissections.

Hollis Hall was used as barracks by George Washington's troops during the American Revolution.

Massachusetts Hall, built in 1720, is Harvard's oldest building.

★ Old Harvard Yard
This leafy yard dates from the founding of the college in 1636. Freshman dormitories dot the yard, and throughout the year it is a focal point for students.

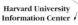
Harvard University Information Center ✓

★ John Harvard Statue
This statue celebrates Harvard's most famous benefactor. Almost a place of pilgrimage, graduates and visitors invariably pose for photographs here.

University Hall, designed by Charles Bulfinch, was built in 1816.

★ Widener Library
This library memorializes Harry Elkins Widener, who died on the Titanic *in 1912. With more than 3 million volumes, it is the third largest library in the US.*

★ **Memorial Church**
*This church was built
in 1931 and copies
earlier styles. For
example, the steeple
is modeled on that
of the Old North
Church (see p87) in
Boston's North End.*

VISITORS' CHECKLIST

Massachusetts Ave. Ⓣ *Harvard.*
◯ *24 hrs.* ◉ *2nd Thu in Jun
(Commencement).* ♿ 🚻 🎧
Lectures, concerts and films.
Harvard Information Center
📞 *(617) 495-1573.* **Harvard
Box Office** 📞 *(617) 496-2222.*
Harvard Film Archive 📞 *(617)
495 4700. Films shown nightly.*
🌐 *www.harvard.edu*

Memorial Hall, a
Ruskin Gothic building,
memorializes Harvard's
Union casualties from
the Civil War.

**Sackler and Peabody
Museums, and Harvard
Museum of Natural
History** *(see pp116–17)*

Sever Hall
*One of the most distinctive
of Harvard's Halls, this
Romanesque style-building
was designed by Henry
Hobson Richardson.*

**Fogg Art and Busch-Reisinger
Museums** *(see pp114–15)*

Tercentenary Theater

STAR SIGHTS

★ **Old Harvard Yard**

★ **John Harvard Statue**

★ **Widener Library**

★ **Memorial Church**

Carpenter Center for Visual Arts
*Opened in 1963, the Carpenter
Center is the only building in the
US designed by the avant-garde
French architect Le Corbusier.*

0 meters   50

0 yards   50

The Harvard University Museums

Harvard's museums were originally conceived to revolutionize the process of education; students were to be taught by allowing them access to artifacts from around the world. Today, this tradition continues, with the museums housing some of the world's finest university collections: art from Europe and America in the Fogg Art and Busch-Reisinger Museums, archaeological finds in the Peabody Museum, Near and Far Eastern art in the Sackler Museum, and a vast collection of artifacts in the Harvard Museum of Natural History.

Main entrance to the Fogg Art and Busch-Reisinger Museums

Fogg Art and Busch-Reisinger Museums

32 Quincy St. ☎ *(617) 495-9400.*
◐ *10am–5pm Mon–Sat, 1–5pm Sun.* ● *Jan 1, July 4, Thanksgiving, Dec 25.* 🎫 ♿ ☑ W *www.art museums.harvard.edu*

Until the Fogg Museum was created by a surprise bequest in 1891, Harvard, like most universities, used prints of famous paintings and casts of sculptures to teach art history. Both the Fogg and the Busch-Reisinger, which was grafted onto the Fogg in 1991, have small but select collections of art from Europe and America.

The Fogg building was completed in 1927 and is a red-brick Georgian building similar to other buildings at Harvard. The collections, which focus on Western art from the late Middle Ages to the present, are organized around a central courtyard modeled on a 16th-century church in Montepulciano, Italy. The ground-floor corridors surrounding the courtyard feature 12th-century capitals from Moutiers St-Jean in Burgundy, France.

Two small galleries near the entrance and the two-story Warburg Hall display the Fogg's collections that

prefigure the Italian Renaissance. The massive altarpieces and suspended crucifix in the Warburg are particularly impressive. The ground-floor galleries on the left side of the entrance are devoted to 17th-century Dutch, Flemish, and English painting, 17th- and 18th-century Neapolitan painting, and European and North American art of the 18th century. Among the English and American 18th-century paintings are a series of unfinished studies made by John Singleton Copley.

The museum's second level is dominated by a collection of Pre-Raphaelite painting and a few select works by John Singer Sargent. The small galleries along the front of the building change exhibitions frequently but tend to focus on drawings and graphic arts, and on 19th-century French and American art. The highlight of the second level is the Maurice Wertheim Collection of Impressionist and Post-Impressionist art,

most of it collected in the late 1930s. With a number of important paintings by Renoir, Manet, and Degas, the Wertheim gallery is the Fogg's most popular. An adjacent gallery displays American art from after 1950, such as works by the minimalist painter Frank Stella, one of the more important exponents of color-field painting.

The museum also houses rotating displays from its collection of 19th- and 20th-century African art.

Werner Otto Hall, which contains the Busch-Reisinger Museum, is entered through the second level of the Fogg. The museum's collections focus on Germanic art and

Copley Studies
These unfinished studies by John Singleton Copley were made for his 1787 painting The Siege of Gibraltar.

First floor

Main entrance

GUIDE TO THE FOGG ART AND BUSCH-REISINGER MUSEUMS

Art from the Middle Ages to the 18th century is on the first floor of the Fogg Art Museum. French and American art from the 19th and 20th centuries and 20th-century American art are on the second floor. The Busch-Reisinger Museum focuses on Germanic art.

Light-Space Modulator (1923–30) by the Hungarian Moholy-Nagy

design from after 1880, with an emphasis on German Expressionism. Harvard was a safe haven for many Bauhaus artists, architects, and designers who fled Nazi Germany, and both Walter Gropius and Lyonel Feininger chose the Busch-Reisinger as the depository of their personal papers and drawings. Periodic exhibitions explore aspects of the work and philosophy of the Bauhaus movement. Although small, the museum owns major paintings and sculptures by 20th-century masters such as Max Beckmann, Lyonel Feininger, Wassily Kandinsky, Moholy-Nagy, Paul Klee, Oskar Kokoschka, Emil Nolde, and Franz Marc.

Central Courtyard of the Fogg Art Museum

Red River Valley (1958)
This painting by Frank Stella is typical of his minimalist style, which he often achieved using house painters' techniques.

Entrance to Busch-Reisinger Museum

Reading room

To study room

Second floor

Key

☐ Fogg Art Museum

☐ Hammer Galleries (within the Fogg Art Museum)

☐ Busch-Reisinger Museum

☐ Special exhibition gallery (within the Busch-Reisinger Museum)

☐ Nonexhibition space

Skating (1877)
This portrait, by Edouard Manet, shows elegantly attired Parisians at a skating rink. It is from the Fogg's famed collection of French Impressionist paintings.

Peabody Museum of Archaeology and Ethnology

11 Divinity St. [C] (617) 496-1027.
[O] 9am–5pm Mon–Sat, 1–5pm
Sun. [●] Jan 1, Jul 4, Thanksgiving,
Dec 25. [🖼] [♿] [🎫]
[W] www.peabody.harvard.edu

The Peabody Museum of
Archaeology and Ethnology
was founded in 1866 as the
first museum in the
Americas devoted
solely to anthro-
pology. The many
collections, which
include several
million artifacts and
more than 500,000
photographic images,
come from all around
the world. Initially, in
the 19th century, the
museum's pioneering
archaeological and
ethnological research
began relatively
close to home with
excavations of
Mayan sites in
Central America.
The Peabody also
conducted some of
the first and most
important research
on the precontact
Anasazi people
of the American
Southwest and on
the cultural history   **Native American**
of the later Pueblo   **totem pole,**
tribes of the same   **Peabody Museum**
region. Joint expedi-
tions sponsored by the
Peabody Museum and the
Museum of Fine Arts (see
pp106–9) also uncovered
some of the richest finds of
dynastic and predynastic
Egypt. Research continued
in all these areas well into
the 20th century and later

broadened to embrace the
cultures of the islands of
the South Pacific.
    The Hall of the North
American Indian on the
ground level was com-
pletely overhauled in the
1990s. Most of the artifacts
are displayed in a way that
puts them in the context of
the time when they were gathered, when European
and Native cultures
first came into contact.
For example, the
Native American tribes
of the Northern Plains
are interpreted largely
through an exhibition
detailing the Lewis
and Clark expedition
of 1804–06; these two
explorers undertook
to find a route, by
water, from East to
West Coast, and on
their way collected
innumerable artifacts.
Other outstanding
exhibits include
totem carvings by
Pacific Northwest
tribes and a wide
range of historic
and contemporary
Navajo weavings.
The third floor is
devoted to Central
American anthropol-
ogy, with casts of
some of the ruins
uncovered at Copán
in Honduras and
Chichen Itza in Mexico. The
fourth floor concentrates on
Polynesia, Micronesia, and
other islands of the Pacific.
    A gift shop sells outstanding
folk art, music, and decorative
items made by the modern-
day descendants of the peoples
detailed in the museum.

**Triceratops skull in the Harvard
Museum of Natural History**

Harvard Museum of Natural History

26 Oxford St. [C] (617) 495-3045.
[O] 9am–5pm Mon–Sat, 1–5pm Sun.
[●] Jan 1, Jul 4, Thanksgiving, Dec
25. [🖼] [♿] [🎫]
[W] www.hmnh.harvard.edu

The Harvard Museum of
Natural History is actually
three museums rolled into
one, all displayed on a single
floor of a turn-of-the-century
classroom building. It includes the collections of the
Mineralogical and Geological
Museum, the Museum of
Comparative Zoology, and
the Botanical Museum. The
straightforward presentation
of labeled objects exudes
an infectious, old-fashioned
charm, yet their initial appearance belies the fact that these
are some of the most com-
plete collections of their kind.
    The mineralogical galleries
include some of Harvard
University's oldest specimen
collections, the oldest of
which dates from 1783.
Virtually every New England
mineral, rock, and gem type
is represented here, including
rough and cut gemstones and
one of the world's premier
meteorite collections.
    The zoological galleries
owe their inception to the
great 19th-century biologist
Louis Agassiz and include his
personal arachnid collection.
The collection of taxidermied
bird, mammal, and reptile
specimens is comprehensive,
and there is also a collection
of dinosaur skeletons. Children are most fascinated by
the giant kronosaurus (a type
of prehistoric sea serpent)
and the skeleton of the first
triceratops ever described in

Frog mask fom Easter Island in the South Pacific, Peabody Museum

scientific literature. There are also fossil exhibits of the earliest invertebrates and reptiles, as well as skeletons of still-living species, including a collection of whale skeletons.

The collections in the botanical galleries include the Ware Collection of Blaschka Glass Models of Plants, popularly known as the "glass flowers." Between 1887 and 1936, father and son artisans Leopold and Rudolph Blaschka created these 3,000 exacting models of 850 plant species. Each species is illustrated with a scientifically accurate lifesize model and magnified parts. While the handblown models were created as teaching aids, they are a unique accomplishment in the glassblowers' art and are as prized for their aesthetic qualities as their scientific utility.

Amethyst specimen in the Harvard Museum of Natural History

Sackler Museum
485 Broadway, Cambridge.
((617) 495-9400. **⬤** 10am–5pm Mon–Sat, 1–5pm Sun. **⬤** Jan 1, Jul 4, Thanksgiving, Dec 25. **⬤ ⬤ ⬤**
W www.artmuseums.harvard.edu

Named after a famous philanthropist, physician, and art collector, the Arthur M. Sackler Museum is home to Harvard's collection of ancient, Asian, Indian, and Near Eastern art. Opened in 1985, it is housed in a modern building designed by James Stirling and his firm of architects based in London, England, and is itself a bold artistic statement. Aware that Harvard University had long embarked on a tradition of erecting many unique buildings in the area just north and east of Harvard Yard, Stirling was prompted to introduce the innovatively

designed building to the world as "the newest animal in Harvard's architectural zoo." The exterior borrows details and decorative devices from several surrounding buildings, while the starkly modern interior galleries provide optimal display space. The 30-ft (10-m) entrance lobby features a 1997 wall-painting by the Conceptual artist Sol Lewitt, whose trademark is colorful geometric shapes, which appear to float in space.

The Sackler is best toured by ascending to the permanent collections on the fourth floor and working back down to the lobby. The head of the stairwell terminates at gallery 10, where changing exhibitions highlight aspects of Harvard's collections of ancient Greek art, including a coin collection from the empire of Alexander the Great and unusually extensive selections of red and black pottery with decorative friezes. A small adjacent gallery displays Egyptian, ancient Near Eastern, Etruscan, and Bronze Age art. Most of Harvard's early Egyptian acquisitions were transferred to the Museum of Fine Arts *(see pp106–9)*, the

Southeast Asian Buddha head, Sackler Museum

Sackler's partner in a number of archaeological expeditions. The fourth floor galleries continue to flow, one to another, without a corridor, passing through a large gallery devoted to ancient Roman art, and then continuing eastward through Indian and Southeast Asian collections, much of which consists of Buddhist sculptures and figures from Hindu mythology. The fourth floor ends in three galleries of Chinese art situated at the front of the building: the first houses Chinese sculpture; the next Chinese Buddhist stone sculpture; the last room archaic Chinese bronzes, jades, and ceramics, many of which were the gifts of Harvard-affiliated diplomats. These collections are thought to be among the finest of Chinese art in the West.

The second-floor galleries host changing, thematic exhibitions of the Sackler's extensive collections of Islamic art from the Near East and central Asia. The first-floor gallery, behind the ticket booth, hosts ambitious and thought-provoking special exhibitions.

Buddhist sculptures, part of the Sackler's Asian and Indian collections

Charlestown ❽

SITUATED ON THE NORTH BANK of the Charles River, directly opposite the North End, Charlestown exudes history. The site of the infamous Battle of Bunker Hill, when American troops suffered huge losses in their fight for independence, today the district forms a major part of Boston's Freedom Trail (see pp54–57). As well as sights from the American Revolution, visitors can see USS Constitution, pride of the post-revolutionary American Navy, which took part in the 1812 war with Britain. Also of interest is the Charlestown Navy Yard.

Granite obelisk of the Bunker Hill Monument, erected in 1794

🏛 Bunker Hill Monument
Monument Square. 📞 (617) 242-5641. ◯ 9am–4:30pm daily.
🅆 www.charlestown.ma.us

In the Revolution's first pitched battle between British and colonial troops, the British won but failed to escape from Boston. Following the June 17, 1775 battle, American irregulars were joined by other militia to keep British forces penned up until George Washington forced their evacuation by sea the following March. A Tuscan-style pillar was erected in 1794 in honor of Dr. Joseph Warren, a Boston revolutionary leader who died in the battle, but Charlestown citizens felt something grander was in order. They began raising funds in 1823, laid the cornerstone in 1825 and dedicated the 221-ft (67-m) granite obelisk in 1843. It was the tallest monument in the US until the Washington Monument was erected in 1885. There is no elevator, but 294 steps lead to the top for spectacular views of Boston harbor.

🏛 Bunker Hill Pavilion
Water St. 📞 (617) 241-7575.
◯ Apr–Nov: 9am–6pm daily. ● Thanksgiving. 🎦 🚫 ♿

Next to Charlestown Navy Yard, Bunker Hill Pavilion shows a multimedia presentation The Whites of Their Eyes. The title comes from the purported order that American troops not fire until they could see the whites of the Redcoats' eyes. The show consists of a series of color slides projected on 14 screens, audio effects, and lifesized costumed figures.

🏛 City Square
When John Winthrop arrived with three shiploads of Puritan refugees in 1630, they settled first in the marshes at the base of Town Hill, now City Square. A small public park now marks the site of Winthrop's Town House, the very first seat of Boston government. Today, one of Boston's best-loved restaurants, Olives (see p331), faces onto the square.

Municipal art in City Square

🏛 John Harvard Mall
Ten families founded Charlestown in 1629, a year before the rest of Boston was settled. They built their homes and a palisaded fort on Town Hill, a spot now marked by John Harvard Mall. Several bronze plaques within the small enclosed park commemorate events in the early history of the Massachusetts Bay Colony (see p38), one plaque proclaiming "this low mound of earth the memorial of a mighty nation." A small monument pays homage to John Harvard, the young cleric who ministered to the Charlestown settlers and who left his name, half his estate, and all his books to the fledgling college at Newtowne when he died in 1638 (see pp112–13).

🏛 Warren Tavern
2 Pleasant St. 📞 (617) 241-8142.
◯ lunch and dinner daily, brunch Sat–Sun. 🅆 www.warrentavern.com

Dating from 1780, Warren Tavern was one of the first buildings erected after the British burned Charlestown. It was named after Joseph Warren, president of the Provincial Congress in 1774 and a general in the Massachusetts Army. He enlisted as a private with the Continental Army for the Battle of Bunker Hill, where he was killed. The tavern, once derelict, has been restored to its 18th-century style. By contrast, the food is modern fare.

Old-fashioned clapboard houses on Warren Street

USS *Constitution*, built in 1797, moored in Charlestown Navy Yard

⚓ Charlestown Navy Yard

🅒 (617) 242-5601.
🕐 Sep–Jun: 9am–5pm; Jun–Labor Day: 9am–6pm. ● Jan 1, Thanksgiving, Dec 25. 🐾 🖋 Ⓦ
www.nps.gov/bost/cnyintro.htm
Boston's deep harbor and long tides made Charlestown a logical site for one of the US Navy's first shipyards, established in 1800. For 174 years, as the Navy moved from wooden sailing ships to steel giants, Charlestown

Navy Yard played a key role in supporting the US Atlantic fleet. On decommissioning, the facility was transferred to the National Park Service to interpret the art and history of naval shipbuilding. The yard was designed by Alexander Parris, architect of Quincy Market (see p80), and was one of the first examples of industrial architecture in Boston.

Drydock No. 1, built in 1802, was the one of the first docks that could be drained of water – its first occupant was USS *Constitution*. Rangers also give tours of the World War II destroyer USS *Cassin Young*.

⚓ USS *Constitution*

Charlestown Navy Yard. 🅒 (617) 242-5670. 🕐 9:30am–3:50pm daily. 🐾 🖋 Ⓦ www.USS Con.com.
Museum: 🕐 9am–6pm daily. ● Jan 1, Thanksgiving, Dec 25. 🐾 🐾 Ⓦ www.ussconstitutionmuseum.org
The oldest commissioned warship afloat, the USS *Constitution* was built in the North End and christened in 1797. She saw immediate action in the Mediterranean protecting American shipping from the Barbary pirates. In the War of 1812, she won fame and her nickname of "Old Ironsides" when

cannonballs bounced off her in a battle with the British ship *Guerriere*. In the course of her active service, she won 42 battles, lost none, captured 20 vessels, and was never boarded by an enemy. She was nearly scuttled several times, and at one time was reduced to serving as a floating barracks. In 1830, Oliver Wendell Holmes penned the poem *Old Ironsides* that rallied public support to save the ship, while on another occasion, in the 1920s, schoolchildren sent in their pennies and nickels to salvage her. She underwent her most thorough overhaul in time for her 1997 bicentennial, able to carry her own canvas into the wind for the first time in a century. On July 4 each year, she is taken out into the harbor for an annual turnaround that reverses her position at the Navy Yard pier to insure equal weathering on both sides. A small museum documents her history.

VISITORS' CHECKLIST

Ⓣ Community College.
🚌 93. ⛴ from Long Wharf.
📷 Wed. 🎆 June 24.

CHARLESTOWN TOWN CENTER

Bunker Hill Monument ①
Bunker Hill Pavilion ②
Charlestown Navy Yard ③
City Square ④
John Harvard Mall ⑤
USS *Constitution* ⑥
Warren Tavern ⑦

0 meters 200
0 yards 200

KEY

✠ Church

Wellesley College ❾

106 Central St, Wellesley. **(** *(781) 283-1000.* **Museum** *(781) 283-2051.* ◯ *year-round: call for hours.*

FOUNDED IN 1875, this top college for women has former First Lady Hillary Rodham Clinton (b.1947), now Senator (D) from New York, among its graduates. The grounds of the hilly Gothic campus overlooking Lake Waban are a virtual arboretum, with trees tagged for easy identification.

The main attraction is the **Davis Museum and Cultural Center**, with its collection of 5,000 paintings, prints, photos, drawings, and sculptures spanning the ages from classical to contemporary. The dramatic building was the first US project for noted Spanish architect Jose Rafael Moneo (b.1937).

Broadmoor Wildlife Sanctuary ❿

280 Eliot St, S Natick. **ℹ** *(781) 235-3929.*

NINE MILES (14.5 KM) of walking trails go through field, woodland, and wetland habitats. A boardwalk skirts the bank of Indian Brook before crossing a marsh. The 110-ft (33.5-m) bridge spanning the brook is an ideal lookout from which to photograph beavers, otters, and wood ducks. In winter the sanctuary is popular with snowshoe enthusiasts.

Nature Center ◯ *9am–5pm Tue–Fri, 10am–5pm Sat, Sun & public hols.* 🔊
Trails ◯ *dawn to dusk.* 📷 ♿

Former First Lady Hillary Rodham Clinton, a Wellesley College grad

Lexington ⓫

🏠 *31,500.* **ℹ** *1875 Massachusetts Ave (781) 862-1450.*

LEXINGTON AND NEIGHBORING Concord are forever linked in history as the settings for two bloody skirmishes that acted as catalysts for the Revolutionary War *(see p144)*. It was here on April 19, 1775, that armed colonists, called minutemen, clashed with British troops on their way to Concord in search of rebel weaponry. The *Minute Man* statue stands on the town common, now known as **Lexington Battle Green**. The battle is reenacted each year in mid-April. The local Historical Society maintains three buildings linked to the battle that now display artifacts from that era. **Buckman Tavern** served as both the meeting place for the minute-

men before the confrontation and as a makeshift hospital for their wounded. Paul Revere alerted the colonists of the advancing British troops and is said to have stopped here following his historic ride *(see box below)*. Revere also stopped at the **Hancock-Clarke House** to warn Samuel Adams (1722–1803) and John Hancock (1737–93), two of the eventual signatories to the Declaration of Independence. **Munroe Tavern** served as headquarters for British forces.

🏛 **Historical Society Houses**
Hancock-Clarke House 36 Hancock St. **Buckman Tavern** 1 Bedford St. **Munroe Tavern** 1332 Massachusetts Ave. **(** *(781) 862-1703.* 📷

Lincoln ⓬

🏠 *7,700.* **ℹ** *152 Lincoln Rd (781) 259-1111.*

LOCATED JUST 13 MILES (21 km) from Boston at the midway point between Concord and Lexington, Lincoln was once called "Niptown" because it was comprised of parcels of land that were "nipped" from neighboring towns. Today this wealthy rural community is noted for its interesting array of sightseeing attractions.

Buckman Tavern at Lexington, meeting place of the minutemen

PAUL REVERE'S RIDE

Under the cover of night on April 18, 1775, Boston silversmith Paul Revere (1734–1818) took on a daring mission. Rowing silently past British ships in the harbor, he reached Charlestown, borrowed a horse, and rode to Lexington to spread the alarm: the British were approaching to arrest patriots John Hancock and Samuel Adams in Lexington and seize rebel arms in Concord. Detained by British troops on the way to Concord, he was released just in time to see the first shots fired on Lexington Green. Nearly 100 years later, his heroics were immortalized in the 1860 poem *Paul Revere's Ride* by New Englander Henry Wadsworth Longfellow.

Outdoor sculptures at DeCordova Sculpture Park

The **DeCordova Sculpture Park,** the largest park of its kind in New England, displays some 70 contemporary large-scale American sculptures as part of its changing outdoor exhibition. The estate was bequeathed to the town by wealthy entrepreneur and patron of the arts Julian DeCordova (1850–1945). The museum is famous for its collection of contemporary New England artworks.

Walter Gropius (1883–1969), the founder of the original Bauhaus school of design in Germany – and one of the 20th century's most influential architects – fled Adolf Hitler's regime in 1934 to become a professor at Harvard in 1937. By 1935 Gropius had built his unique home by combining traditional New England elements, such as clapboard and fieldstone, with modern flourishes of chrome banisters and acoustical plaster. **Gropius House** stands as a prime example of Bauhaus design.

Art and architecture are also celebrated at the **Codman House,** built in 1730 and expanded in the 1790s by merchant John Codman. Home to five generations of the Codman family, the structure was expanded again in 1860, adding 18th-century architectural details to the interior and exterior. The three-story house is set on a 16-acre (6.5-ha) estate and contains wonderful neoclassical furnishings.

At **Drumlin Farm,** which is a Massachusetts Audubon Society property, visitors have an opportunity to see a working New England farm in action as well as to enjoy bird-watching and nature walks.

The farm has hands-on learning activities for children.

🏛 DeCordova Museum and Sculpture Park
51 Sandy Point Rd. **📞** *(781) 259-8355.*
Museum ⭘ *11am–5pm Tue–Sun.* 📷
📹 ♿ 🛍 **Sculpture park** ⭘
8am–10pm daily.

⚓ Gropius House
68 Baker Bridge Rd. **📞** *(781) 259-8098.* ⭘ *Jun–mid-Oct: 11am–4pm Wed–Sun; mid-Oct–Jun: 11am–4pm Sat–Sun.* 📷 📹 *hourly.* ♿ *first floor only.* 📷 ⓘ

⚓ Codman House
Codman Rd. **📞** *(781) 259-8843.*
⭘ *Jun–Oct: 11am–4pm Wed–Sun.*
📷 📹 *hourly.*

🦌 Drumlin Farm Education Center and Wildlife Sanctuary
Rte 117. **📞** *(781) 259-9807.*
⭘ *Mar–Oct: 9am–5pm Tue–Sun; Nov–Feb: 9am–4pm Tue–Sun.* 📷 ♿ 🚻

Quincy ⓭

🏙 *84,985.* ℹ *(617) 847-1454.*

NOW A SUBURB south of Boston, Quincy was once home to five generations of the Adams family, among them the second and sixth presidents of the US. The 12.5-acre (5-ha) **Adams National Historical Park** has 12 buildings, including the John Adams Birthplace, where the second president was born in 1735. His son, John Quincy Adams (1767–1848), was born just steps away at what is now called The John Quincy Adams Birthplace. Other structures include the Old House, home to four generations of the family, and a church, where both presidents and their wives are buried. A trolley provides transportation between sites and the visitor center.

⚓ Adams National Historical Park
1250 Hancock St. **📞** *(617) 770-1175.*
⭘ *mid-Apr–mid-Nov: 9am–5pm daily.*
📷 📹 ♿ *partial.*

ENVIRONS: New Bedford, 49 miles (79 km) south on the coast, was once one of the world's major whaling ports. This working-class town lends its name to the **New Bedford Whaling National Historical Park.** The 13-block site was established to commemorate whaling history and heritage. An introductory video, walking maps, and guided tours with rangers are available at the visitor center. Among the town's main attractions is the excellent **New Bedford Whaling Museum.** The museum has one of the finest collections of whaling artifacts in the world, as well as model ships and carved figureheads. Whenever it is in port, the twin-masted wooden schooner *Ernestina,* an 1894 floating National Historic Landmark, offers tours of the deck and day cruises in warm weather.

⚓ New Bedford Whaling National Historical Park
33 William St. **📞** *(508) 996-4095.*
⭘ *9am–4pm daily.* ♿ 🚻

🏛 New Bedford Whaling Museum
18 Johnny Cake Hill. **📞** *(508) 997-0046.* ⭘ *Memorial Day–Labor Day: 9am–5pm Fri–Wed, 9am–8pm Thu; Labor Day–Memorial Day: 9am–5pm daily.* 📷 📹 ♿ 🚻

⚓ Schooner *Ernestina*
State Pier. **📞** *(508) 992-4900.* 📷 *dock tours and day sails May–Oct; call for schedules and reservations.*

Model ships on display at the New Bedford Whaling Museum

BOSTON STREET FINDER

THE KEY MAP BELOW shows the area of Boston covered by the *Street Finder* maps, which can be found on the following pages. Map references, given throughout this guide, for sights, restaurants, hotels, shops,

and entertainment venues refer to the grid on the maps. The first figure in the map reference indicates which *Street Finder* map to turn to (1 to 4), and the letter and number that follow refer to the grid reference on that map.

KEY TO STREET FINDER

- Major sight
- Place of interest
- Other building
- Ferry boarding point
- Train station
- Ⓣ Subway station
- Bus station
- Taxi rank
- P Parking
- Tourist information
- Hospital with emergency room
- Police station
- Church
- Post office
- Railroad
- One-way street
- Pedestrian street

SCALE OF MAPS 1–4

0 meters   1000
0 yards   1000

0 meters   250
0 miles   250

A

A Street	4 F4
Acorn Street	1 B4 & 4 D1
Adams Place	1 B3
African Meeting House	1 C3
Albany Street	4 D5
Anderson Street	1 B3
Appleton Street	3 C3
Arch Street	2 D4 & 4 F1
Arlington Street	1 A4 & 4 D1
Ash Street	2 D4 & 4 F1
Ash Street	4 E3
Athens Street	4 F4
Atlantic Avenue	2 D5 & 4 F2
Avenue De Lafayette	1 C5 & 4 F2
Avery Street	1 C5 & 4 E2

B

B Street	4 F5
Back Bay Station	3 C3
Battery Street	2 E2
Battery Wharf	2 E2
Batterymarch Street	2 D4
Beach Street	1 C5 & 4 E2
Beacon Street	1 A4 & 3 A2
Beaver Place	1 A4 & 4 D1
Bedford Street	2 D5 & 4 F2
Bell Atlantic Building	2 D4
Belvidere Street	3 A3
Benne Street	4 E2
Benton Street	3 A5
Berkeley Street	1 A4 & 3 C1
Blackstone Block	2 D3

Blackstone Square	3 C5
Blackstone Street	2 D3
Blagden Street	3 C3
Blossom Court	1 B2
Blossom Street	1 B2
Bond Street	4 D4
Boston Athenaeum	1 C4
Boston Arena	3 A4
Boston Center for the Arts	4 D3
Boston Globe Store	2 D4 & 4 F1
Boston Public Library	3 C2
Boston Tea Party Ship	2 E5
Bosworth Street	1 C4 & 4 F1
Bowdoin Street	1 C4
Bowker Street	1 C3
Boylston Street	1 A5 & 3 B3
Braddock Parkway	3 B5
Bradford Street	4 D4
Branch Street	1 B4 & 4 D1
Brattle Book Shop	1 C4 & 4 E1
Bridge Court	1 B3
Bristol Street	4 E4
Broad Street	2 E4
Broadway	4 F3
Bromfield Street	1 C4 & 4 F1
Burbank Street	3 A4
Burke Street	3 A5
Byron Street	1 B4 & 4 D1

C

Cambria Street	3 A3
Cambridge Street	1 B3
Camden Street	3 B5
Canal Street	2 D2

Cardinal O'Connell Way	1 B2
Causeway Street	1 C2
Cedar Lane Way	1 B4
Center Plaza	1 C3
Central Wharf	2 E3
Chandler Street	4 D3
Charles Street	1 B2
Charles Street Meeting House	1 B4
Charlesbank Park	1 A2
Charlestown Avenue	1 A1
Charter Street	2 D2
Chatham Street	2 D3
Chauncy Street	1 C5 & 4 F2
Chester Park	3 B5
Chestnut Street	1 A4 & 4 D1
Children's Museum	2 E5
Christian Science Center	3 B3
Christopher Columbus Park	2 E3
Church Street	4 D2
City Square	1 C1
Claremont Park	3 B4
Clarendon Street	1 A5 & 3 C1
Clark Street	2 E2
Clearway Street	3 A3
Clinton Street	2 D3
Clough House	2 D3
Colonial Theater	1 B5 & 4 E2
Columbia	2 D5 & 4 F2
Columbus Avenue	1 B5 & 3 A5
Commercial Avenue	1 A2
Commercial Street	2 D1
Commercial Street	2 E3
Commercial Wharf	2 E3

Commonwealth Avenue	3 B2
Concord Street	3 C5
Congress Street	2 D3
Cooper Street	2 D2
Copley Place	3 C3
Copley Square	3 C2
Copp's Hill Burying Ground	2 D2
Cortes Street	4 D3
Cotting Street	1 C2
Court Houses	1 C3
Court Street	2 D3
Coventry Street	3 A5
Cross Street	2 D3
Cross Street	2 E3
Cunard Street	3 A5
Custom House	2 E3

D

Dalton Street	3 A3
Dartmouth Place	3 C3
Dartmouth Street	3 C2
Davenport Street	3 B5
Dedham Street	4 D4
Derne Street	1 C3
Devonshire Street	2 D5 & 4 F1
Dorchester Avenue	4 F5
Dwight Street	4 D4

E

East Street	2 D5 & 4 F2
East Berkeley Street	4 D3
East Brookline Street	4 D5
East Canton Street	4 D5
East Concord Street	3 C5

NEW ENGLAND
REGION BY REGION

New England at a Glance

T UCKED AWAY IN THE northeasternmost corner of the United States, New England is rich in history and natural beauty. Many of the country's earliest settlements were established within these six states, with the seeds of the Revolutionary War taking root most firmly in Massachusetts. Interspersed along large tracts of rural countryside, heavy forests, and sweeping coastlines, Ivy League universities and college towns bring an influx of modernity to this historically significant region.

Vermont's fall foliage usually peaks in mid-October.

The Towne House in Old Sturbridge Village was built in 1796. Located in Sturbridge, Massachusetts, the village is one of the New England's most popular living-history museums (see p160).

Mark Twain House in Hartford, Connecticut, is where the famous US author penned many of his most beloved works. The house was commissioned in 1873 for the then hefty sum of $45,000 (see pp200–201).

```
0 kilometers      100

0 miles        50
```

Sugarloaf/USA *is one of Maine's premier ski centers. The mountain has the second-largest vertical drop of all New England ski slopes (see p362–3).*

Lobster boats *dot the waters near Isle au Haut at Ferry Landing.*

The Chase House *is featured in the Strawbery Banke restoration project in Portsmouth, New Hampshire (see pp254–5).*

The Breakers *is one of Newport, Rhode Island's most opulent mansions. Designed after 16th-century palaces in Italy, the 70-room masterpiece was used as the summer "cottage" for the wealthy Vanderbilt family (see pp186–7).*

MASSACHUSETTS

....

O F ALL THE NEW ENGLAND STATES, *Massachusetts may have the most diverse mix of natural and man-made attractions. Miles of wide sandy beaches beckon along the eastern seaboard; green mountains and rich culture characterize the Berkshire Hills in the west. America's early architecture has been well protected, from the lanes of Boston to villages dotting coast and countryside.*

Many of America's pivotal events have been played out against the backdrop of Massachusetts. In 1620 a group of 102 British Pilgrims sailing to the Virginia Colony were blown off course and forced to land farther north. Their colony at Plymouth *(see pp150–51)* was the first permanent English settlement in North America. More than 100 years later the seeds of the American Revolution took strongest root in Boston, blossoming into the nation of the United States and forever altering the course of world history.

Massachusetts has always been New England 's industrial and intellectual hub. The machinery of the American Industrial Revolution chugged to life in the early 19th century in Lowell *(see p142)* and other mill towns. Later the high-tech labs in Cambridge *(see pp110–11)* would help lead the nation into the computer age. In 1944 scientists at Harvard University *(see pp112–17)*, the oldest and most prestigious college in the nation, developed the world's first digital computer. Today the venerable university attracts visitors from around the world wanting to tour its beautiful campus and explore the multitude of treasures in its magnificent museums.

Travelers can also tread the same ground as some of the country's most influential leaders. Quincy *(see p119)* honors the father and son team of John Adams (1735–1826) and John Quincy Adams (1767–1848), the nation's second and sixth presidents. Fashionable Hyannis Port on Cape Cod *(see pp154–9)* is home to the Kennedy clan *(see p159)* compound. Of course, the Cape is best known for its expanse of sand dunes and beaches along the Cape Cod National Seashore *(see pp154–5).*

Part of the stunning sculpture collection at Chesterwood in Stockbridge

◁ **Sunset on Duxbury Beach**

Exploring Massachusetts

MASSACHUSETTS IS A WONDERFUL DESTINATION for travelers in that such a diverse array of attractions is squeezed into a relatively small area. Art, music, theater, and dance can be found in abundance in many of the state's larger urban areas and busy college towns. Scenic seascapes, historic villages, and whale-watching junkets await along the coast and Cape Cod *(see pp156–9)*. Understandably, the coastal beaches are popular spots in summer. Venturing inland, visitors will come upon centuries-old towns, verdant forests and meadows, and countless opportunities for antiquing. As is the case with all the New England states, fall is one of the most beautiful times of year to visit.

Blooming wildflowers beside the Deerfield River

GETTING AROUND

Interstate 93 and Interstate 95 are the two largest and most popular north-south routes leading into Boston. Interstate 495 loops outside the perimeter of Boston, thereby bypassing much of the heavy traffic. Highway 2 and Interstate 90 are the two biggest east-west routes. Boston's Logan International Airport is New England's largest airport. Amtrak has rail links between Boston and New York City with stops in between. Bus lines such as American Eagle, Bonanza Bus, Concord Trailways, Greyhound, and Peter Pan service most of Massachusetts. Passenger and car ferries sail year-round from Cape Cod (leaving from Woods Hole) to Martha's Vineyard and from Hyannis to Nantucket. Advance reservations are essential for cars.

Brant Point, at the entrance to Nantucket Harbor

SIGHTS AT A GLANCE

SEE ALSO

**The impressive Minute Man Visitor
Center in Lexington**

KEY

- ▬ Interstate
- ▬ Major road
- ▭ Minor road
- ▬ Scenic route
- �֎ Viewpoint

SALISBURY

NORTH
SHORE

LOWELL

ROCKPORT

GLOUCESTER

MERRIMACK
VALLEY

SALEM

CONCORD

MARBLEHEAD

SUDBURY

CAMBRIDGE

BOSTON

QUINCY

DUXBURY

PROVINCETOWN

PLYMOUTH

CAPE COD
NATIONAL
SEASHORE

Cape
Cod
Bay

ORLEANS

PROVIDENCE

SANDWICH

BREWSTER

DENNIS

BARNSTABLE

HYANNIS

CHATHAM

FALL RIVER

CAPE COD

NEW BEDFORD

FALMOUTH

WOODS HOLE

OAK BLUFFS

Nantucket
Sound

MARTHA'S
VINEYARD

EDGARTOWN

NANTUCKET
ISLAND

AQUINNAH
(GAY HEAD)

0 kilometers   50

0 miles   25

Salem ●

A LTHOUGH IT IS BEST KNOWN for the infamous witch trials of 1692, which resulted in the execution of 20 innocent people, this coastal town has other, less sensational claims to fame. Founded in 1626 by Roger Conant (1592–1679), Salem grew to become one of New England's busiest 18th- and 19th-century ports, its harbor filled with clipper ships carrying treasures from around the globe. Present-day Salem is a bustling, good-natured town that has the ability to celebrate its rich artistic and architectural heritage, all the while playing up its popular image as the witchcraft capital of America.

An 1842 whaling scene from the Peabody Essex Museum

Exploring Salem

Salem's main attractions are situated in clusters in the harbor and downtown areas. The historic waterfront can be explored on foot, as can the busy area along Essex and Liberty streets (*see pp138–9*).

⛫ Peabody Essex Museum

East India Sq. **(** (800) 745-4054. **◯** Mar–Oct: 10am–5pm Mon–Sat, 12pm–5pm Sun. **⌖ ⛫ ⛐ ⛡**
With a collection of more than one million objects,

Photo opportunities for Salem visitors

this museum is one of New England's largest repositories, including what is regarded as the world's most complete holding of Asian export art. The Liberty Street building contains a vast selection of treasures brought back from the Orient, the Pacific, and Africa by Salem's sea captains. Exhibits include jewelry, porcelain figures, ritual costumes, scrimshaw, figureheads, and navigational

instruments. The building on Essex Street traces more than 300 years of New England history with art, displays of furniture, china, silver, and military memorabilia.

⛴ Salem Maritime National Historic Site

174 Derby St. **(** (978) 740-1680. **◯** year-round: 9am–5pm daily. **●** Jan 1, Thanksgiving, & Dec 25. **⛐**
Salem's heyday as a maritime center has been preserved here. At its peak, the town's harbor was serviced by some 50 wharves. Today this waterfront complex maintains three restored wharves that date back to the 1700s, including the 2,100-ft (640-m) Derby Wharf. The *Friendship*, a reconstruction of an East

SALEM CITY CENTER

Bonded Warehouse ⑤
Custom House ④
Derby Wharf ③
House of Seven
   Gables ⑦
Peabody Essex
   Museum ①
Salem Maritime
   Nat. Hist. Site ②
Salem Witch
   Museum ⑧
West India
   Goods Store ⑥

KEY

▦ Street-by-Street map
    see pp138–9

═══ Highway

ℹ Tourist information

🅿 Parking

0 meters   300

0 feet   1000

Blacksmith at the Salem 1630 Pioneer Village

Indiaman sailing ship built in 1797, is moored at the dock.

Buildings at the site include the 1819 Custom House where author Nathaniel Hawthorne (1804–64) worked as a surveyor in the late 1840s. The redbrick structure, described in Hawthorne's novel *The Scarlet Letter* (1850), contains his office and desk. The Public Stores hold vintage dock equipment and items imported from around the world.

🏛 House of Seven Gables Historic Site

54 Turner St. 📞 (978) 744-0991. ⭕ year-round: 10am–5pm daily. ● first 3 weeks Jan, Thanksgiving, & Dec 25. ✎ 📷 obligatory. ♿ partial. 🚻
Fans of author Nathaniel Hawthorne should make a pilgrimage to this 1668 house. The Salem-born writer was so taken with the Colonial-style home that he used it as the setting in his novel *House of Seven Gables* (1851). As well as its famous seven steeply pitched gables, the house also has a secret staircase. The site contains some other early homes, including Hawthorne's birthplace, a gambrel-roofed 18th-century residence moved from Union Street in 1958.

🏛 Salem Witch Museum

19 1/2 Washington Sq N. 📞 (978) 744-1692 or (800) 544-1692. ⭕ Jul–Aug: 10am–7pm daily; Sep–Jun: 10am–5pm daily. ● Jan 1, Thanksgiving, Dec 24, & 25. ✎ ♿ 🚻
Salem's most visited sight commemorates the town's darkest hour. In 1692 150 people were jailed and 20

executed after being charged with practicing witchcraft. According to some, Nathaniel Hawthorne – who was profoundly disturbed by reports of the events – added a "w" to his last name to distinguish himself from descendants of Judge Hathorne, the man who presided over the witch trials. A 30-minute multimedia reenactment of the witch-hunt and subsequent trials gives visitors a chilling look at the frenzy that once gripped Salem. The town capitalizes on its association with witches each year in October with one of the nation's largest and most colorful celebrations of Halloween.

🏛 Salem 1630 Pioneer Village

Forest River Pk. 📞 (978) 745-0525. ⭕ mid-Apr–Nov: 10am–5pm Mon–Sat, 12pm–5pm Sun. ✎ ♿ partial. 🚻
Salem's earliest settlement is re-created at this museum, complete with thatched cottages, workshops, gardens, and animals. Costumed guides demonstrate daily chores and activities common to 17th-century settlers.

ENVIRONS: Just four miles (6 km) from town lies the region's most picturesque

Clock Tower at Abbot Hall in Marblehead

spot: Marblehead. When President George Washington (1732–99) visited the town, he said it had "the look of antiquity." This still holds true today.

Settled in 1629 and perched on a rocky peninsula, this village displays its heritage as a fisherman's enclave and a thriving port. Crisscrossed by hilly, twisting lanes, the historic district is graced with a wonderful mix of merchants' homes, shipbuilders' mansions, and fishermen's cottages. With more than 200 houses built before the Revolutionary War and nearly 800 built during the 1800s, the district is a catalog of American architecture. Included among the historic buildings is the spired **Abbot Hall**, the seat of local government built in 1876, where the famous *The Spirit of '76* painting (1875) by Archibald Willard (1836–1918) is hanging. Built in 1768 for a wealthy businessman, **The 1708 Jeremiah Lee Mansion** has a sweeping entrance hall, mahogany woodwork, and hand-painted wallpaper. A drive along the shoreline will reveal the lighthouse at Point O'Neck that has guided ships since 1835.

🏛 Abbot Hall

Washington Sq. 📞 (781) 631-0000. ⭕ call for hours. ♿

🏛 The 1708 Jeremiah Lee Mansion

161 Washington St. 📞 (781) 631-1768. ⭕ Jun–Oct: 10am–4pm Tue–Sat, 1pm–4pm Sun. ✎ 📷

Street-by-Street: Historic Salem

L IKE MANY NEW ENGLAND TOWNS, Salem has enjoyed
a rebirth in recent years. Downtown renewal
programs have revitalized the city core, particularly
around Essex Street. Specialty shops, cobblestone
walkways, restaurants, and a pedestrian mall offer
visitors an array of diversions, including stores specializing in the occult. Travelers are best served by
stopping by the Visitor Center operated by the
National Park Service, where they can watch a
27-minute film on the region's history and pick
up maps to guide their tour.

Peabody Essex Museum
*houses the 1765 portrait of
Sarah Erving by John S. Copley.*

Old Town Hall
*The red-brick building
is now a popular
venue for concerts.*

Old Burying
Point Cemetery

Salem Witch Village traces
the history of witches by looking
at their traditions, legends, and –
ultimately – their persecution.

| 0 yards | 50 |
| 0 meters | 50 |

KEY

▢ Pedestrian mall

▬ ▬ Suggested route

STAR SIGHTS

★ **Gardiner-Pingree
House**

★ **Essex Street
Pedestrian Mall**

SALEM WITCH TRIALS

In 1692 Salem was swept by a wave of
hysteria in which 200 citizens were
accused of practicing witchcraft. In all
150 people were jailed and 19 were
hung as witches, while another man
was crushed to death with stones. No
one was safe: two dogs were executed
on the gallows for being witches. Not
surprisingly, when the governor's wife
became a suspect, the trials came to an
abrupt and officially sanctioned end.

**Early accused:
Rebecca Nurse**

★ **Essex Street Pedestrian Mall**
Recent renewal programs have turned this cobblestone walkway into a busy mall of shops, cafés, and restaurants.

National Park Service Visitor Center is housed in a renovated armory and shows a short film of the region's history.

★ **Gardiner-Pingree House**
This 1804 house is elegantly decorated and furnished with period pieces.

Salem Witch Museum

LIBERTY STREET

ESSEX STREET

BROWN STREET

WASHINGTON SQ. WEST

HAWTHORNE BOULEVARD

CHARTER STREET

TO WATERFRONT

Statue of Nathaniel Hawthorne honors the Salem-born author of *The Scarlet Letter* (1850).

Crowninshield Bentley House
Built in 1727, this house typifies the architectural style of mid-18th century dwellings.

Tour of the North Shore ❷

Tᴏ HE SCENIC TIP of the North Shore is a favorite escape for harried Bostonians and vacationers who come for the quaint towns, sandy beaches, and whale-watching excursions that are found here in abundance. Ipswich, founded in 1633, still has more than 40 houses built before 1725. It is also known for its sandy beaches, marshes, dunes and seafood, especially clams. The rocky shores of Cape Ann hold diverse pleasures, including artists' colonies, mansions, and opportunities for swimming and boating.

Fisherman's Memorial statue

Fishermen casting into the surf on a North Shore beach

Ipswich ⑧
A wealth of 17th century architecture makes this a fine town to explore.

Antiquing
Antique stores can be found throughout the North Shore region, particularly in Essex along Main Street.

Manchester-by-the-Sea ①
A scenic harbor, luxurious mansions, and a wide beach are town highlights.

Ipswich River ⑧

①A

Castle Neck River

133

Essex

Essex River

133

Chebacco Lake

Magnolia ②
This town is known for magnificent summer homes and the Medieval-style Hammond Castle Museum.

① 127

②

KEY

▬ Tour route

═ Other road

🔆 Viewpoint

0 kilometers   3

0 miles   3

Gloucester ③
Famous for its *Fisherman's Memorial* statue, this is a lively town with a busy harbor

THE WORLD'S FIRST FRIED CLAM

The town of Essex has a proud culinary distinction: it was here that the clams were first fried. In 1916 Lawrence "Chubby" Woodman and his wife were selling

raw clams by the road. Following a friend's suggestion, they tried deep-frying a clam. The popularity of the new-dish snack helped Woodman open his own restaurant – still one of the region's most popular today.

Fried clams to go from Woodman's restaurant in Essex

Wingaersheek Beach ⑦
One of the North Shore's most popular beaches. At low tide visitors can walk to the Annisquam lighthouse.

• Castle Neck

Essex Bay

Rockport ⑥
Settled in 1690, the town is home to art galleries and an often photographed structure, the red fishing shed called Motif No.1.

Lanesville

Halibut Point

Pigeon Cove •

Annisquam

127

⑦
•

128

• Riverdale

Sandy Bay

Eastern Point Light ⑤
The view from the lighthouse takes in the rocky shoreline and, on clear days, Boston's skyscrapers.

⑥

127

③

128

127

127

④

127

Long Beach

Gloucester Harbor

Rocky Neck ④
Home to one of America's oldest art colonies, Rocky Neck lays claim to fine seafood restaurants.

Eastern Point Light

⑤

Power looms on display in the Boott Cotton Mills Museum

Lowell ❸

🏙 103,000. ✈ 30 miles (48 km) S in Boston. 🚌 ℹ 9 Central St, Ste 201 (978) 459-6150.

Lowell has the distinction of being the country's first industrial city, paving the way for the American Industrial Revolution. In the early 19th century, Boston merchant Francis Cabot Lowell (1775–1817) opened a cloth mill in nearby Waltham and equipped it with his new power loom – a vast improvement over the old manual methods. The increase in production was so great that the mill quickly outgrew its quarters and was moved to the town of East Chelmsford (later renamed for Lowell). Set on 400 acres (162 ha) and using power provided by a steep drop in the Merrimack River, the business expanded to include 10 giant mill complexes, which employed more than 10,000 workers.

While the town prospered, it was at the expense of its workers, many of whom were unskilled immigrants exploited by the greedy mill owners. Eventually laborers organized and there were many strikes. The most successful was the 1912 Bread and Roses Strike, which began in neighboring Lawrence and spread to Lowell. While that confrontation helped improve conditions for workers, the relief was temporary. In the 1920s companies began to move south in search of cheaper labor. The death knell came in 1929. The country was rocked by the Great Depression and the mills closed, leaving Lowell a ghost town.

In 1978 the **Lowell National Historical Park** was established to rehabilitate more than 100 downtown buildings and preserve the town's unique history. The Market Mills Visitor Center on Market Street offers a free introductory video show, walking tour maps, guided walks with rangers, and tickets for canal boat tours of the city's waterways. From March to November, antique trolleys take visitors to the **Boott Cotton Mills Museum**, the centerpiece of the park, where 88 vintage power looms produce a deafening clatter. Interactive exhibits trace the Industrial Revolution and the growth of the labor movement. Also in Lowell, the **American Textile History Museum** traces the history of 300 years of American textiles, from early spinning and weaving to mass production.

Lowell has nonindustrial attractions as well. The **New England Quilt Museum** displays both antique and contemporary examples of the quilt-maker's art, and the **Sports Museum of New England** has interactive exhibits on sports in the state. Painter James McNeill Whistler (1834–1903), most famous for his portrait of his mother, was born in Lowell while his father was in charge of the railroad works for the city's mills. Whistler's birthplace is now a museum that displays prints of some of his work, but focuses more on 19th- and 20th-century American art, especially regional artists.

🏛 Lowell National Historical Park
67 Kirk St. 📞 (978) 970-5000. ◯ year-round: 9am–5pm daily. 📷 tours & exhibits. 🎫 call for hours. ♿

🏛 Boott Cotton Mills Museum
400 John St. 📞 (978) 970-5000. ◯ year-round: 9:30am–5pm daily. 📷 ♿

🏛 American Textile History Museum
491 Dutton St. 📞 (978) 441-0400. ◯ year-round: 9am–4pm Tue–Fri, 10am–4pm Sat. ● public hols. 📷 🎫 ♿

🏛 New England Quilt Museum
18 Shattuck St. 📞 (978) 452-4207. ◯ year-round: 10am–4pm Tue–Sat; May–Sep: 12pm–4pm Sun. ● public hols. 📷 ♿

Bedroom display at the New England Quilt Museum in Lowell

Lowell's Jack Kerouac

Lowell native Jack Kerouac was the leading chronicler of the "beat generation," a term that he coined to describe members of the disaffected Bohemian movement of the 1950s. Although he lived elsewhere for most of his adult life, his remains are buried in the town's Edson Cemetery. Excerpts from Kerouac's most famous novel, *On the Road* (1957), and other of his writings are inscribed on granite pillars in the Kerouac Commemorative Park on Bridge Street.

Jack Kerouac (1922–69)

Part of the Fruitlands Museums' Shaker collection

🏛 **Sports Museum**
of New England
25 Shattuck St. 🎫 *(978) 452-6775.*
⭕ *summer: 10am–5pm Tue–Sat,*
12pm–5pm Sun; winter: 10am–5pm
Thu–Sat. 🖼 ♿

🏛 **Whistler House**
Museum of Art
243 Worthen St. 🎫 *(978) 452-7641.*
⭕ *year-round: 11am–4pm Tue–Sat.*
🖼 ♿

Sudbury ❹

🏘 *16,500.* 🚊 *24 miles (39 km)*
E in Boston. 🛈 *(978) 443-7300.*

THE PICTURESQUE TOWN of Sudbury is home to a number of historic sites, including the 1797 First Parish Church and the 1723 Loring Parsonage. Longfellow's Wayside Inn, one of the nation's oldest inns, was built c.1700 and was immortalized in Henry Wadsworth Longfellow's poetry collection entitled *Tales of a Wayside Inn* (1863). In the 1920s the building was purchased by industrialist Henry Ford (1863–1947), who restored it, filled it with antiques, and surrounded it with other relocated structures, such as a rustic gristmill, a schoolhouse, and a general store.

Nashoba Valley ❺

🛈 *43 Buena Vista St, Devens (978)*
772-6976.

FED BY THE NASHOBA RIVER, Nashoba Valley is an appealing world of meadows and orchards and colonial towns built around village greens. The region is particularly popular in May when the apple trees are in bloom, and again in fall when the apples are ripe for picking and the surrounding hills are ablaze in autumn colors.

The **Fruitlands Museums**, the valley's major attraction, is composed of four museums and two outdoor sites on beautiful hilltop grounds that include nature trails and picnic areas with valley views. Founder Clara Endicott Sears (1863–1960), a philosopher, writer, collector, and early preservationist, built her home here in 1910 and began gathering properties of historical significance. Her first acquisition was Fruitlands, the "New Eden" commune based partly on vegetarianism and self-sufficiency initiated by Bronson Alcott (1799–1888) and fellow Transcendentalists.

Fruitlands Museums' rocking horse

Alcott was the father of author Louisa May Alcott (1832–88) and was the model for the character of Mr. March in her book *Little Women* (1868). The restored farmhouse now serves as a museum and includes memorabilia of Alcott, Ralph Waldo Emerson (1803–82), and other Transcendentalist leaders.

Five years later, Sears acquired a building in nearby Shaker Village. The 1790 structure, the first office building in the village, now houses a collection of traditional Shaker furniture, clothing, and artifacts. The American Indian Museum opened its doors in 1928 to display Sears' personal collection of Native American artifacts.

Another of the region's attractions is the **Nashoba Valley Winery**, a beautiful 55-acre (22-ha) orchard that produces wines from fruits such as apples, pears, peaches, plums, blueberries, strawberries, and elderberries. More than 100 varieties of apples are grown here. On weekends the winery offers tours of the facility.

🍷 **Fruitlands Museums**
102 Prospect Hill Rd, Harvard. 🎫
(978) 456-3924. ⭕ *mid-May–Oct:*
10am–5pm daily. 🖼 ♿ *partial.*
🍷 **Nashoba Valley Winery**
100 Wattaquodoc Hill Rd, Bolton.
🎫 *(978) 779-5521.* ⭕ *year-round:*
11am–5pm daily. **Winery tours:** *year-round: 11:30am–4pm Sat–Sun.* 🖼

Henry Wadsworth Longfellow's Wayside Inn, one of the nation's oldest

Concord ❻

THE PEACEFUL, PROSPEROUS suburban look of modern-day Concord masks an eventful past. This small town was at the heart of two important chapters in US history. The first was marked by a single dramatic event, the Battle of Concord on April 19, 1775, which signaled the beginning of the Revolutionary War. The second spanned several generations, as 19th-century Concord blossomed into the literary heart and soul of the US, with many of the nation's great writers establishing homes here. The influence of both important periods is in full evidence today.

North Bridge in Minute Man National Historical Park

Exploring Concord
At Concord's center lies Monument Square. It was also at the center of the battle fought between British troops and Colonists more than 200 years ago. Having seized the gun cache and other supplies of rebel forces, the British soldiers began burning them. Nearby Colonist forces spotted the smoke and, believing the British were torching the town, rushed to Concord's defense, precipitating the Revolutionary War.

🏛 Minute Man National Historical Park
174 Liberty St. ☎ (978) 369-6993 ext 22. ◯ May–Oct: 9am–5pm daily; Nov–Apr: 9am–4pm daily. ● Jan 1, Thanksgiving, & Dec 25. ♿

On April 19, 1775, a group of militia, ordinary citizens, and Colonist farmers known as minutemen confronted British troops who were patrolling the North Bridge. The minutemen fought valiantly, driving three British companies of troops from the bridge and chasing them back to Boston.

This 990-acre (400-ha) park preserves the site and tells the story of the American victory. The Minute Man Visitor Center also features a massive battle mural and a 22-minute multimedia show called "Road to Revolution." The Battle Road Trail traces the five-mile

(8-km) path followed by the British as they advanced from Lexington to Concord – the same route they took in their retreat back to Boston.

The park's North Bridge Unit is the place where the first major engagement was fought. This so-called "shot heard around the world" set off the war. Across the bridge is the famous *Minute Man* statue by Concord native Daniel Chester French (1850–31). A short trail leads from the bridge to the North Bridge Visitor Center. A reenactment of the battle takes place every year in April in Concord and Lexington.

🏛 Concord Museum
Jct of Lexington Rd & Cambridge Tpk. ☎ (978) 369-9763. ◯ Jan–Mar: 11am–4pm Mon–Sat, 1pm–4pm Sun; Apr–Dec: 9am–5pm Mon–Sat, 12pm–5pm Sun. ☒ ♿

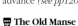

The museum's eclectic holdings include decorative arts from the 17th, 18th, and 19th centuries, such as clocks, textiles, and metalware. History buffs will want to see the lantern in the Old North Church steeple that Paul Revere ordered hung to warn Colonists of the British advance *(see pp120–21)*.

Minute Man statue in Concord

🏛 The Old Manse
Monument St. ☎ (978) 369-3909. ◯ mid-April–Oct: 10am–5pm Mon–Sat, 12pm–5pm Sun. ☒
The parsonage by the North Bridge was built in 1770 by the grandfather of writer Ralph Waldo Emerson (1803–82),

Along the Battle Road, by John Rush, a representation of what a battle of the time might have been like

**Concord's Old Manse: home to
19th-century literary giants**

who lived here briefly. Author
Nathaniel Hawthorne (1804–
64) and his wife rented the
house during the first three
years of their marriage. Several
of their loving inscriptions are
scratched into the windows.
The house got its name from
Hawthorne's *Mosses from an
Old Manse* (1846), the collection of short stories he wrote
here. The house contains
family possessions as well as
period furniture.

🏛 Emerson House

Cambridge Tpk. 📞 *(978) 369-2236.*
⭕ *mid-Apr–late Oct: 10am–4:30pm
Thu–Sat, 2pm–4:30pm Sun & public
hols.* 📷

Ralph Waldo Emerson lived
in this house from 1835 until
his death in 1882, writing
essays, organizing lecture
tours, and entertaining friends
and admirers. Much of
Emerson's furniture, writings,
books, and family memora-
bilia are on display.

🌿 Walden Pond State Reservation

915 Walden St. 📞 *(978) 369-3254.*
⭕ *call for hours.* 📷 📹 ♿
Essayist Henry David Thoreau
(1817–62) lived in relative
isolation at Walden Pond from
July 1845 to September 1847.
During his stay, he compiled
the material for his seminal
work *Walden; or, Life in the
Woods* (1854). In the book,
he called for a return to simplicity in everyday life and a
respect for nature. Because of
Thoreau's deep influence on

future generations of
environmentalists, Walden
Pond is widely considered
to be the birthplace of the
conservationist movement.
The pond itself is sur-
rounded by 333 acres (135
ha) of mostly undeveloped
woodlands. The area is
popular for walking, fishing,
and swimming, and today is
far from the solitary spot that
Thoreau described, even
though the reservation limits
the number of visitors to no
more than 1,000 people at
one time.

Fisherman on the tranquil waters of Walden Pond

CONCORD TOWN CENTER

Concord Museum ⑦	Monument Square ①
Emerson House ⑧	North Bridge ④
Minute Man National	North Bridge
Historical Park ②	Visitor Center ③
Minute Man Statue ⑤	The Old Manse ⑥

KEY

= Highway

ℹ Tourist information

P Parking

0 meters   300
0 feet   1000

Mayflower II, replica of the original Pilgrim sailing ship

Plymouth ❼

🏛 52,000. ✈ 40 miles (64 km) NW in Boston. ⛴ to Provincetown (seasonal). 🛈 130 Water St (508) 747-7533 or (800) USA-1620.

In 1620, 102 PILGRIMS aboard the ship *Mayflower* sailed into Plymouth harbor and established the first permanent English settlement in the New World. Today the town bustles with tourists exploring the sites of America's earliest days, including **Plimoth Plantation** *(see pp150–51)*, 2.5 miles (4 km) from town. The plantation is a realistic reconstruction and living-history museum of the Pilgrim village. Plymouth itself is a popular seaside resort, complete with a 3.5-mile- (6-km-) long beach, harbor cruises, and fishing excursions. In the fall, the surrounding bogs turn ruby red as the annual cranberry harvest gets underway. Plymouth is popular for its "Progress," which takes place each Friday in August at 6pm and on

Thanksgiving Day at 10am. Visitors come to witness the solemn re-enactment of the Pilgrims' slow procession to Burial Hill, where a short service is held.

Most of the historic sights can be accessed on foot by the Pilgrim Path that stretches along the waterfront and downtown areas. A sightseeing trolley connects points of interest and features a 40-minute history of the town. Ensconced in a monument at the harbor is the country's most famous boulder, Plymouth Rock, marking the spot where the Pilgrims are said to have first stepped ashore.

The **Mayflower II**, a replica of the 17th-century sailing ship that carried the Pilgrims over from England, is moored by Plymouth Rock. At just 106 ft (32 m) in length, the vessel seems far too small to have made a transatlantic voyage, especially considering the horrific weather it encountered. Walking along the cramped deck, visitors will marvel at the Pilgrims' courage in undertaking such a risky trip.

Even after surviving the brutal crossing, many Pilgrims succumbed to illness and malnutrition during their first winter in Plymouth. Their remains are buried

across the street on Coles Hill, which is fronted by a statue of Massasoit, the Wampanoag Indian chief who allied himself with the new-comers and aided the survivors by teaching them the growing and use of native corn. It was with Massasoit and his people that the Pilgrims celebrated their famous first Thanksgiving. Coles Hill offers a panoramic view of the harbor.

Burial Hill at the head of the Town Square was the site of an early fort and the final resting place of many members of the colony, including Governor William Bradford (1590–1656). Each Friday in August, citizens dressed in Pilgrim garb walk from Plymouth Rock to the hill to reenact the church service attended by the 51 survivors of the first winter.

Perched on a hilltop overlooking town, the 81-ft (25-m) National Monument to the Forefathers is dedicated to the Pilgrims who made the dangerous voyage to the New World. The Pilgrim Mother Fountain was erected in honor of the women who made the original voyage. Twenty-five set sail from England, but only four of them survived.

Opened in 1824, the **Pilgrim Hall Museum** is one of America's old-est public museums, housing the largest existing collection of Pilgrim-era furniture, decorative arts, and even armor. Some of the personal possessions on display include bibles, cradles, and the sword of one of the most colorful Pilgrims, Myles Standish (c.1584–1656), a former soldier of fortune who went on to found nearby Duxbury *(see p149)*. The museum also contains the only portrait of a *Mayflower* passenger and the hull of the *Sparrow Hawk*, a 1626 sailing ship. For a treatment of the Pilgrims' saga that particularly appeals

Statue of Massasoit

Signing the Mayflower Compact, one of 26 scenes at the Plymouth National Wax Museum

◁ **Cape Cod National Seashore, Head of the Meadow Beach**

Pilgrim Hall exhibits furniture, armor, and art

to children, take in the **Plymouth National Wax Museum**. Some 180 life-size wax figures in 26 settings help trace the Pilgrims' journey from their native England to Holland and then across the Atlantic to the New World. Among the scenes re-created are the landing at Plymouth Rock and the first Thanksgiving. Sound and light effects heighten the drama.

Plymouth has six historic homes of special interest. Among them is the **1677 Harlow Old Fort House**, constructed of timbers from the original Pilgrim fortification. The house is furnished with period pieces and is the setting for demonstrations of early pioneer skills such as carding, spinning, weaving, and candle dipping. Pottery is made on the premises of the town's oldest home, the **Richard Sparrow House**, c.1640. The original house of the **Mayflower Society House** was built in 1754 and extensively renovated in 1898. What was the old kitchen is now the office for the General Society of Mayflower Descendants. Its research library has one of the finest genealogical collections in the country.

Travelers heading west on Route 44 will pass numerous cranberry bogs. Close to the start of Route 44 is the **Ocean Spray Cranberry World**. This one-of-a-kind attraction is the place to go to learn everything there is to know about cranberries. Exhibits outline the evolution of cranberry harvesting through the ages and a variety of cranberry-based dishes are prepared in a demonstration kitchen. Visitors can also sample cranberry products.

🏛 **Mayflower II**
State Pier. 📞 (508) 746-1622.
🕐 Apr–Nov: 9am–5pm daily. 🏷
🏛 **Pilgrim Hall Museum**
75 Court St. 📞 (508) 746-1620.
🕐 year round: 9:30am–4:30pm daily. ● Jan 1. 🏷
🏛 **Plymouth National Wax Museum**
16 Carver St. 📞 (508) 746-6468.
🕐 Jul–Aug: 9am–9pm daily; Jun & Sep–Oct: 9am–7pm daily; Nov–May: 9am–5pm daily. 🏷
🏚 **1677 Harlow Old Fort House**
119 Sandwich St. 📞 (508) 746-0012. 🕐 by appt only. 🏷 🏠
🏚 **Richard Sparrow House**
42 Summer St. 📞 (508) 747-1240.
🕐 Apr–late Dec: 10am–5pm Mon–Tue, Thu–Fri & Sun, 10am–8pm Sat; late Dec–Apr: 10am–5pm Sat. 🏷 ♿ call first. 🏠
🏚 **Mayflower Society House**
4 Winslow St. 📞 (508) 746-2590.
🕐 call for hours. 🏷
🏛 **Ocean Spray Cranberry World**
225 Water St. 📞 (508) 746-2350.
🕐 May–Nov: 9:30am–5pm daily.
🎥 ♿ 🏠

Duxbury ❽

🏙 15,350. 🚗 34 miles (54 km) N in Boston. ℹ 32 Court St, Plymouth (508) 747-0100.

DUXBURY WAS SETTLED in 1628 by a group of Pilgrims who found that the Plymouth colony was getting too crowded. Two who made the move, John Alden (c.1598–1687) and Myles Standish (c.1584–1656), were on the *Mayflower* crossing. Today the town is best known for its nine-mile- (14-km-) long beach.

The last home of Alden and his wife was the 1653 **Alden House**. The structure has several features of note, including gunstock beams and a ceiling plastered with crushed clam and oyster shells.

King Caesar House, the home of another prominent resident, is one of the town's grandest structures. Ezra Weston II, an 18th-century shipping magnate, had a fortune large enough to earn him the nickname "King Caesar." It also allowed him the luxury of building this stately Federal mansion in 1808. Today the house is furnished with period pieces, French wallpaper, and a small museum celebrating the region's maritime history.

Elsewhere in town, the **Art Complex Museum** contains everything from Asian and European art to Shaker furniture and contemporary New England art. A

Shaker piece at Art Complex Museum

Japanese tea hut is the setting for a traditional tea ceremony held on the last Sunday of the month, June through August.

🏚 **Alden House**
105 Alden St. 📞 (781) 934-9092.
🕐 mid-May–mid-Oct: 10am–5pm Mon–Sat, 12pm–5pm Sun. 🏷 🎥 ♿
🏚 **King Caesar House**
King Caesar Rd. 📞 (781) 934-6106.
🕐 mid-Jun–Labor Day: 1pm–4pm Wed–Sun; day after Labor Day–Sep: 1pm–4pm Sat–Sun. 🏷 🎥
🏛 **Art Complex Museum**
189 Alden St. 📞 (781) 934-6634.
🕐 year-round: 1pm–4pm Wed–Sun.

Plimoth Plantation

PLIMOTH PLANTATION is a painstakingly accurate re-creation of the Pilgrim's 1627 village. Encircled by a palisade, the settlement's rudimentary thatched dwellings are furnished with reproductions of 17th-century pieces. Throughout the site, costumed interpreters portraying historically accurate personages from the original colony go about their daily tasks of salting fish, gardening, and musket drills. Even the plantation's livestock have been bred to represent the types of cattle, goats, and chickens common in the 17th century.

Colony Governor William Bradford

Plimoth Plantation
Costumed interpreters mingle with visitors on the village's busy central street.

Vegetable garden

Outer palisade

★ **Hopkins House**
Stephen Hopkins had prior colony experience in Virginia. His wife Elizabeth gave birth to their son, Oceanus, on the Mayflower.

★ **Allerton House**
Issac Allerton was the agent who dealt with the colony's financiers.

STAR FEATURES

★ **Hopkins House**

★ **Allerton House**

★ **Storehouse**

Powder Vials
The bandolier of a costumed interpreter is hung with handcarved gunpowder vials.

KEY

☐ **Illustrated**
☐ **Not illustrated**

1 Fort/Meetinghouse
2 Standish and Alden Houses
3 Winslow and Cooke Houses
4 Bradford House
5 Allerton House
6 Cow Shed
7 Hopkins House
8 Brewster and Browne Houses
9 Dutch Barn
10 Fuller House
11 Forge
12 Storehouse

VISITORS' CHECKLIST

Rte 3A. 🛈 137 Warren Ave
(508) 746-1622. 🔵 Apr–Nov:
9am–5pm daily. 🅿️ ♿ limited
access to certain parts of site;
wheelchairs available upon
request. 🚪
🅦 www.plimoth.org

Palmer
House

★ **Storehouse**
*Everyday provisions were
stored here, along with furs
and other goods to be
shipped to England.*

| 0 meters | | 10 |
| 0 yards | | 10 |

Local Reeds
*Used for thatching,
reeds were long-
lasting, easily
repaired, and vir-
tually waterproof.*

Dutch Barn

The Cow Shed
*Cows and other
livestock were
housed in what
was often called
the "beasthouse."
It opens into an
enclosed paddock.*

Martha's Vineyard scene: fishing boat outside fishing shack

Martha's Vineyard ⑨

🚶 13,900. ✈ West Tisbury.
🚢 Woods Hole; Hyannis; Falmouth;
New Bedford; New London, CT.
ℹ Beach Rd, Vineyard Haven (508)
693-0085.

THE VINEYARD, as the locals call it, is the largest of all New England's vacation islands at 108 sq miles (280 sq km). Just a 45-minute boat ride from shore, it is blessed with a mesmerizing mix of scenic beauty and the under-stated charm of a beach resort. Bicycle trails abound here and opportunities for hiking, surf fishing, and some of the best sailing in the region add to the Vineyard's lure. Each town has its own distinctive mood and architec-tural style, making for inter-esting exploring.

Vineyard Haven
Most visitors arrive on Martha's Vineyard aboard ferries that sail into this waterfront town, which was largely destroyed by fire in the 1800s. Vineyard Haven is sheltered between two points of land known as East and West Chop, each with its own landmark lighthouse.

Edgartown
As the center of the island's whaling industry in the early 1800s, Edgartown was once home to wealthy sea captains and merchants. The streets are lined with their homes.
    The main building of the **Martha's Vineyard**

Victorian home with gingerbread ornamentation in Oak Bluffs

Historical Society complex is the 1765 Thomas Cooke House. The beautiful 12-room structure is filled with antique furniture, ship models, scrimshaw, and gear used by whalers.
    At the eastern end of the waterfront, visitors can catch the ferry to Chappaquiddick Island, a rural outpost that is popular for its beaches and opportunities for bird-watching, surf fishing, canoe-ing, and hiking. This quiet enclave was made famous by a fatal accident in 1969, when a car driven by Senator Edward Kennedy (b.1932) went off the bridge, killing a young woman passenger.

🏛 **Martha's Vineyard Historical Society**
59 School St. ☎ (508) 627-4441.
◯ mid-Jun–Oct: 10am–4pm
Wed–Sat; Oct–mid-June: 1pm–4pm
Wed–Fri, 10am–4pm Sat. ● Sun.
🖼 ♿ 🏠

Oak Bluffs
Tourism began on Martha's Vineyard in 1835 when local Methodists began using the undeveloped area to pitch their tents during their sum-mer revival meetings. The setting proved popular and more people came every year in search of sunshine and salvation. Gradually the tent village gave way to a town of colorful gingerbread cottages, boardinghouses, and stores, and was named Cottage City. In 1907 it was renamed Oak Bluffs. The town is home to the **Flying Horses Carousel**, the oldest continuously oper-ating carousel in the country. Today's children delight in riding on it as much as those of the 1870s.

🎠 **Flying Horses Carousel**
Oak Bluffs Ave. ☎ (508) 693-9481.
◯ Memorial Day–Labor Day: daily,
call for hours. 🖼 🏠

Western Shoreline
Unlike the Vineyard's busier eastern section, the western shoreline is tranquil and rural. The area, which includes the towns of North and West Tisbury, Menemsha, and Aquinnah (the recently renamed Gay Head), is

---

WHALE-WATCHING

Whale off the coast of Martha's Vineyard

From April to mid-October the waters off Nantucket Island and Cape Cod come to life with the antics of finback, right, minke, and humpback whales. These gentle behemoths bang their massive tails, blow clouds of bubbles, and sometimes fling their entire bodies into the air only to come crashing down in mammoth back or belly flops. Whales are most numerous during July and August, and cruises are offered from many ports, including Provincetown and Barnstable on the Cape, Vineyard Haven on Martha's Vineyard, and the Straight Wharf in the town of Nantucket.

Colored cliffs of Aquinnah on western shore of Martha's Vineyard

graced by a number of private homes and pristine beaches, many of them strictly private.

Tiny West Tisbury remains a rural village of picket fences, a white-spired church, and a general store. In Menemsha, a working fishing fleet fills the harbor, and the weathered fishermen's shacks, fish nets, and lobster traps look much as they did a century ago. Windswept Aquinnah at the western edge of the island is famous for its steep multi-hued clay cliffs – a favorite subject of photographers.

Nantucket Island ⓾

🏠 9,000 (year-round).
✈ West Tisbury. ⛴ Hyannis & Oak Bluffs. ℹ 48 Main St (508) 228-1700.

Lying off the southern tip of Cape Cod *(see pp158–9)*, Nantucket Island is a 14-mile- (22-km-) long enclave of tranquility. With only one town to speak of, the island remains an untamed world of kettle ponds, cranberry bogs, and lush stands of wild grapes and blueberries, punctuated by the occasional lighthouse.

In the early 1800s the town of Nantucket was the envy of the whaling industry, with a fleet of about 100 vessels.

Brant Point Light on Nantucket Island

The town's architecture reflects those glory days, with the magnificent mansions of sea captains and merchants – made rich from their whaling profits – lining Main Street. Today the town has the nation's largest concentration of pre-1850s houses.

The **Nantucket Historical Association** (NHA) operates 11 historical buildings in town. One of the most important sites is the Whaling Museum on Broad Street, which sheds light on the whaling industry through exhibits of ship models, tools, ship's logs, portraits, scrimshaw, and an enormous whale skeleton. Also located on Broad Street, the Peter Foulger Museum hosts changing exhibitions that highlight the NHA collection of furniture, baskets, portraits, and other artifacts. The Fair Street Museum, which is attached to the Quaker Meeting House, is a reminder that the island was once a refuge for many Quakers seeking freedom to practice their religion. It now houses the NHA Research Library. The library has a huge collection of diaries and letters, manuscripts, business documents, ships' logs, maps and charts, and genealogical materials, as well as more than 45,000 photographs.

🏛 **Nantucket Historical Association (NHA)**
15 Broad St. 📞 *(508) 228-1894.*
Historic buildings ◯ *call for hours.*
Whaling Museum *only.*

ENVIRONS: Just eight miles (13 km) from the town of Nantucket lies the tiny village of **Siasconset**. The village, which is called "Sconset" by locals, is located on the eastern shore of the island and easily lives up to the description offered by one 18th-century visitor: "Perfectly unconnected with the real world and far removed from its perturbations." Set between cranberry bogs and rose-covered bluffs overlooking the Atlantic Ocean, the village's narrow lanes are lined with miniature cottages that are among the oldest of the island. These are fishermen's shanties, many of them constructed out of wood rescued from shipwrecks, accounting for Sconset's old nickname, "Patchwork Village."

Once Sconset was a summer colony for actors, attracting such luminaries of the American stage as Lillian Russell (1861–1922) and Joseph Jefferson (1829–1905), who made the 35-minute ride from the town of Nantucket via an island railroad. Today there are only a few inns remaining. The majority of Sconset's summer visitors own or rent homes, a fact that serves to keep the beaches uncrowded and the village peaceful.

Cape Cod National Seashore ⓫

National Park sign

STRETCHING MORE THAN 40 miles (64 km) from Chatham in the south to Provincetown in the north, Cape Cod National Seashore is one of the Eastern Seaboard's true gems. With the backing of President John Kennedy (1917–63) the seashore was established in 1961 to protect the fragile sand dunes and beaches, salt marshes, glacial cliffs, and woodlands. While the delicate landscape has been under federal protection since then, certain features have been added, including bike trails, hiking paths, and specially designated dune trails for off-road vehicles. Historical structures are interspersed among the seashore's softly beautiful natural features.

★ Old Harbor Life-Saving Station
This 1897 station houses a museum containing turn-of-the-century rescue equipment and shipwreck paraphernalia. During the summer months, traditional rescue methods are demonstrated.

★ Province Lands Area
The barren, windswept landscape of the Province Lands Area has long been an inspiration for writers and artists. Here beech forests give way to horseshoe-shaped dunes and white sand beaches.

Overview
Visitors get an overview of the area in the park's visitor centers.

KEY

▬▬	Major road
▬▬	Minor road
- -	Walking trail
—	Park boundary
ℹ	Tourist information
P	Parking
⛴	Ferry (seasonal)
🧺	Picnic area
⚜	Viewpoint

0 kilometers 2

0 miles 2

Pilgrims
Heights

Head of the Meadow Beaches

Coast Guard Beach

Highland Light
(Cape Cod Light)

S. Highland Rd

Longnook Rd

Longnook
Beach

N. Pamet Rd.
S. Pamet Rd.

Ballston
Beach

Collins Rd

Newcomb
Hollow Beach

Duck
Harbor
Beach

Gross Hill Road

Chequesset Neck Rd.

Wellfleet

E. Commercial St.

Cahoon
Hollow Beach

White Crest
Beach

Ocean View Drive

LeCount
Hollow
Beach

South Wellfleet

LIEUTENANT
ISLAND

Jeremy
Point

Marconi
Station
Site

Marconi
Beach

**Nauset
Light
Beach**

Nauset Cable Road

Ocean
View
Drive

i   P

Doane Rd.

Coast
Guard
Beach

Nauset
Marsh

Eastham

Orleans
(Nauset)
Beach

Orleans

Beach Road

SIPSON
ISLAND

Pleasant
Bay

STRONG
ISLAND

Chatham

VISITORS' CHECKLIST

Rte 6, Cape Cod. 99
Marconi Site Rd, Wellfleet (508)
349-3785. year-round.
www.nps.gov/caco

★ **Atwood Higgins House**
*This 1730s Colonial-style home
typifies the houses of early settlers
to the region.*

Wildflowers *bloom
throughout the seasons
at the National Seashore.*

★ **Atlantic White
Cedar Swamp Trail**
*A nature trail,
part of which is a
boardwalk over
swamp, leads
through forested
swampland and
stands of scrub oak
and pitch pine to
Marconi Station.*

Marconi Beach,
*a broad and sandy
expanse near South
Wellfleet, is named
after Guglielmo
Marconi (1874–
1937), who transmit-
ted the world's first
wireless message from
this area in 1903.*

STAR FEATURES

★ **Old Harbor
   Life-Saving Station**

★ **Province Lands Area**

★ **Atlantic White Cedar
   Swamp Trail**

★ **Atwood Higgins
   House**

Cape Cod ⑫

MORE THAN 13 MILLION PEOPLE arrive each summer to enjoy the boundless beaches, natural beauty, and quaint colonial villages of Cape Cod. Extending some 70 miles (113 km) into the sea, the Cape is shaped like an upraised arm, bent at the elbow with the Atlantic Ocean and the Cape Cod National Seashore (see pp154–5) and ending with the fist at Provincetown. Crowds are heaviest along Route 28, where beaches edge the warmer waters of Nantucket Sound and Buzzard's Bay. Towns along Route 6A, the old Kings Highway, retain their colonial charm, with many of the old homes now serving as antique shops and inns.

Exploring the Lower Cape

First-time visitors to Cape Cod are almost always confused when they are given directions by locals. This is because residents have divided the Cape into three districts with names that do not make much sense. The Mid- and Upper Cape is actually the southernmost portion closest to the mainland, while the Lower Cape is the northernmost section.

The Lower Cape takes in the long elbow of the peninsula that curls north-ward and forms Cape Cod Bay. The towns of Chatham, Brewster, Orleans, Eastham, Wellfleet, Truro, and Provincetown are all located in this section of Cape Cod.

Provincetown

This picturesque town at the northern tip of the Cape has a colorful history. The Pilgrims first landed here in 1620 and stayed for five weeks before pushing on to the mainland. During that time they drew up the Mayflower Compact, a fore-runner of the American Constitution. "P-Town," as it is called, later grew into a major 18th-century fishing center. By the beginning of the 20th century, P-Town had become a bustling artists' colony. Today this popular and eccentric town is one of New England's most vibrant destinations. Visitors should be warned, however, that in the summer months the

Pilgrim Monument

town's population can swell from 3,500 to more than 80,000.

The place where the Pilgrims first landed is marked by a bronze plaque on Commercial Street and commemo-rated by the tallest granite structure in the US, the 252-ft (77-m) **Pilgrim Monument**. On a clear day, the view from the top extends all the way to Boston. Eclectic displays in the adjacent museum include exhibits of Pilgrim history as well as marine and Arctic artifacts.

The **Whydah Pirate Museum** is named for a ship that sank in a storm off Cape Cod after being captured by pirates. It exhibits artifacts such as gold dubloons, weapons, clothing, and West African gold jewelry. The region's rich cultural history is celebrated in the galleries of the **Provincetown Art Association and Museum**, where works by local artists

Fishermen on their boat in Provincetown harbor

are displayed. One of the town's busiest locales is McMillan Pier, the center of nautical activity, including the jumping-off point for whale-watching cruises (see p152).

🏛 **Pilgrim Monument and Provincetown Museum**
High Pole Hill Rd. 📞 (508) 487-1310. ◯ Apr–Jun & Sep–Nov: 9am–5pm daily; Jul–Aug: 9am–7pm daily. 🌐 🚹

🏛 **Whydah Pirate Museum**
16 MacMillan Wharf. 📞 (508) 487-8899. ◯ May & Sep–Oct: 10am–5pm daily; June–Aug: 8am–9pm daily; Nov–Dec: 10am–5pm Sat–Sun. 🌐 🚹 🚻

🏛 **Provincetown Art Association and Museum**
460 Commercial St. 📞 (508) 487-1750. ◯ call for hours. 🌐 🚹

ENVIRONS: Just 17 miles (27 km) south of Provincetown lies Wellfleet, an early whal-ing center that possesses one of the Cape's largest con-centrations of art galleries.

Busy streets of Cape Cod's Provincetown in the summertime

Farther down the Cape is Eastham, home to the **Old Schoolhouse Museum**, a one-room school built in 1869. Neighboring Orleans is a commercial center with access to the very beautiful Nauset Beach and its much-photographed lighthouse.

🏛 **Old Schoolhouse Museum**
Nauset Rd, Eastham. 📞 *(508) 255-0788.* 🔵 *Jul–Aug: 1pm–4pm Mon–Fri; Sep: 1pm–4pm Sat.*

Chatham
Chatham rests on the very point of the Cape's "elbow," the place where Nantucket Sound meets the Atlantic Ocean. An attractive, upscale community, it offers fine inns, a Main Street filled with attractive shops, and a popular summer playhouse. Housed in an 1887 Victorian train station, the **Railroad Museum** contains models, photos, memorabilia, and vintage trains that can be boarded. Fishing boats unload their catch at the pier every afternoon, and the surrounding waters offer good opportunities for amateur anglers to fish for bluefish and bass.

Chatham is also the best place to plan a trip to the **Monomoy National Wildlife Refuge**. Encompassing two islands, this huge reserve attracts migrating birds and is a nesting habitat for such endangered birds as the piping plover and the roseate tern. Deer are spotted here, as are the numerous gray and harbor seals that bask on the rocks.

🏛 **Railroad Museum**
Depot Rd. 📞 *(508) 945-5199.* 🔵 *mid-Jun–mid-Sep: 10am–4pm Tue–Sat.* ♿

🐾 **Monomoy National Wildlife Refuge**
Wikis Way, Morris Island. 📞 *(508) 945-0594.* 🔵 *call for times of boat service to refuge.*

Brewster
Named for Elder William Brewster (1567–1644), who was a passenger on the *Mayflower*, Brewster is another town graced with lovely 19th-century houses of wealthy sea captains. It is also home to a particularly handsome church, the 1834 First Parish Brewster Unitarian Universalist Church. Some pews are marked with names of prominent captains.

Children will love the interactive exhibits found at the **Cape Cod Museum of Natural History**. An observation area looking out on the salt-marsh habitat of birds allows visitors close-up views of the natural world. The 82-acre (33-ha) grounds are laced with three walking trails with boardwalks that cross salt marshes. The museum also offers interesting guided "eco-treks" and cruises to nearby Nauset Marsh and Monomoy Islands.

The five-building **New England Fire and History Museum** houses a helmet collection, 30 antique fire

engines, and firefighter gear dating back to the 1700s. Elsewhere visitors can tour a blacksmith shop and a Victorian apothecary or view the diorama of the 1871 fire that devastated Chicago.

🏛 **Cape Cod Museum of Natural History**
869 Rte 6A. 📞 *(508) 896-3867.* 🔵 *May–mid-Sep: 9:30am–4:30pm Mon–Fri, 1pm–4pm Sat–Sun; mid-Sep–mid-Oct:12pm–4pm Sat–Sun.* 📷 ♿
🏛 **New England Fire and History Museum**
1439 Main St/Rte 6A. 📞 *(508) 896-5711.* 🔵 *Memorial Day–mid-Sep: 10am–4pm Mon–Fri; mid-Sep–Columbus Day: 12pm–4pm Sat–Sun.* ♿

Red and white Nauset Light on the Lower Cape

PROVINCETOWN ARTIST COLONY

Artists, writers, and poets have long been inspired by the sublime natural beauty of Provincetown. The town's first art school opened in 1901 and Hans Hofmann (1880–1966), Jackson Pollock (1912–56), Mark Rothko (1903–70), and Edward Hopper (1882–1967) are among the many prominent artists who have spent time here. Today the town is famous for its art galleries, both large and small. The roster of resident writers includes John Dos Passos (1896–1970), Tennessee Williams (1911–83), Sinclair Lewis (1885–1951), and Eugene O'Neill (1888–1953), whose earliest plays were staged at the Provincetown Playhouse.

Visitor to one of Provincetown's many art galleries

Exploring the Mid- and Upper Cape

S TRETCHING FROM BOURNE AND SANDWICH in the west to
Yarmouth and Harwich in the east, Cape Cod's Mid-
and Upper sections offer travelers a broad range of
vacation experiences. Be it sunbathing on the tranquil
beaches of Nantucket Sound by day or partaking in
the fashionable nightlife of Hyannis once the sun has
set over Cape Cod Bay, this section of the Cape has a
little something for every taste.

Hyannis boatbuilder and his remodeled Russian torpedo boat

Dennis
This gracious village has
developed into a vibrant
artistic center and is home to
the 1927 **Cape Playhouse**,
America's oldest professional
summer theater, as well as
some of the Cape's finest
public golf courses. The list
of stage luminaries who
started their career here is
impressive. Playhouse grads
include eventual Academy
Award-winners Humphrey
Bogart, Bette Davis, and
Henry Fonda. The Playhouse
complex also includes the
Cape Museum of Fine Arts,
displaying the works of Cape
Cod artists. A short drive to
the east, the Scargo Hill
Tower is open to the public
and offers brilliant views of
the surrounding landscape.

Cape Playhouse
820 Rte 6A. ☎ *(508) 385-3911.*
◯ *call for show times.*

Cape Museum of Fine Arts
60 Hope Lane. ☎ *(508) 385-4477.*
◯ *year-round: 10am–5pm Mon–Sat,
1pm–5pm Sun.* ● *Oct–May: Mon &
public hols.* 🎦 📷 ♿ ⊘

Hyannis
The Cape's largest village is
also a busy shopping center
and the transportation hub for
regional train, bus, and air
service. The harbor is full of
yachts and sightseeing boats.
Surprisingly, one of Hyannis'
most popular forms of transportation does not float. The
Cape Cod Central Railroad
takes travelers for a scenic
two-hour round-trip to the
Cape Cod canal. Hyannis

was one of the Cape's earliest
summer resorts, attracting
vacationers as far back as the
mid-1800s. In 1874 President
Ulysses S. Grant (1822–85)
vacationed here, followed by
President Grover Cleveland
(1837–1908) years later. The
most famous estate is the
Kennedy compound, summer
playground of one of
America's most famous political dynasties. The heavily
screened compound is best
seen from the water aboard a
sightseeing cruise.

After John Kennedy's assassination in 1963, a simple
monument was erected in his
honor: a pool and fountain
and a circular wall bearing
the presidential seal. The
**John F. Kennedy Hyannis
Museum** on the ground floor
of the Old Town Hall covers
the years he spent vacation-
ing here, beginning in the
1930s, and is brought to life
with photos, oral histories,
and Kennedy family videos.

Cape Cod Central Railroad
252 Main St. ☎ *(508) 771-3800
or (888) 797-7245.* ◯ *late May–
late Oct: Tue-Sun; call for trip times.*
🎦 ♿ ◯

John F. Kennedy Hyannis Museum
397 Main St. ☎ *(508) 790-3077.*
◯ *call for hours.* 🎦 ♿

Barnstable
This attractive harbor town is
the hub of Barnstable County,
a widespread region extending
to both sides of the Cape. The
Donald Treyser Museum
contains a potpourri of
exhibits, including ship models, nautical equipment, Native
American artifacts, carpentry

Popular sightseeing mode of transportation: Cape Cod Central Railroad

THE KENNEDY CLAN

The center of the Kennedy compound in Hyannis Port is the "cottage" that multi-millionaire Joseph Kennedy (1888–1969) and his wife Rose (1890–1995) bought in 1926. The much-expanded structure was a vacation retreat for the Kennedys and their nine children. John Fitzgerald Kennedy (1917–63), the country's 35th president, and his brothers and sisters continued to summer here long after they had started families of their own. When JFK's son, John Jr, died in a 1999 plane crash off Martha's Vineyard, the Kennedy clan gathered here to mourn.

John and Jacqueline Kennedy at their cottage in Hyannis Port

tools, and an old wooden jail. The bustling harbor offers whale-watching cruises, and several conservation properties make for fine hiking.

🏛 **Donald Treyser Museum**
Rte 6A, Cobb's Hill. 📞 *(508) 362-2092.* ⬤ *mid-Jun–mid-Oct: 1:30pm–4:30pm Tue–Sun.*

Falmouth
Falmouth, settled by Quakers in 1661, grew into a resort town in the late 1800s. The picturesque village green and historic Main Street reflect a Victorian heritage.

Falmouth's coastline is ideal for boating, windsurfing, and sea kayaking. As well, the town is graced with 12 miles (19 km) of beaches. Old Silver is the most popular beach, but Grand Avenue has the most dramatic views of Vineyard Sound. Nature lovers will find walking and hiking trails, salt marshes, tidal pools, and opportunities for beach-combing and bird-watching. The 3.3-mile (5 km) Shining Sea Bike Path offers vistas of beach, harbor, and woodland on the way to Woods Hole.

Woods Hole
This is home to the world's largest independent marine science research center, the Woods Hole Oceanographic Institution (WHOI).

Visitors to the **WHOI Exhibit Center** can explore two floors of displays and videos explaining coastal ecology and highlighting some of the organization's findings. Exhibits include a replica of the interior of the *Alvin*, one of the pioneer vessels developed for deep-sea exploration.

🏛 **WHOI Exhibit Center**
15 School St. 📞 *(508) 289-2252.* ⬤ *call for hours.* 💰 *donation.* 📷 *Jul–Aug by appt.* ♿

Sandwich
The oldest town on the Cape is straight off a postcard: the First Church of Christ over-looks a picturesque pond fed by the brook that powers the water-wheel of a colonial-era gristmill. The church has what is said to be the oldest church bell in the US, dating to 1675. The **Dexter Grist Mill**, built in 1654, has been restored and is grind-ing again, producing cornmeal that is avail-able at the gift shop.

Antique bottle in Glass Museum

Another industry is celebrated at the **Sandwich Glass Museum**. Between 1825 and 1888, local entrepreneurs invented a way to press glass that was prized for its colors. Nearly 5,000 pieces of Sandwich glass are handsomely displayed here.

The most unique attraction in Sandwich is **Heritage Plantation**, a 75-acre (30-ha) garden and museum built around the eclectic collection of pharmaceutical magnate

and inveterate collector Josiah Kirby Lilly, Jr (1893–1966). The artifacts fill three build-ings. The Military Museum includes military miniatures, antique firearms, and a wing devoted to Native American relics. A collection of 37 antique cars is displayed in a reproduction of a Shaker barn. The Art Museum contains everything from folk art and a collection of Currier and Ives prints to changing exhibits and a working 1912 carousel – a favorite with visitors. Outside the expansive grounds are planted with more than 1,000 varieties of trees, shrubs, and flowers, including a brilliant collection of rhododendrons.

🏭 **Dexter Grist Mill**
Maine & Water Sts. 📞 *(508) 888-1173.* ⬤ *call for hours.* 💰
🏛 **Sandwich Glass Museum**
129 Main St. 📞 *(508) 888-0251.* ⬤ *Feb–Mar: 9:30am–4:30pm Wed–Sun; Apr–Dec: 9:30am–5pm daily.* 💰 📷 ♿
🏭 **Heritage Plantation**
67 Grove St. 📞 *(508) 888-3300.* ⬤ *mid-May–mid-Oct: 10am–5pm daily.* 💰 ♿

Film star Gary Cooper's 1930 Duesenberg at Heritage Plantation

Old Sturbridge Village

A T THE HEART OF THIS OPEN-AIR MUSEUM are about 40 vintage buildings that have been restored and relocated from all over New England. Laid out like an early 19th-century village, Old Sturbridge is peopled by costumed interpreters who go about their daily activities. The village common is ringed by the meetinghouse, a tin shop, a shoe shop, and homes. Elsewhere a blacksmith works the forge, farmers tend crops, and millers work the gristmill. Inside buildings visitors will find re-created period settings, early American antiques, and demonstrations of such crafts as spinning and weaving.

VISITORS' CHECKLIST

Rte 20, Sturbridge. 📞 (508) 347-3362. ⏰ Jan–mid-Feb: 10am–4pm Sat–Sun; mid-Feb– Mar: 10am–4pm daily; Apr–Oct: 9am–5pm daily; Nov–Dec: 10am– 4pm. ● Dec 25. 🅿 ♿ some buildings. 🍴 🛒 ♿
Ⓦ www.osv.org

★ **Towne House**
This Federal-style building has a ballroom and contains period furniture and porcelains.

Bullard Tavern
Visitors can enjoy home-cooked seasonal fare in this authentic tavern setting.

Bank

Center Meetinghouse stands at the foot of the village common.

The Parsonage

0 meters   30
0 yards   30

★ **Knight Store**
Rural stores provided crucial links to the outside world by stocking imported goods.

Home-baked goods
Visitors can watch as costumed interpreters go about such daily activities as preparing food.

STAR SIGHTS

★ **Towne House**

★ **Knight Store**

Worcester ⓭

🏚 *170,000.* ✈ *Worcester Airport.*
🚉 🚌 🛈 *33 Waldo St (508) 753-2920 or (800) 231-7557.*

WORCESTER HAS always been on the cutting edge. During the American Industrial Revolution, local designers developed the nation's first mechanized carpet weavers and envelope folders. This spirit of invention reached its pinnacle in 1926, when Worcester native Dr. Robert Goddard (1882–1945) launched the world's first liquid-fuel rocket.

Not all of Worcester's forward thinking has been reserved for the development of new machines, however. Over time this city, which is built on seven hills, became home to 10 colleges and universities plus a center for biological research that in the 1950s developed the first birth-control pill.

Worcester's most unusual attraction is the **Higgins Armory Museum**, a showcase for more than 70 suits of armor and a multitude of ancient weapons. The artifacts date back to medieval and Renaissance Europe, ancient Greece and Rome, and feudal Japan, and are displayed in a hall adorned with stained glass and tapestries. Young museumgoers are allowed to actually don ancient garb from the try-on costume collection.

Housed in a handsome late 19th-century stone building, the **Worcester Art Museum** has distinguished itself as an important repository. Its impressive collection contains some 35,000 objects spanning 5,000 years, including a 12th-century chapter house that was rebuilt stone by stone on the premises. The museum's holdings of East and West Asian art and Japanese woodblock prints are balanced wonderfully by a good number of works by such Western masters as Claude Monet (1840–1926), Thomas

Higgins Armory Museum display

Gainsborough (1728–88), and Pablo Picasso (1881–1973).

Just two miles (3 km) from downtown, the **Ecotarium** promotes a better understanding of the region's environment and its wildlife. Interactive exhibits invite hands-on learning experiences. The surrounding grounds contain a wildlife center for injured and endangered animals, aquarium exhibits, and a 14-inch (35-cm) sky-watching telescope. A three-story museum, also located on the 60-acre (24-ha) grounds, houses a planetarium.

🏛 **Higgins Armory Museum**
100 Barber Ave. 📞 *(508) 853-6015.* ⏰ *year-round: 10am–4pm Tue–Sat, 12pm–4pm Sun.* 📷 ♿

🏛 **Worcester Art Museum**
55 Salisbury St. 📞 *(508) 799-4406.* ⏰ *year-round: 11am–5pm Wed–Fri & Sun, 10am–5pm Sat.* 📷 ♿

🦌 **Ecotarium**
222 Harrington Way. 📞 *(508) 929-2700.* ⏰ *year-round: 10am–5pm Mon–Sat, 12pm–4pm Sun.* 📷 ♿

ENVIRONS: North Grafton, 10 miles (16 km) southeast, has a long history of clockmaking. In the early 1800s brothers Benjamin, Simon, Ephraim, and Aaron Willard were regarded as the some of New England's best craftsmen, designing new styles for timepieces. The timepieces were given such names as Eddystone Lighthouse, Skeleton, and Act of

Parliament. Today more than 70 Willard timepieces and elegant tall clocks are on display in the family's original 18th-century homestead.

🏛 **Willard House and Clock Museum**
11 Willard St, North Grafton. 📞 *(508) 839-3500.* ⏰ *year-round: 10am–4pm Tue–Sat, 1pm–5pm Sun.* 📷 📷 *obligatory.* ♿ *partial.*

Sturbridge ⓮

STURBRIDGE'S ROOTS are literally in the land. Soon after its founding in 1729, residents planted apple orchards, some of which are still in operation. The town's main attraction is its living-history museum: Old Sturbridge Village *(see p160).*

The 1748 Parsonage in Old Sturbridge Village

ENVIRONS: Located nine miles (14 km) west, the village of Brimfield blossoms three times each year as America's flea market capital. The Brimfield Antique Show attracts hundreds of dealers, filling every field, sidewalk, and front porch in town. Treasure hunters descend to the village by the thousands to shop for wares ranging from valuable antiques to the truly kitsch.

Scraping recent layers of paint off an antique carousel horse at the Brimfield's flea market

Springfield **⑮**

🏛 *153,000.* ✈ *15 miles (24 km)
SW in Windsor Locks, CT.* 🚍 🚇
ℹ️ *1441 Main St (413) 755-1346
or (800) 723-1548.*

Now a center for banking
and insurance, Springfield
owes much of its early
success to guns. The
Springfield Armory – the
first armory in the US – was
commissioned by George
Washington (1732–99) to
manufacture arms for the
Colonial forces fighting in
the Revolutionary War.
Today the historic armory is
part of the National Parks
Service and maintains one
of the most extensive and
unique firearms collections
in the world.

In 1891 Dr. James Naismith
(1861–1939), an instructor
at the International YMCA
Training Center, now
Springfield College, invented
the game of basketball.
Basketball Hall of Fame
traces the development of the
game from its humble begin-
nings, in which peach baskets

**Emblem of the Basketball Hall
of Fame in Springfield**

were used as nets, to its evolution as one of the world's
most popular team sports.

Along with its collection
of basketball memorabilia,
the state-of-the-art museum
features interactive displays.
Children and adults can play
against former stars in virtual
reality games or test their
own shooting skills.

Court Square on Main
Street is the revitalized center
of the city, lined with 19th-
century churches, civic and
commercial buildings, and a
300-ft- (91-m-) high tower

housing carillon bells.
Nearby is **The Quadrangle**,
a collection of four museums
of art, science, and history.
The George Walter Vincent
Smith Art Museum displays a
noted collection of Oriental
decorative arts and Islamic
rugs. Galleries at the Museum
of Fine Arts contain
European and American
paintings, sculpture, and
decorative arts. Children
love the Springfield Science
Museum, with its live animal
Solutia Eco-Center, hands-on
exhibits, Phelon African Hall,
planetarium, and Dinosaur
Hall, with its life-sized
model of *Tyrannosaurus
rex*. The Connecticut Valley
Historical Museum tells
Springfield's story through
changing exhibits. The Dr.
Seuss National Memorial,
commemorating Springfield-
native Theodore Geisel
(1904–91), better known as
popular children's author Dr.
Seuss, is scheduled to open
in June 2002.

🏛 **Springfield Armory
National Historic Site**
One Armory Sq. ℹ️ *(413) 734-8551.*
◯ *year-round: 10am–4:30pm
Tue–Sun.* ● *Jan 1, Thanksgiving, &
Dec 25.* 🎦 🛗

🏛 **Basketball Hall of Fame**
1150 W Columbus Ave. ℹ️ *(413)
781-6500.* ◯ *year-round: 10am–
5pm daily.* ● *Jan 1, Thanksgiving, &
Dec 25.* 🎦 🛗

🏛 **The Quadrangle**
State & Chestnut Sts. ℹ️ *(413) 263-
6800.* **Four museums** ◯ *year-
round: 12pm–5pm Wed–Fri, 11am–
4pm Sat–Sun; Jul–Aug: 12pm–5pm
Tue.* 🎦 🛗 *partial.*

Environs: Some 11 miles
(18 km) north, the hamlet of
South Hadley is home to
Mount Holyoke College
(1837), the nation's oldest
women's college. Poet Emily
Dickinson (1830–86) was
one of Mount Holyoke's most
famous graduates. The 800-
acre (320-ha) campus encompasses two lakes and a series
of nature trails. College sites
worth a visit include the **Art
Museum** and the **Talcott
Arboretum**, located in a
Victorian-style greenhouse.

Farther north in Hadley,
the summit of 954-ft (291-m)

**Dinosaur model dwarfing visitor
in Springfield's Science Museum**

Mount Holyoke in **Skinner
State Park** offers a panorama
of the oxbow bend in the
Connecticut River. The park
is well known for massive
laurel displays in June and
flaming foliage in autumn.

🏛 **Mount Holyoke College
Art Museum**
Mount Holyoke College. ℹ️ *(413)
538-2245.* ● *for renovation; call for
new hours.* 🛗
🌿 **Talcott Arboretum**
Mount Holyoke College. ℹ️ *(413)
538-2116.* ◯ *year-round: 9am–4pm
Mon–Fri, 1pm–4pm Sat–Sun.* 🛗
🏞 **Skinner State Park**
Rte 47. ℹ️ *(413) 586-0350.* ◯
Apr–mid-Nov: 10am–7pm daily.

Amherst **⑯**

🏛 *23,000.* ✈ *41 miles (66 km) S in
Windsor Locks, CT.* 🚍 🚇 ℹ️ *409
Main St (413) 253-0700.*

This idyllic college town is
home to three different
institutes of higher learning.
The most popular with visitors
is Amherst College, with its
central green and traditional
ivy-covered buildings.
Founded in 1821 for under-
privileged youths hoping to
enter the ministry, the school
has grown into one of the
most selective small colleges
in the US. The college's excellent **Mead Art Museum**
includes the Rotherwas Room,
an ornately paneled English
hall c.1600. The varied collection of the **Pratt Museum of
Natural History** includes
dinosaur and woolly mam-
moth skeletons and assorted
mineral displays.

Poet Emily Dickinson was one of Amherst's most famous citizens. In her late 30s, Dickinson withdrew from society and spent the rest of her life in the family home, where she died in 1886. The second-floor bedroom of the **Emily Dickinson Homestead** has been restored to the way it was during the years 1855–86, when the reclusive poet wrote her most important verse. Her work remained unpublished until after her death. Over time critics proclaimed it to be the work of a poetic genius. The **Jones Library** has displays on Dickinson's life and works, as well as collections on poet Robert Frost, who taught at Amherst College in the 1940s.

⬚ Mead Art Museum
Amherst College. 📞 *(413) 542-2335.* ◯ *year-round: 10am–4:30pm Tue–Sun, 10am–9pm Thu.* ⬚ ♿

⬚ Pratt Museum of Natural History
Amherst College. 📞 *(413) 542-2165.* ◯ *mid-June–Sep: 12pm–5pm Sat–Sun; Sep–mid-Jun: 9am–3pm Mon–Fri, 10am–4pm Sat–Sun.*

⬚ Emily Dickinson Homestead
280 Main St. 📞 *(413) 542-8161.* ◯ *call for hours.* ⬚ ⬚ *obligatory.*

⬚ Jones Library
43 Amity St. 📞 *(413) 256-4090.* ◯ *year-round: 9am–5:30pm Mon–Sat, 9am–9:30pm Tue & Thu, 1pm–5pm Sun.* **Special collections** ◯ *year-round: 10am–1pm & 2pm–5pm Mon & Sat, 10am–5pm Tue–Fri.* ♿

Northampton ⓱

🏛 *30,000.* ✈ *36 miles (58 km) S in Windsor Locks, CT.* 🚉 ℹ *99 Pleasant St (413) 584-1900.*

A LIVELY CENTER for the arts and known for its fine dining, Northampton has a well preserved Victorian-style Main Street lined with craft galleries and shops. The town is also home to the 1871 **Smith College**, the largest privately endowed women's college in the nation. The handsome campus has a notable **Museum of Art** and the **Lyman Plant House and Botanic Garden**, known for its flower shows and the arboretum and gardens.

Beautiful bloom at Smith College's Lyman Plant House

South of Northampton in Holyoke, visitors can explore the trails in the 1800-acre (728-ha) **Mount Tom State Reservation**. Nearby is the Norwottuck Rail Trail, a popular walking and biking path that runs along an old railroad bed connecting Northampton to neighboring Amherst.

⬚ Smith College Museum of Art
Elm St, Northampton. 📞 *(413) 585-2760.* ● *for renovation; call for new hours.*

♣ Lyman Plant House and Botanic Garden
College Lane, Northampton. 📞 *(413) 585-2740.* ◯ *year-round: 8am–4:15pm daily.* ● *Thanksgiving & Dec 25.*

✳ Mount Tom State Reservation
125 Reservation Rd, Holyoke. 📞 *(413) 534-1186.* ◯ *year-round: 8am–dusk daily.* **Visitors center** ◯ *Memorial Day–Columbus Day: 8am–4:30pm Wed–Fri, 10am–6:30pm Sat, Sun, & public hols.* ♿ *partial.*

Deerfield ⓲

🏛 *5,300.* ✈ *52 miles (84 km) S in Windsor Locks, CT.* ℹ *18 Miner St, Greenfield (413) 773-9393.*

A ONE-TIME FRONTIER outpost that was almost annihilated by Indian raids in the late 1600s, Deerfield survived and its farmers prospered, building gracious clapboard homes along the mile-long (1.6-km) center avenue known simply as "The Street."

Sixty of these remain within **Old Deerfield National Landmark** and are carefully preserved. Some of the buildings now serve as museums, exhibiting a broad range of period furniture and decorative arts, including silverware, ceramics, and textiles. The Flynt Center of Early New England Life schedules changing exhibitions on early life in western Massachusetts. Visitors seeking a photo opportunity can drive to the summit of **Mount Sugarloaf State Reservation** in South Deerfield for views of the Connecticut River Valley.

⬚ Old Deerfield National Landmark
The Street, Old Deerfield. 📞 *(413) 774-5581.* ◯ *year-round: 9:30am–4:30pm daily.* ● *Thanksgiving, Dec 24 & 25.* ⬚

✳ Mount Sugarloaf State Reservation
US 116, South Deerfield. 📞 *(413) 665-2928.* ◯ *May–Dec: 8am–dusk daily.*

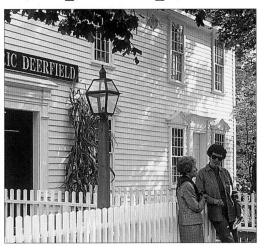
White clapboard house and picket fence in historic Deerfield

Tour of the Mohawk Trail ⑲

ORIGINALLY AN INDIAN WAR PATH, this trail was a popular
artery for early pioneers. In 1914 the trail, which
stretches for 63 miles (100 km) from Orange to North
Adams along Route 2, became a paved road. The choicest
section of the route, from Greenfield to North Adams, was
the first officially designated scenic drive in New England.
This twisting road offers magnificent mountain views, particularly in the sharp hairpin curves leading into North
Adams, and is one of the most popular fall foliage routes.

Charlemont ②
The town is dominated
by the massive statue
Hail to the Sunrise.

Hairpin Turn ③
This sharp bend in
the road offers
soaring views of
Mount Greylock.

*Mount
Greylock*

Hoosic River

KEY

▨ Tour route

≈ Other road

٭ Viewpoint

North Adams ④
Quaint North Adams is near
America's only naturally
formed marble bridge.

Williamstown ⑳

🏠 *8,000.* ✈ *47 miles (75 km) W in
Albany, NY.* 🚌 ℹ *Jct Rtes 2 & 7 (413)
458-9077 or (800) 214-3799.*

ART LOVERS MAKE pilgrim-
ages to Williamstown for
**The Sterling and Francine
Clark Art Institute** to see its
private collection, which features Old Masters and French
Impressionists, including
more than 30 Renoirs. The
**Williams College Museum
of Art** is also notable, with
holdings of everything from
ancient Assyrian stone reliefs
to the last self-portrait by Andy
Warhol (1927– 87). A four-story
skylight now complements the
original 1846 octagonal
structure. Fine art is
not the only show in
town, however.
In summer fans
flock to the
Williamstown
Theater Festival.
Founded in 1954,
the festival is
known for its
high quality
productions
and for
attracting

A 19th-century Steinway at The Sterling and Francine Clark Art Institute

big-name Broadway and
Hollywood stars.

🏛 **The Sterling and
Francine Clark Art Institute**
225 South St. 🚻 *(413) 458-2303.*
◻ *Jul–Aug: 10am–5pm daily; rest of
year: 10am–5pm Tue–Sun.* ▨ 🔧 ♿
🏛 **Williams College
Museum of Art**
Main St. 🚻 *(413) 597-2429.*
◻ *year-round: 10am–5pm Tue–Sat,
1pm–5pm Sun.* ♿

ENVIRONS: More art can be
found 7 miles (11 km) east
in North Adams at the new
**Massachusetts Museum of
Contemporary Art** (MASS

**Degas statue at
Clark Institute**

MoCA). Seven intercon-
nected buildings, part of a
19th-century factory, with
enormous indoor spaces,
elevated walkways, and
outdoor courtyards display
cutting-edge art. The complex is able to house sculptures and paintings that
are too large for most con-
ventional museums.

🏛 **Massachusetts
Museum of
Contemporary Art**
87 Marshall St. 🚻 *(413) 664-4481.*
◻ *Apr–Oct: 10am–6pm daily;
Nov–May: 11am–5pm Wed–Mon.*
▨ ♿ 🅿

Shelburne Falls ①
This small, 19th-century village, with its many original houses, is divided by the Deerfield River. The river is spanned by an old trolley bridge.

TIPS FOR DRIVERS

Tour length: 59 miles (95 km).
Starting point: Rte 2A in Orange.
Stopping-off points: This is a popular route, with no shortage of places to eat. A good start is breakfast at the Deerfield Inn (see p334) just south of Greenfield. At the end of the trip, travelers can head to The Orchards (see p336) in Williamstown, west of North Adams, for lunch.

Connecticut River

② *Charlemont*

Erving

Orange

Deerfield River ①

Deerfield River

Greenfield

0 kilometers 5

0 miles   5

Mount Greylock State Reservation ㉑

Off Rte 7, Lanesborough.
ℹ️ *(413) 499-4263.*

Aroad leads drivers to the top of Mount Greylock, the highest peak in the state at 3,491 ft (1,064 m). Once at the top, visitors can climb the 92-ft (28-m) Summit Veteran's Memorial Tower, commemorating the state's war dead, for a panoramic view of five states. Also at the summit is Bascom Lodge, a 1930s stone and timber structure offering maps, guides, and rustic lodging. The Appalachian Trail *(see pp22–3),* the popular 2,000-mile (3,200-km) hiking path running from Georgia to Maine, crosses Mount Greylock's summit.

Authentic Shaker door latch at Hancock Shaker Village

Summit Veteran's Memorial Tower atop Mount Greylock

Hancock Shaker Village ㉒

Rte 20, outside Pittsfield. 📞 *(413) 443-0188.* ⭕ *late May–late Oct: 9:30am–5pm daily; late Oct–late May: 10am–3pm daily.* ⬤ *Jan 1, Thanksgiving, & Dec 25.* ♿ 🍴

Founded in 1783, this was the third in a series of 19 Shaker settlements established in the Northeast and Midwest as utopian communities. The Shakers, so-called because they often trembled and

shook during moments of worship and prayer, believed in celibacy and equality of the sexes, with men and women living separately but sharing authority and responsibilities. At its peak in the 1830s, there were 300 residents living in the village. Now the community has no resident Shakers.

Twenty of the 100 original buildings have been restored, including the tri-level round stone barn, cleverly designed so that as many as 52 head of cattle could be fed by a single farmhand from a central core. The Brick Dwelling can house up to 100 people, and has a meeting room used for week-day worship and a communal dining room, where traditional Shaker fare is served on select Saturday evenings.

Presentations on the Shaker way of life are offered, including demonstrations of chair-, broom-, and oval box-making. In the Discovery Room visitors may try on reproduction Shaker clothing and also try their hand at crafts such as weaving. An orientation exhibit and videos in several buildings provide historical background.

Picturesque Bish Bash Falls in Mount Washington State Forest

The Berkshires ㉓

⛰ *37 miles (60 km) NE in Albany, NY.* 🚉 *Pittsfield.* 🛈 *Berkshire Common, Plaza Level, Pittsfield (413) 443-9186 or (800) 237-5747.*

VISITORS HAVE LONG been attracted to the peaceful wooded hills, green valleys, rippling rivers, and waterfalls of this western corner of Massachusetts. Among the first tourists were writers such as Henry Wadsworth Longfellow (1807–82), Herman Melville (1819–91), and Nathaniel Hawthorne (1804–64). When the three wrote about the natural beauty of the area, the location caught the attention of many of the region's wealthy people, who began to spend their summers here. Now the region is a year-round playground, popular for its culture as well as for the ample opportunities it provides for outdoor recreation.

The area is speckled with small towns and country villages. Great Barrington to the south and Pittsfield to the north are the commercial centers of the region, while Lenox and Stockbridge are cultural meccas. The old cotton and woolen mills in Housatonic are finding new life as art galleries, and Main Street of Sheffield is lined with interesting little antique shops.

Among the most popular walking and hiking trails in the Berkshires are Bartholemew's Cobble in Sheffield and Bish Bash Falls in the **Mount Washington State Forest**. A trail leads to the summit of Monument Mountain and affords beautiful views. Reputedly, it was on a hike up the mountain that Herman Melville first met Nathaniel Hawthorne, forming a friendship that resulted in Melville's dedicating his novel *Moby-Dick* to his fellow author.

🏞 Mount Washington State Forest
Rte 41 S. 📞 *(413) 528-0330.* ◯ *Memorial Day–Columbus Day.* 🅿

Pittsfield
Although primarily a commercial hub, Pittsfield is central to several interesting sites, most notably Hancock Shaker Village *(see p165).* The town's literary shrine is **Arrowhead**, an 18th-century home in the shadow of Mount Greylock,

Life-sized model of Stegosaurus at Berkshire Museum in Pittsfield

where Herman Melville lived from 1850 to 1863 and where he wrote his masterpiece *Moby-Dick.* Some say the mountain's shape resembles the great white whale in Melville's classic tale.

The **Berkshire Museum** has a large collection of items covering a variety of disciplines, including history, natural science, and fine art. The museum's aquarium is stocked with more than 100 fish and sea creatures. The galleries are notable for their works by such 19th-century American masters as George Inness (1825–94) and Frederic Church (1826–1900).

🏛 Arrowhead
780 Holmes Rd. 📞 *(413) 442-1793.* ◯ *May–Oct: 9:30am–5pm daily; rest of year by appt.* 🅿 🎫 ♿ *first floor only.* 🏠 ∅

🏛 Berkshire Museum
39 South St. 📞 *(413) 443-7171.* ◯ *year-round: 10am–5pm Tue–Sat, 12pm–5pm Sun; Jul–Aug: 10am–5pm Mon.* 🅿 ♿ 🏠 ∅

Lenox
In the late 1800s the gracious village of Lenox became known as the "inland Newport" for the lavish summer "cottages" built by prominent families such as the Carnegies and the Vanderbilts. Before the 1929 Great Depression, there were more than 70 grand estates gracing the area. While some of the millionaires have since moved away, many of their lavish homes remain in service as schools, cultural institutions, resorts, and posh inns. One of the

Gathering hay by oxcart at Hancock Shaker Village

Typical townhouse in the village of Lenox

more prominent mansions is **The Mount**, built in 1902 by Pulitzer Prize-winning author Edith Wharton (1862–1937).

Lenox gained new status as a center of culture in 1937 when the 500-acre (202-ha) Tanglewood estate became the summer home of the Boston Symphony Orchestra. Music lovers flock for concerts to the 1,200-seat Seiji Ozawa Hall or the open

Figures of *Andromeda* and *Memory* at Chesterwood

Music Shed, where many enjoy picnicking and listening to the music on the surrounding lawn. Jazz and popular concerts are interspersed with the classical program. Tanglewood's name is credited to Nathaniel Hawthorne, who lived in a house on the estate at one time and wrote some of his short stories here.

The Mount
2 Plunkett St. ☎ *(413) 637-1899.* ⬤ *Memorial Day–Oct: 9am–3pm daily.* 🖼 ✔ ⛔ 🚻 🚫

Stockbridge
Stockbridge was founded in 1734 by missionaries seeking to educate and convert the local Mohegan Indians. The

simple **Mission House** (c.1739) was built by Reverend John Sergeant for his bride. Today the house contains period pieces and Indian artifacts.

The town's quaint main street, dominated by the 1897 Red Lion Inn, has been immortalized in the popular paintings of Norman Rockwell (1894–1978), one of America's most beloved illustrators. The painter lived in Stockbridge for 25 years, and the country's largest collection of Rockwell originals can be seen at the **Norman Rockwell Museum**.

Stockbridge has been home to its share of prominent residents, including sculptor Daniel Chester French (1850–1931), who summered at his **Chesterwood** estate. It was here that French created the working models for his famous *Seated Lincoln* (1922) for the Lincoln Memorial in Washington, DC. The models remain in the studio along with other plaster casts. During the summer months the grounds are used to exhibit sculpture.

Naumkeag Museum and Gardens is a graceful 1885 mansion built for Joseph H. Choate, US ambassador to Britain and one of the era's leading attorneys. The 26-room house is appointed with its original furnishings and an art collection that spans three centuries. Of note is the exhibit of Chinese porcelains. The grounds are a work of art also, with manicured paths leading visitors through formal gardens.

🚻 Mission House
19 Main St. ☎ *(413) 298-3239.* ⬤ *Memorial Day–Labor Day: 10am–5pm daily.* 🖼 🚫

🏛 Norman Rockwell Museum
9 Glendale Rd. ☎ *(413) 298-4100 ext. 220.* ⬤ *May–Oct: 10am–5pm daily; Nov–Apr: 10am–4pm Mon–Fri, 10 am–5pm Sat–Sun.* 🖼 ✔ ⛔ 🚫

🚻 Chesterwood
4 Williamsville Rd. ☎ *(413) 298-3579.* ⬤ *May–Oct: 10am–5pm daily.* 🖼 ✔ ⛔ *partial.* 🚫

🏛 Naumkeag Museum and Gardens
Prospect Hill. ☎ *(413) 298-3239.* ⬤ *Memorial Day–Labor Day: 10am–5pm daily.* 🖼 🚫

THE ARTS IN THE BERKSHIRES

The Berkshires region has one of America's richest summer menus of performing arts. As well as Boston Symphony Orchestra concerts at Tanglewood, Aston Magna presents baroque concerts at St. James Church in Great Barrington, the Berkshire Opera performs at the Koussevitzky Arts Center in Pittsfield, and the Berkshire Choral Festival is held in Sheffield. The Jacob's Pillow Dance Festival in Becket, the oldest such event in the nation, presents leading international companies. Shakespeare & Company, the Berkshire Theater Festival, and the Williamstown Theater Festival are among the oldest and most respected summer theaters in the nation.

Relaxed setting for the Tanglewood summer concert series

RHODE ISLAND

···

W ITH AN AREA OF JUST OVER *1,200 sq miles (3,100 sq km)*, *Rhode Island is the smallest of the 50 states. However, its historic towns, unspoiled wilderness areas, and a pristine shoreline dotted with inlets and tranquil harbors make the place a lively and easily explored holiday destination.*

For such a small state, "Little Rhody" was founded on big ideals. Driven from the Massachusetts Bay colony in 1636 for his outspoken beliefs on religious freedom, clergyman Roger Williams (1604–83) established a settlement on the banks of Narragansett Bay. He called the town Providence and founded it upon the tenets of freedom of speech and religious tolerance – principles that would be formally introduced in the First Amendment to the US Constitution in 1781. This forward-thinking spirit made Rhode Island the site of America's first synagogue and Baptist church and some of the nation's earliest libraries, public schools, and colleges. In May 1776 Rhode Island followed the lead of New Hampshire and formally declared its independence from British rule.

Although its 400-mile (645-km) shoreline is considered small in comparison to those of neighboring states, Rhode Island has earned its nickname, the Ocean State. In the 17th century, its port towns were primary players in the burgeoning maritime trade with the West Indies. Today some 120 public beaches provide opportunities for swimming, scuba diving, boating, windsurfing, and fishing. Pleasure craft can be seen skimming the waters of Narragansett Bay. Home to the America's Cup yacht races between 1930–85, Newport is well known as one of the world's great yachting centers. But not all of Rhode Island's allure is found on the waterfront. More than 50 percent of the state is covered in woodland. The 11 state parks are ideal for nature walks; three of them allow camping.

Fishing at dusk on beautiful Narragansett Bay

◁ **Linden Place, Bristol, Rhode Island**

Exploring Rhode Island

NOT AN ISLAND AT ALL, the state of Rhode Island does, however, contain dozens of islets and peninsulas along the Atlantic coastline. They dot Narragansett Bay, which takes a huge bite out of the eastern portion of the state. Craggy cliffs, grass-covered bluffs, and golden sand beaches mark the shoreline of the Ocean State, which offers an abundance of opportunities for fishing, swimming, boating, surfing, and other aquatic activities. Inland numerous lakes, reservoirs, and swamps (in South County) maintain the maritime atmosphere. Most activity in Rhode Island centers around its two major cities, Providence *(see pp174–7)* and Newport *(see pp182–7)*, but the smaller roads across the western part of the state are perfect for tranquil country drives.

Vacationers in front of the visitor's pavilion at Point Judith

KEY

▢	Interstate
▢	Major road
▭	Minor road
▢	Scenic route
☼	Viewpoint

0 kilometers   8

0 miles   8

SIGHTS AT A GLANCE

Bristol ❹	Newport pp182–7 ❾	Watch Hill ⓱
Charlestown ⓰	Pawtucket ❸	Wickford ⓫
Great Road ❷	Portsmouth ❻	Woonsocket ❶
Jamestown ❿	Providence pp174–7 ❺	
Little Compton ❼	Saunderstown ⓬	**Tour**
Middletown ❽	South County	Block Island pp192–3 ⓲
Narragansett ⓮	Beaches ⓯	
	South Kingstown ⓭	

SLATERSVILLE
102
Putnam 44 *CHEPACHET*
WEST GLOCESTER 44
HARMONY
Ponaganset Reservoir
S. FOSTER
6 6
Norwich
CLAYVILLE
Scituate Reservoir
Flat River Reservoir
102
95
165 102
3 *EXETEI*
2
138
New London, Connecticut
2 *Great Swamp*
Worden Pond
78 *Watchaug Pond*
WESTERLY *SOUTH COUNTY BEACHES*
CHARLESTOWN ⓰ ⓯
1
1A *Ninigret Pond*
⓱
● *WATCH HILL*

BLOCK ISLAND ⓲

Central Providence, notable for its blend of the historic and modern

GETTING AROUND

Highway 146 follows the Blackstone River Valley south to Providence where it connects with Interstate 95, forming the major north-south artery in the state. For scenery, travelers should stay on Route 1 as it hugs Narragansett Bay and Block Island Sound. An alternative route is 114, which island-hops down the eastern region of the state through Bristol *(see pp172–3)* to Newport.

Amtrak operates rail lines running from Boston through Providence and down as far as Kingston.

Rhode Island Public Transit Authority (RIPTA) provides bus services throughout most of the state, with hourly service between Providence and Newport and a summer service to several South County beaches *(see pp190–91)*.

Year-round ferry services operated by RIPTA are offered from Providence to Newport. Ferries to Block Island also run year-round and depart from Point Judith *(see pp190–91)*.

SEE ALSO

• *Where to Stay* pp313–15

• *Where to Eat* pp336–9

Yachts by the score in the harbor at Newport

Classroom display at the Museum of Work and Culture, Woonsocket

Woonsocket ❶

🏠 44,000. ℹ️ 42 S Main St (401) 769-9675.

A MAJOR MANUFACTURING center located on the busy Blackstone River, Woonsocket was transformed from a relatively small village to a booming mill town by the development of the local textile industry in the 19th and early 20th centuries. Although the textile industry declined after World War II, the city remains one of the major manufacturing hubs.

The **Museum of Work and Culture** focuses on the impact of the Industrial Revolution on the region. The day-to-day lives of the factory owners, managers, and immigrant workers are examined and explained with the help of a re-created 1934 union hall, hands-on displays, models, and multimedia exhibits.

🏛 **Museum of Work and Culture**
42 S Main St. 【 (401) 769-9675. 🔵 9:30am–4pm Mon–Fri, 10am–5pm Sat, 1pm–5pm Sun. 🎫 ♿

The Great Road ❷

ℹ️ (401) 762-0250.

AN OFTEN overlooked gem, the stretch of Great Road (Route 123) between Saylesville and Lime Rock follows the course of the Mosshassuck River for 0.6

Eleazer Arnold House near Lincoln on the Great Road

mile (1 km) and yields eight historically significant buildings. Four of these buildings are open by appointment and include the 1680 **Eleazer Arnold House** and the 1704 **Friends Meetinghouse**, New England's oldest Quaker meeting house in continuous

use. Constructed in 1807 as a toll station and later serving as a hotel, **North Gate,** just off the Great Road, now contains a small museum room decked out with early 18th-century furniture. Farther along the road, **Hannaway Blacksmith Shop** is a one-story, 19th-century structure recently restored for blacksmith demonstrations and special events.

🏛 **Eleazer Arnold House**
487 Great Rd. 【 (617) 227-3956. 🔵 1pm–5pm Sun. 🎫 obligatory; call for appt.
🏛 **Friends Meetinghouse**
374 Great Rd. 【 (401) 723-2515. 🎫 obligatory; call for appt.
🏛 **North Gate**
Rte 246. 【 (401) 725-2847. 🎫 obligatory; call for appt.
🏛 **Hannaway Blacksmith Shop**
671 Great Rd. 【 (401) 333-1100 ext 249. 🎫 obligatory; call for appt.

Pawtucket ❸

🏠 73,000. ℹ️ 175 Main St (401) 724-2200.

THIS BUSTLING INDUSTRIAL CITY, built on hills sliced by the Blackstone, Moshassuck, and Ten Mile rivers is generally acknowledged to be the birthplace of America's Industrial Revolution. It was here in 1793 that mechanical engineer Samuel Slater (1768–1835) built the country's first water-powered cotton-spinning mill.

A major historic landmark, the **Slater Mill Historic Site** includes the restored Slater Mill and the 1810 Wilkinson Mill, complete with an authentic 19th-century machine shop and the only 8-ton (7-tonne) waterwheel in the US.

Pawtucket's Slater Mill Historic Site, home of the first water-powered cotton-spinning mill in the US

McCoy Stadium, playing field of the Pawtucket Red Sox baseball team

Also on the site, the 1758 Sylvanus Brown House is furnished with the machinery and personal effects of Sylvanus Brown, a millwright and pattern-maker.

At the 200-acre (81-ha) **Slater Memorial Park** on the Ten Mile River, there are hiking trails, paddleboats, tennis courts, picnic areas, sunken gardens, and a functional 1894 Looff carousel. The park is also home to the city's oldest dwelling, the 1685 **Daggett House**, which contains exhibits of 17th-century furnishings and antiques.

The **Pawtucket Red Sox** baseball team plays games at McCoy Stadium. This minor league team has players who, once they have honed their skills, may move on to play in baseball's major league for the Boston Red Sox – one of the game's most storied teams.

Pawtucket Red Sox logo

🏟 **Slater Mill Historic Site**
Roosevelt & Slater Aves. ☎ *(401) 725-8638.* ○ *call for hours.* ● *Jan 1, Thanksgiving, & Dec 25.* 🖼 🗎 ♿
🍃 **Slater Memorial Park**
Newport Ave. ☎ *(401) 728-0500 ext 252.* ○ *year-round: 8:30am–9pm daily.* ♿
🏟 **Daggett House**
Slater Park off Rte 1A. ☎ *(401) 724-5748.* 🗎 *obligatory; call for appt.* 🖼
Pawtucket Red Sox
McCoy Stadium, Columbus Ave.
☎ *(401) 724-7300.* ○ *Apr–early Sep; call for schedule.* 🖼 ♿

Bristol ❹

🏛 *21, 650.* ℹ *Thames St (401) 245-0750.*

BRISTOL BLOSSOMED in the late 18th century when its status as a major commercial, fishing, whaling, and ship-building center made it the nation's fourth-busiest port.

The many elegant Federal and Victorian mansions lining Hope, High, and Thames streets attest to those prosperous days. One such fine home is the 1810 **Linden Place**, where scenes from *The Great Gatsby* (1974) were filmed. The Federal-style mansion was built by General George DeWolf (1772–1844) with money he had made from his sugar plantations in Cuba and the slave trade. Regular concerts and tours are offered.

The tasteful trappings of wealth are also in evidence at **Blithewold Mansion and Gardens**. Built in 1907 for Pennsylvania coal baron Augustus Van Wickle (1856–98), the mansion has many flower gardens, a rock garden, and trees from the Far East. The grounds offer spectacular views of Narragansett Bay (*see pp177–8*).

Boating has always been popular with the rich and famous, and Bristol's history as the producer of America's greatest yachts is traced at the **Herreshoff Marine Museum/America's Cup Hall of Fame**.

Photos, models, and a variety of restored ships are displayed in the large warehouse.

A branch of Brown University (*see pp174–5*), the **Haffenreffer Museum of Anthropology** has exhibits of artifacts from indigenous peoples around the world. The museum's North American Indian collection is of particular interest to visitors.

Colt State Park, a 460-acre (186-ha) shoreline park features a three-mile (5-km) shoreline drive along Narragansett Bay, a bicycle trail, many picnic areas, and playing fields. Also on the park grounds is the **Coggeshall Farm Museum**, a replica of a 1790s coastal farm with barn, weaver shed, blacksmith shop, and domesticated animals. Cyclists and inline skaters can tour the picturesque East Bay Bike Path, leading some 14.5 miles (23 km) from Bristol to Providence along the coast-hugging route of an old railroad line.

Art from the Haffenreffer

🏟 **Linden Place**
500 Hope St. ☎ *(401) 253-0390.* ○ *May–Columbus Day: 10am–4pm Thu–Sat, 12pm–4pm Sun.* 🖼 🗎 ♿
🏟 **Blithewold Mansion**
101 Ferry Rd. ☎ *(401) 253-2707.* **Mansion** ○ *April–Oct: 11am–3:30pm Wed–Sun; Nov–Dec: 12pm–8pm Wed–Sun.* ● *public hols.* **Grounds** ○ *10am–5pm daily.* 🖼 ♿
🏛 **Herreshoff Marine Museum/America's Cup Hall of Fame**
1 Burnside St. ☎ *(401) 253-5001.* ○ *May–Oct: 10am–5pm daily.* 🖼 🗎 ♿
🏛 **Haffenreffer Museum of Anthropology**
300 Tower St. ☎ *(401) 253-8388.* ○ *Jun–Aug: 11am–5pm Tue–Sun; Sep–May: 11am–5pm Sat & Sun.* 🖼
🍃 **Colt State Park**
Rte 114. ☎ *(401) 253-7482.* ○ *daily.* ♿
🏛 **Coggeshall Farm Museum**
Poppasquash Rd off Rte 114.
☎ *(401) 253-9062.* ○ *Mar–Sep: 10am–6pm daily; Oct–Feb: 10am–5pm daily.* 🖼 ♿

Providence ●

First Unitarian Church bell

SANDWICHED BETWEEN Boston and New York on busy I-95, Providence is often overlooked by hurried travelers. This is a pity, since the city is blessed with a rich history well worth exploring. Perched on seven hills, Providence started life as a farming community before taking advantage of its location on the Seekonk River to develop into a flourishing seaport in the 17th century. The city then evolved into a hub of industry in the 19th century, with immigrants from Europe pouring in to work in the burgeoning textile mills.

Interior courtyard at Rhode Island School of Design's Museum of Art

🏛 **RISD Museum of Art**
224 Benefit St. ((401) 454-6500.
🔘 year-round: 10am–5pm Tue–Sun,
10am–8pm Fri. ● public hols. 🎦 🔇
🏛 **Providence Athenaeum**
251 Benefit St. ((401) 421-6970.
🔘 year-round: 10am–6pm Mon–Thu,
10am–5pm Fri–Sat, 1pm–5pm Sun.
● weekends during summer.
🚪 **First Unitarian Church**
310 Benefit St. ((401) 421-7970.
🔘 daily. 🔇

🚪 **First Baptist Church in America**
75 N Main St. ((401) 454-3418.
🔘 year-round: call for hours.
🎦 call for times. 🔇

Stately buildings along Benefit Street's Mile of History

Exploring Providence

Providence is bisected by the Providence River, with the Downtown district *(see pp176–7)* on the west bank and College Hill to the east. Walking through College Hill, visitors will pass a large number of 18th-century buildings, including the redbrick colonial Market House, built along the waterway in the 1770s and now part of Rhode Island School of Design (RISD).

🚪 Benefit Street's Mile of History
Benefit St. ((401) 274-1636.
Along Benefit Street's Mile of History there are more than 100 houses ranging in style from Colonial and Federal to Greek Revival and Victorian. This lovely, tree-lined street passes RISD's **Museum of Art**, which houses a small but comprehensive collection of artworks from Ancient Egyptian to contemporary American. Also on Benefit Street is the 1838 Greek

Revival **Providence Athenaeum**. This is where author Edgar Allen Poe (1809–49) courted Sarah Whitman, the woman who was the inspiration for his poem *Annabel Lee* (1849). The library, one of the oldest in America, has a collection dating back to 1753. Other architectural gems include the **First Unitarian Church**, which possesses a 2,500-lb (1,350-kg) bell, the largest ever cast by silversmith and Revolutionary War hero Paul Revere *(see p120)*.

KEY

═	Interstate
═	Highway
🚉	Train station
━	Railroad
ℹ	Tourist information
🅿	Parking

To Federal Hill →

Founded in 1638 by Roger Williams and built in 1774–5, the First Baptist Church in America is noted for its Ionic columns, intricately carved wood interior, and large Waterford crystal chandelier.

🏛 Governor Stephen Hopkins House

15 Hopkins St. **[**401) 331-2134. ◯ Apr–Dec: 1pm–4pm Wed & Sat. 🎟 obligatory.

The 1707 **Governor Stephen Hopkins House** belonged to one of Rhode Island's two signatories to the Declaration of Independence, and contains fine 18th-century furnishings.

🏛 Brown University

45 Prospect St. **[**401) 863-1000. ◯ call for hours. 🎟 ♿ 🏠 🛍 🅿

Founded in 1764, Brown is the seventh-oldest college in the US and one of the prestigious Ivy League schools *(see pp28–9)*. The campus, a rich

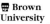

Statue on Brown University campus

blend of Gothic and Beaux Arts styles, is a National Historic Landmark. The John Hay Library has an eclectic collection that includes artifacts and memorabilia relating to President Abraham Lincoln (1809–65), 5,000 toy soldiers and miniatures, and vintage sheet music. Other buildings of note include University Hall, where French and colonial troops were quartered during the American Revolution; Manning Hall, which houses the University Chapel; the John Carter Brown Library, with its fascinating collection of Americana; and the List Art Center, a striking building designed by Philip Johnson (b.1906) and featuring classical and contemporary art.

🏛 John Brown House

52 Power St. **[**401) 331-8575. ◯ Jan–Feb: 10am–5pm Fri & Sat, 12pm–4pm Sun; Mar–Dec: 10am–5pm Tue–Sat, 12pm–4pm Sun. ⬤ Mon & public hols. 🎟 🎟 🛍

This three-story Georgian mansion was built in 1786 for John Brown (1736–1803) by his brother Joseph (1733–85). A successful merchant

VISITORS' CHECKLIST

🏙 160,000. ✈ TF Green State Airport, Warwick, 12 miles (19 km) S. 🚉 Providence Station, 100 Gaspee St. 🚌 1 Bonanza Way. ⚓ Point St (to Newport). 🛈 1 W Exchange St (401) 274-1636 or (800) 233-1636. 🎭 Festival of Historic Houses (Jun–Dec); International Film Festival (Aug). 🌐 www.providencecvb.com

and shipowner, John played a lead role in the burning of the British customs ship *Gaspee* in a pre-Revolutionary War raid in 1772. The John Brown House was the most lavish of its era, introducing Providence to many new architectural elements, including the projecting entrance, Doric portico, and the Palladian window above it. There are Neoclassical pediments over paired doorways, a grand staircase with twisted balusters, ornate plaster ornamented ceilings, and intricate detailing inside arches over windows and mantels.

Sparing no expense, Brown ordered wallpapers from France and furniture from famed cabinetmakers Townsend and Goddard. The 12-room house has been impeccably restored and is a repository for some of the finest furniture and antiques of that period.

The 1786 John Brown House, an excellent example of Georgian architecture

PROVIDENCE CITY CENTER

To Roger Williams Park and Zoo

0 meters 250

0 yards 250

Downtown Providence

DOWNTOWN PROVIDENCE, to the west of the Providence River, has undergone several recent renewal phases. In all, $1 billion has been pumped into the rejuvenation project since 1983. Keeping a balance with the old and the new, Providence municipal officials have managed to clean out previously blighted areas by restoring historic buildings, installing more green spaces, and building pedestrian malls and markets. The reclaimed waterfront and developing arts and entertainment district have helped inject new vitality into the city's core. Visitors are best served by exploring on foot so they are free to poke into the numerous shops, cafés, and restaurants.

Exploring Downtown Providence

Providence's rebirth is more than just physical; it is also cultural. The Trinity Repertory Company on Washington Street is home to one of the best theater groups in the country and has performances year-round. Just a block away, the Providence Performing Arts Center, a 1928 movie palace, features Broadway shows, concerts, entertainment for children, and big-screen films, with free organ recitals in the fall.

The Trinity Repertory Company, housed in a 1917 historic theater

♣ Waterplace Park and Riverwalk

Memorial Blvd. *(401) 751-1177.*
◯ *9am–4:30pm daily.* ● *Jan 1, Thanksgiving, & Dec 25.*
One of the newest and brightest additions to the downtown area is this 4-acre (1.6-ha) walkway at the junction of the Moshassock, Providence, and Woonasquatucket rivers. Visitors can stroll the park's cobblestone paths, float under footbridges in rented kayaks,

canoes, or gondolas, or enjoy the free concerts at the amphitheater during the summer months.

🏛 The Arcade

65 Weybosset St. *(401) 598-1199.*
◯ *Jun–Aug: 10am–6pm Mon–Fri, 10am–4pm Sat; Sep–May: 10am–5pm Mon–Fri, 11am–4pm Sat.* ● *Sun & public hols.* ⟨symbols⟩
Known as the "Temple of Trade," this 1828 Greek Revival building has the distinction of being the first indoor shopping mall in the US. The massive, three-story stone complex covers an entire block in Providence's old financial district and has been acclaimed as "one of the three finest commercial buildings in 19th-century America" by New York's Metropolitan Museum of Art. Similar columns on the Westminster entrance match the six 22-ft- (6.7-m-) high Ionic granite columns on Weybosset. Inside a skylight extends the entire length of the building, providing light even on rainy days. Restored in 1980, this lively marketplace contains specialty shops, clothing boutiques, and restaurants.

🚩 Federal Hill

Visitors will know they are in Little Italy once they pass through Federal Street's impressive arched gateway, decorated with a traditional bronze pine nut. A stripe down the center of the street – in the colors of the Italian flag – confirms that this lively neighborhood in the Federal Hill district is truly Italian in spirit. Bordered by Federal and Broadway streets and

Atwells Avenue, the area is marked by Italian groceries, restaurants, bakeries, import shops, and a pleasant old-world plaza.

The 1828 three-story Arcade, lined with boutiques and restaurants

🚩 Rhode Island State House

82 Smith St. *(401) 222-2357.*
◯ *8:30am–4:30pm Mon–Fri.* ● *public hols.* ⟨symbol⟩ *self-guided, others by appt.* ⟨symbols⟩
Dominating the city landscape, this imposing building was constructed in 1904 by the prominent New York firm McKim, Mead, & White. The white Georgian marble dome is one of the largest self-supported domes in the world. A bronze statue called *Independent Man*, a longtime symbol of Rhode Island's free spirit, tops the magnificent dome. Among the displays in the statehouse are a full-length portrait of President George Washington (1732–99) by Gilbert Stuart (1755–1828),

Rhode Island State House, with its white marble dome

ROGER WILLIAMS (1603–1683)

More than an exponent of religious freedom, Roger Williams was also a friend and champion of the area's indigenous inhabitants. He defied the strict restraints of the Massachusetts Bay Colony, believing that all people should be free to worship as they liked without state interference. Banished from Massachusetts for his outspoken views, he established his own colony of Rhode Island and Providence Plantations, obtaining the land from the Narragansett Indians so that "no man should be molested for his conscience sake." It became the country's first experiment in religious liberty.

a portrait of Providence resident and Civil War General Ambrose Burnside (1824–81) by Emanuel Leutze (1816–68), and the original state charter of 1663.

🐾 Roger Williams Park and Zoo

1000 Elmwood Ave. 📞 *(401) 785-3510.* 🚌 *Kennedy Plaza.* **Park** ◯ *7am–9pm daily.* **Zoo** ◯ *May–Oct: 9am–5pm Mon–Fri, 9am–6pm Sat–Sun; Nov–Apr: 9am–4pm daily.* ● *Dec 25.* 🔖 *zoo.* ✔ 🚻 🎁 🍴

In 1871 Betsey Williams, a direct descendant of Roger Williams, donated 102 acres (41 ha) of prime real estate to the city for use as parkland. Since that time, another 320 acres (130 ha) of property have been added to the site. Once farmland, the park now

Historic cookbooks from the Culinary Archives and Museum

holds gardens and greenhouses, ponds, a lake with paddleboats and rowboats for rent, jogging and cycling paths, and a tennis center. Children especially love the carousel and train, the planetarium, and the Museum of Natural History.

Without a doubt, the highlight of the park is the zoo, which has more than 900

animals and 156 species. Dating back to 1872, the zoo is one of the oldest in the nation, but this has not stopped it from keeping up to date. Exhibits include the Plains of Africa, with elephants, zebras, giraffes, and cheetahs; a Madagascar exhibit of endangered lemurs; the Australasia area, with open-air aviary; and an underwater window for viewing penguins and polar bears as they cavort in the water.

🏛 Culinary Archives and Museum at Johnson & Wales University

315 Northup St. 📞 *(401) 598-2805.* ◯ *10am–4pm Tue–Sat.* ● *public hols.* ✔

This one-of-a-kind museum contains half a million items relating to the culinary arts – hardly surprising since Johnson & Wales University is devoted to training chefs. The museum was created in 1979, when Chicago chef Louis Szathmary donated his vast collection of culinary oddities, including a cannibal eating bowl from Fiji and rings worn by bakers that had been excavated at Pompeii. Exhibits include hotel and restaurant finery and a gallery of famous chefs.

Roger Williams Park and Zoo, a highlight of downtown Providence

Boats moored at the Sakonnet Wharf near Little Compton

Portsmouth ❻

🏠 16,850. 🛈 23 America's Cup Ave, Newport (401) 845-9123 or (800) 976-5122.

PORTSMOUTH figures greatly in Rhode Island history. It was the second settlement in the old colony, founded in 1638 just two years after Providence. The town was also the site of the 1778 Battle of Rhode Island, the only major land battle fought in the state during the American Revolution. Bad weather and fierce British resistance forced the US troops to retreat. With the British in hot pursuit, only the courage of the American rear guard enabled most of

Delightful denizens of the Green Animals Topiary Garden

the soldiers to escape to the sanctuary of Butts Hill Fort. Today some of the fort's redoubts are still visible from Sprague Street, where plaques recount the battle.

The **Green Animals Topiary Garden** is a more

whimsical attraction. Located on a Victorian estate, this lighthearted garden is inhabited by a wild array of topiary creations. In all, some 80 animal shapes – including elephants, camels, giraffes, bears, birds, even a dinosaur – have been trimmed and sculpted from a selection of yew, English boxwood, and California privet. Elsewhere on the grounds, formal flower gardens, a rose arbor, and a museum with an extensive collection of Victorian-era toys delight even the very youngest visitors.

🌷 **Green Animals Topiary Garden**
Cory's Lane. 📞 (401) 847-1000. 🕐 May–Oct: 10am–5pm daily. 🏷

Little Compton ❼

🏠 3,350. 🛈 23 America's Cup Ave, Newport (401) 845-9123 or (800) 976-5122.

RESIDENTS OF Little Compton relish their isolated nook at the end of a peninsula that borders Massachusetts with good reason: Little Compton is one of the most charming villages in the entire state, protected from the outside world by the surrounding farmlands and woods.

The white-steepled United Congregational Church stands over Little Compton Commons. Beside the church lies the old Commons Burial Ground,

with the gravesite of Elizabeth Padobie (c.1623–1717). The daughter of *Mayflower* Pilgrims Priscilla and John Alden, Padobie was the first white woman born in New England. The 1680 **Wilbor House** was home to eight generations of the Wilbor family. The house is furnished with period pieces and antique household items. Elsewhere on the grounds visitors can explore a one-room schoolhouse and artist's studio. An 1860 barn displays old farm tools, sleighs, a one-horse shay, oxcart, and buggies.

Nearby **Sakonnet Vineyards** is the largest winery in New England. There are free daily wine tastings and guided tours. Beyond the vineyard on Route 77 is Sakonnet Wharf, where the curious can watch fishermen arrive with their catches.

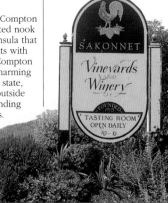

Sakonnet Vineyards in Little Compton

◁ **Old Harbor, Block Island**

♙ Wilbor House
548 W Main Rd. 🔲 *(401) 635-4035.*
◯ *Jul–Aug: 2pm–5pm Thu–Sun;
Sep: 2pm–5pm Sat–Sun.* 📷

🎋 Sakonnet Vineyards
162 W Main Rd. 🔲 *(401) 635-8486.*
◯ *Memorial Day–Columbus Day:
10am–6pm; rest of year: 11am–5pm.*
📷 *on the hour, last tour at 5pm.* ♿

ENVIRONS: Four miles (6 km)
northeast is Adamsville.
Gray's Store dates back to
1788 making it the oldest
general store in the country.
It contains the first post office
(1804) in the area and still
has its original soda fountain,
candy and tobacco cases,
and ice chest.

**Gray's Store, built in 1788, on
Main Street in Adamsville**

♙ Gray's Store
4 Main St. 🔲 *(401) 635-4566.*
◯ *9am–5pm Mon–Sat, 12pm–4pm
Sun & public hols.*

Middletown ❽

🚶 *19,950.* 🚉 *23 America's Cup
Ave, Newport (401) 845-9123 or
(800) 976-5122.*

Nestled between Newport
(see pp182–7) and
Portsmouth on Aquidneck
Island, Middletown is known
primarily for its two popular
beaches. **Third Beach** is
located on the Sakonnet River
and is outfitted with a boat
ramp. A steady wind and relatively calm water make the
beach a favorite among wind-
surfers and families with
young children.

Third Beach runs into the
largest and most beautiful
beach on the island.
Sachuest, or
Second Beach,
is widely con-
sidered one of
the best places
to surf in south-
ern New England.
This spacious strand is
rippled with sand dunes
and equipped with
campgrounds. Purgatory
Chasm, a narrow cleft in the
rock ledges on the east side
of Easton Point, provides a
scenic outlook over both the
beach and 50-ft- (15-m-) high
Hanging Rock.

Second Beach has yet
another advantage; it is adjacent to the **Norman Bird
Sanctuary**, a 450-acre

Middletown's popular Third Beach

(182-ha) wildlife area with
seven miles (11 km) of walking trails that are ideal for
birding. Some 250 species
have been sighted at this
sanctuary, including herons,
egrets, woodcocks, thrashers,
ducks, and swans. The
refuge is home to numerous
four-legged animals, such as
rabbits and red foxes. A
small natural history
museum is also
located on the
site, and during
the winter
months the
sanctuary trails
are used by cross-
country skiers.
Amateur entomolo-
gists will enjoy pay-
ing a visit to the
Newport Butterfly Farm.
Colorful species from all
around the world can be
found in a giant, specially
designed, screened-in greenhouse. Visitors are free to
walk among the flowers and
observe the beautiful insects
as they feed on nectar and
lay eggs.

**Inhabitant of
Newport
Butterfly Farm**

🏖 Third Beach
Third Beach Rd. 🔲 *(401) 849-2822.*
◯ *Memorial Day–Labor Day: lifeguards on duty 8am–6pm daily.* 📷
🏖 Second Beach
Third Beach Rd. 🔲 *(401) 849-2822.*
◯ *Memorial Day–Labor Day: lifeguards on duty 8am–6pm daily.* 📷
🦋 Norman Bird Sanctuary
583 Third Beach Rd. 🔲 *(401) 846-
2577.* ◯ *June–Aug: 9am–5pm
daily; rest of year: 9am–5pm
Tue–Sun.* ⬤ *Thanksgiving & Dec 25.*
📷 🎫
🦋 Newport Butterfly Farm
594 Aquidneck Ave. 🔲 *(401) 849-
9519.* ◯ *May–Sep: 11am–4pm daily.*

Waterfowl in Middletown's Norman Bird Sanctuary

Newport

A CENTER OF TRADE, culture, wealth, and military activity for more than 300 years, Newport is a true sightseeing mecca. Historical firsts abound in this small city. America's first naval college and synagogue are here, as are the oldest library in the country and one of the oldest continuously operating taverns. Any visit to the city should include a tour of the mansions from the Gilded Age of the late 1800s, when the rich and famous flocked here each summer to beat New York's heat. These summer "cottage" retreats of the country's wealthiest families, the Vanderbilts and Astors among them, are some of America's grandest private homes.

Advertisement for carved whalebone, or whale ivory

Exploring Newport

Like Italy, Newport has a distinctly boot-shaped outline. The city's famous mansions are located on the southeastern side, or the heel of the boot. Newport's harborfront is to the west, where the laces would be. The city's most interesting streets, America's Cup Avenue and Thames Street, are found here. Pedestrians will find restaurants, shops, and colonial buildings, including the 1726 Trinity Church.

⛪ Museum of Newport History

127 Thames St. ☎ *(401) 846-0813.*
⊙ *Apr–Oct: 10am–5pm Mon & Wed–Sat, 1pm–5pm Sun; Nov–Mar: 10am–4pm Fri–Sat, 1pm–4pm Sun.*
● *Tue.* ⬛ ⊘
The Brick Market, a commercial hub during the 18th century, is now a museum that provides an excellent introduction to the city's history and architecture. Self-guided tours include an audiovisual exploration of the downtown in a 19th-century omnibus.

🔲 Touro Synagogue

85 Touro St. ☎ *(401) 847-4794.*
⊙ *call for times.* ☑ *every half hour.*
🔲 *Shabbat and all Jewish hols.* ⬛ ⊘
America's oldest synagogue, Touro was erected in 1763 by Sephardic Jews who had fled Spain and Portugal in search of religious tolerance. Designed by architect Peter Harrison (1716–75), it is considered one of the country's finest examples of 18th-century architecture. Services still follow the Sephardic rituals of its founders.

⚓ Fort Adams State Park

Harrison Ave. ☎ *(401) 847-2400.*
⊙ *sunrise to sunset daily.* ☑ **Museum of Yachting** ☎ *(401) 847-1018.*
⊙ *mid-May–Oct: 10am–5pm daily; Nov–mid-May: by appt.* ⬛ 🔲 ⬛

Fort Adams, centerpiece of Fort Adams State Park

Fort Adams is one of the largest military forts in the country. Completed in 1857 at a cost of $3 million, it was designed to house 2,400 troops. The property surrounding the fort is equipped with facilities for swimming, soccer, rugby, and picnicking. Each year Newport's world-famous music festivals *(see p33)* are held here.

The park also is home to the Museum of Yachting, which chronicles Newport's famed yachting history. One

Public grass courts at the International Tennis Hall of Fame

of the museum's highlights is its collection of classic luxury boats in its outdoor basin.

⛪ International Tennis Hall of Fame

194 Bellevue Ave. ☎ *(401) 849-3990.* ● *9:30am–5pm daily.* ●
Thanksgiving & Dec 25. 🔲 *courts available to public.* ⬛ ⬛ ⬛
The hall is housed in the Newport Casino, once a private club for Newport's elite. Founded in 1880, the club installed grass tennis courts to introduce its members to the latest sports rage. The first US National Lawn Tennis Championship, later known as the US Open, was held here in 1881. Today the hall displays everything from antique rackets to the "comeback" outfit worn by Monica Seles (b.1972). The grass courts are the only ones in the US open to the public.

⛵ Cliff Walk

Begins at Memorial Blvd. ☎ *(401) 849-8048.* ⊙ *year-round: dawn–dusk daily.* ☑
This 3.5-mile (5.5-km) walk along Newport's ragged cliffs offers some of the best views of the Gilded-Age mansions. Local fishermen preserved public access to the trail by going to court when wealthy mansion-owners tried to have it closed. The walk was designated a National Recreation Trail in 1975. The Forty Steps, each step named for someone lost at sea, lead to the ocean.

The breathtaking Cliff Walk, popular with residents as well as visitors

⚓ International Yacht Restoration School

449 Thames St. 📞 *(401) 848-5777.* ⏰ *10am–5pm daily.* ⬤ *Jan–Mar: Sun.* 🎫 ♿

Students at work at International Yacht Restoration School

Founded in 1993, this small school provides a fascinating look at yacht restoration. Visitors can observe students from the mezzanine, and tour the waterfront campus and the *Coronet*, built in 1885. It is the world's oldest grand yacht and is slated for restoration by the school.

⚓ Redwood Library and Athenaeum

50 Bellevue Ave. 📞 *(401) 847-0292.* ⏰ *9:30am–5:30pm Mon & Fri–Sat, 9:30am–8pm Tue & Wed–Thu, 1pm–5pm Sun.* ⬤ *public hols.* 🎫 ♿

Completed in 1750, the Redwood is the oldest continuously operating library in America and is one of the country's earliest examples of temple-form buildings. Apart from books, the library also contains a fine colonial portrait collection.

⚓ Newport Mansions

Preservation Society of Newport County, 424 Bellevue Ave. 📞 *(401) 847-1000.* ⏰ *May–Oct: 10am–5pm daily; winter: call for hours.* ⬤ *Dec 24 & 25.* 🎫 *obligatory.* ♿ *partial.* 🚫

Redwood Library and Athenaeum's stately interior

Built between 1748 and 1902, 12 of these summer "cottages," most of them along Bellevue Avenue, are open

VISITORS' CHECKLIST

🏠 *28,000.* ✈ *TF Green Airport, Warwick, 27 miles (43 km) NW.* 🚌 *Gateway Center, 23 America's Cup Ave.* ⛴ *Perrotti Park (to Providence).* 🛈 *Newport County Convention & Visitor's Bureau, 23 America's Cup Ave (401) 845-9123 or (800) 976-5122.* 🎭 *Newport Tennis Week (Jul), JVC Jazz Festival (Aug).* Ⓦ *www.GoNewport.com*

for guided tours. Modeled on European palaces and decorated with the finest artworks, the mansions were used for only 10 weeks of the year. The Breakers *(see pp186–7)* is one of the finest examples.

🏛 Naval War College Museum

686 Cushing Rd. 📞 *(401) 841-4052.* ⏰ *10am–4pm Mon–Fri, 12pm–4pm Sat–Sun.* ⬤ *Oct–Jun: Sat–Sun.* 🎫 ♿

This site preserves the history, art, and science of naval warfare and the heritage of Narragansett Bay. Founded in 1885, the college is the oldest naval institute of higher learning in the world. The museum houses ship models and maritime art.

NEWPORT CITY CENTER

Museum of Newport History ①
Redwood Library and Athenaeum ④
Touro Synagogue ②
Trinity Church ③

0 meters   300
0 yards   300

KEY

🟦 Street-by-Street map see pp184–5

═ Highway

⛴ Ferry

🚌 Bus station

🅿 Tourist information

🛈 Parking

Around Washington Square

NEWPORT'S FIRST SETTLERS were religious moderates fleeing persecution at the hands of Puritans in the Massachusetts Bay colony. With its accessible harbor, the town quickly developed into a thriving seaport. However, its location also made it vulnerable. When Rhode Island declared independence from colonial rule in 1776, British forces occupied the city. Before they were driven out in 1780, the occupying army destroyed much of the town. Thanks to preservation efforts, a number of colonial buildings survive. Several of them can be seen on this tour around historic Washington Square, the center of Newport's political and economic life during colonial times.

Historic marker

Architectural detail *is typical of the Washington Square district.*

White Horse Tavern
Granted its liquor license in 1673, the White Horse claims to be the nation's oldest continuously operating tavern. At one time, state legislators gathered here before sitting at Colony House.

St. Paul's Methodist Church was built in 1805. A simple structure, it reflects the continuation of the Colonial style in the decades after independence.

Bank of Newport

Rivera House, currently a bank, was once the home of Abraham Rivera, a prominent member of Newport's Jewish and business communities. Rivera laid the cornerstone of Touro Synagogue.

Statue of Oliver Hazard Perry
Oliver Hazard Perry (1785–1819) defeated British forces in a pivotal naval battle in the War of 1812, securing control of Lake Erie for the US. Perry's former home at No. 29 Touro Street faces the statue.

FAREWELL

MARLBOROUGH ST

DUKE STREET

THAMES STREET

WASHINGTON SQUARE

TOURO STREET

STAR SIGHTS

★ **Museum of Newport History**

★ **Touro Synagogue**

★ **Museum of Newport History**
The Brick Market, once the center of commerce, has been renovated to house this museum (see p182) that brings to life Newport's economic, social, and sporting past.

Colony House
This grand structure from 1739 was the state's main seat of government until 1900. Rhode Island's declaration of independence was read from the balcony in May 1776, two months before the July 4th proclamation in Philadelphia.

Wanton-Lyman-Hazard House (1675) is the oldest surviving home in Newport.

Newport County Court House

★ **Touro Synagogue**
Dedicated in 1763, Touro is the oldest synagogue in the country (see p182).

STONE ST

BROADWAY

HOZIER

SPRING STREET

TOURO ST

DIVISION ST

SPRING STREET

CLARKE STREET

The Newport Historical Society
is a resource center for studies of Newport history. Open to the public, the library holds historic manuscripts and a small art gallery.

THAMES STREET

Artillery Company

KEY

- - - Suggested route

0 meters 25

0 yards 25

PINEAPPLE SYMBOLISM

While on trade missions to Africa and the West Indies, Newport's sailors ate fresh fruit to ward off scurvy. What they did not eat, they brought home to their families. It became tradition in Newport to place a pineapple on the doorstep when the seagoing man of the house had returned safely. In time, the fruit became a local symbol of hospitality and was often incorporated into the door's transom or applied directly to the door itself. Pineapples appear on many old Newport homes.

The Breakers

THE ARCHITECTURE and ostentation of the Gilded Age of the late 1800s reached its pinnacle with the Breakers, the summer home of railroad magnate Cornelius Vanderbilt II (1843–99). Completed in 1895, the four-story, 70-room limestone structure surpassed all other Newport mansions in extravagance. US architect Richard Morris Hunt (1827–95) modeled the building after the 16th-century palaces in Turin and Genoa. Its interior is adorned with marble, alabaster, stained glass, gilt, and crystal.

The Structure
Built in the Italian Renaissance style, the Breakers is alleged to have cost more than $10 million – a huge sum of money in 1895.

Visitors' entrance, west side

The Great Hall
The Great Hall rises 50 ft (15 m), or two full stories, providing a majestic welcome to the mansion.

★ **Mrs. Vanderbilt's Bedroom**
This sumptuous room is decorated in Louis XVI style. Its flowered wall covering and upholstery are reproductions of the original silk and cotton fabrics.

The Music Room
This grand room was the scene of many dances and recitals. The bronze and crystal chandeliers, furniture, and gilt decorative touches were modeled on Italian designs.

STAR FEATURES

★ **Mrs. Vanderbilt's Bedroom**

★ **The Dining Room**

★ **The Morning Room**

A MAGNATE'S LIFE

Cornelius Vanderbilt II inherited the mantle as head of the Vanderbilt empire in 1885. He directed the family businesses, mainly railroads, with his brother William for 11 years before suffering a paralyzing stroke. He convalesced at the Breakers, but died in 1899 at the age of 56. At the time of his death, the local gossip held that he had more money than the US Mint.

Cornelius Vanderbilt II

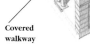

Covered walkway

★ The Dining Room
The most richly adorned room in the mansion, the two-story, 2,400-sq-ft (220-sq-m) dining room has two huge crystal chandeliers and a stunning arched ceiling.

Upper Loggia
The upper loggia offers a view of the sunrise over the Atlantic Ocean. Its ceiling is painted to look like canopies against a clouded sky.

Sculpted Archways
Ornately carved archways are inspired by Italian Renaissance-style palazzos.

The Billiard Room
The Billiard Room features several costly wall marbles; the arches and mantel are decorated with yellow alabaster. The mahogany billiard table was built by Baumgarten of New York. Steel beams were needed to support the huge chandeliers.

★ The Morning Room
The ceiling of this east-facing room is adorned with paintings of the Four Seasons, the mahogany doors with the Four Elements. All cornices, pilasters, and panels were made in France and shipped to Newport.

Sunbathing on the rocks at Beavertail Lighthouse and State Park

Jamestown ⑩

🏛 5,000. ⓘ 23 America's Cup Ave, Newport (401) 845-9123 or (800) 976-5122.

Named for England's King James II (1633–1701), Jamestown is located on Conanicut Island and linked to Newport *(see pp184–9)* and the mainland by a pair of bridges. During the Revolutionary War, British troops torched much of the town, sparing very few of the houses from that era.

The town is best known for the **Beavertail Lighthouse and State Park**, perched at the southernmost tip of the island. The first lighthouse here was built in 1749 and was subsequently replaced by the present structure in 1856. As with many New England lighthouses, the coastal vistas from Beavertail are beautiful. The winds, currents, and surf can be heavy at times, but on calm days hiking, climbing, and sunbathing on the rocks are favorite pastimes.

Situated on the site of an early fort and artillery battery, **Fort Wetherill State Park** offers great scenic outlooks, picnic tables, and a boat ramp. The park is a popular place for saltwater fishing, boating, and scuba diving. Legend has it that notorious privateer Captain Kidd (1645–1701) stashed some of his plundered loot in the park's Pirate Cave.

♣ **Beavertail Lighthouse and State Park**
Beavertail Pt. ⓒ (401) 423-9941. **Park** ⦿ dawn to dusk daily. **Lighthouse** ⦿ call for hours. 🅿 ♿
♣ **Fort Wetherill State Park**
Fort Wetherill Rd. ⓒ (401) 423-9941. ⦿ dawn to dusk daily. 🅿 ♿

Wickford ⑪

🏛 25,000. ⓘ 4808 Tower Hill Rd, Wakefield (401) 789-4422 or (800) 548-4662.

Considered a part of North Kingston, the quaint village of Wickford lies in the northernmost point of Washington County, also known as South County. Wickford's many 18th- and 19th-century houses are a magnet for artists and craftsmen. John Updike *(see pp30–31)*, author of *Rabbit Run* (1960), has family roots here. The 1745 Updike House on Pleasant Street is just one of some 60 buildings constructed before 1804.

Daytrippers hailing from Providence and Connecticut are apt to jam Wickford's picturesque harbor and busy streets. Among the many shops along Brown and Main streets, the Shaker Shop is a favorite for its replicas of old Shaker furniture, quilts, and boxes.

Old Narragansett Church (more commonly called Old St. Paul's) is one of the oldest Episcopal churches in the US, dating back to 1707, with box pews, an organ from 1660, and an upstairs gallery to which plantation slaves were

Wickford's tranquil harbor

relegated. Artist Gilbert Stuart (1755–1828) was baptized here in a silver baptismal font given to the church as a gift by England's Queen Anne (1665–1714).

ENVIRONS: One mile north of town is **Smith's Castle**, one of America's oldest plantation houses. In 1678 settler Richard Smith built a dwelling on the site. Hardly a castle, the structure served as a garrison for

Smith's Castle, just outside of Wickford

the soldiers who had participated in the 1675 Great Swamp Fight against the Narragansett Indians. The battle resulted in a mass slaughter of Indians, which set off a chain of tragic events culminating in the retaliatory destruction of the garrison and the death of 40 soldiers. Later the structure was rebuilt and acquired by the Updike family in 1692. Subsequent additions and renovations transformed the structure into one of the most handsome plantation houses on the Rhode Island shore. The house contains fine paneling, 17th- and 18th-century furnishings, china, and a chair once owned by Roger Williams (*see pp176–7*).

🏛 **Smith's Castle**
55 Richard Smith Dr. (*(401) 294-3521.*) call for hours.

Saunderstown 12

27,000. ℹ 8045 Post Rd, North Kingston *(401) 295-5566.*

LOCATED BETWEEN Wickford and Narragansett, this town has two main attractions. The gambrel-roofed **Gilbert Stuart Birthplace** was built in 1751 along

the Mattatuxet River. Stuart (1755–1828), whose portraits of US presidents were to bring him lasting fame, was born here. His best-known portrait, that of George Washington, graces the US one-dollar bill.

On the first floor of the house, Stuart's father built a large kitchen and snuff mill, the first in America, powered by a wooden waterwheel. The upstairs living quarters are furnished with authentic period pieces.

Also in town is the 18th-century **Silas Casey Farm**. Still in operation, the farm has been occupied by the same family for 200 years. The 360-acre (146-ha) property is ringed by almost 30 miles (48 km) of stone walls. The house contains original furniture, paintings, and prints, and visitors can tour the family cemetery.

🏛 **Gilbert Stuart Birthplace**
815 Gilbert Stuart Rd. (*(401) 294-3001.*) Apr–Oct: 11am–4pm Thu–Mon. ● Nov–Mar.
🏛 **Silas Casey Farm**
2325 Boston Neck Rd. (*(401) 295-1030.*) Jun–Oct: 1pm–5pm Tue, Thu, & Sat. ● Nov–May.
♿

South Kingstown 13

26,700. ℹ 328 Main St *(401) 783-2801.*

SOUTH KINGSTOWN is a 55-sq-mile (142-sq-km) town that encompasses 15 villages,

Plaque at Stuart Birthplace

HERE WAS BORN
DECEMBER 3, 1755
GILBERT STUART
AMERICA'S FOREMOST
PORTRAIT PAINTER
ERECTED BY THE STATE OF RHODE ISLAND 1922

including Kingston, Green Hill, Wakefield, and Snug Harbor. The town is home to the **Museum of Primitive Art and Culture**. Located in an 1856 post office, the museum displays weapons, tools, and implements of aboriginal cultures around the world, including prehistoric New England.

After visiting the museum, travelers can enjoy some of the region's outdoor charms. Sightseers, particularly those with cameras, will want to make the trek to the top of the observation post at Hannah Robinson Rock and Tower, where they are greeted with expansive views of the Atlantic Ocean and the Rhode Island seashore.

The South County Bike Path is a 3.7-mile (6-km) paved trail, starting at the Kingston train station, which takes cyclists through Great Swamp, the scene of the 1675 slaughter of 2,000 Narragansett Indians at the hands of soldiers and settlers – one of the bloodiest battles ever fought in New England. The swamp is now a pristine 3,300-acre (1,335-ha) wildlife refuge called the **Great Swamp Management Area** and is home to creatures such as coyotes, mink, wild turkeys, and ring-necked pheasants. Nature trails lead visitors through dense woodland, past a dike to a boardwalk into a marsh. Birders should pack binoculars and visit the refuge in the spring, when songbirds are spotted during their annual migration.

🏛 **Museum of Primitive Art and Culture**
1058 Kingston Rd. (*(401) 783-5711.*) Labor Day–Memorial Day: 10am–2pm Tue–Thu; rest of year: 11am–2pm Wed; by appt other days.
🦌 **Great Swamp Management Area**
Liberty Lane off Great Neck Rd. (*(401) 222-1267 or (401) 789-0281.*) dawn to dusk daily.

Whale-watching off Point Judith, a popular summer activity

Narragansett **⓭**

🏛 18,000. ✈ TF Green Airport.
ℹ 4 Woodruff Ave (401) 783-7821.

I N THE LATE 19th century this
town's waterfront area
gained national fame as a
fashionable resort, complete
with a large casino. In 1900

a devastating fire razed the
1884 casino and many of the
lavish hotels that lined the
waterfront. All that remains
of the ornate 1884 casino are
The Towers, two stone towers linked by a Romanesque
Revival-style arch.

Today rolling dice have
given way to rolling waves, as
the town beach offers some
of the best surfing on the East
Coast. Nearby the **South
County Museum** depicts
early Rhode Island life with
displays of children's toys,
farm tools, weapons, a cob-
bler's shop, a general store,
and a working print shop.

🚾 **The Towers**
35 Ocean Rd. 📞 (401) 295-5270. ◯
Jul–Aug: 12pm–4pm Sat–Sun. ⬤
Sep–Jun. ◪ call for hours. ♿
🏛 **South County Museum**
On Canochet Farm off Rte 1A.
📞 (401) 783-5400. ◯ May–Oct:
10am–4pm Wed–Mon. ◪
ENVIRONS: Located at the
south end of the Narragansett
peninsula, **Point Judith** and
Galilee are departure points
for numerous whale-watching

cruises, sightseeing boat
tours, ferries to Block Island
(see pp192–3), and charters
for deep-sea fishing. Toward
the end of World War II, a
German U-boat was sunk just
two miles (3 km) off the Point
Judith Lighthouse. Today the
lighthouse affords beautiful
views of the ocean. Galilee is
famous for its Blessing of the
Fleet festival in late July *(see
p33)*. The Galilee Salt Marsh
is popular for birding.

Charlestown **⓰**

🏛 6,000. ✈ 🚉 ℹ 4945 Old Post
Rd (401) 364-3878.

T HIS SMALL TOWN stretches
along four miles (6.4 km)
of lovely beaches, encom-
passing the largest saltwater
marsh in the state and several
parks. It is also a convenient
base for nature lovers. The
2,000-acre (810-ha)
Burlingame State Park on
Watchaug Pond is equipped
with campgrounds, nature
trails, swimming and picnic

South County Beaches **⓯**

D RIVING ALONG Highway 1 between Narragansett and
Watch Hill, travelers will pass some 100 miles (161
km) of pristine white sand beaches. These thin strands
of sand are all that separate Block Island Sound from
a series of tidal salt ponds, some of which have been
designated national wildlife refuges. The ponds are
big lures for bird-watchers hoping to study the egrets,
sandpipers, and herons that swim and wade in the
salty marshes. Many of the beaches are free to the
public, except for parking fees.

KEY

▥	Major road
═	Other road
⛴	Ferry
✈	Airport
☀	Viewpoint

Misquamicut State Beach ⑤
The state's largest beach has gentle surf
and a nearby old-time amusement park
with rides and diversions for children.

To Westerly

78

1A

1

Winnapaug Road

✈ Westerly State
Airport

Watch Hill Road

Winnapaug
Pond

5

Atlantic Avenue

Watch Hill

216

Haversham

1A

Quonochontaug
Pond

Quonochontaug •

Weekapaug

areas, trails for road and mountain bikes, as well as fishing and boating. Birders will enjoy the Audubon Society's **Kimball Wildlife Refuge**, located on the south side of the park. The refuge is a habitat for many kinds of waterfowl and migrating birds, and has a network of easy footpaths.

More outdoor enjoyment can be found at the 172-acre (70-ha) **Ninigret Park**. Maintained trails lead cyclists and hikers through the

grounds, which are graced with a spring-fed swimming pond, tennis courts, and baseball fields. During the winter months, the trails are used by cross-country skiers.

☒ Burlingame State Park
Rte 1A. **(** (401) 322-8910.
◯ Apr–Oct: dawn–dusk daily.
🏕 for camping facilities.
☒ Kimball Wildlife Refuge
Prosser Trail. **(** (401) 231-6444.
◯ dawn–dusk daily.
☒ Ninigret Park
Rte 1A. **(** (401) 364-1222.
◯ dawn–dusk daily. 🅿 ♿

Nature trails through the Kimball Wildlife Refuge

Watch Hill ⓱

ℹ 1 Chamber Way, Westerly (401) 596-7761.

A VILLAGE within the town of Westerly, Watch Hill has been an upscale resort and beach haven for the rich and famous since the 19th century. Strolls along Bay Street yield beautiful views of the many gingerbread-trimmed Victorian houses perched on rocky hills above the beach. Visitors to Watch Hill can enjoy the village's relaxed atmosphere, with a little window shopping or sunbathing down at the beach. Believed to be the oldest carousel in the US, the 1867 **Flying Horse Carousel** on the beach is a favorite of children. The vantage point of the Watch Hill Lighthouse offers views of neighboring Connecticut's Fishers Island.

🎠 Flying Horse Carousel
Bay St. **(** (401) 596-7761.
◯ mid-Jun–Labor Day: 1pm–8pm Sat–Sun. 🅿 🔲 🍴

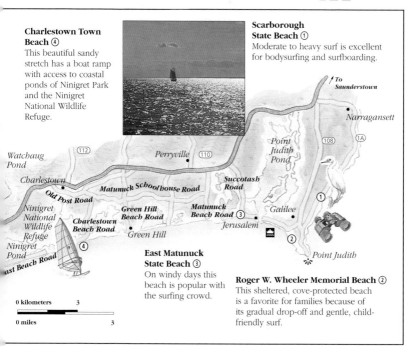

Charlestown Town Beach ④
This beautiful sandy stretch has a boat ramp with access to coastal ponds of Ninigret Park and the Ninigret National Wildlife Refuge.

Scarborough State Beach ①
Moderate to heavy surf is excellent for bodysurfing and surfboarding.

East Matunuck State Beach ③
On windy days this beach is popular with the surfing crowd.

Roger W. Wheeler Memorial Beach ②
This sheltered, cove-protected beach is a favorite for families because of its gradual drop-off and gentle, child-friendly surf.

0 kilometers 3

0 miles 3

Tour of Block Island ⑱

LYING 13 miles (21 km) off the coast, the haven of Block Island has long been a favorite getaway spot for New Englanders. With 25 percent of its wild landscape under protection, Block Island is a wonderful destination for outdoor enthusiasts who enjoy such activities as swimming, fishing, sailing, bird-watching, kayaking, canoeing, and horseback riding. Some 30 miles of natural trails entice hikers and cyclists alike to experience the island's natural beauty firsthand.

Southeast Light

Colorful lobster buoys ashore on Block Island

Great Salt Pond ④
Completely protected from the ocean, Great Salt Pond has three marinas and is an excellent spot for kayaking and fishing. New Harbor is Block Island's prime marina and boating center.

Rodman's Hollow ③
Nature trails lead hikers through the glacial depression of Rodman's Hollow Natural Area. The wildlife refuge is home to hawks and white-tailed deer. One path takes visitors to the beach at Black Rock Point at the southern extremity of the island.

KEY

▬	Tour route
⁼	Other road
⁑	Viewpoint
⛴	Ferry
✕	Airport

0 meters   500

0 yards   500

Great Salt Pond

Dead Man's Cove

Cormorant Point

Champlin Road

Grace Cove Road

West Side Road

Beacon Hill

Beacon Hill Road

Center Road

✕

Cooneymus Road

Cooneymus Swamp

Dickens Road

③

Black Rock Road

Lakeside Drive

Black Rock Point

TIPS FOR DRIVERS

Tour length: 18 miles (29 km).
Getting there: Regularly scheduled flights from Westerly, RI, and chartered flights from other mainland airports. Year-round ferry service from Point Judith, RI. Ferries carry cars by advance reservations only, (401) 783-4613.
Stopping-off point: Old Harbor, the island's only village, has inns and several quaint restaurants overlooking the ocean (see pp335–7).

Settlers Rock ⑥
A plaque honors the 16 Englishmen who landed here in 1661. The rock is at the edge of Sachem Pond, a favorite for swimming and kayaking.

Clayhead ⑤
Offers wonderful views of the Atlantic Ocean and is the starting point for a popular nature trail that goes all the way to Settlers Rock.

Old Harbor ①
This village is the main hub of activity on the island. Victorian houses, hotels, and shops line the streets, and anglers can charter boats to fish for striped bass, bluefish, flounder, and cod.

Mohegan Bluffs ②
The name of the bluffs goes back to 1590, when local Manisses Indians tossed 50 Mohegan invaders off these dramatic 200-ft- (61-m-) high red clay cliffs into the waters below. Built in 1875, the Southeast Light was once the most powerful in New England.

CONNECTICUT

ONNECTICUT IS QUINTESSENTIAL NEW ENGLAND. *Its quiet charm is evident everywhere, in scenic villages replete with white steepled churches, immaculate village greens, covered bridges, and old-fashioned clapboard houses ringed by stone walls. Even the state's most bustling cosmopolitan centers contain enclaves of picturesque serenity that invite visitors to poke about at their leisure.*

The third-smallest state in the US, Connecticut is brimming with history. One of the country's original 13 colonies, Connecticut has always been a trendsetter, beginning with its adoption in 1639 of the Fundamental Orders of Connecticut – the New World's first constitution. It was on Connecticut soil that the nation's first public library, law school, and amusement park were built. Scholars and soldiers can thank the fertile minds of state residents for giving them the first dictionary and pistol, gourmands for the hamburger and corkscrew, and children for the three-ring circus, lollipop, and Frisbee.

Water has played an important role in shaping the state. The Housatonic, Naugatuck, Connecticut, and Thames rivers have been feeding the interior woodlands for thousands of years and acted as the main transportation arteries for early inhabitants. Fueled by waterpower, mill towns sprang up along the rivers, eventually giving way to larger commercial centers. Today these waterways are the arenas of canoeists looking for their next adventure. Houseboats and tour boats offer road-weary passengers unique views of the picturesque towns that hug the banks.

Autumn's annual explosion of color makes it the favorite time of year for visitors to meander along Connecticut's byways, hike the Berkshires, wander the Appalachian Trail (*see pp22–3*), and indulge in the seasonal bounty of country inns. In addition, the state calendar bulges with eclectic events. Old-fashioned county fairs are held concurrently with cutting-edge performing arts showcases and regattas. When people have had their fill of ballooning and antiquing, they can sample the wares in one of the state's late-summer oyster festivals.

Mystic Seaport's calm harbor

◁ **First Church of Christ Congregational, Farmington, built in 1652**

Exploring Connecticut

COMPACT ENOUGH TO CROSS in a few hours, Connecticut has treasures that entice travelers to stay for days. The magnificent shoreline, stretching 105 miles (170 km) from Greenwich on the New York State line northeast to Rhode Island, is scalloped by coves, inlets, and harbors, and dotted with state parks, beaches, and marinas. The coast is punctuated by historically significant houses, culminating in Mystic Seaport *(pp214–15)*, an authentic 18th- and 19th-century seafaring village. The area also attracted America's Impressionist artists. Their works are shown in the state's many museums *(pp202–203)*. Inland hills and valleys are dotted with tiny postcard-perfect villages.

Hartford's Bushnell Park

Beach at Mount Tom State Park

GETTING AROUND

Hugging the coast, Interstate 95 serves as the primary east-west link. Interstate 84 follows a similar route from Danbury through Hartford and beyond. The major north-south artery is Interstate 91. Metro North runs trains from New York City to New Haven. Amtrak's New York-Boston line makes stops along Connecticut's shoreline. Several major bus companies, including Peter Pan Trailways, Bonanza, and Greyhound, offer interstate services. Seasonal ferries operate New London-Block Island, Rhode Island, and year-round services run New London-Orient Point, New York, as well as Bridgeport–Port Jefferson.

0 kilometers   10

0 miles   10

SEE ALSO

SIGHTS AT A GLANCE

WOODSTOCK

OLD NEW-GATE PRISON **10**

NEW ENGLAND AIR MUSEUM **9**

rkhamsted *servoir* **7**

SIMSBURY

WINDSOR **8**

BROOKLYN

FARMINGTON **2**

HARTFORD **1**

STORRS

COVENTRY **11**

CANTERBURY

BRISTOL

NEW BRITAIN **3**

WETHERSFIELD **5**

WILLIMANTIC

DINOSAUR STATE PARK **4**

LEBANON **12**

MIDDLETOWN

NORWICH **13**

Connecticut River

Thames River

EAST HADDAM

GILLETTE CASTLE **19**

FOXWOODS RESORT CASINO **14**

ESSEX **18**

NEW LONDON **15**

GROTON

MYSTIC **16**

NEW HAVEN **23**

MADISON **20**

OLD LYME **17**

STONY CREEK

EAST HAVEN

GUILFORD **21**

THE THIMBLES **22**

Boat tours cruising the 365 picturesque islands of The Thimbles

KEY

▬▬	Interstate
▬▬	Major road
▬▬	Minor road
▬▬	Scenic route
❋	Viewpoint

Hartford ❶

Elizabeth Park sign

S ERVING FIRST AS AN ANCIENT Saukiog Indian settlement and later as a Dutch trading post, Connecticut's capital was founded in 1636 by the Reverend Thomas Hooker (1586–1647) and a group of 100 Englishmen from the Massachusetts Bay Colony. By the late 19th century, Hartford was basking in its Golden Age, thanks to both an economic boom in the insurance industry and a cultural flowering typified by resident authors Mark Twain *(see pp200–201)* and Harriet Beecher Stowe *(see pp30–31)*. In recent decades, an ambitious revitalization program has helped breathe new life into the downtown core.

The imposing facade of the Wadsworth Athenaeum

Exploring Hartford

Approaching the city by car, travelers are greeted by sunlight gleaming off the gold-leaf dome of the hilltop **State Capitol**. Many of Hartford's most popular attractions are easily accessed on foot from the Capitol building, which has an information office for tourists.

🏛 Old State House

800 Main St. **[** *(860) 522-6766.* **○** *year-round: 10am–4pm Mon–Fri, 11am–4pm Sat.* **●** *last two weeks Aug & public hols.* 🎫 ♿ 🚻

The 1796 State House, designed by Charles Bulfinch (1763–1844), is the country's oldest Capitol building. Its graceful center hall, grand staircase, and ornate cupola make the Old State House one of the nation's finest examples of Federal architecture. Of interest are the Great Senate Room and the courtroom where the slave ship *Amistad* trial of 1839 was held. Actors stage reenactments of the trial, which eventually absolved a group of Africans accused of mutiny.

🏠 Center Church and Ancient Burying Ground

675 Main St. **Church [** *(860) 249-5631.* **○** *by appt.* 🎫 *by appt.* **Burying Ground [** *(860) 561-2585.* **○** *10am–4pm daily.*

Five stained-glass windows designed by US artist Louis Comfort Tiffany (1848–1933) grace the 1807 Center Church (First Church of Christ in Hartford). The church's Ancient Burying Ground contains some 415 headstones dating back to 1648, including that of Hartford's founding father Thomas Hooker. Across Main Street is the 527-ft- (160-m-) high Travelers Tower, the tallest man-made observation post in the state.

🏛 Wadsworth Athenaeum

600 Main St. **[** *(860) 278-2670.* **○** *year-round: 11am–5pm Tue–Sun.* **●** *Mon & public hols.* 🎫 *free Thu & before 12pm Sat.* 🎫 ♿ 🖥 🚻

Open since 1844, this museum has the distinction of being

the oldest continuously operating public art museum in the country. Its extensive collection has 45,000 pieces and spans five centuries. It is particularly strong in Renaissance, Baroque, and Impressionist works, as well as in European decorative arts. The museum is especially noted for its extensive collection of American paintings, including works by Thomas Cole (1801–48) and Frederic Church (1826–1900). Outside in the Burr Mall is the monumental red steel sculpture called *Stegosaurus* (1973) by Connecticut resident Alexander Calder (1898–1976).

Alexander Calder's *Stegosaurus*

🏠 Harriet Beecher Stowe House

77 Forest St. **[** *(860) 522-9258.* **○** *year-round: 9:30am–4:30pm Mon–Sat, 12pm–4:30pm Sun.* **●** *Oct–May: Mon & public hols.* 🎫 🎫 *obligatory.* ♿ *first floor.* 🚻 📷

Located next to the Mark Twain House *(see pp200–201)*, this home is adorned with gingerbread ornamentation typical of late 19th-century Victorian design. Stowe's fame as the author of the anti-slavery novel *Uncle Tom's Cabin* (1852) overshadowed her skill as an interior decorator. Evidence of her talent is the upper-class elegance of her 1871 home. The Stowes lived here until Harriet's death in 1896.

East Senate Chambers of Hartford's Old State House

♣ Bushnell Park

Trinity and Elm Sts.
📞 (860) 232-6710. ⬤ year-round. 📷 May–Oct.
⬥ Carousel ⬤ May–Oct:
11am–5pm Tue–Sun. ▨

Shaded by 100 tree
varieties, the 40-acre
(16-ha) park is the
lush creation of noted
landscape architect
and Hartford native
Frederick Law
Olmsted (1822–1903).
Children adore the
park's 1914 Bushnell
Carousel, with its 48
hand-carved horses, ornate
"lovers' chariots," and
refurbished Wurlitzer band
organ. The 115-ft- (35-m-) tall
Soldiers and Sailors Memorial
Arch honors those who saw
duty in the American Civil
War (1861–65).

♣ Elizabeth Park Rose Gardens

Prospect Ave. 📞 (860) 242-0017.
Gardens ⬤ dawn to dusk daily.
Greenhouses ⬤ 10am–4pm daily.
Ninety-acre (28-ha) Elizabeth
Park was the first city-owned
rose garden in the United
States. Each year more than
900 varieties of rose bloom
on approximately 15,000

Soldiers and Sailors Memorial

bushes. The park
also has delightful
herb, perennial, and
rock gardens as well.

⚏ State Capitol

210 Capitol Ave. 📞 (860)
240-0222. ⬤ Apr–Oct:
8am–5pm Mon–Sat;
Nov–Mar: 8am–5pm
Mon–Fri. ⬥ 🖼

The State Capitol
was designed by
Richard Upjohn
(1828–1903) in the
high Victorian-
Gothic style. It is
constructed primarily of
marble and granite and
has a golden dome.
Highlights of the grand
interior are the oak
woodwork and the
ornate oak
charter chair.

🏛 Museum of American Political Life

200 Bloomfield Ave. 📞 (860) 768-
4090. ⬤ Jun–Aug: 11am–4pm
Tue–Fri, 12pm–4pm Sat; Sep–May:
11am–4pm Tue–Fri, 12pm–4pm
Sat–Sun. ⬤ public hols. ▨
West Hartford, 5 miles (8 km)
from Hartford, hosts the
Museum of American Political
Life. It sits on the University
of Hartford campus and has
a huge collection of banners,
campaign buttons,
posters, and artifacts
from George
Washington's day
to the present.

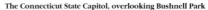

The Connecticut State Capitol, overlooking Bushnell Park

HARTFORD CITY CENTER

Bushnell Park ⑤
Center Church ②
Old State House ①
State Capitol ⑥
Travelers Tower ③
Wadsworth
Athenaeum ④

KEY

═══ Interstate

🚉 Train station

─── Railroad

ℹ Tourist information

🅿 Parking

0 meters 500

0 yards 500

Mark Twain House

Brickwork

MARK TWAIN (1835–1910) lived in this delightful house with his family from 1874 to 1891. During that prolific period, he penned six novels. Based in part on a floor plan sketched out by Twain's wife, Olivia, the 19-room home is a masterpiece of the Picturesque-Gothic style – combining both the sense of high style and playfulness personified by its owners. Legend has it that Twain, a former riverboat pilot, had his architect design the home with expansive upper balconies, peaked gables, and towering turrets in order to give the house the appearance of one of his beloved Mississippi steamboats.

North face of Mark Twain House, showing peaked gable and turret

★ Billiard Room
Twain wrote some of his best-known works, including The Adventures of Tom Sawyer *(1876), in the tranquility of the Billiard Room.*

★ Library
The ornate fireplace mantel was carved in Scotland in 1869 for a castle that burned down before it was installed.

Turret-style bay windows

The Conservatory
houses a statue of Eve by Karl Gerhardt (1853–1940). Twain had helped finance Gerhardt's studies in Europe.

STAR FEATURES

★ Billiard Room

★ Library

★ Master Bedroom

VISITORS' CHECKLIST

351 Farmington Ave. ☎ *(860) 247-0998 ext 26.* 🚌 *all buses marked E Farmington Ave.* ☐ *May–Oct & Dec: 9:30am–4pm Mon–Sat, 12pm–4pm Sun; Jan–Apr & Nov: 9:30am–4pm Mon & Wed–Sat, 12pm–4pm Sun.* ● *Jan 1, Easter Sunday, Thanksgiving, Dec 24 & 25.* 📷 📅 *obligatory, last tour 4pm.* ♿ *first floor only.* W *www.marktwain.org*

★ Master Bedroom
Twain rhapsodized about the Master Bedroom, claiming it possessed "the most comfortable bedstead that ever was [and one that brings] peace to the sleepers."

The decorative treatment of the railings is indicative of the "Stick" style of the 1870s.

Entrance
The massive wooden door leads into the neo-Tudor-style Entrance Hall, famous for its ornamental carvings.

MARK TWAIN

Raised in the frontier town of Hannibal, Missouri, on the banks of the Mississippi River, young Samuel Langhorne Clemens (better known as Mark Twain) was exposed to a strange cast of characters. Steamboat captains, gamblers, circus performers, actors, and minstrel showmen were just some of the people who passed through the town. As an adult, Twain worked as a typesetter, printer, miner, journalist, soldier, lecturer, editor, and even steamboat captain before finally trying his hand at writing full-time in 1870.

Graceful exterior of the Hill-Stead Museum in Farmington

Farmington ❷

🏛 *21,050.* 🚉 *232 Murphy Rd, Hartford (860) 244-8181 or (800) 793-4480.*

PERCHED ON THE BANKS of the surging Farmington River, this quiet enclave has long been the starting point for canoeists, fishermen, and bird-watchers. The skies above the Farmington River Valley are also a busy place, popular with hang gliders and hot-air balloonists taking in the spectacular vistas from on high. Several companies offer champagne flights over the scenic valley, while others offer candlelit tours of the town's historic homes.

The interior of the **Hill-Stead Museum** has remained unchanged since the 1946 death of its original owner Theodate Pope Riddle (1867–1946). Pope, one of the country's first female architects, designed the Colonial–Revival mansion, which was completed in 1901. Her will stipulated that upon her death nothing in the house could be changed, altered, or moved. The result is a fascinating home frozen in the Edwardian period. On display is the Riddle family's fine collection of French and American Impressionist paintings, including works by Edgar Degas (1834–1917), Édouard Manet (1832–83), Mary Cassatt (1845–1926), and James Whistler (1834–1903). The museum also contains splendid examples of American and European furniture and decorative arts. Particularly noteworthy on the grounds of the 150-acre (61-ha) estate is the sunken garden. The **Stanley-Whitman**

House is a well-preserved example of the framed over-hang style of early 18th-century architecture of New England. The house, furnished with Colonial pieces, is often used as a venue for craft demonstrations and exhibits. Elsewhere in Farmington, admirers of old cemeteries will find many markers of interest in the Ancient Burying Ground, with gravestones dating back to 1661. In the Riverside Cemetery, one tombstone marks the grave of Foone, an African slave who drowned in the town's canal after being

freed in the *Amistad* trial (*see pp198–9*).

🏛 **Hill-Stead Museum**
35 Mountain Rd. ☎ *(860) 677-9064.* ⬜ *May–Oct: 10am–5pm Tue–Sun; Nov–Apr: 11am–4pm Tue–Sun.* ⬤ *Mon & public hols.* 📷 🎫 *obligatory.* ♿ *partial.*
🏛 **Stanley-Whitman House**
37 High St. ☎ *(860) 677-9222.* ⬜ *May–Oct: 12pm–4pm Wed–Sun; Nov–Apr: 12pm–4pm Sat–Sun.* 📷 🎫 ♿ *partial.*

ENVIRONS: Twenty miles (32 km) south of Farmington lies the blue-collar town of Waterbury. The town is

Arts of the West by Thomas Hart Benton at the New Britain Museum of American Art

IMPRESSIONIST ART TRAIL

Between 1885 and 1930 Connecticut was a magnet for many American artists. Childe Hassam (1859–1935), J. Alden Weir (1852–1919), Willard Metcalf (1858–1925), and others depicted marshes, seascapes, harbors, and farms in a style called American Impressionism. Their works are in ten museums on a self-guided trail that winds from Greenwich to New London.

SIGHTS AT A GLANCE

Bruce Museum, Greenwich ①
Bush-Holley Historic Site, Cos Cob ②
Florence Griswold Museum, Old Lyme ⑨
Hartford Steam Boiler Company, Hartford ⑧
Hill-Stead Museum, Farmington ⑥
Lyman Allyn Art Museum, New London ⑩
New Britain Museum of American Art, New Britain ⑤
Wadsworth Athenaeum, Hartford ⑦
Weir Farm, Ridgefield and Wilton ③
Yale University Art Gallery, New Haven ④

proud of its ethnic roots, as evidenced by its 240-ft- (73-m-) tall Clock Tower, modeled on the city hall in Siena, Italy. Tools, decorative arts, and reconstructed workers' quarters in the **Mattatuck Museum** help trace Waterbury's rise to fame as the "Brass City" during the 19th and early 20th century.

🏛 Mattatuck Museum
144 W Main St, Waterbury. ☎ (203) 753-0381. ◷ year-round: 10am–5pm Tue–Sat, 12pm–5pm Sun. ● Mon, Sun in Jul & Aug, & public hols. ✇ ✇ ♿ ▣

New Britain ❸

🏙 70,000. 🛈 1 Grove Place, Suite 301 (860) 225-3901.

L YING AT THE GEOGRAPHIC center of the state, New Britain is also the midpoint between Boston to the north and New York to the south. Travelers to either city should stop to visit the **New Britain Museum of American Art**. The repository's 19 galleries house a distinguished collection of art from the Colonial period to the present. Almost every well-known US artist is represented here, including Georgia O'Keeffe (1887–1986), Andrew Wyeth (b.1917), Alexander Calder (1898–1976), and Isamu Noguchi (1904–88). The American Impressionist collection is also important.

🏛 New Britain Museum of American Art
56 Lexington St, New Britain. ☎ (860) 229-0257. ◷ year-round: 12pm–5pm Tue–Fri & Sun, 10am–5pm Sat. ✇

Dinosaur State Park ❹

400 West St, Rocky Hill. ☎ (860) 529-8423. **Park** ◷ 9am–4:30pm daily. **Exhibit center** ◷ 9am–4:30pm Tue–Sun. ● public hols. ✇

D URING THE LOWER JURASSIC period some 200 million years ago, the dinosaurs that roamed this region literally left their mark on the land. Today some 500 prehistoric tracks are preserved beneath this park's huge geodesic dome. Also on display is a life-size model of an eight-

One of 500 ancient tracks at **Dinosaur State Park**

ft- (2-m-) tall *Dilophosaurus*, the creature that most likely left the prints. Two large dioramas tell the story of the Connecticut Valley during the Triassic and Jurassic periods. A highlight of this exhibit is a replica of *Coelophysis*, the bones of which were found in the area. A thrill for children and amateur paleontologists is the chance to make plaster casts of the tracks as part of the interpretive programs. (Call ahead to find out what to bring.) The park also has a picnic area and miles of nature trails that double as cross-country skiing runs.

Farmington

Hartford

New Britain

New Haven

Connecticut River

Thames River

New London

Old Lyme

Interior of Wadsworth Athenaeum

Mary Cassatt's work at Hill-Stead Museum

KEY

━━ Tour route

══ Other road

0 kilometers   15

0 miles   15

Street-by-Street: Wethersfield ❺

NOW AN AFFLUENT Hartford suburb, Wethersfield began as the state's first settlement in 1634. In 1640 its citizens held an illegal public election – America's first act of defiance against British rule. The town also hosted the 1781 Revolutionary War conference between George Washington (1732–99) and his French allies, during which they finalized strategies for the decisive American victory in Yorktown. Preserved within a 12-block area, Old Wethersfield stands as a primer of American architecture, with numerous houses from the 18th to 20th centuries. The centerpiece is the Webb-Deane-Stevens Museum, a trio of dwellings depicting the differing lifestyles of three 18th-century Americans: a wealthy merchant, a diplomat, and a leather tanner.

A Connecticut River-style entrance built in 1767

Church and Main
The house atop the street sign marks the area of one of Connecticut's first suburban communities.

133 Main Street
This 1787 house was the home of Reverend Joseph Emerson, who ran the Female Seminary at the Old Academy at 150 Main.

KEY

– – – Suggested route

Memorial Plaque
This simple plaque pays tribute to the Massachusetts adventurers who settled here in 1634.

STAR SIGHTS

★ **First Church of Christ**

★ **Webb-Deane-Stevens Museum**

★ **Buttolph Williams House**

◁ **Cruising through The Thimbles, a collection of 365 islands and islets**

VISITORS' CHECKLIST

🏛 26,000. ✈ Bradley International Airport, 17 miles (27 km) N in Windsor Locks. 🚌 from Hartford. ℹ Greater Hartford Tourism District, 234 Murphy Rd, Hartford. (860) 244-8181 or (800) 793-4480. W www.enjoyhartford.com

★ First Church of Christ

One of only three Colonial meeting houses left in the state, the 1761 church included presidents George Washington (1732–99) and John Adams (1735–1826) among its worshipers.

Ancient Burying Ground

Legend has it that the graves of nine victims of the 1637 Pequot Massacres are buried here.

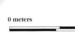

Wethersfield Museum & Visitors' Center

★ Buttolph Williams House

Built c.1720, this house exemplifies the era's austere architecture. The parlor is shown at right.

★ Webb-Deane-Stevens Museum

The Joseph Webb House, built in 1751, is part of the Webb-Deane-Stevens Museum. Shown at right is wallpaper from one of the upstairs bed chambers.

Litchfield Hills ❻

American Clock and Watch Museum

N ESTLED IN THE FOLDS AND FOOTHILLS of the Berkshire Hills and Taconic Mountains in the northwesternmost section of Connecticut, the Litchfield Hills region covers some 1,000 sq miles (2,590 sq km), or one-quarter of the state. Many people consider this to be the most scenic part of Connecticut. Anchored by the Housatonic River, the bucolic landscape of woods, valleys, lakes, and wildlife offers unparalleled opportunities for canoeing, kayaking, white-water rafting, tubing, fly-fishing, and hiking. In autumn, traffic along the winding roads can slow as the brilliant fall foliage entrances sightseers. A steady influx of the wealthy into the area has resulted in the gentrification of Litchfield's 26 towns and villages, with boutiques and bistros popping up beside traditional craft shops and historic homes and gardens.

Fishing at Mount Tom State Park outside Litchfield

Bristol

🏠 62,000. 🛈 10 Main St (860) 584-4718.
Bristol's past as a premier clock manufacturing center is celebrated at the American Clock and Watch Museum on Maple Street. Housed in an 1801 mansion, this vast collection includes 5,000 clocks and watches.

Bristol is also home to the Lake Compounce Theme Park, the nation's oldest amusement park. Complete with the fastest and longest wooden roller coaster on the East Coast, a haunted house, and a white-water raft ride, the park on Lake Avenue has been entertaining families since 1846. More family fun can be found on Riverside Avenue in the form of the New England Carousel Museum. Its collection of antique carousels is one of the finest in the world.

Woodbury

🏠 9,400. 🛈 Litchfield.
With its 45 shops and dealers, this is a popular haunt for antique lovers. Antique furnishings from the late 18th century can also be found at the Glebe House on Hollow Road. This minister's farmhouse is surrounded by the Gertrude Jekyll Garden, the noted English landscaper's only garden on US soil. The

town is also blessed with five churches from various eras that have been wonderfully preserved.

New Preston

🛈 Litchfield.
New Preston offers access to 95-acre (38-ha) Lake Waramaug State Park. The lake is especially beautiful in the autumn, when the glorious colors are reflected on its mirrorlike surface. Visitors can rent canoes for peaceful paddles around the shoreline, and some 80 campsites cater to enthusiasts who want to linger and enjoy the great outdoors. The Hopkins Vineyard, perched

above the lake, offers wine tastings along with tours of its facilities.

Litchfield

🏠 8,850. 🛈 Litchfield Hills Visitors' Bureau, PO Box 968, Litchfield (860) 567-0263.
Picturesque Litchfield has many noteworthy historic buildings, such as South Street's 1784 Tapping Reeve House and Law School, the country's first law school.

Just on the outskirts of town on Route 202, Mount Tom State Park has trails leading to the 1,325-ft (404-m) summit. The lake is ideal for scuba diving, swimming, boating, and fishing.

Elegant Bellamy-Ferriday House and Garden in Bethlehem

Bethlehem

🏛 3,700. ℹ Litchfield.

One of the town's highlights is the Bellamy-Ferriday House and Garden, the 18th-century home of Reverend Joseph Bellamy (1719–90), founder of the first theological seminary in America. Located on Main Street, this 13-room house displays Ferriday family delftware, furniture, antiques, and Oriental art.

West Cornwall

ℹ Litchfield.

Tiny West Cornwall is best known for its covered bridge. The 1841 bridge, which spans the Housatonic River, is only one of two such spans in the state open to car traffic.

Norfolk

🏛 2,000. ℹ Litchfield.

Founded in 1758, this small village is located in the northwest corner of the state. Its village green is known for two key reasons: a monument that was designed by architect Stanford White (1853–1906) and US sculptor Augustus Saint-Gaudens (see pp262–3); and the Music Shed. The latter is an auditorium on the Ellen Batell Stoeckel Estate that hosts the highly acclaimed annual Norfolk Music Festival.

Re-created Algonkian village at the Institute for American Indian Studies

Washington

🏛 3,950. ℹ Litchfield.

At the Institute for American Indian Studies, situated on Curtis Road, those with a bent for history can examine a pre-contact Algonkian village, artifacts from 10,000 years ago, and exhibits of northwest Connecticut's Woodland Indians. The grounds contain a re-created archaeological dig.

Kent

🏛 2,900. ℹ Litchfield.

Art lovers should go out of their way to visit this small community. It is well known for having the highest concentration of galleries in the region. The Bachelier-Cardonsky Gallery on Main Street and the Paris-New York-Kent Gallery on Kent Station Square are two of the most popular. North of town travelers indulge in outdoor fun at Kent Falls State Park. A short hike into the 295-acre (119-ha) park will reward visitors with stunning views of what many people consider the most impressive waterfall in Connecticut. Picnic facilities overlook the idyllic scene.

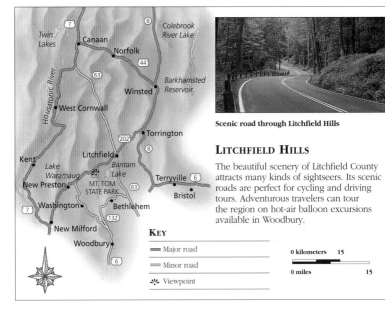

Scenic road through Litchfield Hills

LITCHFIELD HILLS

The beautiful scenery of Litchfield County attracts many kinds of sightseers. Its scenic roads are perfect for cycling and driving tours. Adventurous travelers can tour the region on hot-air balloon excursions available in Woodbury.

KEY

━━ Major road

══ Minor road

�)(Viewpoint

0 kilometers   15

0 miles   15

Picturesque bridge over the Connecticut River outside the town of Windsor

Simsbury **7**

🏠 22,000. ℹ️ 800 Hopmeadow St (860) 658-2500.

Oᴿɪɢɪɴᴀʟʟʏ ᴀ ϙᴜɪᴇᴛ ᴄᴏʟᴏɴɪᴀʟ farming community, Simsbury grew into something of a boomtown in the early 1700s with the discovery of copper in the region. The wheels of US industry started turning here with the opening of the nation's first steel mill in 1728. Three centuries of local history are squeezed into the **Phelps Homestead Museum Complex**. Among the six historic buildings located on the site are a one-room 1740 schoolhouse, a Victorian carriage house, a colonial-era barn, and the fully furnished home of an 18th-century sea captain. Exhibits outlining 300 years of agriculture in the region stand next to displays of industrial tools and antique farm implements.

🏛 **Phelps Homestead Museum Complex**
800 Hopmeadow St. 📞 (860) 658-2500. 🕐 mid-May–Columbus Day: 10am–4pm Tue–Sat; rest of year: call for hours. 🔵 public hols. 🦽 🎫 summer: 1pm–4pm.

Windsor **8**

🏠 27,800. ℹ️ 96 Palisado Ave (860) 688-3813 or (800) 248-8283.

Wɪɴᴅsᴏʀ ᴡᴀs sᴇᴛᴛʟᴇᴅ in the early 1630s by Pilgrims from Plymouth (see pp148–9), making it the oldest permanent English settlement in the state — a claim that is disputed by the residents of nearby Wethersfield (see pp206–207). A drive along Palisado Avenue passes several historic houses.

The 1758 **John & Sarah Strong House** is an old surviving frame structure named after the newlyweds who built it and lived in it for four years before heading west to settle. It has an excellent collection of furnishings reflecting the history of Windsor. Across the street is the **Dr. Hezekiah Chaffee House**, a three-story brick Georgian-Colonial built in the mid-1700s. The home is appointed with period furniture and features changing exhibits. Visitors may also tour the adjoining Palisado Green. Here nervous settlers built a walled stockade during the 1637 war with the Pequot Indians. Further down the road stands the 1780 Georgian

home of the state's first senator, Oliver Ellsworth (1745–1807). Today the **Oliver Ellsworth Homestead** contains interior design details from the era, including the original wallpaper.

🏛 **John & Sarah Strong House**
96 Palisado Ave. 📞 (860) 688-3813. 🕐 year-round: 10am–4pm Tue–Sat. 🔵 Sun–Mon & public hols. 🦽 includes admission to Dr. Hezekiah Chaffee House. 🎫

🏛 **Dr. Hezekiah Chaffee House**
96 Palisado Ave. 📞 (860) 688-3813. 🕐 year-round: 10am–4pm Tue–Sat. 🔵 Sun–Mon & public hols. 🦽 includes admission to John & Sarah Strong House. 🎫

🏛 **Oliver Ellsworth Homestead**
778 Palisado Ave. 📞 (860) 688-8717. 🕐 mid-May–mid-Oct: 12pm–4:30pm Tue–Wed & Sat. 🦽

Eɴᴠɪʀᴏɴs: Fifteen miles (24 km) north of Windsor, the **Connecticut Trolley Museum** takes visitors on a nostalgic journey. A round-trip through the grounds on an antique trolley highlights permanent displays of classic trolley cars dating from 1894 to 1949. The Connecticut Fire Museum is annexed to the museum and has antique fire trucks and tells the colorful history of state firefighting.

🏛 **Connecticut Trolley Museum**
58 North Rd, East Windsor. 📞 (860) 627-6540. 🕐 Apr–Memorial Day: 10am–5pm Sat, 12pm–5pm Sun; Memorial Day–Labor Day: 10am–5pm Wed–Sat, 12pm–5pm Sun. 🦽 access to both museums.

Sea captain's home, Phelps Homestead Museum Complex

New England Air Museum **9**

Bradley International Airport, Windsor Locks. **📞** *(860) 623-3305.* **⏰** *10am–5pm daily.* **●** *Jan 1, Thanksgiving, & Dec 25.* 🅰 🗹 🚻 🔒

AVIATION FANS can indulge their flights of fancy at the largest aviation museum in the Northeast. The impressive collection of 80 aircraft spans the complete history of aviation beginning with pre-Wright Brothers flying machines right up to present-day jets and rescue helicopters. Located near Bradley International Airport, the museum is housed in and around two cavernous hangars. Highlights include a Bunce-Curtiss Pusher, a vintage 1909 Blériot and a Sikorsky VS-44 Flying Boat, the last of the four-engined flying boats.

To experience the thrill of flying, visitors can strap themselves into a simulator of the Grumman Tracer, where pilots were trained to fly.

Old New-Gate Prison and Copper Mine insignia

Old New-Gate Prison and Copper Mine **10**

ℹ *115 Newgate Rd, East Granby.* **📞** *(860) 653-3563.* **⏰** *mid-May–Oct: 10am–4:30pm Wed–Sun.* 🅰 🗹 🚻 🔒

WHEN FINANCIAL WOES forced the sale of this less than prosperous 18th-century copper mine, its new proprietors found a novel but grim use for the dark hole in the ground. In 1773 the local government transformed the nation's first chartered copper mine into the state's first colonial prison. Over the course of

One of the planes on display at the New England Air Museum

its infamous career, the jail held everyone from horse thieves to captured British soldiers. New-Gate represented a particularly brutal form of punishment, with prisoners living and sleeping in damp, sunless tunnels. Mercifully, the prison was abandoned in 1827, although tours of its lower chamber still inspire shivers.

Coventry **11**

👥 *11,350.* **ℹ** *1195 Main St (860) 742-1085.*

COVENTRY IS THE BIRTHPLACE of Nathan Hale (1755–76), one of the inspirational heroes of the American Revolution (1775–83). Just minutes before he was to be hanged by the British for being a spy, the 21-year-old Coventry schoolteacher uttered his now famous last words, "I only regret that I have but one life to lose for my country."

The **Nathan Hale Homestead** is an anomaly in that its

namesake never actually lived in the house. The existing structure, located on the site where Hale was born, was built by Hale's brothers and father in 1776, the same year he was executed.

Some of Hale's belongings are on display, including his Bible, army trunk, silver shoe buckles, and boyhood "fowling piece," which is hung above the fireplace in the dining room.

Coventry is also home to the **Caprilands Herb Farm**, a 20-acre (8-ha) operational farm with more than 30 herb gardens. The greenhouse and grounds are open to the public, as is the restored 18th-century barn. At the end of a visit, some of the more than 300 types of herbs grown here can be purchased.

🏛 **Nathan Hale Homestead** 2299 South St. **📞** *(860) 742-6917.* **⏰** *mid-May–mid-Oct: 1pm–4pm Wed–Sun & by appt.* 🅰 🗹 🚻 *partial.*
🏛 **Caprilands Herb Farm** 534 Silver St. **📞** *(860) 742-7244.* **⏰** *year-round:10am–5pm daily.* **●** *public hols.*

The 10-room Nathan Hale Homestead in Coventry

Lebanon

🏠 6,500. ✈ Hartford. 🚌 🚉 New London. ❓ 856 Trumbull Hwy (860) 642-6579.

Tʜɪs ᴇᴀsᴛᴇʀɴ Connecticut community is steeped in American Revolution history. It was here on the 160-acre (65-ha) common that French hussars trained before joining their American allies in Yorktown for the climactic battle of the conflict. Lebanon native and artist John Trumbull (1756–1843), whose paintings can be seen in Hartford's Wadsworth Athenaeum *(see pp198–9)*, put down his paintbrush long enough to design the town's 1807 Congregational Church.

Also overlooking the green is the **Governor Jonathan Trumbull's House**. The 1740 house has a secret room where Trumbull's father, an ardent Patriot, hid from the English during the American Revolution. Further along the common are such stops as the **Doctor William Beaumont Homestead**, where one of the world's pioneers of gastric medicine was born, as well as the neoclassical Wadsworth Stable, where George Washington (1732–99) kept his horses.

🏛 Governor Jonathan Trumbull's House
169 W Town St. ☎ (860) 642-7558. ○ mid-May–mid-Oct: 1pm–5pm Tue–Sat. ◙

🏛 Doctor William Beaumont Homestead
169 W Town St. ☎ (860) 642-6579. ○ May–Oct: 1pm–5pm Sat. ◙

Eɴᴠɪʀᴏɴs: Twelve miles (19 km) to the east, Canterbury is home to the

Prudence Crandall House. Crandall (1803–90) raised the ire of citizens when, in 1832, she admitted a young black student to her private school for girls. Undaunted by threats of boycotts, Crandall kept the school open and attracted students, many of whom were black, from other states. Public outcry was such that the local government pushed through a law forbidding private schools to admit black children from out of state. Crandall was subsequently jailed and brought to trial. It was only after an angry mob attacked the school in 1834 that the heroic Quaker woman reluctantly closed its doors forever. Today the museum commemorates Crandall's struggle and traces local black history.

🏛 Prudence Crandall House
Canterbury Green. ☎ (860) 546-9916. ○ year-round: 10am–4pm Wed–Sun. ◙

Norwich ⑬

🏠 35,000. ❓ 69 Main St. (860) 886-4683.

Nᴏʀᴡɪᴄʜ ʜᴀs the dubious distinction of being the birthplace of Benedict Arnold (1741–1801), forever synonymous with traitor for betraying Colonial forces during the American Revolution. In contrast, the Colonial Cemetery contains graves of soldiers, both American and French, who died fighting for the American cause during the war.

A two-story colonial structure consisting of a pair of annexed saltboxes, the **Christopher Leffingwell House**, is named after a financier of the Colonial side in the

American Revolution. During the war, Leffingwell's house and tavern were used for secret meetings. The interior, full of late 17th- and 18th-century furniture, has never been remodeled, making it of special interest.

🏛 Christopher Leffingwell House
348 Washington St. ☎ (860) 889-9440. ○ Apr–Dec: 1pm–4pm Tue–Sun & by appt. ● public hols. ◙ 🅿

Eɴᴠɪʀᴏɴs: Located five miles (8 km) south of Norwich is the **Shantok Village of Uncas**, final resting place of Native American leader Uncas (d.1683). Inspiration for James Fenimore Cooper's novel *Last of the Mohicans* (1826), Uncas provided early colonists with the plot of land for the original Norwich settlement and sided with them during the Pequot War of the 1630s. An obelisk memorializing Uncas was erected here in 1840.

A Leffingwell sculpture

🏛 Shantok Village of Uncas
Rte 32 S of Norwich. ☎ (888) 226-7711. ○ dawn to dusk daily. 🅿

Foxwoods Resort Casino ⑭

Rte 2. ☎ (800) PLAYBIG. **Casino** ○ 24 hrs daily. ♿ 🅿 🍴 ⊟ ∅ ☕ 🛍

Fɪʀsᴛ ᴏꜰ ᴛʜᴇ ɴᴀᴛɪᴠᴇ American-operated casinos, this gaming facility has hundreds of games tables, more than 5,800 slot machines, and high-stakes bingo and poker. In addition, the 1,500-seat Fox Theater attracts entertainment headliners from around the world.

Also on casino grounds is the **Mashantucket Pequot Museum**, a state-of-the-art research and exhibition center of Native American history. Multimedia displays and touch-screen computers provide a detailed study of the natural history of the area

Jonathan Trumbull's War Office in Lebanon

Life-size Native American figures at the Mashantucket Pequot Museum

and its earliest inhabitants. Walking through a replica Pequot Village c.1500, visitors come upon life-size figures depicting aspects of local Native American life.

⛪ Mashantucket Pequot Museum
110 Pequot Trail. ((860) 396-6800 or (800) 411-9671. ◯ Memorial Day–Labor Day: 10am–7pm daily; rest of year: 10am–6pm Wed–Mon. ● Jan 1, Thanksgiving, & Dec 25. ☒ ☑ 🔊 ▢ ▥

New London ⑮

🏠 26,000. 🚋 ⓘ 470 Bank St (860) 444-2206 or (800) 863-6569.

BRITISH FORCES LED by traitor Benedict Arnold razed New London during the American Revolution. Rebounding from the attack, the town enjoyed new-found prosperity during the whaling industry during the 19th century. The four colonnaded Greek Revival mansions along Whale Oil Row attest to the affluence of that era.

Remarkably, many homes survived Arnold's torching, including the **Joshua Hempsted House**. Built in 1678, the dwelling is insulated with seaweed and represents one of the few 17th-century homes left in the state.

Connecticut College houses the **Lyman Allyn Art Museum**, a repository of decorative arts and a dollhouse collection. Also on campus, the 750-acre (303-ha) college Arboretum encompasses a variety of ecosystems, native trees and shrubs, trails, and ponds. At the edge of town is **Monte Cristo Cottage**, boyhood home of Nobel Prize-winning playwright Eugene O'Neill (1888–1953). The two-story cottage, which served as the setting for his Pulitzer Prize-winning play *Long Day's Journey into Night* (1957), is now a research library, with some of O'Neill's belongings on display.

⛪ Joshua Hempsted House
Jct of Hempstead, Jay, & Truman Sts. ((860) 443-7949. ◯ mid-May–mid-Oct: 12pm–4pm Thu–Sun. ▨ ▢ obligatory.

⛪ Lyman Allyn Art Museum
625 Williams St. ((860) 443-2545. ◯ year-round: 10am–5pm Tue–Sat, 1pm–5pm Sun. ● public hols. ▨ ▢ by appt. 🔊

⛪ Monte Cristo Cottage
325 Pequot Ave. ((860) 443-0051. ◯ Memorial Day–Labor Day: 10am–5pm Tue–Sat; mid-Sept–Oct: call for hours. ● public hols. ▨

ENVIRONS: Directly across the river from New London is Groton. The USS *Nautilus*, the world's first nuclear-powered

submarine is berthed at the **Submarine Force Museum** on the Naval Submarine Base. **Fort Griswold Battlefield State Park** is where British troops under Benedict Arnold killed surrendered American soldiers in 1781. A 134-ft (41-m) obelisk memorial and a battle diorama mark the event.

⛪ Submarine Force Museum
Crystal Lake Rd. ((860) 694-3174. ◯ mid-May–mid-Oct: 9am–5pm Wed–Mon, 1pm–5pm Tue; rest of year: 9am–4pm Wed–Mon. 🔊

⛵ Fort Griswold Battlefield State Park
Monument & Park Aves. ((860) 445-1729. **Museum** ◯ May–Labor Day: 9am–5pm daily. **Park** ◯ year-round: 8am–sunset daily.

Sea lion sculpture on the rocks at Mystic Aquarium

Mystic ⑯

🏠 2,600. ⓘ 28 Cottrell St (860) 572-9578.

WHEN SHIPBUILDING waned, Mystic turned to tourism. Today Mystic Seaport (see pp214–15) and **Mystic Aquarium**, a world-class venue, make the town bustle. Seals and sea lions cavort in the outdoor Seal Island; indoors is a colony of African black-footed penguins and 3,500 sea creatures. The world's largest outdoor beluga tank and a huge gallery of stingrays and sharks as well as a coral display are fascinating. The 14,000-seat theater has daily shows.

⛪ Mystic Aquarium
55 Coogan Blvd. ((860) 572-5955. ◯ Jul–Labor Day: 9am–6pm daily; rest of year: 9am–5pm daily. ● Jan 1, Thanksgiving, & Dec 25. ▨ 🔊 ▥

World's first nuclear-powered sub, USS *Nautilus*, berthed at Groton

Mystic Seaport

Town welcome

WHAT BEGAN AS A MODEST collection of nautical odds and ends housed in an old mill in 1929 has grown into the world's largest maritime museum. The 17-acre (7-ha) working replica of a 19th-century port is a complex of more than 40 buildings open to the public, including a bank, chapel, tavern, rope-making shops, and one-room schoolhouse from the 1800s. Despite its fascinating exhibits of ship models and authentic scrimshaw, Mystic Seaport's main attraction remains its preservation shipyard and its fleet of antique ships, including the *Charles W. Morgan*, the last remaining vessel in the nation's fleet of 19th-century whalers.

Seagoing Connection
Almost every building in town sports a nautical motif.

Whaleboat Exhibit
A fully equipped whaleboat contains all the gear carried in such vessels in the late 1800s. It is housed in a shed on Chubb's Wharf.

Burrows House
The early 1800s home of a shopkeeper and his milliner wife re-creates coastal domestic life.

Middle Wharf

Shipcarver's Shop
Independent craftsmen carved figureheads and other decorations, such as this American eagle, for shipbuilders.

★ The *Charles W. Morgan*
The last wooden whaling ship in the world was built for a Quaker merchant in 1841. Visitors can tour the quarters of officers and crew.

STAR FEATURES

★ **Mystic River Scale Model**

★ **The *Charles W. Morgan***

Thomas Oyster House
Initially used as a culling shop to sort oysters by size, the 1874 building was later used to shuck oysters before shipping them on ice.

Village Green Bandstand
Sometimes used as a concert venue, especially for July 4th celebrations.

The *L.A. Dunton*
This 1921 schooner is the last existing example of the once-popular New England round-bow fishing vessels.

The *Sabino*
Built in 1908 in East Boothbay, Maine, the coal-fueled steamship Sabino takes passengers on cruises along the Connecticut coast.

The *Joseph Conrad*
Built in Denmark in 1882, this is one of the museum's three largest ships. It serves as a training vessel.

★ Mystic River Scale Model
Inside is a 50-ft- (17-m-) long model giving a bird's-eye view of Mystic in 1870. It has more than 250 detailed buildings.

Lighthouse
This structure is a copy of the 1746 Brant Point Lighthouse on Nantucket, the second lighthouse to be built in New England.

The Harpist by Alphonse Jongers
at the Florence Griswold Museum

Old Lyme ⑰

🏃 6,800. ℹ️ 470 Bank St, New
London (860) 444-2206.

O NCE A SHIPBUILDING center,
Old Lyme is home to
numerous 18th- and 19th-
century houses. Originally
built for merchants and sea
captains, many became residences of the artists who
established a colony here
in the early 1900s.
The **Florence Griswold
Museum** is intimately linked
to the arts. Not only are the
walls of this 1817 mansion
adorned with some of the
country's great paintings,
but some of the walls are
works of art themselves.
The mansion became the
home of Captain Robert
Griswold and his daughter
Florence. An art patron,
Florence began letting rooms
in the 1890s to New York
artists looking for a summer
by the sea. She hosted Henry
Ward Ranger (1858–1916),
Childe Hassam (1859–1935),
and Clark Voorhees (1871–
1933), spawning the Old
Lyme Art Colony.
Now a featured stop on the
American Impressionist Art
Trail *(see pp202–203)*, the
museum has more than 900
works by artists who at one
time lived in the house or
nearby. Many of Griswold's
guests painted on the wall
panels of the dining room as
thanks for her generosity.

🏛 Florence Griswold
Museum
96 Lyme St, Old Lyme. 📞 (860)
434-5542. 🕐 Jan–Apr: 1pm–5pm
Wed–Sun; May–Dec: 10am–5pm
Tue–Sat, 1pm–5pm Sun. 🎨 🎟 🚹

Essex ⑱

🏃 2,500. ℹ️ 393 Main St,
Middletown (860) 347-0028.

I N A RECENT SURVEY naming
America's top small town,
Essex was at the head of the
list. Sited on the Connecticut
River, the village is surrounded by a series of sheltered
coves and has a bustling
marina and tree-lined, virtually crime-free streets.
The **Connecticut River
Museum**, a restored 1878
warehouse, is perched on a
dock overlooking the water.
Its collection and exhibits
of maritime art and artifacts
tell the story of this once-
prominent shipbuilding
town, where the *Oliver
Cromwell* – the first warship
built for the American
Revolution (1775–83) – was
constructed. The museum's
conversation piece is a replica of the world's first submersible craft, the *Turtle*, a
squat, single-seat vehicle
built in 1776. Transportation
is also the focus at the **Essex
Steam Train & Riverboat
Ride**, where guests take an
authentic, coal-belching
steam engine for a 12-mile
(19-km) scenic tour. At the
midpoint, passengers can
take a 90-minute cruise down
the river aboard a riverboat.

🏛 Connecticut
River Museum
67 Main St. 📞 (860) 767-8269.
🕐 year-round: 10am–5pm Tue–Sun.
⬤ Labor Day, Thanksgiving, & Dec 25.
🎨 🎟 🚹
🚂 Essex Steam Train
& Riverboat Ride
Exit 3 off Rte 9. 📞 (860) 767-0103.
🕐 call for ride times. 🎨 🎟 🚹

ENVIRONS: Five miles (8 km)
north of Essex is Chester,
home to **Goodspeed-at-
Chester**, a theater that presents new musicals. Across
the Connecticut River the
town of East Haddam offers
spectacular views of river
traffic from the **Goodspeed
Opera House**. This late-
Victorian "wedding cake"
gem is the setting for new
musicals and revivals, which
are presented from April
to December.

🚂 Goodspeed-at-Chester
N Main St / Rte 82, Chester.
📞 (860) 873-8668. 🕐 call for
show times. 🎨 🚹
🚂 Goodspeed
Opera House
Rte 82, East Haddam. 📞 (860) 873-
8668. 🕐 call for show times. 🎨 🚹

**Replica of the first submersible at
Connecticut River Museum**

Gillette Castle ⑲

See pp218–19.

Madison ⑳

🏃 16,000. ℹ️ 22 Scotland Ave
(203) 245-7394.

M ADISON IS A RESORT TOWN
full of antique stores
and boutiques, including a
specialty store that stocks
British kippers, bangers, and
pork pies. Several historic
homes are open for viewing,
including the 1685 **Deacon
John Grave House**. The
structure has served as tavern, armory, courthouse, and
infirmary, but has always
belonged to the Graves. One
of the oldest artifacts on display is the family's book-
keeping ledger, with entries
from 1678 to 1895.
Madison is also home to
**Hammonasset Beach State
Park**, the largest shoreline
park in the state. Poking into
Long Island Sound, the
peninsula has a two-mile- (3-
km-) long beach that attracts
swimmers, sailors, scuba

divers, and sunbathers. The park has baseball diamonds, picnic areas, and a 541-site campground.

♛ Deacon John Grave House

581 Boston Post Rd. 🔴 *(203) 245-4798.* ○ *May–Sep: 1pm–4pm Wed–Sat.* 🔷

✗ Hammonasset Beach State Park

I-95, exit 62. **Park** 🔴 *(203) 245-2785.* **Campground reservations** 🔴 *(877) 668-2267.* **Park** ○ *8am–dusk daily.* 🔷 🔷 🔷

Guilford ㉑

🏛 *20,000.* 🚏 *393 Main St, Middletown (860) 347-0028.*

In 1639 REVEREND Henry Whitfield (1597–1657) led a group of Puritans from Surrey, England, to a wild parcel of land near the West River. There they established the town of Guilford. A year later, fearing an attack by local Mennuncatuk Indians, the colonists built a three-story stronghold out of local granite. The Tudor Gothic-style fort, the oldest stone dwelling of its type in New England, now serves as the **Henry Whitfield State Historical Museum**. The austere interior is notable for its 33-ft- (10-m-) long great hall and 17th-century furnishings.

Guilford is graced by dozens of historic 18th-century homes. Both the **Hyland House**, a classic early saltbox *(see p26)*, and the 1774 **Thomas Griswold House** are open to view. **Dudley Farm**, a 19th-century working farm and

The boardwalk at Hammonasset Beach State Park in Madison

living history museum, demonstrates agricultural techniques of the era. In mid-July craftsmen gather on Guilford Green for the Guilford Handcraft Exposition *(see p33).*

🏛 Henry Whitfield State Historical Museum

248 Old Whitfield St. 🔴 *(203) 453-2457.* ○ *Feb–mid-Dec: 10am–4:30pm Wed–Sun; mid-Dec–Jan by appt.* 🔷

♛ Hyland House

84 Boston St. 🔴 *(203) 453-9477.* ○ *Jun–Labor Day: 10am–4:30pm Tue–Sun; mid-Sep–mid-Oct: 10am–4:30pm Sat–Sun.* ● *Columbus Day.* 🔷 🔷 *obligatory.*

♛ Thomas Griswold House

171 Boston St. 🔴 *(203) 453-3176.* ○ *Jun–Labor Day: 11am–4pm Tue–Sun; mid-Sep–Oct: 11am–4pm Sat–Sun.* 🔷 🔷 *obligatory.* 🔷

♛ Dudley Farm

2351 Durham Rd. 🔴 *(203) 457-0770.* ○ *year-round: 10am–2pm Mon–Fri.* ● *Sat–Sun.*

The Thimbles ㉒

🚊 *from Stony Creek Dock.* 🚏 *(203) 488-9878.*

From STONY CREEK, travelers can cruise to the Thimble islands aboard one of several tour boats that operate in the area. Many of the 365 islands are little more than large boulders visible only at low tide. Some of the privately owned islands sport small communities. One colorful legend about this clutch of islands centers on circus midget General Tom Thumb (1838–83) courting a woman on Cut-In-Two Island. Another has the privateer Captain Kidd (1645–1701) hiding plundered treasure on Money Island while being pursued by the British fleet. Today cruisers watch seals or take in glorious fall colors.

The Thimbless, home to seals, whales, and colorful legends

Gillette Castle ⓳

Entrance sign

OSTENTATIOUS AND BIZARRE, Gillette Castle is the antithesis of New England architectural grace. However, visitors to the 24-room granite mansion always leave with a smile. Actor William Gillette (1853–1937) based the design of his 1919 dream home on medieval castles, complete with battlements and turrets. The castle is rife with such oddities as Gillette's homemade trick locks, furniture set on wheels and tracks, a cavernous 1,500-sq-ft (139-sq-m) living room, and a series of mirrors starting in his bedroom that permitted him to see who was arriving downstairs in case he wished to be "indisposed" or make a grand entrance.

Park and goldfish pond, a pleasing vista

221 Baker Street Secret Room

Servants' quarters

The View
The castle has a view of the Connecticut River and its traffic. Gillette lived on a houseboat for five years while the castle was constructed.

ROCKY HILL

The Study
Gillette spent much of his time in the Study. The chair at his desk is on a set of small tracks so it can be easily moved back and forth.

Castle Grounds
Following Gillette's death, the castle and its 117 acres (47 ha) became a state park. His railroad with its two locomotives used to carry guests on a three-mile (5-km) tour through the property. Now visitors walk the trails.

STAR FEATURES

★ The Great Hall

★ Library Museum

Main Entrance
The huge oak door through which visitors must pass is equipped with an elaborate homemade lock.

WILLIAM GILLETTE

An eccentric playwright and actor who reputedly made $3 million playing Sherlock Holmes on the stage, William Gillette paid homage to his literary meal ticket by re-creating the fictional sleuth's London sitting room as described in Sir Arthur Conan Doyle's books. Gillette spent $1 million to build his folly and in his will stipulated that it never fall into the hands of "any blithering saphead."

VISITORS' CHECKLIST

67 River Rd off Rte 82, Hadlyme.
(860) 526-2336. slated for reopening spring 2002.
for renovations in 2001.
first floor and terrace.

★ Library Museum
Gillette's gallery of pastoral artwork and seascapes is housed here.

Mezzanine

Castle Exterior
Constructed on a steel framework, the castle is built of fieldstone bought from local farmers and lifted up the hill on an aerial tram designed by Gillette.

Outdoor terrace

Outdoor terrace

★ The Great Hall
Exposed stone walls are five feet (1.5 m) thick in some places, and heavy oak covers steel beams. Gillette had a generator installed to provide power, but the castle is still dark and baronial.

New Haven ㉓

The land on which Connecticut's third most populous city stands was purchased from the Quinnipiac Indians in 1638 for a few knives, coats, and hatchets. The city's location on the coast where the West, Mill, and Quinnipiac rivers flow into Long Island Sound has helped make it one of the state's major manufacturing centers. Over the centuries, items ranging from clocks and corsets to musical instruments, carriages, and Revolutionary War cannonballs have been made here. In 1717 Yale University (see pp222–5) moved from Saybrook to New Haven, establishing the city as a center for education, technology, and research. Today New Haven also offers opportunities for attending theater, opera, dance performances, and concerts.

Amistad Memorial

Exploring Downtown New Haven

The 16-acre (6-ha) New Haven Green is the central section of the original nine symmetrical town squares the Puritans laid out in New Haven, the first planned city in America. The Green has been the focal point of local life ever since, serving as the setting for many of New Haven's activities and festivals. Three churches, all built between 1812 and 1815, sit on the Green on Temple Street. United Church on the Green (often called North Church for its northern location) is in the style of London's St. Martin-in-the-Fields. Graced by a beautiful Tiffany stained-glass window, the First Church of Christ (Center Church) is considered an architectural masterpiece of the American Georgian style. The crypt beneath the church holds the remains of some of the city's original

colonists. Among the notables buried here are Benedict Arnold's first wife, Margaret, and James Pierpont (1659–1714), one of the founders of Yale University. Trinity Church on the Green was one of the first Gothic-style churches in America.

Looming on the corner of Court and Church streets is the monumental Greek

Tiffany stained-glass window at First Church of Christ

Revival post office, now the Federal District Court, designed in 1913 by James Gamble Rogers (1867–1947), architect of many of Yale University's Gothic Revival buildings. City Hall faces the Green on Church Street and epitomizes high Victorian style, with its polychrome limestone-and-sandstone facade. In front of City Hall, the 14-ft- (4-m-) tall bronze Amistad Memorial, which honors Senghe Pieh (also known as Joseph Cinque), leader of the *Amistad* revolt (see p198), is on the exact site of the jail where the mutinous slaves were held.

In late April the Green becomes the stage for Powder House Day, a reenactment of one of Benedict Arnold's few celebrated moments. At the start of the American Revolution, Arnold, then a captain in the militia, seized control of municipal arsenal and led his troops to Boston to help bolster the sagging Colonial forces.

Church spires around New Haven Green

⛩ New Haven Colony Historical Society

114 Whitney Ave. 📞 *(203) 562-4183.* ◯ *year-round: 10am–5pm Tue–Fri, 2pm–5pm Sat–Sun.* ● *public hols.* 📷 🚻

This handsome Colonial Revival house traces the city's cultural and industrial growth from 1638 to the present. Exhibits include such items as Eli Whitney's cotton gin, the sign that hung over Benedict Arnold's George Street shop, a fine collection of colonial pewter and china, and permanent galleries on the *Amistad* and the city's maritime history.

⛩ Grove Street Cemetery

227 Grove St, gate at N end of High St. 📞 *(203) 787-1443.* ◯ *year-round: 8am–4pm daily.* ✔ 🚻

Established in 1797 and covering 18 acres (7 ha), this was the first cemetery in the US to be divided into family plots. Walking through its 1848 Egyptian Revival gate, visitors will find a veritable who's who of New Haven. Eli Whitney (1765–1825), Noah Webster (1758–1843), Charles Goodyear (1800–1860), and Samuel F.B. Morse (1791–1872) are just some of the distinguished citizens buried in this cemetery.

The colorful 1916 carousel at Lighthouse Point Park

New Haven Parks

Among New Haven's many attractive parks, the 84-acre (34-ha) **Lighthouse Point Park** on Long Island Sound is a standout. The park has nature trails, a picnic grove, a bird sanctuary, swimming facilities, a 1916 Coney Island-style carousel, and an 1840 lighthouse. **East Rock Park**

offers a spectacular view of Long Island Sound, New Haven, and the harbor and is crisscrossed by 10 miles (16 km) of nature trails. The 123-acre (50-ha) **Edgewood Park** has a duck pond, nature trail, in-line skating rink, and playground. Black Rock Fort, from the Revolutionary War period, and Fort Nathan Hale, vintage Civil War era, offer splendid views of New Haven Harbor.

🦅 Lighthouse Point Park

2 Lighthouse Rd. 📞 *(203) 946-8790.* **Park** ◯ *year-round: dawn–dusk daily.* **Beach** ◯ *Memorial Day–Labor Day: dawn–dusk daily.* 📷 ✔

🦅 East Rock Park

E Rock Park. 📞 *(203) 946-6086.* ◯ *year-round: 8am–dusk daily.*

🦅 Edgewood Park

Edgewood Ave. 📞 *(203) 946-8028.* ◯ *year-round: dawn–dusk daily.* ✔

🏛 Eli Whitney Museum

915 Whitney Ave, Hamden. 📞 *(203) 777-1833.* ◯ *May–Oct: 11am–4pm daily; Nov–Apr: 12pm–5pm Wed–Fri & Sun, 10am–3pm Sat.* ● *public hols.* 📷 ✔

On the northern outskirts of New Haven in the suburb of Hamden is the Eli Whitney Museum. One of the nation's earliest inventors, Whitney (1765–1825) was best known for developing the cotton gin, thereby automating the labor-intensive task of separating cotton from its seeds. Another of Whitney's inventions, a musket with interchangeable parts, revolutionized manufacturing and helped fuel the Industrial Revolution. The museum contains examples of Whitney's innovations and explanations of how they changed the way people work.

🦅 Connecticut Audubon Coastal Center

1 Milford Point Rd, Milford. 📞 *(203) 878-7440.* **Center** ◯ *year-round: 10am–4pm Tue–Sat, 12pm–4pm Sun.* ● *gate closed at dusk.* 📷 ✔ 🚻

Just 15 miles (16 km) southwest of New Haven, travelers come upon the Connecticut Audubon Coastal Center, one of the state's best birding sites. This 8.4-acre (3-ha) bird and wildlife sanctuary and nature center is situated on Long Island Sound at the mouth of the Housatonic River. Visitors can take nature walks along the beach or around the salt marsh and climb a 70-ft (21-m) tower overlooking Long Island Sound.

Eli Whitney Museum in Hamden, just north of New Haven

🏛 Shore Line Trolley Museum

17 River St, East Haven. 📞 *(203) 467-6927.* ◯ *call for hours.* 📷 ✔ *partial.* 🚻

Five miles (8 km) to the east of New Haven in East Haven is the Shore Line Trolley Museum. The oldest rapid-transit car and first electric freight locomotive are among 100 vintage trolleys from 1878 onward on display. The museum also offers a three-mile (5-km) trolley ride through salt marshes and woods on the oldest suburban trolley line in the country.

The 1840 lighthouse at Lighthouse Point Park

Yale University

FOUNDED IN 1701, THIS IVY LEAGUE SCHOOL is one of the most prestigious institutions of higher learning in the world. The list of Yale's distinguished alumni includes Noah Webster (1758–1843), who compiled the nation's first dictionary, Samuel Morse (1791–1872), inventor of Morse code, and four US presidents, including Bill Clinton (b.1946). While its law and medical schools attract much of the attention, Yale's other graduate programs (ranging from divinity to drama) are no less demanding. In some ways avant-garde, in others staunchly traditional, Yale admitted its first female Ph.D. student before the turn of the 20th century, but didn't become fully co-educational until 1969.

Wrexham Tower, Branford College, on the Yale campus

Exploring Yale Campus

Yale's campus comprises much of New Haven's down-town core, with the main section located on the west-ern flank of the New Haven Green. Campus buildings reflect the architectural eclec-ticism that runs through the university. Connecticut Hall is Yale's oldest building and the only one left of a row of Georgian buildings on the Old Campus, Yale's original quadrangle. Nathan Hale (see pp216–17) and US President William Howard Taft (1857–1930) had rooms here when they were students.

Yale's oldest building, Connecticut Hall, constructed in 1717

After World War I, James Gamble Rogers (1867–1947) designed the Memorial Quadrangle, a beautiful Gothic complex that is now the heart of the campus. Another Rogers design, Harkness Tower, completed in 1921, was modeled on St. Botolph's Tower in Boston, England, and has a facade covered with sculptures celebrating Yale's history and traditions. Each day at noon and again at 6pm the beautiful sounds of the bell tower's carillon can be heard throughout New Haven. On the Memorial Gate near the tower, the school's motto is inscribed: "For God, for country, and for Yale."

Post-World War II architects have left their mark on cam-pus, too. The Yale School of Art and Architecture is as controversial today as when it was built in the 1960s. From

VISITORS' CHECKLIST

Across from New Haven Green.
🛈 149 Elm St (203) 423-2300.
Call individual sites for hours.
🎭 ♿ 🎨 International Festival
of Arts and Ideas (Jun).
🅦 www.yale.edu

the outside this 36-level build-ing seems to stand only seven stories tall. The collection of buildings that makes up Ezra Stiles and Morse Colleges at Broadway and Tower is by architect Eero Saarinen (1910–61), who based the design on an Italian mountain village. Philip Johnson's Kline Biology Tower, Yale's skyscraper, was completed in 1965.

🏛 Yale Center for British Art

1080 Chapel St. 📞 (203) 432-2800.
⊙ year-round: 10am–5pm Tue–Sat, 12pm–5pm Sun. ● public hols. 🎫
♿ 🛈
In 1966 philanthropist Paul Mellon (1907–99) donated his collection of British art to the university. This was no small gift, considering it consisted of more than 50,000

KEY

🛈	Tourist information
P	Parking

Library Court in the Yale Center for British Art

paintings, prints, drawings, watercolors, and rare books and documents. Needing the right space to display its artistic windfall, the university hired American architect Louis Kahn (1901–74) to design an elegant new center. Thus was born this important collection covering the major art schools and masters from Tudor times to the present.

The museum has the largest collection of British art outside the UK. Included among the paintings are works by William Hogarth (1697–1764), Thomas Gainsborough (1727–88), and Joseph Turner (1775–1851). The fourth floor of the museum is arranged chronologically so that visitors are given an overview.

Statue of Elihu Yale (1649–1721)

YALE UNIVERSITY CAMPUS

Beinecke Library ②
Connecticut Hall ⑦
Harkness Tower ⑤
Memorial Quadrangle ④
Old Campus ⑥

Sterling Memorial Library ③
Yale Center for British Art ⑧
Yale School of Architecture ⑩
Yale University Art Gallery ⑨
Yale Visitor's Center ①

🏛 Sterling Memorial Library

128 Wall St. 📞 (203) 432-2798.
🕐 year-round: 8:30am–12am Mon–Fri, 10am–5pm Sat, 1pm–12am Sun. ⬤ Sat in Aug.
This striking library with stained-glass windows and Gothic arches is the largest on campus. It contains some 4 million items, including rare Babylonian tablets.

Gothic entrance to the Sterling Memorial Library

🏛 Beinecke Rare Book and Manuscript Libraries

121 Wall St. 📞 (203) 432-2977.
🕐 year-round: 8:30am–5pm Mon–Fri, 10am–5pm Sat. ⬤ Sat in Aug & public hols.
American architect Gordon Bunshaft (1909–90) built the walls of this library out of translucent marble. This unique design helps filter the sunlight, which could harm the library's illuminated medieval manuscripts and 7,000 books. The library owns a host of rare books and manuscripts, but its prized possession is one of the world's few remaining Gutenberg Bibles.

🏛 Yale University Art Gallery

1111 Chapel St. 📞 *(203) 432-0611.*
⬤ *year-round: 10am–5pm Tue–Sat,*
1pm–6pm Sun. ⬤ *public hols.* ▮
♿ ▯

This top collection of Asian, African, European, American, and pre-Columbian art reflects the generosity and taste of Yale alumni and benefactors. The museum, founded in 1832, has approximately 100,000 objects in its huge collection, including many in the sculpture garden.

Housed in two units and divided over four floors, the gallery's vast collection highlights art as far back as ancient Egypt. The gallery is one of the finest medium-size museums in the US and is famous for its collection of American paintings, furniture,

Entrance to the Peabody Museum of Natural History

and decorative arts. Among its prized American pieces is John Trumbull's *The Battle of Bunker's Hill* (1786). Visitors can view more contemporary works, including paintings by

Pablo Picasso, Vincent Van Gogh, Édouard Manet, Claude Monet, and Jackson Pollock.

🏛 Peabody Museum of Natural History

170 Whitney Ave. 📞 *(203) 432-5050.* ⬤ *year-round: 10am–5pm Mon–Sat, 12pm–5pm Sun.* ⬤ *public hols.* 🖼 ▮ ♿ ▯

Visitors entering the museum are dwarfed by the imposing skeleton of a 67-ft- (20-m-) high *Brontosaurus* – an apt introduction to this outstanding museum, famous for its collection of dinosaurs.

Children migrate to the Great Hall of Dinosaurs, where they can mingle with the mastodon and socialize with the *Stegosaurus*. Included among the many fossils and realistic dioramas is a 75-million-year-old turtle.

Tour of Coastal Fairfield County

P.T. Barnum

TRAVELERS FOLLOWING Interstate 95 are bound to strike it rich along the "Gold Coast," so nicknamed because of the luxurious estates, marinas, and mansions concentrated between Greenwich and Southport. This, the southernmost corner of the state, has attractions sure to meet everyone's taste. The shoreline is dusted with numerous beaches offering a variety of summer recreation opportunities. Nature preserves, arboretums, planetariums, and the state's only zoo will appeal to naturalists of all ages. People of a more artistic bent can visit the area's numerous small galleries or visit some of its larger, well-established museums.

New Canaan Historical Society building

Stamford's First Presbyterian Church has the largest mechanical-action organ in the state.

Greenwich ⑥
Blessed with a stunning coastline, this town is home to the Bush-Holley Historic Site, the state's first Impressionist art colony.

Stamford ⑤
This major urban area has a lively downtown and the First Presbyterian Church, which is shaped like a fish.

Putnam Lake

Horseneck Brook

Mianus River

106

Stamford
⑤

⑥ *Greenwich*

1

Archelon, at 10 ft (3 m), ranks as the largest turtle that ever roamed the planet.

The Peabody's third floor has a slightly more contemporary feel, with displays of mounted animals that range from the very large – bison, bears, and musk oxen – to the very small – snakes, birds, and mice. Elsewhere visitors can examine the Peabody's exhibits on the cultures of ancient Egypt, Mesoamerica, Polynesia, and the Plains Indian.

⛫ Yale Collection of Musical Instruments

15 Hillhouse Ave. **C** *(203) 432-0822.*
☐ *Sep–Jun: 1pm–4pm Tue–Thu. Call for concert times.* ● *Jul–Aug.* 🎫 🚫 *by appt.* ♿ *partial.*
A must stop for the musically inclined, this stunning

collection of instruments, considered among the top ten of its kind, has 800 objects, including historic woodwind and stringed instruments. The collection was started by New Haven piano manufacturer Morris Steinert (1831–1912). Steinert's love of music (he also founded the New Haven Symphony) saw him travel to Europe to

collect and restore antique instruments, especially claviers and harpsichords, forerunners to his beloved piano. Some of the collection's violins and harpsichords date back centuries. The museum holds a series of concerts from September to April. Many of the concerts are performed using the historic instruments.

Angelic detail on Yale's graceful High Street Bridge

KEY

▬▬ Tour route

▭▭ Other road

New Canaan ④
The drive into town, which is set in a bucolic landscape of woods, streams, and rolling fields, is spectacular in fall.

Bridgeport ①
Circus impresario P.T. Barnum was once mayor of this city, home to such attractions as the Beardsley Zoo, the Barnum Museum, and the Discovery Museum.

Saugatuck River

Mill River

④ New Canaan

② Westport

① Bridgeport

124

Norwalk ③

95

136

95

Darien

136

Fairfield

8

1

0 kilometers　3

0 miles　　　3

Westport ②
A charming town on the banks of the Saugatuck River; home to the Sherwood Island State Park.

Norwalk ③
The trendy South Norwalk waterfront district has historic buildings, restaurants, shops, and cafés, as well as the Maritime Aquarium at Norwalk.

TIPS FOR DRIVERS

Tour length: 44 miles (71 km), including detour to New Canaan. **When to go:** To avoid the summer traffic, it is best to go in June or September. Fall foliage usually peaks in mid-October. **Stopping-off points:** There are a number of seaside restaurants in Greenwich and Norwalk.

VERMONT

······················

V ERMONT WAS GIVEN ITS NAME BY EXPLORER *Samuel de Champlain in 1609. The word means "Green Mountain" in French, and must have seemed most suitable when he gazed upon the fertile landscape. Almost 400 years later, Vermont is still very much an enclave of unspoiled wilderness, with thick forests blanketing the rolling hills and the valley lowlands.*

In all there are just over a half a million people living in Vermont, one of the most rural states in the Union. The countryside is replete with manicured farms where the state's trademark black and white Holstein cattle graze against a backdrop of natural beauty. The pastoral landscape, dotted with pristine villages and covered bridges, evokes the idealized images found in paintings by longtime resident Norman Rockwell *(see p241)*. An anti-billboard law ensures that the countryside is not blighted by obtrusive advertisements.

Vermonters may be small in number, but they are nationalistic and often have led the country's conscience on social and political issues. The Stars and Stripes are a familiar sight in Vermont; the American flag, "Old Glory" as is it known, decorates many a front porch.

It is hardly surprising that people from around the world are attracted to this green corner of the US. Each season brings new opportunities to enjoy nature. When the countryside is covered in a blanket of snow, picturesque towns are transformed into bustling ski centers. Outdoor enthusiasts have long known that Vermont possesses some of the best boating, hiking, camping, and fishing in the country. Vermont is also a magnet for painters, writers, musicians, and poets who enrich the cultural life of the state. Regional theaters, museums, and art galleries are prominent attractions. But Vermont is at its scenic best in the fall, when thousands of "leaf peepers" come to see the natural phenomenon of leaves changing color *(see pp20–21)*. What makes the season so special here is the variety of colors that the trees manifest, from the palest mustard to flaming scarlet.

Grazing Holstein cows, a favorite breed in Vermont, in a typical state setting

◁ **Vermont's trademark rural landscape**

Exploring Vermont

UNLIKE NEW ENGLAND'S coastal states, with attractions most often found along the water's edge, Vermont's highlights are sprinkled liberally throughout the state. The northeastern region boasts mountains, forests, and the fjordlike Lake Willoughby (*see pp230–31*). Snaking down the western border, Lake Champlain and its islands (*see p236*) provide the backdrop for the collegial spirit of Burlington (*see pp235–7*) and the one-of-a-kind Shelburne Museum (*see pp238–9*). Pre–Revolutionary War villages grace the south and provide good base camps for hikers looking to trek the Appalachian Trail (*see pp22–3*) or enjoy the natural splendor of the Green Mountain National Forest (*see p244*).

Burlington's waterfront, well used by sailors and boaters

SEE ALSO

• *Where to Stay* pp317–19

• *Where to Eat* pp342–3

KEY

▬	Interstate
▬	Major road
▭	Minor road
▬	Scenic route
☼	Viewpoint

SIGHTS AT A GLANCE

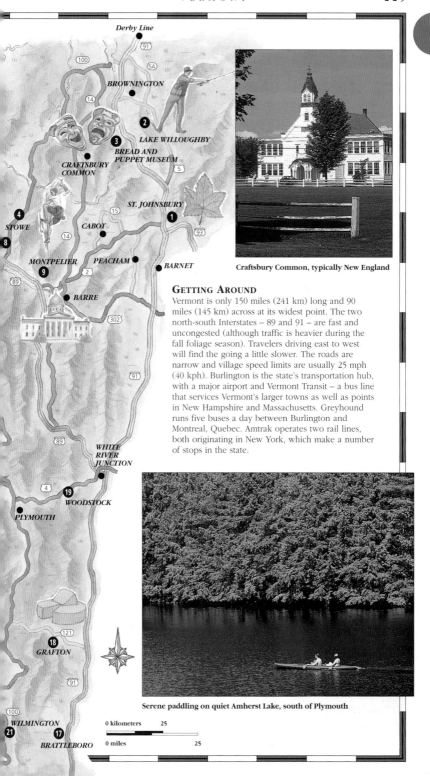

Derby Line

BROWNINGTON

② LAKE WILLOUGHBY

③ BREAD AND
PUPPET MUSEUM

CRAFTSBURY
COMMON

ST. JOHNSBURY

①

④
STOWE
⑧

CABOT

MONTPELIER PEACHAM

⑨ BARNET

BARRE

WHITE
RIVER
JUNCTION

⑲
WOODSTOCK

PLYMOUTH

⑱
GRAFTON

WILMINGTON
㉑ ⑰
BRATTLEBORO

Craftsbury Common, typically New England

GETTING AROUND

Vermont is only 150 miles (241 km) long and 90
miles (145 km) across at its widest point. The two
north-south Interstates – 89 and 91 – are fast and
uncongested (although traffic is heavier during the
fall foliage season). Travelers driving east to west
will find the going a little slower. The roads are
narrow and village speed limits are usually 25 mph
(40 kph). Burlington is the state's transportation hub,
with a major airport and Vermont Transit – a bus line
that services Vermont's larger towns as well as points
in New Hampshire and Massachusetts. Greyhound
runs five buses a day between Burlington and
Montreal, Quebec. Amtrak operates two rail lines,
both originating in New York, which make a number
of stops in the state.

Serene paddling on quiet Amherst Lake, south of Plymouth

0 kilometers   25

0 miles   25

St. Johnsbury ❶

🏘 7,800. ✈ 77 miles (125 km)
W in Burlington. 🚍 ℹ 357 Western
Ave (802) 748-3678 or (800) 639-
6379.

THIS SMALL industrial town,
which is the unofficial
capital of Vermont's northeast
region – also called the
"Northeast Kingdom" – sits
atop a promontory at the
convergence of the Moose,
Sleeper, and Passumpsic
rivers. The town is named
for Saint Jean de Crèvencour,
who was a friend of
Revolutionary War hero Ethan
Allen. It was the Frenchman
who suggested that "bury" be
added to the name because
there were too many towns
called St. John.
    It was here in 1830 that
Thaddeus Fairbanks (1796–
1886), a mechanic, invented
the platform scale, an easier
and more accurate method
of weighing than the balances
of the time. The Fairbanks
scale, as it came to be
known, put St. Johnsbury
on the map and boosted the
growth of other pioneer
industries, notably the manufacturing of maple products.
    The Fairbanks family col-
lected art and antiques, which
now are housed in the
**Fairbanks Museum and
Planetarium** – one of the
area's finest natural history
museums. This Romanesque-
style brick Victorian building,
now on the National Historic
Register, contains over 150,000
artifacts, including 4,500

Art on walnut wall panels at St.
Johnsbury Athenaeum Art Gallery

Tranquil waters of Lake Willoughby

stuffed birds and animals, and
tools, dolls, and toys.
    Also on Main Street is the
**St. Johnsbury Athenaeum
Art Gallery**, a Victorian gem
with gleaming woodwork,
paneled walls, and circular
staircase. The gallery highlights the landscapes of the
Hudson River School of painting. Popular in the 1800s, the
movement was the first native
school of American art, and
focuses on the beauty of the
natural world. Albert Bierstadt
(1830–1902), whose massive
canvas *Domes of Yosemite*
(1867) hangs here, was one
of its leaders.

🏛 **Fairbanks Museum and
Planetarium**
1302 Main St. ℂ (802) 748-2372.
Museum ◯ Jul–Aug: 10am–6pm
Mon–Sat, 1pm–5pm Sun; Sep–Jun:
10am–4pm Mon–Sat, 1pm–5pm Sun.
● Jan–Mar: Sun. **Planetarium**
◯ call for show times. 🎫 ♿ 🚹
🏛 **St. Johnsbury
Athenaeum Art Gallery**
1171 Main St. ℂ (802) 748-8291.
◯ year-round: 10am–8pm Mon &
Wed, 10am–5:30pm Tue & Thu–Fri,
9:30am–4pm Sat. 🎫 ♿ 🚹

ENVIRONS: Nineteen miles
(30 km) to the west is Cabot,
where one of the state's best-
known agricultural products –
cheddar cheese – is made. The
Cabot Creamery, a farmers'
cooperative, was started in
1919 and now produces a
mind-boggling 100 million lbs
(45.5 million kg) of cheese a
year. The creamery offers
tours and free tastings.

🏠 **Cabot Creamery**
Main St., Cabot, Rte 215. ℂ (802)
563-3393 or (800) 837-4261. ◯
Jun–Oct: 9am–5pm daily; Nov–May:
9am–4pm Mon–Sat. ● Jan 1, Sun in
Jan, Thanksgiving, & Dec 25. 🎫 ♿

Lake Willoughby ❷

Rte 5A near Barton. ℂ (802) 525-
1137.

TRAVELERS HEADING east
from Barton climb a crest
on the road only to be met
with the breathtaking view of
this beautiful body of water.
The narrow glacial lake,
which plunges 300 ft (90 m)
in certain areas, is flanked by
two soaring cliffs: Mount
Pisgah at 2,750 ft (840 m)
and Mount Hor at 2,650 ft
(810 m). Jutting straight out of
the water, the mountains give
the lake the appearance of a
rugged Norwegian fjord
or a resort in Switzerland,
garnering it the nickname
the "Lucerne of America."
    With trails leading around
both promontories, this is a
haven for hikers and swimmers looking for a secluded
spot. There are wonderful
picnic and camping areas
along the beaches at either
end of the five-mile (8-km)
lake. Several resorts and bed
and breakfast establishments
ring the shores. The lake itself
offers plenty of recreational
opportunities – fishing, boating, scuba diving – and there
are three nearby golf courses.

ENVIRONS: Because of its
isolated location 11 miles
(18 km) northwest of Lake
Willoughby, Brownington
has retained the look of an
18th-century village, with few
modern touches. The **Old
Stone House** museum documents the history of the
region. Twenty-two miles (35
km) to the north of the lake
lies Derby Line – really two
communities in one. The
northern half, which is in
Quebec, Canada, is called

Rock Island. The border between Canada and the US runs through the middle of the **Haskell Free Library and Opera House**, a stately granite and brick building constructed in 1904.

Part of the audience sits in the US, but the stage is in Canada. The building's wealthy benefactor, Mrs. Martha Stewart Haskell (1831–1906), wanted both communities to enjoy her gift.

🏛 **Old Stone House**
28 Old Stone House Rd. 📞 *(802) 754-2022.* ⏰ *call for hours.* 🎥 *obligatory.* ♿ 📷
🏛 **Haskell Free Library and Opera House**
93 Caswell Ave. 📞 *(802) 873-3022.*
Library ⏰ *year-round: 10am–5pm Tue–Wed & Fri–Sat, 10am–8pm Thu.*
Opera House ⏰ *May–Oct: call for hours.* ⬛ *Sun–Mon.* 🎥

Bread and Puppet Museum ❸

Exit 25 Rte 122 near Glover. 📞 *(802) 525-3031 or (802) 525-6972.* ⏰ *May–Oct: 10am–6pm daily; call for show times.* 📷

AN EXTRAORDINARY place down a quiet rural road, this museum is a century-old, two-story building, which once served as a barn to shelter dairy cattle. The cattle

A selection of fanciful creatures at the Bread and Puppet Museum

The Austrian-style Trapp Family Lodge

have gone, but every inch of space is taken up by paintings, masks, and other theatrical knickknacks, most notably puppets of all shapes and sizes, dressed in outlandish costumes in every style. The props belong to the internationally famous Bread and Puppet Theater company, founded in 1962. The troupe members live communally on the surrounding farm. Their productions are notable for the masterful use of giant puppets and are made even more fun by enlisting the help of the local population.

Typical Vermont church in Craftsbury Common

ENVIRONS: Small and graceful Craftsbury Common, just 14 miles (22 km) southwest, is pure Americana. Gnarled old trees, planted in 1799 to commemorate the death of George Washington (1732–99), the first president of the US, line the main street. The village green is flanked by handsome clapboard homes with black shutters, and is anchored at one corner by a typical New England church with a white wooden steeple. In winter the area is popular with cross-country skiers.

Stowe ❹

🏚 *3,500.* ✈ *40 miles (64 km) W in Burlington.* ℹ *51 Main St (802) 253-7321, (877) 467-8693 or (800) 247-8693.*

IT IS HARDLY SURPRISING that the Von Trapp family, whose daring escape from Austria during World War II was the inspiration behind the 1965 movie *The Sound of Music*, chose Stowe as their new home. The pretty village is ringed by mountains, which reminded them of the Alpine region they had left behind. Their Trapp Family Lodge *(see p319)* is part of the 2,700-acre (1,092-ha) estate. The giant wooden chalet is one of the area's most popular hotels.

The village has been a major ski and outdoor activity center since the 1930s. In winter it draws hordes of skiers looking to enjoy the region's best slopes *(see pp362–3)*. Mountain Road begins in the village and is lined with chalets, motels, restaurants, and pubs; it leads to the area's highest peak, 4,393-ft (1,339-m) Mount Mansfield. Many local spas and resorts offer gourmet meals, and massages and other health treatments.

In summer there are still opportunities to enjoy the outdoors. Visitors can hike, rock-climb, fish, and canoe, or walk, cycle, or inline skate along the paved, meandering 5.5 mile (8.5 km) Stowe Recreational Path. It winds from Stowe's village church across the West Branch River, then through woodlands.

Burlington ⑤

BURLINGTON IS ONE OF VERMONT'S most popular tourist destinations. It is a lively university town with almost half of its population of just over 40,000 made up of students or people associated with the University of Vermont (UVM) and the city's four colleges. One of the oldest universities in the country, UVM was founded in 1791, the same year that Vermont officially joined the United States. Burlington's strategic location on the eastern shore of Lake Champlain *(see p236)* helped it prosper in pioneer times, and today it is Vermont's center of commerce and industry. The town is also rich in grand old mansions, historic landmarks, interesting shops, and restaurants and has an attractive waterfront. The famed American Revolution patriot Ethan Allen (1738–89), omnipresent throughout the state, has his final resting place here in Greenmount Cemetery.

The restored Flynn Theater, close to City Hall Place

Exploring Burlington

The center of Burlington is compact and easy to explore on foot. Battery Street, near the waterfront, is the oldest, most historic part of the city and a jumping-off point for ferries to New York State and sightseeing trips around Lake Champlain. More than 200 buildings in the downtown core have been renovated in recent years, and visitors will find many architectural landmarks, including the First Unitarian Church *(see pp234–5)*.

Battery Park, at the north end of Battery Street where it meets Pearl Street, was the site of a battle between US soldiers and the British Royal Navy. Burlington saw several skirmishes during the War of 1812, and scuba divers have found military artifacts at the bottom of the lake. Five shipwrecks, three lying close to Burlington, can be explored by divers who register with the Waterfront Diving Center on Battery Street.

These days Battery Park is a much more peaceful place. Lake Champlain is at its widest point here, and visitors who stroll through the park are rewarded with lovely views of Burlington Bay and the backdrop

of the Adirondack Mountains on the other side of the lake. Entertainment is presented in the park on Thursday and Sunday evenings in summer.

Burlington's cultural life comes to the fore during its annual jazz festival in June. Venues for this popular concert series include City Hall Place, Waterfront Park, the Church Street Marketplace *(see pp234–5)*, and the Flynn Theater. A former vaudeville theater and movie palace, the Flynn has had its Art Deco interior carefully restored, and now stages a variety of cultural events throughout the

Statue in Battery Park

KEY

▨	Street-by-Street map *see pp234–5*
═	Highway
✿	Viewpoint
⛴	Ferry
ℹ	Tourist information
P	Parking

0 meters   250

0 yards   250

Spirit of Ethan Allen II with a full complement of sightseers

VISITORS' CHECKLIST

🏙 40,700. ✈ Burlington
International Airport, 3 miles
(5 km) E of town. 🚌 345 Pine
St. ⛴ King St Dock. 🛈 Suite
100, 60 Main St (802) 863-3489
or (877) 686-5253. 🎷 Discover
Jazz Festival (Jun).
Ⓦ www.vermont.org

year. A Mozart festival, which started here at the University of Vermont, runs for three weeks in the summer and has spread to other communities. Concerts are held in St. Paul's Cathedral, UVM's Recital Hall, City Hall Park, and Shelburne Farms south of the city.

⛴ *Spirit of Ethan Allen II*
Burlington Boat House, College St.
📞 (802) 862-8300. ⭕ May–Oct:
9am–7pm daytime and sunset dinner
cruises (reservations necessary). 🎫 🅿
♿ 🍴

Tall-stack steamers used to ply the waters of Lake Champlain. Today visitors can board the three-decker cruise ship, *Spirit of Ethan Allen II*, which holds 500 passengers. Its 90-minute trip gives a good historical overview as the captain narrates entertaining tales of the Revolutionary War.

🏛 Robert Hull Fleming Museum
61 Colchester Ave. 📞 (802) 656-0750. ⭕ May–mid-Sep: 12pm–4pm Tue–Fri; mid-Sep–May: 9am–4pm Tue–Fri; year-round: 1pm–5pm Sat–Sun. ● public hols. 🎫 ♿ 🛈

The museum is located on the campus of the University of Vermont, up on a hillside overlooking the city. Built in 1931, the elegant Colonial Revival building houses a huge collection of artifacts – more than 19,000 items – ranging from ancient Mesopotamia to modern times. Some of the items on display include European and American

Statue of Penelope in the Fleming Museum

paintings and sculptures, Native Indian crafts, costumes, textiles, glassware, and numerous archeological remains.

🏛 Shelburne Farms
1611 Harbor Rd. 📞 (802) 985-8686. ⭕ May–mid-Oct: 9am–5pm daily. 🎫 🅿 ♿ partial.
Seven miles (11 km) south of town are Shelburne Museum (*see pp238–9*) and Shelburne Farms, a historic 1,400-acre (566-ha) estate. The parklike grounds of the latter include rolling pastures, woodlands, and a working farm. Tours are given of the dairy. Children can pet the animals in designated areas.

TO
COLCHESTER

COLCHESTER AVENUE →

PEARL STREET

SOUTH WILLARD STREET

PROSPECT STREET

UNIVERSITY PLACE

COLLEGE STREET

MAIN STREET

MAIN STREET

TO WILLISTON

MAPLE STREET

PROSPECT STREET

TO SHELBURNE MUSEUM
TO SHELBURNE FARMS

BURLINGTON TOWN CENTER

Battery Park ⑦
Church Street
 Marketplace ④
City Hall Place ⑤
First Unitarian
 Church ③
Flynn Theater ⑥

Robert Hull Fleming
 Museum ②
*Spirit of
 Ethan Allen II* ⑨
University of
 Vermont ①
Waterfront Park ⑧

Part of the stately University of Vermont campus

Street-by-Street: Historic District

THE FOUR-BLOCK SECTION known as the Church Street Marketplace is located at the center of the city's historic district. The neighborhood has been converted into a pedestrian mall complete with trendy boutiques, patio restaurants, specialty stores, factory outlets, craft shops, and, naturally, a Ben & Jerry's *(see p236)*. The marketplace, thronged with shoppers and sightseers at the best of times, is at its most vibrant in the summer months, with numerous street performers and musicians adding color and action. The district also has its share of historical attractions, including the 1816 First Unitarian Church.

Richardson Building
This 1895 chateau-style building was a 19th-century department store.

The Masonic Temple is Church Street's tallest structure.

★ First Unitarian Church
Standing at the head of Church Street, the First Unitarian Church was built in 1816 and stands as the oldest house of worship in Burlington.

The Burlington Montgomery Ward Building, built in 1929, is on the National Register of Historic Places. Its graceful lines and colorful facade typify pre-Depression architecture.

Central-Union Blocks
This was the first major development on upper Church Street. It now houses restaurants and pubs.

STAR SIGHTS

★ City Hall

★ First Unitarian Church

Pedestrian Mall
This section of the mall – particularly lively on weekends – is popular among students and tourists for its many shops and terraces. Cafés, pubs, and restaurants are housed in Queen Anne-style buildings from the late 1800s.

Second Merchants Bank
was built in 1895 by Burlington architect Sydney Greene.

★ City Hall
This 1928 building marks the southern boundary of the marketplace and is made of local brick, marble, and granite.

KEY

☐	Pedestrian mall
– –	Suggested route

0 meters 25
0 yards 25

WINOOSKI AVENUE

ANK STREET

COLLEGE STREET

MAIN STREET

Abraham Block was once considered the most striking commercial block in the state.

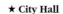

City Hall Park
The park is a popular outdoor concert venue. It features a poured concrete fountain and two granite monuments. One honors those who died in the Civil War; the other, soldiers who died in World War II.

Sailing and boating, popular on beautiful Lake Champlain

Lake Champlain **❻**

Vermont-New York border from Whitehall to Alburg. 🚶 *Burlington.*
🚍 ℹ️ *60 Main St, Burlington (802) 863-3489.*

SAID TO BE THE HOME OF "Champ," a water serpent that could be a distant cousin of the Loch Ness Monster, Lake Champlain was named for French explorer Samuel de Champlain (1567–1635). He discovered and explored much of the surrounding region. Some 120 miles (190 km) long and 12 miles (19 km) wide, the lake has its western shore in New York State, while the eastern sector is in Vermont. Scenic hour-long ferry rides run regularly between Burlington and Port Kent, New York.

Sometimes called the sixth Great Lake because of its size, Champlain has 500 miles (800 km) of shoreline and is sprinkled with about 70 islands. At the lake's northern end, the Alburg Peninsula and a group of thin islands (North Hero, Isle La Motte, and Grand Isle) give glimpses of the region's colorful past.

At Ste. Anne's Shrine on Isle La Motte is a statue of Champlain. Grand Isle is home to America's oldest log cabin (1783). The villages of North and South Hero were named in honor of brothers Ethan and Ira Allen. Their volunteers, the Green Mountain Boys, helped secure Vermont's status as a separate state.

Some of Lake Champlain's treasures are underwater, preserved in a marine park where scuba divers can explore shipwrecks resting on sandbars and at the bottom of the lake.

The **Lake Champlain Maritime Museum** at Basin Harbor gives an overview of the region's marine history. On display are ship models, old divers' suits, and photographs of Lake Champlain steamers, the most famous of which was the SS *Ticonderoga*, built in 1906 and now part of the collection of Americana at the nearby Shelburne Museum *(see pp238–9).*

Ben & Jerry's bus, gaily decorated with dairy cows

🏛 **Lake Champlain Maritime Museum**
4472 Basin Harbor Rd, Vergennes.
📞 *(802) 475-2022.* 🕐 *May–mid-Oct: 10am–5pm.* 🚫 ♿

Shelburne Museum **❼**

See pp238–9

Gold dome of the Vermont State House in Montpelier

Ben & Jerry's Ice Cream Factory **❽**

Rte 100, Waterbury. 📞 *(802) 244-5641 or (866) BJTOURS.*
🕐 *Jun: 9am–5pm daily; Jul–Aug: 9am–8pm daily; Sep–Oct: 10am–6pm daily; Nov–May: 10am–5pm daily.*
🚫 ♿ 🍴 🛍

ALTHOUGH BEN COHEN and Jerry Greenfield hail from Long Island, New York, they have done more than any other "flatlanders" to put Vermont's dairy industry on the map. In 1977 these childhood friends paid $5 for a correspondence course on making ice cream and parlayed their knowledge into a hugely successful franchise.

Ben and Jerry use the richest cream and milk from local farms to produce their ice cream and frozen yogurt. The Ben & Jerry trademark is the black and white Holstein cow, embellishing everything in the gift shop.

Tours of the factory start every 15 minutes and run for 30 minutes. Visitors learn all there is to know about making ice cream. They are given a bird's-eye view of the factory floor, and at the end of the tour a chance to sample from more than 50 flavors of ice cream, frozen yogurt, and sorbet.

Montpelier **❾**

👥 *8,400.* 🚶 *40 miles (64 km) NW in Burlington.* 🚍 🚍 ℹ️ *134 State St (802) 828-0587.*

MONTPELIER is the smallest state capital in the US, but its diminutive stature is advantageous: The city is impeccably clean, friendly, and easily seen on foot. Despite its size, Montpelier has a grand, imposing building to house its state politicians and legislators. The **Vermont State House,** which dates back to 1859, replaced an earlier building that was destroyed by fire. It is now a formidable Greek Revival structure, complete with a gilt cupola and giant fluted pillars of granite that were hewn from one of the quarries at neighboring Barre.

The **Vermont Historical Society Museum**, run by the local historical society, is housed in a replica of a 19th-century hotel. The impressive lobby is well furnished with Victorian memorabilia, and the museum has changing themed exhibits dealing with the history of Vermont.

🏛 Vermont State House
115 State St. (*(802) 828-2228.*
☐ *year-round: 8am–4pm Mon–Fri.*
● *public hols.* 🚫 ♿ 🏛
🏛 Vermont Historical Society Museum
109 State St. (*(802) 828-2291.*
☐ *year-round: 9am–4:30pm Tue–Fri, 9am–4pm Sat, 12pm–4pm Sun.* 🚫
🚫 ♿

ENVIRONS: Seven miles (11 km) to the south, Barre (pronounced "berry") is the self-proclaimed granite capital of the world. In the 19th century, Italian and Scottish stonemasons came here to work the pale, white and blue-gray rock.

The region still is a hive of granite-related activity, with several large plants producing stone for tombstones (many have ended up in Barre's Hope Cemetery on Merchant Street), statues, and monuments. In nearby Graniteville, the **Rock of Ages Quarry** is the biggest such operation. Visitors can watch – from the safety of an observation deck – as the stone is being hewn from the huge 475-ft (134-m) pit. Shuttle buses run regularly, taking visitors between the quarry and the Graniteville visitor center.

🔍 Rock of Ages Quarry
773 Main St, Graniteville. (*(802) 476-3119.* ☐ *May–Oct: 8:30am–5pm Mon–Sat, 12pm–5pm Sun.* 🚫 🚫 ♿

Mad River Valley 🔟

Central VT along Rte 100. 🚹
Rte 100, Waitsfield (802) 496-3409.
🚩 *Waitsfield, mid-May–Columbus Day: 9:30am–1pm Sat.*

LOCATED IN central Vermont, Mad River Valley is most famous for outdoor activities that include hiking, cycling, hunting, and especially skiing. In fact, the area's motto is "Ski it if you can."

One popular stop is the Mad River Glen ski area *(see p362)*, which attracts die-hard traditionalists who enjoy their sport the old-fashioned way – without fancy high-speed gondolas (though there are four chairlifts) and snow-making equipment. With only a couple of dozen trails, Mad River Glen caters to the country's most skilled skiers.

Sugarbush *(see p362)*, on the other hand, has more than 100 trails and a vertical drop of 2,650 ft (800 m). It is the polar opposite of Mad River Glen. This trendy resort, which caters to beginners and intermediate skiers as well as those who are more

Moss Glenn Falls near Warren in Mad River Valley

advanced, has the most modern snowmaking facilities and lifts. It was very popular with the 1960s "jet set," but now a more "retro" crowd who own time-share condos frequents the slopes. A state-of-the-art express "people mover" connects what used to be two separate ski areas: Lincoln Peak and Mount Ellen.

Activities in and around Waitsfield, the small, fashionable, and wealthy community that is the center of this tourist region, include hiking, hunting, and – of all things – polo. The local landmark is a round barn, which is one of only a dozen remaining in the state. It is a venue for cultural functions and art exhibits. It sits next to an elegant inn and restaurant that has been converted from an 1806 farmhouse.

Bucolic scenery outside of Waitsfield, a popular summer destination

Shelburne Museum ❼

ORE THAN JUST an eclectic repository, the Shelburne Museum celebrates three centuries of American ingenuity, creativity, and diversity. Here folk art, antique tools, duck decoys, and circus memorabilia are displayed on the same grounds as scrimshaw, Native American artifacts, and paintings by such US artists as Winslow Homer (1836–1910) and Grandma Moses (1860–1961). Established in 1947 by collector Electra Webb (1888–1960), the museum's 37 historic structures and their contents constitute one of the nation's finest museums.

Big Chief statue

★ Circus Building
The horseshoe-shaped building houses a 500-ft- (152-m-) long miniature circus parade. The west entrance foyer features this 3,000-piece miniature circus.

Vintage 1920s carousel

Museum Store
Handicrafts by New England artisans are sold here.

McClure Visitor Center and Round Barn
The first two floors of this 1901 barn fea-ture changing exhibits. The visitor center is located on the top floor.

★ **Railroad Station**
The station was built in 1890 in Shelburne, Vermont, and relocated here. It houses a variety of railroad memorabilia, including telegraphy systems, vintage railroad maps, a restored stationmaster's office, and men's and women's waiting rooms.

Beach Lodge contains a variety of big-game trophies and Native American artifacts.

Locomotive 220, a 1915 10-wheel steam locomotive, hauled freight and passenger trains. Engine 220 could pull 12.5 tons (11 tonnes) of dead weight.

1871 Lake Champlain Lighthouse
Built to warn ships off reefs in the lake, the building now tells of the life led by lighthouse keepers.

★ **SS *Ticonderoga***
A National Historic Landmark, the SS Ticonderoga was rescued from the scrap heap by Webb in 1950. Today the former Lake Champlain steamship is open for visitors to explore.

STAR FEATURES

★ **Railroad Station**

★ **Circus Building**

★ **SS *Ticonderoga***

Middlebury ⓫

🏃 8,500. ✈ 36 miles (58 km)
N in Burlington. 🚊 🛈 2 Court St
(802) 388-7951 or (800) 733-8376.

Middlebury, founded in 1761, is the archetypal New England town. It has not one, but two village greens, or "commons," tall-spired churches, a prestigious college, and a collection of Colonial-era homes. In all Middlebury lays claim to more than 300 buildings that were constructed during the 18th and early 19th centuries. Chief among them are the Congregational Church, the Battell and Beckwith commercial blocks, and the Middlebury Inn, a classic brick Georgian-style hostelry with shuttered windows that dates back to 1827.

The town, which sits on Otter Creek, gets its name from the days of stage coaches when Middlebury served as the transit point on Vermont's main north-south and east-west routes. Morgan horses, one of the first US native breeds, were often seen on this route. Today visitors can tour the **UVM Morgan Horse Farm** for a look at this versatile and historic breed.

At one time Otter Creek powered the machinery for a thriving wool and grain industry. The restored Frog Hollow Mill is now the home of the **Vermont State Craft Center**, which exhibits the work of more than 250 local artists and craftspeople. History buffs will enjoy the **Henry Sheldon Museum of Vermont History**, an 1829 house that documents the early 19th century through its collection of furniture, textiles and clothing, and portraits.

Folk art and folk ways are the themes running through the exhibits at the **Vermont Folklife Center**, a former Masonic Hall. Until recently, the Folklife Center was housed in a home dating back

Peaceful campus of Middlebury College

to the early 1800s in which Gamaliel Painter (1743–1819), the founder of **Middlebury College**, once lived. The college's 500-acre (200-ha) campus is a delightful place to explore, with graceful architecture, an art gallery, and green spaces.

The college's Bread Loaf campus in nearby Ripton is nestled in the Green Mountain National Forest (see p244) and allows access to the scenic Robert Frost Interpretive Trail. Named for the famous American poet who drew his inspiration from the landscapes of New England, the path is flanked with quotations from Frost's poems set on plaques.

◐ UVM Morgan Horse Farm
Rte 23 NW of Middlebury in Weybridge. 📞 (802) 388-2011. ◐ May–Oct: 9am–5pm daily. 📷 🅿 🅳
🟦 Vermont State Craft Center at Frog Hollow
Main & Mill Sts. 📞 (802) 388-3177. ◐ call for hours. 🅳
🏛 Henry Sheldon Museum of Vermont History
1 Park St. 📞 (802) 388-2117. ◐ year-round: 10am–5pm Mon–Sat. 📷 🅳
🏛 Vermont Folklife Center
3 Court St. 📞 (802) 388-4964. ◐ year-round: 11am–4pm Tue–Sat. 🅳
🎓 Middlebury College
College St. 📞 (802) 443-5000. ◐ year-round: Mon–Fri. 📷 🅳

Killington ⓬

🏃 1,000. ✈ 5 miles (8 km) W in Rutland. 🛈 Rte 4, West Killington (802) 422-3333.

Sporty types who like outdoor adventure and a lively social life head for this year-round resort. Killington has a highly developed tourism infrastructure, with hundreds of condominiums, vacation homes, ski lodges and B&Bs, golf courses, hiking and bike trails, and an adventure center with water slides and a climbing wall. It operates the largest ski center (see p262) in the eastern United States, with 200 runs for alpine skiing and snowboarding spread across seven peaks including nearby Pico Mountain. Killington itself is the second-highest peak in Vermont at 4,240 ft (1,295 m). Two of the best cross-country ski centers in the eastern US – Mountain Top Inn (see p317) and Mountain Meadows (see

One of the numerous trails at Killington, Vermont

Morgan Horse Farm

p318) – are also situated in the Killington area.

The ski season here usually lasts eight months, longer than anywhere else in Vermont, and one of the gondolas that ferry skiers to the peaks runs during the summer and fall as well. It is worth taking a ride to the top for the spectacular views. On a clear day, visitors can glimpse parts of five states and distant Canada. Killington also keeps busy throughout the summer with arts and crafts shows, barbecues, and music festivals.

Manchester ⓭

🏨 3,860. ✈ 33 miles (53 km) N in Rutland. 🚌 🛈 Suite 1, 5046 Main St (802) 362-2100.

Mᴀɴᴄʜᴇsᴛᴇʀ is actually made up of three separate communities: Manchester Depot and Manchester Center, the outlet centers of New England, and Manchester Village. The sum of these parts is a picturesque destination surrounded by mountains, typical of scenic southern Vermont. There are two major ski areas: Stratton *(see p363)*, a recently enlarged complex with more than 90 trails and a hillside ski village with shops and restaurants; and Bromley *(see p363)*, a busy, family-oriented ski area.

Manchester has been a popular vacation resort since the 19th century, when wealthy urbanites used to head to the mountains to escape the summer heat. The town's marble sidewalks fringed by old shade trees, the restored Equinox hotel *(see p318)*, and several stately homes evoke that era. Today's tourists take pleasure in following the Equinox Skyline Drive, with its panoramic view of the countryside from the crest of Mount Equinox. Many visitors enjoy spending their time hunting for brand-name bargains in the designer outlets and factory stores.

One of Manchester's largest and most elegant houses is **Hildene**, a 24-room Georgian Revival manor house built by Robert Lincoln (1843–1926), a lawyer, diplomat, and the son of President Abraham Lincoln (1809–65). Among the mansion's most notable features are its 1,000-pipe Aeolian organ and Lincoln family memorabilia. The grounds are graced with an impeccable formal garden, based largely on a pattern taken from a stained-glass window.

Also housed in a stately Georgian mansion, the **Southern Vermont Art Center** rotates its permanent collection of 700 paintings and photographs. The hilly 400 acres (160 ha) also contain a striking sculpture garden. Elsewhere the **American Museum of Fly Fishing** claims to house the largest collection of fly-fishing paraphernalia in the world.

Antique kitchenware on display at elegant Hildene

The collection, which often travels to other museums, includes hundreds of rods, reels, and flies used by famous people such as singer Bing Crosby, literary giant Ernest Hemingway, and former president Jimmy Carter.

🛖 **Hildene**
Rte 7A. 📞 (802) 362-1788. ⏰ mid-May–Oct: 9:30am–4pm daily. 🚫 🅿 every 30 mins. ♿

🏛 **Southern Vermont Art Center**
West Rd. 📞 (802) 362-1405. ⏰ May–Oct: 10am–5pm Tue–Sat, 12pm–5pm Sun; Dec–Mar: 10am–5pm Mon–Sat. 🚫 ♿ 🔤

🏛 **American Museum of Fly Fishing**
Seminary Ave. 📞 (802) 362-3300. ⏰ year-round: 10am–4pm Mon–Fri. ⏰ public hols. 🚫 ♿

Eɴᴠɪʀᴏɴs: Nine miles southwest lies little Arlington, with two major claims to fame: angling and art. Nearby Batten Kill River is considered by experienced fishermen to be one of the best trout rivers in the state, if not the whole of New England. Local anglers may have served as subjects for artist Norman Rockwell (1894–1978) during the years that he lived here. The **Norman Rockwell Exhibition** houses a collection of his work and photographs of some of the townsfolk he used as models.

🏛 **Norman Rockwell Exhibition**
Rte 7A. 📞 (802) 375-6423. ⏰ May–Oct: 9am–5pm daily; Nov–Apr: 10am–4pm daily. ⏰ Jan, Thanksgiving, & Dec 25. 🚫 ♿

Nᴏʀᴍᴀɴ Rᴏᴄᴋᴡᴇʟʟ ɪɴ Vᴇʀᴍᴏɴᴛ

Painter and illustrator Norman Rockwell, famous for idealized depictions of small-town America, lived in Arlington at the height of his career, from 1939 to 1954. His paintings were so detailed they looked almost like photographs, and the magazine covers that he designed for publications such as

Norman Rockwell surveys his work surrounded by friends and his son c.1944

Saturday Evening Post, the *Ladies' Home Journal,* and *Look,* have become collectors' items. Admirers of his work should be sure to visit the Norman Rockwell Museum in Stockbridge, Massachusetts *(see pp166–7),* and Arlington *(see right).*

Green Mountain National Forest ⓮

ℹ️ *Forest Supervisor, Green Mountain National Forest, 231 N Main St, Rutland.* 📞 *(802) 747-6700.* **Hapgood Campground** 📞 *(877) 444-6777 for reservations (all other campgrounds on first-come, first-served basis).* ⭕ *year-round.* ♿ *to campgrounds.*

THIS HUGE SPINE of greenery and mountains runs for 350,000 acres (142,850 ha) – almost the entire length of the state – along the Green Mountain range. The mountains, many more than 4,000 ft (1,200 m) high, have some of the best ski centers in the eastern United States, including Sugarbush *(see p237)* and Mount Snow *(see p246).* A large network of snowmobile and cross-country ski trails are also maintained throughout the winter months.

The National Forest is divided into northern and southern sectors, and encompasses six wilderness areas; sections of the forest have remained entirely undeveloped – no roads, no electricity, and even paths may be poorly marked or non-existent. While hard-core backcountry hikers and campers may enjoy this

Woodward Reservoir in the Green Mountain National Forest

challenge, the majority of travelers will prefer to roam the less primitive areas of the forest. Picnic sites and camp-grounds are found through-out, along with more than 500 miles (805 km) of hiking paths, including the challeng-ing Long and Appalachian trails *(see pp22–3).*

Many lakes, rivers, and, reservoirs offer excellent boating and fishing opportu-nities. On land, bike paths (both mountain and road) are numerous and specially designated paths are open to horseback riders. Regardless of their mode of transporta-tion, visitors are encouraged to stay on the paths in order to preserve the delicate ecosystem. Markers indicate designated lookout points and covered bridges. The

town of Stratton in the southern portion of the Green Mountain range offers recreational activities such as golf, horseback riding, sail-ing, and fly fishing, as well as alpine and cross-country skiing in winter. The Stratton Arts Festival is held in the fall. Nearby Bromley Mountain Ski Center *(see pp363)* has been a popular family resort since the 1930s.

Bennington ⓯

🧗 *16,800.* ✈ 🚌 ℹ️ *100 Veterans Memorial Dr (802) 447-3311 or (800) 229-0252.* 🛍 *Wed & Fri.*

ALTHOUGH IT IS TUCKED away in the southwest corner of the Green Mountain National Forest bordering Massachusetts and New York

Dense woodlands of the Green Mountain National Forest

◁ **Paper Mill Village Bridge, originally built in 1889, near Bennington**

State, Bennington is no backwoods community. The third-largest city in the state, Bennington is an important manufacturing center and home to Bennington College, the faculty of which once included cutting-edge engineer Buckminster Fuller (1895–1983).

Three covered bridges (just off Route 67) herald the approach to town. These 19th-century wooden structures, built with roofs to protect them against the harsh Vermont winter, were nick-named "kissing bridges" because in the days of horses and buggies they provided a discreet shelter for courting couples to embrace.

Bennington was established in 1749 and a few decades later Ethan Allen arrived on the scene to lead the Green Mountain Boys, a citizen's militia originally created to protect Vermont from the expansionist advances of neighboring New York. Allen would later make his name as a patriot during the Revolutionary War by leading his men into battle and scoring several decisive victories against British forces.

The revolutionary era comes alive during a walking tour of the **Old Bennington Historic District** just west of the downtown core, where a typical New England village green is ringed by pillared Greek Revival structures and Federal-style brick buildings. The 1806 **First Congregational Church**, with its vaulted plaster and wood ceilings, is a striking and much-photographed local landmark. Next to it is the Old Burying Ground, resting place of five Vermont governors

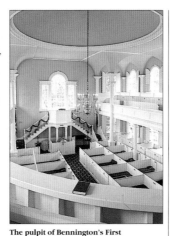

The pulpit of Bennington's First Congregational Church

and the beloved poet Robert Frost *(see pp30–31)*.

Looming over the Historic District is the 306-ft- (93-m-) high **Bennington Battle Monument**, a massive stone obelisk that, when it was built in 1891, was the tallest war monument in the world. It commemorates a 1777 battle in nearby Willoomsac Heights, when the colonial forces defeated the British army and their allies, leading to the surrender of their commander, General John Burgoyne (1722–92). An elevator takes visitors to an observation area that affords panoramic views of Vermont and the neighboring states of New York and Massachusetts.

The turbulent times of the Revolutionary and Civil wars are also recalled at the **Bennington Museum and Grandma Moses Gallery**. The museum houses several dozen paintings by famed folk artist Anna Mary "Grandma" Moses (1860–1961), who lived in the Bennington area. A farmer's wife with no formal training in art, Moses started

The 1891 Bennington Battle Monument

painting landscapes as a hobby when she was in her mid-70s. She was "discovered" by the critics in 1940, when a collection of her art was shown at a private exhibition in the Museum of Modern Art in New York City. At that time the 79-year-old primitive artist was being hailed as an important new talent. By the time she died in 1961 at the age of 101, Grandma Moses had produced some 1,600 works of art, including a series of tiny country scenes painted on mushrooms. The collection in Bennington includes her only known self-portrait.

The Museum's comprehensive collection of Americana also includes uniforms, furniture, and examples of pottery from Bennington's ceramics industry, which reached its peak in the mid-1800s. The display of American glassware includes examples of the decorative Art Nouveau style that was popularized by Louis Comfort Tiffany (1848–1933).

Portrait of Governor Paul Brigham in Bennington Museum

🏛 **Old Bennington Historic District**
📞 *(802) 447-3311 or (800) 229-0252.*
⛪ **First Congregational Church**
Monument Ave. 📞 *(802) 447-1223.*
🚪 *11am Sun.* 🅿
🏛 **Bennington Battle Monument**
15 Monument Circle. 📞 *(802) 447-0550.* ⏱ *mid-April–late Oct: 9am–5pm daily.* 📷 ♿
🏛 **Bennington Museum and Grandma Moses Gallery**
W Main St. 📞 *(802) 447-1571.*
⏱ *Jun–Oct: 9am–6pm daily; Nov–May: 9am–5pm daily.* 📷 ♿ 🚻

Wilmington ⑯

🏠 *1,950.* ✈ *8 miles (13 km) NW in West Dover.* ℹ *21 W Main St (802) 464-8092 or (877) 887-6884.*

WILMINGTON is the largest village in the Mount Snow Valley, with several dozen restaurants and stores catering to the tourists who come to enjoy outdoor sports at the nearby mountain. Like so many of Vermont's small towns, its Main Street is lined with restored 18th- and 19th-century buildings, many listed on the National Register of Historic Places.

Standing 3,600 ft (1,100m) tall, **Mount Snow** is named after the original owner of the land, farmer Reuben Snow, although most visitors believe the name refers to the abundance of white stuff that during winter is the resort's *raison d'être.*

In the late 1990s, more than $35 million was spent on upgrading the ski center *(see p363),* which now has 134 trails, many of them wooded, spread over 765 acres (310 ha). Mount Snow was one of the first ski resorts in the US to provide facilities for snowboarders, with dedicated learning areas for beginners and facilities for advanced surfers. The center also opened the first mountain-bike school in the country. Outdoor summer attractions include 45 miles (72 km) of challenging bike trails (some are also ski runs), hiking

Verdant farmlands around the town of Wilmington

routes, an inline skate and skateboard park, and a climbing wall. The 18-hole **Mount Snow Golf Course** awaits those looking for a more sedate diversion.

🎿 **Mount Snow**
Rte 100. 📞 *(802) 464-3333 or (800) 245-7669.* ⏰ *year-round.* 🎿 ♿
⛳ **Mount Snow Golf Course**
Rte 100. 📞 *(802) 464-4254; call for tee times.* ⏰ *7am–dusk Mon–Fri, 6am–dusk Sat–Sun & public hols.* 🎿

Brattleboro ⑰

🏠 *12,500.* ✈ *20 miles (32 km) NE in Keene, NH.* 🚌 🚉 ℹ *180 Main St (802) 254-4565.* 🎪 *May–Oct: Wed & Sat.*

PERCHED ON THE BANKS of the Connecticut River on the New Hampshire border, Brattleboro is the first major town that northbound travelers encounter as they enter the state. Fort Dummer was originally established here in 1724, making it the state's first European settlement. For that reason, Brattleboro has adopted the slogan "Where Vermont Begins."

A bustling center of commerce and industry, the town is also a hub of tourism. As is the case with so many other Vermont towns, there is a historic district with many Colonial-era buildings of architectural interest. In the 1840s, after the Vermont Valley Railroad was laid to provide a vital link to the outside world, natural springs were discovered in the area and Brattleboro took on a new personality as a spa town where people came for "cures" and health treatments.

The former railroad station is now home to the **Brattleboro Museum and Art Center**, which contains a collection of organs manufactured by the entrepreneurial Estey family, whose instruments were exported around the world. The Brattleboro

Antique organ in the Brattleboro Museum and Art Center

Music Center, which is located on Walnut Street, stages an annual Bach Festival and a summer Jazz Festival.

🏛 **Brattleboro Museum and Art Center**
Main & Vernon Sts. 📞 *(802) 257-0124.* ⏰ *mid-May–early Nov: 12pm–6pm Tue–Sun.* 🎿 ♿

Grafton ⑱

🏠 *600.* ✈ *47 miles (76 km) N in Rutland.* ℹ *56 Townshend Rd (802) 843-2255.*

A THRIVING INDUSTRIAL center 200 years ago, Grafton suffered a steady decline until by the 1960s it was almost a ghost town. But in 1963 Dean Mathey (1890–1972), a wealthy investment banker, established a foundation with the mandate to restore historic structures and revitalize commercial life. Today the village is an architectural treasure trove of 19th-century buildings.

Two tourist attractions are also thriving commercial enterprises: the **Grafton Village Cheese Company**, with its hearty cheddars, and the Old Tavern at Grafton *(see p318),* a hostelry since 1801. Over the years, the inn has hosted author Rudyard Kipling (1865–1936), and President Theodore Roosevelt (1858–1919).

Grafton mailbox

Grafton Village Cheese Company

533 Townshend Rd. ☎ *(802) 843-2221 or (800) 472-3866.* ○ *year-round: 8am–4pm Mon–Fri, 10am–4pm Sat–Sun.* ✉ ♿

ENVIRONS: Eighteen miles (29 km) to the north lies the hamlet of Plymouth Notch. The tiny community was the birthplace of Calvin Coolidge (1872–1933), the 30th president of the US. The **Calvin Coolidge State Historic Site** encompasses an 1850s general store and post office once run by Coolidge's father, a cheese factory, a schoolhouse, and the Coolidge family home.

In Weston, 21 miles (34 km) west of Plymouth Notch, visitors will find the **Vermont Country Store**. The store is famous for its enormous and eclectic array of merchandise, personally selected by its owner, Lyman Orton. Not only are these items highly original – be they badger-hair shaving brushes or hand-blown glasses that sea captains once used to forecast the weather – they are also always of the highest quality.

♛ Calvin Coolidge State Historic Site

Rte 100A. ☎ *(802) 672-3773.* ○ *late May–mid-Oct: 9:30am–5pm daily.* ✉ ♿ ▯

One of the many beautiful homes in the village of Woodstock

⬛ Vermont Country Store

Rte 100, Weston. ☎ *(802) 824-3184.* ○ *year-round: 9am–5pm Mon–Sat.*

Woodstock ⑲

🚶 *1,000.* ✈ *31 miles (50 km) W in Rutland.* 🚌 ⓘ *18 Central St (802) 457-3555 or (888) 496-6378.*

E VEN IN VERMONT, a state where historic, picturesque villages are commonplace, Woodstock stands out. Founded in 1761, the town is an enclave of renovated brick and clapboard Georgian houses. The restoration of the town came about as a result of the generosity of philanthropists such as the Rockefeller family and

railroad magnate Frederick Billings (1823–90). An early proponent of reforestation, Billings personally financed the planting of 10,000 trees throughout the village.

Billings Farm & Museum is still a working entity. The 1890 farmhouse has been restored and there are seasonal events open to the public, such as plowing competitions in the spring and apple-cider pressing in the fall. The museum also traces Vermont's agricultural past with old photographs and exhibits of harvesting implements, butter churns, and ice cutters.

The **Vermont Raptor Center** is a reserve where injured birds of prey are cared for until they can be returned to the wild. As well as operating conservation programs and summer day camps for children, the naturalists here give frequent presentations about the owls, falcons, and eagles that have come under their care.

🏛 Billings Farm & Museum

River Rd. ☎ *(802) 457-2355.* ○ *late May–Oct: 10am–5pm daily.* ✉ ♿ ▯

🦅 Vermont Raptor Center

Church Hill Rd. ☎ *(802) 457-2779.* ○ *year-round: 10am–4pm daily.* ● *Sun.* ✉ ✉ ♿

ENVIRONS: Six miles (10 km) east of town is the stunning Quechee Gorge. The best view of the chasm is on Route 4, which crosses the gorge via a steel bridge. A short hiking trail leads from the parking lot on the east side down to the Ottauquechee River below.

THE RISE OF CALVIN COOLIDGE

Calvin Coolidge was born in tiny Plymouth to parents who ran a general store. His humble upbringing endowed him with traits that would carry him to the presidency in the 1920s: honesty, frugality, and industry. Known as "Silent Cal," because he wasted little time on small talk, Coolidge guided the US to a period of economic prosperity before the onset of the Great Depression of 1929.

Boyhood home of Calvin Coolidge

NEW HAMPSHIRE

NEW HAMPSHIRITES ARE KNOWN *for their fiercely independent nature, born of necessity in the early 1600s when European settlers established outposts in this mountainous and heavily forested region. This natural beauty is still in evidence, in the soaring peaks of the White Mountains Range, the pristine water of Lake Winnipesaukee, and the small, but scenic coastline.*

There can be no better expression of New Hampshire's individualistic spirit than the state motto, "Live Free or Die," which is stamped on every state license plate. Six months before the July 4, 1776 signing of the Declaration of Independence, New Hampshire became the very first state to formally declare its separation from Great Britain. Ever cautious of centralized government, modern New Hampshirites proudly point out that they pay no personal income tax, nor is sales tax levied on most consumer goods in the state – a boon for tourists looking for bargains.

The landscape that helped forge the determined mindset of early settlers has changed little in the ensuing centuries. It is estimated that more than 90 percent of the state is undeveloped, with dense forest covering more than three-quarters of its land.

The northern part of the state is wild country, its woodlands bisected by the mighty Connecticut River and rippled by the tall peaks of the White Mountains Range *(see p265)*. Campers, climbers, and canoeists reign here. The hundreds of lakes and ponds that quilt central New Hampshire attract vacationers year-round looking to boat, fish, cross-country ski, and snowmobile. In the southwest, sightseers drive across rolling farmland that is punctuated by scenic villages and covered bridges. Even the industrial heartland of the Merrimack Valley is predominantly rural. A mere 15-minute drive from the downtown cores of the state's major commercial centers of Concord *(see pp258–9)* and Manchester *(see p259)* will transport travelers to the tranquility of dairy farms or quiet country roads.

Early October view of the Presidential Range in the White Mountains

◁ Canterbury Shaker Village, founded in 1792

Exploring New Hampshire

NEW HAMPSHIRE'S COMPACT BORDERS make it ideal for sightseeing. Some attractions can be enjoyed on foot, as with the spectacular board-walked chasm of Franconia Notch (see pp272–3), or by car, as with a breathtaking fall-foliage tour along the Kancamagus Highway (see p270). The remains of colonial battlements, the Shaker villages at Enfield (see p262) and Canterbury (see pp260–61), and the historic homes of poets, politicians, and presidents are sprinkled throughout the state. Called the Granite State for its extensive granite formations and quarries, New Hampshire's rough edges are softened somewhat in its many fine muse-ums. The Currier Gallery of Art (see p258) is one such establishment, giving visitors the chance to view work by some of the world's great masters.

Bridge over the Flume Gorge in Franconia Notch State Park

GETTING AROUND

Interstate 93 is the largest and most popular north-south route in the state, with numerous smaller roads branching off to more remote areas. Drivers should be aware of two New Hampshire realities: heavier traffic during peak fall-foliage season, especially on the weekends; and moose crossings. While moose sightings are thrilling, collisions with the huge animals can be extremely dangerous. Travelers should drive with caution at all times. Currently the only Amtrak train stop in the state is in Claremont. Travelers may also take Amtrak to White River Junction, Vermont, or to Boston and link up with a bus line from there. Commercial bus lines servicing the area include C&J Transport, Concord Trailways, and Greyhound bus lines (see p375). The state's largest airport is found in the south in Manchester (see p258), although Maine's Portland International Airport is a good jumping-off point for northeastern New Hampshire.

KEY

▨ Interstate

▨ Major road

▭ Minor road

▨ Scenic route

❉ Viewpoint

17 WHITE MOUNTAIN NATIONAL FOREST

112

15 HANOVER

Newfound Lake

13 ENFIELD SHAKER MUSEUM

SAINT-GAUDENS NAT. HISTORIC SITE

14

4

120

103

12 NEW LONDON

LAKE SUNAPEE REGION 10

❉

89

HENNIKER

Connecticut River

202

KEENE

7

9

MONADNOCK STATE PARK 5 ❉

RHODODENDRON STATE PARK 6

119

101

Lengthy Cornish-Windsor Bridge outside Cornish

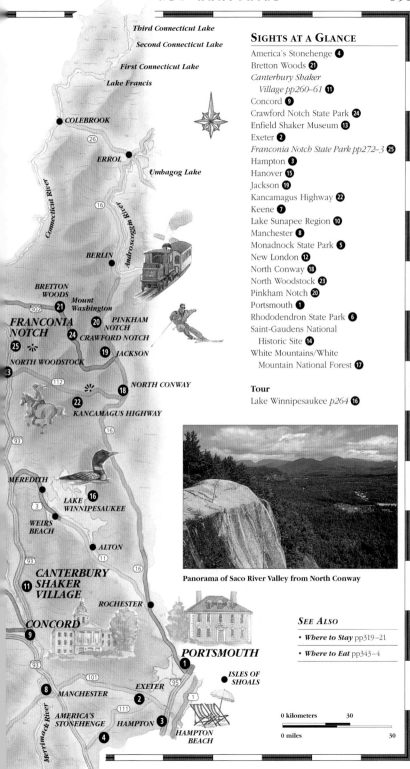

Third Connecticut Lake

Second Connecticut Lake

First Connecticut Lake

Lake Francis

● COLEBROOK

(26)

● ERROL

Umbagog Lake

(16)

BERLIN

BRETTON
WOODS
(302) **21** Mount
FRANCONIA Washington
NOTCH **20** PINKHAM
24 NOTCH
CRAWFORD NOTCH
25 ✴ **19** JACKSON
NORTH WOODSTOCK
3
(112) **18** NORTH CONWAY
22
KANCAMAGUS HIGHWAY
(16)
(93)

MEREDITH
16
LAKE
WINNIPESAUKEE
3
WEIRS
BEACH
● ALTON
(11)
(93) (16)
CANTERBURY
SHAKER
VILLAGE
11 ROCHESTER ●
CONCORD
9
(93) PORTSMOUTH
(101) **1**
ISLES OF
8 EXETER SHOALS
MANCHESTER **2**
(111)
AMERICA'S HAMPTON
STONEHENGE **3**
4 HAMPTON
BEACH

Connecticut River
Androscoggin River
Merrimack River

Panorama of Saco River Valley from North Conway

SEE ALSO

• *Where to Stay* pp319–21
• *Where to Eat* pp343–4

0 kilometers 30

0 miles 30

Portsmouth ❶

W HEN SETTLERS ESTABLISHED a colony here in 1623, they called it Strawbery Banke *(see pp254–5)* in honor of the berries blanketing the banks of the Piscataqua River. In 1653 the name was changed to Portsmouth, a reflection of the town's reputation as a hub of maritime commerce. First a fishing port, the town enjoyed prosperity in the 18th century as a link in the trade route between Great Britain and the West Indies. During the years leading up to the American Revolution, the town was a hotbed of revolutionary fervor and the place where colonial naval hero John Paul Jones (1747–92) built his warship, the *Ranger*.

Favorite with tourists: Portsmouth's Market Street

Exploring Portsmouth

Girded by the Piscataqua River and the North and South Mill ponds, compact Portsmouth is easily explored on foot. The town's past permeates the downtown core, especially along busy Market Street. Historic buildings, some constructed in the 19th-century by wealthy sea captains, have been restored and turned into museums, boutiques, and restaurants. The city also has a number of brew pubs and microbreweries that produce local ales. More than 70 historic sites, including houses and gardens, can be found along the Portsmouth Harbour Trail, a walking tour of the Historic District.

Beautiful exterior of Moffat-Ladd House in Portsmouth

🏛 Governor John Langdon House

143 Pleasant St. 🄲 (603)-436-3205. ⬜ Jun–mid-Oct: 11am–5pm Wed–Sun. ⬤ Labor Day. 🎟 🄲 ♿

The son of a farmer of modest means, John Langdon (1741–1819) became one of Portsmouth's most prominent citizens. Langdon enjoyed great prosperity as a ship captain, merchant, and shipbuilder before becoming the governor of New Hampshire and a US senator. In 1784 he built this imposing Georgian mansion. The house is known for its ornate Rococo embellishments. The grounds feature a grape arbor and a large rose garden.

🏛 Moffat-Ladd House

154 Market St. 🄲 (603) 742-7745. ⬜ mid-Jun–mid-Oct: 10am–4pm Mon–Sat, 2pm–5pm Sun. 🎟 🄲 ♿

One of Portsmouth's first three-story homes, this elegant 1763 mansion was built for wealthy maritime trader and sea captain John Moffatt. The house's boxy design was a precursor to the Federal style of architecture that would later become popular

throughout the country. The house, located on the Portsmouth Harbour Trail, is graced by a grand entrance hall, a series of family portraits, and period furnishings.

🏛 Wentworth-Gardner House

50 Mechanic St. 🄲 (603) 436-4406. ⬜ mid-Jun–mid-Oct: 1pm–4pm Tue–Sun. ⬤ public hols. 🎟 ♿

Also located on the Portsmouth Harbour Trail, this 1760 house is considered to be one of the best examples of Georgian architecture in the country. The house's beautiful exterior has rows of multi-paned windows, symmetrical chimneys, and a pillared entrance. The interior has 11 fireplaces, hand-painted wallpaper, and graceful carvings that took artisans a year to complete.

TO CHAMBER OF COMMERCE USS ALBACORE ISLES OF SHOALS STEAMSHIP CO.

Piscataqua River

MARKET STREET
BOW STREET
PENHALLOW
MARKET STREET
HANOVER STREET
P
FLEET STREET
CONGRESS STREET
PLEASANT STREET
STATE STREET
COURT STREET
ROGERS AVENUE
PARROTT AVENUE
South Mill Pond

JOHN PAUL JONES

Born in Scotland, John Paul Jones (1747–92) went to sea as a cabin boy when he was only 12 years old. He worked his way up to being the first mate on a slave ship, then later the commander of a merchant vessel in Tobago. A hard taskmaster, Jones escaped to America before he was to go on trial for the deaths of several sailors he had punished. Regarded as an outlaw by the British, Jones went on to become an illustrious naval commander for the US. During the American Revolution, Jones led a series of daring raids up and down the British coast for which he was awarded a gold medal by Congress.

USS *Albacore*

Albacore Park, 600 Market St.
[(603) 436-3680. ☐ May–Oct: 9:30am–5:30pm daily; Nov–Apr: 9:30am–5:30pm Thu–Mon. 🖏
This sleek submarine was the fastest underwater vessel of its type when it was launched from the Portsmouth Naval Shipyard in 1953. It gives visitors access to the cramped quarters of submariners and an idea of what life was like for the submarine's 55 crew members. Exhibits in the visitor center trace the vessel's history.

🏛 Children's Museum of Portsmouth

280 Marcy St. [(603) 436-3853. ☐ Jul–Aug: 10am–5pm daily; Sep–Jun: 10am–5pm Tue–Sat. 🖏 🖢
This museum features a series of interactive exhibits that invite participation. Kids can command a submarine or fly in the replica of a space shuttle. Elsewhere aspiring paleontologists are invited to don lab coats and help with the excavation of dinosaur fossils, while budding musicians can play instruments from around the world.

🌊 Water Country

Rte 1 S of Portsmouth. [(603) 427-1111. ☐ Jun–Labor Day: call for hours. 🖏 🖫
Eighteen water rides, a huge wave pool, a pirate ship, and a man-made lagoon await visitors to New England's largest water park. Smaller children can enjoy the slides and fountains in designated areas, while the more adventurous thrill-seekers can careen down looping water slides.

Popular destination on summer days: Water Country

PORTSMOUTH CITY CENTER

Children's Museum
of Portsmouth ⑤
Gov. John Langdon House ②
Moffat-Ladd House ①
Strawbery Banke Museum ③
Wentworth-Gardner House ④

KEY

🟩	Street-by-Street map *see pp254–5*
▬	Highway
🚹	Tourist information
🅿	Parking

Street-by-Street: Strawbery Banke

Aldrich Garden bloom

THIS OUTDOOR MUSEUM near the waterfront is located on the very spot on which Portsmouth was founded. Tracing the history of the town, this 10-acre (4-ha) site contains more than 40 buildings that depict life from 1695 to 1955. Those houses open to the public are furnished in period style and contain interesting collections of decorative arts, ceramics, and assorted artifacts. Many of the buildings are set amid gardens cultivated according to their eras, from early pioneer herb gardens to formal Victorian flower beds.

Traditional transport
Visitors can tour Strawbery Banke on authentic horse-drawn carriages.

Family Activity Center is housed in an 1821 building and is now used for youth and family programs.

COURT STREET

ATKINSON STREET

JEFFERSON STREET

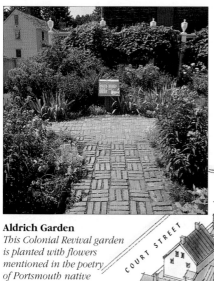

COURT STREET

WHIDDEN PLACE

Aldrich Garden
This Colonial Revival garden is planted with flowers mentioned in the poetry of Portsmouth native Thomas Bailey Aldrich (1836–1907).

WASHINGTON STREET

0 meters   50

0 yards   50

★ Chase House
Built c.1762, this elegant home is furnished with sumptuous pieces from several periods.

STAR SIGHTS

★ Chase House

★ Jones House

★ Sherburne House

Jackson House
Displays in this late 18th-century home feature the various trends of interior decor that have come and gone over the last 160 years.

VISITORS' CHECKLIST

Marcy St. (603) 433-1100.
May–Oct: 10am–5pm daily.
limited access to some buildings.
www.strawberybanke.org

★ **Sherburne House**
Built in 1695, the home now serves as an exhibit on 17th-century house design and construction.

MARCY STREET

RSE LANE

JEFFERSON STREET

MAST LANE

PUDDLE LANE

Winn House exhibit of traditional house construction

Dinsmore Shop
A cooper makes barrels and casks while visitors observe in this craft workshop, built in 1800.

KEY

– – – Suggested route

WASHINGTON STREET

★ **Jones House**
Housed in a 1790 structure, the Exhibit and Archaeology Center displays a variety of artifacts excavated on the site.

Exeter ❷

🏛 14,500. ✈ 15 miles (24 km)
E in Portsmouth. ℹ 120 Water St
(603) 772-2411.

T HE QUIET LITTLE town of
Exeter southwest of
Portsmouth was much less
tranquil during the century
and a half leading up to
the American Revolution
(1775–83). The community
sprang up around the falls
linking the freshwater Exeter
River and the salty Squamscott
River. It was founded in 1638
by the Reverend John
Wheelwright (1592–1679),
an outspoken cleric who
was thrown out of the
Massachusetts colony for
his radical views.

During the turbulent years
leading up to American
Independence, outraged
townspeople openly defied
the British government. They
drove off officials who had
been dispatched to cut down
trees for the British Navy,
burned their leaders in effigy,
and finally declared independence from Britain, setting a
precedent for the
rest of the colonies.

Dominating the
center of town,
Phillips Exeter
Academy stands as
one of the country's
most prestigious
preparatory schools.
The complex of
more than 100 ivy-
clad brick buildings
fronted by manicured lawns
was founded in 1781.

Other points of interest
include the **Gilman Garrison**

House, a fortified log
building dating back to the
mid-17th century, and the
**American Independence
Museum,** which houses
an original copy of the
Declaration of Independence
as well as a draft of the
American Constitution.

🏚 **Gilman Garrison House**
12 Water St. 📞 (603) 436-3205.
⭕ Jun–mid-Oct: 12pm–5pm
Sat–Sun. 🎫 📷 obligatory. ♿
🏛 **American Independence
Museum**
1 Governors Lane. 📞 (603) 772-
2622. ⭕ May–Oct: 12pm–5pm
Wed–Sun. 🎫 📷 obligatory. 🛍 🚫

Hampton ❸

🏛 15,000. ✈ 12 miles (19 km)
N in Portsmouth. ℹ 1 Park Ave
(603) 926-8718.

O NE OF NEW HAMPSHIRE'S
oldest towns, Hampton
is situated at the geographic
center of the many state
parks and public beaches
that line Highway 1A, the
coast road. Public recreation
areas stretch from
Seabrook Beach, a
sandy shore dotted
with dunes, to the
rugged shoreline of
**Odiorne Point State
Park** in Rye to the
north. The park has
biking trails, tidal
pools, and a board-
walk spanning a salt-
water marsh. The
park's Science Center also
runs interpretive nature programs that are especially
appealing to young visitors.

**Exeter farmers
market sign**

**Exterior of the American
Independence Museum in Exeter**

Ten miles (6 km) to the south
of the factory outlet shopping
mecca of North Hampton,
travelers will come upon the
popular **Hampton Beach**.
This miniature version of
Atlantic City comes complete
with a casino that hosts big-
name entertainers and an old-
fashioned boardwalk lined
with video arcades, ice-cream
shops, and stalls selling
T-shirts and tacky souvenirs.
Open year-round, Hampton
Beach is busiest during hot
summer months, when
vacationers come to enjoy
the miles of clean, golden
beaches, including a separate
area designated for surfers.
Swimmers and jet skiers test
the waters, para-sailers soar
overhead, and deep-sea
fishing and whale-watching
charter boats are available
from Hampton Harbor.
Hampton Beach is not the
place for people looking to
get away from the crowds,
but it is geared toward family
fun, with game arcades,
water slides, magic shows,
and a series of free concerts
and fireworks.

Away from the casino and busy boardwalk, the blue skies and tranquil surf of Hampton Beach

**🏃 Odiorne Point
State Park**
Rte 1A, Rye Beach. 📞 (603) 436-
8043. **Science Center** ⬜ year-
round: 10am–5pm. ⬤ Jan 1,
Thanksgiving, & Dec 25. 🖼 ♿
Park ⬜ year-round: 8am–dusk. 🖼
🚻 Hampton Beach
📞 (800) 438-2826 or
(603) 926-8717.

America's Stonehenge ❹

Haverhill Rd, North Salem. 📞 (603)
893-8300. ⬜ mid-Feb–mid-Jun:
9am–5pm daily; mid-Jun–Aug: 9am–
7pm daily; Sep–Oct: 9am–5pm daily;
Nov–Jan: 9am–4pm daily. 🖼

A LTHOUGH NOT NEARLY AS
imposing as its British
namesake, this is an intriguing place nonetheless.
Believed to be one of the
oldest man-made complexes
this side of the Atlantic, the
30-acre (12-ha) grounds of
America's Stonehenge are
scattered with standing
stones, walls, and stone
chambers. Archeologists,
historians, and astronomers
have argued for decades
about the origins of the site,
with credit going to everyone
from ancient Greeks to way-
ward aliens. Today one of the
most popular theories has
Native American tribes con-
structing this megalithic complex as a giant calendar to
measure the movements of
the sun and the moon.
Excavations have turned up a
wealth of ancient remains,
including stone pottery, tools,
and petroglyphs that have
been carbon-dated to
between 3,000 and 4,000
years old. One of the more
gruesome parts of the site is
the five-ton (4.5-
tonne) Sacrificial
Table, carved
with grooves that
researchers believe
may have been
troughs for collect-
ing the blood of
victims. Special
events are held at
the site during the
spring and fall
equinox and at
the winter and
summer solstice.

Mount Monadnock, popular with climbers and hikers

Monadnock State Park ❺

Off Rte 124, W of Jaffrey. 📞 (603)
532-8862. ⬜ year-round. 🖼 🅿

S TANDING SOME 3,165 ft
(965 m) high, Mount
Monadnock has two claims to
fame. It is said to be one of
the most climbed mountains
in the world (it is not unusual
to find several hundred hikers
milling around its peak) and it
has spawned a term used in
geology. A "monadnock" is an
isolated hill or mountain of
resistant rock rising above a
plain that has been created
by glacial activity.
    The mountain's popularity
has a lot to do with its campsites, scenic picnic areas, and
numerous hiking trails. Within
the 5,000-acre (2,000-ha) park,
there are 40 miles (64 km) of
trails, many of which lead to
the summit. The climb to the
peak of the metamorphic
schist pinnacle takes more
than three hours, but on clear
days intrepid hikers are
rewarded with gorgeous
views of all six New England
states. Markers along the trails
have been erected in memory
of such men of letters as
Ralph Waldo Emerson

(1803–82) and Henry David
Thoreau (1817–62), both of
whom climbed to the peak.
The visitor's center gives an
overview of the hiking trails,
the history of the mountain,
and information about the
local flora and fauna. The
campsites are open year-
round and in the winter
months the trails are popular
with cross-country skiers.

Rhododendron State Park ❻

Off Rte 119, W of Fitzwilliam. 📞
(603) 532-8862. ⬜ year-round:
dawn–dusk daily. 🖼 ♿ partial.

N EW ENGLAND'S LARGEST
grove of wild rhododen-
drons bursts into a celebration
of pink and white in June
through mid-July. The 450-
acre (180-ha) park has more
than 16 acres (6 ha) of giant
rhododendron bushes.
Walking through the rhododendrons, some of which
grow to more than 20 ft (6 m)
high, is a feast for the senses
in summer, but there are flo-
ral highlights in other seasons
as well. In the spring the
woodland park is carpeted
with trilliums. By May the
apple trees are heavy with
blossoms. During
summer, visitors
will find flowering
mountain laurel and
wildflowers such as
jack-in-the-pulpit
and delicate pink
lady slippers. The
park is equipped
with picnic areas
and hiking trails that
offer spectacular
views of Mount
Monadnock and the
surrounding peaks.

Ancient ruins of America's Stonehenge

Keene ❼

🏠 *25,350.* ✈️ *58 miles (93 km) E in Manchester.* 🚉 🛈 *48 Central Sq (603) 352-1303.*

K EENE IS THE LARGEST town in southern New Hampshire's Monadnock region. The nation's first glass-blowing factory was founded in nearby Temple in 1780, and soon after Keene became one of the region's hotbeds of arts and crafts. By the 19th century the town was famous for the production of high-quality glass and pottery and for its thriving wool mill. The **Horatio Colony Museum** is the former home of a descendant of the mill-owning family. Its period furnishings give a good idea of upper-class life in the mid-1800s. Today the focus of Keene's thriving cultural life is Keene State College, located on what is reputed to be the widest Main Street in the world. The college has several theaters and art studios where events are staged throughout the year.

🏛️ **Horatio Colony Museum**
199 Main St. 📞 *(603) 352-0460.*
⭕ *May–Oct: 11am–4pm Wed–Sun.*
📷 *obligatory.*

ENVIRONS: Half a dozen covered bridges *(see p263)* lie within a 10-mile (16-km) radius of Keene, giving the region the nickname "Currier and Ives country." Road markers direct drivers to each span. These "kissing bridges," where young couples would steal secret embraces as they rode their buggy through them, have long been favorite subjects of photographers.

W. Swanzey Thompson Covered Bridge near Keene

Manchester ❽

🏠 *105,250.* ✈️ *1 Airport Rd.* 🚉
🛈 *889 Elm St (603) 666-6600.* 📷
(603) 622-7531.

I N 1805 A MODEST MILL was built on the east bank of the Merrimack River. Fueled by waterpower, the Amoskeag Mill continued to expand until by the beginning of the 20th century it claimed the title as the largest textile mill in the world. At its peak, the operation employed some 17,000 people and its complex of brick buildings stretched for more than one mile (1.5 km). Today the structures that once held workers and heavy machinery are used for restaurants, college classrooms, and even residential housing.

This former industrial center is now known for the **Currier Gallery of Art**, New Hampshire's premier art museum. The museum's diverse collection of over 12,000 items includes works by such European masters as John Constable (1776–1837), Claude Monet (1840–1926), and Henri Matisse (1869–1954).

The museum's west wing houses an extensive collection of the works of 20th-century American painters such as Andrew Wyeth (b.1917) and Georgia O'Keeffe (1887–1986), famous for her surrealistic renditions of New Mexico's landscapes. The decorative arts section displays a large selection of period furniture, silverware, and 18th- and 19th-century glassware, including a collection of rare glass paperweights from France.

The museum's largest piece is the nearby Zimmerman House. The single-story home was built in 1950 by pioneering American architect Frank Lloyd Wright (1867–1959). The simple, elegant lines of its exterior are typical of Wright's Usonian style of utilitarian design. Shuttles take visitors from the museum to the house, and guided tours (by advance reservation) of its interior highlight textiles and furniture designed by Wright.

🏛️ **Currier Gallery of Art**
201 Myrtle Way. 📞 *(603) 669-6144.*
⭕ *year-round: 11am–5pm Mon, Wed–Thu, & Sun, 11am–8pm Fri, 10am–5pm Sat.* 📷 🎫 ♿ 🏠 🖥️ 🚫

Concord ❾

🏠 *37,500.* ✈️ *25 miles (49 km) S in Manchester.* 🚉 🛈 *40 Commercial St (603) 224-2508.*

N EW HAMPSHIRE'S CAPITAL is a quiet little town, but thanks to its prominent political position, it has been associated with a number of important historical figures. Mary Baker Eddy (1821–1910),

Painting in the Currier Gallery of Art in Manchester

CONCORD COACHES

In 1827 Concord-based wheelwright Lewis Downing and coach builder J. Stephens Abbot built the first Concord Coach, designed to withstand the unforgiving trails of the undeveloped West. The 1-ton (1-tonne) stagecoaches were, in their own way, as revolutionary as the Internet is today because they helped facilitate communications across the vast emerging hinterland. Wells Fargo, the famous transportation company, relied heavily on the coaches during the California Gold Rush (1848–55) to carry mail and passengers on parts of the route between New York City and San Francisco.

founder of the Christian Science Church, spent much of her life here. The **Pierce Manse** was the one-time home of Franklin Pierce (1804–69), the 14th president of the US.

The 1819 **State House**, built from New Hampshire granite and Vermont marble, is one of the oldest in America. Inside the building are several hundred paintings of the state's better known residents and political figures. In its heyday, the Eagle Hotel on Main Street, now an office building, hosted the likes of presidents Andrew Jackson and Benjamin Harrison, aviator Charles Lindbergh, and former first lady Eleanor Roosevelt.

Concord schoolteacher Christa McAuliffe (1948–86) unfortunately gained her fame through tragedy. On January 28, 1986, McAuliffe boarded the *Challenger* space shuttle as the first civilian to be launched into space by NASA. Seventy-three seconds after the lift-off, with her husband and children watching from the ground, the shuttle exploded

into a fireball and crashed, killing McAuliffe and her six fellow astronauts.

McAuliffe's memory lives on in the form of **The Christa McAuliffe Planetarium**. Capped by a giant glass pyramid, this futuristic museum was opened on June 21, 1991, to teach people about astronomy and the exploration of space. Visitors can enjoy such rotating multimedia shows as "Through the Eyes of Hubble" – the universe as seen through the powerful telescope used by NASA – and "Destination Mars."

THE CHRISTA McAULIFFE PLANETARIUM

Entrance to Christa McAuliffe Planetarium

🚩 **Pierce Manse**
14 Penacook St. 📞 *(603) 225-2068 or 224-7668.* 🕐 *mid-Jun–mid-Sep: 11am–3pm Mon–Fri.* 🎟 ✅ 🚻

🚩 **State House**
107 N Main St. 📞 *(603) 271-2154.*
Visitor center 🕐 *year-round: 8am–4:30pm Mon–Fri.* ♿ 🚻

🏛 **The Christa McAuliffe Planetarium**
3 Institute Dr. 📞 *(603) 271-7827.* 🕐 *year-round: 10am–2pm Mon–Wed, 10am–5pm Thu–Sat, 12pm–5pm Sun. Call for show times.* 🎟 ♿ 🚻

Lake Sunapee Region ❿

ℹ️ *143 Main St, New London (603) 763-2495 or (800) 258-3530.*

THIS SCENIC REGION, dominated by 2,743-ft- (835-m-) high Mount Sunapee and the 10-mile- (16-km-) long lake at its feet, is a major drawing card for outdoor enthusiasts, particularly boaters and skiers. Many locals have vacation and weekend homes here, and an increasing number of retirees are also moving to the region, attracted not only by the scenery but also by the activity-oriented lifestyle.

Lake Sunapee (its name is said to be derived from the Penacook Indian words for "wild goose water") has been attracting visitors for well over a century. In the mid-1800s, trains and steamships used to transport tourists to hotels that rimmed the lake. The steamships have long since gone, but vacationers can rent canoes, picnic on the beach, or take a narrated trip on a sightseeing boat. **Mount Sunapee State Park**'s namesake peak attracts hikers and climbers during the summer months and skiers during the winter. The chairlifts, which run year-round, transport sightseers to the peak. An observation platform affords lovely views of the lake and the surrounding countryside.

🎿 **Mount Sunapee State Park**
Rte 103. 📞 *(603) 763-2356.* 🕐 *year-round.* ♿

Sightseeing boat on Lake Sunapee

Canterbury Shaker Village ⓫

FOUNDED IN 1792, THIS VILLAGE was occupied for 200 years, making it one of the longest-lasting communities of the religious group in the country. Shakers also lived in nearby Enfield *(see pp262)*. Their belief in strict isolation from the rest of the world and in celibacy eventually led to their demise. The last member of this colony died in 1992, and now 25 of the original buildings are open to the public. Millponds, nature trails, and traditional gardens punctuate the 690-acre (280-ha) site. Skilled artisans re-create Shaker crafts, known for their workmanship.

Canterbury Shaker Village
The village is dominated by the central Dwelling House (below).

The belfry
is a distinctive shape and contains a bell made by Revolutionary War hero Paul Revere.

Shaker Brooms
The common flat broom was invented in 1798 by Shaker Brother Theodore Bates. Shakers believed that cleanliness mirrored spiritual purity.

THE CREAMERY RESTAURANT

Creamery Restaurant
This 1905 creamery serves traditional Shaker fare in season for lunch.

Brethren's Retiring Room

STAR FEATURES

★ **Dining Room**

★ **Old Library and Museum**

★ **Sisters' Retiring Room**

★ **Dining Room**
This area once held as many as 60 Shakers per sitting.

KEY

☐ **Illustrated building**

1 Trustees' Office
2 The Infirmary
3 Meeting House
4 Dwelling House
5 Sisters' Shop
6 Carriage House
7 The Creamery
8 Carpenter Shop
9 Fire House/Power House
10 Laundry
11 Horse Barn
12 School House
13 Syrup Shop

VISITORS' CHECKLIST

288 Shaker Rd, Canterbury. 📞
*(603) 783-9511 or (800) 982-
9511.* 🕐 *May–Oct: 10am–5pm
daily; Apr, Nov–Dec: 10am–5pm
Fri–Sun.* 📷 🚌 🚻 🛍 🚻
🌐 *www.shakers.org.*

Dormer rooms were used for summer sleeping and as clothes cupboards.

Popular Stop
Historic buildings, a restaurant, and a gift shop make Canterbury a favorite tourist destination.

★ **Sisters' Retiring Room**
Men and women had separate sleeping quarters. Each one is equipped with traditional Shaker furniture.

★ **Old Library and Museum**
The library contains 1,500 Shaker books and documents and a museum.

The Infirmary
Built in 1811, this building served as the hospital, pharmacy, dental office, and morgue.

New London

🏛 *3,700.* ✈ *28 miles (45 km) NW in Lebanon.* 🚌 ℹ *Main St (603) 526-6575 or (877) 526-6575.*

NEW LONDON'S PERCH atop a crest gives it an enviable view of the surrounding forests during the fall foliage season. The bucolic setting also serves as a wonderful backdrop for the town's rich collection of colonial and early 19th-century buildings. Of these, the architectural centerpiece is **Colby-Sawyer College**, an undergraduate liberal arts school founded in 1837. The college organizes numerous cultural programs, including plays, lectures, films, concerts, and art exhibitions. More cultural fun can be had farther down the street at the **New London Barn Playhouse**. Housed in a refurbished 1820s barn, the theater stages popular plays and musicals during the summer months.

🎭 **Colby-Sawyer College**
Main St. ℹ *(603) 526-2010.* ○ *year-round: 9am–5pm Mon–Fri.*
♿ 🚻 🏛
📷 **New London Barn Playhouse**
209 Main St. ℹ *(603) 526-4631 or (603) 526-6710.* ○ *mid-Jun–Sep: call for hours.* 📷

Enfield Shaker Museum ⑬

Rte 4A, Enfield. ℹ *(603) 632-4346.* ○ *mid-May–mid-Oct: 10am–4pm Mon–Sat, 12pm–5pm Sun; mid-Oct–mid-May: 10am–4pm Sat, 12pm–4pm Sun.* 📷 🚻 ♿ 🏛

FACING RELIGIOUS persecution in Britain in the mid-18th century, several groups of Shakers, a sect that broke away from the Quakers, fled to North America under the spiritual guidance of Mother Ann Lee (1736–84). The Shaker village at Enfield was founded in 1793, one of 18 such communities in the US.
Between the founding of Enfield and the 1920s, the Shakers constructed more than 200 buildings, of which 13 remain. And while they

Colby-Sawyer College in New London

farmed more than 3,000 acres (1,200 ha) of land, property was under the ownership of the community, not individuals. Members were celibate and they were strict pacifists, devoting their "hands to work and hearts to God." At one time the Enfield Shakers numbered over 300, but, as in similar communities, their numbers gradually dwindled. In 1923 the last 10 members moved to the Canterbury Shaker Village *(see pp260–61)* north of Concord. The last Canterbury Shaker died as recently as 1992 at the age of 96.
The exhibits at the museum illustrate how the Shakers lived and worked. Visitors will come across fine examples of Shaker ingenuity, including one of their many inventions: sulfur matches. The buildings are filled with the simple but practical wooden furniture for which the Shakers, who were consummate craftspeople, were famous. The 160-year-old

Great Stone Dwelling, the largest such structure ever built by these industrious people, has been turned into a 24-room inn.

Saint-Gaudens National Historic Site ⑭

Rte 12A N of Cornish-Windsor Bridge. ℹ *(603) 675-2175.* ○ *Jun–Oct: 9am–4:30pm daily.* 📷 ✓ 🏛

THIS NATIONAL HISTORIC SITE celebrates the life of Augustus Saint-Gaudens (1848–1907), the preeminent US sculptor of his time. When Saint-Gaudens moved to Cornish in 1885, it marked the beginning of the town's evolution into an art colony. Artists, writers, and musicians alike were attracted to the town by the talent of Saint-Gaudens, whose family had emigrated to the US from Ireland when he was just a baby. Something of a world traveler, Saint-Gaudens became an apprentice cameo cutter in New York and later studied at the École des Beaux-Arts in Paris. He also won several commissions in Rome. By the time that he returned to New York, his reputation as a brilliant sculptor had been well established. His work, usually of heroic

Saint-Gaudens' angel

Great Stone Dwelling in the Enfield Shaker Museum

subject matter, can be found throughout the country. New England is home to many Saint-Gaudens masterpieces, including Boston's Shaw Memorial (1897).

Eventually Saint-Gaudens grew tired of the big-city pace, buying an old tavern near the Connecticut River and turning it into a home and studio. Many of his greatest works were created here, including the famous statue of Abraham Lincoln (1809–65) in Lincoln Park, Chicago. Today this historic 1805 structure is filled with the sculptor's furniture and samples of his small, detailed sketches for large bronzes. A number of his sculptures are scattered around the 150-acre (61-ha) property, which is laid out with formal gardens and pleasing walking trails flanked by tall pines and hemlocks.

ENVIRONS: Just two miles (3 km) south of the Saint-Gaudens site, visitors will come upon the Cornish-Windsor Bridge. Spanning the Connecticut River

Model for Boston's Shaw Memorial

between New Hampshire and Vermont, the structure is the longest covered bridge in New England at 460 ft (140 m). Three other covered bridges can be found in the vicinity of Cornish.

Hanover ⑮

🏘 *9,200.* ✈ *6 miles (10 km) SE in Lebanon.* 🚌 🚉 *216 Nugget Building (603) 643-3115.*

HANOVER, with a traditional village green ringed by historic brick buildings, is the archetypal New England college town. Situated in the upper valley region of the Connecticut River, it is a pleasant stop for visitors following the Appalachian Trail, which goes right

through the center of town. Hanover is the home of **Dartmouth College**, the northernmost of the country's Ivy League schools. The college was originally known as Moor's Indian Charity School, and was founded in 1769 to educate and convert Abenaki Natives. Today some 4,500 students participate in programs that include one of the oldest medical schools in America, the Thayer School of Civil Engineering (1867), and the Amos Tuck School of Business Administration (1900). The school's famous graduates include statesman Daniel Webster (1782–1852) and former vice president Nelson Rockefeller (1908–79).

The college has a number of noteworthy sights. The **Baker/Berry Memorial Library** is decorated by a series of thought-provoking murals tracing the history of the Americas painted by Mexican artist José Clemente Orozco (1883–1949) in the early 1930s. The **Hood Museum of Art** has a diverse collection that includes Native American and African art, early American and European paintings, and works by such noted modern artists as Pablo Picasso (1881–1973).

🏫 **Dartmouth College**
🎟 *(603) 646-2875.* 📷 ♿
🏫 **Baker/Berry Memorial Library**
Dartmouth College. 🎟 *(603) 646-2560.* ◷ *year-round: call for hours.* ♿
🏛 **Hood Museum of Art**
Dartmouth College. 🎟 *(603) 646-2808.* ◷ *year-round: 10am–5pm Tue & Fri–Sat, 10am–9pm Wed, 12pm–5pm Sun.* 📷 ♿ ⊘ 🚻

Gallery in Dartmouth's Hood Museum of Art in Hanover

COVERED BRIDGES

American bridge builders began covering their wooden spans in the early 19th-century to protect the truss work and planking from the harsh weather. Originally the bridges were built by locals, meaning that each one had design elements specific to its region. Covered bridges built in farming communities were wide enough and tall enough to accommodate a wagon loaded with hay. Bridges leading into town had the added luxury of pedestrian walkways. The bridges, though, were more than just river crossings. Fishermen cast their lines beneath the spans, children used them as platforms from which to dive into the water below, birds nested among the rafters, and social dances were sometimes held beneath their roofs.

One of New Hampshire's covered bridges outside Cornish

Tour of Lake Winnipesaukee ⑯

Flashy sign at Weirs Beach

THIS STUNNING LAKE has a shoreline that meanders for 240 miles (386 km), making it the biggest stretch of waterfront in New Hampshire. Ringed by mountains, Winnipesaukee is scattered with 274 islands. Around its shores are sheltered bays and harbors, with half a dozen resort towns where visitors can enjoy activities ranging from canoeing to shopping for crafts and antiques.

TIPS FOR DRIVERS

Tour length: 70 miles (113 km).
Starting point: Alton, at junction of Hwys 11 & 28.
Stopping-off points: Popular Weirs Beach eateries include Paradise Beach Club and Patio Garden Restaurant. Center Sandwich's Chequers Harbor and Corner House Inn are popular. Wolfeboro has many places to eat, including Loves Quay Restaurant, Rumors Café, and West Lake Asian Cuisine.

Squam Lake ④
This pristine body of water was where the movie *On Golden Pond* (1981) was filmed. The lake is ideal for boating and fishing.

Center Sandwich ⑤
The surrounding woodland makes this town a favorite destination during fall foliage season.

Castle in the Clouds ⑥
The mansion looms on the crest of a hill some 750 ft (229 m) above the lake.

Meredith ③
Upscale Meredith has beautiful lakeside homes and is the starting point for a scenic train trip between Meredith and Weirs Beach.

Weirs Beach ②
This bustling holiday town has a sandy beach, a boardwalk, fairground rides, souvenir shops, and water parks with slides.

Wolfeboro ①
One of the country's oldest vacation spots, Wolfeboro is the largest community on the lake and one of the prettiest.

KEY

▬▬ Tour route

— Other road

❊ Viewpoint

0 kilometers 5

0 miles 5

White Mountains/ White Mountain National Forest ⑰

ℹ 719 Main St, Laconia (603) 528-8721. **Camping** ⛺ (877) 444-6777 or in Canada (518) 885-3639. Call for availability and reservations. ♿

Brightly colored engine of the Conway Scenic Railroad

NEW HAMPSHIRE'S heavily forested northland is an outdoor paradise, encompassing a national forest, several state parks, more than 1,200 miles (1,900 km) of hiking trails, several dozen lakes, ponds and rivers, and 23 campgrounds. The White Mountain National Forest, a small portion of which lies in neighboring Maine, sprawls over 770,000 acres (311,600 ha).

The most beautiful wilderness area in the state, the National Forest is home to an abundance of wildlife, including a large population of moose. These giant members of the deer family are very shy, but they can be seen from the road at dawn or dusk, lumbering back and forth from their feeding grounds or standing in a swampy pond.

This region offers all manner of outdoor activities – from bird-watching and skiing to rock climbing and kayaking – but even less sporty travelers will revel in the spectacular scenery visible from their car. More than 20 summits soar over 4,000 ft (1,200 m). Driving through the White Mountains,

Saco RANGER STATION WHITE MOUNTAIN *National Forest*

Ranger station marker

visitors encounter one scenic vista after another: valleys flanked by forests of pine, waterfalls tumbling over rocky outcrops, and trout rivers hissing alongside the meandering roads.

In 1998 a stretch of road, the 100-mile- (161-km-) long White Mountains Trail, was designated as a National Scenic and Cultural Byway. The trail loops across the Mount Washington Valley, through Crawford Notch (see p271), North Conway, and Franconia Notch (see pp272–3).

Brilliant fall foliage colors, interspersed with evergreens, transform the rugged countryside into a living palette. The leaves of different trees manifest a rich variety of shades – flaming red maples, golden birch, and maroon northern red oaks. Driving during the fall can be a beautiful but slow-moving experience since thousands of "leaf peepers" are on the

roads. Accommodations can also be difficult to find unless they are booked well in advance.

North Conway ⑱

🏘 2,500. ✈ 70 miles (112 km) SE in Portland, ME. ℹ Main St (603) 356-3171 or (800) 367-3364.

THE GATEWAY TO the sublime beauty of the White Mountains, North Conway is, surprisingly, also a bustling shopping center. This mountain village now has more than 200 factory outlets and specialty shops lining its Main Street. Prices are low in the first place, even for designer names such as Calvin Klein, Ralph Lauren, and L.L. Bean, but because there is no sales tax in New Hampshire, all purchases become even better bargains.

Locals are quick to point out that there are many other attractions in and around North Conway, including canoe trips on the Saco River and a ride into the mountains in an old-fashioned train aboard the **Conway Scenic Railroad**. Family fun can be found at the **Story Land** theme park, where children can ride on an antique German carousel, a pirate ship, or Cinderella's coach.

🚂 **Conway Scenic Railroad**
Rte 16 in North Conway. ⛺ (603) 356-5251 or (800) 232-5251. ⏰ call for schedule. 🎫 ☑ ♿
🎡 **Story Land**
Rte 16 in Glen. ⛺ (603) 383-4293. ⏰ mid-Jun–Labor Day: 9am–6pm daily; Labor Day–Columbus Day: 10am–5pm Sat–Sun. 🎫 ♿

Breathtaking view from Cathedral Ledge just outside North Conway

Red and white covered bridge leading into Jackson

Jackson ⑲

🏠 750. ✈ *77 miles (125 km) SE in Portland, ME.* **ℹ** *Rte 16B (603) 383-9356 or (800) 866-3334.*

THIS MOUNTAIN VILLAGE is tucked away on a back road off Route 16B, but drivers will not miss it because the entrance is marked by its distinctive red and white covered bridge. The picturesque 200-year-old community is, along with the nearby villages of Intervale, Bartlett, and Glen, the main center for accommodation in the Mount Washington area.

Jackson was at one time a favorite getaway spot for big-city Easterners, but the hard times of the Great Depression of the 1930s saw the town slip into disrepair. Developers rediscovered this quiet corner of New Hampshire in the 1980s and began restoring several of the town's best hotels.

Jackson is a popular base camp for winter sports enthusiasts because the region is blessed with more than 110 downhill ski runs and a network of more than 200 miles (320 km) of cross-country trails. The main ski centers are Black Mountain, the Wildcat Ski Area, and the recently enlarged Attitash Bear Peak *(see p363).* With 273 acres (113 ha) of skiable terrain served by 12 lifts, Attitash is the state's biggest ski center.

Summer sports abound here as well. The region's numerous peaks and valleys make this prime hiking and mountain-biking country, and a restored 18-hole course gives golfers the chance to play a round against one of the most scenic backdrops in New England. After having worked up a sweat, bikers and hikers can cool off under the waterfalls of the Wildcat River in Jackson Village.

Pinkham Notch ⑳

ℹ *Rte 16 N of North Conway (603) 466-2721.* ⏰ *6:30am–10pm daily.*

NAMED AFTER Joseph Pinkham, who according to local lore explored the area in 1790 with a sled drawn by pigs, this rocky ravine runs between Gorham and Jackson. The lofty Presidential Range girds the western flank of Pinkham Notch, while the 4,415-ft (1,346-m) Wildcat Mountain looms to the east.

Backcountry adventurers love this part of the state because of its great variety of activities. Skiing at the Wildcat Ski Area is among the best in the state, and its high elevation makes for a long season, running from November to April. In the summer, visitors can ride to the summit aboard the aerial gondola. Picnic areas at the top offer great views of Mount Washington and the Presidential Range.

Hiking trails lace Pinkham Notch, including a section of the fabled Appalachian Trail *(see pp22–3).* These well-maintained paths range from less demanding nature walks suitable for whole families to lung-testing climbs best attacked by serious hikers. Along the way, visitors are led past some of the region's most captivating sights, including waterfalls, rivers, scenic overlooks, and pristine ponds tucked away

Sublime beauty of the Presidential Range from Pinkham Notch

Striking exterior of the Mount Washington Hotel and Resort

in thick woodland. Lucky travelers may spot raccoons, beaver, deer, and even the occasional moose.

Bretton Woods ㉑

🏨 550. ✈ 96 miles (155 km) SE in Portland, ME. ℹ (603) 278-1000. 🖼

THIS TINY ENCLAVE situated on a glacial plain at the base of the Presidential Range has an unusual claim to fame: it hosted the United Nations Monetary and Financial Conference in 1944. The meetings established the International Monetary Fund and laid the groundwork for the World Bank, a response to the need for currency stability after the economic upheavals of World War II. The delegates also set the gold standard at $35 an ounce and chose the American dollar as the international standard for monetary exchange.

The setting for this vital meeting was the **Mount Washington Hotel and Resort** (see p319). It is easy to imagine the reaction of delegates when they first caught sight of this grand Spanish Renaissance-style hotel from a sweeping curve in the road. Opened in 1902, the hotel's sparkling white exterior and crimson roof stand out in stark contrast to Mount Washington, looming 6,288 ft (1,917 m) skyward behind the edifice.

The hotel has entertained a host of distinguished guests, including British Prime Minister Sir Winston Churchill (1874–1965), inventor Thomas Edison (1847–1931), baseball star Babe Ruth (1895–1948), and three presidents.

Apart from its sublime setting, what makes the hotel so impressive is its sheer size. Designated a National Historic Landmark, the 200-room structure was built by 250 skilled craftsmen from Italy. Today the hotel is surrounded by more than 17,300 acres (7,000 ha) of parkland, and its numerous facilities include a 27-hole golf course laid out by the famous Scottish designer Donald Ross (1872–1948). Nearby Bretton Woods ski area (see p362) offers alpine skiing along with 62 miles (100 km) of cross-country trails.

Sir Winston Churchill, a Mount Washington visitor

🏨 Mount Washington Hotel and Resort

Rte 302, Bretton Woods. ℂ (603) 278-1000 or (800) 258-0330. ♿ 🏠

ENVIRONS: The Mount Washington Valley, in which Bretton Woods is located, is dominated by the 6,288-ft (1,917-m) peak of Mount Washington, the highest in the northeastern United States. Other imposing peaks belonging to the Presidential Range – Adam, Jefferson, Madison, Monroe, and Eisenhower – surround Mount Washington, which has the dubious distinction of having the worst weather of any mountain in the world. Unpredictable snowstorms are not unusual, even during the summer months; the highest wind ever recorded on Earth was clocked here in April 1934: 230 mph (370 kph). During the last century, the mountain has claimed the lives of almost 100 people caught unaware by Mount Washington's temperamental climate.

On clear days, however, when the mountain is in a good mood, nothing compares to the panoramic view from the top. Brave souls hike to the summit by one of the many trails, drive their own cars up the winding Mount Washington Auto Road, or puff their way slowly to the top in the deservedly famous **Mount Washington Cog Railroad**. Billed as "America's oldest tourist attraction," the railroad started operating in 1869.

The train, powered by steam locomotives, chugs its way up the cog track to the top of the mountain belching steam. The 3.5-mile (5.6-km) route to the top is one of the steepest tracks in the world, climbing at a heart-stopping 37 percent grade at some points. At the top, passengers can visit the Sherman Adams Summit Building, with the Summit Museum, and Mount Washington Observatory, one of the world's leading mountain weather stations.

🏨 Mount Washington Cog Railroad

Off Rte 302, Marshfield Base Station. ℂ (603) 278-5404 or (800) 922-8825. ◯ May–Oct: call for hours. 📷 ♿ 🏠 🍴

Mount Washington Cog Railroad

Perfect spot to stop along the Kancamagus Highway for the view of Mount Chocorua

Kancamagus Highway ❷

Rte 112 between Lincoln & Conway.
🅸 *Saco District Ranger Station, 33 Kancamagus Hwy (603) 447-5448.*

TOUTED BY MANY as the most scenic fall-foliage road in New England, this stretch of highway runs through the White Mountain National Forest *(see p265)* between Lincoln and Conway. The road covers about 34 miles (55 km) of Route 112 and offers exceptional vistas from the Pemi Overlook as it

Sabbaday Falls, a highlight of the Kancamagus Highway

climbs 3,000 ft (914 m) through the Kancamagus Pass. Descending into the Saco Valley, the well-traveled road joins up with the Swift River, following the aptly named waterway into Conway. The highway provides fishermen with easy access to the river, home to brook and rainbow trout.

Campgrounds and picnic areas along the entire length of highway give travelers ample opportunity to relax and eat lunch on the banks of cool mountain streams. Maintained by the US Forest Service, the campgrounds are equipped with toilets and one has shower facilities; all are operated on a first-come, first-served basis. Well-marked trails also allow drivers to stretch their legs in the midst of some of the most beautiful scenery in the state. One of the most popular trails is the short loop that leads travelers to the oft-photographed Sabbaday Falls. Closer to Conway, road signs guide drivers to several scenic areas that afford views of cascades, rapids, and rivers.

The area is home to a wide variety of wildlife, including resident birds such as woodpeckers and chickadees, as well as migratory songbirds who breed here in the summer. Larger inhabitants include deer, moose, and the occasional black bear.

Clark's Trading Post in North Woodstock

North Woodstock ❷

🏠 *1,300.* ✈ *66 miles (106 km) SW in Lebanon.* 🅸 *Rte 112 & Connector Rd, Lincoln (603) 745-6621 or (800) 227-4191.*

NOT INCLUDING ITS convenient location near the White Mountains *(see p265)*, the town's main attraction is **Clark's Trading Post,** a strange combination of circus acts, amusement park rides, and museums. Children especially love the trained bears and the over-the-top performers. A session at Clark's "bumper boat" marina, in which participants try to ram each other's boat, is where the younger set can blow off the steam that may have built up on a leaf-peeping drive.

🎪 **Clark's Trading Post**
Rte 3, North Woodstock. 🄲 *(603) 745-8913. Call for hours & show times.* 🖼

◁ **Silver Cascades, Crawford Notch State Park, in the autumn**

ENVIRONS: Tiny Lincoln is located just three miles (5 km) northwest of North Woodstock. The town's location at the western end of the Kancamagus Highway and at the southern entrance of Franconia Notch State Park *(see pp272–3)* have turned it into a base camp for both backwoods adventurers and stick-to-the-road sightseers. Nearby **Loon Mountain** *(see p363)* is one of the state's premier ski resorts. However, in the summer it offers a number of activities, from guided nature walks and tours of caves to horseback riding, mountain biking, and a gondola ride to the summit.

Loon Mountain
E of I-93, near Lincoln. **(** *(603) 745-6281.*

View from the Willey House in Crawford Notch State Park

Challenging climbing wall at Loon Mountain outside of Lincoln

Crawford Notch State Park ㉔

Rte 302 between Twin Mountains & Bartlett. **(** *(603) 271-3556.* **Camping (** *(603) 271-3678; call for reservations.* year-round.

THIS NARROW PASS, which squeezes through the sheer rock walls of Webster and Willey mountains, gained notoriety in 1826. One night a severe rain sent tons of mud and stone careening into the valley below, heading straight for the home of innkeeper Samuel Willey and his family. Alerted by the sounds of the avalanche, the family fled outdoors, where all seven were killed beneath falling debris. Ironically the lethal avalanche bypassed the house, leaving it unscathed. Several writers, including New Englander Nathaniel Hawthorne *(see p30),* have immortalized the tragedy in literature. The house still stands today and is now in service as a visitors center.

Once the notch was threatened by over-logging. However, the establishment of the state park in 1911 has ensured protection of this rugged wilderness. Today white-water boaters come here to test their mettle on the powerful Saco River, which carves its way through the valley. Fishermen ply the park's more tranquil ponds and streams in search of sport and a tasty dinner of trout or salmon.

People who prefer to keep their feet dry can still enjoy the water on a short hiking trail leading to the Arethusa Falls. Towering more than 200 ft (61 m) in the air, this magnificent cascade is New Hampshire's tallest waterfall. Elsewhere drivers will get wonderful views of the Silver Cascades and Flume Cascades waterfalls without leaving the comfort of their car.

ROBERT FROST AND NEW HAMPSHIRE

The natural beauty of New Hampshire was an inspiration to one of America's best-loved poets: Robert Frost (1874–1963). Born in San Francisco, California, the four-time winner of the Pulitzer Prize moved to Massachusetts with his family when he was 11. After working as a teacher, a reporter, and a mill hand, Frost moved to England in 1912. Upon his return to the US in 1915, Frost settled in the Franconia Notch area *(see pp272–3).* The majestic setting inspired him to pen many of his greatest works, including his famous poem *Stopping by Woods on a Snowy Evening* (1923).

Robert Frost farm in Derry, New Hampshire

Franconia Notch State Park ㉕

Canoeing on Profile Lake

THIS SPECTACULAR mountain pass carved between the Kinsman and Franconia ranges is graced with some of the state's most spectacular natural wonders. Foremost among them is the Old Man of the Mountain, a rocky outcropping on the side of a cliff that resembles a man's profile. The huge granite face is the unofficial state symbol, a perfect choice considering residents' reputation for being stoic. Elsewhere a boardwalk and stairways lead visitors through the Flume Gorge, a narrow, granite chasm slashed in two by the Flume Brook, while an aerial tramway carries passengers to the summit of Cannon Mountain. Also within the park is Boise Rock, a picnic area by a mountain spring that offers views of the Cannon Cliffs and Echo Lake.

Glacial Boulder
This glacial boulder is one of the sights on the Flume Trail.

KEY

▨▨▨	Interstate
▬▬▬	Major road
▭▭	Minor road
– –	Walking trail
ℹ️	Tourist information
🅿️	Parking
– –	Aerial tramway
- - -	Bus shuttle
🅰️	Camping
☽	Viewpoint

★ The Basin
The waterfall at the Basin empties into a large granite pothole.

Fishin' Jimmy Trail

Kinsman Pond Trail

Cascade Trail

Basin-Cascade Trail

Mount Pemigewasset Trail

Indian Head Trail

Cascade Brook Trail

The Basin

Pemi Trail

Recreational Trail

TO CONCORD

93

TO PLYMOUTH

3

P

ℹ️

The Pool

The Flume

Flume Slide Trail

Liberty Spring Trail

🅰️

93

★ Flume Gorge
The granite walls of this narrow gorge tower more than 90 ft (27 m) above visitors walking along the boardwalk. A two-mile (3-km) self-guided trail leads hikers past points of interest.

0 miles   1

0 kilometers   1

Scenic Views
Hikers are rewarded with many beautiful panoramas along the park's trails.

Wild Bunchberrys
This fruit can be found throughout the lush Franconia Notch region.

★ Old Man of the Mountain
Seen from the right angle, this cliff face looks like a man's profile.

STAR FEATURES

★ The Basin

★ Flume Gorge

★ Old Man of the Mountain

★ Profile Lake

★ Profile Lake
This lake is often called the Old Man's Washbowl because it is located directly below the Old Man of the Mountain. It is a favorite among fly-fishermen looking for brook trout.

MAINE

....

MAINE TRULY IS THE GREAT OUTDOORS. *More than 5,500 miles (8,850 km) of inlets, bays, and harbors make up its spectacular coastline. Inland deep forests and jutting mountain peaks complement 32,000 miles (51,500 km) of rivers and 6,000 glacial lakes. However, for all its wild mystique, Maine also includes quaint villages, appealing cities, and discount shopping meccas.*

Maine has a long and rich history. While some historians maintain that the Vikings probed the rocky coast as early as the 11th century, European settlement began in earnest 500 years later, beginning with the Popham Beach colony of 1607. Although this original colony was short-lived, it spawned a succession of similar settlements at Monhegan (1622), Saco (1623), and Georgeana (1624). The last – renamed York *(see p278)* in 1652 – became the English America's first chartered city in 1642.

While Maine has always been one of the more sparsely populated states in the Union, it has been at the center of numerous territorial disputes, beginning with its abrupt seizure by Massachusetts in 1652 (an unhappy forced marriage, which ended in 1820 when Maine was granted statehood). Between 1675 and 1748 a series of four bloody wars was fought between British colonials and their French counterparts in Quebec. At the outset of the Revolutionary War (1775–83), Portland *(see pp280–83)* was bombarded and burned by the British as an example to other colonies harboring similar anti-Loyalist sentiments.

Traveling through Maine it is easy to see what all the fuss was about. The state's trove of unspoiled wilderness is interspersed with wonderfully preserved relics of its past. Beautiful Colonial homes can be found throughout the state. The importance of seafaring in the region's history is evident in the lighthouses *(see p279)*, maritime museums, and the sea captains' mansions found up and down the coast. And although tourism is now Maine's number one industry, the state has remained remarkably undeveloped, retaining much of the natural splendor that first attracted settlers so many centuries ago.

Hot summer shoreline along Old Orchard Beach

◁ **Cape Neddick Lighthouse at York Beach**

Exploring Maine

MAINE'S MOST POPULAR attractions are found dotted
along its coast, beginning in the southeast with
the beach playgrounds of Ogunquit *(see pp278–9)*,
Old Orchard *(see p279)*, and the resort towns of the
Kennebunks *(see p279)*. The scenery gets more dra-
matic as travelers move north through Boothbay
Harbor *(see p285)*, Pemaquid Point *(see p285)*, and
Muscongus Bay. The tiny villages are perfect starting
points for sailing and kayaking excursions. Yachts
and windjammers ply the waters of the Penobscot
Bay region *(see pp286–7)*, while Acadia National
Park *(see pp288–9)* stands as Maine's coastal jewel.
Farther north, the rising sun first strikes the US at
Cobscook Bay. World-class hiking, boating, and
mountain-biking opportunities are found inland
among the state's many mountains, lakes, and rivers.

**Stone fortifications at Fort William
Adams Park in Portland**

GETTING AROUND

Interstate 95 is the only major artery in the
state. As a result, the smaller scenic routes
along the coastline are often congested with
summer traffic. Many coastal towns can be
reached from Boston by Concord Trailways
bus lines. Maine State Ferry Service has
numerous routes to and from various
seashore destinations. Both Portland and
Bangor have international airports. The
scarcity of public roads in northern Maine
means that drivers occasionally have to
resort to logging roads, which are operated
much like toll roads. Carved out of the
rough wilderness, these dirt roads are best
tackled with four-wheel drive vehicles.

0 kilometers   30

0 miles   30

ALLAGASH
WILDERNESS
WATERWAY

*Allagash
Lake*

MOOSEHEAD
LAKE

㉑

ROCKWOOD

THE FORKS

EUSTIS

STRATTON

SUGARLOAF
SKI RESORT
⑲

⑳

RANGELEY
LAKES REGION

GRAFTON
NOTCH
STATE PARK

MOUNT BLUE
STATE PARK

NEWRY

RUMFORD

⑱
BETHEL

AUGUSTA

⑰

Long Lake

FRYEBURG

Sebago
Lake

BRUNSWICK

BATH

⑦

⑥ FREEPORT

⑤ PORTLAND

④

③

② THE KENNEBUNKS

KITTERY   OGUNQUIT

①

PEMAQUID
POINT

⑧
BOOTHBAY
HARBOR

OLD ORCHARD
BEACH

Kennebec River

View of Mount Katahdin, centerpiece of Baxter State Park

SIGHTS AT A GLANCE

SEE ALSO

KEY

▬	Interstate
▬	Major road
▭	Minor road
▬	Scenic route
☀	Viewpoint

Picturesque Stonington village on Deer Isle

Kittery ❶

🏃 9,500. ✈ 49 miles (78 km)
NE in Portland. ℹ 306 Rte 1
(207) 439-7545.

T HE SOUTHERN COAST of
Maine begins at the
Piscataqua River and Kittery,
a town with a split personality. Founded in 1647, Kittery
boasts the oldest church in
the state, the 1730 **First
Congregational Church**.
Many fine old mansions line
the streets, including the John
Bray House, one of the oldest
dwellings in Maine. **Fort
McClary**, now a state historic
site, has fortifications dating
to the early 1800s and a
hexagonal blockhouse, and
the **Kittery Historical and
Naval Museum** is filled with
ship models and exhibits
explaining maritime history.
Despite its wealth of historical
attractions, Kittery is best
known for a more contem-
porary lure – the more than
100 factory outlet stores
promising bargains along
Route 1, where shoppers can
browse for name brands at
discount prices.

🛉 **First Congregational
Church**
23 Pepperrell Rd. 📞 (207) 439-0650.
🕐 8am & 10am Sun.
🏯 **Fort McClary State
Historic Site**
Rte 103 E of Kittery. 📞 (207) 384-
5160. 🕐 late May–Oct: 9am–dusk
daily. ♿
🏛 **Kittery Historical and
Naval Museum**
Rogers Rd. 📞 (207) 439-3080.
🕐 Jun–Oct: 10am–4pm Tue–Sat.
♿ & partial.

**Hexagonal Fort McClary block-
house in Kittery**

ENVIRONS: Four miles (6 km)
from Kittery, visitors will come
upon York Village. Settled in
the 1630s, the village later grew
into an important trading center, its wharves and warehouses
filled with treasures from the
lucrative West Indies trade.
A collection of seven historic
buildings maintained by the
Old York Historical
Society, **Old York**
traces town history
over three centuries.
A repository for his-
torical items, Old York
has a superb collec-
tion of regional deco-
rative arts housed in
more than 30 period
rooms and galleries.
Tours begin at
Jefferds' Tavern, a
colonial hostelry, and
include two historic
homes, a 1745 one-
room schoolhouse, and the
John Hancock Warehouse,
named after its owner, an
original signatory of the
Declaration of Independence.
Down the street, the 1719 Old
Gaol (jail) stands as one of the
country's oldest public buildings. Dark, foreboding dun-
geons tell of harsh conditions

**Lobster trap
buoys**

faced by the felons who served
their sentences within the jail's
three-ft- (1-m-) thick walls.

🏯 **Old York**
Lindsay Rd. 📞 (207) 363-4974.
🕐 June–mid-Oct: 10am–5pm
Tue–Sat, 1pm–4pm Sun. ♿ 📷 last
tour at 4pm. 🚫 ∅ indoors.

Ogunquit ❷

🏃 900. ✖ 36 miles (58 km)
NE in Portland. ℹ 36 Rte 1 S
(207) 646-2939.

I T IS EASY TO SEE why the
Abenaki Indians called
this enclave Ogunquit, or
"Beautiful Place by the Sea."
Maine beaches do not come
any better. From mid-May to
Columbus Day, trolleys shuttle
visitors to this powdery three-
mile (5-km) stretch
of sand and dunes
that curves around
a backdrop of
rugged cliffs. Atop
the cliffs is the
1.25-mile (2-km)
Marginal Way, a
footpath that offers
walkers dramatic
vistas of the ocean.
Perkins Cove,
home of the only
pedestrian draw-
bridge in the US, is
a quaint jumble of
fishermen's shacks now transformed into shops, art galleries, restaurants, and docks
with fishing and cruise boats.
This picturesque outpost
attracted an artist's colony as
early as 1890, establishing it
as a haven for the arts. The
handsome **Ogunquit Museum
of American Art** was built in

Scenic ocean vista at Marginal Way in Ogunquit

1952 by the eccentric but wealthy Henry Strater, who served as its director for more than 30 years. Constructed of wood and local stone, the museum has wide windows to allow views of the rocky cove and meadows. A three-acre (1-ha) sculpture garden and lawns also make the most of the breathtaking setting. The permanent collection includes art by many notable American painters.

🏛 **Ogunquit Museum of American Art**
183 Shore Rd. 📞 *(207) 646-4909.*
🅾 *Jul–mid-Oct: 10:30am–5pm Mon–Sat, 2pm–5pm Sun.*
⬤ *Labor Day.*

The Kennebunks ❸

🔼 *30 miles (48 km) NE in Portland.*
ℹ️ *17 Western Ave, Kennebunk (207) 967-0857.*

FIRST A THRIVING PORT and busy shipbuilding center, then a summer retreat for the wealthy, the Kennebunks are made up of two villages, Kennebunkport and Kennebunk.

The profusion of fine Federal and Greek Revival structures in Kennebunkport's historic village is evidence of the fortunes made in shipbuilding and trading from 1810 to the 1870s. With its 100-ft- (30-m-) tall white steeple and belfry, the 1824 South Congregational Church is a favorite subject for photographers. History of a different sort can be found at the **Seashore Trolley Museum**, where some 200 antique streetcars are housed, including one vehicle from New Orleans named "Desire." Visitors can embark on a tour of the countryside aboard one of the restored trolleys.

The scenic drive along Route 9 offers views of surf along rocky Cape Arundel. At Cape Porpoise hungry travelers can sample lobster pulled fresh from

Kennebunkport signpost

MAINE'S LIGHTHOUSES

For centuries mariners have been guided to safety by Maine's picturesque lighthouses. The coast is dotted with 63 such beacons, some accessible from the mainland and others perched on offshore islands. Portland Head Light was commissioned by the country's first president, George Washington (1732–99), and built in 1791, making it the oldest lighthouse in the state. It, like several other beacons, is open to the public and houses a small museum focusing on local marine and military history.

Nubble Lighthouse near Old York

the Atlantic. Kennebunk is famous for its beaches, most notably Kennebunk Beach, which is actually three connected strands. One of the town's most romantic historic homes is the 1826 Wedding Cake House. According to the local lore, George Bourne was unexpectedly called to sea before his marriage. Although a very hastily arranged wedding took place, there was no time to bake the traditional wedding cake. Instead, the shipbuilder vowed to his bride that upon his return he would remodel their home to look like a wedding cake. Today the Gothic spires, ornate latticework, and gingerbread trim offer proof that Bourne was a man of his word. Housed in four restored 19th-century buildings, **The Brick Store Museum** offers glimpses into the past with displays of decorative arts. It also offers

interesting architectural walking tours of the town's historic area.

🏛 **Seashore Trolley Museum**
195 Log Cabin Rd, Kennebunkport.
📞 *(207) 967-2800.* 🅾 *mid-Jun–mid-Oct: 10am–5pm daily.* ♿
🏛 **The Brick Store Museum**
117 Main St, Kennebunk. 📞 *(207) 985-4802.* 🅾 *Apr–late Dec: 10am–4:30pm Tue–Sat.* ⬤ *public hols.*

Old Orchard Beach ❹

🏘 *9,000.* 🔼 *13 miles (21 km) NE in Portland.* 🚌 ℹ️ *First St (207) 934-2500 or (800) 365-9386.*

ONE OF MAINE'S OLDEST seashore resorts, Old Orchard Beach's seven miles (11 km) of sandy shoreline and low surf make it a favorite spot for swimming. Children love the pier lined with game booths and food stands, a roller coaster, a 60-ft (18-m) water slide, and a 36-hole miniature golf course complete with pools and waterfalls. A new floating marina caters to water sports.

Fresh lobster from the Cape Porpoise area in southern Maine

Portland ⑤

Children's Museum banner

POET AND PORTLAND NATIVE Henry Wadsworth Longfellow (1807–82) described Maine's largest city as "the beautiful town that is seated by the sea." Longfellow was inspired by Portland's fortunate location on the crest of a peninsula with expansive views of Casco Bay and the Calendar Islands on three sides. Once a prosperous port and an early state capital, Portland has been devastated by no less than four major fires, resulting in a preponderance of sturdy stone Victorian buildings that line many of its streets today.

Exploring Portland

A thriving arts community and a downtown with interesting shopping and dining are all part of a stroll along Congress Street and through the restored Old Port Exchange area *(see pp282–3)*. The West End has fine homes and a splendid Western Promenade overlooking the water. The working waterfront and nearby beaches add to the city's charm.

🏛 Portland Museum of Art

7 Congress Sq. 【 *(207) 775-6148.*
◯ *year-round: 10am–5pm Sat–Wed, 10am–9pm Thu–Fri.* ● *Oct–May: Mon.* 📷 ♿
Portland's premier fine art collection is housed in a building that is itself a masterpiece. The redbrick facade of the award-winning building features striking arches. The elegant interior uses natural light filtered through skylights to help illuminate the collection of such important American artists as Andrew Wyeth (b.1917) and Winslow Homer (1836–1910). Works by such European masters as Paul Gauguin (1848–1903) and Pablo Picasso (1881–1973) are also on display.

🏛 Children's Museum of Maine

142 Free St. 【 *(207) 828-1234.*
◯ *year-round: 10am–5pm Wed–Sat, 12pm–5pm Sun; May–Sep: 10am–5pm Mon–Tue.* ● *public hols.* 📷 ♿
This historic brick building houses three floors of interactive exhibits designed for youngsters. Displays include Toddler Park, Ship Ahoy!, Climbing Wall, Star Lab, and Camera Obscura.

🏛 Wadsworth-Longfellow House

489 Congress St. 【 *(207) 879-0427.*
◯ *Jun–Oct: 10am–4pm daily.* 📷 ♿
⬆ *first floor.* ♿
Poet Henry Wadsworth Longfellow grew up in this 1785 house. The materials for the Georgian home were

The distinctive Hay Gallery in Portland's downtown arts district

transported from Philadelphia on a barge. The house contains family mementos, portraits, and furnishings.

🏛 Victoria Mansion

109 Danforth St. 【 *(207) 772-4841.*
◯ *mid-Jun–Sep: 10am–4pm Tue–Sat, 1pm–5pm Sun; Dec: 11am–5pm Wed–Sun.* ● *Jan–May, Nov, Jul 4, & Dec 25.* 📷 📷 *every half hour.* ♿

```
0 meters          400
0 yards           400
```

Dahlov Ipcar's *Blue Savannah* in the Portland Museum of Art

PORTLAND CITY CENTER

Children's Museum of Maine ④
Neal Dow Memorial ①
Old Port ⑥ *(see pp282–3)*
Portland Museum of Art ③
Victoria Mansion ②
Wadsworth-Longfellow House ⑤

Coastal fishing on the outskirts of Portland

This sumptuous brownstone villa was completed in 1860 to serve as the summer home of Ruggles hotelier Sylvester Morse (c.1816–93). The interior has extraordinary interior detail, such as painted *trompe l'oeil* walls and ceilings, wood paneling, marble mantels, and a flying staircase.

🏠 George Tate House
1270 Westbrook St. ((207) 774-
9781. ◯ year-round: 10am–4pm
Tue–Sat, 1pm–4pm Sun. ◑ Oct–Jun,
Jul 4, & Labor Day. 🖼 ✔ ⛪

In 1755 George Tate, an agent of the British Royal Navy, constructed an elegant gambrel-roofed home with rich wood paneling, patterned floors, a dogleg staircase, and eight fireplaces. Now a National Historic Landmark, the house has fine period furnishings and an 18th-century garden where tea is served on summer Wednesdays.

🏠 Neal Dow Memorial
714 Congress St. ((207) 773-7773.
◯ year-round: 11am–4pm Mon–Fri.
Neal Dow (1804–97), one of Portland's prominent citizens, built this Federal-style mansion in 1829. Twice serving as the city's mayor, Dow was an abolitionist and prohibitionist who also championed the causes of women's rights and prison reform. The Dow family's original furnishings, paintings, china, and silver are displayed along with memorabilia of Dow's career.

🏛 Maine Narrow Gauge Railroad Co. & Museum
58 Fore St. ((207)
828-0814. ◯ year-
round: 10am–4pm
daily. ⛪ **Train ride** ◯
mid-May–mid-Oct on the
hour; call for other times. 🖼
Scenic trips along a three-mile (5-km) stretch of the waterfront are the highlight of this museum dedicated to the railroad that served much of Maine from the 1870s to the 1940s. Exhibits include vintage locomotives, a restored caboose, and a parlor car.

🏠 Portland Observatory
138 Congress St. ((207) 774-5561.
◯ call for hours. 🖼 ✔ ⛪ ⛪

Constructed in 1807, this octagonal landmark is the last surviving 19th-century signal tower on the Atlantic. Visitors willing to make the 102-step climb to the upper deck are rewarded with far-ranging views through the telescope.

🏛 Museum at Portland Head Light at Fort Williams Park
12 Captain Strout Circle. ((207)
799-2661. ◯ call for hours. 🖼 ⛪
First illuminated in 1791 by order of President George Washington (1732–99), the lighthouse has been the subject of poetry, postage stamps, and photographs. The keeper's house is now a museum with exhibits on the history of the world's beacons. The large surrounding park, just four miles (6.5 km) from downtown, features a beach and picnic areas.

Portland Observatory atop Munjoy Hill

KEY

🟦 Street-by-Street map
see pp282–3

═ Highway

ℹ Tourist information

🅿 Parking

Street-by-Street: Old Port

THIS ONCE-DECAYING NEIGHBORHOOD near the harbor has been restored and is now the city's liveliest area, filled with shops, art galleries, restaurants, and bars. The Old Port's narrow streets are lined with classic examples of Victorian-era commercial architecture. From the docks, ships take passengers out for deep-sea fishing excursions and harbor tours; ferries to Nova Scotia, Canada, save travelers some 850 miles (1,370 km) of driving. Cruises include mailboat rides and excursions to the Calendar Islands, where visitors can enjoy everything from cycling to sea kayaking.

Lively District
The Old Port has numerous pubs and outdoor terraces.

Centennial Block
has a facade made of Maine granite.

Charles Q. Clapp Block
This distinctive building was designed by self-taught architect Charles Quincy Clapp in 1866.

First National Bank
is a typical example of Queen Anne commercial style. Its sandstone and brick exterior features a corner tower and tall chimneys.

Dolphins Statue
The statue is situated in the small cobblestone area in the middle of the Old Port district.

Mary L. Deering Block,
built for the prominent Deering family, is a mix of Italian and Colonial Revival styles.

FORE STREET

Seaman's Club
Built after the devastating fire of 1866, the building is known for its striking Gothic windows.

★ United States Custom House
Built following the Civil War (1861–5), this regal building contains gilded ceilings, marble staircases, and chandeliers.

Antique shops *can be found throughout the Old Port district.*

0 meters   50

0 yards   50

KEY

‑ ‑ ‑   Suggested route

State of Maine Armory
was designed to resemble a fortress and once was home to several units of the reserve militia known as the National Guard.

★ Mariner's Church
Built in 1828, the building is an eclectic mix of Greek Revival and Federal styles, and is now used to house a variety of shops and businesses.

Freeport ❻

🏠 7,000. ✈ 17 miles (31 km)
SW in Portland. ℹ 23 Depot St
(207) 865-1212 or (800) 865-1994.

ALTHOUGH FREEPORT dates
back to 1789, shoppers
would argue that it did not
arrive on the scene until
1917, when the first L.L.
Bean clothing store opened
its doors. Today this retail
giant is open 24 hours a day,
365 days a year, and, with
more than 3.5 million customers annually, L.L. Bean
is easily Maine's biggest
man-made attraction. Since
the 1980s more than 150
other brand-name outlets
have opened here.

Travelers who make it
past the shops will discover
a working harbor in South
Freeport, where seal-watching
tours and sailing cruises
depart. The shoreline includes
**Wolfe's Neck Woods State
Park**, 233 acres (94 ha) of
tranquility wrapped along
Casco Bay.

Freeport's most unusual
sight is the **Desert of Maine**.
Originally a late-1700s farm,
the area was severely over-
tilled and over-logged. The
topsoil eventually disappeared
altogether, giving way to
glacial sand deposits and creating a 40-acre (16-ha) desert
of sand dunes. Visitors can
walk the nature trails with a
guide who narrates the history
of the area, or ride on an open
cart. The farm museum is
housed in a 1783 barn.

L.L. BEAN AND OUTLET SHOPPING

Leon Leonwood Bean (1872–1967) likely
would be amazed if he could see the result
of his dislike for cold, wet feet. The hunting shoe he developed in 1912 with leather
uppers on rubber overshoe bottoms began
a company that now claims more than a
billion dollars in sales worldwide and
carries anything needed for outdoor
excursions. Bean's showroom has
grown into a mammoth flagship store
that includes a 785-sq-ft (73-sq-m-)
pond stocked with trout.

Bust of L.L. Bean

🌿 **Wolfe's Neck Woods
State Park**
Wolfe's Neck Rd. ℹ (207) 865-
4465. ⬤ year-round: May–Sep:
9am–dusk daily; Sep–May: 9am–
6pm daily. 📷 ✗ ♿
🏜 **Desert of Maine**
95 Desert Rd. ℹ (207) 865-6962.
⬤ May–mid-Oct: 8:30am–6pm
daily. 📷 ♿

**Peary-MacMillan Arctic Museum
on Bowdoin College campus**

Brunswick ❼

🏠 21,000. ✈ 33 miles (53 km) SW
in Portland. 🚌 ℹ 59 Pleasant St
(207) 725-8797.

BRUNSWICK IS best known as
the home of Bowdoin
College and as the land entry
for the scenic panoramas of
the town of Harpswell – a
peninsula and three islands
jutting out into Casco Bay.

Founded in 1794, the col-
lege claims a number of
distinguished alumni, including explorers Robert Peary
(1856–1920) and Donald
MacMillan (1874–1970). The
Peary-MacMillan Arctic

Museum honors the two,
who in 1909 became the first
to reach the North Pole.
Exhibits trace the history of
polar exploration and display
the journals of both men.

The **Pejepscot Historical
Society** offers displays of
Brunswick history in its three
museums and offers tours of
both Skolfield-Whittier House,
a 17-room Italianate mansion
built in 1858 by a shipyard

Seemingly endless acres of sand in Desert of Maine, Freeport

owner, and the Joshua L. Chamberlain House, a Civil War museum.

🏛 Peary-MacMillan Arctic Museum

9500 College Station, Bowdoin College. 📞 *(207) 725-3416.* ◻ *year-round: 10am–5pm Tue–Sat; 2pm–5pm Sun.* ● *public hols.* ♿

🏛 Pejepscot Historical Society

159 Park Row. 📞 *(207) 729-6606.* ◻ *call for opening hours and tour times for each museum.*

Boothbay Harbor's busy boardwalk area

ENVIRONS: Nine miles (14 km) east lies Bath, long a ship-building center. Its stately homes were built with the profits from this lucrative industry. In 1608 colonists constructed the *Virginia*, the first British boat produced in the New World. Since then, some 4,000 ships have been constructed here. The **Maine Maritime Museum** operates the country's only surviving wooden shipbuilding yard. The modern Maritime History Building annex is a repository of nautical models, paintings, and memorabilia.

Nautical art from the Maine Maritime Museum in Bath

🏛 Maine Maritime Museum

243 Washington St. 📞 *(207) 443-1316.* ◻ *9:30am–5pm daily.* ● *Jan 1, Thanksgiving, & Dec 25.* 📷 📹 *call for times.* ♿ *partial.* 🏠

Boothbay Harbor ❽

🏞 *2,500.* ✈ *38 miles (61 km) N in Augusta.* 🏢 *192 Townsend Ave (207) 633-2353 or (800) 266-8422.*

THE BOATING CAPITAL of the mid-coast, Boothbay Harbor bustles with the influx of summer tourists. Dozens of boating excursions cast off from the dock. Visitors might choose to take an hour's sail along the coast aboard a majestic windjammer, a 41-mile (66-km) cruise up the

Kennebec River, or the popular day trip to the artists' retreat on Monhegan Island *(see p287)*. Sightseers can participate in a wide range of activities, including puffin and whale-watching expeditions. The harbor is at its best in late June, when majestic tall ships parade in under full sail for the annual Windjammer Days festival.

The town itself is chock-a-block with shops and galleries. **Marine Resources Aquarium**, a haven for parents of restless children on rainy days, is equipped with a large touch tank filled with sea creatures, which can be touched – including a dogfish head shark.

Boothbay WHALE WATCH

Boothbay Harbor whale watch sign

🐋 Marine Resources Aquarium

194 McKown Point Rd. 📞 *(207) 633-9559.* ◻ *late May–Sep: 10am–5pm daily.* 📷 📹 ♿

ENVIRONS: A scenic 30-mile (48-km) drive up the coast brings travelers to Pemaquid Point, complete with shelves of granite cliffs that jut from the sea. Rising dramatically above a bluff and offering panoramic views of the coastline, the 1827 **Pemaquid Point Light** houses the **Fisherman's Museum** in the old light-keeper's home. The **Pemaquid Art Gallery** is on the grounds and shows the work of local artists. There is a bonus for history buffs at the 8-acre (3-ha) **Colonial Pemaquid State History Site**, which

includes a 1695 graveyard and a replica of **Fort William Henry**. English colonialists fought French invaders at this spot in several forts that date from the early 17th century onward. A small museum contains a diorama of the original 1620s settlement and displays a collection of tools, pottery shards, and household items that reflect the rustic and often very difficult lives of the early settlers.

🚨 Pemaquid Point Light

Rte 130. 📞 *(207) 677-2494.* ◻ *May–Oct: call for hours.* 📷 ♿ **Fisherman's Museum** ◻ *May–Oct: call for hours.* ♿ **Pemaquid Art Gallery** ◻ *May–Oct: call for hours.*

🚨 Colonial Pemaquid State History Site/ Fort William Henry

Off Rte 130. 📞 *(207) 677-2423.* ◻ *late May–early Sep: call for hours.* 🍴

Pemaquid Point Light and the Fisherman's Museum

Penobscot Bay 9

PENOBSCOT BAY IS PICTURE-BOOK MAINE, with high hills seemingly rolling straight into the ocean, wave-pounded cliffs, sheltered harbors bobbing with fishing boats, and lobster traps piled high on the docks. Windjammer sailboats, ferries, and numerous cruise ships carry passengers to offshore islands, setting sail from ports such as Rockland, Camden, and Lincolnville, popular stops on the bay's western shore. The former shipbuilding centers of Searsport and Bucksport lie beyond. The more remote eastern shore leads to serene, perfectly preserved villages such as Castine and Blue Hill.

Sailboats moored in the safe confines of Camden Harbor

Secluded cliff-top view of Penobscot Bay

Exploring Penobscot Bay

To sail across Penobscot Bay covers a mere 35 miles (56 km) from its southernmost outpost of Port Clyde to its northern tip at Stonington. However, typical of Maine's ribboned coast, the same voyage takes almost 100 miles (160 km) by car. Either mode of transportation will offer stunning views of one of Maine's coastal highlights.

Rockland

⛝ *1 Harbor Pk (207) 596-0376.*
Long a fishing town and commercial center, Rockland is now evolving into a tourist destination. These days lobster boats share the harbors with excursion boats, state ferries, and the graceful schooners of Maine's windjammer fleet.

On land the Farnsworth Art Museum on Main Street showcases some of the giants of US art, including Rockwell Kent (1882–1971), and Edward Hopper (1882–1967). The new $10-million Wyeth Center

is devoted to the works of N.C. (1882–1945), Andrew (b.1917), and Jamie (b.1946) Wyeth, three generations of talented artists who painted in Maine for many years.

Two miles (3.2 km) south of Rockland on Route 73, the Owls Head Transportation Museum makes an interesting stop. It houses aircraft, cars, bicycles, and carriages. Every other weekend from May to October vintage planes take wing and fly as part of shows hosted by the museum.

Camden

⛝ *Commercial St, Public Landing (207) 236-4404.*
The compact village is ideal for exploring on foot. Shady streets are lined with elegant homes and spired churches, and a host of shops border the waterfront. Among the fine inns on High Street is the Whitehall, with a room dedicated to Pulitzer Prize-winning poet Edna St. Vincent Millay (1892–1950), who went to school in Camden.

Fans of Millay might also want to visit Camden Hills State Park on Route 1, where a short road leads to the top

of 796-ft (242-m) Mount Battie. Standing on this point overlooking Penobscot Bay, Millay was inspired to write her first volume of poetry.

Searsport

⛝ *Main & Steamboat (207) 548-7255.*
Searsport was once a major shipbuilding port. Now a handful of restored sea captains' homes on Church Street house the collection of the Penobscot Marine Museum. An extensive collection of maritime art, ship models, navigational instruments and imported goods and displays of shipbuilding tools help tell the story of those glory days.

Considered to be the antiques capital of Maine, the town is chock-a-block with shops and has large and busy flea markets on weekends in the summer.

Bucksport

⛝ *263 Main St (207) 469-6818.* ⛝
Bucksport looks across the Penobscot River to New England's biggest stronghold, the 125-acre (51-ha) Fort Knox State Park. Built in

Vintage aircraft at Owls Head Transportation Museum

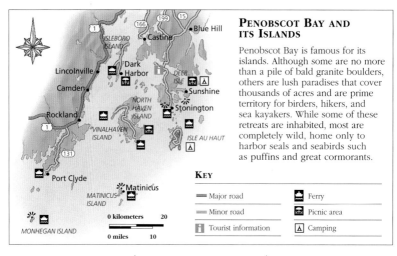

PENOBSCOT BAY AND ITS ISLANDS

Penobscot Bay is famous for its islands. Although some are no more than a pile of bald granite boulders, others are lush paradises that cover thousands of acres and are prime territory for birders, hikers, and sea kayakers. While some of these retreats are inhabited, most are completely wild, home only to harbor seals and seabirds such as puffins and great cormorants.

KEY

Major road		Ferry	
Minor road		Picnic area	
Tourist information		Camping	

0 kilometers 20

0 miles 10

---

the mid-1800s, the huge octagonal structure is found on Route 174. It was used as a training facility for troops during the Civil War (1861–5). Visitors can explore barracks, storehouses, and even some underground passages.

Castine

i *Emmerson Hall, Court St* *(207) 326-4502.*
Founded in the early 17th century and coveted for its strategic location overlooking the bay, Castine has flown the flags of France, Britain, Holland, and the US.

Relics of Castine's turbulent past can still be seen at Fort George on Wadsworth Cove Road, the highest point in town. Fort George was built by the British in 1779 and witnessed the American Navy's worst defeat during the Revolutionary War, a battle in which more than 40 colonial ships were either captured or destroyed. The fort is always open. Across from Fort George on Battle Avenue is the Maine Maritime Academy.

On Perkins Street, the two-story Wilson Museum houses a collection that includes everything from Balinese masks and pre-Inca pottery to minerals and farm tools. It is closed during the fall and winter months.

Blue Hill

i *Blue Hill Town Hall* *(207) 374-3242.*
Surrounded by fields of blueberries and with many of its white clapboard buildings listed on the National Historic Register, Blue Hill is a living postcard. Visitors will get a great view if they climb up Blue Hill Mountain.

Deer Isle

i *Rte 15 at Eggemoggin Rd* *(207) 348-6124.*
Deer Isle, reached from the mainland via a graceful suspension bridge, is actually a series of small islands linked by causeways. Island highlights include the towns of Deer Isle and Stonington, and the famous Haystack Mountain School of Crafts.

Isle au Haut

i *Rte 15 at Eggemoggin Rd* *(207) 348-6124.*
A mail boat from Stonington covers the eight miles (13 km) to Isle au Haut. Almost half the island, some 2,800

White-tailed deer, a common sight throughout the Penobscot Bay area

wooded acres (1,133 ha), belongs to Acadia National Park (*see pp288–9*) and offers 20 miles (32 km) of hiking.

Monhegan Island

i *(207) 596-0376.*
This unspoiled enclave has no cars, no commotion, and until recently no electricity. Only a half mile (0.8 km) wide and 1.7 miles (2.7 km) long, this island is smaller than New York City's Central Park, and is a favored retreat for birders and hikers who enjoy rough trails along rocky cliffs and through deep forest. Painter Jamie Wyeth is one of the prominent current residents of a summer artists' colony. Cruise companies operate round-trip excursions from Port Clyde, Boothbay Harbor, and New Harbor.

North Haven Island

i *(207) 867-4433.*
Eight miles (13 km) long and 3 miles (5 km) wide, North Haven is a refined summer colony and home to 350 hardy year-round residents. Much of the island remains open fields and meadows filled with wildflowers.

Vinalhaven

i *(207) 863-4826.*
Tiny Vinalhaven is a perfect place for a swim or a hike. Inland moors and green spaces are balanced by a granite shoreline and a harbor bustling with lobster boats.

Acadia National Park ⑩

LOCATED PRIMARILY ON Mount Desert Island, the 35,000-acre (14,164-ha) Acadia National Park is a wild, unspoiled paradise. Wave-beaten inland forests await travelers. The park's main attraction is the Loop Road, a 27-mile (43-km) drive that climbs and dips with the pink granite mountains of the east coast of the island before swinging inland past Jordan Pond, Bubble Pond, and Eagle Lake. Visitors who want a closer, more intimate look at the flora and fauna can do so on foot, bike, or horseback.

Vintage Carriage Roads
Forty-five miles (72 km) of old broken-stone carriage roads can be used for hiking and cycling.

Acadia's Wildlife
The park is home to numerous animals including woodchucks, white-tailed deer, red foxes, and the occasional black bear.

★ **Bass Harbor Head**
Craggy Bass Harbor Head exemplifies Maine's rock-bound shoreline. The 1858 Bass Harbor Head lighthouse affords magnificent views of the ocean.

KEY

▬ Major road	
▬ Minor road	
▬ Scenic route	
— Park boundary	
🛈 Tourist information	
P Parking	
⛴ Ferry	
🎪 Picnic area	
Ⓐ Camping	
🚻 Men's and women's toilets	
🍴 Oceanarium	

0 kilometers 2

0 miles 2

STAR FEATURES

★ **Bass Harbor Head**

★ **Thunder Hole**

★ **Sand Beach**

★ **Cadillac Mountain**

VISITORS' CHECKLIST

ℹ️ *Hulls Cove Visitor Center, off Rte 3 in Hulls Cove.* 📞 *(207) 288-3338.* 🕐 *year-round.* 🚌 *Bangor-Bar Harbor.* 🅿️ 🛥️ *at Hulls Cove.* ♿
W *www.nps.gov/acad/home.htm*

★ Cadillac Mountain

The 1,527-ft- (465-m-) tall Cadillac Mountain is the highest point on the Atlantic Coast. Hiking trails and an auto road lead to spectacular panoramas at the summit.

Jordan Pond

Many visitors stop at beautiful Jordan Pond, where a restaurant serves lunch, afternoon tea, and dinner from late May to late October.

★ Sand Beach

Sand Beach is one of only two lifeguarded beaches in the park, but the ocean water, which rarely exceeds 55° F (15° C), discourages many swimmers.

★ Thunder Hole

The ocean's relentless pounding on the island's cliffs has created the natural phenomenon known as the Thunder Hole. When the tide rises during heavy winds, air trapped in this crevice is compressed and expelled with a resounding boom.

Rolling hills near Eagle Lake on the outskirts of Bar Harbor

Bar Harbor ⑪

🏃 5,000 ✈ 11 miles (17 km) NW in Trenton. 🚌 Island Explorer (free). 🛈 93 Cottage St (207) 288-5103.

WITH A COMMANDING location on Frenchman Bay, Bar Harbor is Mount Desert Island's lively tourist center. Artists Thomas Cole (1801–48) and Frederic Church (1862–1900) discovered the area's beauty in the 1840s and their brilliant work attracted the wealthy. In the 19th century, the town was a summer haven for some of America's richest people, including the Astors and the Vanderbilts.

Today Bar Harbor is a thriving waterside resort that attracts 5,000,000 visitors each year. From here people can explore Acadia National Park (see pp288–9) or the mid-Maine coastline, or grab a ferry to Nova Scotia, Canada.

🏛 Bar Harbor Historical Society Museum
33 Ledgelawn Ave. 【 (207) 288-0000. ⓞ Jun–Oct: 1pm–4pm Mon–Sat.
In 1947 a fire destroyed 17,000 acres (6,880 ha) of wilderness and a third of Bar Harbor's

lavish summer homes, all but ending the village's reign as a high-society enclave. A display of early photographs shows the grand old days and the devastating effects of the fire. Happily for visitors, several of the remaining summer showplaces have been turned into gracious inns (see pp321–2).

🎭 Criterion Theater
35 Cottage St. 【 (207) 288-3441. ⓦ
A perennial favorite, the Criterion Theater is an Art Deco gem that is listed on the National Register of Historic Places. The theater shows both popular and art films.

🏛 Abbe Museum
Rte 3. 【 (207) 288-3519.
ⓞ mid-May–June: 10am–4pm daily; July–Aug: 9am–5pm daily; Sep–mid-Oct: 10am–4pm daily. ⓦ ⓑ
Just outside the village, this museum celebrates Maine's Native American heritage with exhibits of tools, crafts, art, and archaeology. Hands-on programs and workshops are taught by Native artists. Next to the museum are the Wild Gardens of Acadia, with some 300 species of local plants.

🐟 Bar Harbor Oceanarium & Lobster Hatchery
Rte 3. 【 (207) 288-5005. ⓞ mid-May–mid-Oct: 9am–5pm Mon–Sat.
ⓦ ⓒ ⓑ ⓓ
Bar Harbor Oceanarium, 8.5 miles (14 km) northwest of town, is where to see harbor seals, explore a salt marsh on Thomas Bay Marsh Walk, or visit the Maine Lobster Museum, which has demonstrations of lobstering by real fishermen. The hatching and raising process is explained at the separate Lobster Hatchery.

🐾 Acadia Zoo
Rte 3 in Trenton. 【 (207) 667-3244. ⓞ May–Jun & Sep: 10am–4pm daily; Jul–Aug: 9:30am–8pm daily. ⓦ ⓑ
A popular family attraction, the Acadia Zoo is located in Trenton across the bridge from Mount Desert Island, where pastures, streams, and woods shelter some 45 species of animals, including reindeer, wolves, monkeys, and moose. A barn has been converted into a rain-forest habitat for monkeys, birds, reptiles, and other denizens of the Amazon.

Northeast Harbor ⑫

✈ 12 miles (19 km) N in Trenton. 🛈 Harbor Dr (207) 276-5040.

NORTHEAST HARBOR IS the center of Mount Desert Island's social scene. The village has a handful of upscale shops, a few dining places, many handsome but rambling summer mansions, and a scenic harbor where boats set sail for nearby Cranberry Islands.

Chartered cruise boat in Bar Harbor

🍁 Asticou Terrace and Thuya Lodge and Gardens

Rte 3 S of Rte 198 jct. 📞 *(207) 276-5130.* ⏰ *Jul–Sep: 7am–7pm.* 🅿️ *for gardens.*

The harbor can best be admired from the stunning Asticou Terraces. A granite path snakes along the hillside, yielding ever-wider vistas as it ascends, with benches and a gazebo placed at strategic viewpoints. At the top of the hill are Thuya Lodge, with collections of paintings and books, and Thuya Gardens, with flowers beds and a reflecting pool that descends to the harbor's edge.

ENVIRONS: Somes Sound, a finger-shaped natural fjord that juts five miles (8 km) into Mount Desert Island, separates Northeast Harbor from quiet Southwest Harbor.

Whimsical sculpture in Asticou Gardens

The village's close ties to the sea are celebrated at the **Mount Desert Oceanarium**. Located in a former ship's chandlery, the oceanarium features 20 tanks teeming with live coastal sea animals and exhibits on scallops, whales, lobsters, tides, fishing gear, and the weather. Children enjoy getting acquainted with the horseshoe crabs, sea snails, starfish, and other inhabitants of the touch tank. A drive or bike ride beyond Southwest Harbor leads to unspoiled villages, including Bass Harbor, where tourists are few and visitors can explore the 1858 Bass Harbor Head Light.

🦌 Mount Desert Oceanarium

172 Clark Point Rd. 📞 *(207) 244-7330.* ⏰ *mid-May–mid-Oct: 9am–5pm Mon–Sat.* 🅿️ ✔️ ♿ 🚻

Machias ⓭

🏘️ *2,900.* ✈️ *91 miles (146 km) W in Bangor.* ℹ️ *112 Dublin St (207) 255-4402.*

Sᴵᴛᴜᴀᴛᴇᴅ ᴀᴛ ᴛʜᴇ ᴍᴏᴜᴛʜ of the river of the same name, Machias retains many of the handsome old homes that sprang up during its days as a prosperous 19th-century lumber center. The town's name comes from the Micmac Indians and means "bad little falls," a reference to the waterfall that cascades in the center of town. There is a good view of the falls from the footbridge in Bad Little Falls Park, a mid-town oasis.

Machias proclaims itself as the wild blueberry capital of Maine. It also lays claim to the region's oldest building, the 1770 **Burnham Tavern**, now a museum with period furnishings, paintings, and historic photographs. It was here that plans were made for the first naval battle of the Revolutionary War in 1775 *(see pp40–41).* Following that heated meeting, local men sailed out into Machias Bay on the small sloop *Unity* and captured the British man-of-war HMS *Margaretta.* Models of the two ships can be seen at

THE LOBSTER INDUSTRY

Harbors filled with lobstering boats and piers piled high with traps are familiar sights in the state that is America's undisputed lobster capital. Maine harvests over 40 million lbs (18 million kg) of this tasty crustacean each year. No visit is complete without a trip to a lobster pound, where patrons pick a live lobster from the tank, wait for it to be steamed, and savor the sweet meat at a picnic table overlooking the ocean.

Lobster fishermen

the **Gates House**, a restored 1807 Federal-style home in nearby Michiasport.

The town is set on the Machias River, a demanding canoeing route. **Rogue Bluffs State Park** to the southwest of town offers swimming in a 60-acre (24-ha) freshwater pond and a one-mile- (1.6-km-) long sweep of beach. The park has a launching ramp for sea kayaks, which are popular in Machias Bay. Birders go to nearby Cutler for boat trips to Machias Seal Island, home to puffins, Arctic terns, and razorbill auks.

🏛️ **Burnham Tavern**
Main St. 📞 *(207) 255-4432.* ⏰ *mid-Jun–Sep: 9am–5pm Mon–Fri.* 🅿️ ✔️

🏠 **Gates House**
Rte 92, Michiasport. 📞 *(207) 255-8461.* ⏰ *mid-Jun–mid-Sep: 12:30pm–4:30pm Tue–Sat.* 🅿️

🍁 **Rogue Bluffs State Park**
Rogue Bluffs Rd, Rogue Bluffs. 📞 *(207) 255-3475.* ⏰ *mid-May–mid-Sep: 9am–dusk.* 🅿️ ♿

Footbridge in Bad Little Falls Park in Machias

Campobello Island ⓮

I N 1964 2,800 ACRES (1,133 ha) of Campobello Island was designated as a memorial to President Franklin Delano Roosevelt (1882–1945). The main settlement of Welshpool was where the future president spent most of his summers, until 1921 when he contracted polio. Undaunted, Roosevelt went on to lead the US through the Great Depression and World War II. The highlight of the park – which actually lies in Canada and is the only international park in the world – is Roosevelt Cottage, a 34-room summer home that displays Roosevelt's personal mementos.

KEY

▬▬ Major road

▬▬ Minor road

▬▬ Scenic route

— Park boundary

- - Walking trail

🛈 Tourist information

🅿 Parking

🏕 Picnic area

🅰 Camping

🌿 Viewpoint

★ Roosevelt Cottage
Built in 1897, the sprawling wood-frame structure is one of a cluster of cottages that once belonged to wealthy families.

Mulholland Point
has an 1885 lighthouse and a waterfront picnic site that offers good views of the FDR Memorial Bridge and Lubec.

WELSHPOOL, N.B.

774

Dicks Pond

Eastern Pond

Herring Cove Road

Roosevelt Cottage

Snug Cove

HERRING COVE PROVINCIAL PARK

774

Cranberry Point Drive

Glensevern Road

ROOSEVELT CAMPOBELLO INTERNATIONAL PARK

Lake Glensevern

HERRING COVE BEACH

LUBEC, ME.

FDR. INTL. MEMORIAL BRIDGE

Fox Farm

Lily Pond

Eagle Hill

Deep Cove

Fox Hill Drive

0 kilometers　　　1

0 miles　　　1

Fox Hill

RACCOON BEACH

Raccoon Point

Cranberry Point

Upper Duck Pond

Lower Duck Pond Bog

Liberty Point Drive

Owen Head

Lower Duck Pond Bog is a prime habitat for such birds as killdeer, American black duck, and great blue heron.

Mink Point

Gooseberry Point

Lower Duck Pond

Yellow Bank

Ragged Point

STAR FEATURES

★ Roosevelt Cottage

★ Liberty Point

★ Liberty Point
A pair of observation decks perched on the rugged cliffs afford far-ranging views of the coastline and the ocean.

🌿 Liberty Point

Privately owned Hamilton's Folly mansion in Calais

Calais ⑮

🏠 4,000. ✈ 229 miles (424 km) W in Bangor. ℹ 7 Union St (207) 454-2211.

PERCHED ON the west bank of the St. Croix River opposite St. Stephen, New Brunswick, Calais is Maine's busiest border crossing to Canada. The two countries share jurisdiction over nearby St. Croix Island, where in 1604 explorers Samuel de Champlain (1567–1635) and the Sieur de Monts (c.1560–1630) established the first white settlement in North America north of Florida. The island is accessible only by boat, a difficult trip due to strong currents and tides that can run as high as 28 ft (8.5 m).

Calais was devastated by a gigantic fire in 1870. One of the few buildings that survived the conflagration is Hamilton's Folly mansion at No. 78 South Street. The Victorian house was so dubbed by locals because of its ostentatious design – a tribute to excess that bankrupted its owner.

Outdoor activities abound here. The St. Croix River is a challenging waterway for canoeists and a prime spot for salmon fishing. Three miles (5 km) southwest of Calais is the Baring Unit of the **Moosehorn National Wildlife Refuge**, 12,000 acres (4,856 ha) of wilderness that beckons hikers, bird-watchers, and naturalists. Man-made eagle nesting platforms have been erected along Route 1 north of town. Visitors should watch for the 400-sq-ft (120-sq-m) observation deck on this road for the best views. Also, there are a number of commercial farms that allow visitors to pick their own blueberries.

🦌 Moosehorn National Wildlife Refuge

Charlotte Rd S of Calais. ☎ (207) 454-7161. **Park** ◯ year-round: 9am–sunset. **Office** ◯ year-round: 7:30am–4pm Mon–Fri. ♿

Bangor ⑯

🏠 33,200. ✈ 287 Godfrey Blvd. 🚌 ℹ 519 Main St (207) 947-0307.

THE WORLD'S LEADING lumber port in the 1850s, Bangor remains the commercial center of northern Maine. The town's Penobscot River harbor was once loaded with ships carrying pine logs from nearby sawmills. This past is saluted with a 31-ft (9.5-m), 3,200-lbs (1,450-kg) statue of the mythical lumberjack Paul Bunyan on Main Street. Industrial might aside, Maine's second-largest city also draws visitors because of its ideal location as a base camp for treks to Acadia National Park (see pp288–9) and the forestlands that stretch to the north.

The city has a number of noteworthy residences from both the past and the present. The stately homes spared by a 1911 fire still line the West Market Square Historic District and the Broadway area. Maine-born horror author Stephen King lives in a mansion at No. 47 West Broadway, complete with a wrought-iron fence festooned with iron bats and cobwebs. The Greek Revival 1836 Thomas Hill House is headquarters for the **Bangor Historical Society Museum** and is elegantly furnished with period rooms and changing exhibits.

One of Bangor's most pleasant green spaces is the **Mount Hope Cemetery**. Established in 1834, the cemetery is gardenlike and beautifully landscaped with ponds, bridges, and paved paths that attract strollers and inline skaters. This spirit of movement is also celebrated at the **Cole Land Transportation Museum**. The museum's collection contains more than 200 vehicles dating from the 19th century, ranging from fire engines and horse-drawn logging sleds to antique baby carriages.

🏛 **Bangor Historical Society Museum**
159 Union St. ☎ (207) 942-5766. ◯ Apr–Dec: 12pm–4pm Tue–Sat. 📷 ☎
🎏 **Mount Hope Cemetery**
State St. ◯ 7:30am–dusk Mon–Fri. 📷 ♿
🏛 **Cole Land Transportation Museum**
405 Perry Rd. ☎ (207) 990-3600. ◯ May–early Nov: 9am–5pm daily. 📷

Ripe blueberries in Calais

Bangor's West Market Historic District

Augusta ⓱

🏠 20,0300. ✈ 75 Airport Rd. 🚇
ℹ 21 University Dr (207) 623-4559.

MAINE'S STATE CAPITAL is a relatively quiet city of 20,000. The 1832 **Maine State House**, the centerpiece of the government complex on the Kennebec River, was built of granite quarried from neighboring Hallowell. Major expansions have left only the center block from the original design by Boston architect Charles Bulfinch (1763–1844). Exhibits include political portraits and battle flags. Across the street, the **Blaine House** has been serving as the governor's mansion since 1919. The 28-room Colonial-style home was built in 1832 for a local sea captain.

Costumed interpreter at Old Fort Western in Augusta

The **Maine State Museum** has exhibits spanning "12,000 years of Maine history." One highlight is the "Made in Maine" exhibit, which re-creates a water-powered woodworking mill. The **Old Fort Western** is a restoration of one of New England's oldest surviving wooden forts, dating from 1754. The fort was built on the site where the Plymouth Pilgrims (see pp150–51) had established their trading post the previous century.

🏛 Maine State House
State & Capitol Sts. 📞 (207) 287-1400. ◯ year-round: 8am–5pm Mon–Fri. 🅿 9am–1pm Sat. 🚻

Imposing facade of the Maine State House in Augusta

🏛 Blaine House
192 State St. 📞 (207) 287-2121.
◯ year-round: 2pm–4pm Tue–Thu & by appt. 🅿 call to arrange (207) 287-2301. 🚻

🏛 Maine State Museum
State Capitol Complex, State St.
📞 (207) 287-2301. ◯ year-round: 9am–5pm Mon–Fri, 10am–4pm Sat, 1pm–4pm Sun. ● public hols. 🅿 🚻

🏛 Old Fort Western
16 Cony St. 📞 (207) 626-2385.
◯ call for hours. 🅿 🚻

ENVIRONS: Heading southwest from Augusta, travelers will get a rare look at the last active Shaker community in the US. Established in the 18th century, the Sabbathday Lake Shaker Community is home to a mere handful of residents who still adhere to their traditional beliefs of simplicity, celibacy, and communal harmony. Tours of the 17-building village include a stop at the **Shaker Village Museum** to see the beautiful furniture and ingenious inventions that became Shaker trademarks.

Nestled at the feet of Maine's western mountain ranges, Poland Springs is famous for the water taken from its spring. Continuing west, travelers will come upon Sebago Lake, a favorite among fishermen because of its delicious salmon.

Lifeguard's chair on the shore of tranquil Sebago Lake

🏛 Sabbathday Shaker Village Museum
707 Shaker Rd, New Gloucester.
📞 (207) 926-4597. ◯ late May–mid-Oct: 10am–4:30pm Mon–Sat.
🖼 🅿 🚻

Bethel ⓲

🏠 2,500. ✈ 70 miles (113 km) S in Portland. ℹ 30 Cross St (207) 824-2282 or (800) 442-5826.

A PICTURESQUE HISTORIC district, a major New England ski resort, and proximity to the White Mountains give Bethel year-round appeal. First settled in 1796, the town grew into a farming and lumbering center, and with the coming of the railroad in 1851 quickly became a popular resort. The line-up of classic clapboard mansions on the town green includes the Federal-style **Moses Mason House** (c.1813), which has been restored and furnished with period pieces.

Scenic drives are found in all directions, taking in tiny, unspoiled colonial hamlets such as Waterford to the south and beautiful mountain terrain to the north. **Sunday River Ski Resort** (see p362), six miles (10 km) north of town in Newry, has eight mountains and more than 100 ski trails. Evans Notch, a natural pass through the White Mountain peaks, offers many memorable views, including the Roost, a suspension bridge high above the Wild River and a favorite with photographers. **Grafton Notch State Park** has even more spectacular scenery along its drives and hiking trails. The park's special spots include waterfalls bearing such fanciful names as Screw Auger and Mother Walker, and sweeping views from Table Rock and the top of Old Speck Mountain.

🏛 Moses Mason House
10–14 Broad St. 📞 *(207) 824-2908.* ◻ *Jul–early Sep: 1pm–4pm Tue–Sun.*
🎟 🅿 ♿

⛷ Sunday River Ski Resort
Off Rte 2 in Newry. 📞 *(207) 824-3000 or (800) 5432-SKI.* ◻ *9am–4pm Mon–Fri, 8am–4pm Sat–Sun.* 🅿

🌿 Grafton Notch State Park
Rte 26 NW of Newry. 📞 *(207) 824-2912.* ◻ *mid-May–mid-Oct.* 🅿

Sugarloaf ⑲

ℹ *(207) 237-2000 or (800) 843-5623.*

MAINE'S HIGHEST ski mountain, Sugarloaf is the centerpiece of this touristic village packed with hotels, restaurants, and hundreds of condominiums. Downhill skiers have been flocking to the **Sugarloaf/USA** ski center *(see p362)* for years, attracted by the more than 100 trails and a vertical drop of 2,800 ft (870 m). The center also offers cross-country skiing, snow-shoeing, and ice skating.

In summer, the emphasis shifts to the resort's 18-hole golf course, boating on the lakes and rivers, and hiking in the surrounding Carrabassett Valley. The resort is also famous for a network of more than 50 miles (80 km) of mountain-biking trails through terrain ranging from flat trails to challenging circuits full of steep climbs and descents.

Screw Auger Falls in Grafton Notch State Park

⛷ Sugarloaf/USA
Carrabassett Valley. 📞 *(207) 237-2000 or (800) 843-5623.* ◻ *8:30am–3:50pm daily.* 🅿 📷 ♿ *in lodge.* 🍴

Rangeley Lakes Region ⑳

ℹ *1 Park Rd (207) 864-5364 or (800) 685-2537.*

SET AGAINST a backdrop of mountains, this rustic area encompasses a series of pristine lakes that have long been a magnet for any kind of outdoor enthusiast. In summer fishermen ply the waterways for trout and salmon, while canoeists frequently spot a moose or two lumbering along the shoreline. While the area has become

Moose crossing sign

popular with mountain bikers recently, the beauty of the place is no secret. Hikers have been enjoying the vistas from the summit of **Bald Mountain** and tramping the section of the Appalachian Trail running along **Saddleback Mountain** for decades.

Elsewhere, the popular **Rangeley Lake State Park** provides vacationers with facilities for swimming, fishing, birding, boating, and camping, and 1.2 miles (2 km) of lakefront. Toward the southeast, **Mount Blue State Park** is home to Lake Webb, a favorite haunt of fishermen because of its plentiful population of black bass, trout, and salmon. The park is dominated by the towering 3,187-ft (971-m) Mount Blue.

🎿 Bald Mountain
📞 *(207) 864-7311.*
🎿 Saddleback Mountain
📞 *(207) 864-5671.* ◻ *9am–4pm daily.*
🌿 Rangeley Lake State Park
South Shore Dr, Rangeley. 📞 *(207) 864-3858.* ◻ *mid-May–Sep: 9am–dusk.* 🅿
🌿 Mount Blue State Park
West Rd, Weld. 📞 *(207) 585-2347.* ◻ *mid-May–Sep: daylight hours.* **Camping** 📞 *(207) 585-2261.* 🅿 🅿 ♿

Challenging snowboarding on Sugarloaf, Maine's second-highest mountain at 4,237 ft (1,290 m)

The dramatic 1,800-ft- (550-m-) high cliffs of Mount Kineo on Moosehead Lake

Moosehead Lake ㉑

ℹ️ *Rte 15, Greenville (207) 695-2702 or (207) 695-2026.*

FORTY MILES (64 KM) long and blessed with 320 miles (515 km) of mountain-rimmed shoreline, Moosehead Lake is one of the largest bodies of freshwater within any state in the Northeast. A popular destination for hunters, fishermen, hikers, and canoeists since the 1880s, the region is attracting a whole new breed of outdoor enthusiasts: mountain bikers, skiers, and snowmobilers.

Greenville, the region's largest town, is the starting point for excursions into the deep boreal forests known as the Great North Woods, including seaplane services that fly visitors to remote fishing camps. **Big Squaw Mountain Resort** *(see p322)* in Greenville offers affordable skiing and its chairlift provides panoramic views of the countryside all year.

The **Moosehead Marine Museum** tells of the history of the steamboat in Greenville, beginning in 1836 when the town was a logging center. One of the museum's prized possession is the *Katahdin*, a restored 1914 steamboat and the last of a fleet of 50 such boats that plied the lake during the peak lumbering years. The *Katahdin* offers lake cruises and excursions to Mount Kineo, the sheer cliff face of which is the most prominent landmark on the lake. Local Native Americans considered the mountain sacred. The tiny settlement of Rockwood, the closest town to Mount Kineo, provides views of the mountain from rustic lakeside lodgings *(see p323)*.

🎿 Big Squaw Mountain Resort
Rte 15 between Greenville & Rockwood. 📞 *(207) 695-1000.* **Chairlift** ◯ *ski season: 9am–4pm; weekends in summer and fall.* 🏔️ ♿

🏛️ Moosehead Marine Museum
N Main St, Greenville. 📞 *(207) 695-2716.* **Museum** ◯ *Jun–mid-Oct: 10am–2pm Tue–Thu & Sat–Sun.* 🚢 **Cruises** ◯ *call for times and reservations.* ♿

Baxter State Park ㉒

ℹ️ *64 Balsam Dr, Millinocket (207) 723-5140.* **Office** ◯ *8am–4pm Mon–Fri.* **Park** ◯ *mid-May–mid-Oct.* 🚗

THIS PARK was named for Governor Percival Proctor Baxter (1876–1969). Baxter was instrumental in the effort to preserve this magnificent land, purchasing more than 200,000 acres (81,000 ha) and donating it to the state over 30-odd years with the stipulation that it was never to be developed. The park encompasses 46 mountain peaks, 18 of them over 3,000 ft (900 m), including Katahdin, Maine's tallest.

The park's 200 miles (320 km) of hiking trails are unsurpassed, and range from demanding climbs to easy family walks. Henry David Thoreau *(see p30)* tried the trek in 1846, but never made it to the 5,267-ft (1,605-m) summit of Katahdin. However, thousands of hikers are successful each year, and the trails are crowded with climbers in summer and fall. Some hardy souls can be seen completing the last steps of the famous Appalachian Trail *(see pp22–3)*, which runs from Springer Mountain, Georgia, to its terminus atop Katahdin.

Deer, bear, raccoons, and other wildlife are abundant in this pristine park, and ponds such as Grassy, Sandy Stream, and Russell are favorite watering spots for Maine's official state animal: the moose.

Majestic Mount Katahdin, a popular hiking destination

◁ **Monhegan Harbor, with Manana Island in the distance**

Autumn colors in Aroostook State Park

Aroostook County ⓴

ℹ️ *302 Main St, Caribou (207) 498-8736.*

MAINE'S LARGEST and most northern county, Aroostook covers an area greater than the combined size of Connecticut and Rhode Island. The region is best known for agriculture, with some one million acres (405,000 ha) producing nearly two billion lbs (907 million kg) of potatoes each year, plus lush crops of clover, oats, barley, and broccoli. In summer endless acres of potato fields are covered with blossoms, a vision in pink and white. Another four million acres (1,620,000 ha) of land is forested, mostly owned by paper companies that process the lumber in 50 local pulp and paper mills.

In summer hikers trek the trails in **Aroostook State Park**, fly fishermen plumb the streams for salmon and trout, and canoeists and kayakers paddle the Allagash River. When the heavy winter snows come, snowmobilers arrive in large numbers to explore the entire 1,600 miles (2,500 km) of the Interstate Trail System.

Aroostook County begins in the south in Houlton, a quiet town with a Market Square Historic District of 28 19th-century buildings. A French dialect can be heard in the northern St. John Valley, the legacy of Acadians who settled here in 1785. The **Acadian Village** consists of 16 original and reconstructed buildings from the early days. **The New Sweden Historical Museum** remembers a Swedish colony that settled not far from Caribou in the late 19th century.

🌿 **Aroostook State Park**
87 State Park Rd, S of Presque Isle.
🅲 (207) 768-8341. ⃝ mid-May–mid-Oct: daylight hours; accessible for cross-country skiing and snowmobiling in winter. 🖼 🅿 ♿

🏛 **Acadian Village**
Rte 1, Van Buren. ⃝ mid-Jun–mid-Sep: 12pm–5pm. 🖼

🏛 **The New Sweden Historical Museum**
Capitol Hill & Station Rds., New Sweden. 🅲 (207) 896-3018. ⃝ Jun–mid-Sep: 12pm–4pm Tue–Sat, 2pm–5pm Sun.

Finely crafted tools of the trade for fly fisherman

ENVIRONS:
Starting at Lake Chamberlain and extending north for more than 90 miles (145 km), the **Allagash Wilderness Waterway** is one of New England's most stunning natural areas. The waterway and its many lakes and streams have been protected since 1966. The Allagash has also been designated a National Wild and Scenic Rivers System.

The state owns the land flanking the waterway for 500 ft (150 m) on each side, assuring a protected habitat for dozens of animals and more than 120 bird species. Anglers will find a healthy population of brook trout and whitefish.

A trek up or down the Allagash system is the ultimate canoe trip in the state, and one that generally takes between five and ten days. Especially beautiful spots are Allagash Lake, a tranquil side trip where no motors are allowed, and Allagash Falls, a dramatic 40-ft (12-m) drop that necessitates carrying the canoe (called "portaging") for about a third of a mile (0.5 km). The canoeing season runs from late May to early October.

🛶 **Allagash Wilderness Waterway**
ℹ️ *Maine Bureau of Parks and Lands, 106 Hogan Rd, Bangor (207) 941-4014.* ⃝ year-round. 🖼

Frog in the protected habitat of the Allagash Wilderness Waterway

---

MAINE'S GREAT RAFTING RIVERS

Maine is famous for three whitewater rivers, the Kennebec, the Dead, and the west branch of the Penobscot. The first two rivers meet near the town called The Forks, southwest of Moosehead Lake, where more than a dozen rafting companies offer equipment and guided trips (*see p.357*). The Millinocket area services paddlers bound for the Penobscot, famed among rafters for its challenging drop through a vertical walled canyon below the Ripogenus Dam.

Kennebec River rafters in the challenging whitewater

TRAVELERS' NEEDS

WHERE TO STAY

THE INCREDIBLY varied accommodations of the New England states are tailored to suit virtually all tastes and budgets. If

Sign for rustic inn in Cape Cod

you are looking to commune with nature and save a few dollars at the same time, you can take your pick of campsites *(see pp356–9)* sprinkled liberally throughout the six states. Rustic country inns and bed and breakfasts (B&Bs) are plentiful, offering travelers quaint facilities and a more personal touch. Hotels and motels are also popular choices, conveniently located in or around busy tourist destinations. From the most posh hotel in Boston to a historic Vermont B&B or a rugged backcountry camping experience in Maine, New England has a place for everyone. During the summer vacation season, lodgings can sometimes be hard to come by, so it is always best to book in advance. This is also true during the fall-foliage season.

Luxurious Foxwoods Resort Casino near Mystic, Connecticut

HOTELS

NEW ENGLAND HAS NO shortage of hotel chains. The majority of the large chains, such as Holiday Inn, Hilton, Hyatt, Marriott, and Ramada, offer standard amenities that include such things as a bar, dining room, and exercise facilities. Although one hotel room is generally indistinguishable from the next, they are all impeccably clean and come equipped with a television, room service, and a private bathroom – comforts not always found in B&Bs.

The luxury hotels, usually found in city centers, can be very lavish. Lush decor, fine dining, and valet services are the earmarks of such establishments. The area's large casinos and resorts are also known for their lavishness.

It is always best to notify the reservation clerk should you be arriving late. Most hotels will hold your reservation only until 6pm, especially during the tourist season.

MOTELS

IF YOU ARE ON a budget, motels offer you the best and most flexible value for your money. Often found on the outskirts of cities and towns, motels also dot the New England roads most frequented by travelers. While you will not find the same amenities as in the big hotels, motels will offer you convenience and comfort at significantly lower prices. The standard motel room is equipped with a private bathroom, color TV, and heat and air conditioning. The more modern places usually have two double beds, making it easier to accommodate your whole family in a single room.

BED AND BREAKFASTS AND INNS

AMERICAN B&BS can differ greatly from their European counterparts. Very often they are not the cozy one- or two-room guest lodgings located in the owner's personal residence like those you would come across in Europe. Increasingly, New England B&Bs are professionally operated businesses in which guests live in separate accommodations from the owner or caretaker. This style of B&B tends to be larger in size and have more rooms than its more traditional counterpart. The loss of intimacy usually comes with the added bonus of private bathrooms and added services. Of course, traditionalists can still find small, cozy B&Bs throughout New England. Regardless of the size, all B&Bs offer distinctive lodgings and a breakfast, which may vary in size and style from one establishment to another.

Like B&Bs, inns come in all shapes and sizes, from the very rustic to the large resort-style lodging. Not only do inns serve breakfast and

Antiques and antique furnishings, a typical feature of New England B&Bs

Mount Washington Hotel and Resort in Bretton Woods, New Hampshire

dinner, the larger ones can come with such "extras" as swimming pools, gardens, and taverns. Depending on their location, many inns are affiliated with local tennis or golf clubs.

Because some B&Bs and inns are historic homes appointed with beautiful antique furniture, they usually prohibit smoking and often do not allow children. The **New England Innkeepers Association**, or one of its state branches, is a good lodging resource.

Vine-covered exterior of Daggett House in Edgartown, Massachusetts

PRICES AND RESERVATIONS

Rates and availability can fluctuate from season to season. Prices are generally highest in the peak tourist periods (July–August and mid-September–late October) and in the cities, coastal areas, and other prime vacation destinations. The reverse is true with ski resorts, when winter months are the most expensive. Booking your accommodations well in advance is always the safest way to avoid complications. This is especially true if you are looking forward to staying at a B&B or inn in which rooms are limited.

To save money you should try booking in cities on the weekend and in the country during the week. Many hotels in urban areas such as Boston cater to business travelers and may offer reduced rates from Friday to Sunday. Conversely, many of the rural lodgings, popular with the weekend crowd, slash their prices substantially during the week.

Always inquire about package deals offered by motels and hotels. Discounted meals and free passes to local attractions are sometimes thrown in as added incentive for you to stay with them. Some inns and B&Bs also work in conjunction with each other to promote inn-to-inn tours for cyclists and cross-country skiers, offering special rates for accommodations along the tour route.

To avoid unpleasant surprises, it is always prudent to ask about any restrictions, including those on children, pets, and smoking.

HOW TO BOOK

Most of the major hotels have toll-free reservation numbers, and it is fairly common practice now to take reservations by fax or via the Internet. Room rates are usually quoted for two people sharing a room, including tax or breakfast; all B&Bs, of course, provide a morning meal. Local tourist offices are also excellent sources of information regarding accommodations.

Beautiful room at the Inn by the Sea in Cape Elizabeth, Maine

HIDDEN EXTRAS

You should be aware that the prices quoted for many accommodations are not entirely accurate in terms of what you will be greeted with on your final bill. Often the quoted rates do not include taxes, which can increase the bill significantly – even in the haven of New Hampshire, which has no sales tax, but does have lodging and restaurant taxes. Hotels in large urban areas often charge for their parking facilities, sometimes substantially. If you are staying in Boston, for example, parking costs could amount to $20–$25 per day.

BUSINESS TRAVELERS

Outside of the major hotels, most New England accommodations are ill-equipped for the modern business traveler. The big chains, however, have the technology to send and receive faxes and provide Internet access. Some of Boston's newly refurbished properties offer multi-line phones, in-room fax machines, and private voice mail. If you are planning on booking into an older property, you should always make sure that it has been upgraded with the facilities you might require.

DISABLED TRAVELERS

Although federal law requires that all businesses provide access and facilities for the disabled, the practical reality is that this is not always the case. The vast majority of large private and chain hotels are modern enough to be equipped with the necessary facilities, including visual notification of the fire alarm, incoming phone calls, and the doorbell. Many also have some suites designated specifically for the disabled. However, many of New England's older buildings and B&Bs have narrow hallways that can obstruct wheelchairs and have no ramps. As always, it is best to check in advance.

WHERE TO STAY IN BOSTON

The centrally located Back Bay has the greatest concentration of hotels, convenient for tourists as well as

B&B bedroom at Arlington, Vermont's Inn on Covered Bridge Green

for business travelers. In the gentrifying South End, an increasing number of restored Victorian townhouses have been converted into B&Bs. Accommodations in the downtown financial district near the waterfront cater to business people during the week, but often offer good value to vacationers on the weekends. Across the Charles River, Cambridge has a large number of hotels, particularly around Harvard Square and among the Kendall Square office towers. In more suburban Brookline along the Green Line Trolley routes west of the Back Bay, several guesthouses as well as more upscale B&Bs offer additional alternatives. One plus for travelers: Boston hotels now house many of the city's top restaurants, including Clio in the Eliot Hotel, the Federalist at Fifteen Beacon, Julien at the Hotel Meridien Hotel, and Aujourd'hui at the Four Seasons Hotel.

Boston hotels are particularly busy in May and June for college graduations, July and August for summer vacations, and September and October for the fall-foliage season. Throughout the course of a year, many Boston hotels cater to business travelers, including the hotels downtown around the Hynes Convention Center, and in Cambridge's Kendall Square. This means that the rates are often lowest on weekends.

The city does have a good selection of smaller hotels and B&Bs, often offering more personal service and charm than the big convention hotels. If you are looking for a classic B&B – a room or two in the owner's home – you should contact one of the B&B booking agencies, such as the **Bed and Breakfast Agency of Boston**, **Host Homes of Boston**, or the **Bed and Breakfast Associates Bay Colony, Ltd.** A recent trend is the "boutique" hotel, a small, elegantly appointed accommodation with solicitous service. Be warned: these luxury boutiques are among the most expensive lodging options.

Like most American cities, Boston has its share of chain hotels in all price categories. There are few budget chain properties within the city itself, although visitors will find lower-priced chains, such as **Susse Chalet**, in

Boston's Seaport Hotel, busy during the summer

surrounding communities. In fact, this chain is popular throughout the New England region. While short on charm, these accommodations offer functional budget lodgings. Good-value B&B accommodations near Boston can be found in the North Shore towns of Rockport *(see p141)* and Salem *(see pp138–9)*. Both of these attractive seaside towns have good selections of mid-priced B&Bs, and are easily accessible by the MBTA commuter rail. Contact the **North of Boston Convention and Visitors Bureau** for more detailed information.

The stylish Hotel Pemaquid in New Harbor, Maine

Middlebury Inn in Vermont

HOSTELS

HOSTELS HAVE LONG been a way for people – especially students – to slash their traveling budget. However, unlike the more extensive European model, New England's hostel network is somewhat underdeveloped. Rhode Island, for example, has no facilities at all. The good news is that some of the region's prime locations (including Boston and Cape Cod) do have hostels. A list of member hostels and their locations is available from **Hostelling International– American Youth Hostels (HI/AYH)**. **HI/AYH Eastern New England Council** provides information on hostels in New Hampshire, Maine, and Massachusetts. Connecticut and Vermont are covered by the **HY/AYH Yankee Council**. A short walk from the Hynes Convention Center, the **Boston International Youth Hostel** offers a variety of rooms, including some very affordable six-bed dormitories and several private doubles.

Choosing a Hotel

THESE HOTELS have been selected across a wide price range for their excellent facilities, good location, character, and value. They are listed by area and then by price category, with symbols highlighting some of the amenities that may influence your choice of where to stay. Map references for Boston hotels help you locate the hotels on the Street Finder (pp122–7).

	CREDIT CARDS	NUMBER OF ROOMS	RECOMMENDED RESTAURANT	CHILDREN'S FACILITIES	GARDEN OR TERRACE

BOSTON

BEACON HILL AND THE THEATER DISTRICT

JOHN JEFFRIES HOUSE $$$
14 David G. Mugar Way. **Map** 1 B3. 【 (617) 367-1866. **FAX** (617) 742-0313.
Redbrick inn at the foot of Beacon Hill overlooking the Charles River.
Rooms are Victorian in style, and while some are tiny, the two-room suites
are a good value. Most of the rooms have kitchenettes. 🎿 ⊞ 📺 🔒 ♿

AE DC MC V D	46 (23)			●

MILNER HOTEL $$
78 Charles St S. **Map** 4 E2. 【 (800) 453-1731 or (617) 426-6220.
FAX (617) 350-0360. �W www.milner-hotels.com
Modest European-style budget hotel with basic rooms. Avoid the tiny
standard rooms. Close to the heart of the Theater District. 🎿 ⊞ 📺 P

AE MC V D	64			

COACH HOUSE BED & BREAKFAST $$$
16 Lime St. **Map** 3 B4. 【 (617) 227-5013. **FAX** (617) 227-9517.
@ CoachBandB@aol.com
This traditional antique-filled home has two small guest rooms.
In the Captain's Room there is a built-in nautical twin bed, while
the more elegant red-and-cream Toile Room has a queen bed.

	2			

RADISSON BOSTON $$$
200 Stuart St. **Map** 4 D2. 【 (800) 333-3333 or (617) 482-1800.
FAX (617) 451-2750. �W www.radisson.com
Comfortable mid-range hotel with lots of amenities. Standard rooms have
no particular charm, but the location near theaters and Back Bay is
convenient for tourists and business travelers. 🎿 ⊞ 📺 Y ⬚ 📺 🔒 P ♿

AE DC MC V D			●	

BEACON HILL BED & BREAKFAST $$$$
27 Brimmer St. **Map** 1 A4. 【 (617) 523-7376. @ bhillbb@aol.com
The three large bedrooms in this six-story Victorian townhouse are
furnished with a mix of antiques and more contemporary furnishings.
The rates are high, but the location near the Public Garden is excellent. 🎿

	3			

HOLIDAY INN SELECT GOVERNMENT CENTER $$$$
5 Blossom St. **Map** 1 B3. 【 (800) 465-4329 or (617) 742-7630.
FAX (617) 742-4192. �W www.basshotels.com/holiday-inn
A modern, 15-story, business-class chain hotel. On the north side of
Beacon Hill near Massachusetts General Hospital, a short walk from
Government Center. 🎿 ⊞ 📺 Y ⬚ 📺 🔒 P ♿

AE DC MC V D	303 (2)		●	

TREMONT BOSTON WYNDHAM HOTEL $$$$
275 Tremont St. **Map** 4 E2. 【 (800) 996-3426 or (617) 426-1400.
FAX (617) 338-1893. �W www.wyndham.com
The refurbished lobby of this imposing 1925 brick and stone building is
decorated with pillars and carved granite. Rooms are more simple but have
greater flair than those in a standard chain hotel. 🎿 ⊞ 📺 Y 📺 🔒 P ♿

AE DC MC V D			●	

BOSTON PARK PLAZA $$$$$
64 Arlington St. **Map** 4 D2. 【 (800) 996-3426 or (617) 426-2000.
FAX (617) 426-5545. �W www.bostonparkplaza.com
Opened in 1927, this grand luxury hotel is classically Bostonian.
Elegantly appointed, the spacious rooms also boast many modern
amenities, such as voice mail and dataports. 🎿 ⊞ 📺 Y 📺 🔒 P ♿

AE DC MC V D			●	

CHARLES STREET INN $$$$$
94 Charles St. **Map** 1 B4. 【 (877) 772-8900 or (617) 314-8900.
FAX (617) 371-0009. �W www.charlesstreetinn.com
Deluxe boutique hotel in an 1860s townhouse. All the sumptuous
antique-filled rooms have working fireplaces, as well as whirlpool tubs,
two-line telephones, internet connections, and CD players. 🎿 ⊞ 📺 🔒

AE DC MC V D	8			

Price categories for a standard double room per night, inclusive of breakfast, service charges, and any additional taxes:

$ under $100
$$ $100–$150
$$$ $150–$200
$$$$ $200–$250
$$$$$ over $250

CREDIT CARDS
Major credit cards accepted: *AE* American Express; *DC* Diners Club; *MC* MasterCard/Access; *V* Visa, *D* Discover Card.

NUMBER OF ROOMS
Number of rooms in the hotel (suites shown in parentheses).

RECOMMENDED RESTAURANT
Good restaurant within the hotel.

CHILDREN'S FACILITIES
Hotel has various facilities for young children.

GARDEN OR TERRACE
Hotel has a garden, courtyard, or terrace.

	CREDIT CARDS	NUMBER OF ROOMS	RECOMMENDED RESTAURANT	CHILDREN'S FACILITIES	GARDEN OR TERRACE
FOUR SEASONS $$$$$ 200 Boylston St. **Map 4 D2.** ((800) 332-3442 or (617) 351-2036. FAX (617) 423-0154. W www.fourseasons.com The ultimate in service and luxury, and consistently ranked among the top hotels in the city. It has grand reception rooms and sumptuous bedrooms, many overlooking the Public Garden.	AE DC MC V D	288 (72)	■	●	
SWISSÔTEL $$$$$ One Ave de Lafayette. **Map 4 D2.** ((800) 621-9200 or (617) 451-2600. FAX (617) 451-0054. W www.swissotel.com A high-rise tower houses this modern, well-appointed hotel that caters to business travelers but also offers good-value weekend specials. The area is a bit seedy but close to Downtown Crossing.	AE DC MC V D	471 (30)		●	

OLD BOSTON AND THE FINANCIAL DISTRICT

	CREDIT CARDS	NUMBER OF ROOMS	RECOMMENDED RESTAURANT	CHILDREN'S FACILITIES	GARDEN OR TERRACE
SHAWMUT INN $$ 280 Friend St. **Map 1 C2.** ((800) 350-7784 or (617) 720-5544. FAX (617) 723-7784. W www. shawmutinn.com Simply furnished rooms, all with kitchenettes, in a former state office building one block from North Station. A fine budget choice; suites are a good value for families.	AE MC V	65 (11)		●	
HARBORSIDE INN $$$ 185 State St. **Map 2 E3.** ((617) 723-7500. FAX (617) 670-2010. W www.hagopianhotels.com The small guest rooms in this old mercantile warehouse have exposed brick walls, Victorian-style furniture, and wooden floors with Oriental rugs. Near Faneuil Hall but surrounded by the "Big Dig."	AE DC MC V D	54 (2)			
OMNI PARKER HOUSE $$$$ 60 School St. **Map 2 D4.** ((800) 843-6664 or (617) 227-8600. FAX (617) 742-5729. W www.omnihotels.com Home of the Parker House Roll and Boston Cream Pie, this traditional and comfortable hotel has been open since 1885.	AE DC MC V D	551 (21)		●	
FIFTEEN BEACON $$$$$ 15 Beacon St. **Map 1 C4.** ((877) 982-3226 or (617) 670-1500. FAX (617) 670-2525. W www.xvbeacon.com Coolly opulent boutique hotel in a former office building. Chic rooms all have a high-style mix of traditional and contemporary furnishings, with facilities including CD players and fax machines.	AE DC MC V D	61 (2)	■		
LE MERIDIEN $$$$$ 250 Franklin St. **Map 2 E4.** ((800) 543-4300 or (617) 451-1900. FAX (617) 423-2844. W www.lemeridienboston.com In a former Federal Reserve Bank building, this deluxe hotel in the heart of the Financial District pampers business travelers and often offers affordable weekend getaway packages.	AE DC MC V D	326 (26)	■	●	
REGAL BOSTONIAN $$$$$ Faneuil Hall Marketplace. **Map 2 D3.** ((800) 343-0922 or (617) 523-3600. FAX (617) 523-2454. W www.regal-hotels.com/boston Three mazelike redbrick former warehouse buildings opposite Faneuil Hall are home to this upscale traditional hotel. Rooms have small balconies. Complimentary airport limousine service.	AE DC MC V D	201 (13)	■		■
WYNDHAM BOSTON $$$$$ 89 Broad St. **Map 2 E4.** ((800) 996-3426 or (617) 556-0006. FAX (617) 556-0053. W www.wyndham.com This Art Deco former office building was converted to a hotel in 1999. The classy lobby and the bathrooms retain original marble floors; rooms are traditionally furnished with modern facilities.	AE DC MC V D	362 (66)		●	

For key to symbols see back flap

		Credit Cards	Number of Rooms	Recommended Restaurant	Children's Facilities	Garden or Terrace
Price categories for a standard double room per night, inclusive of breakfast, service charges, and any additional taxes: $ under $100 $$ $100–$150 $$$ $150–$200 $$$$ $200–$250 $$$$$ over $250	**CREDIT CARDS** Major credit cards accepted: *AE* American Express; *DC* Diners Club; *MC* MasterCard/Access; *V* Visa, *D* Discover Card. **NUMBER OF ROOMS** Number of rooms in the hotel (suites shown in parentheses). **RECOMMENDED RESTAURANT** Good restaurant within the hotel. **CHILDREN'S FACILITIES** Hotel has various facilities for young children. **GARDEN OR TERRACE** Hotel has a garden, courtyard, or terrace.					

NORTH END AND THE WATERFRONT

GOLDEN SLIPPER B&B AFLOAT $$$ Lewis Wharf. **Map 2 E3.** (781) 545-2845. This is a 40-foot Chris Craft boat, docked at Lewis Wharf in Boston Harbor. Well equipped, it sleeps up to four and is available to guests from May through October. Owners provide a Continental breakfast.		2			
SEAPORT HOTEL $$$$ One Seaport Lane. **Map 2 F5.** (877) 732-7678 or (617) 385-4000. FAX (617) 385-4001. W www.seaporthotel.com A modern, towering business hotel next to the World Trade Center, every room has an internet hookup, plus in-room conferencing facilities. Weekend specials are attractive.	AE DC MC V D	426	■	●	
BOSTON HARBOR HOTEL $$$$$ 70 Rowes Wharf. **Map 2 E4.** (800) 752-7077 or (617) 439-7000. FAX (617) 345-6799. W www.bhh.com This opulent hotel with classically elegant furnishings overlooks the harbor. Although the "Big Dig" construction rumbles nearby, the hotel and its fine contemporary restaurant are oases of calm.	AE DC MC V D	230 (15)	■	●	■
MARRIOTT LONG WHARF $$$$$ 296 State St. **Map 2 E3.** (800) 228-9290 or (617) 227-0800. FAX (617) 227-2867. W www.marriott.com An upscale, modern chain hotel in a great harborfront location. All rooms have at least partial harbor views.	AE DC MC V D	402 (14)		●	■

BACK BAY AND SOUTH END

463 BEACON STREET GUEST-HOUSE $ 463 Beacon St. **Map 3 A2.** (617) 536-1302. FAX (617) 247-8876. W www.463beacon.com This stately five-story guest house is good value. Rooms vary, but some have bay windows, fireplaces, and other original features, plus microwaves and fridges. Most rooms have a private bath. Weekly maid service only.	DC MC V D	20			
CHANDLER INN $$ 26 Chandler St. **Map 4 D3.** (800) 842-3450 or (617) 482-3450. FAX (617) 542-3428. W www.chandlerinn.com A simple but friendly inn in a former Coast Guard station, two blocks from most of the South End's restaurants. The small rooms with floral bedspreads and simple motel-style furnishings sleep up to two people.	AE DC MC V D	56			
COLLEGE CLUB $$ 44 Commonwealth Ave. **Map 3 C2.** (617) 536-9510. FAX (617) 247-8537. W www.thecollegeclubofboston.com A hidden gem and excellent value, this ornate Victorian town house near the Public Garden is home to a private club. It rents six lovely double rooms, and five more austere singles that share bathrooms.	MC V D	11			
COPLEY HOUSE APARTMENTS $$ 239 West Newton St. **Map 3 B3.** (800) 331-1318 or (617) 236-8300. FAX (617) 424-1815. W www.copleyhouse.com Studio and one-bedroom apartments in a group of restored buildings. Ask for details, as apartments vary significantly in style and quality.	AE DC MC V D	65		●	
NEWBURY GUEST HOUSE $$ 261 Newbury St. **Map 3 B2.** (617) 437-7666. FAX (617) 262-4243. W www.hagopianhotels.com In Boston's chic shopping neighborhood, this brownstone guest house caters to business people and fashionable vacationers. Tasteful rooms are furnished with Victorian-style reproductions. Book well in advance.	AE DC MC V D	32			■

82 CHANDLER STREET B&B $$$ — 5
82 Chandler St. **Map 4** D3. *(888) 482-0408 or (617) 482-0408.*
FAX *(617) 482-0659.* W *www.channel1.com/82chandler*
Located on a residential South End street, this long-established B&B in a four-story row house has three guest rooms, plus two studio apartments. All units are well furnished and have kitchenettes; only two have TVs.

CLARENDON SQUARE INN $$$ — AE MC V — 3
198 West Brookline St. **Map 3** C4. *(617) 536-2229.*
W *www.clarendonsquare.com*
A stylish B&B in an elegantly restored 1860s South End townhouse. Rooms all have fireplaces. There is a roof deck with hot tub.

MIDTOWN HOTEL $$$ — AE DC MC V D — 159
220 Huntington Ave. **Map 3** B4. *(800) 343-1177 or (617) 262-1000.*
FAX *(617) 262-8739.* W *www.midtownhotel.com*
Family-friendly 1960s hotel near Symphony Hall. Simple, clean rooms. Front and side rooms are more spacious than those in rear.

UNION PARK GUEST HOUSE $$$ — AE MC V — 3
12 Union Park. **Map 4** D4. *(617) 421-1821.* FAX *(617) 421-1821.*
W *www.unionparkguesthouse.com*
One block from Tremont Street and its many restaurants, this Victorian town house has large rooms furnished with queen-sized beds. No breakfast served, but rooms have fridges, and there are several cafés nearby.

BACK BAY HILTON $$$$ — AE DC MC V D — 385
40 Dalton St. **Map 3** A3. *(800) 874-0063 or (617) 236-1100.*
FAX *(617) 867-6104.* W *www.hilton.com*
Modern 26-story tower hotel behind the Hynes Convention Center with well-equipped rooms. Prices are often lower than at comparable Back Bay hotels, especially on weekends.

COPLEY SQUARE HOTEL $$$$ — AE DC MC V D — 143 (11)
47 Huntington Ave. **Map 3** C3. *(800) 225-7062 or (617) 536-9000.*
FAX *(617) 236-0351.* W *www.copleysquarehotel.com*
The rooms in this comfortably appointed older hotel have traditional reproduction furnishings and more character than many nearby high-rise hotels.

ELIOT HOTEL $$$$$ — AE DC MC V D — 95 (95)
370 Commonwealth Ave. **Map 3** A2. *(800) 443-5468 or (617) 267-1607.* FAX *(617) 536-9114.* W *www.eliothotel.com*
Graciously furnished, all-suite hotel, built in 1925. Rooms have separate sitting rooms, plus business amenities including fax machines and dataports. Home of the fine contemporary restaurant Clio.

FAIRMONT COPLEY PLAZA BOSTON $$$$$ — AE DC MC V D — 379 (60)
138 St. James Ave. **Map 3** C2. *(800) 527-4727 or (617) 267-5300.*
FAX *(617) 247-6681.* W *www.fairmont.com*
The gold lions guarding the hotel entrance are a city landmark. Known as the "grande dame" of Boston, this ornately appointed, palatial hotel is the epitome of luxury.

THE JEWEL OF NEWBURY $$$$$ — AE DC MC V D — 8 (8)
254 Newbury St. **Map 3** B2. *(617) 536-5523.* FAX *(617) 424-8798.*
W *www.jewelboston.com*
Victorian town house turned opulent boutique hotel. Spacious, romantic suites feature ornate antique furniture, rugs, and decorative fireplaces. Cozy North African restaurant on lower level with outdoor terrace.

LENOX HOTEL $$$$$ — AE DC MC V D — 212 (12)
710 Boylston St. **Map 3** B2. *(800) 225-7676 or (617) 536-5300.*
FAX *(617) 267-1237.* W *www.lenoxhotel.com*
This highly regarded and recently refurbished 100-year-old hotel has sumptuously appointed rooms with all manner of luxuries. It is also home to the excellent Anago restaurant.

RITZ-CARLTON HOTEL $$$$$ — AE DC MC V D — 275 (42)
15 Arlington St. **Map 4** D2. *(800) 241-3333 or (617) 536-5700.*
FAX *(617) 536-9340.* W *www.ritzcarlton.com*
Large luxury hotel, built in 1927, overlooking the Public Garden. Beautifully appointed, with traditional French Provincial furnishings and elegant reception and dining rooms.

For key to symbols see back flap

	Price categories for a standard double room per night, inclusive of breakfast, service charges, and any additional taxes: $ under $100 $$ $100–$150 $$$ $150–$200 $$$$ $200–$250 $$$$$ over $250	**CREDIT CARDS** Major credit cards accepted: *AE* American Express; *DC* Diners Club; *MC* MasterCard/Access; *V* Visa, *D* Discover Card. **NUMBER OF ROOMS** Number of rooms in the hotel (suites shown in parentheses). **RECOMMENDED RESTAURANT** Good restaurant within the hotel. **CHILDREN'S FACILITIES** Hotel has various facilities for young children. **GARDEN OR TERRACE** Hotel has a garden, courtyard, or terrace.	CREDIT CARDS	NUMBER OF ROOMS	RECOMMENDED RESTAURANT	CHILDREN'S FACILITIES	GARDEN OR TERRACE

	CREDIT CARDS	NUMBER OF ROOMS	RECOMMENDED RESTAURANT	CHILDREN'S FACILITIES	GARDEN OR TERRACE
WESTIN COPLEY PLACE $$$$$ 10 Huntington Ave. **Map 3 C3.** ☎ *(800) 228-3000 or (617) 262-9600.* **FAX** *(617) 424-7483.* W *www.westin.com* This 36-story hotel buzzes with business traffic. Comfortable and upscale, it has excellent facilities and great views. 🏋 ⌨ ♨ ↑ ♉ ≋ ♈ �'⃨ P ♿	AE DC MC V D	800 (45)	■	●	
FARTHER AFIELD					
CONSTITUTION INN $ 150 Second Ave, Charlestown. ☎ *(617) 241-8400.* **FAX** *(617) 241-2856.* An economy inn run by the Y.M.C.A., most of the basic rooms have two twin beds, although several have queen-sized ones. ⌨ ♨ ↑ ≋ ♈ P ♿	AE MC V	200 (2)			
LONGWOOD INN $ 123 Longwood Ave, Brookline. ☎ *(617) 566-8615.* **FAX** *(617) 738-1070.* @ *lwdin@tiac.net* Turn-of-the-century Arts and Crafts-style mansion, now a budget inn. It retains an air of faded elegance, although the rooms are quite basic. ♨ P		22		●	■
BROOKLINE MANOR INN $$ 32 Center St, Brookline. ☎ *(800) 535-5325 or (617) 232-0003.* **FAX** *(617) 734-5815.* W *www.brooklinemanorinn.com* This tastefully refurbished Victorian guest house has simple but comfortable rooms, all with modern bathrooms. ⌨ ♨ P	AE MC V	35		●	■
IRVING HOUSE $$ 24 Irving St, Cambridge. ☎ *(877) 547-4600 or (617) 547-4600.* **FAX** *(617) 576-2814.* W *www.irvinghouse.com* This wooden-framed Victorian house inn has simple rooms (some are quite small) and an attractive terrace. Some rooms share baths. ⌨ ♨ �'⃨ P ♿	AE MC V	44		●	■
A CAMBRIDGE HOUSE BED AND BREAKFAST $$$ 2218 Massachusetts Ave, Cambridge. ☎ *(800) 232-9989 or (617) 491-6300.* **FAX** *(617) 868-2848.* W *www.acambridgehouse.com* This bright yellow 1892 house is now an exquisitely restored Victorian fantasy, with four-poster beds and working fireplaces. ⌨ P	AE DC MC V D	15			■
BERTRAM INN $$$ 92 Sewall Ave, Brookline. ☎ *(800) 295-3822 or (617) 566-2234.* **FAX** *(617) 277-1887.* W *www.bertraminn.com* A meticulously restored 1907 Arts and Crafts-style home, with an elegant parlor, sunporch, and cozy, antique-filled rooms. ⌨ ♨ �'⃨ P	AE MC V	14 (4)			■
HARVARD SQUARE HOTEL $$$ 110 Mt. Auburn St, Cambridge. ☎ *(800) 458-5886 or (617) 864-5200.* **FAX** *(617) 864-2409.* W *www.doubletreehotels.com* Location is the best feature of this refurbished hotel in the heart of Harvard Square. The rooms are basic but comfortable. Ask for a room at the front, as the rear rooms have no view. ⌨ ♨ ↑ �'⃨ P ♿	AE DC MC V D	73		●	
MARY PRENTISS INN $$$ 6 Prentiss St, Cambridge. ☎ *(617) 661-2929.* **FAX** *(617) 661-5989.* W *www.maryprentissinn.com* An antique-filled B&B in a Greek Revival-style house. There is a spacious sundeck and modern amenities include dataports and fridges. ⌨ �'⃨ P	AE MC V	20 (5)			■
GRYPHON HOUSE $$$$ 9 Bay State Rd, Boston. ☎ *(877) 375-9003 or (617) 375-9003.* **FAX** *(617) 425-0716.* W *www.gryphonhouseboston.com* This five-story 1895 bowfronted boutique hotel has gracious antiques-filled public rooms and large guest suites furnished in a variety of styles. Bathrooms have whirlpool tubs, and some rooms have river views. ⌨ ♨ �'⃨ P	AE DC MC V D	8 (8)			

INN AT HARVARD $$$$
1201 Massachusetts Ave, Cambridge. 📞 (800) 458-5886 or
(617) 491-2222. FAX (617) 492-4896. W www.theinnatharvard.com
Modern four-story hotel built around a sunny atrium, which blends well
with the nearby Harvard University buildings. The rooms are comfortably
appointed and filled with period furniture.

AE DC MC V D | 113 (1)

SHERATON COMMANDER $$$$
16 Garden St, Cambridge. 📞 (800) 535-5007 or (617) 547-4800.
FAX (617) 868-8322. W www.sheratoncommander.com
Chic, old-fashioned hotel opposite Cambridge Common. Rooms are
decorated in traditional colonial style.

AE DC MC V D | 175 (14)

UNIVERSITY PARK HOTEL $$$$
20 Sidney St, Cambridge. 📞 (800) 222-8733 or (617) 577-0200.
FAX (617) 494-8366. W www.univparkhotel.com
This contemporary hotel, owned by Massachusetts Institute of Technology,
is filled with technology such as ergonomically designed furniture, in-room
internet access, and phones with voice mail.

AE DC MC V D | 210 (28)

CHARLES HOTEL $$$$$
One Bennett St, Cambridge. 📞 (800) 882-1818 or (617) 864-1200.
FAX (617) 864-5715. W www.charleshotel.com
This contemporary luxury hotel has rooms appointed with Shaker-style
furnishings and quilts. Home of the excellent modern-Mediterranean Rialto
restaurant and the Regatta-bar jazz club.

AE DC MC V D | 293 (44)

HYATT REGENCY CAMBRIDGE $$$$$
575 Memorial Dr, Cambridge. 📞 (800) 233-1234 or (617) 492-1234.
FAX (617) 491-6906. W www.hyatt.com
Modern pyramid-shaped hotel on the Charles River with a revolving
restaurant and great views of the Boston skyline. Slightly inaccessible for
those without a car, but there is a shuttle service for guests. Room rates
drop by as much as 50 percent on weekends.

AE DC MC V D | 469 (10)

MASSACHUSETTS

CONCORD: *Colonial Inn* $$$$
48 Monument St. 📞 (978) 369-9200. FAX (978) 369-2170.
@ info@concordscolonialinn.com W www.concordscolonialinn.com
This historic site was built in 1716 and has been operating as a hotel
since 1889. Beautiful Colonial-style rooms.

AE DC MC V D | 56 (7)

CONCORD: *North Bridge Inn* $$$$
21 Monument St. 📞 (888) 530-0007 or (978) 371-0014. FAX (978) 371-6460.
W www.northbridgeinn.com
A charming bed-and-breakfast with six suites, each named after a New
England author. The building was constructed in 1885 and has recently
undergone extensive renovations.

AE MC V | 6 (6)

EDGARTOWN: *The Daggett House* $$$$
59 North Water St. 📞 (800) 946-3400 or (508) 627-4600. FAX (508) 627-4611.
W www.mvweb.com/daggett
Delightful inn, comprised of four historic buildings, featuring rooms
decorated in a warm country style. The garden leads right down to the
harbor, where chairs are set out for use by the guests.

AE D MC V | 31 (10)

HYANNIS: *Captain Gosnold Village* $$
230 Gosnold St. 📞 (508) 775-9111. W www.captaingosnold.com
Close to beaches and Hyannis Harbor, this family-oriented resort has
motel rooms, studios, and cottages. No air-conditioning.

AE MC | 35 (28)

LENOX: *The Mayflower Motor Inn* $$$
474 Pittsfield Rd. 📞 (413) 443-4468
A standard motel that provides comfortable lodging. Coffee and
doughnuts served in the morning.

AE DC MC V D | 21

LENOX: *Cranwell Resort and Golf Club* $$$$
55 Lee Rd. 📞 (800) 272-6935 or (413) 637-1364. FAX (413) 637-4364.
@ info@cranwell.com W www.cranwell.com
This luxurious resort offers accommodations in a number of magnificent
lodgings. The rooms include a variety of amenities, and there is an
18-hole championship golf course.

AE DC MC V D | 107 (25)

For key to symbols see back flap

Price categories for a standard double room per night, inclusive of breakfast, service charges, and any additional taxes:

$ under $100
$$ $100–$150
$$$ $150–$200
$$$$ $200–$250
$$$$$ over $250

CREDIT CARDS
Major credit cards accepted: *AE* American Express; *DC* Diners Club; *MC* MasterCard/Access; *V* VISA, *D* Discover Card.

NUMBER OF ROOMS
Number of rooms in the hotel (suites shown in parentheses).

RECOMMENDED RESTAURANT
Good restaurant within the hotel.

CHILDREN'S FACILITIES
Hotel has various facilities for young children.

GARDEN OR TERRACE
Hotel has a garden, courtyard, or terrace.

		CREDIT CARDS	NUMBER OF ROOMS	RECOMMENDED RESTAURANT	CHILDREN'S FACILITIES	GARDEN OR TERRACE
NANTUCKET: *The Nesbitt Inn* 21 Broad St. ☎ (508) 228-0156 or (508) 228-2446. FAX (508) 228-2446. Located right in town, this Victorian bed-and-breakfast is operated by the exceptionally friendly hosts, Mr. and Mrs. Noblit, and is decorated with antiques and Oriental carpets. No television or air conditioning. Shared bath.	$	MC V	14 (2)		●	■
NANTUCKET: *Union Street Inn* 7 Union St. ☎ (508) 228-9222. FAX (508) 325-0848. @ unioninn@nantucket.net W www.union-street-inn.com The recently restored Union Street Inn exemplifies Nantucket architecture and is located in the historic district. The rooms are tastefully decorated; many have fireplaces.	$$$$	AE MC V	12 (1)			■
NORTH ADAMS: *Blackinton Manor Bed and Breakfast* 1391 Massachusetts Ave. ☎ (800) 795-8613 or (413) 663-5795. FAX (413) 663-3121. @ donaldhaines@hotmail.com W www.blackinton-manor.com Built in 1849, this elegant bed-and-breakfast is well known for the musical events that take place here throughout the year. It has a spacious living room with a fireplace and grand piano. Television in some rooms.	$$	MC V	6 (2)			■
OAK BLUFFS: *The Nashua House* 30 Kennebec Ave. ☎ (508) 693-0043. FAX (508) 693-6283. @ calebcaldwellmv@hotmail.com W www.nashuahouse.com A Victorian house, built in 1873 and located in the center of town. The affordable rooms are sunny and offer a nice view, but do not have television or air-conditioning units. All the rooms have shared baths.	$$	AE MC V	16			
OAK BLUFFS: *The Island Inn* Beach Rd. ☎ (800) 462-0269 or (508) 693-2002. FAX (508) 693-7911. @ innkeeper@islandinn.com W www.islandinn.com Located on extensive lawns, very near the beach. The resort has cottages, studios, and suites, most of which offer spectacular views.	$$$$	AE DC MC V D	51 (27)	■	●	■
PLYMOUTH: *Ellisville Harbor House Bed and Breakfast* 159 Ellisville Rd. ☎ (888) 738-2337 or (508) 888-3692. FAX (508) 888-5978. @ kathy@ellisville.com W www.ellisville.com Full breakfasts are served either in the dining room or on the large sundeck. This historic site has a private beach. Swans, deer, and seals can be seen on the grounds in the various seasons.	$$	MC V	3			■
PLYMOUTH: *Pilgrim Sands Motel* 150 Warren Ave. ☎ (800) 729-SAND or (508) 747-0900. FAX (508) 746-8066. @ thebeach@pilgrimsands.com W www.pilgrimsands.com Located across the street from Plimoth Plantation, this motel has a private beach and large, modern rooms. Breakfast is not included.	$$	AE DC MC V D	64 (2)		●	■
PROVINCETOWN: *Three Peaks* 210 Bradford St. ☎ (800) 286-1715 or (508) 487-1717. FAX (508) 487-3164. @ dana@threepeaks.com W www.threepeaks.com B&B with a large wraparound porch set on beautiful grounds. No children. Only some of the rooms have air conditioning.	$$	AE MC V D	6			■
ROWLEY: *Country Garden Inn and Motel* 101 Main St, Rte 1A. ☎ (800) 287-7773 or (978) 948-7773. FAX (978) 948 7947. @ reserve@countrygardenmotel.com W www.countrygardenmotel.com Beautiful gardens, picnic areas and hammocks surround the various lodgings. There is a gazebo, heated pool and a spa. Breakfast not included.	$	AE DC MC V D	25 (10)		●	■

SALEM: *Hawthorn Hotel* — $$$
18 Washington Sq W. (800) SAY-STAY or (978) 744-4080.
FAX (978) 745-9842. @ sales@hawthornhotel.com W www.hawthornhotel.com
This upscale Federal-style hotel combines tasteful decoration with modern amenities. The Hawthorne is centrally located in downtown Salem and hosts annual Halloween festivities.
AE MC V D — 89 (6)

STURBRIDGE: *Colonel Ebenezer Crafts Inn* — $$
Fiske Hill. (800) 782-5425 or (508) 347-3313. FAX (508) 347-1254.
@ info@publickhouse.com W www.publickhouse.com
A delightful inn offering a great view of the countryside. It has a large backyard with a patio, swimming pool, and swings. Tea is served in afternoon. No television.
AE MC V D — 8 (2)

STURBRIDGE: *Comfort Inn and Suites* — $$
215 Charlton Rd, Rte 20. (800) 228-5150 or (508) 347-3306.
FAX (508) 347-3514.
@ comfortinnsturb@cs.com W www.sturbridgecomfortinn.com
Surrounded by immaculate grounds and beautiful landscaping, this Comfort Inn has an impressive array of amenities and is located less than 1 mile (1.6 km) from Old Sturbridge Village.
AE DC MC V D — 77 (44)

WEST DENNIS: *The Barnacle Motel* — $
219 Main St. (508) 394-8472. W www.sunsol.com/barnacle
Clean comfortable accommodations for very reasonable rates. Breakfast is not included.
AE DC MC V D — 36

WILLIAMSTOWN: *The Williams Inn* — $$$
On the Green. (800) 828-0133 or (413) 458-9371. FAX (413) 458-2767.
W www.williamsinn.com
Situated on the campus of Williams College, this inn has elegant rooms and offers meal plans for breakfast and dinner.
AE DC MC V D — 103

RHODE ISLAND

BLOCK ISLAND: *Rose Farm Inn* — $$
Roslyn Rd. (401) 466-2034. FAX (401) 466-2053.
W www.blockisland.com/rosefarm
Set in a peaceful sea and country setting, this inn was a working farm until 1963. The 20 acres (8 ha) of farmland are now home to marsh hawks, ring-neck pheasants, and white-tail deer. Some rooms have a shared bath. Closed October to April. Children 12 and older welcomed.
AE DC MC V D — 19 (4)

BLOCK ISLAND: *1661 Inn and Hotel Manisses* — $$$
Spring St. (401) 466-2421. FAX (401) 466-3162.
@ biresorts@riconnect.com W www.blockisland.com/biresorts/
This historic inn, animal farm, and Victorian hotel is a perfect base from which to explore Block Island. No air-conditioning. Some rooms have no television, and some have shared bathrooms.
MC V — 38 (3)

BRISTOL: *King Philip Inn* — $
400 Metacom Ave. (800) 253-7610 or (401) 253-7600. FAX (401) 253-1857.
Located on Route 136 in Bristol, the King Philip Inn is minutes away from Newport beaches and naval facilities, Providence nightspots, museums and historic homes, and Battleship Cove in Massachusetts.
AE DC MC V D — 30

CHARLESTOWN: *General Stanton Inn* — $$
4115A Old Post Rd, Rte 1A. (401) 364-8888. FAX (401) 364-3333.
One of the oldest continuously run inns in North America, the General Stanton still has some of the old atmosphere, with its low ceilings, fireplaces, brick ovens and hand-hewn timbers. The weekend flea market is one of South County's best. Breakfast not included.
AE MC V — 16

NEWPORT: *The Black Duck Inn* — $$
29 Pelham St. (401) 841-5548. FAX (401) 846-4873.
@ marya401@aol.com W www.blackduckinn.com
Situated in the heart of downtown Newport. Each room is distinctly decorated in the romantic Laura Ashley tradition. Two rooms have a joint washroom for families or two couples traveling together.
AE MC V — 8

For key to symbols see back flap

Price categories for a standard double room per night, inclusive of breakfast, service charges, and any additional taxes:

$ under $100
$$ $100–$150
$$$ $150–$200
$$$$ $200–$250
$$$$$ over $250

CREDIT CARDS
Major credit cards accepted: AE American Express; DC Diners Club; MC MasterCard/Access; V Visa, D Discover Card.

NUMBER OF ROOMS
Number of rooms in the hotel (suites shown in parentheses).

RECOMMENDED RESTAURANT
Good restaurant within the hotel.

CHILDREN'S FACILITIES
Hotel has various facilities for young children.

GARDEN OR TERRACE
Hotel has a garden, courtyard, or terrace.

	CREDIT CARDS	NUMBER OF ROOMS	RECOMMENDED RESTAURANT	CHILDREN'S FACILITIES	GARDEN OR TERRACE
NEWPORT: *Beech Tree Inn* $$$ 34 Rhode Island Ave. (800) 748-6565 or (401) 847-9794. FAX (401) 847-6824. @ beechtreeinn@hotmail.com W www.beechtreeinn.com/beech.htm Victorian home built in 1887. Many rooms have fireplaces and Jacuzzis. Noted for "the biggest breakfast in Newport," with a variety of eggs, pancakes, five juices, and more. Older children welcome. ▨ ▥ ▤ P	AE MC V D	16 (2)			■
NEWPORT: *Best Western Mainstay Inn* $$$ 151 Admiral Kalbfus Rd. (401) 849-9880. FAX (401) 849-4391. @ themainstayinn@aol.com Located near all the main attractions in Newport, including the historic harbor, the Newport Mansions, and the beaches. Just across the street from the Jai Alai Fronton/Casino. Breakfast not included. ▨ ▥ ▤ ▧ ▤ P ▤	AE DC MC V D	165 (5)		●	
NEWPORT: *Castle Hill Inn and Resort* $$$$$ 590 Ocean Ave. (888) 466-1355 or (401) 849-3800. FAX (401) 849-3838. W www.castlehillinn.com This resort with a private beach includes several houses. The restaurant has repeatedly won the Wine Spectator Award of Excellence. Children over 12 are welcome. ▨ ▥ ▤ P ▤	AE MC V D	35 (2)	■		■
PROVIDENCE: *C.C. Ledbetter Bed and Breakfast* $$ 326 Benefit St. (401) 351-4699. FAX (401) 351-4699. Located opposite John Brown House, a block from Brown University. Charming rooms with handmade quilts Breakfast included. ▨ P	MC V	4			■
PROVIDENCE: *The State House Inn* $$ 43 Jewett St. (401) 351-6111. FAX (401) 351-4621. @ statehouseinn@edgenet.net W www.providence-inn.com Built in 1889, the inn is a bit of country charm minutes away from downtown Providence. The artful blend of antiques and early American furnishings creates a warm and inviting atmosphere. Shared bath. ▨ ▥ P	AE MC V D	10			
PROVIDENCE: *Holiday Inn Downtown Providence* $$$ 21 Atwells St. (401) 831-3900. FAX (401) 751-0007. W www.basshotels.com In the heart of downtown, walking distance to Federal Hill and College Park. Indoor pool and whirlpool. The well-known Black Swan restaurant serves delicious steaks and seafood. Breakfast not included. ▨ ▥ ▧ ▤ ▧ ▤ P ▤	AE DC MC V D	274	■	●	
PROVIDENCE: *The Westin Providence* $$$$$ One West Exchange St. (800) WESTIN1 or (401) 598-8000. FAX (401) 598-8200. Four-time Pinnacle Award winner. The Agora restaurant was named by Esquire magazine as one of the best new restaurants in America. Connected to Providence Place Mall and the Rhode Island Convention Center. Breakfast not included. ▨ ▧ ▤ ▧ ▤ ▤ P ▤	AE DC MC V D	364 (28)	■	●	
WARWICK: *Master Hosts Inn* $$ 2138 Post Rd. (401) 737-7400. FAX (401) 739-6483. Located across from T.F. Green Airport, but away from the noise. Features eight different types of rooms, from economy class singles to executive suites with refrigerators and bars. Five minutes from Providence and 20 minutes from Newport. Pets allowed. ▨ ▥ ▧ P ▤	AE DC MC V D	103 (10)		●	
WESTERLY: *Sand Dollar Inn* $ 171 Post Rd. (800) 910-SAND or (401) 322-2000. FAX (401) 322-1590. W www.visitri.com/sanddollarinn Two miles from the coast, the inn is comprised of three buildings, including a cottage for four. The grounds contain many species of flowers and ornamental plantings. Closed from December to March. ▨ ▥ P ▤	AE MC V D	33		●	■

WESTERLY: *Andrea Hotel* ⑤⑤ MC V 25
89 Atlantic Ave. 【 *(401) 348-8788*. 𝗙𝗔𝗫 *(401) 596-1790*.
ⓦ *www.andreahotel.com*
A local landmark for more than 50 years, the hotel is located directly on a 300-foot private stretch of Misquamicut Beach. Nightly entertainment is a magnet for area locals, and there is a game room for youngsters. The restaurant is also well known. Breakfast not included.

WESTERLY: *The Villa* ⑤⑤⑤ AE MC V D 7
190 Shore Rd. 【 *(800) 722-9240 or (401) 596-1054*. 𝗙𝗔𝗫 *(401) 596- 6268*.
ⓦ *www.thevillaatwesterly.com*
A romantic hideaway of flower gardens, Italian porticos, and private terraces. Features an outdoor Jacuzzi and a Mediterranean designer pool. Each room has its own decorative theme. Near Newport and the ferry to Block Island. No children.

WOONSOCKET: *Pillsbury House* ⑤⑤ AE MC V 4 (1)
341 Prospect St. 【 *(800) 205-4112 or (401) 766-7983*. 𝗙𝗔𝗫 *(401) 762-0442*.
ⓐ *ngzu61a@prodigy.com* ⓦ *www.pillsburyhouse.com*
Built in 1875 on historic Prospect Street in Woonsocket's fashionable north end. Breakfast includes a choice of juices, fresh fruit, homemade breads or muffins with an entree and fresh coffee. Children over 12.

CONNECTICUT

BROOKLYN: *Friendship Valley B&B Inn* ⑤⑤ AE MC V 6 (1)
60 Pomfret Rd, Rte 169. 【 *(860) 779-9696*. 𝗙𝗔𝗫 *(860) 779-9844*.
ⓐ *friendshipvalley@snet.net* ⓦ *www.friendshipvalleyinn.com*
A quintessential New England inn with history. Each room is named after one of the previous families who owned the house, some of them prominent locally or nationally. No air-conditioning.

COVENTRY: *Special Joys B&B* ⑤ MC V 3
41 North River Rd. 【 *(860) 742-6359*. 𝗙𝗔𝗫 *(860) 742-9343*.
The owners' special devotion to antique toys is reflected throughout the premises, conservatory, and gardens. There is an antique doll and toy shop and museum on the premises, along with flower gardens and a solarium-lit dining area. Children over 6.

COVENTRY: *Bird-in-Hand B&B* ⑤⑤ AE DC MC V D 4 (3)
2011 Main St. 【 *(888) 426-9080 or (860) 742-0032*. 𝗙𝗔𝗫 *(860) 742-0032*.
ⓐ *info@thebirdinhand.com* ⓦ *www.thebirdinhand.com*
A historic building operating as an inn since 1800. A secret closet in one of the rooms is believed to have hidden slaves traveling on the Underground Railroad. Television in some rooms. Children over 10.

EAST HADDAM: *Bishopsgate Inn* ⑤⑤ DC MC V 6 (1)
7 Norwich Rd. 【 *(860) 873-1677*. 𝗙𝗔𝗫 *(860) 873-3898*.
ⓐ *ctkagel&assoc@bishopsgate.com* ⓦ *www.bishopsgate.com*
Built in 1818. Each floor has its own sitting area. Breakfast is ample, and a candlelight dinner in the room can be arranged. The suite has a sauna. Children over 5. Television in common rooms only.

GREENWICH: *Cos Cob Inn* ⑤⑤ AE DC MC V D 14 (5)
50 River Rd. 【 *(877) 549-4063 or (203) 661-5845*. 𝗙𝗔𝗫 *(203) 661-2054*.
ⓐ *innkeeper@coscobinn.com* ⓦ *www.coscobinn.com*
A country inn built in the 1800s and located in equally historic Greenwich. Every room has its own theme, with names like Captain's Quarters and The Parisian Room. Two rooms have a Jacuzzi.

GROTON: *The Clarion Inn* ⑤⑤⑤ AE DC MC V 70
156 King's Hwy. 【 *(800) 443-0611 or (860) 446-0660*. 𝗙𝗔𝗫 *(860) 445-4082*.
ⓦ *www.clarionhotels.com*
Located close to the USS *Nautilus* Memorial, Mohegan Sun Casino, and the beaches. Pets allowed for a charge. Free fitness facilities down the street.

HARTFORD: *Red Roof Inn* ⑤ AE DC MC V D 115
100 Weston St. 【 *(860) 843-7663*. 𝗙𝗔𝗫 *(860) 742-0433*.
ⓦ *www.redroof.com*
Hacienda design, 2 miles (3 km) from downtown. Movies and video games available in all rooms. Free papers in the morning. Pets allowed.

For key to symbols see back flap

		CREDIT CARDS	NUMBER OF ROOMS	RECOMMENDED RESTAURANT	CHILDREN'S FACILITIES	GARDEN OR TERRACE

Price categories for a standard double room per night, inclusive of breakfast, service charges, and any additional taxes:

$ under $100
$$ $100–$150
$$$ $150–$200
$$$$ $200–$250
$$$$$ over $250

CREDIT CARDS
Major credit cards accepted: *AE* American Express; *DC* Diners Club; *MC* MasterCard/Access; *V* Visa, *D* Discover Card.

NUMBER OF ROOMS
Number of rooms in the hotel (suites shown in parentheses).

RECOMMENDED RESTAURANT
Good restaurant within the hotel.

CHILDREN'S FACILITIES
Hotel has various facilities for young children.

GARDEN OR TERRACE
Hotel has a garden, courtyard, or terrace.

HARTFORD: *Crowne Plaza Hartford Downtown* $$$$
50 Morgan St. ((860) 549-2400. FAX (860) 549-7844.
@ cjohnston@bristolhotels.com W www.basshotels.com/hotels/bdlcc
A full-service hotel with simple elegance and luxury touches. There is a free shuttle within 3-mile (5-km) radius of the hotel. Walking distance to all the major attractions.

AE DC MC V D — 350 (5) — ●

HARTFORD: *Goodwin Hotel* $$$$$
One Haynes St. ((888)212-8380 or (860)246-7500.
FAX (860)247-4576. W www.goodwinhotel.com
The turn-of-the-century Goodwin serves guests with poise and style, but without pretension. The restaurant has been voted Best Hotel Dining by Connecticut Magazine for 10 years running.

AE DC MC V D — 124 (11) ■ ●

KENT: *Constitution Oak Farm* $
36 Beardsley Rd. ((860) 354-6495. @ constitutionoak@hotmail.com
Rustic environment on a 200-acre (80-ha) farm built in the 1830s. Rooms feature period furnishings and ceiling fans. two rooms have private baths. Television upon request. One mile from Lake Waramaug.

— 4 — — ■

LEDYARD: *Stonecroft Country Inn* $$
515 Pumpkin Hill Rd. ((860) 572-0771. FAX (860) 572-9161.
@ stoncrft@concentric.net W www.stonecroft.com
A former estate, the 1807 inn is listed on the National Register of Historic Places. Features rooms with whirlpools and fireplaces. The restaurant has been well reviewed. No children.

AE MC V D — 10 (2) ■ — ■

LITCHFIELD: *Litchfield Inn* $$
432 Bantam Rd. ((860) 567-3444 or (860) 567-4503. FAX (860) 567-5358.
@ litchfieldinn@compuserve.com W www.litchfieldinnct.com
A quaint country inn located just west of Litchfield. Features a gigantic chandelier, delicately carved main staircase, and four working fireplaces. Eight luxurious theme rooms.

AE DC MC V — 32 (8) ■ ● ■

MYSTIC: *Seaport Motor Inn* $$
Coogan Blvd. ((860) 536-2621. FAX (860) 536-4493.
Overlooking Olde Mistick Village and the Mystic Aquarium. Intimate dining at Jamm's Restaurant and adjoining Captain's Lounge. Close to all the major attractions, including beaches and USS *Nautilus*.

AE MC V D — 118 — ●

MYSTIC: *Foxwoods Resort Casino* $$$$
Rte 2. ((800) 369-9663 or (860) 312-3000. W www.foxwoods.com
Five casinos, 24 restaurants, and three hotels. The Great Cedar Hotel and the Grand Pequot Tower are above the casino. The Two Trees Inn, smaller and less expensive, is located half a mile away from the casino; shuttle bus service is provided.

AE DC MC V D — 1392 ■ ● ■

MYSTIC: *Zéphirine Boat & Breakfast* $$$$
Fort Rachel Marina. ((860) 572-0771. FAX (860) 572-9161.
@ stoncrft@concentric.net W www.stonecroft.com
An out-of-the-ordinary lodging alternative. This restored 40-foot antique wooden yacht, docked on the Mystic River, sleeps two. Large sitting room and afterdeck. Open June–October.

AE MC V D — 1 (1)

MYSTIC: *Steamboat Inn* $$$$$
73 Steamboat Wharf. ((860) 536-8300. FAX (860) 536-9528
@ sbwharf@aol.com W www.visitmystic.com/steamboat
Spacious rooms are named after famous Mystic ships from the schooner days. All rooms have whirlpool baths and antique furnishings. Magnificent views of the river and the dock.

AE MC V D — 10 (1) — ●

NEW CANAAN: *Village Inn of New Canaan* $$
122 Park St. **C** *(800) 370-2224 or (203) 966-8413.* **FAX** *(203) 966-8413.*
@ *frontdesk@villageinnnc.com* W *www.villageinnnc.com*
The 18th-century inn combines great atmosphere with up-to-date
comfort. Adjoining rooms and family apartments with kitchen are
available. Individual voice mail for each guest.

AE DC MC V D	32 (7)	●

NEW LONDON: *Lighthouse Inn* $$$
6 Guthrie Place. **C** *(888) 443-8411 or (860) 443-8411.* **FAX** *(860) 437-7027.*
W *www.lighthouseinn-ct.com*
The former home of steel magnate Charles S. Guthrie, this 1902
Mediterranean-style mansion has beautiful views of Long Island Sound
and is located close to major attractions in the area.

AE MC V	52 (5)	● ■

SIMSBURY: *Iron Horse Inn* $
969 Hopmeadow St. **C** *(800) 245-9938 or (860) 658-2216.* **FAX** *(860) 651-0822.*
W *www.ironhorseofsimsbury.com*
A small inn located in the heart of Simsbury, close to a scenic walking
path leading behind the old estates. Each room has a voice mailbox
and a private balcony. Ideal for traveling families. Pets are allowed in
some rooms.

AE MC V	27 (1)	● ■

WINDSOR: *Residence Inn by Marriott* $$
100 Dunfey Lane. **C** *(800) 331-3131 or (860) 688-7474.* **FAX** *(860) 683-8457.*
Complimentary beverages and hors d'oeuvres Monday through Thursday.
All rooms have kitchens, movies, VCRs, coffeemakers, microwaves, and
refrigerators. Fifteen minutes from downtown Hartford. Pets allowed.

AE DC MC V D	96 (96)	● ■

VERMONT

ARLINGTON: *Inn on Covered Bridge Green* $$$
3587 River Rd. **C** *(802) 375-9489 or (800)726-9480.* **FAX** *(802)-375-1208.*
@ *cbg@sover.net* W *www.coveredbridgegreen.com*
In this 1792 farmhouse, the former home of Norman Rockwell, each
room has its own bath and fireplace. Rockwell's former studio as well as
what was once the barn have been turned into fully equipped cottages.
Walking trails. Mountain bikes and canoe rides offered.

MC V	10 (1)	■

ARLINGTON: *The West Mountain Inn* $
144 West Mountain Inn Rd. **C** *(802) 375-6516* **FAX** *(802) 375-6553*
@ *info@westmountaininn.com* W *www.westmountaininn.com*
Situated on 150 acres (60 ha) of woodland, complete with skiing
and hiking trails, a bird sanctuary, and even llamas, the seven-gabled
West Mountain Inn is for those seeking outdoor activities and
relaxation. Inside, expect hearty country cuisine and charming
decor.

AE MC V D	18 (6)	● ■

BRATTLEBORO: *Days Inn* $
959 Putney Rd. **C** *(800) 544-8313 or (802) 254-4583* **FAX** *(802) 254-4585*
A modern and comfortable chain hotel. Good value with some extra
amenities, such as a free movie channel.

AE DC MC V D	48	●

BURLINGTON: *Radisson Hotel* $$$$
60 Battery St. **C** *(800) 333-3333 or (802) 658-6500.* **FAX** *(802) 658-4659.*
@ *rhbguest@hotmail.com* W *www.radisson.com*
The Radisson is Burlington's most upscale hotel and is right in the heart of the
downtown core. The best rooms have breathtaking views of Lake Champlain
with the Adirondacks rising behind.

AE DC MC V D	256 (10)	■ ● ■

CHITTENDEN: *Mountain Top Inn* $$$$$
195 Mountain Top Rd. **C** *(800) 445-2100 or (802) 483-2311.* **FAX** *(802) 483-6373.*
@ *info@mountaintopinn.com* W *www.mountaintopinn.com*
Intimate country inn set in central Vermont, the 35 rooms of the main
inn are supplemented by 12 separate cottages and chalet units. Closed
between Columbus Day and Christmas, and again from mid-March to
Memorial Day. TVs in main lodge common rooms.

AE MC V	47	■ ● ■

COLCHESTER: *Fairfield Inn* $
15 South Park Dr. **C** *(800) 228-2800 or 802-655-1400.* **FAX** *(802) 338-9158.*
@ *figm@writemail.com* W *www.fairfieldinn.com*
The Fairfield Inn is part of the Marriott Hotels chain of affordable
accommodations. It is good value, especially since it is located close to
downtown Burlington.

AE D MC V	117	

For key to symbols see back flap

<table>
<tr><td>

Price categories for a standard double room per night, inclusive of breakfast, service charges, and any additional taxes:

$ under $100
$$ $100–$150
$$$ $150–$200
$$$$ $200–$250
$$$$$ over $250

</td><td>

CREDIT CARDS
Major credit cards accepted: *AE* American Express; *DC* Diners Club; *MC* MasterCard/Access; *V* VISA, *D* Discover Card.

NUMBER OF ROOMS
Number of rooms in the hotel (suites shown in parentheses).

RECOMMENDED RESTAURANT
Good restaurant within the hotel.

CHILDREN'S FACILITIES
Hotel has various facilities for young children.

GARDEN OR TERRACE
Hotel has a garden, courtyard, or terrace.

</td></tr>
</table>

	CREDIT CARDS	NUMBER OF ROOMS	RECOMMENDED RESTAURANT	CHILDREN'S FACILITIES	GARDEN OR TERRACE
CRAFTSBURY COMMON: *The Inn on the Common* $$$$$ 1162 North Craftsbury Rd. (800) 521-2233 or (802) 586-9619. FAX (802) 586-2249. @ info@innonthecommon.com W www.innonthecommon.com Three restored Federal homes nestled in an idyllic village setting, Features elegantly decorated rooms, beautiful views, and outstanding cuisine as well as excellent cross-country skiing. One television in sitting room. Rooms do not have air-conditioning. ▣	AE MC V	16 (1)	■	●	■
GRAFTON: *Old Tavern at Grafton* $$$$ 92 Main St. (800) 843-1801 or (802) 843-2231. FAX (802) 843-2245. @ oldtavern@vermontel.net W www.old-tavern.com Along with 11 rooms in the main building, the Old Tavern rents out a number of charming cottages and guest houses around town. The Old Tavern is a place of peace and quiet—there are no televisions or telephones in the rooms. Only the executive suite is air-conditioned. ▣	AE MC V	58 (10)	■	●	■
KILLINGTON: *Mountain Meadows Lodge* $$ 285 Thundering Brook Rd. (800) 370-4567 or (802) 775-1010. @ havefun@mtnmeadowslodge.com W www.mtmeadowslodge.com Vermont's only mountain lodge set on both a lake and the famous Adirondack Trail, the lodge is perfect for outdoor types. It features excellent family services, including a state-licensed children's center and baby-sitting (with advance notice). ▣	AE MC V	16 (1)	■	●	■
MANCHESTER: *The Equinox Resort* $$$$$ 3567 Main St. (802) 362-4700. FAX (802) 362-1595. @ postmaster@equinox.com W www.equinoxresort.com This historic 18th-century resort has stunning public spaces and spacious, country-style rooms. Guests can also take advantage of the resort's activities including golf, falconry, fishing, and off-road driving (separate charges apply for most activities). ▣	AE DC MC V D	183	■	●	■
MIDDLEBURY: *The Middlebury Inn* $$ 14 Court House Sq. (800) 842-4666 or (802) 388-4961. FAX (802) 388-4563. @ midinnvt@sover.net W www.middleburyinn.com The town's main hostelery since 1827, this historic inn offers well-equipped rooms furnished with reproduction antiques, all with private baths, some with whirlpool tubs. Two-room suites with shared bath are geared to families. ▣	AE DC MC V D	75 (8)		●	
MONTPELIER: *Econo Lodge* $ 101 North Hill St. (802) 223-5258. FAX (802) 223-0716. @ gitndra101@cs.com W www.econolodge.com Comfortable, clean, and basic, the EconoLodge is located less than a mile from downtown Montpelier. ▣	AE DC MC V D	54			
MONTPELIER: *The Inn at Montpelier* $$ 147 Main St. (802) 223-2727. FAX (802) 223-0722. @ mail2inn@aol.com W www.innatmontpelier.com These two beautifully renovated adjacent Federal-style homes are the capital city's most stately lodgings. A large veranda wraps around the brick Lamp Langdon house. If it's winter, ask for one of the six rooms with fireplaces. ▣	AE DC MC V D	19 (2)		●	■
NORTH HERO: *North Hero House Inn & Restaurant* $$ 3643 Rte 2. (888) 525-3644 or (802) 372-4732. FAX (802) 372-3218. @ nhhlake@aol.com W www.northherohouse.com Three of this inn's four buildings front on beautiful Lake Champlain. The main house, complete with library and pub, sits just across the road. Guests have access to the a private beach. ▣	AE MC V	26 (2)	■	●	■

RICHMOND: *The Richmond Victorian Inn* $
191 East Main St. ((888) 242-3362 or (802) 434-4410. FAX (802) 434-4411.
@ gailclar@together.net W www.richmondvictorianinn.com
Located in the foothills of the Green Mountains, this inexpensive inn's six
guest rooms are furnished in a country Victorian style with antiques and
quilts. No televisions or air-conditioning in rooms. 🛏 🎯 P

AE DC MC V — 6 (1)

ST. JOHNSBURY: *Comfort Inn and Suites* $$$
703 Rte 5 S. ((800) 228 5150 or (802) 748-1500. FAX (802) 748-1243.
@ vermonttajmahal@aol.com W www.vtcomfortinnsuites.com
A deluxe hotel with a full range of services and elegant interior decor.
All rooms have separate sitting area with extra amenities such as in-room
iron, coffeemaker, hair dryer, and movies. 🛏 🎯 🔲 ♨ 🍴 🚿 P ♿

AE DC MC V D — 107 (5)

SHELBURNE: *Inn at Shelburne Farms* $$
1611 Harbor Rd. ((802) 985-8498. FAX (802) 985-1233.
W www.shelburnefarms.org
Built in 1899 on a bluff overlooking Lake Champlain, the inn is situated
on a 1,000-acre (400-ha) property, landscaped by Frederick Law
Olmstead. Guests can enjoy the private beach, views of the lake, and the
sumptuous bedrooms, 17 of which have private baths. No televisions or
air-conditioning. 🛏 🎯 🍴 P

AE DC MC V D — 24

STOWE: *Wood Chip Inn* $
4492 Mountain Rd. ((800) 676 9181 or (802) 253-9080. FAX (802) 253-7873.
@ wdchipinn@aol.com W www.gostowe.com
Charming and economical, the Wood Chip Inn offers traditional Vermont
breakfasts as well as homemade breads and soups. Not all rooms have
air-conditioning and television. 🛏 🎯 P ♿

AE MC V — 9

STOWE: *Trapp Family Lodge* $$$$$
700 Trapp Hill Rd. ((800) 826-7000 or (802) 253-8511. FAX (802) 253-5740.
@ info@trappfamily.com W www.trappfamily.com
World-famous 93-room resort on 2,700-acre (1.092-ha) property. Along
with large Austran-style main lodge, the resort features 100 guest houses,
nightly entertainment, a range of recreational activities, and exquisite
cuisine. Some rooms air-conditioned. 🛏 🎯 🔲 🍴 ♨ 🍴 🚿 P ♿

AE DC MC V D — 116 (18)

WATERBURY: *Holiday Inn & Spa* $$$
45 Blush Hill Rd. ((800) 621-7822 or (802) 244-7822. FAX (802) 244-7822.
@ holidays@together.net W www.holiday-inn.com/waterburyvt
Situated on a plateau in the heart of the Green Mountains central to
Burlington, Montpelier, and Stowe, this is the perfect launching point for
day trips around north and central Vermont. 🛏 🎯 🍴 ♨ 🍴 P

AE DC MC V D — 79 (1)

NEW HAMPSHIRE

ALTON BAY: *Bay Side Inn on Lake Winnipesaukee* $
Rte 11D. ((603) 875-5005. @ bsi@worldpath.net W www.baysideinn.com
Open May to October, this lovely inn on the shores of Lake Winnipesaukee
offers complimentary sailboats, a lakeside sundeck, and a breathtaking view
of the White Mountains. Cottages available. No air-conditioning. 🛏 🎯 P ♿

MC V — 18

BRETTON WOODS: *Mount Washington Hotel and Resort* $$$$$
Rte 302. ((800) 258-0330 or (603) 278-1000. FAX (603) 278-8838.
@ hotelinfo@mtwashington.com W www.mtwashington.com
Since 1902, this elegant resort has offered high quality service in a beautiful
natural setting. Dinner at any of the five restaurants is included, and the
cool mountain air keeps the rooms comfortable during the summer season.
Air conditioning in Tower Suites only. 🛏 🎯 🔲 🍴 ♨ 🍴 🚿 P ♿

AE MC V D — 200 (24)

CONCORD: *The Centennial Inn* $$$
96 Pleasant St. ((603) 225-7102. FAX (603) 225-5031.
@ centennialinn@totalnet.nh.net W www.someplacesdifferent.com
Housed in a restored 1876 Victorian mansion, this centrally located inn
provides handsomely furnished rooms and suites for the business and
pleasure traveler. 🛏 🎯 🔲 🍴 🚿 P ♿

AE DC MC V D — 32 (5)

ENFIELD: *Mary Keane House Bed and Breakfast* $$
98 Chosen Vale Lane. ((603) 632-4241.
@ mary.keane.house@valley.net W www.marykeanehouse.com
A wonderful 1929 residence that is a romantic, relaxing home away from
home on a huge waterfront property. Ideally located within walking
distance of restaurants and the Shaker Village. 🛏 🎯 P

AE DC MC V — 4 (3)

For key to symbols see back flap

Price categories for a standard double room per night, inclusive of breakfast, service charges, and any additional taxes:

$ under $100
$$ $100–$150
$$$ $150–$200
$$$$ $200–$250
$$$$$ over $250

CREDIT CARDS
Major credit cards accepted: *AE* American Express; *DC* Diners Club; *MC* MasterCard/Access; *V* VISA, *D* Discover Card.

NUMBER OF ROOMS
Number of rooms in the hotel (suites shown in parentheses).

RECOMMENDED RESTAURANT
Good restaurant within the hotel.

CHILDREN'S FACILITIES
Hotel has various facilities for young children.

GARDEN OR TERRACE
Hotel has a garden, courtyard, or terrace.

	CREDIT CARDS	NUMBER OF ROOMS	RECOMMENDED RESTAURANT	CHILDREN'S FACILITIES	GARDEN OR TERRACE
EXETER: *The Inn and Conference Center of Exeter* $$$ 90 Front St. (603) 772-5901. FAX (603) 778-8757. @ sales@innofexeter.com W www.someplacesdifferent.com Georgian style inn with good restaurant. Rooms have four-poster beds and antique furnishings.	AE DC MC V D	46 (3)	■		■
FRANCONIA: *Lovett's Inn* $$ 1474 Profile Rd. (800) 356-3802 or (603) 823-7761. FAX (603) 823-8802. For 70 years the distinctive hospitality of this former country estate has attracted such guests as movie star Bette Davis and members of the Kennedy clan. Some rooms have television and air-conditioning.	DC MC V D	21 (5)	■	●	■
FRANCONIA: *The Franconia Inn* $$$$ 1300 Easton Rd. (603) 823-5542. FAX (603) 823-8078. @ info@franconiainn.com W www.franconiainn.com Cozy turn-of-the-century inn, surrounded by stunning scenery. This place has enough sports and activities keep outdoor enthusiasts satisfied year round. No air-conditioning or television.	AE MC V	34 (4)	■	●	■
HAMPTON: *Ashworth by the Sea* $$ 295 Ocean Blvd. (800) 345-6736 or (603) 926-6762. FAX (603) 926-2002. A year-round beachfront hotel with an air of old-fashioned elegance and relaxation. Spacious rooms with ocean views.	AE DC MC V D	105 (1)			■
HANOVER: *Hanover Inn* $$$$$ Wheelock & Main. (800) 443-7024 or (603) 643-4300. FAX (603) 646-3744. @ info@hanoverinn.com W www.hanoverinn.com Attentive service and excellent dining mark this elegant inn, which has been operating for more than 200 years. All guest rooms are decorated in Colonial-style. The restaurant has an award-winning selection of wines.	AE DC MC V D	92 (22)	■	●	■
KEENE: *Carriage Barn Bed and Breakfast* $$ 358 Main St. (603) 357-3812. @ carriagebarn@carriagebarn.com W www.carriagebarn.com Cheerfully decorated with local antiques, this home offers a relaxed and peaceful environment in the heart of town. No television.	AE MC V D	4		●	
MANCHESTER: *The Highlander Inn* $$$ 2 Highlander Way. (800) 625-6426 or (603) 548-9248. FAX (603) 625-6466. W www.highlanderinn.com A popular resort for Bostonians since the turn of the century. Its proximity to the airport is a great convenience for both business and pleasure travelers.	AE DC MC V D	66 (8)	■	●	■
MEREDITH: *Meredith Inn Bed and Breakfast* $$ 2 Waukewan St. (603) 279-0000. FAX (603) 279-4017. @ inn1897@meredithinn.com W www.meredithinn.com A recently restored Victorian home refurbished with all the modern amenities. Convenient to Lake Winnipesaukee activities. No air conditioning.	MC V D	8			
NEW LONDON: *The New London Inn* $$ 140 Main St. (800) 526-2791 or (603) 526-2791. FAX (603) 526-2749. @ nlinn@kear.net W www.newlondoninn.com Federal-style 1792 inn furnished with European and American antiques. It has a library, a tavern, and dining room overlooking the common. No air-conditioning; some rooms have television.	AE MC V	24 (1)	■	●	■

NORTH CONWAY: *Junge's Motel* $$ | AE MC V D | 28 (2) | ● ■
1858 White Mountain Hwy. ((603) 356-2886. W www.jungesmotel.com
Affordable accommodations offering the outdoor enthusiast year-round
access to sports and activities. 🏊 ♨ 🌊 P 🏄

PORTSMOUTH: *The Inn at Christian Shore* $$ | MC V | 5 | ■
335 Maplewood Ave. ((603) 431-6770. FAX (603) 431-7743.
A well-preserved early 1800s home furnished with a mix of antiques,
African art, and contemporary paintings. The gourmet breakfasts offer
vast choice. 🏊 P 🏄

PORTSMOUTH: *Sheraton Harborside Portsmouth* $$ | AE DC MC V D | 202 (21) | ■ ●
250 Market St. ((603) 431-2300. FAX (603) 431-7805.
@ info@sheratonportsmouth.com W www.starwood.com
A modern hotel ideally located in the historic waterfront district. Rates
vary according to level of occupancy. 🏊 ♨ 🏊 Y 🌊 🍴 🛏 P 🏄

ROCHESTER: *The Governor's Inn* $ | AE MC V D | 20 (3) | ■
78 Wakefield St. ((603) 332-0107. FAX (603) 335-1984.
W www.governorsinn.com
A 1920s Georgian Colonial home, now an inn and restaurant. Meals are
served in the courtyard in the summer months. 🏊 ♨ Y 🛏 P

SUNAPEE: *The Inn at Sunapee* $ | AE MC V D | 16 | ■
125 Burkehaven Hill Rd. ((800) 327-2466 or (603) 763-4444. FAX (603) 763-9456.
@ innatsunapee@kear.net W www.innatsunapee.com
An 1875 New England home overlooking beautiful Lake Sunapee.
Country style hospitality with a touch of Asia in the food and decor.
No television or air-conditioning. 🏊 ♨ Y 🌊 P 🏄

TROY: *The Inn at East Hill Farm* $$$$$ | MC V D | 63 | ● ■
460 Monadnock St. ((603) 242-6495. FAX (603) 242-7709.
@ info@east-hill-farm.com W www.east-hill-farm.com
Set on 150 acres (60 ha), this year-round resort has farm activities for
children and pleasing amenities for adults. Above rates are based on a
family of four; weekly rates are much lower. All meals are included.
Some rooms have television and air-conditioning. 🏊 ♨ 🌊 🛏 P 🏄

WEIRS BEACH: *Lake Winnipesaukee Motel* $ | AE MC V D | 16 | ● ■
350 Daniel Webster Hwy. ((603) 366-5502. FAX (603) 366-2388.
W www.lakewinnipesaukeemotel.com
This small motel takes prides in its warm hospitality, peaceful
surroundings, and 45 years of experience. A private, two-bedroom house
is also available for larger groups. 🏊 ♨ 🌊 P 🏄

WOLFEBORO: *The Wolfeboro Inn* $$ | AE MC V | 44 (3) | ■ ■
90 Main St. ((800) 451-2389 or (603) 569-3016. FAX (603) 569-5375.
@ webmaster@wolfeboroinn.com W www.wolfeboroinn.com
Historic inn on the waterfront of America's oldest summer resort, offering
tastefully decorated rooms, fine dining, a private beach, and a solid
reputation for comfort and service. 🏊 ♨ Y 🛏 P 🏄

MAINE

BANGOR: *Fairfield Inn* $ | AE DC MC V D | 153 | ●
300 Odlin Rd. ((800) 228-2800 or (207) 990-0001. FAX (207) 990-0917.
W www.marriott.com
A modern, fully equipped hotel, conveniently located less than 1 mile
(1.6 km) from downtown Bangor. Continental breakfast, juice, and coffee
available 24 hours a day. 🏊 ♨ 🌊 🍴 🛏 P 🏄

BAR HARBOR: *Mill Brook House* $$ | MC V D | 3 | ■
Mill Brook Rd. ((877) 288-3860 or (207) 288-3860.
@ millbrook@acadia.net W www.BarHarborLodging.com
Set on 4.5-acre- (1.8-ha-) property with brook, waterfalls, and swimming
hole, this inn offers quiet country accommodations near Acadia National
Park. Rooms do not have televisions or air-conditioning. 🏊 ♨ P

BAR HARBOR: *Mira Monte Inn and Suites* $$$ | AE DC MC V D | 16 (3) | ■
69 Mount Desert St. ((800) 553-5109 or (207) 288-4263.
FAX (207) 288-3115. @ marian@miramonte.com W www.miramonte.com
Constructed in 1864, this is one of only two B&Bs in town owned by Bar
Harbor natives. It features two formal gardens. All rooms have air-
conditioning, private bath, fireplace and/or balcony. 🏊 ♨ 🛏 P 🏄

For key to symbols see back flap

Price categories for a standard double room per night, inclusive of breakfast, service charges, and any additional taxes:

$ under $100
$$ $100–$150
$$$ $150–$200
$$$$ $200–$250
$$$$$ over $250

CREDIT CARDS
Major credit cards accepted: *AE* American Express; *DC* Diners Club; *MC* MasterCard/Access; *V* VISA, *D* Discover Card.

NUMBER OF ROOMS
Number of rooms in the hotel (suites shown in parentheses).

RECOMMENDED RESTAURANT
Good restaurant within the hotel.

CHILDREN'S FACILITIES
Hotel has various facilities for young children.

GARDEN OR TERRACE
Hotel has a garden, courtyard, or terrace.

	CREDIT CARDS	NUMBER OF ROOMS	RECOMMENDED RESTAURANT	CHILDREN'S FACILITIES	GARDEN OR TERRACE
BETHEL: *Bethel Inn and Country Club* $$$$$ On the Common. (800) 654-0125 or (207) 824-2175. FAX (207) 824-2233. @ info@bethelinn.com W www.bethelinn.com A premier Maine resort, the property has its own championship golf course, two dining rooms, a fitness center, tennis course and private meeting facilities. Price includes free golf and dinner.	AE DC MC V D	138 (12)	■	●	■
CAPE ELIZABETH: *Inn by the Sea* $$$$$ 40 Bowery Beach Rd. (800) 888-4287 or (207) 799-3134. FAX (207) 799-4779. @ innmaine@aol.com W www.innbythesea.com Every room in this luxurious inn is a suite, each with an ocean view from the porch or deck. Minutes away from Portland, the inn has a gourmet restaurant, private beach, and tennis courts.	AE MC V D	43 (43)	■	●	■
CARIBOU: *Caribou Inn and Convention Center* $ 19 Main St. (800) 235-0466 or (207) 498-3733. FAX (207) 498-3149. @ cicc3733@aol.com W www.caribouinn.com With low rates and wide range of facilities and in-room amenities, this inn offers great value. The Greenhouse Restaurant is known for the best and least expensive breakfasts in the area.	AE DC MC V D	73 (3)	■	●	■
CARRABASSETT VALLEY: *Sugarloaf/USA Resort* $$$ Rte 27. (800) THE-LOAF or (207) 237-2000. FAX (207) 237-2718. @ info@sugarloaf.com W www.sugarloaf.com One of New England's most renowned ski resorts. Guests may use health club and take ski or snowboard lessons with no extra charge. Golf course consistently ranks as one of America's most picturesque. More than 200 one- to five-bedroom condo units also available.	AE MC V D	162 (24)	■	●	■
EAST MACHIAS: *Riverside Inn and Restaurant* $$ Rte 1. (207) 255-4134. FAX (207) 255-3580. @ riversideinn@nemaine.com W www.riversideinn-maine.com Situated on the East Machias River, this serene getaway features rooms individually decorated with antiques. All have private baths. The inn's terraced perennial garden is a great place for evening strolls.	AE MC V	4 (2)	■		■
FRYEBURG: *Oxford House Inn* $$$ 105 Main St. (800) 261-7206. FAX (207) 935-7046. @ innkeeper@oxfordhouseinn.com W www.oxfordhouseinn.com A charming bed-and-breakfast located in the activity-filled White Mountains and Western Lakes region of Maine. The inn has a gourmet restaurant and four beautifully decorated rooms.	AE DC MC V D	4	■		■
GREENVILLE: *Big Squaw Mountain Resort* $ Rte 15. (207) 695-1000. FAX (207) 695-4384. Economical accommodation for skiers and outdoor enthusiasts visiting Big Moose Mountain. Some dorm-style rooms accommodate up to eight people. Tennis courts are also available.	AE MC V D	52		●	
GREENVILLE: *Greenville Inn* $$ Norris St. (888) 695-6000 or (207) 695-2206. FAX (207) 695-0335. @ gvlinn@moosehead.net W www.greenvilleinn.com Along with the four rooms in the main building, this beautifully appointed Victorian inn has six cottages, all with porches or decks. Televisions in some rooms. No air-conditioning.	MC V D	4 (2)	■		■
KENNEBUNK: *The Beach House Inn* $$$$ 211 Beach Ave. (207) 967-3850. FAX (207) 967-4719. @ innkeeper@beachhseinn.com W www.beachhseinn.com A luxurious bed-and-breakfast located on the oceanside at Kennebunk Beach, featuring a large wraparound porch. All rooms have views of the ocean or of the manicured garden and private bath.	AE MC V	35 (1)			

KENNEBUNKPORT: *The Colony Hotel* ⑤⑤⑤⑤⑤ AE MC V │ 123
140 Ocean Ave. 【 *(800) 552-2363 or (207) 967-3331.*
FAX *(207) 967-8738.* @ *reservations@thecolonyhotel.com*
W *www.thecolonyhotel.com*
A short walk from Kennebunkport, the majestic Colony Hotel is perched
overlooking the ocean. This environmentally responsible resort offers a
heated saltwater pool, private beach, and extensive gardens. Closed from
mid-October to mid-May. 〓 〓 〓 〓 〓 〓 P 〓

MILLINOCKET: *Best Western Heritage Motor Inn* ⑤ AE DC MC V D │ 48
935 Central St. 【 *(800) 528-1234 or (207) 723-9777.* FAX *(207) 723-9777.*
W *www.bestwestern.com*
Air-conditioned rooms at a reasonable cost. The property connects to most
cross-country and snowmobile trails heading to northern Maine. A
swimming pond is steps away. 〓 〓 〓 〓 P 〓

NEW HARBOR: *Hotel Pemaquid* ⑤ │ 28 (4)
3098 Bristol Rd. 【 *(207) 677-2312.* W *www.hotelpemaquid.com*
A classic Maine inn, decorated with antiques, this former farmhouse first
welcomed guests in 1888. A short walk from the coast and near the
Pemaquid Point lighthouse. Some rooms have shared bath. Breakfast not
served. No air conditioning. Closed mid-Oct to mid-May. 〓 〓 P 〓

NEWRY: *Sunday River Inn* ⑤⑤⑤ AE MC V D │ 24
23 Skiway Rd. 【 *(207) 824-2410.* FAX *(207) 824-3181.*
@ *info@sundayriverinn.com* W *www.sundayriverinn.com*
Family-oriented inn located .5 miles (.8 km) from Sunday River ski hill.
Cross-country ski center and skating and sliding areas located at the inn.
Closed from April 1 to the end of November. 〓 〓 〓 P 〓

OGUNQUIT: *The Cliff House* ⑤⑤⑤⑤ AE MC V D │ 168 (2)
Shore Rd. 【 *(207) 361-1000.* FAX *(207) 361-2122.*
@ *cliffhouse@maine.com* W *www.cliffhousemaine.com*
Oceanside resort built in 1872 with full floor devoted to recreation. A licensed
masseuse is on staff. All rooms are air-conditioned and have balconies. Cliff
House Trolley takes guests to spots of interest in the area. Closed from early
December to late March. 〓 〓 〓 〓 〓 〓 〓 P 〓

PORTLAND: *Inn at St. John* ⑤ AE DC MC V D │ 37
939 Congress. 【 *(800) 636-9127 or (207) 773-6481.* FAX *(207) 756-7629.*
@ *info@innatstjohn.com* W *www.innatstjohn.com*
Century-old inn just minutes from Portland's Old Port, Waterfront, and
Arts districts. Rooms are tastefully decorated and all are air-conditioned.
〓 〓 P 〓

PORTLAND: *Portland Regency Hotel* ⑤⑤⑤⑤ AE DC MC V D │ 95 (8)
20 Milk St. 【 *(800) 727-3436 or (207) 774-4200.* FAX *(207) 775-2150.*
@ *publicpublic@the regency.com* W *www.theregency.com*
Situated in the heart of the Old Port district, the Regency is Portland's
premiere full-service hotel. The hotel's fitness center is free for guests.
〓 〓 〓 〓 〓 P 〓

RANGELEY: *North Country Inn Bed and Breakfast* ⑤ MC V │ 4
Maine St. 【 *(800) 295-4968 or (207) 864-2440.*
@ *info@northcountrybb.com* W *www.northcountrybb.com*
This 19th century Colonial bed and breakfast has a huge porch that looks
out onto Rangeley Lake and surrounding mountains. No air conditioning.
Children under eight not welcome. 〓 〓 P

RANGELEY: *Rangeley Inn* ⑤⑤ AE MC V D │ 50 (1)
51 Main. 【 *(800) 666-3867 or (207) 864-3341.* FAX *(207) 864-3634.*
@ *rangeinn@rangeley.org* W *www.rangeleyinn.com*
Rooms available in either the Main Inn or the Motor Lodge (prices nearly
the same) as well as two lakeside cabins. Located two miles from public
beach. Jacuzzis in some rooms in Main Inn. 〓 〓 〓 〓 P 〓

ROCKWOOD: *The Birches Resort* ⑤ AE MC V D │ 25
Birches Rd. 【 *(800) 825-9453 or (207) 534-7305.* FAX *(207) 534-8835.*
@ *wwld@aol.com* W *www.birches.com*
The Birches offers accommodation in cabins (15), lodge rooms (4), and
private rental homes (6). The 11,000-acre (4,450-ha) resort is launching
point and host for wilderness expeditions. Meal plans are offered. Also
has outdoor Jacuzzi and sauna. Television in common room.
〓 〓 〓 〓 P 〓

For key to symbols see back flap

WHERE TO EAT

To MANY OUTSIDERS, New England is synonymous with simple, hearty, somewhat boring fare. While it is true that a traditional meal of the past often consisted of cod or boiled beef and cabbage served with potatoes, the regional menu is substantially more varied and tempting. Local cheeses and produce from rural areas complement the exquisite seafood, often caught fresh the same day, that is found up and down the coast. In recent years, the New England dining experience has been expanded to include a host of ethnic flavors, thanks to a steady stream of immigrants into the large urban areas. As well as bringing with them new dishes from their homeland, these chefs are finding novel ways to prepare some old New England standbys. Boston's restaurant scene is particularly vibrant. The city's top restaurants serve a medley of styles, such as French and Italian, often using other Mediterranean and Asian accents. Boston was once called "Bean Town" because of the popularity of its baked beans; now it has good Indian, Southeast Asian, Latin American, and Caribbean restaurants.

Fanciful Maine eatery sign

EATING THROUGH THE DAY

MOST RESTAURANTS usually serve breakfast from 6 or 7am until 11am or noon. Some establishments will serve you breakfast at any hour of the day. The choice is varied, with some spots offering little more than a bagel and a coffee and others whipping up portions of eggs, bacon, and sausages hefty enough to keep you going almost all day.

Lunch can run anytime from 11:30am until 3pm, and is equally varied. In busy Boston, businessmen can be seen gulping down a sandwich at the counter of a local deli or sitting down to enjoy a

An Italian atmosphere at Boston's Caffè Vittoria

sumptuous meal at one of the city's many fine restaurants. In many places, the lunch menu is the same as it is for dinner, with smaller portions and significantly lower prices.

Traditionally New Englanders serve up large dinners. You can usually sit down between 6 and 10pm. Some restaurants, notably those in Boston's Chinatown and Kenmore Square, stay open late, supported mostly by the hungry crowds heading home from the dance clubs and bars.

It is not uncommon for restaurants to be closed on Mondays or during select hours between lunch and dinner. Some of the finer establishments may serve dinner exclusively. As always, you should check in advance.

Restaurant in Connecticut

PAYING AND TIPPING

WAITERS ARE generally paid fairly low wages, meaning they earn the bulk of their income through tips. This means that all restaurants with table service expect some sort of gratuity at the end of the meal. Each state charges a different meal tax, but it is standard practice to leave between 15 and 20 percent of the pre-tax bill as the tip. If the service is good or bad, adjust the tip rate accordingly. If you are paying by credit card, you may include the tip in the charged amount on the space provided on the receipt. Some fast-food restaurants have optional tip-jars next to the cashier.

Relaxed ambience of a typical beachfront seafood eatery

Rustic charm of the Grist Mill Restaurant in Killington, Vermont

ALCOHOL AND SMOKING

ALMOST ALL restaurants have strictly defined smoking and non-smoking sections, and an increasing number are banning smoking all together. Be sure to specify where you wish to be seated when making your reservation. Bars, on the other hand, almost always allow smoking.

Twenty-one is the legal drinking age, so underage travelers should be aware that they will be denied access to most bars. They will also not be allowed to order wine with dinner in restaurants. The majority of places are very strict about this and will often require you to show photo ID before you are served. Passports are generally the best form of identification, as many people are unfamiliar with driver's licenses from abroad.

DRESS CODES

NEW ENGLAND is a relaxed place where, for the most part, people dress on the casual side when they are dining out. This is especially true along the coast, where the casual beach atmosphere carries over into restaurants. There, shorts and T-shirts are commonplace. However, some establishments do have very strict dress codes. For the top dining rooms, a jacket and tie are required for gentlemen and the equivalent is expected for women. Formal evening wear is uncommon, but in some of the finest restaurants it is not out of place.

TRADITIONAL NEW ENGLAND FOOD

COASTAL NEW ENGLAND is all about seafood, pure and simple. Of the many types of fish served up fresh from the fisherman's net, swordfish, bluefish, tuna, and striped bass are among diners' favorites. Shellfish are also plentiful. You will find just about every method under

Outdoor dining in the summer in Portsmouth, New Hampshire

the sun for preparing mussels, clams, and oysters – and all of them delicious. On chilly autumn days, nothing is quite as fortifying as a bowl of thick clam chowder.

Lobster, however, is the quintessential meal in maritime New England. Although they are found off Rhode Island and Massachusetts, the lobsters from Maine are most coveted. Eating a lobster can be a messy undertaking, which is why all seafood restaurants stock plastic bibs and a large supply of napkins for their customers. The more rudimentary eateries, tiny little shacks dotting the coastline and serving fresh seafood on paper plates, may not be as well equipped, which is why it is always a good idea to carry a roll of paper towels in your car.

Not all New England delicacies are pulled from the sea, however. Vermont is the dairy capital of the region, producing high-quality yogurt and cheese, especially cheddars.

Throughout the spring, summer, and fall, area restaurants and markets take advantage of the fresh produce being harvested locally. Delicate fiddleheads make a brief appearance on menus during the spring – though the uninitiated should eat them sparingly – as do fresh strawberries in the early summer. The region, particularly Maine, is also known for its delicious blueberries that are used in any number of pies, muffins, and pancakes. In the late summer, visitors can indulge in sweet New England corn.

NEW ENGLAND'S MAPLE SYRUP

During the spring thaw in late March and early April, New England farmers hammer spigots into the trunks of their sugar maple trees in order to collect the trees' clear, slightly sweet sap in buckets. Traditionally sap is then poured into vats back at the "sugarhouse" and boiled for hours. When most of the excess water has been evaporated, an amber-colored syrup is left – a highly concentrated, thoroughly delicious product that is distinctly New England. The finest quality syrup goes best on pancakes and waffles and over ice cream.

What to Eat in New England

Ice cream

NEW ENGLAND'S CUISINE reflects the many cultures that have settled since the 17th century, when English pilgrims first adapted their tastes to include local ingredients. Ethnic foods are common; the Irish brought corned beef and potatoes, the Italians pasta, and all adopted native ingredients. Many traditional dishes depended on foods that kept well – both beans and cod, for instance, lasted well through winter. Today it is not surprising to find elegant dining rooms, strongly influenced by tradition, serving variations on classical dishes.

Wild Blueberry Pancakes
Served in a stack with butter and blueberry syrup. Tiny wild blueberries from Maine are mixed in with the batter.

Deep Filled Sandwich
Huge, deep filled sandwiches are a Boston specialty. The choice of breads and fillings is almost endless.

Boston Baked Beans
White beans slow-baked with salt pork and mustard are served with codfish cakes, brown bread, and beets.

Mustard seasoning

Beets

Small whole onions

Beef

Cabbage

Carrots

Pickles

Boiled potatoes

New England Boiled Dinner
Originally an Irish dish, this home-style favorite consists of a large piece of beef, which is slow-boiled with cabbage, potatoes, carrots, and onions. It is served with mustard seasoning and pickled beets and cucumbers on the side.

Chicken Pot Pie
Served as individual pies or by the wedge, the filling contains chunks of chicken and vegetables in a creamy sauce.

Calamari Italian Style
Whole baked squid stuffed with bread crumbs, herbs, and garlic are served in a rich tomato and herb sauce.

Sushi
Seasoned rice topped with thin-sliced raw fish such as tuna, yellowfin, and salmon, form nigiri sushi. Maki sushi is rolled in seaweed to enclose the fish and rice. Both types come with horseradish and pickled ginger.

Italian salami

SAUSAGES

Cured hard sausages, such as Italian salami, are eaten cold and are often found in sandwiches. Semi-cured and fresh sausages, including German *wurst* and Irish bangers, are served hot. Polish *kielbasa* can be chopped into omelets, while *linguica* is found in Portuguese soup.

Semi-cured Polish *kielbasa*

Semi-cured Portuguese *linguica*

German *wurst*

Irish banger

Boiled lobster

Steamer clams

Corn on the cob

Baked potato

Melted butter

Clam Chowder
This creamy soup contains chunks of potato and chopped clams. Corn, fish, and other chowders are also popular.

Clambakes
A boiled lobster and clams steamed with seaweed are served with fresh corn on the cob and baked potatoes. The lobster and clams are dipped into melted butter and eaten, usually, with the fingers.

Wilted Spinach Salad
This side dish consists mainly of wilted spinach with crisp fried bacon crumbled on top. A light dressing may be added.

Pretzel

Cookies

Muffin

Bagels

Baked Goods
Bagels and muffins are common breakfast foods. Cookies tend to be large, chewy, and hearty, with flavors such as oatmeal and chocolate chip. Large soft pretzels are a ballpark treat.

Squash
Summer squashes come in two varieties – green zucchini and yellow squash. They are a common side dish in late summer.

Indian Pudding
Served with ice cream or cream, this slow-baked soft pudding is made of cornmeal, sugar, molasses, spices, and milk.

Pumpkin Pie
This pumpkin, milk, egg, and spice custard pie is often eaten at Thanksgiving and typically served with whipped cream.

DRINKS

As well as simple brewed cups of American-style coffee, espresso, cappuccino, and latte have become New England favorites; decaffeinated coffee is also widely available. A host of micro-breweries that brew beer to sell only in their restaurants have sprung up in the area. Samuel Adams, on the other hand, is on tap everywhere. Sakonnet Vineyards produces New England wines found in some restaurants. Fruit juices and frappés, a blend of ice cream and milk, are a refreshing alternative to alcoholic drinks.

Cranberry juice

Fruit frappé

Back Bay and John Harvard microbrewery beers

Samuel Adams beer

Sakonnet wine

Choosing a Restaurant

RESTAURANTS HAVE been selected across a wide range of price categories for their value, good food, atmosphere, and location. The chart below highlights some of the factors that may influence your choice of where to eat. Restaurants are listed by area, and within these by price. Opening times are indicated by a "B" for breakfast, "L" for lunch, and "D" for dinner.

		CREDIT CARDS	OUTDOOR TABLES	VEGETARIAN	GOOD WINE	LATE OPENING
BOSTON						
BEACON HILL AND THE THEATER DISTRICT						
EAST OCEAN CITY 25-29 Beach St. **Map** 4 F2. 〖 *(617) 542-2504.* Tanks full of fish destined for diners' plates welcome visitors here. The menu includes seafood and much more, in portions meant to be shared. L, D. 🔨	⑤	MC V		■		■
CHINA PEARL 9 Tyler St. **Map** 4 F2. 〖 *(617) 426-4338.* Boston's best dim sum, including seasonal favorites such as steamed dumplings and sesame balls. The atmosphere is noisy and exuberant. B, L, D. 🔨	⑤⑤	AE MC V D		■		
IMPERIAL SEAFOOD RESTAURANT 70 Beach St. **Map** 4 F2. 〖 *(617) 426-8543.* Friendly Cantonese restaurant serving tasty seafood, vegetable, and meat dishes, as well as dim sum, selected from a roving trolley. L, D. 🔨	⑤⑤	AE MC V		■		
PANIFICO 144 Charles St. **Map** 1 B3. 〖 *(617) 227-4340.* Bakery and restaurant that serves a variety of unusual and delicious sandwiches, pizza, salads, and pastries. They also offer a few larger entrées, which are served through until dinner. B, L, D.	⑤⑤			■		
BREW MOON 115 Stuart St. **Map** 4 E2. 〖 *(617) 742-2739.* Thriving brew-pub serving very good modern American cuisine and a wide range of snacks to eat while sampling the award-winning beers. Also has a branch in Harvard Square. L, D, Brunch Sun. 🍸 🔨 ♿	⑤⑤⑤	AE DC MC V	●	■		■
JACOB WIRTH COMPANY RESTAURANT 31-37 Stuart St. **Map** 4 E2. 〖 *(617) 338-8586.* Built by German Jacob Wirth, the 19th-century decor remains unaltered. Delicious *wursts* and *schnitzel*. Great selection of beer. L, D. 🎵 🍸 🔨 ♿	⑤⑤⑤	AE DC MC V D				
LEGAL SEAFOODS 26 Park Square. **Map** 4 E2. 〖 *(617) 426-4444.* Legal has many locations throughout the city, all serving the freshest and best prepared seafood available. Try their raw bar for oysters, then an entrée created by famed Boston seafood chef Jasper White. L, D. 🅿 🍸 🔨 ♿	⑤⑤⑤	AE DC MC V D		■	●	■
PARAMOUNT DELI-RESTAURANT 44 Charles St. **Map** 1 B4. 〖 *(617) 720-1152.* Imagine a diner-turned-gourmet, and you have the Paramount. The urban "home cooking" from their open kitchen includes chicken *picatta* and *farfalle* with sun-dried tomatoes, feta, and garlic. B, L, D. 🔨	⑤⑤⑤	AE MC V		■		
FIGS 42 Charles St. **Map** 1 B4. 〖 *(617) 742-3447.* A side project of famed chef Todd English. The Mediterranean influence shows in the huge array of pizza, pasta, and appetizers. L (Sat, Sun), D. 🔨	⑤⑤⑤⑤	AE MC V		■	●	
NO. 9 PARK 9 Park St. **Map** 1 C4. 〖 *(617) 742-9991.* The jazz-influenced retro decor in this restaurant puts diners in a light-hearted mood. Carefully considered and well-executed modern American menu, including lobster, seafood, and game. L, D. 🅿 🍸 🔨 ♿ ⬤ Sun.	⑤⑤⑤⑤	AE DC MC V			●	
75 CHESTNUT 75 Chestnut St. **Map** 1 B4. 〖 *(617) 227-2175.* The dark wood interior suggests an age-old private club; the menu, though, is anything but traditional. The focus is on seafood prepared in deliciously unusual ways, such as their pistachio-crusted salmon. D. 🅿 🍸 ♿	⑤⑤⑤⑤	AE DC MC V D		■	●	

Price categories include a three-course meal for one, half a bottle of house wine and all unavoidable extra charges such as sales tax and service.

- Ⓢ under $20
- ⓈⓈ $20–30
- ⓈⓈⓈ $30–45
- ⓈⓈⓈⓈ $45–60
- ⓈⓈⓈⓈⓈ over $60

CREDIT CARDS
Major credit cards accepted: *AE* American Express; *MC* Master Card/Access; *DC* Diners Club; *V* Visa; *D* Discover Card.

OUTDOOR TABLES
Garden, courtyard, or terrace with outside tables.

VEGETARIAN
A good selection of vegetarian dishes available.

GOOD WINE
Extensive list of good wines, both local and international.

LATE OPENING
Full menu or light meals served after 11pm.

	CREDIT CARDS	OUTDOOR TABLES	VEGETARIAN	GOOD WINE	LATE OPENING
THE HUNGRY I ⓈⓈⓈⓈⓈ 71 Charles St. **Map** 1 B4. ℂ *(617) 227-3524.* Chef-owner Peter Ballarin has given this beloved institution a sophisticated facelift. The inventive food has French influences and features fish and game. The enclosed terrace is a romantic oasis. L, D, Brunch Sun.	AE DC MC V	●	■	●	
LOCKE-OBER ⓈⓈⓈⓈⓈ 3 Winter Place. **Map** 1 C4. ℂ *(617) 542-1340.* Once the bastion of upstanding Boston male society, the men's club surroundings are retained, but women are now welcome. Cuisine is European with American influences. Reservations recommended. L, D. 🅿 🔴 🔴 ♿	AE DC MC V			●	
OLD BOSTON AND THE FINANCIAL DISTRICT					
DURGIN-PARK ⓈⓈ 340 North Market St. (Faneuil Hall Marketplace). **Map** 2 D3. ℂ *(617) 227-2038.* A Boston institution, serving all the New England standards that no one else seems to cook any more – Indian pudding, baked beans, and baked scrod, dished up by a sharp-tongued staff. L, D. 🔴 🔴 🔴	AE DC MC V D				
UNION OYSTER HOUSE ⓈⓈⓈ 41 Union St. **Map** 2 D3. ℂ *(617) 227-2750.* Boston's oldest restaurant, the Union Oyster House has managed to keep up with the times and features a respected updated menu of traditional New England seafood and more. Oyster bar is the best part. L, D. 🅿 🔴 🔴	AE DC MC V D			●	
THE VAULT ⓈⓈⓈⓈ 105 Water St. **Map** 2 D4. ℂ *(617) 292-9966.* Relaxed wine bar with impeccable French cuisine, right in the heart of the business district. The menu ranges from hearty oyster stew with buttermilk crackers to melon soup with crème fraîche. B, L, D. 🔴 🔴 Sun.	AE DC MC V D	●	■	●	■
JULIEN ⓈⓈⓈⓈⓈ 250 Franklin St. (Hotel Meridien). **Map** 2 D4. ℂ *(617) 451-1900.* Unadulterated French haute cuisine, exquisitely prepared. Julien has the comfort and grace of a classic dining room that is confident of its quality. Reservations are recommended. L, D. 🔴 🔴 🅿 🔴 ♿	AE DC MC V D			●	
MAISON ROBERT ⓈⓈⓈⓈⓈ 45 School St. **Map** 2 D4. ℂ *(617) 227-3370.* This is the beloved home of French cuisine in Boston, unfussy yet *au courant*. The café serves bistro fare for many budgets; the dining room is more expensive and requires reservations. L, D. 🅿 🔴 ♿ 🔴 Sun.	AE MC V D	●	■	●	
NORTH END AND THE WATERFRONT					
ERNESTO'S PIZZERIA Ⓢ 69 Salem St. **Map** 2 D4. ℂ *(617) 523-1373.* Absolutely nothing fancy here, just a few tables, sawdust on the floor, and an excellent variety of fresh pizza. Perfect for lunch in a rush. L, D.			■		
MONICA'S Ⓢ 143 Richmond St. **Map** 2 E3. ℂ *(617) 227-0311.* An attractive pizza parlor in the North End, Monica's serves gourmet pizzas with seafood, chicken, vegetables, and scores of other combinations at cozy little tables. Good salads, too. D. ♿	MC V		■		
RUDI'S Ⓢ 30 Rowes Wharf (Boston Harbor Hotel). **Map** 2 E4. ℂ *(617) 330-7656.* Large delicatessen, where patrons order portions from the serving counter and seat themselves at café tables. Rudi's also sells beautiful pastries and gourmet food gifts to take home. B, L, D. 🅿 ♿	AE MC V D	●	■		

For key to symbols see back flap

Price categories include a three-course meal for one, half a bottle of house wine and all unavoidable extra charges such as sales tax and service. $ under $20 $$ $20–30 $$$ $30–45 $$$$ $45–60 $$$$$ over $60	**CREDIT CARDS** Major credit cards accepted: *AE* American Express; *MC* Master Card/Access; *DC* Diners Club; *V* VISA; *D* Discover Card. **OUTDOOR TABLES** Garden, courtyard, or terrace with outside tables. **VEGETARIAN** A good selection of vegetarian dishes available. **GOOD WINE** Extensive list of good wines, both native and international. **LATE OPENING** Full menu or light meals served after 11pm.	CREDIT CARDS	OUTDOOR TABLES	VEGETARIAN	GOOD WINE	LATE OPENING
ANTICO FORNO $$ 93 Salem St. **Map** 2 D2. 📞 *(617) 723-6733.* Menu featuring meals cooked in the large brick oven in the rear of the dining room. Pizza is excellent, as are the roasted meats. D. 🚻 ♿		MC V		▣		
BARKING CRAB $$ 88 Sleeper St. **Map** 2 E5. 📞 *(617) 426-2722.* Boston's classic shoreside seafood joint, facing the city from across a channel in the harbor. Lobster, steamers, clamrolls, and chowder, all served along with plenty of paper napkins. L, D. 🎵 🅿 🍸 🚻 ♿		AE MC V	●	▣		
LA FAMIGLIA GIORGIO'S $$ 112 Salem St. **Map** 2 D2. 📞 *(617) 367-6711.* Huge portions of well-prepared pasta are the order of the day here, and La Famiglia is always ready to help you choose. Good value – you will leave full and happy. L, D. 🚻		AE DC MC V D		▣		
POMODORO $$$ 319 Hanover St. **Map** 2 E2. 📞 *(617) 367-4348.* Crowded, raucous, and aromatic, the small storefront housing Pomodoro brims with patrons at all hours. The menu has real Italian dishes that are always well prepared. Try the monkfish with saffron risotto. L, D. 🚻				▣		
RABIA'S $$$ 73 Salem St. **Map** 2 D2. 📞 *(617) 227-6637.* Romantic Italian restaurant, with helpful staff who combine with a talented chef to create a relaxed and convivial evening. D. 🎵 🚻 ♿		AE DC MC V D		▣	●	
TAVERNA TOSCANA $$$ 63 Salem St. **Map** 2 D2. 📞 *(617) 742-5233.* Frescoes and subtle, golden-hued walls create a comfortable setting in this intimate Italian restaurant. Good choice of seasonally inspired entrées. D.		AE MC V		▣		
THE CHART HOUSE $$$ 60 Long Wharf. **Map** 2 E3. 📞 *(617) 227-1576.* A steak and seafood dining room frequented by tourists wandering the waterfront. Decor is quaintly old-fashioned, with ships' wheels and other nautical paraphernalia. Only snacks are served outside. D. 🅿 🍸 🚻 ♿		AE DC MC V D	●	▣		
ROWES WHARF RESTAURANT $$$$ 70 Rowes Wharf (Boston Harbor Hotel). **Map** 2 E4. 📞 *(617) 439-3995.* Elegant dining room overlooking the Boston Harbor. Serves excellent seafood and meats, prepared in a classical style with contemporary influences. Reservations recommended. D. 🅿 🍸 🚻		AE DC MC V D		▣	●	
TERRAMIA $$$$$ 98 Salem St. **Map** 2 D2. 📞 *(617) 523-3112.* Boisterous and mixed clientele line up nightly to dine on the trademark *gnocchi*, prepared daily, as well as on the sublime lobster fritters. Casual, friendly service and setting. D. 🚻		AE DC MC V D		▣		
TRATTORIA A SCALINATELLA $$$$$ 253 Hanover St. **Map** 2 E2. 📞 *(617) 742-8240.* A refreshingly original take on the age-old Italian trattoria. Diners may choose to eschew the menu in favor of host and owner Paolo's recommended progression of courses, chosen to suit your tastes. D.		AE MC V			●	
BACK BAY AND SOUTH END						
MEN TEI NOODLE HOUSE $ 66 Hereford St. **Map** 3 A2. 📞 *(617) 425-0066.* Osaka-style *udon* noodles and an array of snack foods and entrées that any budget can afford. Efficient staff and mixed, lively clientele. L, D.				▣		

THE OTHER SIDE COSMIC CAFE   ⑤
407 Newbury St. **Map** 3 A3. **(** (617) 536-9477.
Avant-garde juice bar and sandwich restaurant with cheerful staff.
Beverages dominate, from health-conscious wheat grass to potent
black coffee. Hip artsy crowd makes anyone feel at home. L, D. 👫 🚶

THE POUR HOUSE   ⑤
907-909 Boylston St. **Map** 3 B3. **(** (617) 236-1767.
Casual and popular place, with typical bar menu and simple, well-cooked
food. Burgers, fries, and beer are the things to have here. B, L, D. 🅿 🍸 👫

HAZEL'S COUNTRY KITCHEN   ⑤⑤
130 Dartmouth St. **Map** 3 C3. **(** (617) 262-4393.
Quirky coffee shop and modern American restaurant with several tasty
daily specials and an extensive sandwich menu. Menu has many grilled
options, and the breakfast selection has something for everyone. B, L, D.

STEVE'S   ⑤⑤
316 Newbury St. **Map** 3 A3. **(** (617) 267-1817.
This casual Greek restaurant is a bargain among its more glamorous neighbors. All the Greek classics, and retsina to wash it down with. B, L, D. 🚶

CHARLEY'S SALOON   ⑤⑤⑤
284 Newbury St. **Map** 3 B2. **(** (617) 266-3000.
Typical American food, well prepared, is what Charley's does best.
Large outdoor seating area is cool and shady in the afternoon. The
bar is busy from after work onward. L, D, Brunch Sun. 🍸 🚶

GYUHAMA OF JAPAN   ⑤⑤⑤
827 Boylston St. **Map** 3 B3. **(** (617) 437-0188.
One of the best sushi bars in Boston, with both tables and chairs and tatami
rooms. Drop by late-night for the surreal Rock-n-Roll Sushi, when waitresses
change from kimonos to dancing gear, with music to match. L, D. 🍸 🚶

RAY'S   ⑤⑤⑤
552 Tremont St. **Map** 4 D4. **(** (617) 426-0008.
Lively restaurant open from lunch to late-night, serving pastries and
quality sandwiches; fillings include marinated red peppers, artichoke
hearts, and cold cuts. Popular with locals. L, D, Brunch Sun. 🍸

SAMUEL ADAMS BREW HOUSE   ⑤⑤⑤
710 Boylston St. **Map** 3 B2. **(** (617) 536-2739.
Brew-pub outlet for the national microbrewed beer, it attracts a big after-
work and tourist crowd. Good burgers, plenty of appetizers. L, D. 🅿 🍸 👫

AMBROSIA ON HUNTINGTON   ⑤⑤⑤⑤
116 Huntington Ave. **Map** 3 B3. **(** (617) 247-2400.
The warm-toned decor and high ceilings lend a spacious feel that is
rare in urban restaurants. The chef uses classic French methods fused
with Asian flavors; sorbets are his signature dish. L, D. 🅿 🍸

SONSIE   ⑤⑤⑤⑤
327 Newbury St. **Map** 3 A3. **(** (617) 351-2500.
If you are a supermodel or aspiring actor, this is the terminally hip place to
go. The open-front dining room is good for people-watching while you sip a
cocktail and nibble on gourmet pizza or tequila-battered shrimp. L, D. 🍸 👫

TAPEO   ⑤⑤⑤⑤
266 Newbury St. **Map** 3 B2. **(** (617) 267-4799.
A wonderfully earthy tapas bar in the middle of pretentious Newbury Street.
Regulars are devoted to the sangria and a dinner of tiny dishes, though
there is a menu of full entrées and wines if you prefer. L, D. 🅿 🍸 🚶

THE JEWEL OF NEWBURY   ⑤⑤⑤⑤
254 Newbury St. **Map** 3 B2. **(** (617) 536-5523.
An elegant, friendly, and charming restaurant serving beautiful
Moroccan cuisine, especially the couscous and tagine. L, D. 🅿

TREMONT 647   ⑤⑤⑤⑤
647 Tremont St. **Map** 3 C4. **(** (617) 266-4600.
Pushing the boundaries of new and old American food alike, this youthful
and unpretentious restaurant enjoys innovation, and succeeds. Try the sea
bass on jasmine rice or the spice-rubbed steak. Sundays' Pajama Brunch
is a must, if solely for the cinnamon rolls. D, Brunch Sun. 🅿 🍸 🚶 👫

For key to symbols see back flap

<table>
<tr><td colspan="2">

Price categories include a three-course meal for one, half a bottle of house wine and all unavoidable extra charges such as sales tax and service.
ⓢ under $20
ⓢⓢ $20–30
ⓢⓢⓢ $30–45
ⓢⓢⓢⓢ $45–60
ⓢⓢⓢⓢⓢ over $60

</td></tr>
</table>

CREDIT CARDS
Major credit cards accepted: *AE* American Express; *MC* Master Card/Access; *DC* Diners Club; *V* VISA; *D* Discover Card.
OUTDOOR TABLES
Garden, courtyard, or terrace with outside tables.
VEGETARIAN
A good selection of vegetarian dishes available.
GOOD WINE
Extensive list of good wines, both native and international.
LATE OPENING
Full menu or light meals served after 11pm.

	CREDIT CARDS	OUTDOOR TABLES	VEGETARIAN	GOOD WINE	LATE OPENING
ANAGO ⓢⓢⓢⓢⓢ 65 Exeter St. **Map** 3 B2. (*(617) 266-6222.* This bistro is host to the cuisine of a top American chef. The "global" menu is both fresh and creative, while avoiding being too trendy. The carpaccio of beef, tuna, and scallops is delicious. L, D. **P ▼ ⌘ ⌂**	AE MC V		■	●	
AUJOURD'HUI ⓢⓢⓢⓢⓢ 200 Boylston St. (Four Seasons Hotel). **Map** 4 D2. (*(617) 451-1392.* Possibly one of the best dining experiences in Boston, the excellent contemporary cuisine includes rack of lamb and medallions of veal. This is complemented by a lovely ambience and a view of the Public Garden. There is also an alternative healthy cuisine menu. B, L, D.	AE MC V		■	●	
CLIO ⓢⓢⓢⓢⓢ 370A Commonwealth Ave. (Eliot Hotel). **Map** 3 A2. (*(617) 536-7200.* It is hard to say whether the wonderful food or the Parisian dining-club ambiance is responsible for the popularity of this French-inspired modern American restaurant. *Foie gras,* caramelized swordfish, and seared spiced steak are highlights. Reservations suggested. B, D, Brunch Sun. **P ▼ ▼ ⌂**	AE DC MC V			●	
L'ESPALIER ⓢⓢⓢⓢⓢ 30 Gloucester St. **Map** 3 B2. (*(617) 262-3023.* In the absolute top tier of Boston restaurants, with impeccably classic decor, excellent service, and New England-influenced European cuisine. Reservations recommended. D. **P ▼ ▼ ●** Sun.	AE DC MC V		■	●	
METROPOLIS ⓢⓢⓢⓢⓢ 584 Tremont St. **Map** 4 D4. (*(617) 247-2931.* A very pleasant environment in which to dine. The Sunday brunch is festive, and dinner unassuming and tasty. Modern American cuisine with Mediterranean influences. D, Brunch Sun. **P ▼ ⌘**	AE MC V				
MISTRAL ⓢⓢⓢⓢⓢ 223 Columbus Ave. **Map** 3 C3. (*(617) 867-9300.* Like the wind in the south of France, Mistral's waiting list shows no sign of dwindling. The cellar is as thoughtfully assembled as the menu, and the fashionable wine bar is always busy. Reservations essential. D. **P ▼ ▼ ⌂**	AE MC V		■	●	■
STEPHANIE'S ON NEWBURY ⓢⓢⓢⓢⓢ 190 Newbury St. **Map** 3 B2. (*(617) 236-0990.* A large patio offers good people-watching potential, the favorite pastime on Newbury Street. Menu mainly has lighter fare, such as salads, inventive sandwiches, and good pizzas. L, D. **▼ ⌂**	AE MC V D	●		●	
VOX POPULI ⓢⓢⓢⓢⓢ 755 Boylston St. **Map** 3 B2. (*(617) 424-8300.* French-American food, eclectic in style, in a comfortably sophisticated and intimate atmosphere. Several dining areas and bars give diners choice of moods. The food is exquisite, with dishes such as tamarind-glazed quail and creamy slat cod. D, Brunch Sun. **P ▼ ▼ ⌂**	AE DC MC V D	●	■	●	
FARTHER AFIELD					
CAMPO DE FIORI ⓢ Holyoke Center Arcade, 1350 Massachusetts Ave., Cambridge. (*(617) 354-3805.* Serves Roman flatbread made into the most subtly delicious sandwiches. Fillings include avocado, grilled mushrooms, fresh mozzarella, and *prosciutto.* Excellent lunch stop, great value. L. **⌘ ⌂ ●** Sun.	AE MC V D		■		
DELI HAUS ⓢ 476 Commonwealth Ave., Kenmore Square. (*(617) 247-9712.* Crowded, noisy basement deli, popular with post-nightclub crowds in search of sandwiches, milkshakes, fries, and burgers. B, L, D.		●	■		■

Ma Soba — ⑤

30 Dunster St., Cambridge. **☎** *(617) 868-7878.*
The menu here reads like a list of East Asia's greatest soups and is
wildly popular with hungry, discerning students on budgets. L, D. ✗

Mr. Bartley's Burger and Salad Cottage — ⑤

1246 Massachusetts Ave., Cambridge. **☎** *(617) 354-6559.*
Hamburgers in such glorious profusion and variety that you will dwell
over their chalk-board menu despite the reigning chaos around you.
Excellent burgers and great sweet potato fries. L, D. ✗ ● Sun.

One Arrow St. Crêpes — ⑤

1 Arrow St., Cambridge. **☎** *(617) 661-2737.*
Nestled off Massachusetts Avenue and serving sweet and savory crêpes.
Sip homemade lemonade and try a spiced pear, blue cheese, arugula,
and walnut crêpe, or stick with something more simple. L, D. ● Mon.

Pinocchio's — ⑤

74 Winthrop St., Cambridge. **☎** *(617) 876-4897.*
Excellent value and terrific pizza – Sicilian style pizza rectangles come
heaped with toppings and are an unbeatable fast meal, night or day. L, D.

South Street Diner — ⑤

178 Kneeland St., Boston. Map 4 F2. **☎** *(617) 350-0028.*
A true American greasy spoon, in the most endearing sense possible.
This 24-hour diner next to the transportation hub of South Station serves
sandwiches, and omelets fresh from the grill. B, L, D. ✗

John Harvard's Brew House — ⑤⑤

33 Dunster St., Cambridge. **☎** *(617) 868-3585.*
Features their excellent microbrewed beer on tap. Publike decor and a
menu of inspired American staples, such as buttermilk-fried chicken with
spiced cornbread. Try the beer sampler if indecisive. L, D. ☕ ✗ ♿

Pho Pasteur — ⑤⑤

35 Dunster St., Cambridge. **☎** *(617) 864-4100.*
Pho is a Vietnamese noodle dish, prepared with sublime complexity at
this stylish restaurant in Harvard Square. While other dishes are excellent,
the grilled pork *pho*, with mint and a delicate sauce, is definitive. L, D. ✗

Chez Henri — ⑤⑤⑤

1 Shepard St., Cambridge. **☎** *(617) 354-8980.*
The offspring of French bistro and Cuban café, the relaxed and
romantic Chez Henri mixes classical methods with fresh Caribbean
and local ingredients. Try the nightly fixed-price menu. D. ☕ ✗ ♿

House of Blues — ⑤⑤⑤

96 Winthrop St., Cambridge. **☎** *(617) 491-2583.*
Music hall and restaurant devoted to bringing the beauty of Southern
music and food to the rest of the country. Succulent barbecue fare and
moist cornbread, adapted to Northern tastes. L, D, Brunch Sun. ♫ ☕

Les Zygomates — ⑤⑤⑤

129 South St., Boston. Map 4 F2. **☎** *(617) 542-5108.*
Wine is the *raison d'être* here, with delicious bistro fare, such as rabbit
pâté and venison *vol-au-vents* to complement it. L, D, Brunch Sun. ☕ ☕

Olive's — ⑤⑤⑤⑤

10 City Square, Charlestown. **☎** *(617) 242-1999.*
Mediterranean-influenced cuisine by local celebrity chef Todd English,
served in a bistro-like setting. Perpetually crowded, they do not accept
reservations. Dress well to minimize your wait. D. 🅿 ☕ ☕ ♿ ● Sun.

Rialto — ⑤⑤⑤⑤⑤

1 Bennett St. (Charles Hotel), Cambridge. **☎** *(617) 661-5050.*
Rarely do the top restaurants create an atmosphere so down to earth. The
menu of seasonal dishes may include *foie gras* with dried fruit compote,
tender roast duckling, or simple tomatoes with fresh mozzarella. D. 🅿 ☕ ♿

The Harvest — ⑤⑤⑤⑤⑤

44 Brattle St., Cambridge. **☎** *(617) 868-2255.*
A favored haunt of university professors, The Harvest is one of the finest
restaurants in Harvard Square. Modern American cuisine bursting with
fresh flavors and local produce. Reservations suggested. L, D. ☕ ☕ ♿

For key to symbols see back flap

Price categories include a three-course meal for one, half a bottle of house wine and all unavoidable extra charges such as sales tax and service.
Ⓢ under $20
ⓈⓈ $20–30
ⓈⓈⓈ $30–45
ⓈⓈⓈⓈ $45–60
ⓈⓈⓈⓈⓈ over $60

CREDIT CARDS
Major credit cards accepted: *AE* American Express; *MC* Master Card/Access; *DC* Diners Club; *V* VISA; *D* Discover Card.

OUTDOOR TABLES
Garden, courtyard, or terrace with outside tables.

VEGETARIAN
A good selection of vegetarian dishes available.

GOOD WINE
Extensive list of good wines, both native and international.

LATE OPENING
Full menu or light meals served after 11pm.

	CREDIT CARDS	OUTDOOR TABLES	VEGETARIAN	GOOD WINE	LATE OPENING

MASSACHUSETTS

AMHERST: *Judie's* ⓈⓈ 51 N. Pleasant St. 📞 *(413) 253-3491.* Giant popovers are a signature here, along with eclectic food served in a sunny greenhouse or quieter back room. Good place for afternoon tea or snack. L, D. 🍸 🏃 ♿ ⬤ Thanksgiving & Dec 25.	AE MC V D	■			
CAPE COD: *The Beehive Tavern* Ⓢ 406 Rte 6A, Sandwich. 📞 *(508) 833-1184.* A Cape legend for its rustic charm, friendly staff, lobster pie, and Bee Sting ice cream. L, D. 🅿 🍸 🏃 ♿	MC V				
CAPE COD: *Jack's Outback* Ⓢ 161 Main St., Yarmouth Port. 📞 *(508) 362-6690.* "Good food, lousy service" is the motto in this "cutesy" place with better food than Mom used to make. Breakfasts are models of Americana. B, L, D. 🍸 🏃					
CAPE COD: *Scargo Cafe* ⓈⓈ 700 Rte 6A, Dennis. 📞 *(508) 385-8200.* Warm and welcoming ambience with fireplace is matched by . creative cuisine and excellent service, handy location across from the Cape Playhouse. L, D. 🅿 🍸 🏃 ♿	AE MC V D				
CAPE COD: *Belfry Inne & Bistro* ⓈⓈⓈ 6-8 Jarves St., Sandwich. 📞 *(508) 888-8550.* Inside an old de-sanctified church is some of the best so-called "fusion" food on the Cape, a feast for eye and palate. L, D. 🅿 🍸 🏃 ♿ ⬤ Sun & Mon.	AE MC V	■			
CAPE COD: *Regatta of Falmouth By-The-Sea* ⓈⓈⓈ 217 Clinton Ave., Falmouth. 📞 *(508) 548-5400.* Lovely view of the harbor in this stylish place with subtle French decor complements the creative French-American seafood menu. D. 🅿 🍸 ♿ ⬤ Oct-Memorial Day.	AE MC V			●	
CAPE COD: *Chillingsworth* ⓈⓈⓈⓈⓈ 2449 Main St., Brewster. 📞 *(508) 896-3640.* The epitome of fine dining served in a 300-year-old house. The place exudes charm, has seamless service, and an elegant French prix fixe menu. Casual fare available in the Garden Room. D. 🅿 🍸 ⬤ Dec-Apr.	AE DC MC V			●	
CONCORD: *Aigo Bistro* ⓈⓈⓈ 84 Thoreau St. 📞 *(978) 371-1333.* Exotic food (with Mediterranean accent) and fine service are "givens" in this sophisticated bistro upstairs in Concord depot. D. 🅿 🍸 🏃 ⬤ Sun.	DC MC V	■			
DEERFIELD: *Deerfield Inn* ⓈⓈⓈ 81 Old Main St. 📞 *(413) 774-5587.* The inn's Colonial decor suits the traditional menu of seafood, rack of lamb, and veal dishes. B, L, D. 🅿 🏃 ♿ ⬤ Dec 25.	AE DC MC V				
ESSEX: *Woodman's of Essex* ⓈⓈ Rte 133. 📞 *(978) 768-6057.* This old summer favorite with families is known for clam *everything*, including clam bakes, and huge portions. L, D. 🅿 🏃					
GLOUCESTER: *White Rainbow* ⓈⓈⓈ 65 Main St. 📞 *(978) 281-0017.* Sauteed lobster, seafood, and continental dishes are the fare in this 19th-century landmark building. D. 🍸 ♿ ⬤ Dec 24 &25.	AE DC MC V D			●	

LENOX: *Bistro Zinc* $$$ AE MC V
56 Church St. 📞 *(413) 637-8800.*
Strengths of this sophisticated cafe are wood-fired pizzas, fig-roasted quail, olive-crusted tuna, other contemporary dishes. L, D. 🅿 🛆 ⏧ ● Tue.

LENOX: *Blantyre* $$$$ AE DC MC V
Blantyre Rd. 📞 *(413)637-3556.*
This formal English-style country house offers prix fixe special-occasion dining at its most elegant. French menu features seafood and game, such as saddle of rabbit with Oregon truffles. Exceptional wine list.
L, D. 🅿 🍷 ⏧ 🎵 ● Mon., also Nov-Apr.

MARTHA'S VINEYARD: *Black Dog Tavern* $$$ AE MC V
Beach St. Extension, Vineyard Haven. 📞 *(508) 693-9223.*
With crowded rustic quarters facing the harbor, this place is a hit for its steamers, grilled bluefish sandwiches, other fresh seafood.
B, L, D. 🛆

MARTHA'S VINEYARD: *Sweet Life Cafe* $$$ AE MC V D
Upper Circuit Ave., Oak Bluffs. 📞 *(508) 696-0200.*
Three cozy dining rooms in an old Victorian house and tented garden set the stage for unusual New American-Asian fusion menu.
D. 🍷 ⏧ to garden only ● Jan-Feb.

NANTUCKET: *Atlantic Cafe* $$ AE DC MC V D
15 S.Water St. 📞 *(508) 228-0570.*
Rowboats hung from the ceiling convey the nautical theme. As you might expect, seafood and snacks are the specialties.
L, D. 🛆 ⏧ ● late Dec-early Jan.

NANTUCKET: *21 Federal* $$$ AE MC V
21 Federal St. 📞 *(508) 228-2121.*
Four stylish minimalist dining rooms in an old house feature elegant New American fare. There's also a lighter, less expensive bistro menu.
L, D. 🍷 🛆 ⏧ ● Jan-Mar.

NANTUCKET: *Chanticleer* $$$$ AE DC MC V
New St., Sconset. 📞 *(508) 257-6231.*
In a country cottage with garden setting, this premier French restaurant has a special way with local seafood.
L, D. 🅿 🍷 ⏧ ● Mon, also late Oct-mid-May.

NORTHAMPTON: *Eastside Grill* $$ AE MC V
19 Strong Ave. 📞 *(413) 586-3347.*
Unprepossessing exterior, but loyal fans love the Cajun specialties – especially the fabulous New Orleans pudding. D. 🍷 ⏧

NORTHAMPTON: *Northampton Brewery* $$ AE MC V D
11 Brewster Court. 📞 *(413) 584-9903*
A popular college hangout for its snacks, vegetarian dishes, sandwiches, casual meals and the well-sampled house-brewed microbeers. L, D. 🍷 🛆 ⏧

PLYMOUTH: *Lobster Hut* $ MC V
Town Wharf. 📞 *(508)746-2270.*
Fried clams, fish & chips, clam chowder, huge portions, all are notable at this self-serve waterfront spot.
L, D. 🅿 🛆 ⏧ ● Jan.

PLYMOUTH: *McGrath's* $$ AE DC MC V D
Water St. 📞 *(508) 746-9751.*
A longtime casual waterfront hangout, this place offers fresh seafood and other standards. L, D. 🍷 🛆 ⏧

ROCKPORT: *The Glass Verandah at the Yankee Clipper Inn* $$ AE MC V D
96 Granite St. 📞 *(978) 546-7795*
You dine on regional American dishes -- seafood, duck, steak -- on a glass-enclosed porch overlooking the ocean.
B, D. 🅿 🍷 🛆 ● Jan-Feb

SALEM: *Red Raven's Love Noodle* $$
75 Congress St. 📞 *(978) 745-8558.*
Tops for creative flair, both in funky decor and original dishes, including intriguing vegetable specials. D. 🅿 ● Sun & Mon.

For key to symbols see back flap

	CREDIT CARDS	OUTDOOR TABLES	VEGETARIAN	GOOD WINE	LATE OPENING
Price categories include a three-course meal for one, half a bottle of house wine and all unavoidable extra charges such as sales tax and service. **⑤** under $20 **⑤⑤** $20–30 **⑤⑤⑤** $30–45 **⑤⑤⑤⑤** $45–60 **⑤⑤⑤⑤⑤** over $60 · **CREDIT CARDS** Major credit cards accepted: *AE* American Express; *MC* Master Card/Access; *DC* Diners Club; *V* VISA; *D* Discover Card. · **OUTDOOR TABLES** Garden, courtyard, or terrace with outside tables. · **VEGETARIAN** A good selection of vegetarian dishes available. · **GOOD WINE** Extensive list of good wines, both native and international. · **LATE OPENING** Full menu or light meals served after 11pm.					
SALEM: *Lyceum Bar & Grill* ⑤⑤⑤ 43 Church St. (*(978) 745-7665.* In this historic building, where Alexander Graham Bell gave the first phone demo in 1877, you'll find a good assortment of New American and grilled dishes. L, D. 🍴 ⛓ ♿	AE MC V				■
SPRINGFIELD: *Hofbrauhaus* ⑤⑤⑤ 1105 Main St. (*(413) 737-4905.* Longtime favorite for its Bavarian gemutlichtheit, German specialties, and seafood. L (Fri.only), D. 🅿 🍴 ⛓ ♿	AE DC MC V D				■
STOCKBRIDGE: *Truc Orient Express* ⑤⑤ 1 Harris St. (*(413) 232-4204.* Oriental decor and Vietnamese specialties are a natural here and make a nice change when you've had enough lobster and seafood. L, D. 🅿 🍴 ⛓ ♿ ⬤ Tue.Nov-Apr.	AE DC MC V	●	■		
STURBRIDGE: *Publick House* ⑤⑤⑤ 295 Main St. (*(508) 347-3313.* In the Sturbridge spirit, this atmospheric 1771 Colonial house with open hearths features Americana, such as lobster pie, prime rib. B, L, D. 🅿 🎵 ⛓ ♿	AE DC MC V	●	■		
SUDBURY: *Longfellow's Wayside Inn* ⑤⑤ 72 Wayside Inn Rd. (*(978) 443-1776.* Historic surroundings make this a favorite for simple fare: prime rib, fresh seafood, and the like. L,D. 🅿 🍴 ⛓ ⬤ Christmas.	AE DC MC V D				
WALTHAM: *The Watch City Brewery* ⑤⑤ 262 Moody St. (*(781) 647-4000.* Once an old bank, this is a fun place for microbrewery beer aficionados, with pleasing ambience, snacks, meals. L, D. 🍴 ⛓ ♿	AE DC MC V				■
WALTHAM: *The Tuscan Grill* ⑤⑤⑤ 361 Moody St. (*(781) 891-5486.* This stylish trattoria features some of the best northern Italian fare in the area, with open kitchen, wood-grilled specialties. D. 🅿 🍴 ♿ ⬤ major holidays.	MC V D			●	
WELLESLEY: *Blue Ginger* ⑤⑤⑤ 583 Washington St. (*(781) 283-5790.* Foodies consider this East-West bistro unique in the this part of the state for its blend of Asian cuisines, extensive wine list, and blue-accented minimalist decor. It is worth a detour. L, D. 🍴 ⛓ ♿ ⬤ Sun.	AE MC V		■	●	
WILLIAMSTOWN: *The Orchards* ⑤⑤⑤⑤ 222 Adams Rd. (*(413) 458-9611.* Continental food with contemporary touches is served in a romantic setting. Desserts are special. B, L, D. 🅿 🍴 ⛓ ♿	AE DC MC V	●		●	

RHODE ISLAND

ADAMSVILLE: *Abraham Manchester Restaurant & Tavern* ⑤ Main Rd., Adamsville. (*(401) 635-2700.* The wholesome food in this former general store, with its enclosed patio, is mostly Italian. There is some seafood here, but nothing fancy. L, D. 🅿 ⛓	MC V				
BLOCK ISLAND: *Eli's* ⑤⑤ Chapel St. (*(401) 466-5230.* Deceptively simple, Eli's features very good Italian dishes in ordinary surroundings of knotty pine walls and tables. Pesto-baked ziti in cream sauce is one of many delights. L, D. 🍴 ⛓ ♿	MC V		■		

BLOCK ISLAND: *Finn's Seafood Restaurant* $$ AE MC V
Water St. (401) 466-2473.
Location facing the harbor makes ferry-watching a cinch. Nothing fancy here, but steamed mussels, clam rolls, broiled swordfish are all tasty. Finn's is as casual as the island itself. L, D. 🚻 ♿ ◐ Nov-Apr.

BLOCK ISLAND: *Atlantic Inn* $$$ MC V D
High St. (401) 466-5883.
A formal favorite of urbane locals for the spectacular ocean views and prix fixe menu with numerous sophisticated choices, such as grilled monkfish with truffled littleneck risotto.
D. 🅿 🍸 ◐ Columbus Day weekend–Apr.

BLOCK ISLAND: *Gazebo* $$$ AE MC V
Hotel Manisses, Spring St. (401) 466-2421.
New American dishes with a seaward lilt served in an airy octagonal romantic room. Grilled local swordfish and striped bass are beautifully done. The Gatsby Room has a more casual, less expensive menu and is also good. D. 🅿 🍸 ◐ Dec–mid-Feb, weekdays mid-Feb–Apr.

BRISTOL: *Lobster Pot Inc.* $$ AE MC V
119-121 Hope St. (401) 253-9100.
Unsurpassed ocean views in this casual waterfront spot, known for its fresh seafood. L, D. 🎵 🍸 🚻 ◐ Mon.

CHARLESTOWN: *Wilcox Tavern* $$ AE MC V
5153 Post Rd., Rte 1. (401) 322-1829.
Fresh seafood, roast beef, and steaks are specialties in this attractive vintage 1730 house. D. 🅿 🍸 🚻 ◐ Mon.

GALILEE: *George's of Galilee* $$ MC V
25 Sand Hill Cove. (401) 783-2306.
A bustling, wildly busy waterfront landmark, famous in the area for its seafood platters, chowder, and clam cakes. L, D. 🍸 🚻 ◐ Dec.

KINGSTON: *Larchwood Inn* $$ AE DC MC V D
521 Main St. (401) 783-5454.
Traditional old inn in pretty setting is still going strong, with standbys such as prime rib, seafood dishes. B, L, D. 🅿 🍸 🚻 ♿

MIDDLETOWN: *The Glass Onion* $$ AE MC V D
909 E. Main St., Rte 138. (401) 848-5153.
Located in the same building as Newport Vineyards, this perky place with its diverse menu also serves a popular Sunday brunch. L, D. 🅿 🍸 🚻 ♿

MIDDLETOWN: *Sea Shai* $$ AE DC MC V D
747 Aquidneck Ave. (401) 849-5180.
Sushi is ocean-fresh at this, the state's only Korean restaurant. The menu carries Korean grilled BBQ meats and seafood and such Japanese specialties as shabu-shabu, sukiyaki, and tempura. L, D. 🍸 🚻 ♿

NARRAGANSETT: *Coast Guard House* $$ AE DC MC V D
40 Ocean Rd. (401) 789-0700.
This renovated 1888 Coast Guard station has ocean views, good swordfish, and prime rib and is known especially for its Sunday brunch.
L, D. 🎵 🅿 🍸 🚻 ♿

NEWPORT: *Le Bistro* $$ AE DC MC V D
41 Bowen's Wharf. (401) 849-7778.
Tiny, French, and romantic, with water views, this gem is known for its seafood prepared with Gallic flair. L, D. 🅿 🍸

NEWPORT: *The Black Pearl* $$ AE DC MC V
Bannister's Wharf. (401) 846-5264.
Justifiably famous for its clam chowder, this landmark blends classic French fare in the sedate Commodore Room with casual dining in the tavern and bar. Don't miss the apple-raisin bread pudding. L, D. 🍸 🚻

NEWPORT: *La Petite Auberge* $$$ AE MC V
19 Charles St. (401) 849-6669.
In five cozy rooms of a 1714 house, this charmer offers authentic French fare, such as snails with cepes, oysters gratinée, and lobster with truffles, all impeccably prepared and served. The attached café is more casual, less pricey. D. 🍸

For key to symbols see back flap

<table>
<tr><td colspan="2">

Price categories include a three-course meal for one, half a bottle of house wine and all unavoidable extra charges such as sales tax and service.

⑤ under $20
⑤⑤ $20–30
⑤⑤⑤ $30–45
⑤⑤⑤⑤ $45–60
⑤⑤⑤⑤⑤ over $60

</td><td>

CREDIT CARDS
Major credit cards accepted: *AE* American Express; *MC* Master Card/Access; *DC* Diners Club; *V* VISA; *D* Discover Card.

OUTDOOR TABLES
Garden, courtyard, or terrace with outside tables.

VEGETARIAN
A good selection of vegetarian dishes available.

GOOD WINE
Extensive list of good wines, both native and international.

LATE OPENING
Full menu or light meals served after 11pm.

</td></tr>
</table>

	CREDIT CARDS	OUTDOOR TABLES	VEGETARIAN	GOOD WINE	LATE OPENING
NEWPORT: *White Horse Tavern* ⑤⑤⑤ 26 Marlborough St. 【 *(401) 849-3600.* The oldest operating tavern in America, with low-beamed ceilings, wide hearth fires, colonial bric-a-brac, and candlelit dining rooms. Good American food, updated with modern touches: wood-grilled rack of lamb, sauteed shrimp and scallops with wasabi aioli. L, D. 🄿 🅈 🄴 🅃 Jacket (dinner only)	AE DC MC V D			●	
NORTH KINGSTOWN: *Red Rooster Tavern* ⑤⑤ 7385 Post Rd., North Kingston. 【 *(401) 295-8804.* Long a popular magnet, this traditional New England tavern specializes in seafood and Continental dishes. It has an exceptional wine list. L, D. 🄿 🅈 🄴 🄳 ● Mon.	AE DC MC V D			●	
PORTSMOUTH: *Seafare Inn* ⑤⑤⑤ 3352 E.Main St. 【 *(401) 683-0577.* A rejuvenated, slightly starchy Victorian mansion plays host to a menu that is strong on seafood and regional specialties. Everything is well presented. D. 🄿 🅈 🅃 ● Sun.	AE MC V			●	
PROVIDENCE: *Al Forno* ⑤⑤⑤ 577 S.Main St. 【 *(401) 273-9760.* Wood-fire grilled meats, pizzas from stone floor pizza ovens, and baked pasta dishes are signatures of this popular, informal, no-reservations-taken place. The chef-owners keep inventing new and fabulous dishes, using fresh local ingredients. D. 🅈 🄴 🄳 ● Sun & Mon.	AE DC MC V	■			
PROVIDENCE: *Capriccio* ⑤⑤⑤ 2 Pine St. 【 *(401) 421-1320.* Old-time Italian restaurant with a dark grotto-like dining room. It has livened up its menu and features light modern Italian dishes, the likes of grilled octopus and pastas with mascarpone cheese and sun-dried tomatoes. Impressive wine list. L, D. 🎵 🅈 🄴	AE MC V D	■	●		
PROVIDENCE: *Empire* ⑤⑤⑤ 123 Empire St. 【 *(401) 621-7911.* Across from the Trinity Repertory Co., this former auto showroom sports some breezily eclectic food.The thin-crusted pizzas are crowd-pleasers with the hip young clients the café attracts. L, D. 🄿 🅈 🄴 🄳 ● Sun.	AE MC V	●	■		■
PROVIDENCE: *New Rivers* ⑤⑤⑤ 7 Steeple St. 【 *(401) 751-0350.* Some of the best New American food can be found in this intimate town house. Look for dishes such as five-spice chicken, grilled pork tenderloin, and sweet local scallops. D. 🅈 ● Mon.	AE MC V				
PROVIDENCE: *Pot au Feu* ⑤⑤⑤ 44 Custom House St. 【 *(401) 273-8953.* Elegant, formal dining in top level Salon; brick-walled Bistro is at lower level. Both serve consistently excellent classic and regional French food. L, D. 🅈 ● Sun June–Aug and most most major holidays.	AE DC MC V			●	
WARWICK: *Legal Sea Foods* ⑤⑤⑤ 2099 Post Rd. 【 *(401) 732-3663.* A welcome outpost of the famous Boston chain, with similar nautical theme and freshest of fresh seafood, prepared a variety of ways. There's a sizeable raw bar. L, D. 🄴 🄳 ● Thanksgiving, Dec 25.	AE DC MC V D				
WATCH HILL: *Olympia Tea Room* ⑤⑤⑤ Bay St. 【 *(401) 348-8211.* This octogenarian has had a facelift in recent years, and now features an eclectic menu that roams the globe, with American regional dishes, Spanish, Asian, and others. L, D. 🅈 🄳 ● Mon & Tue and Jan–Apr.	AE MC V	●		●	

WESTERLY: *Three Fish* $$$ AE MC V
37 Main St., Westerly. (*(401) 348-9700*.
For serious diners, this charming place is worth a detour for creative food, presented artistically. Dishes such as pan-seared Atlantic salmon and grilled double cut pork chops are always artfully embellished. Lighter fare and prices at the attached River Pub. L, D. 🅿 🍷 ⛄

CONNECTICUT

BROOKLYN: *Golden Lamb Buttery* $$$$
499 Wolf Den Rd. (*(860) 774-4423*.
Prepare for a unique dining experience: lovely American food, hay ride, strolling musicians, in a restored barn on a working farm. Dinner prix fixe. Reservations are essential.
L, D. 🎵 🅿 ⛄ ⬤ Sun & Mon.

CANAAN: *The Cannery* $$ AE MC V
85 Main St. (*(860) 824-7333*.
Creative chef-owner and reliable food make this bistro a favorite spot with locals, featuring items such as ravioli with roasted eggplant, toasted walnuts, and caramelized onions. D. ⛄ ⬤ Nov–Apr: Tue & Wed.

DARIEN: *Coromandel* $$ AE DC MC V D
25-11 Old Kings Highway N. (*(203) 662-1213*.
This may be the state's best Indian restaurant, with South Indian specialties served amiably in limited, well-decorated space.
L, D. 🅿 ⛄

EAST HADDAM: *Gelston House River Grill* $$$ AE MC V
8 Main St. (*(860) 873-1411*.
Views of the river from this hilltop Victorian-Italianate house even outshine the tasty New American food. Proximity to Goodspeed Opera House makes this a tourist favorite. L, D. 🅿 ⛄

FARMINGTON: *Ann Howard's Apricots* $$$ MC V D
1593 Farmington Ave. (*(860) 673-5405*.
An airy two-story restored trolley barn overlooks river and sets the stage for creative New American cooking. L, D. 🎵 🅿 🍷 ⛄

GREENWICH: *Penang Grill* $$ AE MC V
55 Lewis St. (*(203) 861-1988*.
Young and old crowd into this cozy, Malayan-Chinese restaurant for the squid salad, sesame chicken, and other delights. L, D. 🍷 ⛄

GREENWICH: *Restaurant Jean-Louis* $$$$ AE DC MC V D
55 Lewis St. (*(203) 622-8450*.
In this tiny nationally acclaimed, chef-owned French restaurant, you may dine a la carte or on the menu dégustation. Either way, the food is memorable. L, D. 🍷 ⬤ Sun.

GUILFORD: *Quattro's* $$ AE DC MC V
1300 Boston Post Rd. (*(203) 453-6575*.
Crowded and popular, this attractive Italian restaurant does wonders with pasta and veal dishes. L, D. 🅿 ⛄ ⬤ Sun.

HARTFORD: *Shish Kebab House of Afghanistan* $ AE MC V
360 Franklin Ave. (*(860) 296-0301*.
Several small dining areas decorated with Afghan artifacts are a backdrop for well-seasoned Afghan specialties, a rarity in CT. D. 🍷 ⛄

HARTFORD: *Max Downtown* $$$ AE DC MC V
City Place, 185 Asylum St. (*(860) 522-2530*.
Smart, modern, bustling, this favorite-with-locals downtown spot features excellent Modern American dishes. L, D. 🍷 ⛄

HARTFORD: *Peppercorn's Grill* $$$ AE DC MC V
357 Main St. (*(860) 547-1714*.
In this stylish, two-level dining room, look for creative American and Italian dishes, with a few Asian accents. L, D. 🅿 🍷 ⛄ ⬤ Sun.

HARTFORD: *The Savannah* $$$ AE DC MC V D
391 Main St. (*(860) 278-2020*.
An eclectic American menu has sparks of Asia and Italy, served in a quietly romantic room punctuated with African artifacts. L, D. 🍷 ⛄ ⬤ Sun.

For key to symbols see back flap

Price categories include a three-course meal for one, half a bottle of house wine and all unavoidable extra charges such as sales tax and service.
$ under $20
$$ $20–30
$$$ $30–45
$$$$ $45–60
$$$$$ over $60

CREDIT CARDS
Major credit cards accepted: *AE* American Express; *MC* Master Card/Access; *DC* Diners Club; *V* VISA; *D* Discover Card.

OUTDOOR TABLES
Garden, courtyard, or terrace with outside tables.

VEGETARIAN
A good selection of vegetarian dishes available.

GOOD WINE
Extensive list of good wines, both native and international.

LATE OPENING
Full menu or light meals served after 11pm.

	CREDIT CARDS	OUTDOOR TABLES	VEGETARIAN	GOOD WINE	LATE OPENING

LEDYARD: *Stonecroft* $$$
515 Pumpkin Hill Rd. ((860) 572-0771.
Surprising to find such urbane fare, careful service, and high style dining room out in the woods. Save room for the luscious desserts.
L, D. **P & ●** Tue.

Credit Cards	Outdoor Tables	Good Wine
AE DC MC V D	●	●

LITCHFIELD: *West Street Grill* $$$
43 West St. ((860) 567-3885.
The area's most popular gathering place for big-name New Yorkers who weekend in the vicinity offers pace-setting food in a comfortably casual setting. L, D **Y & &**

Credit Cards: MC V · Vegetarian: ■ · Good Wine: ●

MANCHESTER: *Cavey's* $$$
45 E, Center St. ((860) 643-2751.
Schizophrenic place where one floor is casual Northern Italian fare, the other fancy formal French (jackets, pricier, and dinner only), with separate kitchens. Rest assured, both are terrific.
L, D. **♫ P Y ⻑ & ●** Sun & Mon.

Credit Cards: AE MC V · Good Wine: ●

MYSTIC: *Mystic Pizza* $
56 W. Main St. ((860) 536-3700.
Immortalized by Julia Roberts' movie, this pizza-and-pasta parlor is a "must-stop" for most Mystic visitors. L, D. **P ⻑ &**

Credit Cards: DC MC V · Late Opening: ■

NEW BRITAIN: *Fatherland* $
450 S. Main St. ((860) 224-3345.
This spic-and-span no-frills storefront piles on Cyclopean portions of hearty, home-style Polish cooking. L, D. **⻑ &**

Credit Cards: MC V D

NEW HAVEN: *Bentara* $$
76 Orange St. ((203) 562-2511.
Authentic Malaysian food is served in spacious, high-ceilinged rooms decorated with Asian artifacts. Note the exceptional wine and beer lists. L, D. **&**

Credit Cards: AE MC V D · Outdoor Tables: ■ · Vegetarian: ● · Good Wine: ■

NEW HAVEN: *Frank Pepe Pizzeria* $$
157 Wooster St. ((203) 865-5762.
Go early to avoid the lineups for white clam and other pizzas, long considered the state's best. No frills here is an understatement.
L, D. **& ●** Tue.

NEW HAVEN: *Pika Tapas* $$
39 High St. ((203) 865-1933.
Cheerful spot, well suited to eating light, Spanish style, from a menu of small plates (tapas). L, D. **⻑ & ●** Mon.

Credit Cards: AE MC V · Outdoor Tables: ■ · Vegetarian: ● · Good Wine: ■

NEW HAVEN: *Union League Cafe* $$$
1032 Chapel St. ((203) 562-4299.
An historic building plays second fiddle to superb French food, impeccably prepared and served. L, D. **P Y & ●** Sun

Credit Cards: AE DC MC V · Good Wine: ●

NEW HAVEN: *Zinc* $$$
964 Chapel St. ((203) 624-0507.
Stunning minimalist decor suits the vibrant food, a stylish blend of New American with Asian influences, producing unique results.
L, D. **Y & ●** Sun.

Credit Cards: AE MC V D · Outdoor Tables: ■ · Vegetarian: ● · Good Wine: ■

NEW PRESTON: *The Birches Inn* $$$
233 West Shore Rd. ((860) 868-1735
Overlooking Lake Waramaug, the deck in warm weather is considered "the" place to enjoy grilled corn husk stuffed with seafood sausage and other of the chef-owner's surprising specialties.
D. **P ⻑ & ●** Tue.

Credit Cards: AE MC V · Outdoor Tables: ● · Good Wine: ●

NOANK: *Abbott's Lobster in The Rough* ⑤
117 Pearl St. ((860) 536-7719.
Fresh lobsters, clam rolls, and other seafood at plain picnic-style tables facing marina on Mystic River. L, D. 🅿 🚹 ♿ ⬤ Oct–May.

AE MC V

NORTH STONINGTON: *Randall's Ordinary* ⑤⑤⑤
Rte. 2, ((860) 599-4540.
A landmark inn highlights 18th-century recipes, with dishes cooked over an open hearth. A unique experience, prix fixe. B, L, D. 🅿 🍸 🚹

AE MC V

NORWALK: *Meson Galicia* ⑤⑤⑤
Wall St. ((203) 866-8800.
Elegant Spanish food is served in a setting resembling a country inn. A well-chosen Spanish wine list and superlative service are signatures.
L, D. 🍸 ♿ ⬤ Mon.

AE DC MC V

NORWALK: *The Restaurant at Rowayton Seafood* ⑤⑤⑤
89 Rowayton Ave. ((203) 866-4488.
Crowded quarters facing a marina don't deter enjoyment of fresh clams, oysters, and other seafood. L, D. 🍸 ♿

AE DC MC V D

NORWALK: *Silvermine Tavern* ⑤⑤⑤
194 Perry St. ((203) 847-4558.
Vintage New England inn overlooking river, features American classics like chicken pot pie, with a popular Thurs. buffet and Sun. brunch.
L, D. 🎵 🅿 🍸 🎵 🚹 ⬤ Closed Tue.

DC MC V

OLD LYME: *The Bee & Thistle Inn* ⑤⑤⑤
100 Lyme St. ((860) 434-1667.
Old-time setting belies the sophisticated New American menu with many extra touches. L, D. 🅿 🍸 🚹 ♿ ⬤ Tue.

DC MC V

OLD SAYBROOK: *Terra Mar Grille* ⑤⑤⑤
Saybrook Point Inn, 2 Bridge St. ((860) 388-1111.
Serene marina views compete with a menu of American and Northern Italian dishes. Wild game is a specialty. B, L, D. 🅿 🚹 ♿

AE DC MC V D

PLAINVILLE (BRISTOL): *Confetti* ⑤⑤
393 Farmington Ave. ((860) 793-8809.
In an area where good restaurants are hard to find, this is an oasis of hearty well-prepared Italian dishes, good seafood. L, D. 🍸 🚹 ♿

AE MC V D

RIDGEFIELD: *Gail's Station House* ⑤⑤
378 Main St. ((203) 438-9775.
Yeoman portions of well-prepared, eclectic American food make this funky old storefront a popular local hangout. Desserts are really special.
B, L, D. 🚹 ♿

AE MC V D

SIMSBURY: *Metro Bis* ⑤⑤⑤
928 Hopmeadow St. ((860) 651-1908.
Lively bistro setting offers inspired Asian-accented American food.
L, D. 🅿 🍸 🚹 ♿ ⬤ Sun.

AE MC V

SOUTH NORWALK: *Ocean Drive* ⑤⑤⑤
128 Washington St. ((203) 855-1665.
A cool South Beach Miami look combines with inventive seafood dishes in this "happening" new scene. L, D. 🅿 🍸 🚹 ♿

AE DC MC V

STAMFORD: *Bank Street Brewery* ⑤⑤
65 Bank St. ((203) 325-2739.
Favorite after-work hangout for the young, in handsomely restored old bank, now a bustling brew pub, more noted for the scene than the food.
L, D. 🎵 🍸 🚹

AE DC MC V

STONINGTON: *Boom* ⑤⑤
194 Water St. ((860) 535-3925.
Marina dining in a boatyard on seafood prepared with a light touch.
L, D. 🅿 🚹 ♿ ⬤ Mon.

AE DC MC V D

WOODBURY: *Carole Peck's Good News Cafe* ⑤⑤
694 Main St. ((860) 266-4663.
This cheerful place is much loved by foodies for Peck's honest food with innovative twists. Homemade breads and desserts are notable.
L, D. 🎵 🅿 🍸 🚹 ♿ ⬤ Tue.

AE DC MC V

For key to symbols see back flap

Price categories include a three-course meal for one, half a bottle of house wine and all unavoidable extra charges such as sales tax and service.

$ under $20
$$ $20–30
$$$ $30–45
$$$$ $45–60
$$$$$ over $60

CREDIT CARDS
Major credit cards accepted: *AE* American Express; *MC* Master Card/Access; *DC* Diners Club; *V* Visa; *D* Discover Card.

OUTDOOR TABLES
Garden, courtyard, or terrace with outside tables.

VEGETARIAN
A good selection of vegetarian dishes available.

GOOD WINE
Extensive list of good wines, both native and international.

LATE OPENING
Full menu or light meals served after 11pm.

	CREDIT CARDS	OUTDOOR TABLES	VEGETARIAN	GOOD WINE	LATE OPENING

VERMONT

		CREDIT CARDS	OUTDOOR TABLES	VEGETARIAN	GOOD WINE	LATE OPENING
BURLINGTON: *India House Restaurant* $$$ 207 Colchester Ave. 🄲 *(802) 862-7800.* Specializing in traditional North Indian food, with both vegetarian and non-vegetarian choices. Authentic tandoori cooking. Good choice of beers. Reservations are recommended. L, D. 🄿 🄷 ♿		AE DC MC V D		■	●	
BURLINGTON: *Isabel's on the Waterfront* $$$ 112 Lake Sr. 🄲 *(802) 865-2522* Housed in a historic lumber mill overlooking Lake Champlain, the bike path, and Waterfront Park, this establishment serves eclectic American cuisine, and is especially known for the delicious Sunday brunches. L (except Sun), D, Brunch Sun. 🄿 🄨 🄷 ♿ ● Mon.		AE DC MC V D	●	■	●	
BURLINGTON: *New England Culinary Institute at NECI Commons* $$$ 25 Church St. 🄲 *(802) 862-6324.* On the Church Street Marketplace, run by the students of the Culinary Institute. High-quality eclectic American food with some French touches and emphasis on fresh, local ingredients. Reservations recommended. L, D, Brunch Sun. 🄨 🄨 🄷 ♿ ● Thanksgiving, Dec 25, Jan 1.		AE DC MC V D	●	■	●	
BURLINGTON: *Trattoria Delia* $$$ 152 St. Paul St. 🄲 *(802) 864-5253.* Family-run Old-World style restaurant. Good regional Italian specialties in a rustic setting: stone walls, exposed beams, and fireplace. Homemade pasta and a fine selection of Italian wines. Award of excellence from *Wine Spectator.* Reservations recommended. D. 🄿 🄨 🄨 🄷 ♿		DC MC V		■	●	
CRAFTSBURY: *Inn on the Common* $$$$$ 1165 North Craftsbury Rd. 🄲 *(800) 521-2233 or (802) 586-9619.* Famous restaurant in a charming Federal inn in ski country. Cuisine is contemporary American. The prix fixe menu changes daily and includes such dishes as baked cherry planked salmon and sauteed breast of duck. Award-winning wine cellar. Reservations required. D. 🄿 🄨 🄨		AE MC V		■	●	
GRAFTON: *Old Tavern at Grafton* $$$ 92 Main St. 🄲 *(800) 843-1801 or (802) 843-2231.* Housed in an inn built in 1801. Classic gourmet cooking with seasonal and cross-cultural influences. Only the freshest produce is used, including herbs from the inn's garden, and local meat and dairy products. Reservations required. B, L, D. 🄿 🄨 🄨 🎵 🄷 ♿ ● Mar–May		AE MC V		■	●	
KILLINGTON: *The Grist Mill Restaurant* $$$ Killington Rd. 🄲 *(802) 422-3970.* Designed to look like an old mill, this award-winning building has a dining room and separate entertainment lounge. The menu offers a wide range of reasonably priced New England-style food. Smoking is allowed in the lounge, which features live music and a signature cocktail called the "Goombay Smash". L, D, Brunch Sun. 🄿 🄨 🎵 🄷 ♿		AE D MC V	●	■	●	
LOWER WATERFORD: *The Rabbit Hill Inn* $$$$ 48 Lower Waterford Rd. 🄲 *(800) 762-8669 or (802) 748-5168* New American cuisine served in a tranquil 1795 country inn near St. Johnsbury. Prix fixe five-course meal, with local specialties. Reservations required; children 13 and over. D. 🄿 🄨 🄨 🎵 ♿		AE MC V		■	●	
MANCHESTER CENTER: *Up For Breakfast* $ 4935 Main St. 🄲 *(802) 362-4204* Delicious, nutritious breakfasts, with many varieties of eggs, pancakes, French toast, waffles, fruit plates, and tofu "eggs vegetarian." Choice of coffees, including a maple latte, fresh-squeezed orange or grapefruit juice or a champagne-and-OJ mimosa. B. 🄷		MC V		■		

MARLBORO: *The Skyline Restaurant* $$$ MC V

Rte 9. 📞 *(802) 464-5535*

High up on Hogback Mountain, between Wilmington and Brattleboro, this establishment offers its diners a splendid 100-mile view and American cooking, including steak, chicken, seafood, and pasta. Accessible by snowmobile in the winter.

B, L, D, Brunch Sun. 🅿 🍸 🍴 ♿ &

NORTH HERO: *North Hero House Inn and Restaurant* $$$$ AE MC V

3643 US Rte 2. 📞 *(888) 525-3644 or (802) 372-4732*

An 1891 inn located in the picturesque Champlain Islands. Chefs serve up a wide range of American food, from herb-roasted chicken with sauteed apples, raisins, cranberries, and maple syrup to rainbow trout stuffed with crabmeat. A glassed- or screened-in porch overlooks the lake. B, L (summer only), D, Brunch Sun. 🅿 🍸 🎵 ♿ &

SHELBURNE: *Sirloin Saloon* $$$ AE DC MC V D

2545 Shelburne Rd. 📞 *(802) 985-2200*

This restaurant is famous for its aged, hand-cut steaks and prime rib, as well as Maine lobster and fresh fish. Outstanding salad bar with fresh produce from local farms; some organic products. Children's menu is an excellent value. Warm, western-style decor and friendly service. Reservations recommended. D. 🅿 🍸 ♿ &

SHELBURNE: *Restaurant at the Inn at Shelburne Farms* $$$$ AE DC MC V D

1611 Harbor Rd. 📞 *(802) 985-8498*

Creative Continental cuisine in an historic mansion overlooking Lake Champlain. Some produce comes straight from their market garden; the farms produce cheese and bread for the restaurant as well. Free-range chicken, lamb, beef, fish and seafood, with menu changing a few times per season. Reservations required.

B, D, Brunch Sun. 🅿 🍸 🍴 🎵 ♿ & ● mid-Oct–mid-May

STOWE: *Maxwell's* $$$$$ AE DC MC V D

4000 Mountain Rd. 📞 *(800) 451-8686 or (802) 253-8585*

The fine dining option at the Top Notch Spa, Maxwell's serves gourmet New England cuisine with many health-conscious options. Menu includes seared tuna and free-range breast of chicken. This is an elegant room with beautiful views from large windows. It has received the Award of Excellence from *Wine Spectator*. B, D, Brunch Sun. 🅿 🍸 🍴 🎵 ♿ &

STRATTON: *Sage Hill* $$$$ AE MC V

61 Middle Ridge Rd. 📞 *(877) 887-3767 or (802) 297-2500*

In the Stratton Mountain Inn, a short walk from the base of the ski hill and the Village Square. Continental cuisine in a dining room with a fireplace and scenic views. Menu includes rack of lamb, filet mignon, chicken, fish, and pasta. B, D. 🅿 🍸 ♿ & ● mid-Nov.

NEW HAMPSHIRE

CENTER SANDWICH: *Corner House Inn* $$$$ AE MC V D

22 Main St. 📞 *(800) 501-6219 or (603) 284-6219.*

Local residents have been dining at this country inn for more than a century. Traditional American country cuisine served in four cozy rooms.

L, D, Brunch Sun. 🅿 🍸 🎵 ♿ & ● Mon during winter

CONCORD: *Cat'n Fiddle* $$$ AE MC V D

118 Manchester St. 📞 *(603) 228-8911.*

This 26-year-old family business is a Concord institution. The traditional American fare includes prime rib, steak, seafood, a huge salad bar, and shish kebabs. Casual setting. Reservations on weekends.

L, D, Brunch Sun. 🅿 🍸 ♿ &

DURHAM: *The Three Chimneys Inn* $$$$$ AE DC MC V D

17 Newmarket Road. 📞 *(603) 868-7800*

Fine American and European cuisine such as New England bouillabaise and duck confit, in a beautiful colonial mansion dining room. Vegetarian dishes upon request. L, D. 🅿 🍸 🍴 ♿ & ● Dec 24-25

EXETER: *The Terrace Restaurant at The Inn of Exeter* $$$$ AE MC V D

90 Front St. 📞 *(603) 772-5901.*

A deliciously elegant dining experience in an equally elegant inn. A recipient of 2000's Seacoast Chef of the Year Award.

B,L,D,Brunch Sun. 🅿 🍸 🍴 ♿ &

For key to symbols see back flap

Price categories include a three-course meal for one, half a bottle of house wine and all unavoidable extra charges such as sales tax and service. ⑤ under $20 ⑤⑤ $20–30 ⑤⑤⑤ $30–45 ⑤⑤⑤⑤ $45–60 ⑤⑤⑤⑤⑤ over $60	**CREDIT CARDS** Major credit cards accepted: *AE* American Express; *MC* Master Card/Access; *DC* Diners Club; *V* VISA; *D* Discover Card. **OUTDOOR TABLES** Garden, courtyard, or terrace with outside tables. **VEGETARIAN** A good selection of vegetarian dishes available. **GOOD WINE** Extensive list of good wines, both native and international. **LATE OPENING** Full menu or light meals served after 11pm.	**CREDIT CARDS**	**OUTDOOR TABLES**	**VEGETARIAN**	**GOOD WINE**	**LATE OPENING**

Restaurant	Price	Credit Cards	Outdoor Tables	Vegetarian	Good Wine	Late Opening
HANOVER: *The Daniel Webster Room* Main St. █ *(603) 643-4300.* The Hanover Inn's Edwardian style dining room specializes in seafood with a French influence. Recipient of a *Wine Spectator* Award. B, L, D, Brunch Sun. ▣ ▮ ▥ ▣ ● Sun & Mon dinner, Sat lunch	⑤⑤⑤⑤	AE DC MC V D	●		●	
KEENE: *Elm City Brewing Company* 222 West St. █ *(603) 355-3335.* This renovated 19th-century woolen mill turned restaurant/brewery offers freshly prepared creative American cuisine and eight homemade beers on tap in a lively atmosphere. Above price includes a pint of beer. L, D. ▣ ▮ ▥ ▥	⑤⑤	MC V D	●	■		■
LEBANON: *Sweet Tomatoes Trattoria* 1 Court St. █ *(603) 448-1711.* A popular spot for authentic Italian food in a friendly relaxed environment across from the Lebanon Green. L,D. ▣ ♫ ▥ ▥	⑤⑤⑤	AE MC V	●	■	●	
MEREDITH: *Hart's Turkey Farm Restaurant* Rte 3 & 104 Jct. █ *(603) 279-6212.* The farm was sold but the country-style turkey dinner remains a staple of this family business. A huge selection of non-turkey dishes are also available. ▣ ▮ ▥ ▥ ● Dec 25	⑤⑤	AE DC MC V D		■	●	
PORTSMOUTH: *The Blue Mermaid World Grill* 409 The Hill █ *(603) 427-2583.* A wonderful selection of internationally flavored dishes that include spiced pork, marinated lamb, and a great choice of seafoods prepared on a wood burning grill. Beverage list has 12 different Margaritas, tropical coolers, martinis, and a good wine list. L, D, Brunch Sun. ▣ ▮ ♫ ▥	⑤⑤⑤	AE DC MC V D	●	■	●	
PORTSMOUTH: *Cafe Mirabelle* 64 Bridge St. █ *(603) 430-9301.* Creatively original country-style French cuisine prepared by a classically trained chef in an elegant yet casual environment. Reservations required. L, D. ▣ ▥	⑤⑤⑤	MC V		■	●	
PORTSMOUTH: *Dunfey's Aboard the John Wanamaker* 1 Harbour Place. █ *(603) 433-3111.* This beautifully refurbished 1923 tug boat is New Hampshire's only floating restaurant. An emphasis on the freshest seafood means the New American cuisine changes with the season. Reservations recommended on weekends. L, D. ▣ ▮ ♫ ▥ ● Nov-late May: Sun-Mon.	⑤⑤⑤	AE DC MC V	●	■	●	
PORTSMOUTH: *The Oar House* 55 Ceres St. █ *(603) 436-4025.* A museum restaurant in a restored 1803 waterfront warehouse. Both the decor and mainly seafood menu reflect Portsmouth's maritime heritage. L,D,Brunch Sun. Reservations recommended. ▣ ▮ ♫ ▥ ▥ ● Thanksgiving, Dec 25.	⑤⑤⑤	AE DC MC V D	●		●	
PORTSMOUTH: *The Old Ferry Landing* 10 Ceres St. █ *(603) 431-5510.* From mid-April to September this predominately outdoor restaurant serves moderately priced seafood dinners, soups, and salads on a dock overlooking Portsmouth harbor. ▮ ▥ ▥	⑤⑤	AE MC V	●		●	
SUGAR HILL: *Sunset Hill House* 231 Sunset Hill Road. █ *(800) 786-4455 or (603) 823-5738.* Combine a talented chef with the phenomenal effect of sunset on the White Mountains to the east and the result is a memorable dining experience. Reservations required. B, D, ▣ ▮ ▮ ▥ ▥ ● Nov-Apr: Mon to Wed (except Christmas week)	⑤⑤⑤	AE MC V D	●	■	●	

MAINE

BAR HARBOR: *George's Restaurant* $$$$
7 Stephens Lane. (207) 288-4505.
Mediterranean cuisine with a New England twist is the best way to describe this culinary adventure. There is a fixed price, three-course meal. No air-conditioning. D. Nov–May.
AE, DC, MC, V, D

BETHEL: *Bethel Inn and Country Club* $$$$
Broad St. (207) 824-2175.
The formal dining room offers fine dining in lovely surroundings. A glassed-in veranda allows for year-round views. No air-conditioning. B, D. Nov–mid-Dec and Apr.
AE, DC, MC, V, D

CARIBOU: *Greenhouse Restaurant* $$
US 1 Rte 164. (207) 498-3733 or (800) 253-0466
Located in the Caribou Inn and Convention Center, this restaurant offers good home cooking at reasonable prices. Known for its inexpensive breakfast menu and the for the full turkey dinners served every Sunday. B, L, D.
AE, DC, MC, V, D

EUSTIS: *The Porter House Restaurant* $$$
Rte 27. (207) 246-7932.
The Porter House features a high quality of food at quite reasonable prices. The restaurant is a converted 1908 farmhouse with several dining rooms. Partially air-conditioned. D. Mon and Tue.
MC, V

GREENVILLE: *The Greenville Inn* $$$$$
Norris St. (888) 695-6000 or (207) 695-2206.
Housed in an 1895 Victorian mansion, the Greenville is a gourmet restaurant hidden away in remote Northern Maine. The chef will cater to vegetarian and other special requests. No air-conditioning. D. Sun mid-May–mid-Oct.
MC, V, D

KENNEBUNKPORT: *The Clam Shack* $
2 Western St. (207) 967-3321
Run by Richard and Jo-Anne Jacques, this take-out stand is the quintessential seaside experience. The menu consists of the some of the best fast food seafood you'll find, including fried and steamed clams, scallops, and a truly remarkable lobster roll. L, D. Columbus Day–May

OGUNQUIT: *Barnacle Billy's* $$$
Peking Cove. (207) 646-5575.
This is a classic, bare-bones Maine lobster house. A casual atmosphere and seaside surroundings set the tone for this spot. The more full-service Barnacle Billy's Etc. is right next door. L, D. Oct–Apr.
AE, MC, V

OGUNQUIT: *Arrows Restaurant* $$$$$
Berwick Rd. (207) 361-1100.
Considered one of the best restaurants in New England, the Arrows has won many awards, including *Bon Appetit* magazine"s restaurant of the month. The menu consists of innovative American cuisine, with fresh produce taken from the vegetable garden located on the grounds. Reservations required. D. mid-Dec–mid-Apr and some days. Call for details.
MC, V

PORTLAND: *Katahdin* $$$$
106 High St. (207) 774-1740.
The Katahdin features an eclectic but laid back setting matched by a wide variety of high quality fusion dishes. They don't take reservations, so be sure to get there early. D. Sun, Mon.
MC, V

PORTLAND: *Back Bay Grill* $$$$$
65 Portland St. (207) 772-8833.
The Back Bay Grill has a seasonal menu and offers elegant food in a modern setting. A *Wine Spectator* Award of Excellence winner, this restaurant has an enormous selection of wine and also is known for superb desserts. D. Sun.
AE, DC, MC, V, D

RANGELEY: *People's Choice Restaurant* $$$
Main St. (207) 864-5220.
Family dining in a casual environment. On weekends, the lounge offers live music and a rockin' dance floor. B, L, D.
AE, MC, V, D

For key to symbols see back flap

SHOPPING IN NEW ENGLAND

WHILE MOST PEOPLE seldom equate New England with shopping sprees, the region certainly offers a wide and ever-growing variety of high-quality stores and merchandise. Tourists looking for gifts with a regional flavor should sample the maple syrup and maple sugar candy, especially plentiful in the northern states of Vermont, New Hampshire, and Maine. Many coastal souvenir shops carry beautiful replicas of whalebone scrimshaw carvings. Regional arts and crafts can be found everywhere,

Outlet banner in Kittery

particularly in places such as Provincetown, Massachusetts. In Boston shoppers have a choice of shops, from out-of-the-way second-hand bookstores to trendy fashion boutiques. Of course, some of New England's most well-known shopping experiences happen at the factory outlet stores in Freeport and Kittery, Maine, and Worcester, Massachusetts, where brand name clothing can be found at a discount. These pages offer information for people seeking serious shopping while in New England.

OPENING HOURS

MOST STORES' HOURS are from 9 or 10am to 6pm Monday through Saturday and from 12pm to 5 or 6pm on Sunday. Many retail stores stay open until 9pm on Thursday night and the major department stores often stay open until 9 or 10pm during the week. It is always good to keep in mind that the larger malls, department stores, and factory outlet shops are usually busiest Saturdays, lunch hours, and evenings. Weekday mornings are the best times to shop.

SALES

THERE ARE TWO major sale seasons in New England, particularly in the major urban centers such as Boston. In July many summer clothes are offered at reduced prices in order to make room for the fall fashions. In January clothing and merchandise are cleared after the holidays. In general, the best bargains – and the most frenzied shopping – can be found in the two weeks immediately following Christmas Day.

PAYMENT AND TAXES

MAJOR CREDIT CARDS are accepted at most stores, and many are equipped to handle direct payment transactions with your bank card. Traveler's checks with the proper ID are also accepted at

Large glass atrium of busy Prudential Center shopping mall

many stores in the larger urban areas. In general, the prices on tags in New England stores do not include sales tax. This tax varies from state to state (see p367), ranging from 5 to 7 percent in all states except New Hampshire, which charges no sales tax on retail goods. It is always prudent to keep your bill or credit card receipt as proof of purchase should your merchandise be defective. Most stores will offer a full refund or replace the item.

SHOPPING MALLS

SHOPPING MALLS – clusters of shops, restaurants, and cinemas all within one large complex – have become top destinations for shoppers, offering variety, dining, and entertainment. The practical beauty of malls is that they gather under one expansive roof a wide range of retail stores, from the major department stores to

smaller specialty shops. New England's long, cold winters make malls a popular place for residents. Most malls also offer free parking, and even out-of-town shopping centers are located on public bus lines.

Boston has its share of popular malls. **Copley Place** has more than 100 shops and restaurants, and an 11-screen cinema complex, all centered

New England T-shirts, popular and ubiquitous

Filene's, a Boston shopping mecca for more than a century

around a dazzling 60-ft (18-m) atrium and waterfall. The **Shops at Prudential Center** include two department stores, a huge food court, and many smaller specialty shops. The upscale **Heritage on the Garden** overlooks Boston's Public Garden and features the boutiques of top designers, fine jewelers, and stores selling other luxury goods. Across the Charles River, **Cambridgeside Galleria** has over 100 shops and a waterfront food court.

Travelers looking for a shopping experience of a different kind should visit **Olde Mistick Village** in Mystic, Connecticut. Designed to look like a village from the 1700s, this 26-building complex houses a variety of restaurants and stores selling everything from handmade arts and crafts to fine imported wine.

DEPARTMENT STORES

THE LARGE DEPARTMENT stores are shopping complexes in their own right, offering a host of goods and services, from free gift-wrapping to assistants who will help customers with their shopping.

In general, the major chains are found throughout the US, with each having a particular reputation. For example, Bloomingdale's is known for the latest fashions. Popular discount chains such as K-Mart and Wal-Mart are the places to go for no-frills shopping for just about everything. Sears and JC Penny also deal in general merchandise. These stores are found throughout New England.

There are five major department stores in Boston, each offering a large and varied selection of clothing, accessories, cosmetics, and gifts. They also have restaurants and beauty salons, and provide a

variety of personal shopping services. For those wanting to shop at several stores, **At Your Service Concierge** provides shopping tours in Boston.

At Boston's **Downtown Crossing** (see p70), a bustling shopping district between Boston Common and the Financial District, generations of Bostonians have shopped at **Filene's**, a store that was founded in 1881. Featuring apparel from some of the best known American designers, as well as brand labels for women, men, and children, Filene's offers six floors of high-quality merchandise. It is famous for its bargain basement, now owned and operated separately. The store reduces basement items by 25 percent after 14 days, 50 percent after 21 days, and 75 percent after 28 days. After 35 days the clothes go to charity. Across the street, **Macy's**, the legendary New York emporium, offers an equally impressive array of fashions, cosmetics, and furnishings.

The Prudential Tower houses a complex of shops, including **Lord and Taylor**. The store is well known for its classic American designer labels, juniors and children's department, and men's wear, but it also carries crystal, china, and gifts. Next door, **Saks**

Fifth Avenue caters to a more upscale clientele.

However, for the ultimate high-fashion, high-profile shopping experience, visitors should stop by **Neiman Marcus**, which specializes in haute couture, precious jewelry, furs, and gifts. The store is famous for its Christmas catalog, with presents that have included authentic Egyptian mummies and vintage airplanes.

DISCOUNT AND OUTLET STORES

DEDICATED BARGAIN hunters will want to pay a visit to some of New England's famed outlet centers, where many top designers and major brand manufacturers offer late-season and over-stocked clothing and goods at big discounts. Generally sold at 20 to 30 percent less than regular retail prices, some items can be found reduced by as much as 75 percent.

In Wrentham, Massachusetts, 33 miles (53 km) southwest of Boston, are the **Wrentham Village Premium Outlets**. The stores here sell designer clothing, housewares, and accessories from many leading manufacturers.

Kittery (see p278), Maine, is an even larger outlet destination, with more than 125 shops selling everything from footwear and designer clothes to sports equipment, perfume, books, china, glass, and gifts. There are also numerous restaurants. Also in Maine, **Freeport** (see p284) is home to one of the largest and most famous outlet centers, the outdoor equipment specialist **L.L. Bean**.

L.L. Bean discount outlet, purveyor of outdoor equipment and clothing

ANTIQUING

Nᴇᴡ ᴇɴɢʟᴀɴᴅ ɪѕ an antique hunter's dream, with a multitude of stores offering a wide array of furniture, accessories, and collectibles. From the sprawling antique markets, collectives, and fairs to the smaller specialty shops, there are abundant opportunities to indulge a passion for the past.

Included among the prime antiquing areas in Massachusetts is the Charles Street section of Boston's Beacon Hill (*see p62*). One of the larger stores is **Antiques at 80 Charles**, which has two floors of merchandise ranging from silver tea sets to jewelry, paintings, clocks, and collectibles. Collectors of fine Asian antiques should not bypass **Alberts-Langdon, Inc.**, **Judith Dowling Asian Art**, or **Polly Latham Antiques**.

Boston visitors will also find several antique markets and dealers' collectives, such as the **Boston Antique Cooperative I and II**, which carries everything from antique quilts to candlesticks.

Well-made and distinctive gifts from shop in Sabbathday Lake Shaker Community, Maine

Antique carved whalebone, called scrimshaw

The Berkshires region (*see pp166–7*) is known for its antiquing, particularly in the town of Sheffield. Shops such as **Antiques Center of Sheffield** and **Darr Antiques** cover a broad range of Americana. Perhaps the state's most famous antiquing event is the **Brimfield Antique Show** (*see p161*), which is held three times a year in Brimfield. On the coast, scenic Route 6 through Cape Cod (*see pp156–9*) is peppered with antique shops, especially in the charming towns of Brewster and Dennis.

Connecticut's Litchfield Hills area is another antiques hotbed. The town of Woodbury has dozens of high-quality shops lining its Main Street, including **Wayne Pratt Antiques**, with its collection of impeccable 18th-century furniture. For antiques in Rhode Island, go to Spring Street and lower Thames Street in Newport.

In Maine, Route 1 between Kittery and Scarborough is loaded with shops that carry an eclectic selection of antiques and collectibles. New Hampshire's antiquing areas include Route 4 east of Concord, Route 101A in

Arts and crafts, a regional specialty

Milford, and Route 119 in Fitzwilliam. In Vermont, a large selection of antique shops can be found within the "Southern Circle" bounded by Route 9, Route 7A, and Route 30.

BOSTON FASHION

A ѕᴛᴀᴛᴇʟʏ ɪɴᴛᴇʀɴᴀᴛɪᴏɴᴀʟ city, Boston has many stores featuring fine clothes from Italy, France, England, and Japan, along with fashions from top American designers. Many offer quality clothing for both men and women. **Louis Boston** has long been known as the city's most exclusive men's outfitter. It now also features similarly beautiful clothing for women. Nearby on Newbury Street, **Giorgio Armani** and **Gianni Versace** carry extravagantly stylish and outrageously expensive clothing and accessories. **Alan Bilzerian** attracts celebrities looking for his label and the latest in fashion apparel from Europe and Japan.

Still on Newbury Street, women will find a wide range of stores catering to their every taste, be it the haute mode of **Chanel** in Boston's Ritz-Carlton Hotel or the colorful prints and youthful designs of the Dutch boutique **Oilily**. The street is filled with sumptuous, high-fashion boutiques, including **Bijoux** and **Max Mara**, Italy's most luxurious ready-to-wear manufacturer.

Men seeking the perfect Boston look need go no farther than **Brooks Brothers**, longtime purveyors of traditional, high-quality men's and boys' wear. America's foremost fashion house, **Polo/Ralph Lauren** offers top-quality and highly priced sports and formal attire.

Elsewhere **Abercrombie and Fitch** is favored by teenagers and college students, as is the original **Levi's Store**.

DIRECTORY

SHOPPING MALLS

Copley Place
100 Huntington Ave,
Boston, MA.
[(617) 369-5000.

Heritage on the Garden
300 Boylston St,
Boston, MA.
[(617) 426-9500.

Shops at Prudential Center
800 Boylston St,
Boston, MA.
[(617) 267-1002

DEPARTMENT STORES

At Your Service Concierge
23 St Sauveur Court, Cambridge,
Boston, MA.
[(781) 849-3560.

Filene's
426 Washington St,
Boston, MA.
[(617) 357-3000.

Lord and Taylor
Prudential Center,
Boston, MA.
[(617) 262-6000.

Macy's
450 Washington St,
Boston, MA.
[(617) 357-3000.

Neiman Marcus
5 Copley Place,
100 Huntington Ave,
Boston, MA.
[(617) 536-3660.

Saks Fifth Avenue
Prudential Center,
Boston, MA.
[(617) 262-8500.

DISCOUNT AND OUTLET STORES

Kittery Outlets
Kittery, ME.
[(888) KITTERY.

North Conway Factory Outlets
North Conway, NH.
[(800) 367-3364.

L.L. Bean
Freeport, ME.
[(800) 441-5713

Westbrook Factory Stores
Westbrook, CT.
[(888) SHOP-333

Vermont Factory Outlets
Manchester, VT.
[(802) 362-2100.

Wrentham Village Premium Outlets
Wrentham, MA.
[(508) 384-0600.

ANTIQUES

Alberts-Langdon, Inc.
126 Charles St,
Boston, MA.
[(617) 523-5924.

Antiques at 80 Charles
80 Charles St,
Boston, MA.
[(617) 742-8006.

Antiques Center of Sheffield
33 S Main St,
Sheffield, MA.
[(413) 229-3400.

Boston Antique Cooperative I and II
119 Charles St,
Boston, MA.
[(617) 227-9811.

Darr Antiques
S Main St,
Sheffield, MA.
[(413) 229-7773.

Judith Dowling Asian Art
133 Charles St,
Boston, MA.
[(617) 523-5211

Polly Latham Antiques
96 Charles St,
Boston, MA.
[(617) 723-7009.

Wayne Pratt Antiques
346 Main St,
Woodbury, CT.
[(203) 263-5676.

New Hampshire Antique Dealers' Association
[(603) 434-0449.

Vermont Antique Dealers' Association
[(802) 484-7799.

BOSTON FASHION

Abercrombie and Fitch
4 Faneuil Hall Marketplace,
Boston, MA.
[(617) 536-1001.

Alan Bilzerian
34 Newbury St,
Boston, MA.
[(617) 536-1001.

Bijoux
141 Newbury St,
Boston, MA.
[(617) 424-8877.

Brooks Brothers
46 Newbury St,
Boston, MA.
[(617) 267-2600.

Chanel
5 Newbury St,
Boston, MA.
[(617) 859-0055.

Gianni Versace
12 Newbury St,
Boston, MA.
[(617) 262-6100.

Giorgio Armani
22 Newbury St,
Boston, MA.
[(617) 267-3200.

Levi's Store
Prudential Center,
Boston, MA.
[(617) 375-9010.

Louis Boston
234 Berkley St,
Boston, MA.
[(617) 262-6100.

Max Mara
69 Newbury St,
Boston, MA.
[(617) 267-9775.

Oilily
32 Newbury St,
Boston, MA.
[(617) 247-2386.

Polo/Ralph Lauren
100 Huntington Ave,
Boston, MA.
[(617) 266-4121.

ENTERTAINMENT IN NEW ENGLAND

Nᴇᴡ ᴇɴɢʟᴀɴᴅ is a traveler's dream because it offers a wide range of entertainment opportunities. The sports-minded can take advantage of the region's plethora of outdoor activities *(see pp356–63)*. Those looking for a less strenuous afternoon or evening will never be at a loss. Free concerts and festivals abound throughout the New England summer, and there is no shortage of bars and nightclubs in which to slake, or build,

Carousel at Bushnell Park

your thirst. Mellow jazz lounges and smoky blues bars attract a devoted clientele, while elsewhere, sometimes just across the street, the younger set dances the night away to the rhythms of today's most popular music. Theater, dance, and classical music have long been the mainstays of the region's cultural identity, although pro sports may attract more fervent fans. Family activities and events fill out the range of possibilities.

A waltz evening at the Fairmont Copley Plaza Boston

Pʀᴀᴄᴛɪᴄᴀʟ Iɴꜰᴏʀᴍᴀᴛɪᴏɴ

Tʜᴇ ʙᴇꜱᴛ ꜱᴏᴜʀᴄᴇꜱ for listings of films, concerts, theater and dance performances, and exhibitions in New England are the Thursday and Friday editions of local newspapers, such as the *Providence Journal,* in Providence, Rhode Island, and the *Newport Daily News* in Newport, Rhode Island. In Boston check the Thursday "Calendar" of the *Boston Globe* and the entertainment weekly *The Boston Phoenix.* Even more up-to-the-minute listings can be found on the Internet at Ticketmaster's boston.city search.com, the *Boston Globe*

site www.boston.com, and the *Boston Phoenix* site www.bostonphoenix.com.

Bᴏᴏᴋɪɴɢ Tɪᴄᴋᴇᴛꜱ

Tɪᴄᴋᴇᴛꜱ ᴛᴏ ꜱᴏᴍᴇ of New England's most popular shows, especially some of Boston's popular musicals and theater productions, can be hard to come by, sometimes selling out months in advance. Your best bet is to book early, even for extended events such as the Boston Symphony Orchestra's summer-long Tanglewood concert series *(see p166).*

Two advance ticket agencies dominate New England for concerts, plays, and sports events: **Ticketmaster** and **NEXT Ticketing**. However, tickets for many of Boston's

Seiji Ozawa, conductor of the Boston Symphony Orchestra

concerts and sporting events can also be booked online at CitySearch by using your credit card. Half-price tickets to most non-commercial events as well as some commercial productions are available beginning at 11am on the day of the performance at **BosTix** booths. However, purchases must be made in person and only with cash.

Oᴘᴇɴ-Aɪʀ Fʀᴇᴇ Eɴᴛᴇʀᴛᴀɪɴᴍᴇɴᴛ

Tʜᴇ ᴡᴏɴᴅᴇʀꜰᴜʟ thing about New England is that there are so many free events to keep you entertained throughout the spring, summer, and fall. Revolutionary War reenactments, Native American celebrations, numerous regattas along the coast, and a host of free concerts offer something for everyone. Local newspapers are usually the best source of free show listings.

Boston's Harvard Square has been famous for four decades for its nightly and weekend scene of street performers. Many recording stars paid their dues on Brattle Street and Massachusetts Avenue, and many more flock there in the hope of being discovered – or at least picking up the cost of dinner by passing the hat. The best free outdoor summer entertainment in Boston is found at the Hatch Memorial Shell on the Charles River Esplanade. The Boston Pops

Independence Day fireworks display over Boston Harbor

performs there frequently during the week of July 4, culminating in a huge Independence Day concert complete with booming cannons and a stunning fireworks display. During July and August, the venue resonates with classical music on Wednesday nights, jazz on Sunday afternoons, and pop and rock on select Saturday evenings. On Friday evenings from late June through the Friday before Labor Day, the Hatch Memorial Shell shows big-screen family films.

College towns in New England, such as Burlington in Vermont, Hanover in New Hampshire, and New Haven in Connecticut, also host a wide variety of concerts and events. Many of them have no admission charge.

POPULAR MUSIC

A NUMBER OF LARGER CITIES, such as Worcester, Massachusetts, Providence and Newport, Rhode Island, Hartford and New Haven, Connecticut, and Burlington, Vermont, have vibrant music scenes. Bands and musicians can be found year-round playing everywhere from small clubs to large concert venues. The smaller concerts, especially if they are free, often fill up quickly, so it is wise to arrive a little early.

As you might expect, Boston's cosmopolitan spirit

and lively nightlife lend themselves to a wide range of musical influences, be it pop, punk, or smoky blues. One of Boston's leading venues for name rock bands and up-and-coming groups is **Avalon Ballroom**. The musicians at this Lansdowne Street club play early in order to clear the house out for a stylish late-night dance crowd. The two stages of the **Middle East** in Cambridge's Central Square lead the alternative rock scene, featuring both local bands and touring newcomers. Larger rock venues are the **Orpheum Theatre** and the stadium seating of the **FleetCenter**, which is otherwise occupied by hockey and basketball games.

Elsewhere Providence, Rhode Island, is home to **Lupo's Heartbreak Hotel**, a legendary spot for acts ranging from rock to R&B. In New Haven, Connecticut, **Toad's Place** is one of the city's hottest nightclubs and an intimate setting for pop, country, and folk concerts.

Boston has been particularly hospitable to jazz since the 1920s. The **Berklee Performance Center** in Back Bay is Boston's premier large concert venue for jazz. More intimate settings include **Scullers Jazz Club**

overlooking the Charles River in Brighton and the upscale martini-Scotch-cigar scene of the **Oak Bar** at the Fairmont Copley Plaza Boston.

The musical parent of jazz, blues is also alive and well in Boston. The charter room of the **House of Blues** chain at Harvard in Cambridge has a Hollywood ambience, but the music is genuine and the Sunday gospel-music brunch is legendary. The **Cantab Lounge** in Cambridge's Central Square is a blues-lover's gem, a bar where the owner "Little" Joe Cook plays his 1950s R&B three nights a week and sits in on the Sunday and Wednesday blues jams. The Cantab also runs Wednesday night poetry slams in a downstairs room.

Of course, Boston does not have a lock on blues and jazz. Newport, Rhode Island, has a number of famous spots, including **The Red Parrot**, a two-floor jazz bar, and the **Newport Blues Café**, a popular R&B club.

Boston's musical pastiche is rounded out by a host of top-rate folk and world music clubs. Harvard Square's **Club Passim** is a folk music legend. The club was the late-1950s and early-1960s hangout for the likes of Joan Baez and Van Morrison, and is still one of North America's key clubs in the touring life of singer-songwriters. To catch some local Caribbean tunes and dancing, the best bet is a weekend night at **Rhythm & Spice Caribbean Grill** in Cambridge's Central Square.

The Puerto Rico Festival at Salem, Massachusetts

An evening at the Axis, a dance club in Boston, Massachusetts

BARS AND NIGHTCLUBS

VIRTUALLY EVERY fair-sized city or town you come upon in New England has some type of bar or club. Often there is live entertainment on tap, be it music or stand-up comedy. This usually means having to pay some sort of cover charge.

Boston has a club for just about every dance scene, though little happens before 11pm. **Axis** is one of the edgier Lansdowne Street choices, with several nights of trance, techno, and house music, and gay male night on Sundays. At the other end of the spectrum, **The Big Easy** in the Theater District spins popular music for urban professionals. The surprisingly high-style **Lava** lounge in Kenmore Square draws a well-heeled Euro-crowd for its Versace kind of ambience.

Boston bars come in all shapes and sizes. Located in the basement of the Wilbur Theatre, the extravagantly decorated **Aria** is one of the chic places to be seen. Far more earnest, the venerable **Jacob Wirth Co. Restaurant** is the place to be on Friday for piano bar singalongs. Over the years, **Jillian's of Boston** has had a personality transplant, going from the city's best pool hall to a three-level entertainment complex complete with dart boards, video games, and 50 pool tables.

GAY CLUBS AND BARS

NEW ENGLAND HAS some areas that cater to gays and lesbians. Boston's gay scene comes into sharpest focus in the South End and Bay Village. You should consult the weekly *Bay Windows* magazine for entertainment listings. The perpetually packed **Fritz Lounge** attached to the Chandler Inn is a stalwart bar of the South End. Boston's longest-running gay bar, **Jacques**, features rock acts Friday through Monday and female-impersonator acts the rest of the week.

In Massachusetts, Cape Cod's Provincetown is the real center of the region's gay scene, particularly in the summer. Bars such as **Pied Piper** and **Atlantic House** cater almost exclusively to either an all-male or all-female crowd.

In the summer, a mixed gay and lesbian crowd gathers at the **Crown & Anchor** for the daily afternoon tea dance.

SPECTATOR SPORTS

NEW ENGLANDERS love their sports, as can be seen in the wide array of professional and semi-professional teams found throughout the region. Boston alone has three pro teams. The **Boston Red Sox** is one of the most storied teams in Major League Baseball. Baseball's regular season lasts from early April until early October, and the "Bosox" play their home games in Fenway Park.

The **Boston Bruins** hockey team has five Stanley Cup titles to its credit. During the regular season, running from September to April, the Bruins play in the FleetCenter. Tickets for their games are hard to come by, especially when their long-time rivals, the Montreal Canadiens, skate into town. The most successful Boston sports franchise is undoubtedly the **Boston Celtics**, a team that has won a remarkable 16 National Basketball Association (NBA) championships. The Celtics' regular season extends from October through April, during which time they often play to sold-out crowds at the 19,600-seat FleetCenter.

New England Patriots helmet

The region's only major sports team that does not call Boston home is the **New England Patriots**. The "Pats" bang heads with their National Football League (NFL) opponents in Foxboro Stadium, which is about an hour's drive south of downtown Boston. Most NFL games are played on Sunday during the autumn and early winter, although they also play some Monday night games.

Washington Capitals' Andrei Nikolishin taking a shot at Boston Bruins' goaltender Byron Dafoe

DIRECTORY

BOOKING TICKETS

BosTix
Faneuil Hall Marketplace,
Boston, MA.
((617) 482-2849.

NEXT Ticketing
((617) 423-NEXT.
w www.nextticketing.com

Ticketmaster
((617) 931-2000 (Boston).
((413) 733-2500 (Western MA).
((207) 775-3331 (ME).
((603) 868-7300 (NH).
((401) 331-2211 (RI).
((802) 862-5300 (VT).
w www.ticketmaster.com

POPULAR MUSIC

Avalon Ballroom
15 Lansdowne St,
Boston, MA.
((617) 262-2424.

Berklee Performance Center
Berklee College of Music,
136 Massachusetts Ave,
Boston, MA.
((617) 266-7455.

Cantab Lounge
738 Massachusetts Ave (Central Sq),
Cambridge, MA.
((617) 354-2685.

Club Passim
47 Palmer St (Harvard Sq),
Cambridge, MA.
((617) 492-7679.

FleetCenter
Off Canal St,
Boston, MA.
((617) 624-1050.

House of Blues
96 Winthrop St (Harvard Sq),
Cambridge, MA.
((617) 491-BLUE.

Lupo's Heartbreak Hotel
239 Westminster St,
Providence, RI.
((401) 272-5876.

Middle East
427/480 Massachusetts Ave
(Central Sq),
Cambridge, MA.
((617) 864-EAST.

Newport Blues Café
286 Thames St,
Newport, RI.
((401) 841-5510.

Oak Bar
Fairmont Copley Plaza Boston,
138 St James Ave,
Boston, MA.
((617) 267-5300.

Orpheum Theatre
One Hamilton Place,
Boston, MA.
((617) 679-0810.

The Red Parrot
348 Thames St,
Newport, RI.
((401) 847-3140.

Rhythm & Spice Caribbean Grill
315 Massachusetts Ave (Central Sq),
Cambridge, MA.
((617) 497-0977.

BARS AND NIGHTCLUBS

Aria
264 Tremont St,
Boston, MA.
((617) 338-7080.

Axis
13 Lansdowne St,
Boston, MA.
((617) 262-2437.

The Big Easy
One Boylston Place,
Boston, MA.
((617) 351-2560.

Jacob Wirth Co. Restaurant
31 Stuart St,
Boston, MA.
((617) 338-8586.

Jillian's of Boston
145 Ipswich St,
Boston, MA.
((617) 437-0300.

Lava
575 Commonwealth Ave,
Boston, MA.
((617) 267-7707.

Scullers Jazz Club
400 Soldiers Field Rd,
Boston, MA.
((617) 562-4111.

Toad's Place
300 York St,
New Haven, CT.
((203) 624-8623.

GAY CLUBS AND BARS

Atlantic House
4 Masonic,
Provincetown, MA.
((508) 487-3821.

Crown & Anchor
247 Commercial St,
Provincetown, MA.
((508) 487-1430.

Fritz Lounge
26 Chandler St,
Boston, MA.
((617) 482-4428.

Jacques
79 Broadway,
Boston, MA.
((617) 426-8902.

Pied Piper
193A Commercial St,
Provincetown, MA.
((508) 487-1527.

SPECTATOR SPORTS

Boston Bruins Hockey
FleetCenter,
Boston, MA.
((617) 931-2000
(Ticketmaster).
w www.bostonbruins.com

Boston Celtics Basketball
FleetCenter,
Boston, MA.
((617) 931-2000
(Ticketmaster).
w www.nba.com/Celtics

Boston Red Sox Baseball
Fenway Park,
Boston, MA
((617) 931-2000
(Ticketmaster).
w www.redsox.com

New England Patriots Football
Foxboro Stadium, Rte 1,
Foxboro, MA.
((617) 931-2000
(Ticketmaster).
w www.patriots.com

The Arts in New England

CULTURAL ACTIVITIES are a hallmark of New England. The larger towns and cities (especially Newport and Providence, Rhode Island, and New Haven, Connecticut) all have good symphony orchestras, dance companies, and playhouses. The hub of New England performing arts is Boston, with its world-famous symphony orchestra and bustling theater district.

CLASSICAL MUSIC AND OPERA

WHEN IT COMES to classical music, New Englanders are of one mind. The **Boston Symphony Orchestra** (BSO) and its popular music doppleganger, the Boston Pops, are cherished institutions with a long history of being led by some of America's finest conductors. The BSO performs a full schedule of concerts at Symphony Hall from October through April. The Pops moves in for May and June. In the summer, the BSO takes up residence at the **Tanglewood** (see pp166–7) estate in Lenox.

Boston's oldest musical organization is the Handel & Hayden Society (H&H), founded in 1815. As the first producer of such landmark works as Handel's Messiah (performed annually since 1818), Bach's B-Minor Mass and St. Matthew Passion, and Verdi's Requiem, H&H is one of the country's musical treasures. The organization gives regular performances at Symphony Hall, Jordan Hall, and Old South Church in Copley Square.

Classical music is ubiquitous in Boston. Emmanuel Music, for example, performs the entire Bach cantata cycle at services at Emmanuel Church on Newbury Street. The Isabella Stewart Gardner Museum (see p97) hosts a series of chamber music concerts, continuing a 19th-century tradition of professional chamber concerts in the homes of the social elite.

Boston once had a proud opera tradition, and retains a dormant major company and a grand opera house that remains shuttered. **Boston Lyric Opera** has jumped into the breach, performing small-cast and light opera at a number of places. In Great Barrington, Massachusetts, the **Berkshire Opera Company** produces two operas every July and August.

DANCE

THE REGION'S BEST dance is found in Boston. The city's largest and most popular resident company, the **Boston Ballet** performs a five-ballet season of classics and new choreography at the **Shubert Theatre** and **Wang Center for the Performing Arts**. The annual Nutcracker performances during the Christmas season are a Boston tradition. The more modest **José Mateo's Ballet Theatre** has built a strong body of repertory and choreography. Modern dance in Boston is represented by many small companies, collectives, and independent choreographers who often perform in the **Dance Complex** and **Green Street Studios** in Cambridge. **Dance Umbrella** is the city's principal producer and promoter of dance, presenting programs as varied as tap, ethnic dance, wheelchair dance, and avant-garde choreography. Touring companies often perform at the **Emerson Majestic Theatre**.

From late June to late August, **The School at Jacob's Pillow** in Becket, Massachusetts, hosts the famous Jacob's Pillow Dance Festival. This brilliant celebration attracts some of the world's top performers and highlights all styles of dance.

THEATER

THEATER IS ALIVE and well on stages throughout New England's six states. The epicenter of this dynamic world is, of course, Boston. The city's Theater District (see pp58–9) remains the most architecturally eminent group of early theaters in the US. Moreover, the active houses were largely restored to their original grandeur during the 1990s. Commercial theaters such as the Wilbur, Colonial, and Shubert and the Wang Center generally program road shows of Broadway productions.

The most avant-garde contemporary theater in Boston is found at the **American Repertory Theatre** (ART). ART often premiers new plays, but is best known for often-radical interpretations of traditional and modern classics. By contrast, the **Huntington Theatre** is widely praised for its traditional interpretations.

Several smaller companies, including **Lyric Stage**, devote their energies to showcasing local actors and directors and often premiere the work of Boston-area playwrights. Many of the most adventurous companies perform on one of the three stages at the **Boston Center for the Arts**.

Cape Cod has a number of decent theater companies, notably the **Provincetown Repertory Theatre** and the **Provincetown Theatre Company**. Some of the Cape's best summer theater is staged at the **Cape Playhouse** in Dennis.

Lenox, Massachusetts, is home to The Mount (see p167), the beautiful estate of author Edith Wharton. Each year **Shakespeare & Company** stages productions in the estate's various buildings and amphitheaters.

In Connecticut, at New Haven, the **Yale University Theatre** and **Yale Repertory Theatre** run acclaimed programs from October to May. Providence, Rhode Island, is home to another company with a deservedly sterling reputation, the **Trinity Repertory Company**, which has an interesting mix of programs.

DIRECTORY

STATE ARTS COUNCILS

Connecticut
CT Commission on the Arts
(860) 566-4770.
www.ctarts.org

Maine
Maine Performing Arts Network
(207) 942-7589.
www.maineperforming arts.org
www.mainemusic.org

Massachusetts
Massachusetts Cultural Council
(617) 727-3668.
www.massculturalcouncil.org

New Hampshire
NH State Council on the Arts
(603) 271-2789.
www.state.nh.us/nharts/

Rhode Island
RI State Council on the Arts
(401) 222-3880.
www.risca.state.ri.us

Vermont
Vermont Council on the Arts
(802) 828-3291.
www.vermontartscouncil.org

CLASSICAL MUSIC AND OPERA

Berkshire Opera Company
297 North St,
Pittsfield, MA.
(413) 443-1234.
www.berkop.org

Boston Lyric Opera
Various venues,
Boston, MA.
(617) 542-4912.
www.blo.org

Boston Symphony Orchestra
Symphony Hall,
301 Massachusetts Ave,
Boston, MA.
(617) 266-1492.
www.bso.org

Tanglewood Music Festival
Tanglewood Estate,
Lenox, MA.
(413) 637-5165) (estate).
(617) 266-1492 (for listings).
www.bso.org

DANCE

Boston Ballet
Various venues,
Boston, MA.
(617) 695-6950.
www.boston.com/bostonballet

Dance Complex
536 Massachusetts Ave,
Boston, MA.
(617) 547-9363.
www.dancecomplex.org

Dance Umbrella
Various venues,
Boston, MA.
(617) 482-7570.
www.danceumbrella.org

Emerson Majestic Theatre
219 Tremont St,
Boston, MA.
(617) 824-8000.
www.maj.org

Green Street Studios
185 Green St,
Cambridge, MA.
(617) 864-3191.
www.greenstreetstudios.com

José Mateo's Ballet Theatre
Emmerson Majestic Theatre,
Boston, MA.
(617) 354-7467.
www.btb.org

The School at Jacob's Pillow
358 George Carter Rd,
Becket, MA.
(413) 243-0745.
www.jacobspillow.org

Shubert Theatre
265 Tremont St,
Boston, MA.
(617) 482-9393.

Wang Center for the Performing Arts
270 Tremont St,
Boston, MA.
(617) 484-9393.
www.wangcenter.com

THEATER

American Repertory Theatre
Loeb Drama Center,
64 Brattle St,
Cambridge, MA.
(617) 547-8300.
www.amrep.org

Boston Center for the Arts
539 Tremont Ave,
Boston, MA.
(617) 426-2787.
www.bcaonline.org

Cape Playhouse
Dennis, MA.
(508) 385-3838 or
(508) 385-3911.

Colonial Theatre
106 Boylston St,
Boston, MA.
(617) 426-9366.

Huntington Theatre
264 Huntington Ave,
Boston, MA.
(617) 266-0800.
www.bu.edu/huntington

Lyric Stage
140 Claredon St,
Boston, MA.
(617) 437-7172.
www.lyricstage.com

Provincetown Repertory Theatre
Provincetown, MA.
(508) 487-0600.

Provincetown Theatre Company
Provincetown, MA.
(508) 487-8673.

Shakespeare & Company
The Mount,
Lenox, MA.
(651) 779-5818.
www.shakespeare-company.org

Trinity Repertory Company
201 Washington St,
Providence, RI.
(401) 521-1100 or
(401) 351-4242.

Wilbur Theatre
246 Tremont St,
Boston, MA.
(617) 423-4008.

Yale Repertory Theatre
222 York St,
New Haven, CT.
(203) 432-1234.
www.yale.edu/yalerep

Yale University Theatre
222 York St,
New Haven, CT.
(203) 432-1234.

Outdoor Activities

SQUEEZED WITHIN NEW ENGLAND's relatively compact borders there is a wealth of outdoor activities. Mountain ranges, forests, rivers, and miles of coastline have been preserved as natural playgrounds for outdoor enthusiasts ranging from people just looking for a quiet afternoon in the sun to serious backcountry trekkers. While the majority of unspoiled wilderness is found in northern New England, the much more densely populated south has plenty of adventures in store for visitors as well.

Boston's Swan Boats awaiting those looking for gentle cruises

Camping in White Mountain National Forest, New Hampshire

CAMPING

ALWAYS A POPULAR activity in New England, camping can also save you money on accommodations – depending on how much you are willing to rough it. While there are designated primitive camping areas in the backcountry of selected national forests, the more established campgrounds make up the majority of sites. Standard campgrounds, usually found in state and national forests, are equipped with facilities such as toilets, garbage disposal, and often facilities for hot showers. The tent sites at such places are usually spaced well apart and cost between $12 and $20 a night. For the

hardcore camper, primitive campsites found in national forests offer only the bare minimum: rudimentary cooking areas, pit toilets, and cold running water. These sites are perfect for the frugal outdoor enthusiast, usually costing no more than $10 a night.

On the opposite end of the spectrum, private campgrounds are models of luxury. Most cater to large recreational vehicles (RVs) and motor homes, with running water and electrical hookups. Hot showers and sewage hookups are often provided as well. Many upscale campgrounds have a host of recreational facilities that range from swimming to miniature golf courses. These sites are somewhat more expensive, costing $20 to $40 dollars or so a night.

Government-run campgrounds usually follow the summer season from the end of May through to early October. For the most part, private campgrounds have a much longer season, with some staying open year-round. Regardless of the type of camping that will be

Friendly welcome sign typical of campsites in New England

done, it is always a good idea to reserve a campsite early, especially during the busy summer months. Contact the **National Park Service** or the **National Recreation Reservation Service** for campground information and reservations. Always remember to notify someone of your itinerary and your approximate time of arrival at your destination should you decide to camp or hike by yourself.

HIKING

HIKING TRAILS crisscross almost all of New England, with the two most popular being the New England section of the Appalachian Trail *(see pp22–3)* and Vermont's 265-mile (426-km) Long Trail. Both trails can be quite challenging in spots, with extremely steep mountain climbs to stunning vistas. Maine's Baxter State Park *(see p298)* and New Hampshire's White Mountain National Forest *(see p265)* are both well known for their extensive networks of demanding trails. Not all nature walks need be difficult, however. Acadia National Park *(see pp288–9)* in Maine has an excellent system of easier hiking trails that lead past some of the most breathtaking coastal scenery. The **Rails-to-Trails Conservancy** provides information and maps on the almost 500 miles (800 km) of abandoned railroad tracks that have been converted into paths for cyclists and pedestrians alike. These paths stretch across a vast portion of New England. Companies such as **New England Hiking Holidays** organize excursions that last from two to five days.

Easy biking amid New England wildflowers

Hiking at Center Sandwich, New Hampshire

BIKING

IN ADDITION TO the more formal bike paths, the region possesses hundreds of miles of quiet back roads that are a cyclist's paradise. The pastoral scenery is beautiful, but the distances between towns are rarely so great that you will feel isolated. Cape Cod (see pp154–59) is famous for its wonderful bike paths, as is Nantucket (see p153) with its network of easy trails leading to pristine beaches. Many people believe that the best way to see Martha's Vineyard (see pp152–3), Block Island (see pp192–3), and the Litchfield Hills (see pp208–209) is by bike. Outfitters such as **Vermont Bicycle Touring** can help organize bike tours for some of New England's most scenic regions, supplying everything from bicycles and protective gear to maps and accommodations.

Mountain bikers also have plenty to choose from. Some ski areas let bikers use their lifts and slopes in the summer, and many of the region's forests are open to biking. Acadia National Park, Mount Desert Island (see pp188–9), and the White (see p265) and Green (see p244) mountains all have excellent facilities. To avoid damaging the surrounding environment, mountain bikers should stick to the marked trails. Cyclists should wear helmets and other protective gear.

FISHING

IF YOU LIKE TO FISH, you will love New England. Deep-sea fishing is best at Point Judith in Rhode Island, where you can rent boats through the **Rhode Island Party and Charterboat Association**. Farther up the coast at Cape Cod, surfcasters test the waters for striped bass and bluefish, which are most plentiful between July and October. Brook trout, walleye, and bass are plentiful in the inland streams and lakes, especially in Maine. Contact the **Maine Sporting Camp Association** for information regarding the state's top fishing camps and lodges. Fly-fishermen seeking to hone their skills can do so in one of the highly regarded programs run by **Orvis** in Manchester, Vermont. Fishing licenses are mandatory throughout New England and can be obtained at fishing supply stores.

Turbulent rapids in one of New England's mountain rivers

CANOEING, KAYAKING, AND WHITE-WATER RAFTING

MAINE IS THE premier destination for paddlers, beginning with sea kayakers who flock here each summer to ply the waters along the 3,500-mile (5,630-km) coast. One of the state's most popular excursions is the 325-mile (525-km) Maine Island Trail, which goes from Portland to Machais.

Maine's latticework of rivers is ideal for canoeing, with its most famous trek being down the challenging Allagash Wilderness Waterway (see

Large striped bass, trophy from Woods Hole, Massachusetts

p299). New Hampshire's Androscoggin River is another demanding waterway best tested by experienced paddlers. Canoeists looking for a more leisurely ride can skim across the calm waters of northern New England's lakes and ponds.

White-water rafting is the paddler's roller-coaster ride and, once again, Maine is the region's best theme park. The state's three major rivers, the Penobscot, Kennebec, and Dead, offer gut-wrenching tests of rafters' skills. **Raft Maine** will put you in touch with the proper outfitter. New Hampshire's Saco River is another favorite among the white-water set.

BOATING

NEW ENGLAND'S reputation as one of the world's great cruising areas is well deserved. The thousands of miles of shoreline are dotted with hundreds of anchorages. Penobscot Bay, Maine, and Newport, Rhode Island, are both considered sailing meccas. For those who want something a little calmer than the Atlantic Ocean, New England has countless lakes, large and small, including popular cruising destinations such as Sebago Lake, Lake Champlain, and Lake Winnipesaukee. Boat rentals are available at many seaside and lakeside resorts in New

England. A few outlets will rent a large sailboat for a day or night. These so-called "bareboat charters" are only for experienced sailors, particularly in Maine, where water and weather conditions can be treacherous. **Hinckley Yacht Charters** in Southwest Harbor, Maine, is one of New England's larger companies, with 25 crafts available. This company will also provide fully crewed yacht charters.

Top-notch windsurfing sites and rentals are also available at many locations up and down the coast.

CRUISES

WHALE-WATCHING cruises have become one of the region's most popular activities, with more and more coastal towns trying to cash in. Not quite an exact science, a successful whale-watching trip relies both on the experience of the ship's captain and on the guidance offered by high-tech sounding gear to find these majestic mammals. Most companies will offer a rain check if no whales are sighted.

Plan whale-watching trips carefully. Choose a calm day. Choppy water causes most people to become seasick. If you fear you will get sick, buy some ginger capsules at a health food store and take the recommended dose just before boarding.

Sightseeing and nature cruises are also available throughout New England. For a different view of the city, **Boston Harbor Cruises**

Group rafting run on the Cold River at Charlemont, Massachusetts

DIRECTORY

BIRD-WATCHING

**United States
Fish and
Wildlife Service**
Regional Office,
300 Westgate Center Dr,
Hadley, MA 01035-9589.
(413) 253-8200.
http://northeast.fws.gov/

**Connecticut
Audubon
Society**
2325 Burr St,
Fairfield, CT 06430.
(203) 259-6305 or
(800) 996-8747.
www.ctaudubon.org

**Maine Audubon
Society**
20 Gilsland Farm Rd,
Falmouth, ME 04105.
(207) 781-2330.
www.maineaudubon.org

**Massachusetts
Audubon Society**
208 S Great Rd,
Lincoln, MA 01773.
(800) AUDUBON (283-8266).
www.massaudubon.org

**New Hampshire
Audubon Society**
3 Silk Farm Rd,
Concord, NH 03301.
(603) 224-9909.
www.nhaudubon.org

**Audubon Society of
Rhode Island**
12 Sanderson Rd,
Smithfield, RI 02917-2600.
(401) 949-5454.
www.asri.org

Audubon Vermont
255 Sherman Hollow Rd,
Huntington, VT 05462.
(802) 434-3068.
www.audubon.org/chapter/vt/

BOATING

**Hinckley Yacht
Charters**
Greater Harbor Marina,
PO Box 950,
Southwest Harbor, ME 04679.
(800) HYC-SAIL or
(207) 244-5008.
www.acadia.net/hyc/

CAMPING

**National Park Service
Northeast Region**
Custom House, 200 Chestnut St,
Philadelphia, PA 19106.
(800) 365-2267.
www.nps.gov

**National Recreation
Reservation Service**
40 South St,
Balliston Spa, NY 12020.
(518) 885-3639.
www.reserveusa.com

**Connecticut Campground
Owners Association**
14 Rumford St,
West Hartford, CT 06107.
(860).521-4704.
www.campconn.com

**Maine Campground
Owners Association**
655 Main St,
Lewiston, ME 04240.
(207) 782-5874.
www.campmaine.com

**New Hampshire
Campground Owners
Association**
PO Box 320,
Twin Mountain, NH 03595.
(800) 822-6764.
www.ucampnh.com

**Bureau of Outdoor
Recreation, State Parks
Division**
79 Elm St,
Hartford, CT 06106.
(860) 424-3200.
www.dep.state.ct.us/rec/

**Maine Bureau of
Parks and Lands**
22 State House Station,
Augusta, ME 04333.
(207) 287-3821.
www.state.me.us/doc/parks.htm

**Massachusetts Division
of Forests and Parks**
251 Causeway St, Suite 600,
Boston, MA 02114.
(617) 973-8700.
www.state.ma.us/dem/
forparks.htm

**New Hampshire Division
of Parks and Recreation**
PO Box 1856,
Concord, NH 03302.
(603) 271-3556.

**Rhode Island Department
of Parks and Recreation**
2321 Hartford Ave,
Johnston, RI 02919-1719.
(401) 222-2632.
www.riparks.com

**Vermont Department
of Forests, Parks
and Recreation**
103 S Main St,
Waterbury, VT 05671.
(802) 241-3655.
www.vtstateparks.com

CRUISES

**Bar Harbor Whale
Watch Company**
1 West St,
Bar Harbor, ME, 04609.
(800) WHALES-4.

Boston Harbor Cruises
One Long Wharf,
Boston, MA 02110.
(617) 227-4320.
www.bostonharborcruises.com

FISHING AND
HUNTING

**Maine Sporting
Camp Association**
PO Box 89,
Jay, ME 04249.
www.mainesportingcamps.com

**Rhode Island Party and
Charterboat Association**
44 Obowen Briggs Ave,
Warwick, RI 02886.
(401) 739-6028.
www.rifishing.com

Orvis
Orvis Rd, Sunderland,
Manchester, VT 05254.
(802) 362-1300 or
(800) 235-9763.
www.orvis.com

HANG GLIDING
AND PARAGLIDING

**Vermont Hang-gliding
Association**
www.vhga.org

Morningside Flight Park
357 Morningside Lane,
Charlestown, NH 03603.
(603) 542-4416.
www.flymorningside.com

Boats at pier in Edgartown Harbor, Martha's Vineyard

offers sunset tours throughout the summer. River cruises are available on several New England waterways, including both the Charles and the Connecticut rivers in Massachusetts and Connecticut's Mystic River.

Windjammer cruises are also popular at many coastal towns in Massachusetts, Rhode Island, and Maine.

BIRD-WATCHING

WITH ITS DIVERSE habitats, ranging from mountains to coastal marshes and sand flats to conifer and mixed hardwood forests, New England offers some of the most interesting birding in the United States.

Massachusetts, home to the first Audubon Society in America, is famous for several areas, most notably the northeast coast at Newburyport, Cape Cod, and around the Berkshires. At Machias Seal Island, Maine, birders have a good opportunity to sight nesting colonies of Atlantic puffins. Special boat excursions to the island are offered by local charters.

National parks along with national wildlife refuges and protection areas are often the best places to bird since they are protected and unspoiled. **The US Fish and Wildlife Service** can provide

information on the location of refuges and the birding opportunities at each. Every state's **Audubon Society** will provide information on birding in the state as well as on Audubon field trips to various hotspots.

GOLF

NEW ENGLAND has more than its share of outstanding golf courses – in all price ranges and at all levels of difficulty.

Dedicated golf vacationers have a choice between some stunning coastal and mountain resorts. Of the former, Samoset Resort, located in Rockport, Maine, stands out above all the rest.

With ocean views on 14 holes, Samoset has been called the most visually appealing course in New England. Two other terrific coastal links, the Seaside course at New Seabury and the Ocean Edge Resort and Golf Club, are located on Cape Cod. For a full-fledged mountain golf holiday, consider the Equinox resort in Manchester, Vermont.

It features a championship 1927 Walter J. Travis design surrounded by the Green Mountains. Some famous ski destinations offer great golf as well. In western Maine, Sugarloaf/USA Golf Club presents a memorable Robert Trent Jones, Jr. layout that *Golf Digest* has ranked among the top ten for both memorability and aesthetics. Mount Snow is ranked as one of Vermont's top five courses. Both courses also offer summer golf schools, as does Quechee in Vermont. Other worthwhile mountain courses include The Balsams in north-

Signature of New England: a beautiful golf course

eastern New Hampshire and Cranwell Resort and Golf Club in the Berkshires.

TECHNICAL OR ROCK CLIMBING

WITH NEW ENGLAND's Green Mountains and White Mountains, it's little surprise that this part of the country offers some great climbing.

In Maine the vast majority of cliff climbing falls along its rugged south coast, with high-quality routes in a setting that is truly stunning. Acadia National Park is the most popular destination. Alpine climbers will also find a worthy test in Maine. Mount Katahdin, the state's highest peak, has some of the longest routes in New England.

New England's best climbing, however, is found in New Hampshire, where Cannon Cliff, Cathedral Ledge, and Whitehorse Ledge make up a triumvirate of diverse, challenging peaks. New Hampshire also offers bouldering and sport climbing at several sites, the best of which is Rumney in the center part of the state.

Connecticut and Rhode Island are not especially famed for their climbing, but both offer several quite good bouldering sites, most notably at Lincoln Woods, Rhode Island.

Climbing in Massachusetts is varied, with the central area of the state offering longer scenic routes and Boston providing some of the country's best urban cragging.

Vermont has few developed sites, though the treacherous sport of ice climbing is practiced at Smuggler's Notch and Lake Willoughby.

HUNTING

WITH ITS WIDE range of game spread across its diverse woodlands, New England offers something for every hunter. The hunting seasons are concentrated in the late summer and fall, with limited exceptions. Hunters in

Climber in bold ascent of New Hampshire's White Mountains

all six states require licenses. In most cases, the fees are significantly higher for out-of-state hunters. Guns must be kept unloaded during transport in all states, and in some of them, a secure transport case is mandatory. There are also regulations that govern transport of game out-of-state. For specific information on regulations in each state, contact the government department responsible for wildlife management in that state.

Ruffed grouse

HANG GLIDING AND PARAGLIDING

GOOD HANG gliding and paragliding sites abound in New England. That's no surprise, considering the large number of accessible places throughout the Green Mountains and the White Mountains. The best place to start is Morningside Flight Park in Charlestown, New Hampshire. It is the only full-time flight school and flying center in New England, and it has a 450-ft (137-m) summit launch site on the premises. Not far away in Vermont, Mount Ascutney is known as the premier cross-country hang-gliding site in New England, with flights having reached the Atlantic coast.

Southern New England is not without its advantages, however. Two of the best sand cliff launches are located in Cape Cod, Massachusetts, and Block Island, Rhode Island. Training is essential before attempting these sports. It is important to check local regulations before making any flight. You will find that many sites require memberships or have strict guidelines about landing areas. At state sites in Vermont, gliders must sign a waiver before making any flight. Contact the state association or a local club before making any jump.

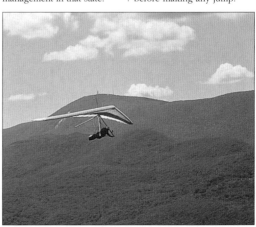

Daring way to view the Berkshires at North Adams, Massachusetts.

Winter Activities

Snowmobile

FAR FROM LAMENTING the end of the stunning fall foliage season, New Englanders instead begin readying themselves for winter activities. Skis and snowboards are pulled out and dusted off, snowmobiles are tuned up, and skates are sharpened in anticipation of cold weather and the slate of outdoor fun it brings. In New England top-notch ski hills and cross-country ski and snowmobiling trails are never far away. This is especially true in the region's northernmost reaches, where the annual blanket of snow is thickest and, for outdoor enthusiasts, most inviting.

Sleigh ride through Hancock Shaker Village in Pittsfield, Massachusetts

SKIING

PEOPLE HAVE been downhill skiing on New England's rounded peaks for more than a century. While the region does not have the elevation of the Rockies, it does offer many large hills, some with a vertical rise of more than 2,000 ft (610 m). The best skiing and snowboarding is concentrated in the three northern states. Vermont has the most high-quality peaks, with **Killington** offering the most trails at 200. But it is **Stowe** that can claim the title of New England's ski capital. A world-famous resort set in the quaint village of the same name, Stowe has the state's highest peak and offers excellent trails for skiers of all levels. For the experienced skier, **Mad River Glen** near Waitsfield provides a stern test in one of the most pristine settings in the world. It also forbids snowboarding.

The White Mountains in New Hampshire have a plethora of good ski hills; downhill, alpine, and cross-country trails are arguably the best in the Northeast. In Maine, **Sugarloaf/USA** and **Sunday River** are considered to be the best hills in the state.

Downhill ski trails in New England are accurately rated following a standard code: Easier = green circle; More Difficult = blue square; Most Difficult = black diamond; and Expert = double diamond. Rental equipment is available at all resorts, as are skiing and snowboarding lessons for all levels. Where price is concerned, in general, the larger, more famous resorts charge more for lift tickets. If you have time, look for off-site sellers. They typically offer reduced prices. Also ask about package deals and senior or child discounts.

Cross-country ski trails are also plentiful in New England. Towns such as Craftsbury Common, Vermont, and **Jackson, New Hampshire** have miles of groomed trails. State parks also often provide good trails. These are good areas for other winter activities such as sliding and snowshoeing. **Catamount Trail**, set aside for skiers and snowshoers, runs 300 miles (482 km) down the length of Vermont. Many renowned downhill resorts also offer cross-country trails. The trails at the **Trapp Family Lodge Ski Center** in Stowe are considered among the best in New England.

Low in the turn at Vermont's majestic Stowe resort

SNOWMOBILING

S NOWMOBILING is extremely popular all across New England, but Maine is truly the mecca for this activity. The state is interconnected by 12,500 miles (20,000 km) of trails and has more than 85,000 registered snow-mobiles using them. Resorts such as **Northern Outdoors** in The Forks and the **New England Outdoor Center** in Millinocket will rent snow-mobiles and accommodations, and supply guides for excursions. Most agencies require that renters have a valid driver's license.

SKATING

I N WINTER, New England has plenty of frozen lakes and rivers for skating. Always check with local authorities to be sure the ice is safe.

Winter also brings droves of bundled-up skaters to the Public Gardens lagoon and Boston Commons Frog Pond in Boston. Rentals are available in the warm-up shed or at the **Beacon Hall Skate Shop**. The **Metropolitan District Commission** also runs 23 indoor rinks in Boston, Cambridge, and surrounding communities.

Freestyle skiing, common at New England ski resorts

SURVIVAL
GUIDE

PRACTICAL INFORMATION

NEW ENGLAND OFFERS a wide variety of recreational activities within a relatively small area. Vacationers can hike the White Mountains of New Hampshire in the morning, swim at Maine's Ogunquit Beach in the afternoon, and take in the Boston Symphony Orchestra at night. Because tourism is such an important part of the regional economy, visitors will find numerous agencies and facilities geared toward making their stay an enjoyable one. Accommodations and restaurants (see pp302–345) come in all price ranges, allowing you to sleep and eat in comfort while staying on budget. For people without cars, transportation is readily available in Boston and throughout the six states (see pp375–9). The following pages offer some practical advice for people traveling in the New England states. Personal Security and Health (see pp370–71) outlines some general guidelines, while Banking/Currency and Communications (see pp372–3) answers some basic financial and media queries.

Acadia welcome sign

WHEN TO GO

NEW ENGLAND IS a four-season vacation destination but is particularly popular in the summer and fall. Generally speaking, the peak tourist period is from mid-June, when schools let out, through October. During this time accommodations and restaurant reservations can be hard to come by, especially in the busy resort towns along the coast. There is another rush during fall-foliage season (see pp20–21), which lasts from sometime in mid-September to late October. During this month-long stretch the hotels and B&Bs farther inland near the woods are booked solid. The length of the ski season depends entirely on the weather. It is not unheard of for New England winters to run from late November right

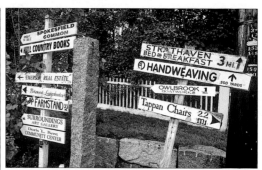

Enough signs to keep visitors busy in Center Sandwich, New Hampshire

through March, during which time New Hampshire and Vermont, which possess the bulk of New England's ski centers (see pp362–3), are busiest. If you are planning a backwoods vacation, it is prudent to avoid wooded areas in April and May, when the ground can be extremely muddy and swarms of hungry black flies fill the air. Don't be fooled by their small size; they have a big bite.

ENTRY REQUIREMENTS

ALL TRAVELERS to New England and the rest of the US should have a passport valid for six months longer than their intended period of stay. Those holding citizenship in the UK, most western European countries, Australia, New Zealand, and Japan require a passport, but do not need a visa if their stay is less than 90 days and

Snowboarding, popular with the young, daring, and fit

they hold a return ticket. Canadian residents require only proof of residence with a photo ID. Citizens of all other countries require a valid passport and a tourist visa, which can be obtained at a US consulate or embassy for a charge of $45. Always make sure to have your passport with you in a secure place, such as a money belt.

CUSTOMS ALLOWANCES

VISITORS OVER THE age of 21 are permitted to enter the US with two pints (1 l) of alcohol, 200 cigarettes, 50 cigars or four lbs (2 kg) of smoking tobaccos, and gifts worth up to $100. Prohibited items include meat products, cheese, and all fresh fruit. Travelers entering the country with more than $10,000 in cash or in traveler's checks must declare the money to customs officials upon entry.

TAXES IN NEW ENGLAND

State	Lodging	Meal	Sales
Connecticut	12%	6%	6%
Maine	7%	7%	5%
Massachusetts	12.5%	5%	5%
New Hampshire	8%	8%	–
Rhode Island	12%	7%	7%
Vermont	9%	9%	5%

TOURIST INFORMATION

STATE TOURISM offices are excellent sources of information and are happy to send road maps, brochures, and listings of accommodations, seasonal events, and attractions free of charge. Some offices also carry discount vouchers for lodging, restaurants, and admission fees. Tourist information booths or welcome centers are equipped with toilets and rest areas are usually found upon entering states on major highways. Many towns maintain a visitors' bureau that dispenses information on local activities, lodgings, and restaurants.

OPENING HOURS

OFFICES ARE generally open from 9am to 5pm Monday to Friday and do not close for lunch. Most stores keep hours from 9 or 10am to 6pm Monday to Saturday, although they often stay open until 9 or 10pm on Thursday and Friday. More and more stores are opening on Sunday. Most New England banks are open from 9am to 3 or 4pm Monday to Thursday and stay open later on Friday. Many banks are open on Saturday. The larger museums are usually open 10am to 5pm Tuesday through Sunday, but

Making the most of summer weather at outdoor cafés

check with the hours listed in this guide. Smaller museums may have seasonal hours and often shut down during the winter. An increasing number of gas stations and convenience stores now stay open 24 hours a day.

ALCOHOL AND CIGARETTES

THE LEGAL drinking age throughout New England is 21, and most young people will be asked to produce a photo ID as proof of age in order to buy alcohol or enter a bar. Your passport is usually your best bet. Drinking in public spaces is against the law, and the

penalties for driving under the influence of alcohol are severe, including the loss of your driver's license.

Cigarettes can be sold only to people 18 years of age or older. It is against the law to smoke in public buildings, such as hospitals, and on public conveyances, including subways and buses. Most restaurants still permit smoking in designated sections, although more and more are completely "smoke-free."

ELECTRICITY

ELECTRICITY FLOWS at the standard US110-120 volts AC (alternating current). Foreign-made electrical appliances may require a US-style plug adapter and a voltage converter.

TAXES

TAXES VARY ON a state-by-state basis. There is no federal sales tax, but all New England states, with the exception of New Hampshire, levy their own sales tax. All states charge taxes on hotel rooms and restaurant meals. Travelers should be aware that many accommodations tack on additional surcharges such as housekeeping and parking fees to bills that can increase the total by up to 15 percent. To avoid unpleasant surprises at the end of a stay, visitors should inquire about extra service charges before they check in.

TIPPING

ALTHOUGH THERE are no set guidelines for tipping, a gratuity is usually given for most services. Travelers should give waiters 15 to 20 percent of the bill, bartenders 50¢ to $1 per drink, barbers 15 percent of the bill, and taxi drivers between 12 and 18 percent of the fare. Porters usually get $1 per piece of luggage and hotel maids $1 per night of stay. Tipping is not usually required at fast-food restaurants, although there is sometimes a jar by the cash register for tips that will be shared by employees.

Mopeds, a popular form of transportation for visitors on the go

HOLIDAYS

WHILE EACH STATE may have its own set of holidays, some major public holidays are celebrated throughout the US. Visitors should keep in mind that on these days schools, banks, and government offices are closed. Museums and transportation services operate on limited schedules, but many retail stores and restaurants maintain regular business hours.

New Year's Day
Jan 1.
Martin Luther King, Jr. Day
3rd Mon in Jan.
President's Day
3rd Mon in Feb.
Memorial Day
Last Mon in May.
Independence Day
Jul 4.
Labor Day
1st Mon in Sep.
Columbus Day
2nd Mon in Oct.
Veterans' Day
Nov 11.
Thanksgiving
4th Thu in Nov.
Christmas Day
Dec 25.

Patriotic decorations for Independence Day

Youngsters taking a break from sightseeing on a New England wharf

TRAVELING WITH CHILDREN

NEW ENGLAND is a fairly child-friendly place. Many museums, zoos, and aquariums offer hands-on and interactive exhibits that encourage younger participants. The multitude of state parks and forests and public beaches give children lots of space to burn excess energy.

Many establishments and services cater to families by having children's menus and reduced admission rates. Most hotels and motels will charge $10 to $20 per cot so that children can stay in the same room as their parents. The same is generally not true for inns and bed and breakfasts (B&Bs), some of which will not take children under a certain age.

STUDENT TRAVELERS

STUDENTS FROM abroad should buy an **International Student Identification Card** (ISIC) before traveling to New England. Numerous discounts are available to cardholders at such places as hostels, museums, and theaters. This is especially true in Boston. The **Student Advantage Card** is a similar card and is available to all American university students. It is advisable for young travelers to carry their passports or driver's license for entry into bars or to buy alcohol in restaurants.

SENIOR CITIZENS

SENIORS ARE ELIGIBLE for a myriad of discounts ranging from car rentals and lodgings to national parks and museums. Depending on the place, the minimum qualifying age for seniors can be as low as 50. Visitors should contact the **American**

Easy bird-watching at Claremont Hotel, Southwest Harbor, Maine

Association of Retired Persons (AARP) for more information. Also, travelers should try the Boston-based, international senior travel organization **Elderhostel**. The organization offers discount lodgings, educational programs, and field trips throughout New England and the US for travelers over the age of 55.

DISABLED TRAVELERS

WHILE US FEDERAL LAW requires that businesses are accessible to the disabled, some historic buildings have limited access for wheelchairs. Most hotels and restaurants are equipped for people with special needs, and more and more small inns are retrofitting some of their rooms. Many outdoor recreation areas, including all national parks, now provide rest rooms and facilities for the disabled, including tour buses and wheelchair-friendly trails. The best advice for disabled travelers is to call ahead or to contact organizations such as the **Society for the Advancement of Travel for the Handicapped** or Mobility International. Both groups provide information and comprehensive guides on the issues of accessibility for the disabled.

Celebration of the first same-sex civil union in Vermont

GAY AND LESBIAN TRAVELERS

N EW ENGLAND has a number of vibrant gay communities. Most notable is Provincetown (see pp156–7) on northernmost Cape Cod. Other gay enclaves include Ogunquit (see pp278–9), Maine, and Boston's South End. *Bay Windows*, New England's largest gay and lesbian weekly, includes arts and cultural listings for all six states, as well as local and regional news. Vermont, which became the first state in the US to legally acknowledge same-sex civil unions, has a well regarded monthly news-letter called *Out in the Mountains*.

DIRECTORY

TOURIST INFORMATION

Connecticut Office of Tourism
505 Hudson St,
Hartford, CT 06105.
☎ (860) 270-8080 or
(800) 282-6863.

Greater Boston Convention and Visitors Bureau
2 Copley Place, Suite 105,
Boston, MA 02116.
☎ (888) SEE BOSTON or (617) 426-3115 or (617) 536-4100.
🌐 www.bostonusa.com

Maine Office of Tourism
59 State House Station,
Augusta, ME 04333-0059.
☎ (207) 287-5711.
🌐 www.visitmaine.com

Massachusetts Office of Travel & Tourism
10 Park Plaza, Suite 4510,
Boston, MA 02116.
☎ (617) 973-8500 or
(800) 447-6277.
🌐 www.massvacation.com

New Hampshire Division of Travel & Tourism Development
172 Pembroke Rd, PO Box 1856,
Concord, NH 03302.
☎ (603) 271-2666.
🌐 www.visitnh.gov

Rhode Island Tourism Division
1 West Exchange St,
Providence, RI 02903.
☎ (401) 222-2601 or
(800) 556-2484.
🌐 www.visitrhodeisland.com

Vermont Department of Tourism and Marketing
6 Baldwin St, Drawer 33,
Montpelier, VT 05633-1301.
☎ (802) 828-3237 or
(800) VERMONT.
🌐 www.1-800-vermont.com

STUDENTS

International Student Identity Card (ISIC)
6 Hamilton Place,
4th floor, ID Dept,
Boston, MA 02108.
☎ (800) 2CANCIL.
🌐 www.canciltravel.com

Student Advantage Card
280 Summer St,
Boston, MA 02210.
☎ (877) 256-4672.
🌐 www.studentadvantage.com

SENIOR CITIZENS

American Association of Retired Persons (AARP)
601 E St NW,
Washington, DC 20049.
☎ (800) 424-3410.
🌐 www.aarp.org

Elderhostel
11 Ave de Lafayette,
Boston, MA 02111.
☎ (617) 426-7788.
🌐 www.elderhostel.org

GAY AND LESBIAN

Bay Windows
631 Tremont St,
Boston, MA 02118.
☎ (617) 266-0393.
🌐 www.baywindows.com

Out in the Mountains
PO Box 1078,
Richmond VT 05477.
☎ (802) 434-6486.
🌐 www.mountainpridemedia.org

DISABLED VISITORS

Society for the Advancement of Travel for the Handicapped
347 Fifth Ave, Suite 610,
New York City, NY 10016.
☎ (212) 447-1928.
🌐 www.sath.org

USEFUL WEBSITES

NewEngland.com
🌐 www.newengland.com

Visit New England.com
🌐 www.visitnewengland.com

Boston Globe Online
🌐 www.boston.com

Boston Citysearch
🌐 boston.citysearch.com

Personal Security and Health

Park Ranger

NEW ENGLAND'S COMPARATIVELY low crime rate makes it a safe vacation destination. Even its largest metropolitan area, Boston, has seen crime on a steady decrease since the early 1990s. Nonetheless, it is always a good idea for travelers to take a few simple precautions to make sure that their trip is a safe one. This same rule of thumb applies to the wilderness areas. Almost free of crime, these areas possess a number of natural hazards that can be minimized.

Motorized police patrol on Surfside Beach, Nantucket, Massachusetts

LAW ENFORCEMENT

THREE AGENCIES share law enforcement duties: city police, sheriffs (who patrol county areas), and the state Highway Patrol, which deals with traffic accidents and offenses outside city boundaries. New England law enforcement officials are friendly and helpful.

EMERGENCIES

SHOULD YOU require emergency medical, police, or fire services, call 911. The call is free from public phones. Emergency phone boxes are located along major highways. **The Travelers' Aid Society** specializes in providing assistance for those travelers who find themselves stranded.

LEGAL ASSISTANCE

TRAVELERS FROM outside the US who are in need of legal assistance should immediately contact their nearest consulate or their embassy in Washington, D.C. Should you be arrested you have the right to remain silent and are given the right to make one phone call. The police will provide you with the embassy and consulate telephone numbers upon request.

GUIDELINES ON SAFETY

AS WITH ALL large urban centers, New England's major cities, including Boston, Burlington, Worcester, Springfield, New Haven, Hartford, Providence, and Portland, have pockets of crime. Generally speaking, the main tourist areas are safe as most of the problems occur in neighborhoods not usually frequented by travelers. While the numbers of street people or "panhandlers" in cities is on the rise, they are almost always harmless.

It is a good policy to avoid wandering into city neighborhoods that are off the beaten track. Pickpockets are sometimes at work in the busy centers and will target anyone who looks like a tourist. Your best defense is common sense. Avoid wearing expensive jewelry and carry cameras and camcorders securely. As well, you should carry only small amounts of cash. Credit cards and traveler's checks are the most secure options. Money belts or pouches worn under clothing provide maximum security against pickpockets, especially in crowded areas such as buses and malls. While theft in hotels is not common, it is prudent to store valuables in the safe when you are out.

Always lock your car when you leave it and store bags and valuables in the trunk. Valuables left in the open in unattended cars are easy targets for smash-and-grab thieves. In major urban areas it is best to avoid walking through parks or strange neighborhoods at night. Always use automatic teller machines (ATM) on busier, well-lit streets.

Before you leave home, make a photocopy of important documents, including your passport and visa, and keep them with you, but separate from the originals. Also make a note the numbers of your traveler's checks and credit cards, in the event they are stolen.

Fire engine and equipment

Lost and Stolen Property

A̲ LTHOUGH THE chances of retrieving lost or stolen property are very slim, report all missing items to the police and make sure you get a copy of the police report for your insurance claim. In the event of a loss or a theft, it is useful to have a record of your valuables' serial numbers and receipts as proof of possession. If you have misplaced something, retracing your steps can also help: try to remember the taxi companies and bus or train routes you were using when the item went missing. Most taxi and transport companies have Lost and Found departments which can be reached by phoning the general access phone number.

Passport

A stolen passport should be reported immediately to your country's embassy or consulate. Most credit card companies have toll-free numbers to report a lost or stolen card, as do Thomas Cook and American Express for lost traveler's checks *(see right)*, which can often be replaced within a few hours.

Travel Insurance

T̲ HE US DOES not have a national health program and, as a result, emergency medical and dental care, though excellent, can be very expensive. Medical travel insurance is highly recommended in order to defer some costs related to an unscheduled stop in a US hospital. Even with medical coverage you may have to pay for ser-

Passports, easily stolen from careless visitors

vices when you reeive them, then claim reimbursement from your insurance company later. Make sure the insurance policy you choose covers trip cancellation and baggage or document loss, emergency medical care, and accidental death.

Outdoor safety

N̲ EW ENGLAND offers a wide variety of outdoor recreational activities, some of which entail certain risks. These risks can be minimized, however, if the proper precautions are taken. Helmets and other protective items are essential, and often mandatory, for such activities as white-water rafting and mountain biking, as are life jackets for all types of boating. Hikers should always stay on marked trails; those who are hiking or camping alone should notify someone of their destination and estimated time of arrival. Campers should never feed animals and should suspend food from a tree branch to avoid visits from bears. If you see a bear in the distance, yell and wave your arms so as not to surprise it, then back away. If the bear is

Hiking trail marker

Directory

Emergencies

Police, Fire, Medical (all emergencies)
📞 Call 911 (toll-free, or dial 0 for the operator.)

Area Hospitals
📞 Call 411 for directory assistance

Travelers' Aid Society
17 East St,
Boston, MA 02111.
📞 (617) 542-7286.
(For branches in other cities in Massachusetts, Connecticut, or Rhode Island, look in the Yellow Pages or dial 411 for directory assistance).
🌐 www.travelersaid.org

Lost or Stolen Credit Cards and Traveler's Checks

American Express
📞 (800) 528-4800 (cards)
📞 (800) 221-7282 (checks)

Diners Club
📞 (800) 234-6377

Discover
📞 (800) DISCOVER

MasterCard
📞 (800) 826-2181

Thomas Cook
📞 (800) 223-7373 (checks)

Visa
📞 (800) 336-8472

close, don't look it in the eyes. Back away slowly, while talking softly. Do not run. Campfires should be carefully extinguished with water. Mountain hikers and rock climbers should always be prepared for sudden changes in the weather, especially in higher elevations. Ocean swimmers are advised to use beaches with lifeguards and should ask about undertows. Wear a hat and apply sun block in summer. Hikers would be smart to wear bright-colored clothes and avoid forests and fields during hunting season.

Ambulance

Banking/Currency and Communications

BECAUSE MANY New England banks outside of Boston do not exchange foreign currency, travelers from abroad should plan to use their credit cards, US-dollar traveler's checks, or, most conveniently, Automatic Teller Machine (cash machine) cards. Never carry all your money and credit cards with you at the same time, and keep in mind that most banks and foreign currency exchanges are closed on Sundays.

A dollar bill ($1), a quarter (25¢), pennies (1¢), and a nickel (5¢)

BANKING

MOST NEW ENGLAND banks are open from 9am to 3 or 4pm Monday to Thursday and stay open later on Friday. Many banks are open on Saturday. All banks are closed on Sunday and public holidays.

Traveler's checks can usually be cashed at banks with a recognized photo ID, such as a passport. Main branches of national banks are located in the large urban areas and will exchange foreign currency for a small fee. It is always a good idea to ask about hidden service charges or commissions before you make a transaction. In general, you will get the best rates at big city banks or private exchange bureaus in larger centers.

The most commonly accepted credit cards in New England

AUTOMATIC TELLER MACHINES

AUTOMATIC TELLER MACHINES (ATMs) are found throughout New England, even in tiny country villages. Look for them in bank foyers or just outside the entrances. ATMs are also found in airports, train stations, shopping malls, supermarkets, large gas stations, and along streets of most major cities. Widely found bank-card networks include Cirrus, Plus, Star Systems, and Interlink. The machines also will dispense money to credit cards such as VISA or MasterCard. Before leaving home, ask your bank if your card can be used in New England. Bank cards can also be used to pay at many hotels, restaurants, retail stores, and gas stations.

CREDIT CARDS

THE MOST commonly accepted credit cards in New England are MasterCard, VISA, and American Express, although Diner's Club and the Discovery Card are gaining popularity. Credit cards can be used at restaurants, shops, and hotels, as well as to reserve tickets over the phone or to book a rental car. The biggest benefit of

credit cards is that they offer you much more security than having to carry around large sums of cash, and they can be very useful in emergency situations.

TRAVELER'S CHECKS

THE MAJOR advantage offered by traveler's checks is that, unlike cash, they can be refunded if they are lost or stolen. American Express and Thomas Cook traveler's checks are accepted in many US shops, restaurants, and hotels, especially in the major tourist centers. It is often easier to pay directly with US-dollar traveler's checks than cashing them in advance, and you will get your change in cash.

Banks and exchange bureaus will exchange your US-dollar traveler's checks directly into cash. Traveler's checks in foreign currency can be cashed at a bank or with a cashier at some major hotels. Exchange rates and commission charges are always posted and sometimes a little shopping around will save you some money. Personal checks drawn on overseas banks are rarely accepted in the US.

FOREIGN EXCHANGE

ONCE YOU ARE outside the major cities, you may find it difficult to exchange your foreign currency. Most foreign exchange offices are open from 9am to 5pm weekdays. Among the best-known agencies are **American**

Imaginative country mailboxes near Grafton, Vermont

Express Travel Agency and **Thomas Cook Currency Services**. For the best rates, avoid exchanging your money at airports or train or bus stations. Banks will usually give you the most favorable rates.

TELEPHONES

WHILE ALL New England pay phones accept coins (5¢, 10¢, and 25¢), more and more are being retooled to take phone and credit cards as well, especially in the major urban areas. Local calls cost between 25¢ and 35¢ for three minutes from pay phones, while long-distance rates vary and include both a fixed call charge and a per-minute charge. The easiest way to find out the ever-changing rates is to dial **0** and ask the operator. Do not get the operator to put the call through, however, as calling direct is substantially cheaper. Of course, dialing direct from your hotel room can carry hefty surcharges, meaning it is usually cheaper to place the call yourself using the pay phone in the lobby. Generally speaking, the least expensive times to make long-distance calls are between 11pm and 8am on weekdays and on weekends (except 5pm to 11pm on Sunday). During these periods, you can benefit from a discount of up to 60 percent.

All numbers with a **1-800** or **1-888** prefix are free of charge, as is directory assistance from a pay phone (dial **411** for local, **00** for international), and emergency services (**911**). Operator assistance (**0** for local, **01** for international) has a charge.

Mobile phones can be rented in many New England centers. Visitors from abroad who wish to bring their mobile phones with them should check with their providers before leaving home. Some plans do have international plans that cover the US, but it may be easier to rent a mobile phone once you are in the US.

POSTAL SERVICE

POST OFFICES ARE open weekdays from 9am to 5pm, with some branches offering service on Saturday. All are closed on Sunday and federal holidays. Letters and small parcels with the proper postage can be placed in any blue mailbox. Domestic mail takes one to five days for delivery – longer if you forget the zip code. You can speed up delivery by several days by paying for **Priority Mail** or **Express Mail**'s next-day delivery for domestic mail. It is faster to send overseas mail via airmail.

Public pay phone

COMMUNICATIONS AND MEDIA

THE MOST POPULAR US newspaper in terms of circulation is the *Wall Street Journal*, followed by *USA Today*, *The New York Times*, and the *Los Angeles Times*. They can be found in virtually all major cities. The *Boston Globe* is the most well-respected and widely read newspaper coming out of New England. The *Boston Herald* is a popular tabloid-style daily. The region has many fine local newspapers.

Game shows, soaps, sitcoms, and talk shows dominate the US television airwaves. Cable channels offer 24-hour access to sports, movies, music videos, and news. Public station PBS offers a more highbrow diet of documentaries, concerts, and classic films. Hotels usually have access to the major networks such as CBS, NBC, and ABC, as well as the more popular cable channels such as ESPN (specializing in sports) and CNN (the top news station).

In general, radio stations follow a specific programming format. Those stations on FM frequencies tend to stick to a particular type of music, be it rock, jazz, Top 40, or country western. AM stations are usually geared toward talk-radio shows in which listeners call in to discuss the issues of the day.

Surfing the Internet is fairly easy. Many New England libraries are plugged into the Internet and have terminals, although you may have to pay at some locations. Cyber cafés are increasingly popular, especially in the larger cities. More and more major hotels also offer Internet access to their clientele.

Some of New England's many fine local newspapers

Getting to New England

WHILE THE MOST COMMON WAYS to get to New England are by plane or by car, train and bus services also provide decent access to many regions, particularly the southern New England states. Many people like to begin their vacation in Boston because the city's Logan International Airport handles international flights. Boston is also the hub for rail and bus services coming in from all over the US and parts of Canada.

Bird's-eye view of Camden Harbor in Maine

ARRIVING BY AIR

BOSTON'S **LOGAN International Airport** (BOS) is the region's busiest, although some domestic and international carriers use **Worcester Airport** (ORH) in Worcester, Massachusetts, **T.F. Green Airport** (PVD) in Warwick, Rhode Island, which serves Providence, and **Bradley International Airport** (BDL) in Windsor Locks, Connecticut, which serves Hartford. A few major commercial airlines also fly into Bangor (BGR) and Portland (PWM), Maine; Manchester (MHT), New Hampshire; and Burlington (BTV), Vermont. Other gateways to New England include Montreal, Quebec, and, of course, New York City's three major airports.

Smaller domestic airlines cover specific geographical regions while also offering a few national flights. Although they have fewer flights than the major carriers, they often have substantially reduced fares. A number of regional commuter airlines shuttle passengers around New England, with small, single-prop planes flying to such destinations as Cape Cod and the various islands off the coast.

International travelers will be given a customs and immigration form during their flight and will be required to hand in the completed form to customs officials in the airport. At the immigration area there are two lines, one for US citizens and another for non-US citizens. If you are entering the country via New York's busy JFK, be forewarned that the immigration lines are often long and the process can be a time-consuming ordeal

AIRFARES

IT IS ALWAYS BEST to plan your vacation early and to shop around for the best airfares; a little research can go a long way in terms of securing a substantial discount. For inexpensive consolidated tickets, contact **Intrepid Traveler** online or **NOW Voyager** online. **Lowestfare.com** gives you instant access to the best published prices on the web. Keep in mind that even with the small fees they may charge, travel agents are often your best allies in your search for savings.

The busiest times of year for travel to New England are June through August, as well as the major holidays of Christmas, Easter, Labor Day, and most especially Thanksgiving. Book flights during these periods well in advance. In general, you will get the lowest airfares if you plan to travel during non-peak periods of the year – for instance, prices drop substantially following Labor Day. It is almost always cheaper to fly in and out of New England on weekdays rather than on weekends.

Passenger jet in flight

AIRPORT	INFORMATION	DISTANCE FROM CITY
Logan International (Boston, MA)	☎ *(617) 568-5600*	3 miles (4.8 km) from Downtown Boston
Worcester Airport (Worcester, MA)	☎ *(508) 799-1741*	5 miles (8 km) from Downtown Worcester
T.F. Green Airport (Warwick, RI)	☎ *(401) 737-4000*	10 miles (16 km) from Downtown Providence
Bradley Intl. (Windsor Locks, CT)	☎ *(860) 292-2000*	12 miles (19 km) from Downtown Hartford

ARRIVING BY TRAIN

THE MAJOR AMERICAN RAILROAD is **Amtrak**. While one of Amtrak's busiest routes services southern and central New England up to Boston, there are relatively few routes to destinations in the northern part of the region. Amtrak recently unveiled its high-speed *Acela Regional* train service between New York and Boston, which has cut 90-minutes off regular travel time of about 6 hours. While it is available at a premium price, it is still less expensive than most airfares and has the added convenience of taking you from downtown to downtown without the added expense of taxis or shuttle buses. At present, negotiations are underway to reestablish rail service north and west of Boston.

Train station in North Conway, New Hampshire

ARRIVING BY CAR

GETTING TO New England by car is relatively easy, and you have several options. Beginning in Florida, I-95, also known as Route 128 in the Boston area, is one of the most popular drives for travelers coming from the South. This major interstate highway sticks close to the coast as it passes through Connecticut and Providence, Rhode Island, en route to the outskirts of Boston. Circumventing the city, the highway continues up through New Hampshire and Maine before crossing the border into Canada. Drivers should note that truck traffic along I-95 can be particularly heavy, especially when approaching Boston.

The two major gateways into New England from the

Wheeled luggage

north are I-89 and I-91. The latter crosses from Canada into Vermont at Derby Line and then follows a relatively straight line south along the Vermont/New Hampshire border, through both central Massachusetts and Connecticut all the way down to New Haven. I-89 starts in Vermont's northwesternmost corner and then from Burlington cuts diagonally to Concord, New Hampshire where it links up with I-93 into Boston. The major western points of entry into New England are I-84 and I-90 from New York state.

ARRIVING BY BUS

AS IT STANDS, you can get just about anywhere in New England via bus, so long as you are not in a hurry. Many of the bus companies serve particular sections of New England. **Concord Trailways** has routes in Maine and New Hampshire, and **Vermont Transit** serves Vermont, Maine, and New Hampshire. **Bonanza** is the main Connecticut bus line, while **Peter Pan** has stops in Connecticut and western Massachusetts. Other parts of Massachusetts, most notably Cape Cod and the South Shore, are served by **Plymouth & Brockton**. **Greyhound Lines** is a nationwide carrier and has stops throughout New

England. Greyhound works in conjunction with Bonanza, Vermont Transit, and Peter Pan lines. Most major bus lines offer discount rates for students and seniors (with proper ID), and offer unlimited travel during a set period.

DIRECTORY

AIRFARES

Intrepid Traveler
PO Box 531,
Branford, CT 06405.
📞 *(203) 448-5341.*
🌐 *www.intrepidtraveler.com*

NOW Voyager
74 Varick St, Suite 307,
New York, NY 10013.
📞 *(212) 431-1616 or*
(212) 219-1753.
🌐 *www.nowvoyagertravel.com*

TRAIN

Amtrak
📞 *(800) 872-7245.*

BUS LINES

Concord Trailways
📞 *(617) 426-8080 or*
(800) 639-3317.

Vermont Transit
📞 *(800) 451-3292 or*
(802) 864-6811.

Bonanza
📞 *(617) 720-4110 or*
(800) 556-3815.

Peter Pan
📞 *(413) 781-2900 or*
(800) 343-9999.

Plymouth & Brockton
📞 *(508) 746-0378.*

Greyhound Lines
📞 *(617) 526-1810 or*
(800) 231-2222.

A Greyhound bus

Getting Around Boston

PUBLIC TRANSPORTATION in Boston and Cambridge is very good. In fact it is considerably easier to get around by public transportation than by driving, with the added benefit of not having to find a parking space. All major attractions in the city are accessible on the subway, by bus, or by taxi. The central sections of the city are also extremely easy to navigate on foot.

MBTA commuter bus, with distinctive yellow paint

FINDING YOUR WAY IN BOSTON

THE MORE PLANNING you do before your trip, the easier it will be to locate sights and find your way around the city. The **Greater Boston Convention and Visitors Bureau** *(see p369)* will be a helpful contact point, and your hotel is also likely to be able to offer advice. To find out about any upcoming cultural events, check web-sites for **Boston Citysearch** and the **Boston Globe** *(see p369)*.

Most of Boston is laid out "organically" rather than in the sort of strict grid found in most American cities. When trying to orient yourself, it helps to think of Boston as enclaves – of neighborhoods around a few central squares. In general, uphill from Boston Common is Beacon Hill, downhill is Downtown. Back Bay begins west of Arlington Street. The North End sticks out from the north side of Boston, while the Waterfront is literally that, where Boston meets the sea.

MBTA SUBWAY AND TROLLEY BUSES

BOSTON'S SUBWAY system is the oldest in North America, but it has been vastly expanded and modernized since the first cars rolled between Park Street and Boylston Street on September 1, 1897. The street trolley system is even older, having begun in 1846 with trolleys drawn along tracks by horses. The system was electrified in 1889. The combined subway and trolley lines (most lines move above ground when they leave the city center) are generally known as the "T." The T operates 5am to 12:45am Monday through Saturday and 6am to 12:45am Sunday. Weekday service is every 3 to 15 minutes, on weekends less frequently. There are four lines. The Red line runs from south of the city to Cambridge. The Green line runs from the Museum of Science westward into the suburbs. The Blue line begins near Government Center and goes to Logan Airport, then on to Revere. The Orange line connects the northern suburbs to southwest Boston. Maps of the system are available at the Downtown Crossing MBTA station.

Admission to subway stations is via turnstiles into which you insert a $1 T token or swipe an electro-magnetic pass card. Visitor's Passport passes for unlimited travel for one, three, or five days ($6/$11/$22) can be purchased at Downtown Crossing and Airport stations or at Greater Boston Convention and Visitors Bureau information booths.

Visitor's Passport, valid on all MBTA services

MBTA BUSES

THE BUS SYSTEM complements the subway system and in effect enlarges the entire transit network to cover more than 1,000 miles (1,600 km). However, buses are often crowded and schedules can be hard to obtain. Two useful routes for sightseeing are Charlestown-Haymarket, (from Haymarket, near Quincy Market, to Bunker Hill) and Harvard-Dudley (from Harvard Square via Massachusetts Avenue through Back Bay and the South End to Dudley Square in Roxbury.) Exact change (75 cents) or a pass is required for the fare.

TAXIS

FINDING A TAXI in Boston and Cambridge is rarely difficult except when it is raining. Taxis can be found at stands in tourist areas and can be hailed on the street. Taxis may pick up fares only in the city for which they are licensed – Cambridge taxis only in Cambridge, Boston taxis only in Boston. If you need to be somewhere on time, it is advisable to call a taxi company and arrange a definite pickup time and place.

Rates are calculated by both mileage and time, beginning with a $1.10 "pick-up" fee when the meter starts running. In general, the taxis in Boston and Cambridge are more

Boston taxis waiting for fares at one of the city's many taxi stands

expensive than those in other US cities, except New York. Taxis to Logan Airport are required to charge an airport use fee ($2); those coming from the airport charge for the harbor tunnel toll ($3). Additional surcharges may apply late at night. A full schedule of fares should be posted inside the vehicle.

Boston parkland, ideal for walking

The driver's photograph and permit and the taxi's permit number will also be posted inside all legitimate taxicabs, along with directions for reporting complaints.

WALKING IN BOSTON

BOSTON IS CONSIDERED North America's premier walking city, partly because it is so compact and partly because virtually all streets are flanked by sidewalks. It is nonetheless essential to wear comfortable walking shoes with adequate cushioning and good support.

Because Boston is principally a city of neighborhoods, it is often best to use public transportation to get to a particular neighborhood, and then walk around to soak up the atmosphere. Walking also allows you to see parts of the city that are impractical to explore by car because streets are too narrow; for example, Beacon Hill, parts of the North End, and Harvard Square.

DIRECTORY

SUBWAY AND BUSES

MBTA
(Route and schedule information)
10 Park Plaza.
((617) 222-3200.
w www.mbta.com

TAXIS

Boston Cab Dispatch, Inc.
((617) 262-2227.

Checker Taxi
(Cambridge)
((617) 497-1500.

Town Taxi
((617) 536-5000.

Yellow Cab
(Cambridge)
((617) 547-3000.

THE BOSTON "Ⓣ"

KEY

■ Red line

■ Green line (including green lines B, C, D, & E)

■ Orange line

■ Blue line

◯ Terminal station

●—● Interchange with other lines

MBTA website: www.mbta.com
© MBTA 2000

Driving in New England

Important road sign

W HILE FLYING IS THE FASTEST and most efficient way to get to New England, driving is by far the best way to explore the region. In fact, much of New England's charm is found along scenic jaunts down the coast and driving tours during fall-foliage season. It is important to remember that large areas of the region are essentially wild, so you should always be prepared for any eventuality, such as a breakdown. This is doubly true in the winter, when sudden blizzards and white-outs caused by blowing snow can leave motorists stranded. Boston's public transit system makes it possible to do without a car *(see pp376–7)*, but once outside the city you will need a vehicle to do your best exploring.

A rented convertible, perfect for exploring in good weather

CAR RENTAL

T HE MAJOR CAR rental chains have outlets in most of New England's major cities and larger airports. These national chains include **Avis**, **Budget**, **Enterprise**, **Hertz**, **National**, **Rent-A-Wreck**, and **Thrifty**. While their rates are somewhat higher than smaller local companies, they usually offer extremely efficient service.

In order to rent a car, you must be 21 and possess a valid driver's license. People under 25 will sometimes have to pay a surcharge. A major credit card is usually required as well, unless you are prepared to put down a hefty cash deposit. Credit cards sometimes provide coverage against damage or theft of the vehicle, but it is wise to check what the terms are with your credit card company. Regardless, make sure that your car

rental agreement includes Collision Damage Waiver (CDW) – also known as Loss Damage Waiver (LDW) – or else you will be liable for any damage to the car, even if it was not your fault. This supplemental insurance can cost between $10 and $20 extra a day.

Sightseeing by car, stopping where and when you want

Country roads beckoning drivers to leave the crowds behind

SPEED LIMITS

I T IS IMPORTANT to pay attention to the signs, as speed limits can vary from one place to the next depending on your proximity to a town or city. In general, the maximum speed on an interstate highway varies from 55 to 65 mph (88–105 km/h). On smaller highways, it can range between 30 and 55 mph (50–88 km/h). Cities and towns set speed limits between 20 and 35 mph (32–56 km/h), drastically lower around hospitals and schools. Police often pick strategic points along highways – often right after a sign for lower speed – to set up their radar equipment in order to catch drivers who are going too fast. Do not try to pay tickets or fines directly to the police officer who pulled you over; this can be interpreted as attempted bribery and can land you deeper in hot water.

DRIVING TOURS

T HERE ARE A number of books on the market listing the best driving tours of the region. Some publications, such as *Yankee* magazine, include a complete itinerary of recommended routes, historic stops, and the best places to eat and stay. Tours vary from a single day to an entire week and take in everything from dramatic coastal scenery and tiny fishing villages to mountainous terrain and country towns.

Of course, the favorite season for drivers is in the fall, when the rural roads are flanked by the brilliant colors of leaves *(see pp20–21)*.

State tourism offices *(see p369)* can give you the contact information for organizations that plan foliage tours. Each state also has a hotline number that gives frequently updated foliage reports. Remember, though, that traffic on New England's roads peaks in the fall.

SAFETY TIPS

If you are planning on spending a lot of time in your car, you should follow these simple procedures to ensure your safety and that of your passengers. The **National Highway Traffic Safety Administration** offers news on everything from school bus safety to road rage and operates an Auto Safety Hotline.

- Passengers should wear their seat belts at all times. Infants and young children should be secured in a car seat in the back seat. Follow child seat instruction manuals precisely. A rear-facing child seat should NEVER be placed in the front seat of a vehicle equipped with an air bag.

- Never leave children unattended in your car.

- Clean your windshield and adjust your mirrors for optimum visibility.

- Check your oil, radiator reservoir, brake fluids, and your fan belt before setting off on a long drive.

- Make sure all your lights and turn signals are working properly.

- Check your tires for undue tread wear and make sure that the air pressure is correct. Also see that your spare tire is roadworthy.

- Be sure that you have a working jack and road flares or reflective triangles in the trunk. Pack extra windshield wipers, and in winter stock salt, a snow brush and an ice scraper, and small shovel.

- Also keep a small medical kit in your trunk, along with a blanket and an emergency flashlight. In winter, make sure you have extra gloves, boots, and warm clothes.

- If you do get stuck in winter in an out-of-the-way place, stay inside your car. Keep the motor running for warmth, but open your window slightly to guard against carbon monoxide buildup. Make sure your exhaust pipe is clear of snow.

- Check road conditions on the radio, especially in winter. Heavy snowfalls can leave many areas impassable. Individual state transportation departments often have hotlines dispensing up-to-date information on road conditions and closures.

- Be wary of deer and moose that may run onto the road. Hitting a moose poses more of a threat to you than it does to the animal.

Sign on a Vermont highway warning drivers to watch for moose

DIRECTORY

CAR RENTALS

Avis
((800) 831-2847.

Budget
((800) 527-0700.

Enterprise
((800) 325-8007.

Hertz
((800) 654-3131.

National
((800) 227-7368.

Rent-A-Wreck
((800) 535-1391.

Thrifty
((800) 367-2277.

DRIVING TOURS

Yankee magazine
W www.newengland.com

FOLIAGE HOTLINES

Connecticut
((800) 252-6863.

Maine
((800) 533-9595.

Massachusetts
((800) 227-6277.

New Hampshire
((800) 258-3608.

Rhode Island
((800) 556-2484.

Vermont
((800) 828-3239.

HIGHWAY MANAGEMENT

National Highway Traffic Safety Administration
55 Broadway-Kendall Sq,
Cambridge, MA 02142
((617) 494-3427.
W www.nhtsa.dot.gov

Acknowledgments

DORLING KINDERSLEY would like to thank the following people whose contributions and assistance have made the preparation of this book possible.

MAIN CONTRIBUTORS

Eleanor Berman is an award-winning travel writer and author of 11 travel guides, including *Away for the Weekend: New England* and *Recommended Bed and Breakfasts: New England*. She was the principal contributor to the *Eyewitness Guide to New York*.

Patricia Brooks, a longtime freelance travel and food writer, has lived in Connecticut since 1956. She has authored or co-authored 16 books and writes frequently for national US magazines. Since 1977 she has been the food critic for *The New York Times'* Connecticut Weekly section and writes its weekly Dining Out column of restaurant reviews.

Helga Loverseed's work has taken her to 165 destinations in her 23 years as a travel journalist and photographer. She has won awards both for her photography and her writing, has contributed to six travel guides, and is a travel columnist for several leading newspapers and magazines.

Pierre Home-Douglas has worked as a travel writer and book editor since the late 1980s. His articles on subjects ranging from bicycling through Vermont to sailing up the Nile have appeared in many newspapers and magazines. He has also written for *Great Railway Journeys of the World* and *Explore America*.

FOR DORLING KINDERSLEY

Senior Publishing Manager Louise Bostock Lang
Publishing Managers Kate Poole, Helen Townsend, Jane Ewart
Project Editor Marcus Hardy
Art Editor Nicola Rodway
Editor Simon Hall
Designers Elly King, Nikala Sim
Map Co-ordinators Dave Pugh, Casper Morris
DTP Maite Lantaron, Jason Little, Conrad van Dyk
Picture Researcher Brigitte Arora
Production Michelle Thomas, Marie Ingledew
Design & Editorial Assistance Sam Borland, Katherine Mesquita, Lynne Robinson
U.S Editor Mary Sutherland
Researcher Timothy Kennard

Contributors Tom Bross, Brett Cook, Patricia Harris, Carolyn Heller, David Lyon, Juliette Rogers, Kem Sawyer
Photographers Demetrio Carrasco, Linda Whitwam (Additional photography: Peter Anderson, Clive Streeter)
Illustrators Stephen Conlin, Gary Cross, Richard Draper, Chris Orr & Associates, Robbie Polley, John Woodcock
Maps Ben Bowles, Rob Clynes, Sam Johnston, James Macdonald (Colourmap Scanning Ltd)

THANKS TO

Philippe Arnoldi, Danny-Pierre Auger, Rosemary Barron, Lorraine Doré, Joey Fraser, Dominique Gagné, Pascale Hueber, Solange Laberge, Rob Lutes, Edward Renaud, Odette Sévigny.

SPECIAL ASSISTANCE

Sam Ankerson, Shelburne Museum; Amy Bassett, New Hampshire Parks and Recreation Division; Janel Blood, Concord Chamber of Commerce; Nancy E. Boone, State of Vermont Division for Historic Preservation; Becky Bovill, R.I. Tourism Division; David Bush, Karen Miller, The Mark Twain House; Andrea Carneiro, Melissa Fanny, Preservation Society of Newport County; Heidi Clarke, South County Tourism Council; Katherine Fox, Destination Salem; Margaret Joyce, New Hampshire Office of Travel and Tourism Development; Lauren Kedski, Providence Warwick Convention and Visitors Bureau; Valerie Kidney, New Brunswick Tourism; Sharon Kotok, Strawbery Banke; Linda Levin, Connecticut Dept. of Environmental Protection-Parks Division; Pierre L'Heureux, Dawson College; Renny Loisel, Greater New Haven Convention & Visitors Bureau; Amanda C. Lowe, Massachusetts Office of Travel & Tourism; Caroline Marshall, Greater Portsmouth Chamber of Commerce; Brenda Milkofsky, Wethersfield Historical Society; Wanda Moran, NPS-Acadia National Park; Mike Morand, New Haven and State Affairs Department of Yale University; Sue Moynahan, Marianne McCaffery - NPS - Cape Cod National Seashore; Dr. Virginia Nixon, Liberal Arts College, Concordia University; Amy O'Brien, Greater Boston Convention and Visitors Bureau; Michele Pecoraro, Plimoth Plantation; Greg Gerdel, Vermont Department of Tourism and Marketing; Janice Putnam, Susanna Bonta, Old Sturbridge Village; Jessica Roy, Maine Office of Tourism; Janet L. Serra, Litchfield Hills Visitors Bureau; Tim Shea, Burlington Chamber of Commerce; Sherry Smardon, Greater Hartford Tourism District; Evan Smith, Jan Hagerstrom, Newport County Convention and Visitors Bureau; James R. Spencer, Connecticut Department of Transportation; Amy Strack, Massachusetts Office of Travel and Tourism; Paulette Weaver, Lakes Region Association; Katrina White, North of Boston Convention and Visitors Bureau; Leah Wiedmann, Portland Convention and Visitors Bureau; Tricia Wood, Sarah Patton, Mystic Seaport Museum; Mary Woods, The Coastal Fairfield County Convention & Visitor Bureau; Janie Young, Canterbury Shaker Village.

PHOTOGRAPHY PERMISSIONS

DORLING KINDERSLEY would like to thank all those who gave assistance and permission to photograph at their churches, museums, hotels, restaurants, shops, galleries, and other sights too numerous to list individually.

PICTURE CREDITS

t = top; tl = top left; tlc = top left centre; tc = top centre; tr = top right; cla = centre left above; ca = centre above; cra = centre right above; cl = centre left; c = centre; cr = centre right; clb = centre left below; cb = centre below; crb = centre right below; bl = bottom left; b = bottom; bc = bottom centre; bcl = bottom centre left; br = bottom right; d = detail.

Every effort has been made to trace the copyright holders and we apologize in advance for any unintentional omissions. We would be pleased to insert the appropriate acknowledgments in any subsequent edition of this publication.

AROOSTOOK STATE PARK/Bruce Farnham: 299tl.

DAVID J. BOOKER: 82; BOSTON SYMPHONY ORCHESTRA: 350bc.

ROBERT CHARTIER: 372bl; BRUCE COLEMAN INC., NEW YORK: Mark Newman 4bl; Gene Ahrens 1, 226, 300/301; John M. Burnley 249; Jeff Foott 268/269; Carolyn Schaefer 364/365; CORBIS: John L. Amos 29c; Archivo Iconografico S.A.: 35 tr; Bettmann: 28tr, 28cl, 28c, 28br, 30c, 30br, 37t, 38t, 42bl, 43cl, 44cr, 44br, 45bc, 47bl, 48 bl, 48br, 71br, 120b, 128/129, 142b, 253t; Burstein Collection: 39br; Steve Jay Crise 41br, 47bl; Edifice, Philippa Lewis 56c; Kevin Fleming 29tl, 352tl, 368cr; George Hall 374b; Historical Picture Archive: 36; Anne Hodalio 29 br; Robert Holmes 31t, 102; Hulton-Deutsch Collection: 29bl, 47t, 48tr, 267c; Todd Gipstein 30tr, 47br; Farrell Grehan 30bl; Kelly-Mooney Photography: 32bc; Lake County Museum: 38b; Magma: 25t, 28bl, 29cl, 37b, 45tl, 46cr, 47c; John-Marshall Mantel 31br; Francis G. Mayer 40-41c; Gail Mooney 347tl; David Muench 40tr; Greg Nikas 351tl; Reuters Newsmedia Inc.: 29cr, 120t, 352b, 352b, 369; Bill Ross 371t; Bob Rowan/Progressive Image: 28cb; Phil Shermeister 34t, 378; Joseph Sohm

40bl, 43bc; Paul A. Souders 41cr; Ted Spiegel 35br; 350cl; Peter Turnley 29tr; Connecticut State Parks Division: 219tl, 219br.

Jacques De Tonnacourt: 181cr.

Mary Evans Picture Library: 8/9, 9c, 31c, 38c, 39t, 39cl, 39bc, 40tl, 41t, 42tl, 42c, 43tc, 43cr, 44t, 44cl, 45cr, 46t, 47tr, 48c, 129c, 301c, 365c.

Foxwoods Resort Casino: 302c.

Granger Collection, New York: 51 (inset); 81b.

Harvard University Art Museums: © President and Fellows of Harvard College, courtesy of the Busch-Reisinger Museum, Gift of Mrs. Gordon Dexter *Colonel Ernst August von Hugo and Lt. Colonel von Schlepegrell*, John Singleton Copley, 1787 - 114cr; courtesy of the Busch-Reisinger Museum, Gift of Sibyl Moholy-Nagy, © DACS, London 2000 Light-Space Modulator, Laszlo Moholy-Nagy, 1930 - 114b; courtesy Fogg Art Museum, Gift of Lawrence Rubin © ARS, N.Y. and DACS, London 2000 *Red River Valley*, Frank Stella, 1958 - 115cl; courtesy Fogg Art Museum, Bequest: Collection of Maurice Wertheim *Skating*, Edouard Manet, 1877 - 115b; Historic Deerfield, Inc./Amanda Merullo: 163b; Dave G. Houser: 130tr, 178/179; Hulton Getty Collection: 76b.
Philip C. Jackson: 131br, 169, 171bl, 180cl, 182tr, 182tl, 182c, 183tl, 184tl, 184tr, 184cr, 184br, 185tl, 185c, 185br, 186tr, 187tr, 187cr.
Killington, Vermont: 366bl.

James Lemass: 70br, 72, 95crb.

Maine Office of Tourism: 21bl, 23tr, 303br; Gary Pearl 23c, 131tr, 295b, 303br; The Mark Twain House: 130bl, 200bl, 201tl.; Massachusetts Office of Travel and Tourism/Kindra Clineff: 20tr, 32t, 303bl, 356tr, 357cr, 358br, 360b, 361b, 362c; Museum of Fine Arts, Boston: HU-MFA Expedition *Shawabtis of Taharka* 52b, 106t; Bequest of Mrs. Beatrice Constance (Turner) Maynard in Memory of Winthrop Sargent *Revere Silver Teapot* 106ca; Egypt Exploration Fund *Inner Coffin of Nes-mut-aat-neru* 106cb; 1951 Purchase Fund *La Japonaise* Claude Monet, 1876 – 107t; Ruth and Carl J. Shapiro Colonnade and Vault *John Singer Sargent Murals* 107c; Henry Lillie Pierce Fund *Ram's Head* 107b; George Nixon Black Fund *Ewer and basin* 108t; M. and M. Karolik Collection of American Paintings, 1815 – 1865, by exchange, *Boston Harbor* Fitz Hugh Lane 108c; Bequest of John T. Spaulding *La Berceuse* Vincent van Gogh, 1889 – 108b; Maria Antoinette Evans Fund *Babylonia: Nebuchadnezzar II* 109t; Gift by Contribution *Horse, early 8th century, China* 109c; Richard Norton Memorial Fund *Fragment of fresco from villa at Contrada Bottaro* 109b; Museum of New Hampshire History/Bill Finney: 259t.

Nantucket Island Chamber of Commerce/Michael Glavin: 32cl. New England Aquarium: Bob Kramer 78t/b, 79t. David Noble: 50–51

Old Sturbridge Village/Thomas Neill: 130cl; Omni Parker House: 74clb.

Laurence Parent Photography, Inc: 2/3, 146/147, 274; Peabody Museum of Archaeology and Ethnology/ Harvard University: © President and Fellows of Harvard College 1976. All Rights Reserved. Photos Hillel Burger 116c/b. Photo Researchers Inc.: Worldsat International Inc. 12br; The Preservation Society of Newport County: 186c, 186b, 187tl, 187b; Providence Warwick Convention & Visitor's Bureau: 367t.

Rockland-Thomaston Area Chamber of Commerce/Richard V. Procopio: 33tr.

Seaport Hotel/Peter Vanderwalker: 304b; Springfield Science Museum, Springfield, Ma./Dinosaur Hall: 162tr; State of New Hampshire Division of Travel and Tourism Development: 362tl; David Brownell 254tr, 356cl; Nancy G. Horton 325c; Craig Alness 357bl; Jeffery E. Blackman 358cl, 361t; Stowe Mountain Resort/Chuck Waskuch: 362b; Don Landwehrle 363tr.

Topham Picturepoint: 53tr.

The Union-News and Sunday Republican/David Molnar: 161br; USFWS Photo: 19tr.

Vermont Department of Travel and Tourism: 49cr, 237b. Yale Center for British Art/Richard Caspole: 223t; Yale University Office of Public Affairs: 222t.

Front Endpaper: All commissioned photography with the exception of Bruce Coleman Inc: Gene Ahrens tl; Laurence Parent Photography, Inc: tr.

Jacket: all special photography except gettyone.stone: Patrick Ingrand F/C top; Robert Harding Picture Library: Rolf Richardson F/C left; Caroline Jones: spine bottom; David Noble: F/C centre right, centre below, bottom left and B/C top left.

DORLING KINDERSLEY SPECIAL EDITIONS

Dorling Kindersley books can be purchased in bulk quantities at discounted prices for use in promotions or as premiums. We are also able to offer special editions and personalized jackets, corporate imprints, and excerpts from all of our books, tailored specifically to meet your own needs.

To find out more, please contact: (in the United Kingdom) – Special Sales, Dorling Kindersley Limited, 9 Henrietta Street, Covent Garden, London WC2E 8PS; Tel. 020 7753 3572; (in the United States) – Special Markets Department, Dorling Kindersley, Inc., 95 Madison Avenue, New York, NY 10016.